CLEMENCEAU
A Life at War

"The Tiger," wearing the felt cap given to him by a soldier.
(Wide World Photos.)

CLEMENCEAU
A Life at War

David S. Newhall

The Edwin Mellen Press
Lewiston/Queenston/Lampeter

Library of Congress Cataloging-in-Publication Data

Newhall, David S.
    Clemenceau : a life at war / David S. Newhall.
      p. cm.
    Includes bibliographical references and index.
    ISBN 0-88946-785-4
    1. Clemenceau, Georges, 1841-1929. 2. Heads of state--France-
-Biography. 3. France--Politics and government--1870-1940.
I. Title.
DC342.8.C6N43   1991
944.081'4'092--dc20
[B]
                                                 90-20994
                                                   CIP

A CIP catalog record for this book
is available from the British Library.

The Edwin Mellen Press   The Edwin Mellen Press
Box 450   Box 67
Lewiston, New York   Queenston, Ontario
USA 14092   CANADA L0S 1L0

The Edwin Mellen Press, Ltd.
Lampeter, Dyfed, Wales
UNITED KINGDOM SA48 7DY

Printed in the United States of America

For Edna

and

Rebecca, John, Jesslyn,

Melissa, and David Chester

———————

In Memory of

Rev. Charles Marion Prestwood, Jr., Ph.D.
(1931-1977)

...a son of the South

who fought for racial justice

Table of Contents

Glossary of Abbreviations

Because of its wide availability I have cited Jean Martet, *Georges Clemenceau*, trans. Milton Waldman (New York: Longmans, Green & Co., 1930) rather than the author's *M. Clemenceau peint par lui-même* and *Le silence de M. Clemenceau*. When the French version is cited it is because the English version lacks the passage. The latter is cited as Martet, *Clemenceau*.

Place of publication is Paris unless otherwise noted.

The following abbreviations are employed:

AU   *L'Aurore*, 1897-99, 1903-6.

FRUS   United States of America. Department of State. *Foreign Relations of the United States. Paris Peace Conference. 1919.* 13 vols. Washington, D.C.: United States Government Printing Office, 1942-47.

GC   Georges Clemenceau.

HE   *L'Homme Enchaîné*, 1914-17.

HL   *L'Homme Libre*, 1913-14.

JOC   France. *Journal Officiel. Chambre des Députés. Débats parlementaires.* Imprimerie Nationale, 1881-93, 1906-9, 1917-20.

JORF   France. *Journal Officiel de la République Française.* Imprimerie Nationale, 1870-80.

JOS   France. *Journal Officiel. Sénat. Débats parlementaires.* Imprimerie Nationale, 1902-20.

JU   *La Justice*, 1880-97.

Preface

A book of less than immoderate length about a personage of such immoderate dimensions as Georges Clemenceau must inevitably run the risks of redundancy or presumptuousness. What to tell? What to pass over? What to say that has not been said already by somebody (or a dozen somebodies) and said better? But great subjects always generate problems of selection; length of treatment only affects the degree of difficulty.

The niagara of print poured forth by modern scholarship creates a need for books now and then to serve as syntheses for general readers and students and for useful, reliable references for specialists in related subjects. Without syntheses, readers and researchers alike would drown under the cataract. To meet this need, in any event, has been my aim in writing this book--that and self-education, if you will, because to study Clemenceau's life and career is to find oneself in contact with a huge share of the history of the nineteenth and twentieth centuries. The passage of six decades since his death in 1929 has supplied ample time for materials relating to him to be found and for an historical perspective on his life and times to mature.

Clemenceau refused to write memoirs despite the enormous financial rewards they surely would have reaped. The closest he came was a collection of short essays and reflections about wartime and postwar controversies entitled *Grandeur et misères d'une victoire*, published posthumously in 1930. As for his personal papers, he burned most of them before he died. The Fonds Clemenceau in the archives of the Service historique de l'Armée at Vincennes contains official documents of little direct biographical interest, not personal papers as the title might suggest. The only substantial published collection of his letters is *Lettres à une amie, 1923-1929* (1970), a correspondence with Marguerite (Mme. Fernand) Baldensperger edited by her son, Pierre Brive [Baldensperger]. Previously, in 1969, it might be noted,

Alfred Krebs quoted extensively from discovered correspondence between Clemenceau and Auguste Scheurer-Kestner in the late 1860s.

A ground-breaking work by an English academician, David R. Watson, *Georges Clemenceau: A Political Biography* (1974), first described the nature and general disposition of what survived. In 1979 the late Georges Wormser, a former *chef de cabinet* of Clemenceau's and long-time president of the Amis de Georges Clemenceau--a society which has maintained his former apartment at 8, rue Franklin (Paris XVI), as a small museum and archive--published some additional texts in *Clemenceau vu de près*, which in a sense was a pendant to his highly important study *La république de Clemenceau* (1961). And in 1988 Wormser's successor and the dean of historians working in contemporary French political and diplomatic history, Jean-Baptiste Duroselle, published through Fayard his long-expected and monumental biography *Clemenceau*, a trove of information and wisdom. Duroselle's work is the first to make extensive use of the Musée Clemenceau's collections of letters and memorabilia, which had hitherto been available only on a very limited basis, and in addition he explored numerous public and private archives, a search already well begun by Watson.

Biographies of Clemenceau are fairly abundant, but their nature and quality deserve a word. Biography unfortunately is not a field which French scholars have cultivated in this century as intensively as their brethren in the English-speaking world, no doubt due in part to the great influence of the *Annales* school's emphasis on social and economic analysis. Happily, this disposition has been changing of late, and one can hope that Duroselle's work on Clemenceau will inspire others to take up this genre. Aside from his contribution, probably the most important single book to date on Clemenceau (with the arguable exception of Watson's mentioned above) is Wormser's *La république de Clemenceau*; and because the author was close to Clemenceau during and after the First World War and had easy access to the Musée Clemenceau's archives, it will have permanent value. Most unfortunately for purposes of reference and general usefulness, however, its lack of an index compounds the problems created by its idiosyncratic organization. The biography by Gustave Geffroy (1926), a prominent art critic who was a long-time friend of Clemenceau, is exceptionally valuable for the years before 1900. Gen. Henri Mordacq, Clemenceau's *chef de cabinet militaire* from 1917 to 1920 and likewise a close friend, published a biography (1939), but his four-volume diary, *Le ministère Clemenceau, journal d'un témoin* (1930-31), and the two-volume account of his last years, *Clemenceau au soir de sa vie, 1920-1929* (1931), are of the highest importance. Georges Gatineau-Clemenceau, an erratic grandson, hung out some family wash in *Des pattes du Tigre aux griffes du destin* (1961), but its reliability is open to question. Gaston Monnerville's *Clemenceau* (1968) is a substantial piece of work by a former president of the Senate and especially valuable for its use of the Parliament's records during the First World War, but it lacks sufficient references to make it highly useful to scholars. The biographies by Georges Michon (1931), a well-informed, non-academic Socialist historian, and Alexander Zévaès (1949), a veteran parliamentarian and prolific writer on Third Republic topics, are worth consulting. The other biographies or sketches are mostly by journalists, essayists, or writers of popular histories and vary considerably in quality, Philippe Erlanger's *Clemenceau* (1968) being one of the best of the lot along with Berthe Bastoul's insightful *Clemenceau vu par un passant inconnu* (1938), which has often been unjustly overlooked. One should also consult a collection of essays by a number of well-known scholars, *Clemenceau et la justice* (1979), which treats various facets of his life and work.

Books or articles based on conversations with Clemenceau comprise a special category. The most important by far are by Jean Martet. A novelist of note who was his secretary from 1916 to 1929, Martet rushed three "spoken memoirs" into print after his death--*Le silence de M. Clemenceau* (1929), *M. Clemenceau peint par lui-même* (1929), and *Le Tigre* (1930)--with most of the first two being translated into English by Milton Waldman. They are indispensable reading. But interpretation is something of a problem because Clemenceau was given to colorful outbursts or witticisms which should not routinely be taken at full face value. One should turn to them seriously only after having become quite well-acquainted with the man and his career. The same must be said of other works in this genre, for example those by Fernand Neuray (1930) and René Benjamin (1930).

In English, the best-known survey, now quite dated but still worth reading because of the author's reputation, has long been that by Geoffrey Bruun (1944), with J. Hampden Jackson's (1946) a polished, though much less informed, second. The books by Henry M. Hyndman (1919), a pioneer of socialism in England, and Wythe Williams (1949), an American journalist, have some value because they knew Clemenceau personally and convey good anecdotal material. More recently (1976), the late Edgar Holt, an English journalist-historian, published a respectable work. In 1974, however, David R. Watson brought out the substantial study mentioned above, the first in any language to make serious use of archival materials and from the moment of its appearance an indispensable work for an understanding of Clemenceau's political activity, as the subtitle announces. Watson has put all students of Clemenceau permanently in his debt. It should be noted, however, that about the time he was finishing his work, the French archives for the First World War, the Peace Conference, and the 1920s had only begun to become available, and subsequent scholarship on these periods has flourished mightily. And, as also noted, he did not enjoy the advantages of full access to the Musée Clemenceau's archives which Duroselle was to have. As for more specialized works, one should also call attention here to Samuel Applebaum's *Clemenceau, Thinker and Writer* (1948) and to a well-done original study by an American historian which emphasizes psychological considerations: Jack D. Ellis's *The Early Life of Georges Clemenceau, 1841-1893* (1980).

As stated above, my aim has been to produce a synthesis--that is, an overview of Clemenceau's life and a consideration of his historical significance in the light of scholarship to date. Although I have written with general readers and students first in mind, thus "writing to be read," I have also sought, at some risk of falling between two stools, to be helpful to professional scholars through the references and by treating selected controversial or little-known episodes more fully than one might expect in a synthesis. Hence the notes and index are much more elaborate than is customary in books of this kind. My study has occupied me over a long period of time dating back to my dissertation on Clemenceau (1963). While perforce I have depended in the main on the research of others, especially as regards archival material, I have read all of Clemenceau's parliamentary record and virtually all his vast written output, the great bulk of which appeared originally as editorials or articles in newspapers.

In surveying a career as long and eventful as Clemenceau's, one finds oneself painting battle scenes on bottle caps, so to speak. Space would not permit, for example, detailed narratives of his two ministries (1906-9, 1917-20); consequently, they are dealt with in what are essentially essays. Anticipating, however, that most readers would be largely unfamiliar with French affairs during his first ministry--the War and the Peace Conference being well-traveled terrain--I have provided a chronology of it (Appendix III) as a way around the difficulty. On the whole I have not sought originality of design. The chapter divisions in biographies of Clemenceau, for example, have assumed a quite fixed form because his career in fact passed through a succession of distinct phases, and I could find no compelling reason to depart from this pattern.

David S. Newhall
Centre College
Danville, Ky.
April 1990

Acknowledgments

Because of space limitations, the notes and bibliography unfortunately must omit mention of a multitude of books and articles I have found enlightening. I wish to thank their authors here and ask their forgiveness.

So many persons have aided and encouraged me over the years, and it is troubling not to be able to mention all of them here by name. Again I ask forgiveness. Especially am I indebted to my dissertation director, H. Stuart Hughes, formerly of Harvard University, who encouraged me to go ahead on Clemenceau and saw the project through with his habitual kindness and cheerful patience; to Clemenceau's son, the late Michel Clemenceau, his grandsons Pierre Clemenceau and the late Georges Clemenceau II, and his great-grandsons Georges Clemenceau III (and his wife, Isabel) and Paul Clemenceau for their gracious hospitality, cordiality, and frank speaking; to the late Georges Wormser and his sons Marcel and André, together with Mme. Lise Devinat and others on the staff of the Musée Clemenceau, where I spent many long and happy hours; to professors Jean-Baptiste Duroselle, David R. Watson, and Jack D. Ellis for their interest, generous acknowledgments, and professional advice; to Dr. Jeanne Gilmore O'Brien for gladly sharing with me her enthusiasm and her unequalled knowledge of Clemenceau's family and the early Republican movement; to Prof. Charles G. Vahlkamp and Linda Leppig of Centre College for assistance with translations; to professors Harold S. Schultz, Robert V. Daniels, Wolfe W. Schmokel, and the late Paul D. Evans of the University of Vermont, mentors and treasured friends; to Prof. Samuel B. Hand of the University of Vermont for helping me through some hard times; to Prof. Patrick H. Hutton, my successor at Vermont and editor-in-chief of the uniquely informative *Historical Dictionary of the Third French Republic* (1986), for his professional support and his valuable suggestions on an earlier version of my manuscript; to Mr. Arthur M. Jester, Jr., and professors Michael F. Hamm, Walter B.

Nimocks, Paul L. Cantrell, Charles R. Lee, Jr., and Carol E. Bastian, all of
Centre College, who read all or portions of the manuscript at various stages
and never ceased to be there when I needed them; to Mr. and Mrs. J.
William Kemper for their friendship and generosity over many years; to John
Rupnow, Alice Rivers, Douglas Flaming and the staff of the Edwin Mellen
Press; and to my students in the Senior Seminar in History for good-
naturedly listening to my ramblings about this project.

I hasten to add that of course all errors of fact, vagaries of
interpretation, or infelicities of style must be laid at my door.

I have also been the beneficiary of institutional support, for which I
give sincere thanks: to the American Philosophical Society's Penrose Fund
for helping to defray microfilming expenses; the Shell Oil Company for
grants under the Shell Assists program; the National Endowment for the
Humanities for travel grants and released-time expenses; the faculty research
committees and deans at Centre College and the University of Vermont for
their patience and repeated grants of money and time, with special thanks to
Dean Leonard M. DiLillo; the librarians of the Bibliothèque Nationale, the
University of Paris--Nanterre, the Library of Congress, the Hoover
Institution on War, Revolution, and Peace, the University of California--
Berkeley, Harvard University, the University of Vermont, the University of
Cincinnati, the University of Kentucky, and the wonderfully efficient and
obliging staff at Centre College under the direction of John R. May, Stanley
R. Campbell, and Robert E. Glass; and to Hilda Hunstad and Patsy McAfee
for secretarial services cheerfully rendered in season and out.

Last in mention but first in my heart I give thanks to my parents, Dr.
and Mrs. Chester A. Newhall, for all their help over the years, and above all
to a good and loving wife, Edna, and five beautiful children, all of whom have
borne with me while I was so often across the Atlantic in another man's life.

Chronology

1841	Born at Mouilleron-en-Pareds (Vendée), 28 September
1852-58	Attends the lycée at Nantes
1858-61	Student and intern at the Nantes Preparatory School of Medicine and Pharmacology
1861-65	Student at the Faculty of Medicine of the University of Paris
1861-62	Contributor to *Le Travail* and *Le Matin*; briefly jailed at Mazas Prison; meets Blanqui
1865	Doctor of Medicine; *De la génération des éléments anatomiques*
1865-69	In America, with occasional visits back to France; articles for *Le Temps*
1869	Marries Mary Elizabeth Plummer; moves back to the Vendée
1870-71	Mayor of Montmartre during the siege of Paris and the outbreak of the Commune
1871-85	Actively practices medicine in Montmartre
1871-76	Member, secretary, and president of the Paris Municipal Council
1876-85	Deputy from Montmartre-Clignancourt
1880-97	Publisher and Political Director of *La Justice*
1882	Helps bring down the Gambetta and Freycinet ministries
1883-85	Opposes Ferry's colonial policy
1885-89	Deputy from the Var; the rise and fall of General Boulanger
1887	The Wilson-Grévy Affair and the "Historic Nights"
1889-93	Deputy from Draguignan (Var)
1892	Divorces wife; accused of corruption and treason by Déroulède

1893	Panama Canal Company investigations; the Norton Affair; defeated for re-election
1894-1902	Journalist; publishes several collections of articles, including *La mêlée sociale* and *Le grand Pan*, a play, and a novel
1897-99	Editorialist for *L'Aurore*; the Dreyfus Case
1898	The Zola trial
1901-2	Publisher of *Le Bloc*
1902-20	Senator from the Var
1903-6	Editor of *L'Aurore*; height of the anticlerical campaign
1905	Fall of Delcassé; separation of church and state
1906	Minister of the interior in Sarrien's cabinet; the Courrières (Pas-de-Calais) mine disaster; Great Debate with Jaurès
1906-9	First ministry: minister of the interior
1907	Midi winegrowers' revolt; trouble with public employees' unions; Moroccan intervention begins; an income tax bill presented
1908	Draveil-Vigneux strike violence; the Casablanca Deserters' crisis
1909	Postal strike; the Bosnian crisis settled; the ministry falls
1910	Lecture tour in Argentina, Brazil, and Uruguay; the Rochette inquiry
1912	Overthrows Caillaux on the Franco-German Morocco treaty
1913	Overthrows Briand; opposes Poincaré's election as president
1913-14	Publisher of *L'Homme Libre*
1914-17	Publisher of *L'Homme Enchaîné*; opposes the government's conduct of the war
1915-17	President of the Senate commissions on foreign affairs and the army
1917	Attacks Malvy and the "defeatists"; spy scandals
1917-20	Second ministry: minister of war

1918	Arrest of Caillaux; the Czernin Affair; last offensives by the Germans, and the Chemin des Dames crisis; intervention in the Russian Revolution; victorious offensives and the Armistice
1919-20	The Paris Peace Conference; the Treaty of Versailles
1920	Defeated for the presidency; trip to Egypt
1920-21	Trip to South and Southeast Asia
1922	Visits the United States to plead against isolation
1926	Open Letter to President Coolidge; *Démosthène*
1927	*Au soir de la pensée*
1928	*Claude Monet: Les nymphéas*
1929	*Grandeur et misères d'une victoire* written; dies in Paris, 24 November; buried at Le Colombier, near Mouchamps (Vendée)

CHAPTER I

Son of the Vendée
(1841-1858)

South of the peninsula of Brittany and the port of Nantes on France's Atlantic coast lies a region still little known by outsiders. Although it contains four distinct sub-regions--Coast, Marsh, Plain, and Bocage (broken granitic hills and hedgerow)--this three thousand square-mile extension of the ancient province of Poitou gradually had assumed an identity of its own well before its official baptism (1790) by the National Assembly during the Great Revolution as the department of the Vendée. The Revolution further intensified this identity, for no part of France was more torn by strife. Stubborn, proud, hard-working, prone to extremes of belief or scepticism, the Vendeans fought the soldiers of the Republic and Napoleon with unsurpassed ferocity, and they fought each other, brother against brother, townsman against peasant, republican "Blues" against royalist "Whites." Today, after two centuries come and gone, it is said that ballots still turn up in elections there, no matter what the issue, marked simply "Le Roi" (The King),[1] humble witnesses to a rear-guard resistance to modern ways still to be found in the outbacks of the old Celtic world of Brittany, Ireland, and Wales.

II

Georges-Eugène-Benjamin Clemenceau was a Blue by inheritance and conviction. By 1841, the year of his birth, the Vendée had ceased to

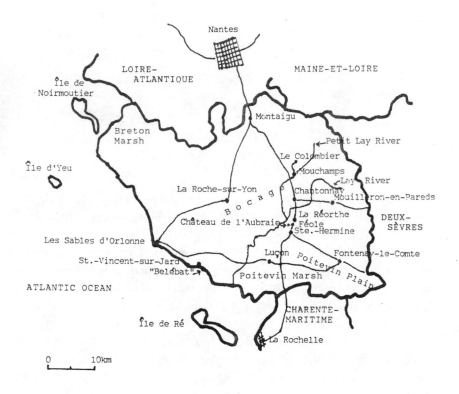

THE DEPARTMENT OF THE VENDÉE

trouble France's rulers.[2] Memories of the Revolutionary Wars smouldered, and around the hearths the old tales could still excite shudders, but the flame had gone out. The child born on 28 September to Benjamin and Emma Clemenceau at the home of Emma's father in the Bocage village of Mouilleron-en-Pareds ("in Paradise") entered a quiet corner of the world during a quiet year. It was a world which would be vastly transformed during his long life, near the end of which he would find himself shaping its destinies as president of the Paris Peace Conference of 1919-20 (the largest such gathering in history) and one of the three most powerful men alive. One can readily make a case that the three--Woodrow Wilson, David Lloyd George, and Clemenceau--and all the other men and women still living who had been born in the middle third of the nineteenth century had witnessed more profound changes in more spheres of life than any generation before or since. If charged with meeting the problems of the day, they could be expected to do so with minds prepared to accept change and to believe that the future held virtually unlimited promise for mankind. On the other hand, it should be no surprise if they were to respond now and again in ways that show they had been forced to digest too much change too soon. Both dispositions were especially true of Clemenceau, easily the senior of the three. (Wilson was born in 1856, Lloyd George in 1863.)

"A time of great change": the phrase has become so banal that it is easy to forget what lies behind it. The generation that passed away in the 1920s and '30s in Europe and North America was living in a world powered by internal-combustion engines and electrical turbines and linked by cable systems, radios, telephones, railway networks, hard-surface roads, automobiles, ocean liners, dirigibles, and airplanes. It was a world boasting motion pictures, phonographs, vaccines for diseases, anesthesia for operations, machine guns, long-range rifled artillery, tanks, submarines, poison gas, chemical pesticides and fertilizers, agricultural power-machinery, refrigerated food, central heating, electric lights, reinforced-concrete skyscrapers, and synthetic fabrics, and assaulted by Freudian psychology, Einsteinian physics, atonal music, jazz, abstract art, and stream-of-consciousness novels. Nothing whatever of this had existed when they were born, or at most the barest beginnings. Moreover, while this physical and cultural upheaval was taking place, the passing generation had seen the West achieve outright domination of all Asia, Africa, and the Pacific isles save for Japan, which had rocketed to Great Power status after two centuries of self-imposed isolation. And the transformation of politics had been nearly as dramatic. Everywhere, self-government was advancing, even in the colonies, and democracy was clearly ascendant, history's greatest war having just been fought to make the world safe for it for all time to come.

All this would have been past imagining in Mouilleron-en-Pareds in 1841, or for that matter in Nantes, where the Clemenceaus lived the better part of the time. Nantes would not see a railroad until 1851; the 230-mile trip to Paris still took a good (really, very bad) forty-eight hours by the best stage, while freight wagons needed sixteen days. But the railroad-building fever had struck, and completed trackage in France would increase from c.350 miles in 1842 to c.1050 in 1847 and c.5,000 in 1860. The industrial revolution was at last making serious headway--well behind England's and very little in western France, though the Société Industrielle de Nantes (1830) was doing what it could to drum up support--with steam engines increasing from 2,450 in 1839 to an encouraging 4,853 by 1847. The French population, more than three-quarters of it living in villages of fewer than two thousand inhabitants, was growing, but at a modest rate, and had reached 34 million, marginally larger than that of the Germanies or the Austrian Empire yet still far ahead of Great Britain's 18.5 million and the United States' 17.1 million (which included 2.5 million slaves) and still the largest in Europe except for the Russian Empire's estimated 57 million. The decline in France's comparative standing in population during his lifetime would be one of the most significant realities Clemenceau would have to confront. The unifications of Italy and Germany in the 1860s--the former containing by 1918 a population only slightly less than France's and the latter's more than two-thirds greater--the surge of Great Britain's population well beyond parity with France, the explosions of the American and Russian populations, and the addition to the club of Great Powers of Japan, whose population surpassed Great Britain's, were facts that would force the French to face some deeply disquieting implications about their country's role in the twentieth century.

But 1841, to return, was a quiet year. A few men of note were born-- Clemenceau, the most eminent, but also a prince of Wales, the future Edward VII, to young Victoria and Albert, wed the previous year; Adm. John ("Jackie") Fisher, prophet and promoter of "dreadnought" fleets; Canada's Sir Wilfred Laurier; Oliver Wendell Holmes, Jr., "the Great Dissenter"; composers Emmanuel Chabrier and Antonin Dvořák; Henry Morton Stanley, who "found" David Livingstone; the fathers of plant ecology (Johannes Warming) and reinforced-concrete architecture (Otto Wagner); and Benoît Coquelin, the first "Cyrano de Bergerac." Notable deaths were even fewer: a president of the United States, William Henry Harrison, a month after his inauguration; a Russian poet and novelist, Mikhail Lermontov; a pioneer in surgery, Sir Astley Cooper; and a ghost from the Reign of Terror, Bertrand de Barère. James Fenimore Cooper published his first Leatherstocking tale, *The Deerslayer*, Emerson his first series of essays, Schumann his first symphony, *Punch* and the *New York Tribune* their first editions, and Dickens another bestseller, *The Old Curiosity Shop*. Thomas Cook arranged his first tour, the first wagon train to use the Oregon Trail lurched out of Lawrence, Kansas, a rapidly rising thirty-two-year-old attorney in Springfield, Illinois, Abraham Lincoln, tried his first case involving the rights of slaves, P. T. Barnum opened a freak and curio show called "The American Museum," Victor Hugo got elected, finally, to the Académie Française, a female was granted a university degree in the United States, Karl Marx received his doctorate, William Ewart Gladstone joined his first cabinet, and John Tyler entered upon four forgettable years as president. The peace of the world was somewhat perturbed, however, when one Adolphe Sax invented the saxophone.

A *tour d'horizon* of politics and international affairs that year would have turned up little to disturb one's sleep. A decade had passed since a spate of revolts had challenged the settlement reached at Vienna a quarter of a century ago. It would be seven more years before a new round of revolts (far more serious this time) would break out and a dozen years before "the Long Peace" among the Great Powers would be ended by the Crimean War.

A nasty crisis provoked by the behavior of Egypt's remarkable governor, Mehemet Ali, toward his lord, the sultan of the ailing Ottoman Empire, had briefly threatened war between France and England a year ago, but France had wisely backed off, and signature of the Straits Convention had proved that the Powers were still determined to compose their disputes peaceably. In England the Chartists and anti-Corn Law leaguers were warming up their agitations for broader suffrage rights and cheaper food but withal setting an example of orderly conduct. If the Irish were restless (nothing new), the potato crop was still good. Portugal and Spain, "ruled" by incompetent queens, had suffered chronic instability and insurrections for a generation, but the Powers much preferred not to get involved in their incomprehensible quarrels. Some Italian states had witnessed abortive Mazzini-inspired disorders of late. But the peninsula seemed unmovable, a desert of reactionary rule by Austrian-connected grand dukes, kings Ferdinand II, *il Bomba* ("the Bomb"), in Naples and Charles Albert in Piedmont-Sardinia, and Pope Gregory XVI, a dyed-in-the-purple medievalist, in the Papal States.

To the east, the Austrian Empire and its white-coated army, "Europe's Fire Brigade," was standing at the ready to keep order, directed as it had been for the past thirty-two years by a man whose very name breathed a promise of changeless security: Prince Klemens Wenzel Nepomuk Lothar von Meternich-Winneburg-Beilstein. The great statesman had put together the coalition that had brought down Napoleon and restored the world to sanity at the Congress of Vienna, and ever since no threat to its stability had escaped his practiced eye. He was aging, however, and his emperor, Ferdinand, was a feeble-minded young man who had announced at his accession in 1835, "I am the emperor now and I want noodles!" The Germanies proper were loosely drawn together under Austria's presidency in the German Confederation, a sprawling legatee of the late Holy Roman Empire comprised of some thirty-five states and four Free Cities. It included most (but, typically, not all) of the Kingdom of Prussia, a Great Power lately fallen on shallow times and from 1840 ruled by a romantic in love with the Middle Ages, Frederick William IV, who honestly believed God vouchsafed to kings a wisdom He withheld from common mortals. Other states in the Bund, a daring five of them rejoicing in timid constitutions graciously bestowed by their rulers, ranged from small kingdoms like Saxony or Bavaria to wafer-sized principalities like Schwartzburg-Sondershausen or Schaumburg-Lippe (not to be confused, of course, with Lippe-Detmold or Lippe-Biesterfeld) governed by princely absolutists with interminable titles, big castles, miniscule armies, and flotillas of marriageable progeny. From the Alps, groaned the poet Heine, one could hear the Germans snoring at their rulers' feet.

In the north, the stubbornest of Dutchmen, William I of The Netherlands, had abdicated the previous year, to general relief, rather than countenance domestic reform after having wasted ten years refusing to recognize the secession of the Kingdom of Belgium, an "independent and perpetually neutral state" the Powers had solemnly sworn to respect. The provincial diets of Denmark as yet had only advisory powers, but the new king since 1839, Christian VIII, was ambling ahead with reforms. The same could not be said of one of Napoleon's former marshals now ruling Sweden and its frontier dependency of Norway as Charles XIV. The Swedes had lost Finland to Russia in the Napoleonic Wars, but long before that they had resigned from the Great Power game.

Next to Metternich, Nicholas I, Tsar of All the Russians, was the staunchest defender of the international status quo. In appearance and action the model autocrat of his day--physically imposing, unbending in principles, hard-working, honest, and when necessary (as it usually seemed to be) ruthless--he ruled an empire nearly as large (and to outsiders nearly as unknown) as the moon. More than 40 million of the some 57 million "souls" in his domains were serfs. Happily for the equanimity of his neighbors, he had confined his territorial expansions to faraway places like the Caucasus or the Khirghiz Steppes, except for a parcel at the mouth of the Danube and an occupation of the principalities of Moldavia and Wallachia (the core of a future Romania) after a short war with the ever-unpopular Turks. All the peoples and powers to the west felt some uneasiness at his looming presence, which his sickening repression of a revolt by his Polish subjects in 1831 had done nothing to abate. But none of his fellow sovereigns would deny that this grandson, son, and husband of German princesses who himself had married off all his six sons and daughters to German royal or princely houses was behaving abroad like a "good European."

The Balkans, destined to be the fount of so much woe during Clemenceau's lifetime, were ruled by the Ottoman and Austrian empires. After a heroic struggle that had roiled international waters through the twenties, the Greeks (some of them, anyhow) had established a small, very shaky state presided over by (inevitably) a German princeling, and the landlocked principality of Serbia, a nest of wondrously complicated feuds, was edging toward full independence from the Turks. But otherwise the exotic peoples of the peninsula were barely beginning to learn their own histories and catch the fever of nationalism. In 1840 a monk translated the Bible into Bulgarian: one had to begin somewhere.

If the Balkans must have seemed remote and unthreatening, how much so the rest of the world. In Africa, France was slowly getting the upper hand against the Bedouin tribes in Algeria in campaigns by Marshal Bugeaud and the fledgling Foreign Legion and starting to penetrate the western and equatorial regions. The British, meanwhile, were establishing themselves at Zanzibar and watching the Boers trek north to the Orange River country and the Transvaal to escape their domination at the Cape. Virtually everywhere else in sub-Saharan Africa, any locale more than a hundred miles from the coast was literally *terra incognita* to whites. In Asia, the United Company of Merchants of England Trading to the East Indies was ruling in desultory fashion by leave of Parliament amidst the debris of the Mogul Empire in India. The Afghans were stoutly resisting British incursion from the Khyber Pass (the First Afghan War), as were, less successfully, the Burmese (between the First and Second Burmese wars), the Manchu rulers of China (the First Opium War), and the Maori chiefs of New Zealand, where the first colonists were scrambling ashore. In the Americas, the Act of Union (1840) had brought Upper and Lower Canada together after some riots and small-scale fighting, and Secretary of State Daniel Webster was waxing hopeful that the debut of Sir Robert Peel's second cabinet at Whitehall boded well for settlement of the Aroostook County War over the Maine-New Brunswick boundary. Admittedly, relations with Mexico were becoming worrisome because of the setting up of an independent state at its expense by Yanqui settlers in Texas. Elsewhere in Latin America, the successors of the liberators from Portuguese and Spanish rule were doing little to enhance the reputation of republicanism.

Indeed, at Clemenceau's birth almost everywhere one turned republicanism was in the doldrums. Even the Swiss Confederation, the sole republic in Europe (unless one counted Andorra, San Marino, and Crakow, which nobody did), was looking as if it would dissolve because of quarrels between Catholic and Protestant cantons over its constitution. True, a brilliant young French aristocrat, Alexis de Tocqueville, had recently (1835) published some acute observations about how democracy was faring in the Great Experiment underway in the United States, a democracy with human slaves, no less, and had had some positive things to say, but he also had questioned some of its reputed virtues and confessed scepticism about its suitability for Europe. In France, republicanism had suffered inglorious defeat in 1830 when the overthrow of the Bourbon monarch Charles X had brought only a substitution of ruling houses instead of a reborn republic. The Orleanist pretender, Louis-Philippe, had been deftly inserted as a "citizen-king" and had survived a ten-year train of bumbling Bourbon, Bonapartist, and Republican plots and assassination attempts which had only earned discredit for their instigators. Not that his own credit had risen so very high: in 1840 he had sought to reflect some light on his colorless regime by having Napoleon's "ashes" brought back from St. Helena in garish pomp to be interred in the Invalides. Shrewd, voluble, corpulent ("the Pear," he was called), and settling into a profound complacency, his government presided over by a Napoleonic relic, Marshal Soult, and run by an intelligent, enlightened, but equally complacent professor of history, François Guizot, Louis-Philippe reigned over a country whose parliament was composed of a chamber of peers named by the king and a chamber of deputies elected by the 200,000 wealthiest men in the land. (Even the Bourbons at least had had to concede a constitution.) Needless to say, in their eyes a democratic republic reeked of demogoguery, guillotines, and blood in the streets.

Yet republicanism was not dead. Every town and city in Europe housed adherents, and in France the Republicans had built up an impressively large underground movement. Despite surface appearances, the early forties in fact were to mark the beginnings of movements which would explode in a wild year of revolts all across the continent in 1848-49 and herald, notwithstanding their universal failures, the coming conquests of democracy. But in 1841 belief still had to be strong indeed merely to survive.

III

Nowhere in France was this more true than in the Vendée. The fact, nevertheless, that republicanism was rejected by the vast majority of its inhabitants did not cause Clemenceau to reject or despise the Vendée.[3] To have done so would have meant at the least an alienation from all his family roots, for both the Clemenceaus and the Gautreaus were Vendeans as far back as the records go. Although he scoffed at genealogies and seemed to know relatively little about his family history, he took an almost perverse pride in his "backward" native region. In 1906 at a banquet during a triumphal tour back home as the new minister of the interior, he rhapsodized (to the wry amusement of the Paris press):

> ...thanks to our combative temperament we were, with our Breton cousins, the last battalion square of the Celts, the Gauls facing out to both the militias of Rome and the hordes of Germany, often defeated, never submissive....It was on our land that the Moorish invasion was stopped [at Tours, in A.D. 732].
> Our life was one of wars against the invader. There are no finer Frenchmen than we....Men of Armorica and Vendée, we are the purest of the Gauls, the sons of those who did not bow down before Caesar....[4]

Needless to say, the earliest notices of the Vendée Clemenceaus begin well after the age of Vercingetorix or Attila the Hun. From the late fifteenth century they show the family acquiring properties from which its branches took their names. Father to son, the Clemenceaus of Le Colombier were country squires, physicians, apothecaries, and office holders. Altogether they became quite typical specimens of a stratum of provincial society which emerged during the Revolution to become the backbone of the country's governing class. Georges' great-grandfather, Pierre-Paul (1749-1825), a squire-physician--son of the sieur du Colombier, Pierre-Benjamin (1709-82) who was also a high-court lawyer (*avocat au Parlement*)--threw in his lot with who was also a high-court lawyer (*avocat au Parlement*)--threw in his lot with the Revolution and served after 1791 as a departmental councilor and mayor of Mouchamps. After participating in the Vendée wars as a physician with the Republic's Army of the West, he was named sub-prefect at Montaigu in 1800 by Napoleon and served for a term (1806-10) as a deputy in the Corps Législatif. His willingness to accept the Napoleonic regime was regarded by the family in later years as an embarrassment, but in the context of the times it was understandable. Like so many Republican patriots, he viewed Napoleon as the Soldier of the Revolution, and as sub-prefect he labored to reconcile Blues and Whites and to repair the physical and moral damage the Vendée had suffered. His son, Georges' grandfather Jean-Paul-Benjamin (1777-1860), likewise a squire-physician, was a longtime mayor of the small township of La Réorthe, but his attitude typified the Restoration years: he had seen enough of the Revolution as a youth and wanted to hear no more of it. Georges recalled him as an odd sort, dour and stilted, who was sometimes to be seen inspecting his lands and cattle in a top hat and white tie.[5]

The Gautreaus, Georges' maternal side, were solid, honorable folk but distinctly below the Clemenceaus in social rank. Artisans, small merchants, and farmers dressed the family tree. François (1790-1872), Georges' grandfather, was a minor landowner and estate manager whose wife, Louise David, had died in 1823 at age thirty-three. He was sufficiently distinguished, however, to have been named mayor of his native village of Mouilleron-en-Pareds in 1832 by Louis-Philippe's regime during the crisis provoked by the madcap attempt of the Bourbon duchesse de Berri to rouse the Vendée royalists to support the claim of her young son ("Henri V") to the throne, and was the first mayor of Mouilleron in two centuries who was not a member of the aristocratic Lattre de Tassigny family. Georges remembered him affectionately as "a gentle soul" who imparted to him a love of country living but who also hoped that he would someday be a deputy in Parliament: "How many times, years later, I thought of him while standing before those six hundred asses' heads. And that memory warmed my heart!"[6]

The Gautreaus added another minority tradition to Georges' inheritance, for they were Protestants, as were most of Mouilleron's inhabitants. Since the Protestants almost unanimously supported the strong in the Vendée, but the Huguenots had struck early roots there and clung on with proverbial Vendean stubbornness despite the fall (in 1636) of La Rochelle, the stronghold on the Vendée's southern border, and the persecutions following Louis XIV's revocation (1685) of the Edict of Nantes, which had granted them legal tolerance. Some Clemenceaus had adopted Protestantism early on, and several had run afoul of the authorities for expressing heretical opinions, but the last Protestant in Georges' direct line had died in 1696 after having been forced to renounce his faith. The Gautreaus, however, stayed firm, and Georges' mother remained devout for life. His father, on the other hand, had been baptized as a Catholic because his mother was a Catholic; but he had become an outspoken atheist and anticlerical--doubtless influenced to some degree by his agnostic father (Georges' grandfather), whose Catholicism finally would become too suspect to earn him a church burial--and exacted a promise from Georges' mother that their children would not be baptized. To his distress, his eldest daughter, Emma, had herself baptized as a Protestant at her marriage, but the rest of the children appear to have stayed untainted.[7]

Paul-Benjamin Clemenceau (1810-97)[*] and Emma-Eucharis-Sophie Gautreau (1817-1903) were married by a Protestant pastor in 1839 after four years of strained negotiations between the two families. Benjamin's father would have had no trouble finding reasons to oppose the match, beginning with the Gautreaus' lower social status, which doubtless translated into a modest or non-existent dowry. But the biggest stumbling block apparently was the Gautreaus' Protestantism. Benjamin's Catholic mother died in 1836, but his mother's mother survived her (to 1849) and stoutly continued the opposition. François Gautreau's Republican sympathies also may have come into the picture because they might only exacerbate a long-existent tension between Benjamin and his apolitical father due to Benjamin's political activity. The marriage finally having been consummated, Benjamin's father remained unfriendly toward Emma until the birth of her third child eleven years later. As for the widower François, on the other hand, he may have dreaded losing his daughter's company, for she and Benjamin intended to

---

[*] He went by the name Benjamin; some sources reverse the names. He had a brother, Paul (Jean-Paul, 1816-58), nicknamed "the Marquis" for his reactionary opinions.

live in Nantes, where he would practice medicine. But they agreed to spend summers and a month in the autumn at Benjamin's father's residence, the Château de l'Aubraie, which was only a half-day's ride from Mouilleron.

IV

Hence it happened that Emma bore Georges and his older sister at her father's home during autumn sojourns in the Vendée rather than in Nantes--nor at l'Aubraie, for it was a custom among bourgeois families for the woman to go to her parents' home to give birth. François' house, a stone building on a side street uphill off the square in Mouilleron, today houses a bakery shop on the ground floor; it bears a plaque, but the upstairs birthplace is closed to the public.

In due course Georges became the natural leader of a decidedly vigorous brood which remained close in loyalty if not in age nor always in harmony. Emma was born in 1840; then followed Georges (1841), Adrienne (1850), Sophie (1853), Paul (1856), and Albert (1861). All married save for Adrienne, who was crippled with a club foot.[8]

Few reminiscences of life in Nantes remain in the record. Instead, family memories and affections centered on l'Aubraie. Located 140 meters down a country lane leading west from the south end of Féole (formerly Féaule)--a village in the *commune* of La Réorthe (pop. 600) some four kilometers north of Ste.-Hermine (pop. 2,300) on the La Rochelle-Chantonnay-Nantes highway--this country home, still a regional landmark, was a striking setting for a childhood: a small castle complete with towers, double wall, moat, and drawbridge, ancient even by French standards, the oldest tower reputed to date from the eleventh century.[9] Today the château, restored at great expense in time and money, is a lovely, comfortable residence, but in Clemenceau's youth it lacked any hint of luxury and was dank and gloomy, with huge cold rooms, crumbling walls, dark passageways, and refuse in the moat. (Clemenceau's grandson Georges II, who carried out the bulk of the restoration, remarked that moats need cleaning out every two hundred years or so.) In compensation, the place invited outdoor pursuits, for in addition to the usual gardens, orchards, and fields there was fine hunting and fishing to be had in a full range of settings--woods and hills nearby, the Grand Lay and its tributaries, the plains which begin at Ste.-Hermine, and ten kilometers farther the Poitevan marshes bordering the ocean.

L'Aubraie had come to the Clemenceaus by marriage.[10] It had belonged to a noble family, the Marsillacs, but after they emigrated during the Revolution, the state confiscated it (making it a *bien national*) and then sold it to Françoise-Henriette Greffard Joubert (1761-1849), Georges' great-grandmother mentioned above as an opponent of his parents' marriage. This remarkable woman was a granddaughter of a manager of the estate, and her late husband, Jean Joubert, who had become the Republican mayor of La Réorthe, had managed it from 1787 until his death early in 1793. In March that year, when the Vendée civil war erupted, she had courageously faced down marauding Blues and Whites and saved the château from burning, though not its furniture and archives. Some time around 1796 she bought it. The Clemenceaus entered the picture in 1809 when her elder daughter, Marie-Thérèse-Gabrielle (1787-1836), married Jean-Paul-Benjamin, Georges' grandfather. When Françoise died in 1849 he inherited it, and on his death in 1860 it passed in entirety to Georges' father, Benjamin, whose younger brother, Paul, had died childless in 1858. Georges remembered Mother Joubert with admiration--a formidable tiny woman in Breton peasant dress lugging around a big stick as she had since the Vendée wars and directing l'Aubraie's daily regime.

That l'Aubraie had come to them by inheritance was something the Clemenceaus emphasized, for as prominent Blues they were sensitive to accusations that they had profited from the Revolution by buying up nationalized properties--which in fact they, like a host of others, had done routinely. Probably as a consequence of this sensitivity, the family's oral tradition about the matter became cloudy. However much the Clemenceaus owed to the Revolution, nevertheless, in point of fact their prosperity had long antedated the Revolution and the Joubert inheritance.

Just how wealthy they were around the time of Georges' birth is not easy to say. In 1982 Jean Estèbe published a tantalizing fragment of evidence to the effect that in 1843 Benjamin Clemenceau, "proprietor of a château-fortress and vast domains," paid a *cens* (property tax) of 1,640 francs.[11] From what is known about the acquisition of l'Aubraie, it would seem highly unlikely that Benjamin was the "proprietor" before his father's death in 1860. The difficulty disappears, however, in light of the fact that Jean-Paul-Benjamin, like his son, went by the name Benjamin, had voting rights because of his own family lands, and thus was listed as a *propriétaire* even if he had not yet inherited l'Aubraie itself as Estèbe implies. The 1640-franc figure, assuming its accuracy, is impressive. Electors under the Orleans regime qualified by paying at least 200 francs and numbered barely 230,000 in the entire country, of whom only 57,000 paid more than 500 francs. In the Vendée about 1840 fewer than 5 persons in 1,000 qualified at 200 francs, and fewer than 200 electors paid more than 1,000 francs. In short, the family (if not Benjamin alone) would have ranked in the highest echelon and with good reason would have been regarded by most Vendeans as "rich." Georges Clemenceau, consciously or not, sought to leave a different impression. As he told Martet late in life, "...my father wasn't rich. With my uncle's money [i.e., Paul's, after his death in 1858], since my father was a good manager and economical, he was able to make ends meet."[12] The truth here was that Benjamin borrowed a great deal of money to restore l'Aubraie, was like many landowners in not being especially "cash rich," and probably "talked poor" because Georges was a poor manager, was always wanting money for his ventures, and over the years borrowed heavily from him and others.

V

Republicanism, undiluted, came to Georges Clemenceau from his father, who himself had probably begun to imbibe it as a youth from his grandfather Pierre-Paul. The latter, after his service to the Napoleonic regime, had withdrawn to the family's old country seat at Le Colombier, near Mouchamps, which during his last decade he turned into a center of Republican activity carried on by a Vendée group, with ties to the strong Republican forces in Nantes, known as the "Blues of Montaigu." His son meanwhile was living with his heiress wife at l'Aubraie, where Benjamin was born in 1810. Benjamin's political estrangement from his father may have taken root as a result of contacts with his grandfather during his schooling in Nantes. At any rate, in 1829, four years after his grandfather's death, he graduated from the lycée in Nantes and promptly set off to Paris to enroll at the Faculty of Medicine to learn the family profession but also, of more immediate interest to him, to immerse himself in Republican politics.

The years in Paris, until he received his degree in 1835, were the most stimulating and, one suspects, the most satisfying of his life. He joined a group of Breton student activists, marched in the July Days revolt of 1830, which overthrew the Bourbons, as a member of university student groups organized under the inspiration of Lafayette--a deed which earned him a Cross of July medal bestowed at a banquet in Nantes on 31 July 1831--joined a Republican organization, Les Associations Nationales, which was soon forced underground, and all in all made contact with a host of ideas and persons (among them the historian Jules Michelet and the Republican conspirator Auguste Blanqui) which were to affect the rest of his life and that, too, of his son Georges. In particular, he came under the influence of the followers of the utopian socialist Henri de Saint-Simon (1760-1825) and of a now mostly forgotten school of philosophy, Ideology, whose destiny was to serve as the link between the ideas of the eighteenth-century philosophes and the new philosophy of Positivism being propounded by Auguste Comte (1798-1857). Neither Saint-Simonianism nor Ideology was necessarily wedded to Republicanism in principle, but Benjamin grafted them to his faith. For him, Republicanism meant not only allegiance to democracy in politics but also to a belief in social and intellectual progress through scientific investigation, medical and technological advances, and a philosophical materialism which rejected all metaphysical or religious speculations, above all any emanating from the Roman Catholic Church.[13]

Benjamin Clemenceau evolved into a truly unique, even strange, man, a character whom Balzac, his contemporary, might have invented. Like his father and grandfather before him, he mostly practiced his profession in a desultory fashion, finally abandoning it altogether for life as a semi-recluse at l'Aubraie, where he settled after his father's death. Gustave Geffroy (1855-1926), one of Georges' closest friends and the author of an important biography of him, knew Benjamin in his later years. He ascribed the retirement to a growing "nervousness" which finally left him unable to bear the spectacle of human suffering before which the science of his day stood all but helpless.[14]

He was not a handsome man, his normally grave features leaving an impression of force, withdrawn and unsympathetic. This appearance, however, was somewhat misleading: his manners were refined, his air and attire even debonaire, and his "keen conversation, forthright opinions, [and] mischievous smile," Geffroy recalled, "were altogether charming." He loved the arts and practiced several (music, painting, lithography) with respectable skill. Much in him bespoke a civilized, sensitive person who carefully guards the inner man. He was a reader and thinker with special skills for acute observation and mercilessly frank, wittily caustic descriptions. Particularly painful to him was the ever-present gap between what men say and what they do, what is and what ought to be. He believed with all his heart in the ideals of the Revolution and resented all the more the successor regimes' betrayals. (Obsessed though he was with the Revolution, he did not collect severed heads as mementos, as rumor has lately alleged. His great-grandson Georges Clemenceau II did discover a number of skulls in a tower Benjamin had used as a study, but it is probable he had acquired them because of his interest in phrenology.[15]) Although personally courageous, he did not find in himself the attributes of a leader, and the stifling political and social conservatism of post-Napoleonic France rendered him misanthropic, disabused, and mordantly sceptical.

Benjamin's influence on his eldest son was profound. Georges testified to it on numerous occasions and in his will directed that he be buried beside his father at Le Colombier. But if father and son were close, the relationship was far from simple. When Georges was not praising him for all he had done for him, he was disposed to remember his severity and brooding rage: "My father was moving and fearsome [*terrible*]....I never saw my father, never, except in one frame of mind--anger. I never entered a room, never, where my father was without his saying to me, 'Georges, get out!' What a man!"[16] According to a story handed down in the family, in a fit of exasperation he once put Georges' misbehaving son, Michel, in a sack which he then hung from a rafter for a few hours.[17] Whatever the literal truth of such testimony, it underscores a central feature in the formation of Georges Clemenceau's personality: the imposing figure of a father whose love could not be truly doubted but who found it difficult to show spontaneous affection or approval. Benjamin gazed down on his son like the portraits of Robespierre and Saint-Just on the dining-room wall, reminding him of the pitiless truths that govern men's lives. Weakness may, perhaps, be forgiven; it can be no excuse.

Hence the leitmotif of Clemenceau's early career has been said to be a protracted struggle to achieve a psychological identity independent of his father.[18] Certainly, such a father could have been the ruination of an intelligent and sensitive boy, which Georges was. Yet, despite unpredictable tackings between harshness and indulgence, Benjamin somehow succeeded in communicating his sincere love. In time he and his son became intimate, if not always congenial, comrades. Benjamin followed his development with intense concern, while Georges looked forward to his letters and to visits back home for hunting trips in the marshes and horseback rides along the mist-filled sunken roads of the Bocage.

In his early years, if probably less importantly later on, Georges' mother supplied the visible affection which his father denied. The ambivalence in his reminiscences about his father is missing in those concerning his mother. In this he conformed entirely with the men of his time and milieu, who almost uniformly, whether sincerely or obeying custom, portrayed their mothers as angelic protectresses from imposing, authoritarian fathers. Probably the only human being about whom he never spoke an unkind word, she was "my dear mother," a saint, the harbor in every storm, the calming presence in the household of a difficult man and his headstrong children. Unselfish to the last degree, she gave herself entirely to those around her, seldom venturing outside the house on her own and permitting herself no indulgences. While gentle to a fault, she nonetheless possessed a trait which strongly marked her progeny: an unbending, undiscourageable will to accomplish her purposes. Her patience was long, and Georges often tested it as a child: "My poor mother, I scared her. Ah! that's because I've always had a rotten character. No sooner born than I wanted what I wanted."[19] He knew she suffered and yet forgave. If he experienced feelings of guilt as a boy because of an often distant, unsympathetic father, he also may have felt some guilt toward a mother whom he tried and who did not deserve an unkindness.

VI

At some point after returning from Paris and medical school, Benjamin fled the constricting atmosphere around his father at l'Aubraie for life at Le Colombier. The marriage to Emma finally won approval, and the couple then settled in Nantes at an apartment at 22, rue Calvaire, in a fashionable downtown quarter. (The locale no longer exists, having been obliterated by Allied bombers in World War II.)

Georges' education, as that of all his brothers and sisters, began at home with his mother, who the family tradition says was passionately fond of teaching and learned Latin for the purpose. In the autumn of 1852, after a year at the Pension Montfort, a private school, he entered the lycée in Nantes (founded in 1808) and until 1858 endured the tiresome rigors of a Victorian classical education. It is indicative of his good fortune that less than five percent of boys his age received some secondary schooling and less than two percent completed the classical curriculum, the sole entryway to the professions. (Girls were denied secondary education until the latter 1860s.) His education also reflected his assured, prominent social standing, though less explicitly, for nearly half the graduates of provincial lycées and municipal *collèges* were from modest and occasionally humble families. And if he attended a lycée rather than a (less prestigious) *collège*, he lived at home, which avoided the expensive board and room costs of the more highly regarded Paris and university-town lycées. It also kept him under his father's eye.[20]

His school records suggest that he was one of the brightest pupils but unsettled and unsettling. Like many boys in the lycées of the time, he rebelled against the inhuman discipline and hidebound curriculum. His professors complained that he was "a very erratic scholar in his work, impetuous at play, and impertinent *[peu sage]* in class."[21] His father upbraided him and sent him off to the Vendée in the summers to work as a clerk-messenger for a notary to keep him out of mischief, but he sympathized enough with the boy's boredom with the antiquated methods of the school to supply him with a forbidden "pony" to help him through struggles with Demosthenes. Time softened Clemenceau's memories of his school days. In 1922 he told the assembled students of the newly renamed Lycée

Clemenceau that he had been "more than glad" to leave the place and that it was only later that he had acquired a passion for the classics he had resisted there: "I realized...that all the little vexations I had encountered were only the result of my own doing....To know for yourselves, without waiting for the future, the fortune of your efforts, resolutely roll up your sleeves and make your destiny."[22]

Georges's political education also began in Nantes.[23] A wall of hostility and recrimination divided a pretentious and still-monied nobility from the commercial and professional classes, and the clergy, thoroughly conservative, was growing in influence. Republicans, or men reputed as such, in fact owned a good deal of property in the Vendée, but they were a small if active minority in the city (whose population numbered about 95,000), where only four "démocrates modérés" and four "démocrates exaltés" sat on the thirty-eight-member municipal council in 1846. The most prominent "exalté" was Dr. Ange Guépin (1805-73), a physician inspired by Saint-Simonianism who was working for economic, social, and educational reforms to benefit the lives of the petit bourgeoisie and the working classes and thus hasten the day of the "final liberation" of mankind. Republicans nationwide, however, tended to be organized at two levels, public and clandestine, and Georges's father was more involved in the latter--indeed, to the point that some claimed, inaccurately, that he was the "chef de résistance" in the West. The most likely candidate, if there was a "chief," was Michel Rocher (1800-61), a kitchenware manufacturer and inventor.[24]

Despite this bubbling activity, the local Republicans did not organize a political banquet as part of the nationwide campaign featuring such protest affairs which finally triggered the insurrection in Paris on 22-24 February 1848. When word arrived of the fall of Louis-Philippe and the proclamation of a republic, however, Rocher formed a "Commission Démocratique" with Guépin, Benjamin Clemenceau, and Victor Mangin, the publisher of the *National de l'Ouest*, which Benjamin was helping to support, and proclaimed the Republic around the city. Emma held young Georges up to the window to see the demonstrators pass, and afterward there was a ceremonial planting of a Liberty Tree, which he recalled many years later for his readers:

> Fournier, curate of the church of Saint-Nicolas and later bishop of Nantes, gravely blessed it. Legend would even have it that later he used a bottle of vitriol to give an edge to his blessing. Both the priest and the tree are dead. I might have predicted it. As for liberty, I have to admit that people continue to talk of it.[25]

The Republic withered too, and in Nantes rather quickly. The municipal council (and the West generally) became more conservative after the revolution than before, with moderate liberal notables tending to combine with conservatives against the Republicans, whose cause had been badly damaged by radical demonstrations in Paris, the bloody June Days insurrection, and the election in December 1848 of Louis-Napoléon Bonaparte, Napoleon's nephew, as president. On 2 December 1851 President Bonaparte finally snuffed out the Republic with a coup, preparatory to reestablishing a Napoleonic empire. In the purge which followed, Benjamin and a Republican journalist, Gallois, publisher of the left-wing *La Démocrate Vendéen*, were briefly detained for spreading "harmful propaganda" even though the local authorities admitted they had remained "politically quiet" and played no part in the scattered uprisings that had greeted the coup.[26] Benjamin was served notice of house arrest in February 1852, which lasted until November when, although he had refused to ask for it, he was pardoned. In 1853 he again was arrested and held overnight, and l'Aubraie was searched and incriminating documents seized.[27] All told, some 25,460 persons were arrested in the post-coup sweeps-- measures which sowed a bitter harvest of hatred for the Bonapartist regime among those of Georges Clemenceau's generation whose fathers had suffered for their beliefs, a hatred which would render them implacable toward their ideological opponents after they brought the Republic back in 1871.

The 1850s, thus, were years of petty persecution and loneliness for the faithful remnant of the Republican cause in Nantes. The tough, able prefect there, Henri Chevreau, would get no argument when he boasted in 1863 that for the past ten years he had been "the absolute master" of his department.[28]

In the meantime, Georges, who had held the center of his parents' attention as a child, suffered at second hand, feeling himself outbid for his father's affection after the birth of Adrienne in 1850 and subjected to cutting words over his school work from a man who was seeing his hopes run into the sand. In 1855 a secret Republican society, La Marianne, was suppressed. Benjamin escaped implication for the time being, but three years later he would not be so lucky. The event would, in effect, end Georges' boyhood.

VII

On 15 March 1858 Benjamin and five workers were arrested in the crackdown following the attempt on Napoleon III's life by Felice Orsini, an Italian patriot. He was confined for a month and then sentenced without trial to transportation to Algeria. The shock of the event was severe. Georges' sister Emma temporarily lost her speech and memory and remained incapacitated for months. Every day the family visited the prisoner for a few minutes, separated from him by a double grill. Watchful parent that he was, Benjamin wrote careful instructions to his wife: Georges should be tutored if necessary, resume his fencing lessons, and be given permission to ride the blooded mare; and he should also read the article on Rome in a recently arrived review. "Finally," he wrote, "you know the promise you made to me and swore on your honor. I remind you of it, and if you go back on it, I will find in me the strength to curse you."[29] The promise was that she would raise the children outside the bonds of religion.

Outright disaster was averted. The prison coach took Benjamin to Marseille, but by then the authorities had decided that resentment in Nantes because of their treatment of him and the pitiful state of his daughter would do more harm than the exile of a respected man was worth. His release was nothing exceptional. The arrests had been widely targeted on "respectable" elements and had aroused great criticism.[30] Benjamin accepted his freedom, but only after warning the prefect in Marseille that his son had taken "the oath of Hannibal." This cryptic (and entirely characteristic) reference concerned an incident which had taken place at the departure from Nantes. As his handcuffed father had moved to climb into the coach, Georges, overcome with repressed rage and grief, stepped forward and murmured, "I will avenge you!" Benjamin turned and said with icy calm, "If you would avenge me, work."[31]

Of all the moments of crisis in a long and stormy life, none struck Georges Clemenceau with greater force and effect than did that farewell to his manacled father at the steps of a prison coach in Nantes.

NOTES
CHAPTER I

[1]   Conversation with Georges Clemenceau II in June 1959 at l'Aubraie. I believe it is still true although doubtless slowly fading.

[2]   On France in this period see David Pinkney, *Decisive Years in France, 1840-1847* (Princeton, NJ: Princeton University Press, 1986), and André Jardin and André-Jean Tudesq, *Restoration and Reaction, 1815-1848*, trans. Elborg Forster (Cambridge: Cambridge University Press, 1983).

[3]   Published genealogies conflict at points. The most reliable are "Les familles Clemenceau et Gautreau," *Société de l'histoire du protestantisme français. Bulletin historique et littéraire* 78 (1929):440-444; and Paul Romane-Musculus, "Généalogie des Gautreau, ascendants maternels de Georges Clemenceau," *Revue du Bas-Poitou*, nos. 2-3 (1952-1953):110-117, and no. 4 (1956):373-374.

[4]   Speech at La Roche-sur-Yon (Vendée), 30 Sept. 1906; in *Le Temps*, 1 Oct. Armorica is the ancient name for Brittany.

[5]   On his forebears here and below, the principal sources are Martet, *Clemenceau*, and Jeanne Gilmore O'Brien, "Les racines républicaines de la famille Clemenceau," *Clemenceau et la justice*. Actes du Colloque de décembre 1979 organisé pour la cinquantenaire de la mort de G. Clemenceau (Publications de la Sorbonne, 1983), pp. 39-44.

[6]   René Benjamin, *Clemenceau dans la retraite* (Librairie Plon, 1930), pp. 61-62.

[7]   Some accounts say the daughters were baptized.

[8]   See Romane-Musculus, "Généalogie des Gautreau," p. 114; and Georges Gatineau-Clemenceau, *Des pattes du Tigre aux griffes du destin* (Les Presses du Mail, 1961), p. 22.

[9]   See especially Abbé Gaillard, "L'Aubraie des Clemenceau," *Revue du Bas-Poitou*, no. 1 (1930):1-11; and Madeleine Clemenceau-Jacquemaire, *Le pot de basilic* (J. Tallandier, 1928), pp. 29-59, *passim*.

[10]   O'Brien, "Les racines républicaines de la famille Clemenceau," on which this account is based, corrects the mistaken version in Martet, *Clemenceau*, pp. 271-272, according to which Pierre-Paul's wife, Charlotte Maillot, was the daughter of "the sieur de l'Aubraie" instead of the sieur de l'Oufraie.

[11]   Jean Estèbe, *Les ministres de la République, 1871-1914* (Presses de la Fondation national des sciences, politiques, 1982), p. 238n.

[12] Martet, *Clemenceau*, p. 297. See André-Jean Tudesq, *Les grands notables en France (1840-1849): Étude historique d'une psychologie sociale*, 2 vols. (Presses Universitaires de France, 1964), 1:91, 98, 99, 135.

[13] On Saint-Simonianism in Paris and Nantes, see Dr. A. Guépin and Dr. É. Bonamy, *Nantes au XIXe siècle: Statistique topographique, industrielle et morale*. Réédition précédéé de "De l'observation de la ville comme corps social," par MM. Ph. Le Pichon et A. Supiot (Nantes: Centre de Recherche Politique, Université de Nantes, 1981), pp. 4-5 and *passim*. On the influence of the Ideologues (Condillac, Helvétius, Cabanis, Destutt de Tracy, *et al.*), see Samuel I. Applebaum, *Clemenceau, Thinker and Writer* (New York: Columbia University Press, 1948), pp. 3-6; and Claude Nicolet, *L'idée républicaine en France (1789-1924). Essai d'histoire critique* (Gallimard, 1982), pp. 115-132.

[14] Gustave Geffroy, *Georges Clemenceau, sa vie, son oeuvre*, new ed. (Librairie Larousse, 1932), pp. 10, 70-72.

[15] Dr. André Carré, "Conférence sur Clemenceau," *Société archéologique et historique de Nantes et de Loire-Atlantique: Bulletin* 116 (1979-80):12. Carré says Benjamin's grandson (more likely his great-grandson Georges Clemenceau II) confirmed this story.

[16] Benjamin, *Clemenceau dans la retraite*, pp. 59-60.

[17] Gatineau-Clemenceau, *Des pattes du Tigre*, p. 35; confirmed to me by Pierre Clemenceau, a son of Michel.

[18] See Jack D. Ellis, *The Early Life of Georges Clemenceau, 1841-1893* (Lawrence, KS: The Regents Press of Kansas, 1980), p. xvi and *passim*; also Pierre de Lacombe, "L'énigme de Clemenceau," *Revue française de psychanalyse* 12 (1948):297-309, *passim*.

[19] Benjamin, *Clemenceau dans la retraite*, p. 65. On Emma see allusions in Clemenceau-Jacquemaire, *Le pot de basilic*, pp. 158, 233, and *passim*; and Dr. A. Raiga-Clemenceau, "Le vrai caractère de Clemenceau," *Nouvelles archives hospitalières*, 1973, no. 2, pp. 45-47.

[20] See Patrick Harrigan, *Mobility, Elites, and Education in French Society of the Second Empire* (Waterloo, Ont.: Wilfred Laurier University Press, 1980), *passim*.

[21] Georges Suarez, *Clemenceau: Soixante années d'histoire de France*, 2 vols. (Les Éditions de France, 1932), 1:24-25. There is some uncertainty about the dates of his attendance. The plaque on the lycée gives 1852-1858, but Martet says he recalled entering in "the fifth form" (1853). Martet, *Clemenceau*, pp. 298-299.

[22] On 27 May 1922; in Général [Jean-Jules-Henri] Mordacq, *Clemenceau au soir de sa vie (1920-1929)*, 2 vols. (Librairie Plon, 1933), 1:213.

The school, next to the Jardin des Plantes and a block from the railroad station, was renamed on 4 Feb. 1919.

23   On the political scene in Nantes below, see especially Tudesq, *Les grands notables en France*, 2:900-1220, *passim*; Guépin and Bonamy, *Nantes au XIXe siècle*, *passim*; Pierre Sorlin, *Waldeck-Rousseau* (Librairie Armand Colin, 1966), pp. 18-54, *passim*; and Xavier du Boisrouvray, "Nantes en 1846, d'après la relation d'un Suédois, le baron Karl Frederick Palmstierna," *Société archéologique et historique de Nantes et de Loire-Atlantique. Bulletin* 116 (1979-80):37-57, *passim*.

24   O'Brien, "Les racines républicaines de la famille Clemenceau," p. 42.

25   GC, *In the Evening of My Thought*, 2 vols., trans. Charles Miner Thompson and John Heard, Jr. (Boston: Houghton Mifflin, 1929), 1:238.

26   L. Morauzeau, *Annuaire de la Société d'Émulation de la Vendée*, Année 1960 (Luçon, 1960), p. 90; as cited in Vincent Wright, "The Coup d'état of December 1851: Repression and the Limits to Repression," in Roger Price, ed., *Revolution and Reaction: 1848 and the Second French Republic* (New York: Barnes & Noble Books, 1975), p. 307. See also David R. Watson, *Georges Clemenceau: A Political Biography* (London: Eyre Methuen, 1974), p. 18; and Roger Price, *The French Second Republic: A Social History* (Ithaca, NY: Cornell University Press, 1972), pp. 291-293. No arrests were listed for Loire-Inférieure and no figures were released for Vendée, presumably where Benjamin was arrested.

27   Conversation with Jeanne Gilmore O'Brien, 8 June 1988.

28   Bernard Le Clère and Vincent Wright, *Les préfets du Second Empire* (Librairie Armand Colin, 1973), p. 45n.

29   Georges Wormser, *La république de Clemenceau* (Presses Universitaires de France,1961), p. 475. Curiously, the letter speaks of "your two children." By March 1858 there were five, two of them sons.

30   Vincent Wright, "La loi de sûreté générale de 1858," *Revue d'histoire moderne et contemporaine* 16 (1969):414-430. See also Eugène Tenot and Antonin Dubost, *Les suspects en 1858. Étude historique sur l'application de la loi de sûreté générale: Emprisonnements-Transportations* (Armand Le Chevalier, 1869), pp. 199-200.

31   Speech at Montaigu (Vendée), 30 Sept. 1906; in *Le Temps*, 2 Oct. See also Martet, *Clemenceau*, pp. 295-296; and Watson, *Georges Clemenceau*, p. 19.

CHAPTER II

Rebel Student
(1858-1865)

Soon after his father's return from Marseille, Georges finished up at the lycée and received his *bachelier ès-lettres* on 24 August 1858. His record was not brilliant, but he had collected some prizes along the way and managed to finish well, taking firsts in Latin translation and the French essay. Although language and literature were his strongest suits, nothing suggests he had seriously considered doing anything but follow his father, grandfather, and great-grandfather into medicine--or, more the case with them, into acquiring a medical degree as a cap to his education.

He began with a three-year stint (1858-61) at the tiny (29 students) but high-quality Preparatory School of Medicine and Pharmacology in Nantes, where at the end of his first year he passed the examinations for his *bachelier ès-sciences* (13 and 16 August 1859).[1] During the following two years of stages and internships in the local hospitals, however, he was twice summoned before the school's administrative council for pranks and disruptive or irregular behavior--absences without proper leave, showing disrespect toward superiors, firing off a gun in the courtyard and garden, scrawling obscene or grotesque pictures and inscriptions on walls, misbehaving in the dining hall, breaking windows, etc.--for which he drew formal public reprimands and a fifteen-day suspension. In short, he was a loose cannon in the place and a pain in the neck to the professoriat. What this conduct betokened is hard to say. No doubt some of it was a sophomoric way of getting back at professors who favored religion and the Bonapartist regime, as Duroselle surmises. But one suspects, too, that some of it also reflected a rebellion against his father or an internal conflict about his choice of a profession which he may have come to feel had been in some sense forced upon him. Be that as it may, the authorities must have sighed with relief when he decided to move on to the Faculty of Medicine at Paris to finish his degree.

His father accompanied him to Paris on the train, a trip he had made on foot in his day, and must have been pleasantly astonished when his erratic offspring won a brilliant 10th place among the 330 candidates applying for the Externate. Only two days before the examination, however, the first issue of *Le Travail* had appeared (22 December 1861) carrying an essay by its "literary and drama critic," Georges Clemenceau.

As had his father, he found politics in Paris more absorbing than medicine, and his father, moreover, encouraged the interest. A double life as medical student and political activist, however, taxed even his extraordinary energy. Sometimes he fought off sleep by clamping a toe with a clothespin or suspending a hand in the air by a string hung from the ceiling over his desk. In the end it was his medical ambitions that paid the price of too many twenty-hour days. Low scores on examinations in 1862 and 1863 earned him unprestigious provisional internships at the Bicêtre (the Paris asylum) and Pitié hospitals, and on impulse he once paid an enrollment fee at the Faculty of Law.[2] At length he decided to forego further competition for the posts required to achieve distinction in medicine and instead obtain a degree by passing a set of prescribed examinations and submitting a thesis.

The examinations--five, which he began to take in April 1864--turned out well for him, and in the spring of 1865 he wrote his thesis. The project occupied him for only a few weeks. Even so, by dint of intense exertion and his facility in writing, he cobbled together a 222-page paper, a more formidable affair than was customary for such offerings but containing no original research. Its nature also accounted for its length, being less scientific than philosophical. Scientific materialism, which his father had poured into him for years, was by now much in vogue among medical students and "advanced" professors and would find a home in medicine more than in any other profession in France well into the twentieth century. Hence Georges's attraction to Prof. Charles Robin (1821-85), nicknamed "the Gendarme of Materialism," an associate of Émile Littré (the leading advocate of Comte's Positivism) and also a friend of the famous Republican historian Jules Michelet, who with Victor Hugo was one of Benjamin's secular gods. Robin advocated theories of "sponteneity" and "heterogeneity" in embryology. Georges used a defense of his mentor's theories in his thesis, *De la génération des éléments anatomiques*, to assert the inanity of searching for "first causes" or "beginnings," enterprises involving *a priori* explanations prohibited by the methods of modern science. Contrary to orthodox Comtean Positivism, nevertheless, he affirmed a sweeping confidence in the explanatory powers of science: "It is to physiology that we must turn henceforth to solve *all* questions relating to origins [*naissance*]."[3]

Georges surely knew of Pasteur, who at that very moment was demolishing "spontaneous generation," but he ignored him and even quoted with approval Robin's refutation of the germ theory of disease. Nor did he cite Darwin, whose *Origin of Species* had just been translated into French. It would be a good fifty years, in fact, before Darwinism would make any headway at all in France against the hold of Lamarck's theory of the inheritance of acquired characteristics.[4] But it didn't really matter. His thesis in effect amounted to an affirmation of a particular intellectual stance to which, as it turned out, he was to remain faithful for the rest of his life. In his philosophical testament he would explain in passing what he had had in mind as a young man: "The once famous hypothesis of 'spontaneous generation' was nothing more than an attempt to minimize the miraculous."[5]

On 13 May 1865 Robin helped him through the defense of his thesis before a board of professors. He had stuck it out and become a duly certified doctor of medicine.

II

That Clemenceau came to politics from an education in science and medicine deserves notice. One result was an interest in public health and hygiene throughout his career.[6] Another was a compassion for suffering humanity; he reminded people sometimes that he had spent nearly six years in hospital wards observing and caring for every kind of physical and mental ailment. Doubtless the experience, too, sharpened his habit of close inspection of and intense concentration on the matter at hand, which intimates noted about him, and tempered his idealism with a gritty realism and a respect for facts. That biology was at the center of his professional education, and not, for example, literature or legal studies, led him in the same direction-- that is, to a distrust of rigid systems and of expectations of any quick fundamental change in mankind. As he remarked a year before his death, basic conditions of existence remain the same--one is born, suffers, and dies: "To hold in hand the nuts and bolts of birth and death, ah! that would be something new!"[7]

In regard to politics as such, republicanism and science--or more accurately, scientism, a belief that the methods of natural science should be the norm for all disciplines--were to Clemenceau and many men of his time interdependent. Science could properly flourish only in the free air of a republic, and a republic could endure only if science were employed to liberate the masses from the thralls of ignorance, degrading social conditions, disease, outworn institutions (e.g., monarchy), and superstition (Roman Catholicism). The appearance of disease in the list was no offhand addition; in France more than in any other country, advocates of democracy regarded attention to public health as a moral obligation.[8] Anticlericalism likewise was thought to be a prerequisite. During Clemenceau's formative years it began a steep rise, the reconciliation of 1848 between the Church and republicanism having amounted to only a fleeting truce. The rise mirrored a growing conservatism out of Rome which reached its apogee under Pius IX (1846-78) with the promulgation of the *Syllabus of Errors* in 1864 and of papal infallibility in 1870. The *Syllabus*, which unequivocally denounced rationalism, socialism, religious toleration, separation of church and state, revolution against "legitimate princes," attacks on the temporal power (the Papal States), and any proposition "that the Roman Pontiff can, and ought to, reconcile himself to...progress, liberalism, and modern civilization" was everything the most rabid anticlericals could have hoped for and kept their arsenals well stocked for a century. The reactionary politics and dogmatism of the Roman church, in short, fed a dogmatic scientism among many of its opponents and branded anticlericalism into the republicanism of Clemenceau's generation. In his case the brand was never to be effaced.

III

Two months after receiving his degree, young Doctor Clemenceau left France. The step resulted from activities having little to do with his professional preparations.[9]

An alert, ambitious young man with a taste for colorful living spiced with intrigue could scarcely have asked for a finer habitat than Paris in the 1860s. Napoleon III's mild police state was oppressive enough to stir contempt among those who cherished the heritage of '89 or '48, but the Paris of Offenbach operettas, Baron Haussmann's building projects, the Crédit Mobilier, famously expensive *grandes horizontales*, and mustachioed swaggerers home from expeditions to the Crimea, Italy, Peking, Mexico City, and the hinterlands of Senegal was light years removed from the gloom of most twentieth-century tyrannies. Luxury paraded unabashed along the new boulevards being hacked through the (literally) medieval slums of the central city, and although its heyday was fading, the Latin Quarter, where Georges settled, accommodated a turbulent population of students, artists, and drifters immortalized in Murger's *Scènes de la vie de Bohème*.

Georges grew to love Paris, although the Vendée was always home. He was no true bohemian even if he did move to less and less comfortable dwellings because of failing newspaper ventures. As he later explained to a journalist, Wythe Williams, "Perhaps I had too much dough, as you Americans say....You see, Papa liked me well enough to send me a decent allowance, especially as I was following his own racket--medicine." (He loved American slang.) There were good times and pretty girls: "The little cocottes were wonderful. They cooked for their boyfriends and darned their socks. But--you see--ahem--I was very busy."[10] No sooner had he arrived in Paris than his father put his connections into play and introduced him to Henri Lefort and Étienne Arago, veteran Republicans, who brought him in touch with elements of future Republican leadership--Eugène Pelletan, Henri Rochefort, Jules Méline, Louis Andrieux. Even before this time, in fact, Georges had had such opportunities: lunch in Paris in 1858 with Léon Gambetta and Arthur Ranc, visits to his father by Michelet in Nantes in 1852 and 1859, and a trip to Brussels in 1859 to do homage to the exiled Victor Hugo.

Le Travail, journal littéraire et scientifique, was the fruit of meetings of a group of young men who were often to be found in the Latin Quarter at the Café de Cluny and the studio of a painter, Jean-Baptiste Delestre (1800-71). Small reviews and newspapers proliferated in the wake of the amnesty of 1859 and of a series of decrees in 1860 designed to bleed off pressure by giving voice to opposition opinion. *Le Travail's* manifesto rang with the self-conscious sincerity of earnest young men striking a blow for liberty:

> Workers, we think that it is from among us, the coming generation, that the men of the future will be drawn and that soon, perhaps, we shall be called to don the manly toga. Sluggards, when the day of combat dawns, what shall we...say to our children when they demand an accounting of what we have done with the heritage of our forefathers?[11]

Georges relished the opportunities afforded by literary and dramatic criticism to mock the regime: "We can be obliged to hide our thought, but not to disguise it, be forced to silence, but not to lie....And besides, the battle is what we live for."[12]

The battle did not stay entirely on the printed page. Faithful to the example of his father, who had taken part in the famous riot in 1830 in support of Victor Hugo's *Hernani*, Georges and the militants of *Le Travail* helped drive Edmond About's *Gaëtana* from the Odéon with four nights (3-6 January 1862) of booing: Monsieur About was said to be basking in the Imperial favor and to have worn aristocratic knee-breeches to a reception. Shortly afterward things got more serious when Georges and several comrades were arrested for inciting a demonstration on 24 February, the anniversary of the birth of the Second Republic. He was apprehended on the 26th at his apartment--which was fortunate, for those arrested at the demonstration were badly beaten by the police. Coincidentally, he had just published an essay, "Les martyrs de l'histoire," on a theme he would make famous thirty years later, that the French Revolution was a "bloc" whose principle must be affirmed or denied as a whole. One could not claim to accept the Revolution while dismissing its methods: "Do they really believe that the triumph of new ideas can be brought about peacefully?"[13]

Georges was incarcerated at Mazas Prison until 12 May. Benjamin went up to see him and wrote to Emma a wry commentary on their son's activities:

> They say that when it comes to their children the vanity of fathers is almost as great as their affection; so if it can console you a little, know that your son had made for himself, I'm told, a kind of position proportionate to his age and the milieu in which he lived; he enthroned himself under the balcony of the Odéon and was a lion in the Latin Quarter; a bit more and his minor notoriety would have perhaps crossed the Pont Neuf had he not been arrested en route.

But when Benjamin told of the beatings at the Place de la Bastille, he admitted he had "wept with rage and bitterness" and hoped he would live to see vengeance rain down for "all these crimes."[14]

Georges disliked prison intensely. Years later he related his experience in a sardonically humorous article on penal reform--"a charming trip in the *panier à salade* while seated on the knees of a butcher's boy who had killed a fellow apprentice," a bath in some coffee-colored water, Mass which could be heard only by putting one's head on the toilet seat, bread called "bran balls" which would "stick to a wall," and for reading matter a turgid epic poem about the "assassination" of Ensign Coulon de Jumonville by George Washington in the 1754 expedition to the Ohio, a piece which he claimed had left him with "an invincible grudge" against Washington.[15] He received a month's sentence on 11 April for "provocation without following effects," evidently a mild charge. After serving his time he recuperated in the Vendée and returned to Paris, unrepentant but more careful. Henceforth the police had him under occasional surveillance.

Apart from participating at the Sorbonne in a sympathy demonstration for Mrs. Lincoln following her husband's assassination and winning election as president of the Society of Medical Students in a protest against a proposed faculty-dominated student association--"The Ministry of the Interior smelled mice and said no dice," he recalled[16]--he confined his overt activity to the printed page while opening a somewhat dangerous line of covert action. *Le Travail* had suspended publication on 2 March 1862, but at the end of June it reappeared as *Le Matin*, which folded in August after eight numbers. Other ephemeral projects followed, but what he contributed has never been catalogued.[17] In any event, he had tasted the delights of journalism and found in it a lifelong love. (An anecdote survived the demise of *Le Travail*. An intense, miserably shabby young man had turned up one day to ask Georges to publish a poem. He agreed, but not before advising the author confidentially that he had best give up literary ambitions. The poem, "Le Doute," was one of the first published works of Émile Zola.[18])

The great boom of the 1850s had faded by 1862. Unemployment in the cities and a floundering stock market threatened serious trouble. The younger radicals saw an opportunity for political gains. They had become critical of the survivors of 1848 for neglecting social reform and contenting themselves with fine speeches instead of hard work. Action became the watchword of the new generation.

They deduced at least two lines of conduct, one which sought to "go to the people" to listen, enlighten, and organize, another which concluded that an elite band of professionals should take the people's cause in hand and make a revolution. For awhile Georges pursued both. He made little progress on the former course. With an oddly assorted group of investors including Augustin Cochin (a Catholic), Alfred Naquet (a Jew), Eugène Pelletan, and Louis Garnier-Pagès (freethinkers), he helped found a "people's bank" specializing in small loans to workingmen's associations; but it soon went broke.[19] Nor was he successful preaching the gospel in cafés in working-class neighborhoods. Articulate, well-attired Republican politicians were at a discount: the bloody June Days of '48 still haunted many memories. Workers, particularly in the growing industrial suburbs, were in the main merely indifferent to Bonapartism. Georges muffled his disappointment. He began to acquire a certain distaste for street-corner politics and the labors of grass-roots organization. He probably could see, too, that the causes of France's failures in self-government and social emancipation might run deeper than conventional Republican doctrine had probed.

Gustave Jourdan stood by to encourage. Georges early on had fallen under the spell of this former official who had converted to republicanism in '48 and had helped to lead a considerable insurrection in Basses-Alpes in 1851. He was a noble, high-minded dedicated man, hopeful, but with no illusions, a social democrat who in the pure tradition of Jacobinism viewed all political opponents as reactionaries, royalists, or bourgeois exploiters.[20] Clemenceau later remembered him as the most eloquent man he had ever heard. Jourdan seemed to understand the impetuous character of his young friend, loved him, but warned him against excesses. Shortly before Clemenceau's death his secretary discovered a packet of letters from Jourdan. Clemenceau was deeply stirred. In late February 1866 the man had died in a cholera epidemic. Sixty years later the pain of that separation was still very much alive.[21]

The other person, aside from his father, who exerted noteworthy influence on him in these years was Auguste Blanqui (1805-81).[22] His theories, which turned on the role of professional revolutionary elites, were more suggestive than coherent, his plots invariably failed, and he spent most of his adult life in prison. Yet few political figures of the nineteenth century had greater long-run influence, for he was a primal source of inspiration for Lenin and his Bolshevik "professionals."

Georges met Blanqui through the intervention of his comrade Ferdinand Taule, who had been confined at the Ste.-Pélagie Prison after the 24 February affair, and Auguste Scheuer-Kestner, also there but on another charge. Blanqui was currently being held at Ste.-Pélagie under the fairly liberal rules of political internment. A reminder to Blanqui of assistance Benjamin Clemenceau had rendered to him in 1848 in obtaining a passport also may have helped gain entrée; in any case, Benjamin did accompany Georges on one of his visits.[23] These visits to Blanqui, which continued almost daily for about a year, probably began around February or March 1863 and were facilitated after July by his internship at the Pitié Hospital across the street from Ste.-Pélagie.

IV

Georges was plainly captivated by the legendary figure. Blanqui was impressed in turn but wondered if Georges and his friends were true revolutionaries. He tested them in a project to smuggle printing presses into the country. One attempt failed when the apparatus had to be dumped into the Seine. Another succeeded, although Georges had to bluff the police at his apartment by shining a light in their eyes to keep the press from view. Shortly afterwards, however, at some point in 1864, Blanqui ordered him to turn over the machine to someone else and broke relations with him. Perhaps it was because Georges had dined with Charles Delescluze, an admirable veteran of '48 but hated by Blanqui as a rival. He may also have been put off by rumors of a scheme allegedly concocted by Scheurer to abduct Napoleon III, an idea which even he, Blanqui, thought harebrained. Probably the real reason was that he had concluded that Georges was not thoroughly converted to his ideas of violent, conspiratorial revolution, and even if converted would not accept the strict discipline he imposed on his lieutenants. His remarks in a letter (6 November 1864) to one of his principal contacts, Dr. Louis Watteau, are suggestive:

> We are not gaining ground in the schools. There is a bourgeois instinct which alienates the young men from our group, even the most outspoken. They sense we are serious about the Revolution and they want no part of it. All this youth which is so hostile to the present government will throw themselves en masse into the Reaction in the wake of a *February catastrophe* absolutely as in 1848....There are at least a score of students who seemed to be with us at the start who have moved very far away as a result of the discoveries they made while with us. As soon as they really understand the basis, the goal, the consequences, they turn their backs and become adversaries, staying in what's called the liberal opposition.[24]

Blanqui's influence on Clemenceau nonetheless outlasted the passing satisfactions of dodging police or of later joining (probably in 1866) a Blanquist-inspired international order, the Société agis comme tu penses (the Act-the-Way-You-Think Society), with a resounding oath to forswear all contact with organized religion. Blanqui very likely confirmed in him certain tendencies and ideas: a belief in action; a distrust of grand socio-economic and historical syntheses, such as were emerging in the writings of Karl Marx; a belief in reason tempered by an appreciation of the role of force; an emphasis, again contrary to Marx, on the power of ideas rather than of material circumstances alone, and a tendency to link economics with ethics-- "Justice is the sole criterion to be applied in human affairs," wrote Blanqui,[25] using a word that was to bulk large in Clemenceau's thought; and a conviction that France, which both men loved passionately, would never be emancipated so long as the Church retained its influence.

More important, however, were the aura of Blanqui's persona and the power of his moral example. Clemenceau was gifted with a formidable intelligence but an even more formidable physical vitality and emotional impulsion. Science, as has been said, contributed much to his philosophical outlook and reinforced habits of concentration and observation, but his other face was that of a romantic moved by, and moving others through, his emotions. He had been raised on the romance of the French Revolution, the Great Days which had opened the doors to Humanity's future and saved France from conquest by foreign despots, the Revolution hymned by Hugo and Michelet. Blanqui had tried to live all that in the flesh. As Clemenceau explained to an interviewer in 1924:

> Blanqui was no theorist, and he remained a stranger to systematic conceptions. On the other hand, he possessed to the highest degree the qualities which make a man of action: courage, sincerity, generosity; it was these things which forced sympathy....Above all, he knew how to create a climate of revolutionary enthusiasm around him: that's what explains, in my opinion, the so-strong hold he exercised on so many of his contemporaries.[26]

That and the moral example. Clemenceau never escaped its spell. In 1896, isolated in defeat, his career at ebb tide, he devoted a moving article to his memory:

> I carry with me unforgettable visions of Blanqui: at Sainte-Pélagie, where I received the first shock of the brilliant black rays which darted forth from the white, emaciated face; during the siege [of Paris, 1870-71], when his voice was not listened to; and later, on the deathbed, in irreparable defeat....Whoever would try not to pass this way in vain will be encouraged by the high, severe lesson of an unshakable soul at grips with the cruelest of destinies, drawing out of constantly renewed defeat the courage that the weak expect of victory, achieving in utter simplicity the absolute sacrifice, and expecting nothing in return, not even, perhaps, the tardy reparation of time, which avenges the victim of the victors.[27]

Dismissed by Blanqui, Georges was to be rejected again a few months later, and far more painfully. The second rejection led to a decision which he believed at the time would irrevocably set a new course for him. He would go to America.

NOTES
CHAPTER II

1   On his medical education see especially Martet, *Clemenceau*, pp. 298-300; Applebaum, *Clemenceau, Thinker and Writer*, pp. 17-27 and *passim*; Watson, *Georges Clemenceau*, p. 25n.; Ellis, *The Early Life of Georges Clemenceau*, pp. 26-28, 210-211; Jean-Baptiste Duroselle, *Clemenceau* (Fayard, 1988), pp. 38-41, 54-63; Charles Coutéla, "Georges Clemenceau, le médecine et les médecins," *Presse médicale* 73 (1965):1435-1438; Gaston Cordier and André Soubiron, "La thèse d'un étudiant en médecine hors série: Georges Clemenceau (13 mai 1865)," *Presse médicale* 73 (1965):3029-3034; David R. Watson, "A Note on Clemenceau, Comte and Positivism," *Historical Journal* [Cambridge] 14 (1971):201-204; and Dr. A. Raiga-Clemenceau, "La thèse de doctorat du docteur Georges Clemenceau (mai 1865)," *Nouvelles archives hospitalières*, 1974, no. 1, pp. 21-24.

2   See HE, 7 Jan. 1915.

3   GC, *De la génération des éléments anatomiques*, par le Dr. G. Clemenceau,...précédé d'une introduction par M. Ch. Robin (G. Ballière, 1867), pp. 106-107 (his italics).

4   On Darwinism and the persistence of the spontaneous generation theory see Denis Buican, *Histoire de la génétique et de l'évolutionisme en France* (Presses Universitaires de France, 1984), pp. 38-39; and John Farley, *The Spontaneous Generation Controversy from Descartes to Oparin* (Baltimore: The Johns Hopkins University Press, 1977).

5   GC, *In the Evening of My Thought*, 1:222.

6   See especially Dr. A. Raiga-Clemenceau, "Le vrai caractère de Clemenceau," *Nouvelles archives hospitalières*, 1973, no. 3, pp, 66-72; and the essay by Michel Valentin in *Clemenceau et la justice*, pp. 59-66.

7   Georges Adam de Villiers, *Clemenceau parle: Conversations inédites* (Éditions Tallandier, 1931), p. 68.

8   See Nicolet, *L'idée républicaine en France*, pp. 310-311.

9   See especially J. [Iouda] Tchernoff, "Georges Clemenceau sous le second empire," *Opinion: Journal de la semaine*, 18 July 1908, pp. 15-17; and *idem*, *Le parti républicain au coup d'état et sous le second empire, d'après des documents et des souvenirs inédits* (A. Pedone, 1906), *passim*.

10   Wythe Williams, *The Tiger of France: Conversations with Clemenceau* (New York: Duell, Sloan & Pearce, 1948), pp. 31-32.

11   *Le Travail*, no. 1 (22 Dec. 1861). "Workers" here means all who labor to aid mankind.

12   *Ibid.*, no. 7 (16 Feb. 1862).

13   *Ibid.*, no. 8 (22 Feb. 1862). The "bloc" speech is in JOC, 29 Jan. 1891, pp. 155-156 (see p. 150 below).

14   Wormser, *La république de Clemenceau*, pp. 475-476.

15   GC, *Le grand Pan* (Bibliothèque-Charpentier, 1919), pp. 294-295.

16   Williams, *The Tiger of France*, p. 34.

17   A list, probably not exhaustive, would include *La Revue Encyclopédique* and *Candide*; ephemeral newspapers; a student paper, *Les Écoles de France*; and a series of books and pamphlets, *La Bibliothèque Démocratique*.

18   Armand Lenoux, *Bonjour Monsieur Zola* (Amiot-Dumont, 1934), pp. 58-59.

19   See Sorlin, *Waldeck-Rousseau*, p. 100.

20   See Philippe Vigier, *La seconde république dans la région alpine: Étude politique et sociale*, 2 vols. (Presses Universitaires de France, 1963), 2:255-256, 317-319, 325.

21   See Martet, *Clemenceau*, pp. 308-310, 317-327 (the letters).

22   See especially Maurice Dommanget, *Blanqui et l'opposition révolutionnaire à la fin du second empire* (A. Colin, 1960), p. 63 and *passim*; Maurice Paz, "Clemenceau, Blanqui's Heir: An Unpublished Letter from Blanqui to Clemenceau Dated 18 March 1879," *Historical Journal* [Cambridge] 16 (1973):604-615; and David R. Watson, "Clemenceau and Blanqui: A Reply to M. Paz," *Historical Journal* 21 (1978):387-397.

23   Gustave Geffroy, *L'enfermé* (Bibliothèque-Charpentier, 1919), pp. 248-49. The passport incident related here, however, is difficult to place in the context of Blanqui's known movements in 1848.

24   Maurice Paz, ed., *Lettres familières d'Auguste Blanqui et du docteur Louis Watteau* (Marseille: Institut historique de Provence, 1976), p. 54.

25   Louis-Auguste Blanqui, *Critique sociale*, 2 vols. (F. Alcan, 1885), 2:58.

26   Sylvain Molinier, *Blanqui* (Presses Universitaires de France, 1948), p. 69.

27   GC, *Au fil des jours* (É. Fasquelle, 1900), pp. 199-200.

CHAPTER III

American Interlude
(1865-1869)

Auguste Scheurer, or Scheurer-Kestner, was the son of an Alsatian chemicals manufacturer (a friend of Georges' father) and married to one of the five brilliant daughters of Charles Kestner, proprietor of another chemicals concern. Georges visited Auguste in Thann in January 1863, was introduced to the Kestners, and instantly fell in love with the youngest and only unmarried daughter, Hortense. She was indeed a prize--beautiful, intelligent, accomplished, vivacious, and wealthy. Suitors pressed on in droves.

Georges' prospects were not good. He was a year her junior and still a student. These were major impediments, as the custom of the age in the upper classes was for men to postpone marriage until at least their early thirties, when they had become "established," and to marry women five to fifteen years younger. Moreover, he had left a quite mixed impression on the girl and her family. Auguste noted that "they found him blunt, which he was, capricious [*fantasque*], which he was not, while appreciating his intellectual qualities...."[1] For most of a year he bided his time, saying little about Hortense. A second visit to Thann, in early 1864, following an overture through Étienne Arago, a friend of Kestner, greatly intensified his passion. He became obsessed with the idea of wringing an answer from the Kestners. Scheurer, the intermediary, found himself in terribly awkward straits. He was certain that the suit was all but hopeless, but his overwrought friend kept bombarding him with letters and finding in his evasive replies reasons to go on hoping. The police contributed to the imbroglio by opening and delaying mail. Georges confided his troubles to his father. As he wrote to Scheurer:

> My father is and always has been before all else a friend to me. Ever since I reached the age of reason, I have never heard an order from his lips, and I have never yet experienced a happiness or a sorrow which we have not shared together....I am on the eve of a great joy or a great sorrow; I want to offer a share of it to my father in advance.[2]

But nothing came of a meeting in May between his father and Victor Chauffour, one of the Kestner sons-in-law, and another visit, in September 1864, likewise failed: "Clemenceau's sojourn in Thann," Scheurer wrote in his diary, "was not favorable to him. His brilliant qualities were all but smothered by his exuberance, which jarred against our very bourgeois Alsatian habits."[3]

On 20 October Georges addressed a final summons to speak to Kestner, all but accusing his friend of going back on his word. The fatal letter from Monsieur Kestner reached Georges a few days later. He reacted with perfect outward calm and wrote to Auguste expressing remorse for his impositions and hasty accusations.

Late in January 1865 during a stopover at the Scheurers', Georges casually mentioned that he was going to America. Auguste tried to dissuade him, but a long letter set him straight:

> You know why I'm leaving. What more do you want from me? What am I going to do? Well, I haven't the slightest idea. I'm leaving, that's all. Chance will do the rest, perhaps a surgeon in the Union army, perhaps something else, perhaps nothing.
> Permit me, my dear friend, not to push any further the psychological study you asked of me. Aside from the fact that it would be useless, the dissection would be painful. Anyhow, I don't want anyone's pity, and I don't need people feeling sorry for me. If I'm cowardly or brave in the face of grief, where I'm going, what I think, what I feel, what I do--all that's a matter between myself and me. I find great fascination (some indefinable mixture of pride and bitterness) in shutting myself up and opening myself to no one. This is my last consolation; he will no longer be my friend who tries to take it from me.[4]

Such a mélange of stoic poses and romantic escapism, testimony both to the severity of his emotional upset and his immaturity, doubtless would not have withstood his father's scrutiny. He put a more acceptable face on the matter by telling him that he wanted to visit the United States to see how democracy worked in the world's only large republic. The separation was eased by making the first stage of the journey (beginning on 26 July) a trip together to England. Georges had agreed with the publisher of his dissertation--he sent the Kestners a copy with his compliments--to finish a translation of J. S. Mill's *A System of Logic* which he had begun in the spring of 1864, perhaps inspired by an article on Mill by Professor Robin;[5] in return for it the publisher would issue a second edition of his dissertation. Benjamin secured interviews with Mill and with the Darwinist philosopher Herbert Spencer, a contact which may have begun to turn Georges toward Darwinism. A bargain was struck with Mill, probably to continue work on the *Logic* but also to translate his recently published articles on Auguste Comte.

II

Father and son parted, and Georges took ship to New York, arriving in mid-August.[6] He described to Gustave Jourdan the pain his departure had caused him. Jourdan wrote back taking him to task for hiding his emotions from his parents: "A word from the heart always does good, and it's no evidence of lofty virtue not to utter it to those who expect it but don't dare ask for it. To your mother at least!" He also chided him about the embarrassing confusion he had left behind regarding an allowance: "Men are made for you to walk beside, not over their heads, aristocrat that you are."[7]

The fact that his father had agreed to provide an allowance suggests again that Georges had not been entirely frank about his intentions. Would he have offered an allowance had he known that he intended to settle permanently in the United States? For it is clear enough--from his correspondence with Scheurer and Madame Jourdan, after her husband's untimely death, and from a remark to Stephen Bonsal in 1922[8]--that he indeed had intended to emigrate, not merely visit for purposes of "study" or whatever. How firm this intention truly was or precisely how long it lasted is impossible to say, for he was back in France in 1866, probably from mid-May until early August, after receiving word of Jourdan's death; and in March 1867 he wrote to Madame Jourdan from New York that he would return, apparently permanently, "in a few years," although his ironic tone in this passage implies that he viewed this eventuality as an humiliating last resort.[9] Certainly his father, for his part, wanted him back home and practicing his profession. Georges continued to equivocate with him, or so one can infer from a crisis later in 1867. In a letter to Madame Jourdan dated 6 September he wrote:

> The conditions which I'm proposing for my return are of the most modest sort, and I hope my father will accept them....I say nothing about myself to you: because I have nothing to tell you. I have finally after a long struggle given up the last of my illusions. I expect nothing more, hope for nothing more and desire nothing more. I'm looking for a cemetery where I can bury myself alive--Paris would be as good a place as any other. If my project materializes we shall converse in our tomb just like the dead in the dialogues of Lucian.[10]

Whatever these "conditions" were--they may have revolved around his father's refusal of money to invest in the developing Midwest[11]--his father rejected them. And unless he had already stopped the allowance--early 1867 seems a more likely point--he surely did so now.

In the wake of this clash, Georges made plans for a short visit to France, presumably to patch things up, but they did not materialize. He did return in the summer of 1868, however. On 11 June before his departure from New York on the 27th, he wrote to Scheurer that he would be visiting for three or four months. But after a couple of weeks at home "under the maternal wing," as he put it, he remarked to Scheurer (27 July) that he planned to return to the United States "if I can, in a year or two."[12] In fact, however, he arrived back in New York on 8 December, but only for a few weeks in connection with his marriage plans (as will appear). In a letter to Scheurer on this occasion he described himself as "an American by profession,"[13] but quite plainly, whether or not he would admit it openly, the intention of settling in America had joined "the last" of his surrendered "illusions."

The obscurities surrounding Georges' mental state in these years are no easier to penetrate than his intentions. His correspondents made no secret of their puzzlement and concern, Scheurer once going so far as to wonder if he had contemplated suicide. Georges replied to that supposition with the calming assurances mixed with ironies and self-mockery with which he customarily met inquiries about his state of mind.[14] The passage from the 6 September 1867 letter to Madame Jourdan quoted above was an exception; if only for a moment, he lifted the curtain masking his innermost feelings. And even then he quickly dropped it, leaving her knowing only that his depression was due to a disagreement with his father. This reference to his father, however, says more than he perhaps intended. As mentioned before, a published study of his psychology in these years rather convincingly makes a struggle with his father its centerpiece.[15]

The frequency of allusions to his progress in "growing up" lends credence to the independence thesis. On the eve of his departure for America in 1865, for example, he wrote to Scheurer that some day they would meet again "when I shall have become a big boy."[16] A letter to Madame Jourdan (10 March 1867) is particularly revealing:

> I admit I have been a dreamer and fanciful like all people whose nervous system is a little too excitable and excited, but experience corrects me a little every day for this defect. You scold me very sharply about my mania for running around the world. Whatever you may think, I nevertheless can assure you that it is contrary to my taste. I should like to live tranquilly and regularly in a little corner. That was my feeling before I left Paris, and the more I go the more I take refuge in the hope of imprisoning myself some day in a calm and regulated life....Nobody is less ambitious than I, but I want to be independent in order to need no one (*except for my friends*) and to be able to scorn [*mépriser*] everyone at will (*except for the aforementioned*)--that is my ideal....I regret more than I can say that my affairs have caused all this worry. I certainly hope that you have not been obliged to sell your bonds....I fear I'll never be able to oblige you as you oblige me. Happily, you are among the small number of those toward whom gratefulness does not weigh on me.[17]

Later the same year he wrote to Scheurer (27 December 1867) in a jocular tone, "What I do, *bon dieu*, it's a mystery....Well, *mon cher*, I study to become wise, upright and moderate, 'respectable' as they say here."[18] Answering (27 July 1868) Scheurer's queries about the "mysteries" of his existence, he protested, "I'm the least mysterious man in the world....In growing I've lost a little of the 'me' habit, that's all."[19] And recalling his behavior during his hapless courtship of Hortense, he expressed to Scheurer (3 February 1869) his chagrin over his "idiocies" and "ridiculous posturings," adding, "You know my excuse, the only one I have: I was young. Since then I've grown a bit older, and I am, if not more modest, at least more moderate."[20]

Many years later, in 1922 in a speech at the Metropolitan Opera in New York during a lecture tour, he referred to his experience in America in terms which, making due allowance for the effects of time and the demands of the occasion, confirm that he was still maturing:

> I was in that happy time a young man of some imagination who thinks everything is possible to him. There is no hard task. What men for hundreds of years and thousands of years have been trying to accomplish and failed--he can do. He has the heart, the mind, the knowledge, and he can do it. So I brought this fresh outlook here. I don't know whether it has been appreciated. I have never been assured of that. But I looked around and I learned what Europe hadn't taught me--to help myself....[I have come today to] express my thanks for the good and practical education that I received. I say practical because of course I do [sic] not come here to learn new things. And so I came with the American spirit and ready to find fault in different ways. But I must confess that I did not find as many faults as I expected.[21]

One may take him at his word and grant that he did indeed grow "a bit older" during these years. But the stress should not be minimized. Clearly there were bouts of depression accompanied by a pronounced restlessness which he made light of but which left his interlocutors uneasy about him. To Madame Jourdan (10 March 1867): "Well, no, today is still not the day when I shall write this famous, often-promised letter in which I'll give you reasons. The *reason* why I abstain from *reasons* is that I will be seen again with a foot in the air and that I still don't know which way the wind is going to turn me."[22] When he has some time on his hands, he told Scheurer (27 September 1867), "I apply myself to losing it, in which I generally succeed."[23] "It is a perpetual amusement to me," he wrote to him again (27 July 1868), "not to know in the evening what I'll do the next day. I live in the unforeseen, and I have the pleasure of offering to myself every morning a bouquet of eternal surprises."[24]

Interspersed with the banter, however, one finds references to fatigue or requests that his haste be excused. There can be little doubt that in fact he kept himself occupied. He habitually worked intensely and rapidly and throughout his life showed a striking capacity to perform under stress. His nature was altogether too active and curious to have tolerated spending over four years applying himself to losing time. His difficulty lay elsewhere. What he probably was feeling at the time was a lack of a clear sense of direction. The context here reminds one of an observation he later made about his father: "...he didn't do a great deal, and like all people who don't do anything, was always very busy."[25] Whatever he appeared to think of himself and tell his correspondents, he nevertheless made a contrary impression on others, at least to judge from the reminiscences of an old French physician in New York who had known him in those years. In an interview on the occasion of the Metropolitan Opera speech, he recalled that young Clemenceau had used the name "Eugène" rather than Georges (an interesting sidelight, without a doubt) and had visited everywhere, especially public facilities such as the courts, forts, and prisons. He seemed particularly interested, too, in the condition of the poor and was an omnivorous reader:

> He was one of the brainiest young men I ever knew. He came to this country without money or friends and by his own exertions supported himself and made a good reputation, too....He never wasted a moment. He parcelled out his time so he could devote so many hours to teaching [see below], so many to study and so many to literary work and the study of our institutions.[26]

Moreover, his need for money had had to act as a considerable stimulus to activity, whatever the truth about his mental or emotional state. From the beginning of his American adventure he had money problems because of his love of travel, his casual record-keeping, and a lifelong habit of spending or lending whatever he had on hand. In his first letter to him (10 September 1865), Jourdan felt moved to warn, "You have too much--for your father has been very generous--to make it necessary to give up any large projects you may have, and you haven't enough to make it unnecessary for you to earn more. What are you going to do?"[27] Before long, in fact, he was borrowing from Jourdan's widow, who was quite well fixed, and from others, among them, curiously, the grandfather of the American author and critic Alexander Woollcott.[28] Fortuitously, the sorry state of his finances encouraged an activity--journalism--which time and again during his life helped him to overcome his interior conflicts and despondency.

III

Soon after he landed in New York, he had begun to send articles to a recently founded (1861) liberal-oriented paper with a great future, *Le Temps*, apparently in hopes it would take him on as a stringer. He did not catch on at first after getting ten articles published, the last dated 10 February 1866. Meanwhile, Jourdan tried without success to find an outlet in Italy. By January 1867, however, Jean Lafont (1835-?), one of his closest friends from the earliest days in Paris, had pried open the door again at *Le Temps*, which finally paid him by the line from 25 September to 15 November and thereafter with a stipend of 150 francs per month.[29] The last piece appeared on 1 August 1870. These articles, ninety-four of them, all told, which he wrote anonymously and forwarded through Lafont lest he arouse the authorities, contain the first mature expressions of attitudes characteristic of him in public life. Since their recovery and reprinting in 1928 they have won a secure reputation among historians of the Reconstruction period--no small achievement for a man newly arrived in a strange land and as a journalist still an amateur.[30]

Journalism gave him an added excuse to travel. After settling in the French quarter near Washington Square with the help of two young Americans he had met in Paris--William Edgar Marshall, the artist, and Eugene Bushe, later a prominent New York lawyer--he took trips along the Atlantic seaboard and to Chicago and St. Louis. To his later regret he turned down a chance to go to California with one of the last wagon trains. Not surprisingly, the South was his first objective. He stepped off a train in Richmond only five months after the Civil War had ended. (He told some American troops during World War I that he had beaten Grant into

Richmond by five minutes. It made a good story, anyhow.[31]) "At the Capitol, where I was welcomed by Houdon's beautiful statue of Washington, I watched the unforgettable spectacle of the first session of a legislature made up of freed slaves."[32] The blatant contradictions of Southern society shocked him, notwithstanding his father's musings on the hypocrisy of men and the memory of childhood tears shed at the theater in Nantes over the misfortunes of Uncle Tom.[33] He listened in polite disbelief while cultured Southern gentlemen defended an institution whose brutalities sickened him. Full thirty years later he would write: "Read in the American newspapers before 1860 the descriptive notices of fugitive slaves. There are only marks of branding irons, shattered jaws, eyes gouged out, limbs mutilated or cut off. Is this not the work of white men, civilized people, Christians?"[34] And in 1917 he recalled his arrival in Fredericksburg and a refusal of a black cabman to accept him when the cab of a white was empty:

> I looked at the man. He had at most a light olive tint to him. It was one of these former slaves whose *liberation* had just caused oceans of blood to be shed in a 'democracy' of the white race. Without waiting until my arrival at the plantation, where a most cordial welcome was prepared for me, I began to ponder this reply and, to tell the truth, after fifty years come and gone I have not reached the end of my reflections.[35]

He devoted his first article (28 September 1865) to the Negro Question, as it was termed, and watched as the country thrashed about for a solution. He thought he saw one in land ownership by the freedmen but admitted dolefully that he expected little from former masters "too blinded by passion to see their own best interests."[36] After years of observing the rise and decline of the reconstructionists' crusade, he drew some wan comfort from a belief that somehow American pragmatism would find a way through. A Darwinian view was settling on him--he was one of only a handful of Frenchmen before the 1870s to use Darwinism as a basis for comments about society--and it inspired somber reflections:

> If, then, the black man cannot successfully compete with the white man, he is fated to become the victim of that natural selection which is constantly operating under our eyes in spite of everything, and he must eventually go under....All are at work, and time alone can show of what the black race is capable.[37]

He found the American political scene immensely stimulating, a far cry from the shoddy, manipulative despotism, as he viewed it, of Napoleon III's regime. But close contact with a functioning democracy tempered his inexperienced idealism; Scheurer thought that "the utilitarian atmosphere of the United States had somewhat deformed the Clemenceau I had known."[38] Action, however, remained the key. Democracy at bottom furnished the opportunity for action, either for good or for evil: no more, no less. He found new heroes--Horace Greeley, Wendell Phillips, Thaddeus Stevens, all of whom he interviewed. Stevens' character and oratory, in which he found a model, especially impressed him. He was present at the reading of the speech calling for President Johnson's impeachment: "Every word counted, and no sentence was without an insinuation. All further discussion was useless after that, and the vote was taken."[39] He saw in him qualities he admired in Blanqui:

> It must be admitted [he wrote on his death in 1868] that Mr. Stevens stands out as a man of only one idea, but that does not matter a whit, since he had the glory of defending that idea when it was trodden in the dust, and the joy of contributing largely to its triumph. That should be accomplishment enough for one man, when the cause to which he devoted his life and soul is that of justice....He was often accused of narrow-mindedness. The truth of the matter is that he put on blinders in order to see more clearly, and he continued to wear them all his life.[40]

His reactions to other elements of the political scene were mixed. He interviewed General Grant, whom he found impressive despite his tobacco-spitting, and he poked a sly lesson to his French readers: "In his [Grant's] opinion, it is the place of Congress to give the impetus, and for the President to receive it. The fact that these views should be honestly and sincerely entertained by a victorious general of immense popularity is a peculiarly American trait."[41] American political campaigns, he explained, are a kind of periodic madness. Torchlight parades, booming cannons, the hyperbolic demagoguery of the Tammany Hall rousers of New York's Irish rabble--he found the spectacle interesting but not worth imitating. The great parties had little to commend them. But he was not fundamentally misled: "Under all the foam and spray, which the wind carries off, the great waves of the sea roll on."[42]

IV

Much as he enjoyed journalism--he confessed he was "crazy about it"[43]--he always needed more money. He took some rooms on Sheridan Square (once allegedly occupied by the future Napoleon III, he was amused to learn many years afterward) and opened a medical practice, but it soon bored him. Patients tired of tardy appointments while he hobnobbed about socially, read at the Cooper Institute and the Astor Library, and ploughed along on his translation of Mill. After finishing one volume of the *Logic*, he had dropped it soon after his arrival upon learning that someone else had done it, but he went on to complete the *Auguste Comte et le positivisme*, a work more to his taste, in April 1867. It was published in Paris in 1868 and went through five subsequent editions to 1898. Perhaps from this period came the outline for a play, *Le Puritain*, which Martet discovered among his effects--a melodramatic tale of stoic fortitude in the face of thwarted love and refusals to follow the easy road to worldly success.[44]

Probably late in the summer of 1867, Eugene Bushe (or by some accounts Horace Greeley) came forward with an introduction to a Miss Catherine Aiken of Stamford, Conn., proprietress of a seminary for Young Ladies.[45] Young doctor Clemenceau was hired as a part-time instructor in French and riding.

There is something incongruous in a picture of Georges Clemenceau leading giggling *jeunes misses américaines* through the intricacies of declensions and dressage, but he appeared to enjoy the work and his spirits improved. A couple of days in Stamford and then, as he put it, "I would beat it back to Broadway,"[46] to the theaters and to work on the next article. The dashing, bearded young Frenchman soon became the talk of Miss Aiken's school. He rode like a dream, told funny stories in a wonderfully accented New York slang, and exhibited a talent for making the rules of grammar simple and logical. "He was a real artist," a pupil recalled, "...and would make sketches on pieces of paper detached from his notes. One day a professor exclaimed, 'Those eyebrows look like Mary Plummer's!' He crumpled the paper in his hand and stopped making sketches for awhile."[47]

Journalism had done much to dissipate his depressions and give some direction to his spirit. And--for a time--so did love. Georges and Mary were drawn to each other but apparently disguised their feelings at first. Eight years older than she, austere but witty, highly principled yet worldly wise, he readily appealed to her late-adolescent imagination. Rides with him and the other girls in shaded lanes and along the shore did the rest. What Georges found in her is less easy to discern. "Beautiful Mary," as she was called, was a slender, dark-eyed charmer, and he was susceptible to feminine attention. She also had money--or at any rate the promise of it in the person of a wealthy uncle, Horace S. Taylor, a self-made man who had come to New York from Springfield, Mass., in 1854 to prosper as a Wall Street banker and a high dignitary of the Masons. He had become her guardian following the premature death of her father, Dr. William K. Plummer, a Springfield, Mass., and Bristol, N.H., dentist who had moved in 1857 to Skinner Prairie, Wisc., near Durand, and died in 1860, leaving three children.[48] But such resemblances as there were to Hortense Kestner--beauty and money--ended there. Although intelligent and a good student, she was basically unsophisticated, uneducated in anything much beyond the social graces expected of marriageable girls of her social standing. Perhaps he saw in her the kind of woman his mother was--quiet, loving, and steady. But Georges Clemenceau required an unusual woman for a wife. He had an extraordinarily large need for unforced, spontaneous affection and support. He needed, too, a woman with a will to match his own, perception to divine his shifting moods, strength to endure them, yet able to pull him up short when necessary. Mary was over her head, while Georges had lost his. They fell in love. It was a misfortune that would cost them dearly.

The courtship went on through the winter and spring of 1868.[49] A day or so before he left for France on 27 June, he got up his courage to propose. But Mary turned him down. Her refusal doubtless hit him hard and helps to account for his ambiguousness about his future plans in the letters he wrote that summer. Not surprisingly, he said nothing to Scheurer about this second disappointment. But all was not lost. A teacher at Miss Aiken's, Mrs. Ada

Chase Dimmick, along with some friends of hers had accompanied Georges back to France, where he showed them around Paris. On her return to New York she found Mary regretting her decision and helped to persuade her to relent. She then cabled the news to Georges, who had been spending time in the Vendée patching things up with his father and was currently planning a trip to Germany to familiarize himself with its culture and language.

The jaunt to Germany would wait. On 8 December Georges was back in New York. At first he pretended to hold out, but that soon ended. The main stumbling block now--though it may very well have been a motivating factor previously in Mary's refusal--was his insistence, true to his Blanquist oath, on a purely civil ceremony, a problem reminiscent of his father's in marrying the girl of *his* choice. It would appear likely, too, that he had by now made up his mind to settle with her in France. These conditions were hard for Mary and Mr. Taylor to accept, and Miss Aiken in the meantime was weighing in with pleas against her marrying an "adventurer" who was probably lying about his château back home.[50] But they finally gave way. (Mr. Taylor afterward repented and cut Mary from his will. A story, widely repeated later on, that Clemenceau had dissipated a huge dowry appears unfounded.[51])

Georges then departed for France on 23 January 1869 to bear the tidings and get some money--a lot of it, in fact. On 13 April, accompanied by an attorney from Nantes, he signed papers in Paris for a loan of 25,000 francs from Joseph-Marie Lafont,[52] with security being provided by a lien on a 34-hectare property at Mourzeuil (Vendée) belonging to his elder sister Emma and her husband, Léon Jacquet. With all now in order he crossed the Atlantic, once again, to fetch his bride, arriving in New York some time before 5 June. On 23 June, after slipping away from the annual school dinner at the Hotel St. Denis,[53] they were married in Mr. Taylor's residence at 333 Fifth Avenue by the Tammany Hall mayor of New York, Okey Hall.[54] And on the 26th, having apparently accomplished some civil formalities in Boston, they set sail from New York on the *Lafayette* to begin their life together.

V

While in France back in February, Georges had written to Auguste Scheurer:

> Two days before receiving your letter, I heard by chance the news you passed on to me....You'll be happy to learn that my state of mind is in every way what you would wish for me. I have long since recognized my folly and fully appreciated your wisdom as well as the patient friendliness with which you listened to my idiocies....[55]

The news was that Hortense had become engaged. On 6 April she married Charles Floquet, a lawyer a dozen years her senior who all agreed was marked for a brilliant future.

NOTES
CHAPTER III

[1] From Scheurer-Kestner's unpublished *Journal*, as cited in Albert Krebs, "Le secret de Clemenceau révélé par les souvenirs de Scheurer-Kestner," *Société industrielle de Mulhouse: Bulletin trimestriel*, 1969, no. 735, p. 71.

[2] *Ibid.*, p. 74 (dated 9 Feb. 1864).

[3] *Ibid.*, p. 80 (some time in Oct. 1864).

[4] *Ibid.*, pp. 81-82 (dated 10 Feb. 1865).

[5] See Duroselle, *Clemenceau*, pp. 60-61.

[6] Assertions that a fellow medical student, Dr. Gustave Dourlen, accompanied him appear erroneous; Dourlen went over in 1866. See Martet, *Clemenceau*, p. 324.

[7] *Ibid.*, pp. 317-319 (dated 10 Sept. 1865, replying to Georges' 21 Aug. letter). The common assertion, derived from Baldensperger (see n. 30 below) that he wrote his first article (dated 28 Sept.) the day he arrived seems altogether unlikely.

[8] Stephen Bonsal, "What Manner of Man Was Clemenceau?" *World's Work* 59 (1930):74. Bonsal knew him from the War and conducted him on his trip to America in 1922.

[9] Georges Wormser, *Clemenceau vu de près* (Hachette-Littérature, 1979), p. 41. For the 1866 sojourn see Duroselle, *Clemenceau*, p. 73.

[10] Léon Treich, *Vie et mort de Clemenceau* (Éditions de Portiques, 1929), p. 65. The letter also contained savage reflections on the death of Emperor Maximilian in Mexico; see p. 320 below. Wormser, in *Clemenceau vu de près*, p. 43n., at last confirmed that this oft-quoted letter was written to Mme. Jourdan.

[11] See Albert Krebs, "Le mariage de Clemenceau," *Mercure de France* 324 (1955):641; and Duroselle, *Clemenceau*, p. 75, regarding a letter to Mme. Jourdan of 10 March 1867.

[12] Krebs, "Le secret de Clemenceau," p. 82 (facsimile); Wormser, *Clemenceau vu de près*, p. 49. See also Duroselle, *Clemenceau*, p. 80.

13   Krebs, "Le secret de Clemenceau," p. 85.

14   *Ibid.*, pp. 85-86. Scheurer may have been referring to the period when he was courting Hortense.

15   Ellis, *The Early Life of Georges Clemenceau*; see p. 18 above.

16   Krebs, "Le secret de Clemenceau," p. 83 (dated 26 July).

17   Wormser, *Clemenceau vu de près*, pp. 40-42 (italics in the original).

18   Wormser, *La république de Clemenceau*, p. 478.

19   Wormser, *Clemenceau vu de près*, p. 49.

20   Krebs, "Le secret de Clemenceau," p. 84.

21   *New York World*, 22 Nov. 1922.

22   Wormser, *Clemenceau vu de près*, p. 40 (italics in the original).

23   Wormser, *La république de Clemenceau*, p. 479.

24   Wormser, *Clemenceau vu de près*, p. 49.

25   Martet, *Clemenceau*, p. 294.

26   *New York World*, 22 Nov. 1922.

27   Martet, *Clemenceau*, p. 319.

28   See "Notes et documents III: Georges Clemenceau à John Durand," *Revue de littérature comparée* 12 (1932):420-422, a letter dated 1 April 1867; and Alexander Woollcott, *While Rome Burns* (New York: The Viking Press, 1934), pp. 64-65.

29   See Duroselle, *Clemenceau*, p. 83.

30   Most of the articles are reprinted in edited versions in GC, *American Reconstruction, 1865-1870, and the Impeachment of President Johnson*, Edited and with an Introduction by Fernand Baldensperger, trans. Margaret MacVeagh (New York: Lincoln MacVeagh-The Dial Press, 1928; repr. Da Capo Press, 1969). Dates of unreprinted articles can be found in Ellis, *The Early Life of Georges Clemenceau*, p. 212. Some were written while he was in France and relying on news reports. The dates given here are of writing, not of publication. In 1868 *Le Temps* was printing 10-11,000 copies; see Pierre Albert, Gilles Feyel, and Jean-François Picard, *Documents pour l'histoire de la presse nationale au XIXe et XXe siècles* (Centre national de la recherche scientifique, 1977), pp. 33-34. Jules Ferry, Charles Floquet, and Henri Brisson were also writing for *Le Temps* at this time. The paper as yet

was not outrightly republican but was distinctly anticlerical. See Louis Girard, "Jules Ferry et la génération des républicains du Second Empire," in François Furet, ed., *Jules Ferry, fondateur de la république.* Colloque de l'École des hautes études en sciences sociales, 1982, présenté par François Furet, Civilisations et Sociétés, no. 72 (Éditions de l'École des hauts études en sciences sociales, 1985), p. 53 and *passim.*

31 George J. Adam, *The Tiger: Georges Clemenceau, 1841-1929* (New York: Harcourt, Brace, 1930), p. 28. Adam was a war correspondent.

32 HE, 14 Feb. 1917. In AU, 29 Nov. 1903, he praised their efforts.

33 HE, 22 April 1916.

34 GC, *La mêlée sociale* (Bibliothèque-Charpentier, 1919), p. 13. See also GC, *In the Evening of My Thought*, 2:399n.

35 HE, 14 Feb. 1917. Conclusion: American thought processes and moral categories are peculiar; probably an "impondérable américaine" will precipitate their entry into the war.

36 GC, *American Reconstruction*, p. 40.

37 *Ibid.*, pp. 298-299; dated 3 Nov. 1865. On his Darwinism see Linda L. Clark, *Social Darwinism in France* (University, AL: University of Alabama Press, 1984), p. 21. In May 1878 he attended a banquet for Herbert Spencer; *ibid.*, p. 45.

38 From Scheurer's *Journal*, in Watson, *Georges Clemenceau*, p. 30n.

39 GC, *American Reconstruction*, p. 161 (dated 6 March 1868).

40 *Ibid.*, p. 226 (dated 13 Aug.). See also pp. 124-125.

41 *Ibid.*, p. 200 (dated 12 June 1868).

42 *Ibid.*, p. 243 (dated 4 Sept. 1868). See also pp. 130-131, 239-242.

43 Williams, *The Tiger of France*, p. 50.

44 Jean Martet, *Le silence de M. Clemenceau* (Albin Michel, 1929), pp. 311-314. He dates it 1867-1868.

45 See "The Clemenceau Case," *New York World*, 14 March 1892, an interview with Mme. Georges Clemenceau.

46 Williams, *The Tiger of France*, pp. 52-53.

47   Mary Walton letter, in Wormser, *La république de Clemenceau*, pp. 99-100.

48   See Alice F. Brown, "The Love Story of Georges Clemenceau," *Mentor* 16 (Oct. 1928):17-19; and Luella M. Kirby and Carolyn B. Lenz, "Wife of Clemenceau Was a Wisconsin Girl," *Wisconsin Then and Now* 16 (1969):6-7. On Taylor see *New York Times,* 31 May 1880 and 22 May 1884. In 1880 he became Grand Master of the Grand Lodge of New York State.

49   The account here is based on Duroselle, *Clemenceau*, pp. 78-82, which contains significant new archival information, above all that concerning the financial arrangement, about which nothing has been published to date. The Woollcott loan (above, p. 48) was also in connection with his marriage.

50   Kirby and Lenz, "Wife of Clemenceau Was a Wisconsin Girl," p. 6.

51   See "The Clemenceau Case," *New York World*, 14 March 1892.

52   Duroselle, *Clemenceau*, p. 82, calls him a "friend." On p. 91 he confirms that he was the father of Jean-Antoine Lafont, his companion mentioned above.

53   According to the French physician cited above, anyhow; in *New York World*, 22 Nov. 1922.

54   Krebs, "Le mariage de Clemenceau," p. 647.   Duroselle, *Clemenceau*, p. 82, gives 20 June and 33 West 31st St., however.

55   Krebs, "Le secret de Clemenceau," pp. 84-85 (dated 3 Feb. 1869).

CHAPTER IV

Baptism
(1869-1871)

Georges and his American bride settled at l'Aubraie during the summer of 1869 for an indefinite stay. Four years of travels, some journalism, and a successful courtship had steadied him, but if he had put some healthy distance between himself and his father, he was back once again under the parental roof. There must have been some delicate moments during this honeymoon *en famille* in a gloomy château in the depths of the Vendée. The strain on Mary doubtless was acute, for in addition to adjusting to marriage and to life in an exotic setting, she was having to learn French in a serious way. Fortunately Georges' mother and sisters treated her with great kindness. One may assume that his father did too--nobody, Mary included, said otherwise then or later--but an absence of references to him in Georges' few surviving letters from this period leaves one suspecting the presence of some lingering covert tension on that side of the household.

As if to deal with it, Georges began to practice medicine in the neighborhood. A letter to Madame Jourdan (26 August 1869) implies that he had planned to set up in Paris after a suitable stay at l'Aubraie.[1] Practice in the provinces, besides, was notoriously unremunerative--hence the search for dowered brides. About the time he wrote, however, Mary became pregnant, and this may have persuaded him to postpone a move. For the present he found the role of country doctor congenial enough, although he would later wonder why he had chosen medicine over law, even to please his father. A pharmacist from Nantes joined him as a professional and hunting companion. "Life was pleasant in those days," he recalled. "Next to the sorcerers and quacks, Grimaux and I held an honorable place in the confidence of the peasants, ever ready to consult us in certain cases of illness which did not respond to the customary absence of any treatment whatsoever."[2]

The months drifted by. On 6 June 1870 a daughter, Madeleine, was born.[3] Perhaps the plan to move to Paris was revived, perhaps not. Six weeks later, however, the plans of millions of obscure persons no longer mattered very much, for France had gone to war with Prussia and her allied German states. It was an event whose repercussions profoundly affected the rest of Georges Clemenceau's life.

II

In two short wars with Denmark (1864) and Austria (1866) and via a diplomatic *tour de force*, the minister-president of Prussia, Otto von Bismarck, had established Prussia's dominance in the Germanies and prepared for a showdown should Napoleon III challenge the new order. Following a coup in Spain he pushed the candidacy of a Hohenzollern for the throne. Napoleon, ill and badly advised, took the bait. The provinces greeted the declaration of war (19 July) mostly with massive indifference. Not so Clemenceau. During the past year the Empire, responding to pressures, had undergone a significant liberalization, a development which had persuaded many hitherto irreconcilable Republicans, Clemenceau included, to take the oath of loyalty, thus signifying their willingness to work within the legal framework.[4] This nevertheless did not prevent him from working against approval of the Liberal Empire in the plebiscite of 8 May 1870, which confirmed the regime by an overwhelming margin of 7,358,786 to 1,571,939. In a speech at Ste.-Hermine in 1921 he wryly recalled making his "debut" in politics in an old room used to store garden tools, addressing an audience of ten including his father, who could not compromise himself and thus had asked him to take over: "I spoke against the plebiscite without obtaining a gesture, a wink of the eyes from the wholly subdued [*effarés*] listeners." The sole convert he won denied afterward that he had supported him; but when the war came a few weeks later, he noted, the laughter at his expense in the villages turned to tears.[5]

The war faced the Empire's opponents with a terrible dilemma: defeat was inadmissible, while victory would consolidate a regime they still despised.[6] Clemenceau, unlike most of his countrymen and contemporary observers, doubted the Empire's ability to win this war. His doubt, however, left a way open to him to escape the dilemma, for like most Republicans of his generation he had an almost mystic faith in the ability of a Republic to save France just as it had during the Great Revolution. A republic could--would--prevent the Empire's defeat from becoming France's defeat. Firm in this belief, responding to the pull of impending events when the news filtering back to the hinterlands began to take an ominous turn, and doubtless feeling he at least should offer his services as a physician, he bade good-bye sometime in early August and went to Paris.[7]

The crisis was not long in coming. Late in August the Empire's two main field armies were surrounded at Metz and Sédan. When news of Napoleon's surrender at Sédan swirled through the city, Clemenceau marched with the throng which broke into the Palais-Bourbon to drive out the Corps Législatif; later that day Floquet took him and some others to close down the Senate. The Republic was duly proclaimed at the Hôtel de Ville, and the "Revolution of September 4th" was over.

Napoleon's war was finished, but not the Republic's. A Government of National Defense hastily prepared for a siege as the Prussians and their German allies bore down on the city. Léon Gambetta, the new minister of the interior, named Étienne Arago mayor of Paris and advised him on appointments of provisional mayors for the city's twenty arrondissements. The XVIIIth (Montmartre-LaChapelle), a difficult assignment,--it had recorded a 74% vote against the regime in May, the second highest in Paris--needed a reliable, preferably left-leaning, incumbent. They settled on a mutual acquaintance, Dr. Georges Clemenceau.

Large windmills on the heights stood as a reminder that Montmartre had only recently come within the city limits. It was inhabited by crowds of poor people displaced by Haussmann's building projects, by artisans, clerks, and (in La Chapelle) some factory and railway workers. Although it was not the most radical district, socialism had made inroads, and suspicion of middle-class lawyers and journalists, erstwhile leaders there, was growing. Clemenceau faced a delicate situation.

The government having left the mayors largely to their own devices, he set out to meet the test by proving that there were no limits to his zeal. Four days after the German ring closed, he summoned his constituents (23 September) to "find our inspiration in the example of our forefathers, and like them we shall conquer."[8] He kept in constant movement, riding herd on the provisioners (price controls were erratic, meat unrationed until October, and bread only near the end of the siege), settling disputes, scrounging fuel, finding space for refugees, treating the sick, browbeating his superiors, and keeping the throngs of newly enrolled National Guards trained, fed, and out of mischief. Although he left the Church schools alone, he cancelled tuitions in the public schools and replaced clerical with lay instructors, among them Louise Michel, "the Red Virgin of Revolution." If the Republic would save France as in '93, the twenty-nine-year-old mayor of Montmartre meant to give it every weapon.

Political problems came to a head in late October. The government, dominated by very moderate lawyers and conventional generals, waffled for weeks on the elections question, but it finally ordered one for Paris after facing down an armed demonstration (31 October) carried out by some National Guards from the "red" districts responding to rumors of a capitulation. Many of the demonstrators were from Montmartre, and Blanqui had been arrested. Clemenceau had found himself in a quandry. A network of vigilance committees and clubs, strongly influenced in Montmartre by socialist and Blanquist elements, had spread through the city. He sympathized with their intentions, promoted the election of Blanqui as a battalion commander in the Guard for inspirational purposes, and allowed the local vigilance committee to use a room at his *mairie*; but he distrusted their methods and judgment and fostered a political club more attuned to his neo-Jacobin leanings, which did not countenance insurrection against a republic or government by committees of patriots however sincere. He posted a protest against any idea of an armistice, joined with the other mayors in the demand for elections, declared (after the fact) his sympathy with the 31 October demonstrators, and resigned his office.[9]

A crackdown cooled off the radicals. Clemenceau reconsidered his resignation and stood for election. He urged the voters, albeit with no enthusiasm, to support the government in a plebiscite it had ordered: "The Government...perhaps reflects better than any other the actual state of opinion."[10] He got sixty-five percent of the vote on 5 November, running against his government-appointed replacement, but the vigilance committee exacted a price: Simon Dereure and Victor Jaclard joined his old friend Jean Lafont as his deputy mayors. The three agreed, however, to sign an appeal for calm and patience. He had won his first election.[11]

The siege continued while Gambetta worked furiously to raise relieving armies in the provinces. Discouragement settled in when a sortie in late November met with bloody failure. Living in a city in which dogs, rats, and even animals from the zoo were fetching good prices, Clemenceau probably was not as hopeful as he appeared in a letter he sent (18 December) to Mary by balloon-post. He described Prussian losses as "enormous" and the besieged as confident, ready to fight "to the very end." He closed with tender words for little Maddie and his wife: "It is so hard not to hear a single word from you....I have not forgotten *one* of the promises I made you. I shall keep them all and I am sure we will see each other soon."[12] His optimism may have stemmed in part from suspicion that the Germans might be the likely ones to read any words from inside the city walls. The letter, in fact, ended up in Bavaria, although most of his others got through. The affair of the "Orsini bombs," however, showed that he was not immune to the unrealistic thinking generated by "siege fever." He approved the manufacture of a large number of homemade bombs, claiming they would be useful "in the hands of women and children" should the Germans break in. The government smelled a plot and confiscated the devices. On Arago's plea that the young mayor was "a good republican," they spared him arrest.[13]

As the suffering increased, exasperation mounted. The government tried to use the mayors to cover its fumblings but only provoked them into making angry charges of incompetence and worse. In an especially stormy meeting of the mayors on 28 December, Clemenceau, seconded by

Delescluze and others from the radical districts, called for more power for the mayors and for sweeping changes in the military leadership, but to no avail. He was also among those most keen for the great breakout attack the National Guard had demanded for weeks. But the army chiefs, and most of the ministry, had little faith in the competence of the Guard and feared its political strength. At length, facing a rapidly deteriorating supply situation and having nothing better to propose, they decided to call its hand. The slaughtered sortie at Buzenval (19 January) was everything the government feared (or hoped) it would be. A day of stunned silence followed, and then a spasm of revolt. Jaclard and Dereure participated, but Clemenceau and the other neo-Jacobins stayed away. The uprising failed. The next day the government, riven by contradictory feelings of relief and discouragement, opened negotiations at Versailles. Clemenceau denounced the parleys in an Open Letter,[14] but most people had had enough. On 28 January an armistice was signed.

III

Declining a plea from Gambetta that he go to Lyon as prefect, Clemenceau stood for election on 8 February to the National Assembly to be convoked in Bordeaux to decide whether to accept the newly proclaimed German Empire's peace terms. He earned a modest twenty-seventh place among the forty-three at-large seats allotted to Paris.[15] Ominously, the lists bearing his name did no better in Montmartre, where both the vigilance committee and the moderates shunned him.

The National Assembly was for Clemenceau a cold shower. The provinces had voted overwhelmingly for local notables, who were mainly monarchist in sentiment and for making peace. Republicans numbered less than a third of the whole, and radicals like Clemenceau comprised barely a quarter of the Republicans. Adolphe Thiers, Orleanist elder statesman, patriot, and bustling power-lover, the "Chief of the Executive Power of the French Republic," received terms from Bismarck which confirmed everyone's worst forebodings: cession of Alsace and part of Lorraine, a huge indemnity (by the standards of the time), and a triumphal march into Paris for the German army. Anguished over the humiliation of his country and apprehensive about the mood in Paris, Clemenceau fought the terms to the end. With a handful of deputies (the "Protestaires")--among them Victor Hugo, Louis Blanc, Sadi Carnot, Édouard Lockroy, Brisson, Ranc, Floquet-- he signed an address (18 February) contesting the legality of the impending cession of Alsace-Lorraine.[16] Shortly before the fatal day of ratification, he returned briefly to Paris with several other deputies to report on the city's mood to the Assembly--he found it calm[17]--and to prepare for the entry of the hated Prussians. His proclamation to Montmartre flirted with demagoguery ("We have been handed over without conditions") but warned that violence would only hurt the Republic and bring useless destruction.[18] The final tally at Bordeaux (1 March) showed 546 to 107 for acceptance. In opposing ratification Clemenceau followed the dictates of his heart, not his head. In 1919 he admitted to Lloyd George and Wilson that Thiers had been right and that "there was absolutely nothing else that could have been done."[19]

Having settled with the Germans, the Assembly turned to Paris. The wretched, shivering city (the winter was one of the century's severest), full of armed men furious at the "sell-out" and fearful that the Republic would be ditched, needed gestures of reconciliation and recognition of its sacrifices. In truth, neither Thiers nor the Assembly (most of it, anyhow) wanted to provoke violence, but they did want to firm up their shaky authority both in Paris and throughout the country. Nevertheless, the measures they took to this end--for example, moving the Assembly back to Versailles rather than to Paris and ending the wartime moratorium on commercial debt collections-- however justified they appeared from the perspective of Bordeaux, inevitably struck Paris with great force and just as inevitably were interpreted there as acts of a crassly insensitive government bent upon provocation.[20]

Clemenceau returned again to Montmartre to try conciliation. He was obviously concerned about the situation there, but to judge from a letter to Madame Jourdan dated 11 March, he was far from pessimistic, dismissing talk of impending trouble as rumors spread by persons with "no other aim than to prevent the Assembly from returning to Paris."[21] Nevertheless, the huge supply of weapons in the city, particularly the more than four hundred cannons and *mitrailleuses* (a kind of Gatling gun) corralled by the National Guard, which had paid for them by public subscription, had become a major breeder of disputes. He tried to arrange a peaceful transfer of the ordnance to the government's control, convinced that it menaced civil peace and authority: the German army, after all, still lay outside the city and might intervene if fighting broke out. Besides, he could hardly remain uninvolved, for 171 pieces, by far the largest of some seventeen concentrations, looked down on the city from the Buttes of Montmartre.

But Clemenceau's authority had waned since February while that of the vigilance committee and the local National Guard committee had grown. Consequently, when he failed as an intermediary in negotiations (10-13 March) between the Montmartre National Guard and the government-appointed chief of the Guard, General d'Aurelle de Paladines--negotiations which resulted in two attempts, aborted by misunderstandings and angry crowds, to transfer the guns peacefully--and when these failures coincided with an order from the government shutting down six radical newspapers, the publication of sentences meted out for the 31 October uprising, and another, more serious, try at getting away some guns, this time at the Place des Vosges (16 March), he was the target of insinuations that he was either an agente of *la Réaction* or its dupe.[22] The only hopeful element in the imbroglio was the Guard's disinclination to take any forceful action on its own. This passivity encouraged Thiers to make a fateful decision.

Exceedingly concerned to placate the money markets which he needed in order to begin paying the German indemnity, convinced by the Place des Vosges failure that negotiations with the Guard were going nowhere, and now fearing that if he could not greet the National Assembly (scheduled to reconvene at Versailles on 20 March) with news that the city was in full control, then the Assembly itself would make things worse by taking more violent measures such as cutting off the Guard's pay--Thiers resolved on the spur of the moment to order a vast, rapid, stealthy operation to seize the cannons and arrest the troublemakers. Reports from government informants indicated that the risks would be small and that "good" Guard units would rally to the government. But generals Vinoy and d'Aurelle, thrice-burned, objected, as did most of the rest of the ministers and officials he convened mere hours before operations would commence. Incredibly, he neither consulted nor warned the mayors.

Early on the night of 17-18 March, an officer went to the Montmartre heights, the most difficult locale, and showed the sleepy, bored sentries an order signed by Clemenceau. The forgery worked; all but seven guards went home to bed. At 2:30 A.M. some fifteen thousand Regulars and three thousand armed police moved out across the fog-shrouded city, reaching the gun parks between 3:00 and 5:00. That marked the end of any coherent movement. By mid-morning the operation had turned into a colossal fiasco, and by late afternoon Thiers had fled to Versailles, leaving orders to the army to evacuate the city.

IV

Clemenceau disdained memoir writing, but he made an exception for the events of the 18th of March.[23] According to his account, written in 1872 shortly after an official inquiry, he first learned of the attempted seizure at 6:00 A.M. when he was awakened by Dereure.

He immediately climbed to the Buttes, where he found General Lecomte's detachment waiting for horses and hitches to come up to move the guns. He berated Lecomte for the government's decision but advised that since the quarter still seemed calm, the pieces should be moved "with the least possible delay." After treating a Guardsman wounded during the seizure, he went down to the *mairie* for a stretcher. But when he returned Lecomte angrily forbade him to move the dying man, evidently suspecting he intended to rouse the quarter by the old ploy of "parading the corpse." At that he gave up in frustration and returned again to the *mairie*.[24]

He remained there for the next nine hours. In the meantime, the troops on the Buttes, pressed by a growing crowd of excited townspeople and Guards angered by Lecomte's heartless decision, mutinied and joined with the Guard to seize Lecomte, some of his officers, and a number of the hated police. A group of police was brought down to the *mairie*, where Clemenceau had them confined to the Guardhouse next door. From this point on he felt obliged to stay close by to protect them with such authority as he still retained. About 10:00 A.M., Captain Mayer of the Guard informed him that Lecomte's party had been taken to the "Château-Rouge," a dancehall nearby on the Buttes. He ordered Mayer back to oversee their safety.[25] He also sent an emissary to contact some of the other mayors. A couple turned up, and he sent them to find others and convoke a meeting at Montmartre. They went off, told the government of Lecomte's capture, but did not return. The mayors met instead about 3:00 P.M. at the *mairie* of the IInd Arrondissement. By 4:00 P.M. Thiers and the government departed for Versailles.

Evidently Clemenceau knew little about the movement in other quarters and in no way anticipated Thiers' withdrawal order. He told Jaclard it seemed "impossible...that the troops will not resume the offensive and the government remain masters of the ground," for he could not imagine any party overlooking the probability of a German occupation of the city if the government were overthrown.[26] He passed the afternoon in tense waiting, an object of suspicion. At one point he found the vigilance committee deliberating in one of the *mairie*'s rooms and ordered them out. After a quarter hour of "extreme anxiety" for him, they left.

Suddenly, at 4:30 P.M., captains Mayer and Garcin burst in with confused reports that generals Lecomte and Thomas had been taken somewhere, probably to the Buttes, and that there was talk that they were to be shot. Gen. Clément Thomas, a hated former commander of the Guard, had been recognized at the Place-Pigalle in civilian clothes and hustled off to No. 6, rue des Rosiers, a local Guard headquarters, where Lecomte's party had been taken (about 3:00 P.M.) on mysterious orders.[27] Clemenceau knew nothing of the transfer nor of Thomas's capture until this moment. With the two captains and an aide, Sabourdy, he set off at once, putting on his tricolor sash as he ran. Before he gained the Buttes he heard reports that the generals had been killed, and when he at last reached the rue des Rosiers the dreadful news was confirmed.[28] He was too late.

Seeing a detachment of Guards leaving with several prisoners perhaps destined for execution, he tried to stop them, but on the plea of one of the prisoners he stepped aside and they departed. What then ensued remained engraved on his memory:

> Suddenly a terrific noise broke out and the mob which filled the courtyard of No. 6 burst into the street in the grip of some kind of frenzy.

Amongst them were chasseurs, soldiers of the Line, National Guards, women, and children. All were shrieking like wild animals without realizing what they were doing. I observed then that pathological phenomenon which might be called blood lust. A breath of madness seemed to have passed over the mob; from a wall children brandished indescribable trophies; women, disheveled and emaciated, flung their arms about uttering raucous cries, having apparently taken leave of their senses....Men were dancing about and jostling one another in a kind of savage fury. It was one of those extraordinary nervous outbursts, so frequent in the Middle Ages, which still occur amongst masses of human beings under the stress of some primeval emotion.[29]

For the next hour Clemenceau lived on a knife edge. Threats hurtled at him from all sides. He started down the street that the detachment had taken but then decided instead to return to the *mairie* by the way he had come, judging, he wrote, that it would be best to face his accusers on the spot rather than risk a demonstration afterward which might result in the massacre of the prisoners at the Guardhouse. With agonizing slowness he and Sabourdy (Mayer and Garcin having vanished) made their way down the streets from the Buttes. More than once Sabourdy got them through, for he was widely respected in the quarter. Counterattack helped, too; several times Clemenceau told a particularly menacing group that they had disgraced the Republic and that the consequences of Lecomte's murder--he still disbelieved the report about Thomas--would be disastrous. "My vigorous attitude," he wrote, "caused them to retreat."[30]

Back at the *mairie* at last, he found Victor Schoelcher and Lockroy waiting for him. They set off to see the vigilance committee, which was now at the rue de la Chausée-Clignancourt.[31] They received assurances there that the officers were again at the "Château-Rouge" and would be released in the evening. Clemenceau then returned to his post. Deciding that he would not attend an emergency meeting of the mayors, he remained alone at the *mairie* and later that night effected a quiet escape of the Guardhouse prisoners.

To the end of his life, Clemenceau met with accusations that he had conspired with the government or, contrarily, that the blood of Lecomte and Thomas was on his hands.[32] His account, whose accuracy has held up well despite charges that it was self-serving, refuted both contentions. Like the other mayors, he was victimized by Thiers' decision: faced with a *fait accompli*, he had no authority to countermand Lecomte's orders, and he had an evident duty to protect the men brought to the *mairie*. Moreover, he learned of the peril to the generals only minutes before their deaths. Once informed, he acted with speed and cool courage, but he was just too late. Therein lies the nub of the criticism of his actions. He was pushed by events, at the mercy of chance informants, and his initiatives were few. He had underestimated the temperature of the city before the 18th and overestimated his prestige in his quarter, and he continued to do so until the capture of Lecomte, which took him by surprise. To protect the men in the Guardhouse meant to leave the important prisoners at the "Château-Rouge" totally at the mercy of erratic National Guards and mutinous Regulars whose mood was more dangerous than he evidently believed. Nevertheless, no one can know what he might have accomplished had he gone about trying to make peace; he was so suspect that he might have made matters worse. He had become intensely aware, and rightly so, of this suspicion, which he found everywhere. Inexperienced, conscientious, he searched in the chaos to find where duty lay.

V

The events of 18 March, it is worth nothing, did not seem to impair his self-confidence. Also, his prominent role in negotiations between Versailles and the insurrectionary Central Committee of the National Guard testified to a recognition of his abilities and trust in his good faith--except, for the time being, in Montmartre, where he was evicted from the *mairie* on 22 March. In essence, the Central Committee wished to legitimize its control of the Guard and hold immediate elections for a municipal council with more powers of home rule for Paris than any government in France has ever been willing to concede to that giant city. Defense of the Republic was the overarching purpose of such proposals. The mayors and deputies of Paris generally supported these desires on the floor of the Assembly. Clemenceau's interventions there showed the strain of day-and-night parleys with intransigent and often unreliable parties. He castigated the government for abandoning Paris and warned that it stood at the brink of a catastrophe, for not just Paris but all France would suffer if it assumed "the terrible responsibility" of refusing to grant immediate elections. His most telling political argument was that a legally sanctioned election would "provide an opportunity for the friends of order in Paris to intervene."[33] But his words of conciliation were drowned in howls provoked by his indictments.

It was no use. He and a handful of mayors, alarmed by rumors that the Orleanists in the Assembly were plotting to oust Thiers and restore the monarchy, "authorized" an election called unilaterally by the Central Committee for 26 March. The hopes of the "friends of order" washed away as the insurgent radicals won and proclaimed the Commune. The following day Clemenceau resigned from the National Assembly.

He did not, however, give up efforts to bridge the chasm now opened between Versailles and the besieged Commune. The first armed clash (3 April) helped provoke organization of the League of Republican Union for the Rights of Paris, composed mainly of former Paris mayors and deputies and led by Floquet, Lockroy, Ranc, and Clemenceau.[34] "Neo-Jacobins," for the most part, who rejected the centralizing authoritarianism of the old Jacobin tradition harking back to the Terror's Committee of Public Safety of 1793-94, they hoped instead to found a decentralized Republic which would unite largely self-governing communes in a participatory democracy--a Republic no longer enthralled by the old visions of revolutionary excess and bloodshed which at the moment in Paris were haunting so many over-excited spirits.[35] The League thought the Commune was legitimate in all but name and that the government should simply recognize the fact, grant Paris full municipal rights, end hostilities, and permit the Guard for the present to retain its arms: as Clemenceau argued, an armed Guard, Republicans all, would be insurance against a move by the Assembly's monarchists to strangle the Republic.[36]

At least six meetings with Thiers followed between 10 April and 20 May. At first Thiers seemed conciliatory, but negotiations foundered, finally, on his determination to send the Regulars into the city to disarm the Guard. This point had such real and symbolic significance that reconciliation proved impossible. Exasperated beyond measure, Clemenceau groaned in a letter to

Scheurer (7 May), "We have given ourselves the delightful task of speaking the language of reason to madmen of every shade who are gaily leading what's left of our country into the abyss." As he succinctly put in a following letter, "The Versaillais are as crazed as the Parisians of the Commune."[37]

The League meanwhile expanded its activities to provincial cities, preaching up republicanism: if the Assembly defeated Paris, it still would not have defeated the Republic. Clemenceau left Paris on May 10 for Bordeaux to attend a congress of delegates from Republican cities which the government had banned. The congress never met, and two of his comrades were arrested, but he escaped and returned to Paris via Strasbourg on the night of 21 May. Early that day the Regulars had broken into the city: "Bloody Week" had begun. He tried to gain entry but fortunately was denied. A man resembling him later escaped summary execution only by proving that he was not the late mayor of Montmartre.[38]

VI

He went home to lie low. Since August he had spent only two-and-a-half days there during brief detours on transits between Paris and Bordeaux. Fearing discovery by the government or the Communards, both of whom were looking for him, he slipped over to Thann to stay with Scheurer awhile and then ventured back again to Paris on 15 June.[39]

Lacerated by humiliating defeat at the hands of the Germans, he had watched in anguished impotence the spectacle of Frenchmen abasing themselves in a savage civil war under the eyes of their conquerors. The impression it made on him was indelible. Nearly half a century later in the midst of the First World War he still could devote most of an article to a bitter indictment of "the little *bourgeoisissimo*....[that] marvelous product of all that human life can admit in its construction in the way of sterility and artificiality": Monsieur Louis-Adolphe Thiers.[40]

NOTES
CHAPTER IV

1   Wormser, *Clemenceau vu de près*, pp. 53-54.

2   GC, *La honte* (P.-V. Stock, 1903), pp. 140-142. Édouard Grimaux, provisional adjunct-mayor in Montmartre, 30 Oct.-4 Nov. 1870, was dismissed from his chair at the École Polytéchnique in 1898 after signing a petition supporting Zola.

3   See Duroselle, *Clemenceau*, p. 91. Other sources give 2 June.

4   See Watson, "Clemenceau and Blanqui," p. 390.

5   GC, *Discours prononcé à Sainte-Hermine le 2 octobre 1921* (Payot, 1921), n.p.

6   See Watson, *Georges Clemenceau*, p. 34, a letter to Scheurer, 23 July 1870.

7   See Duroselle, *Clemenceau*, p. 91.

8   Martet, *Clemenceau*, p. 285.

9   See Étienne Arago, *L'Hôtel de Ville au 4 septembre et pendant le siège* (J. Hetzel, [1874]), p. 313. Henri Arrault replaced him as provisional mayor.

10   Speech at the "Club Reine-Blanche," in Maurice Choury, *Les origines de la Commune, Paris livré* (Éditions Sociales, 1960), p. 97. (The "Reine-Blanche" dancehall was later rebuilt as the famous "Moulin-Rouge.") On his political activity see Robert Wolfe, "The Parisian Club de la Révolution of the Eighteenth Arrondissement, 1870-1871," *Past and Present*, no. 39 (April 1968), pp. 81-119.

11   Manifesto text in Wormser, *La république de Clemenceau*, p. 105. Election results (JORF, 6, 10 Nov. 1870): Clemenceau, 9,409; Arrault (provisional mayor), 4,786; Lafont, 7,293; Dereure, 6,570; Jaclard, 6,350. Jaclard, who was condemned to life at forced labor after the Commune but escaped into exile, became a close friend. He returned after the amnesty of 1880 and was the editorial staff secretary at *La Justice*. See Duroselle, *Clemenceau*, p. 95.

12   Stanley J. Pincetl, Jr., "A Letter of Clemenceau to His Wife by Balloon," *French Historical Studies* 2, no. 4 (Fall, 1962): 511-514.

13   See Ernest Cresson, *Cent jours du siège à la Préfecture de Police* (Plon-Nourrit, 1901), pp. 38-41; and Henri Améline, ed., *Dépositions de témoins de l'enquête sur l'insurrection du 18 mars*, 3 vols. (É. Dentu, 1872), 1:243, 254.

14   Text in Wormser, *La république de Clemenceau*, p. 108.

15   France. *Annales de l'Assemblée Nationale* (Imprimerie Nationale, 1871), 16 Feb. 1871, p. 47; JORF, 21 Feb. 1871.

16   Another protest followed on 2 March; text in Martet, *Clemenceau*, p. 289.

17   See Jean Bruhat, Jean Dautry, and Émile Tersen, *La Commune de 1871*, 2nd ed. (Éditions Sociales, 1970), p. 104.

18   Text in Martet, *Clemenceau*, p. 288.

19   Paul Mantoux, ed., *Les déliberations du Conseil des Quatre (24 mars-28 juin 1919)*. Notes de l'Officier Interprête Paul Mantoux, 2 vols. (Éditions du Centre national de la recherche scientifique, 1955), 1:243. See also AU, 26 June 1905; and HL, 3 Aug. 1914, repr. in GC, *La France devant l'Allemagne*, eds. Louis Lumet and Jean Martet, 2nd ed. (Payot, 1918), p. 113.

20   See David Eugene Griffen, "Adolphe Thiers, the Mayors, and the Coming of the Paris Commune of 1871" (Ph.D. diss., University of California at Santa Barbara, 1971), pp. 107, 112, 157, and *passim*.

21   Wormser, *Clemenceau vu de près*, pp. 59-61.

22   Clemenceau's account is in JORF, 16 May 1876, pp. 3336-3337. See also Robert Tombs, *The War Against Paris, 1871* (Cambridge: Cambridge University Press, 1981), pp. 34-35.

23   Martet, *Clemenceau*, pp. 163-185, contains an abridgement of the still-unpublished memoir. It agrees fundamentally, if not in every detail, with his testimony at the trial of those charged with the Lecomte-Thomas murders and at the Poussargues duel trial. See *Le Temps*, 10, 11, 13, 15 Nov. 1871, 5 Oct., 16 Nov. 1872.

24   Clemenceau testified at the 1871 trial (n. 23 above) that the "call to arms" was not beaten until after he returned to the *mairie*. Others maintained it was being beaten while he was trying to persuade Lecomte to let the wounded man be moved and that he had misled Lecomte with assurances that he could keep order.

25   Captain Garcin said Clemenceau told him regarding the prisoners, "Do what you want about it!" See Georges Soria, *Grande histoire de la Commune*, 5 vols. (Livre Club Diderot, 1970-71), 1:356.

26   Martet, *Clemenceau*, pp. 174-175.

27   The orders probably came from the local Guard committee, but the signatures were illegible.

28   He wrote that when he set out he knew only that the prisoners were not at the "Château-Rouge"; Mayer told him to go to the Buttes. But if Fiaux is correct in saying that Garcin brought the orders (n. 27 above), then why didn't *he* tell him where to go? Louis Fiaux, *Histoire de la guerre civile de 1871* (G. Charpentier, 1879), p. 71.

29   Martet, *Clemenceau*, p. 182.

30   *Ibid.*, p. 184.

31   See Fiaux, *Histoire de la guerre civile de 1871*, p. 77. Jerôme Langlois gave a variant version, in Améline, *Dépositions de témoins*, 2:65-67.

32   Mme. Thomas refused to receive him and hear his explanations, calling him "my husband's murderer." Watson, *Georges Clemenceau*, p. 55n.

33   JORF, 20 March 1871, pp. 195-196, and 21 March, pp. 219 (quoted), 222.

34   See Jeanne Gaillard, "Le radicalisme pendant la Commune d'après les papiers de la Ligue d'Union républicaine des Droits de Paris," *Société d'histoire moderne: Bulletin*, no. 1 (1966), pp. 8-14.

35   See Philip G. Nord, "The Party of Conciliation and the Paris Commune," *French Historical Studies* 15, no. 1 (Spring, 1987), pp. 4-5, 35, and *passim*.

36   See Watson, *Georges Clemenceau*, p. 52.

37   From Scheurer's *Journal*, in Jacques Kayser, *Les grandes batailles du radicalisme des origines aux portes du pouvoir, 1820-1901* (Rivière, 1962), p. 52n.

38   Letter to a woman (Mme. Jourdan?), 26 May 1871, in Léon Treich, *L'esprit de Clemenceau*, 5th ed. (Gallimard, 1925), pp. 102-103.

39   See Duroselle, *Clemenceau*, pp. 103, 111-112.

40   HE, 27 April 1915. He compared him to a Japanese dwarf tree (Thiers was very short) which is pruned to give it the appearance of being distant and powerful. See also Martet, *Clemenceau*, pp. 279, 355.

CHAPTER V

Toward the Heights
(1871-1880)

During the last months before the war, Clemenceau had grown restless with life in the Vendée and his desultory medical practice there.[1] So it is not surprising that when he returned to Paris in mid-June he apparently was soon thinking of settling there permanently. His purpose in the interim, however, had undergone a reorientation. Politics was in his blood now despite the 18th of March; as he ironically observed in old age, "Even that didn't cure me."[2] It was almost, too, as if he felt a need to reenter the arena without delay lest his ideals and hopes for the Republic should be permanently damaged by leaving himself too much time to dwell on the scenes he had witnessed and the disillusioning experiences he had undergone during his baptism. Significantly, he advised his father about this time, with no more than a hint of irony, not to go to Paris for the present if he wished to keep his Republican faith intact.[3] In any case, medicine clearly interested him now less than politics--and vindication.

His fortunes did not mend as quickly as he may have anticipated. By-elections for the National Assembly were held in July 1871. He failed in an attempt to get on the Radical Republican list for Nantes, but he did succeed in Paris, only to be trounced at the polls. The results of this election, which saw about 100 of 114 vacant seats won by Republicans, were highly encouraging nonetheless. He recalled walking along the Seine afterwards with Arthur Ranc and both of them rejoicing, "All is saved, the provinces haven't been scared off!"[4] It had not been the same in 1848; fear that the Republic might be fatally harmed by violence as had been the case after the June Days had helped keep many radical Republicans like Clemenceau from finally throwing in their lot with the Commune.

Lowering his sights, he ran in the Clignancourt district of Montmartre for the Paris Municipal Council, which also conferred membership on the General Council of the Department of the Seine. He was on a ticket sponsored by the Republican Union for the Rights of Paris, successor to the League, and won (30 July), after a run-off ballot, with an undistinguished thirty-seven percent of a very light vote. Thereafter, his reputation in the quarter climbed back steadily, no doubt helped along in the early stages by an encounter (21 November 1871) with a Maj. Noël Poussargues, who had insulted him for his actions on 18 March. He shot the officer in the thigh, served a short sentence (9-24 November 1872) for it in the Concièrgerie Prison following a trial in October 1872, duelling being illegal, and ever after was held in respectful awe on "the field of honor."[5] On 29 November 1874 he was reelected over a Bonapartist opponent by a resounding 5,980 to 1,688 margin.

His standing on the municipal council likewise progressed, and more rapidly than one might expect inasmuch as the Radical Republicans at the outset comprised only a quarter of the eighty-member body and suffered the handicap of being called "the Communards" because of their objections to the government's harsh treatment of the rebels. Furthermore, they were aggressive--"The Finger-in-the-Eye Society" was another nickname--with Clemenceau the most outspoken and obstreperous. Because of, or perhaps in spite of, their views and behavior, they finally gained a working control of the council, symbolized by Clemenceau's elections as secretary on 12 February 1873 and 11 January 1875, vice-president on 5 May, and president on 29 November.

Clemenceau's more than four years on the council served as his springboard back into national politics.[6] He was an active member of committees on finance, public assistance and education, health and hygiene, aid to neglected and abandoned children, and architectural landmarks. He produced three voluminous reports on child assistance, advocating, for example, that unwed mothers be paid subsidies so they could nurse their children themselves rather than have to give them up to state-paid wetnurses. The "stupid bourgeoisie," he wrote later, accused him of thus encouraging vice. He also proposed sending sick children to the country for fresh air instead of to the hospitals, where hygienic measures often left something to be desired; it would be "better to visit them there [in the country] than in the cemetery."[7]

The Commune had made municipal self-government a touchy issue. The new law passed to regulate it (14 April 1871) left Paris as the only city without a mayor and gave the municipal council power only to advise the prefect of the Seine. During his council years Clemenceau was a leader in pushing for municipal liberties. Nothing concrete was won until long after he left the council, but he was the principal proponent of a tactic which had an important effect on national politics. Post-Commune Paris was burdened by a fifty-million-franc debt. He used this as a means to link the issue of control of municipal finance with that of church-state relations, arguing, for example, that, given its scarcity, money should be used to build schools rather than repair churches. Forging on, he proposed refusing on principle to appropriate money for any religious purposes whatever, thus leaving the National Assembly to bear the onus. The upshot was the growth of anticlericalism in Paris, which helped to put himself and the Radical faction in control of the council by 1875 and to thrust the issue to the fore at the national level by the end of the decade, when Jules Ferry would launch a campaign to get the clergy out of public education. When he assumed the council presidency in 1875, Clemenceau, in his widely noted inaugural speech, sounded a trumpet blast which signalled where he stood and where he intended to go:

> The dominant trait of our municipal policy--and especially in that we are the true representatives of Paris--is to be profoundly imbued with a secular spirit; that is to say, consonant with the traditions of the French Revolution, we want to separate the sphere of law, to which everyone owes obedience, from the sphere of dogma, which is espoused by only a fraction of the citizenry. On this basis the great struggle [sic] has been joined, of which we are anxious witnesses and which will characterize the end of the century....We await the shock.[8]

II

During the years on the council and until 1885, Clemenceau carried on a medical practice, and until his election to the Chamber of Deputies in 1876 it apparently was his sole source of income because the councillors were as yet unpaid. (After 1885 he continued for the rest of his life to treat or prescribe for a few old patients and friends.) Since his practice was to all appearances mostly among his constituents, the bulk of whom were decidedly not very well off, he could not have been making very much money; when in 1874 he repaid the 25,000-franc loan from Lafont, he immediately reborrowed 25,000 from five lenders, with the Jacquets still supplying the security.[9]

He kept a two-room office-clinic at 23, rue des Trois-Frères, Montmartre. (This narrow street runs into the rue de Vieuville, which begins by the Métro station at the Place des Abbesses. The old Montmartre *mairie* was located on a dead-end alley, the "Cité de la Mairie," immediately off the rue de Vieuville; it apparently communicated through a back door with the 23, rue des Trois-Frères office, which today is marked with a commemorative plaque.) Patients and petitioners mingled indiscriminately during his semi-weekly open hours. Sometimes the crowd lined up through the courtyard and into the street. To his vast amusement he once confronted a puzzled fellow who had stripped to his underwear before asking for a job at the post office. A reporter from *Le Figaro* paid a visit. After a three-hour wait in the crush, he met the patron:

> A man about thirty-five years old, with close-clipped and graying hair, large black eyes, black, drooping mustache, skin-coloring like a monk's, a frank and open manner, hand always held out, correctly dressed: this is M. Clemenceau. When you have seen him in this office, mingling about, affable, eager, obliging, you wonder how such a man can have ideas which frighten certain people so much.[10]

Impressions from his medical practice in these years remained vivid in his memory. Blind, unmerited suffering, especially of children or animals, affected him deeply:

> I saw from below...everything one can see in the way of infirmities, of sufferings....Those were painful labors, those chases through the worst quarters of the Butte, those visits...in the noisome cells of these pest-ridden hives where, heaped together, enveloped in the stink of rubbish, were so many working-class families who only exchanged the deadly germs of the shop for the infections of the wretched dwelling.
> I complained about going there. But what of those who lived there?[11]

His family recalled that tears invariably welled in his eyes at the mention of a poor child whose death he recounted in "Le Petit Colibri."[12] A passage in another story, however, hinted at rewards he found in climbing "the stairs to some rickety hovel...to indulge in the infinite pleasure of changing misery into joy, of distributing happiness with [one's] own hands."[13]

Amid these labors he renewed relations with Gambetta's circle, and he began mingling with artistic and literary figures more than ever, an activity which was to be an important source of his notoriety while also a welcome relief from the preoccupations and wounds of politics. Plainly he was preparing a return to the national scene. The opportunity came at last when the National Assembly finished its labors on the basic laws comprising the "Constitution of 1875." His inaugural speech as president of the council in effect opened his campaign for a seat in the newly created Chamber of Deputies. His opponent would be Henri Arrault, the man he had defeated in 1870. On 20 February 1876 the XVIIIth Arrondissement (Montmartre-Clignancourt) gave him seventy-six percent of its vote.[14] More than a political triumph, it was the vindication he had sought.

III

Clemenceau's maiden speech, on 16 May 1876, was one of the best of his whole career. He spoke in favor of amnesty for the Communards (thousands of whom were still in prison or exile) as a measure of social reconciliation. The Chamber, impressed, applauded his effort but defeated the bill, 50 to 392--a scenario to be repeated often during his years as a deputy.[15]

He did not make another major speech until 1879, when he emerged to address the amnesty question again and then step out front on others. This self-effacement probably was due somewhat to a need to reassess his life now that he had regained his position at the national level. Quite possibly, however, it may have been the result of a recurrence of fatigue and depression reminiscent of his 1865-67 "withdrawal." His own doctor, in any case, had diagnosed him around 1875 as a "neuropath"--a neurotic.[16] His medical practice in Montmartre was at its peak in these years, and his children--Thérèse (20 June 1972) and Michel (27 November 1873) had joined Madeleine--were in their most demanding stages of growth, so he may have found his energy and nerves unusually taxed.

Also, his marriage probably was starting to unravel under the strain. Mary, whose health was proving delicate and whose pregnancies were difficult, had not lived with him in Paris while he was serving on the municipal council but instead had stayed at l'Aubraie with the children and her in-laws. Georges would come down to visit between the quarterly council sessions, and at other times, too, for he received fairly frequent leaves-of-absence. And in the summer of 1875 she returned to the United States for several months to visit her family. This irregular mode of married life--doubtless due at least initially to her husband's financial situation--surely did not help matters. But when he won election to the Chamber, which carried a yearly salary of 9,000 francs, they settled eventually in a comfortable apartment he had been renting in the fashionable VIIIth Arrondissement at 15, rue de Montaigne (today the site of the Théâtre des Champs-Élysées). Unfortunately, given the state of his mind and his marriage, the Floquets lived only a few doors away. He enjoyed showing off Madeleine to the childless Hortense, who appeared to take a sincere delight in the girl, but his old disappointment would well up occasionally in the form of tasteless, cutting jibes at her. He later described her to an intimate as "beautiful but pretentious" and his sarcasms as "little vengeances."[17] He seems to have felt no shame about this behavior. One wonders what Mary thought.

If these reasons for his effacement were not enough, the general political situation itself would have tended to counsel caution. It was governed by the constitutional struggle begun in 1871. Unable to compose their differences, the National Assembly's monarchists had declared the country a republic in 1875 but had given it institutions appropriate to a constitutional monarchy: a president, elected by Parliament, with extensive, vaguely defined powers; an indirectly elected Senate replete with a cohort of members-for-life as a foil to a popularly elected Chamber of Deputies; and an administration and judiciary clogged with monarchist holdovers. The Republicans nonetheless had steadily won by-elections and in 1876 had taken control of the Chamber. Gambetta persuaded them to mute their differences to show the country that a republic meant stable, responsible government: in due course they would win the Senate and with it the presidency.

Marshal Maurice de MacMahon, Thiers' monarchist replacement (in 1873) as president, unwittingly hastened the day by pushing a dispute with the Chamber in 1877 into a constitutional crisis. Clemenceau served on a steering committee organized by Gambetta after the wild election campaign touched off by MacMahon's dissolution of the Chamber.[18] The committee suspected that the government's Second Empire-style tactics during the campaign presaged a coup d'état; it made plans for armed resistance if necessary. Clemenceau later described Gambetta's "conspiracies" as "screamingly funny," apparently forgetting that he himself had taken the coup rumors more seriously than anyone else and had praised his leadership in glowing terms.[19] But the threat never materialized. "The 363" Republican stalwarts had not returned 400-strong, as Gambetta had predicted, but 326 did, including Clemenceau, who ran unopposed.[20] Their solid presence alone, with the steering committee's leadership, sufficed to win a constitutional point. Never again during the Third Republic (1875-1940) would a president risk a dissolution. Parliament was master, ministers would serve at its pleasure, and presidents would be figureheads, albeit with considerable backstage influence.

As long as the regime was truly at stake, Clemenceau choked down his objections to the constitution. Although a member of Louis Blanc's Extreme Left group and like them unwilling to merge into a comprehensive Republican bloc under Gambetta, like them, too, he generally followed Gambetta's lead, for he sincerely respected him. By early 1879 the Republic belonged to the Republicans: MacMahon had finally resigned and been replaced by a '48ist veteran, Jules Grévy; the Senate had a Republican majority; Paris was again the capital, the "Marseillaise" the national anthem, and Bastille Day the national holiday. Welcome as such victories and gestures were, Clemenceau thought them a mere prelude.

Like Republicans of all shades, he did not conceive of the Republic as merely a constitutional form but as an ideal with political, social, and even spiritual content. As such, it was for him, and would continue to be more or less for the rest of his life, something to be perpetually conquered and defended even after it was no longer seriously contested. (One is reminded of an aged Jaurèsist socialist after World War II who every morning, his daughter said, would come down to breakfast and solemnly announce to the world, "The Republic must be saved!") The *legitimacy*, so to speak, of any *current* version of the Republic was, in short, always contestable. This clashed with a corollary idea: the unity of all Republicans. Division into factions, much less parties, bore the taint of scandal. But given the question of legitimacy, divisions were inevitable and fated to be as wounding as a family quarrel or a divorce.[21]

It was from this context that Clemenceau advocated an amnesty for the Communards, Republicans all, believing that such an act would constitute dramatic proof that the Republicans meant to put the country on a new course. But his full-amnesty counter-proposal to the Waddington ministry's partial amnesty was crushed, 105 to 363 (embarrassed laughter greeted the tally), and his plea for the admission to the Chamber of Blanqui, who had won by-election while still an unamnestied political prisoner, garnered a paltry 33 votes.[22] He did, however, get his first ministerial scalp on a related issue when (at Gambetta's behest, Scheurer suspected) he provoked the resignation of the minister of the interior, Émile de Marcère, with a slashing attack on the operations of the Paris police. At that turn his name began to be heard in very high places as a man to watch, and before the year was out Bismarck, no less, was heard to mention him in the same breath with Gambetta as a threat to President Grévy.[23]

The speeches on the amnesty, Blanqui, the police, and especially one at the Cirque-Fernando in Paris on 11 May which attacked Minister of Education Jules Ferry's policy toward the Catholic teaching orders as weak and inconsistent were taken to be a signal that he had decided to strike out on his own. Probably he was fortified by thanks he received from Blanqui for his efforts on his behalf and a summons from him to seize the torch from the hesitant Gambettists. Louise Michel wrote in the same vein from the New Caledonia prison colony.[24] Ferry, who, while mayor of Paris during the latter weeks of the siege, had come to regard him as a dangerous demagogue, hotly resented his criticism of his proposal to forbid all public or private teaching by unauthorized monastic orders. (The Jesuits were the prime target.) Clemenceau, unlike most anticlericals as yet, wanted outright abolition of the Concordat of 1801, which recognized--but also regulated, to the state's benefit--a privileged status for the Catholic church, and in any event wanted to deal with the congregations by a decree enforcing existing laws (although they had not been enforced for fifty years) rather than go to the trouble of making new laws. In a letter to Scheurer-Kestner, Ferry excoriated Clemenceau's "violent, hateful, arrogant" attack on him (Ferry) at a time when he was under fire from the reactionaries:

> In truth, the frivolousness which reigns over all this [i.e., Clemenceau's proposals] would be unbelievable if one did not clearly perceive here the intent to get to power by successively tossing aside everything which doesn't stem from the sect [of left-wingers] or which doesn't tremble before it....[25]

In the meantime, persistent reports throughout the year that he was a member of combinations trying to found a newspaper or buy into *Le Petit Parisien* further strengthened impressions that he was establishing his own base.[26] Final confirmation came when a small group of investors came forward with funds to found a new, Radical, paper, nominally capitalized at 1.5 million francs in 1,000-franc shares. On 16 January 1880 *La Justice* made its debut with a manifesto that left no doubts about his intentions:

> One sees reappearing the eternal bourgeois race of 1830: doctors of half-measures whom movement frightens and ideas disquiet; the Orleanism of yesterday, the Center-Left of today. The fear of responsibilities, the force of routines, the wastage of minds and of characters: everything which is convenient in indecision and tempting in inertia conspires with them.
> Such we will be, very decided to applaud the first step ahead, but very decided also not to content ourselves with bad excuses in order to call stagnation progress and sterility wisdom; as desirous of seeing the Republicans divide

themselves as little as possible as resolved never to dissimulate a disagreement by abdication; implacable adversaries of the doctrine which consists of abandoning everything in order not to compromise what remains....The Republicans have triumphed. What has become of their flag? We have saluted it in battle; we will serve it in victory.

IV

Clemenceau's newspaper career coincided with the great age of the political press. For a few decades, from the decline of the *images d'Épinal* (colorful crude pictures of current personalities and events) to the advent of television, mass politics in France were more influenced by newsprint than by visual images.[27] It was, for awhile, the heyday of the small-circulation paper filled with weighty editorials, political news, and polemics. No fewer than fifty-nine of them encumbered the Paris newsstands in 1881, and their number waxed into the 1890s. After that they suffered a slow decline. By 1914 three-dozen political dailies together sold a million copies while the Big Five*--using expensive rotary presses and linotype machines, financed by advertising, and catering to the newly literate masses' taste for scandals, features, sports, and pictures--averaged a million apiece. That *La Justice* survived for two decades in such a jungle was a minor miracle. The enterprise demanded heavy infusions of Clemenceau's energies and large amounts of cash which sometimes had to be obtained from persons with dubious motives. When he left the paper in October 1897 he carried debts which tracked him for many years and which cost him his chance to inherit l'Aubraie.[28]

One wonders if *La Justice* was worth the effort. Circulation seldom surpassed ten thousand copies.[29] Ignored by the masses for whom it was intended, it was read only by the political elite and party stalwarts, serious-minded people willing to brave jammed-together columns of eye-straining print to satisfy a taste for analyses of politics, society, and the arts turned out by ill-paid but talented writers. Their pens were sharp, but Clemenceau would allow no mudslinging or unbridled abuse. In the main, however, *La Justice* was read mostly because he and Camille Pelletan (Eugène's son, the lead editorial writer) were men whose opinions counted in a political world

---

* *Le Petit Journal, Le Petit Parisien, L'Écho de Paris, Le Journal* and *Le Matin*.

dominated by personalities, not organized parties. When Clemenceau lost his parliamentary seat in 1893, the paper began a slow slide to oblivion.

Clemenceau loved the newspaper world: at heart he preferred it to life in Parliament. He had allies in politics but few intimate friends, and he kept it that way deliberately. He found his friends instead mainly in journalism and the arts and among his family relations. He savored the late-evening gatherings in the shabby offices clustered around the printing houses where, before putting the papers to bed, the knights of the pen would take their ease, sharing victory or defeat in a masculine atmosphere recking of tobacco, alcohol, and printer's ink. His hat cocked on one ear, a sure sign of good spirits, he would arrive in a gust of mock sarcasms and *boutades*,* greet the assembled faithful, chew over the events of the day, and prepare the "line" for the next. To his admiring staff, save for a few who resented his airs and his sometimes callous jokes about their poverty, he was the Chief, whose vigorous encouragement mixed with patronly rebukes made all those "masterpieces written in the sand"[30] seem worthwhile. He himself did not write for *La Justice* until after his 1893 defeat; his impatient struggles with pen and paper were a standing joke around the office. Apart from an infrequent article or an acerbic note answering an opponent's charges, he confined himself to his titled role of Political Director and left the daily "leader" to Pelletan, a talented editor-in-chief to whom he gave an exceptionally free rein.

V

Clemenceau's battle post in these years was the Palais-Bourbon, his tribune the speaker's rostrum. Before 1914 the business of parliaments was not overwhelmingly complicated, reflecting the still relatively modest role of government. Issues were in some real sense debated, and speeches sometimes could change votes. Given the highly personalized nature of French politics and the emotional ambience of French assemblies, he apparently concluded that the spoken word was the most direct way to influence his colleagues.[31] As for the broader public, *La Justice* customarily

---

* Untranslatable word for a specialty he made famous: whimsical, sometimes brutal, wisecracks or rejoinders which aptly sum up a person or situation.

printed his speeches *in extenso* or issued them in pamphlet form. Whatever the reasons, he became one of the masters in the Western world of an art that has since all but disappeared.

He was a pioneer in developing a distinctively new style. He did not deliver orations in the fashion of the time: he spoke, directly and with few adornments. Ample developments festooned with adjectives and classical or historical allusions, the tricks of the theater--all these he pruned back. His pose was to appear to have none. The marquis de Breteuil, one of his monarchist opponents, commented in his diary:

> [He] is clever and *skilled*. Moreover, I, as a connoisseur, always like Clemenceau's language--no useless phrases--the subject clearly presented--an undeniable logic. At the rostrum he resembles a surgeon who cuts and dissects. His replies are mordant and witty, and his interrupters always have cause for regrets. And although he has a bony face, disagreeable to look at, a jerky manner which is not suited to the rostrum, and sometimes pleasantries in his mouth which are worthy of a Paris street-urchin, it is impossible not to hear him with pleasure.[32]

When not speaking he often would sit motionless, arms and legs crossed, his smooth, almost Mongoloid, face a picture of icy calm. It was the eyes which compelled attention: black-brown, glittering, deep-socketed, and framed by heavy lids, prominent black brows, and high cheekbones, they moved about deliberately, missing nothing, now twinkling, now menacing. At the rostrum he held himself erect, hands resting on the lectern or lightly hooked in the pockets or lapels of his jacket. Since he was barely of medium height (a 1915 identity card listed him at 172cm.--5'7½"--and a 1922 passport at 167cm.--5'5½") and quite thin, though with a muscularity and carriage reminding one of a welterweight boxer--the familiar stoop-shouldered, somewhat heavy appearance dated from his late sixties--the expansive style of a Gambetta or a Jean Jaurès, men of ample chest and girth, might have made him look a trifle ridiculous. He attracted attention without any noticeable effort and had to a surpassing degree the art of keeping a whole assembly under his gaze. Those remarkable eyes defied anyone to take liberties with him. (His physician testified he saw him--at eighty years of age--drop an antelope at two hundred meters with a single shot.[33]) His voice was not especially powerful but carried to large audiences without noticeable strain. It was of medium-high, "second tenor" pitch and capable of expressive inflections, although in time a chronic bronchitis plagued him with hoarseness, and as he aged it took on a harsh, metallic quality which made him embarrassingly audible in social gatherings. Usually he would begin a speech slowly and calmly, but as he warmed up the pace would quicken to what some would compare, especially in the "metallic" years, to the hammering of a machine gun.

He approached the business of speechmaking seriously. Despite his cultivation of a cool outward appearance, he would become nervous at the approach of a major effort. His wife once remarked, "If he has insomnia one night, I know he will make a speech the next day; if the insomnia lasts two nights, I am sure there is going to be a great scene in the Chamber, and if it continues a third night, then a ministry is likely to be overthrown."[34] He did not originally write out his speeches in full, as was the custom, but would note down the chief points and a cluster of key words or phrases, paying particular attention to the closing paragraphs, where he could exercise to great effect his gift for striking summation. Often he would leave the notes in his pocket and not refer to them. The Senate speeches (after 1902) tended to be more literary and labored; he spoke more from a manuscript, appeared more influenced by the written form of his ideas, and when speaking as a member of the government often fumbled about with his papers. But when provoked by interruptions--veteran members customarily warned neophytes of the hazard--he would revert to the style of his younger years, usually regaining lost ground.

He spoke to convince, to prove something, not to entertain, though (as Breteuil admitted) he was undeniably entertaining and doubtless knew it. He observed the courtesies of debate quite scrupulously, even though he was while a deputy one of the most frequent interrupters, and as a rule avoided personal references. If he couched his ideas in simple language and logical from--"the purest dialectic," according to Pelletan[35]--his precision, nevertheless, could be misleading, perhaps even to himself, and his arguments not exempt form sophisms. His philosophy emphasized reason as the tool of progress, but in politics, as he himself observed, the immediate problem is getting men to act. "Not that I seek to diminish the importance of the efforts of the thinkers," he wrote in 1898; "I confine myself to noting that men group themselves en masse around sentiments more than they do around ideas, and that the great secret of getting them to move together is to find the note which causes all souls to vibrate in unison."[36] In a biography of Demosthenes which he wrote shortly before his death, he remarked:

> ...he who wishes above all to carry the vote of an assembly should make up his mind not to care too much for the logic of an argument....He who seeks to convince must first be convinced himself. For him to captivate the intelligence of his listeners is not enough; he fails if he does not cause in them the leap of emotion that carries away the heart....At decisive hours oratory acts like a catapult that shatters the obstacle at a single blow. The effect does not come of calculated artifice; it is ballistic. "Go say to your master...": at that simple phrase of Mirabeau's a whole assembly that had lost itself found itself again.[37]

If Gambetta's favorite weapon may be said to have been the heavy howitzer, Jaurès's the long-range cannon or sometimes the flamethrower, or Aristide Briand's a pleasant toxic gas, Clemenceau's was the rapier. He got to close quarters. In oratory and conversation alike he was served by a verbal facility of phenomenal range and speed. No less an authority than that magician of eloquence David Lloyd George, who could appreciate only the Frenchman's use of English, paid tribute in his memoirs: "Clemenceau was a master of words. No orator of his day had a more perfect command of word and phrase." Likewise, Herbert Asquith: "No Frenchman has a better or quicker gift of expression."[38] Fulsome praise, no doubt, but his speeches and accounts of his conversation basically confirm their testimony: in full flight, and especially when challenged, Clemenceau was a verbal prodigy.

He spoke frequently in the years 1881-85, but after that, until 1893 and later as a senator (1902-20), he reserved himself for large occasions. Unlike an Alexandre Ribot, Joseph Caillaux, or Raymond Poincaré, for whom the Budget debates were the crown of the year, he shunned most financial or technical questions, preferring instead social problems and *la grande politique*. He usually contrived to intervene toward the close of debate when his talent for apt summary could be put to best use. His special device was the use of interruptions as trampolines. As he observed once to a friend, "[It] is rather easy for a public speaker to win back his listeners when they have escaped him. A well-chosen word suffices. But you don't always find the occasion to use it. This occasion can be furnished by the interruptions of members who have hostile intentions."[39] When aroused he was devastating--the short, whirlwind speech on the French Revolution provoked by Joseph Reinach's protest at the banning of Sardou's *Thermidor*, slashing to ribbons the descendants of the Royalists and Girondins and flinging the offal to the roaring lions of the Left; or his reply in March 1918 to poor M. Émile Constant, who had archly invited him to explain his policy, the "I make war" speech.[40]

VI

Armed with formidable talents and in command of a newspaper, Clemenceau set out for the fray. But here arose a conundrum which puzzled his contemporaries and later his biographers--a problem, it might be noted, also found in the case of Lloyd George.[41] His obvious abilities, his driving energy, his drumfire attacks on ministry after ministry signalled to them a raging thirst for office. But to be invited into a ministry an aspirant needs a sizeable bloc of supporters, sympathizers in the swing groups, influential friends outside Parliament, and at least the benevolent neutrality of his potential ministerial colleagues. Taking another tack, he can perhaps win a place through technical expertise. But Clemenceau ignored the rules. So another conclusion was drawn: that he was a "wrecker," a man devoid of constructive talents and devoured by envy. "A malevolent starling," growled Jules Ferry. "Attila the Hun," they called him, and later "the Tiger."[42]

Personal resentments also fed this view. An intimate, deeply admiring friend sadly but accurately put down as one of his principal faults a tendency to make enemies uselessly.[43] Success in politics ordinarily depends on an ability to get along with all manner of men, and French politicians in particular respect the wisdom that today's foe may be tomorrow's ally. But Clemenceau brushed all that aside: "Never fear making enemies. If you don't have any it's because you haven't done anything."[44]

Early naïveté followed by disillusionment no doubt affected him, if not quite to the degree he chose to remember late in life:

> I entered the Chamber in 1871 with the ideas of a child. I admired certain men and believed that one merely had to do as they did, to continue their effort. Political action appeared to me to be simple....And then I became acquainted with political life, this regime. It's appalling, appalling! A world turned upside down.[45]

He came to see politics, at least as he had experienced it, as a jungle, "an implacable conflict of all the passions that, turn and turn about, exchange the vices of power for the virtues of opposition."[46] In his only novel, *The Strongest* (1898), he painted an acid portrait of feckless politicians in the person of Étienne Montperrier, "a precious collection of everything that was not true":

> Étienne was marvelously endowed with the faculties of memory and imitation, and had rapidly acquired the habit of "successful men."...His aptitude for falling into the prescribed attitudes, his art of yielding to all who could serve him, his happy desire to please, and his studied application in order to merit the applause of serviceable mediocrities, made him admired of all, even in his youth. He excelled in all small things and led a cotillion incomparably.
> [He] enrolled himself instinctively on the side of the strongest....Étienne never had the bad taste to disagree with his protectors.[47]

He, Georges Clemenceau, would be no Montperrier. Like the hero of his stillborn play, he would take the hard and lonely road.

Clemenceau did want power--which is, after all, what politics is about: power to influence, power to direct and control. What his critics failed to understand, although in time they began to comprehend, was the way in which he defined the connection between power and the holding of office. The Montperriers in practice equated power with office, where it merged imperceptibly with the formal authority to issue orders, enjoy perquisites, and confer rewards. Obtaining and holding office hence became an all-absorbing pursuit, and if the fortunes of battle changed, they took care to leave behind as many unburned bridges as possible.

Clemenceau contradicted such notions. With a simplicity which disoriented his confreres and which he could (a bit too self-consciously) mock in himself, he persisted in a belief that power is a tool one uses in order to achieve certain public ends. Office merely furnishes a field for action. During cabinet crises he invariably reserved some choice sarcasms for nervous politicans anxiously awaiting a summons to the Élysée--"At the moment [1898] we are attending to the distribution of the ministerial pâté in the parliamentary zoo. Dupuy, Barthou, Poincaré, Méline are hungry...." "To be a minister is vulgar. One can always find men for window-dressing [*oripeaux de théâtre*]."[48] Yet he had no particular quarrel with men's expressed desire for office. What aroused his scorn was their propensity to think they had accomplished something by having "arrived" and "taken power." As much as he enjoyed ticking them off for it, he was intelligent enough to know that in practice ministers must often compromise on their programs, and experience would teach him that great amounts of their time get swallowed up coping with contingencies and answering critics--like the inevitable M. Clemenceau. But the grant of indulgence he customarily issued at the appearance of each new cabinet would soon expire amidst pleas from ministers invoking the heavy burden of their responsibilities: weakness and careerism--or what he took to be such--ranked near the top of his long target-list of human shortcomings.

It goes without saying that more underlay his behavior in this matter than a point of principle. Clemenceau's complex psychology has long attracted a certain interest and, as noted before, has been the subject of a serious study of his early career. In brief, the author of the study concluded that much of his activity, at least down to 1893, was "guilt-engendered" and enhanced his "vulnerability to defeat."[49] He waged a fierce struggle to establish an ego identity independent of his father, and its very intensity gave rise to strong guilt feelings. To prove himself worthy, he wanted to advance his father's ideals, and hence he needed like him to suffer for them. But suffering did double duty, for it also punished him for failing to achieve ego independence. A pattern of self-defeating behavior thus manifested itself which saw him at important junctures refusing or failing to do those things which ordinarily should be done if one expects to succeed in politics.

This analysis has much to commend it. One might add, however, that while this theory (fundamentally Eriksonian) has not been applied to Clemenceau heretofore, other studies of men in politics have shown them to have very similar characteristics: ambivalent feelings toward powerful fathers, cravings for recognition and deference, resort to provocative behavior as a means of goading the environment to inflict punishment on an unworthy self, and so forth. Clemenceau, in sum, may be viewed as an especially marked example of a not-altogether-uncommon type, viz., persons who harbor strong aggressive traits requiring them to punish and be punished and who, in consequence, are drawn to politics.[50]

VII

Whatever the reasons--the combination of which was not simple however simply one may enumerate the parts--Clemenceau refused to join the scramble and would not openly court office. He did work the lobbies sometimes in search of votes for important divisions, but he often left this essential activity to aides and allies. He would ask no favors of a ministry he was combatting and very few of any he supported. He ridiculed the mania for decorations, for example, although he bowed to custom now and then to forward a recommendation for a bit of ribbon. Most important of all, he showed little sustained interest in party organization. To be sure, from about 1880 until 1893 he was the principal leader and acknowledged spokesman of the Radical Republicans. As such he attended caucuses, signed on as a founder of extra-parliamentary associations, and made occasional appearances at rallies. But he had little taste for the day-to-day labors of *la cuisine politique*--the hours spent framing resolutions, cajoling recalcitrants, mingling with the potentates of the Café de Commerce, and buttering up the moneybags. He preferred late-evening suppers with a few lieutenants to the pleasures of the banquet circuit.

His colleagues understandably wondered how this general-sans-army expected to "get into power." His answer was to believe that he *had* power so long as he possessed a voice, a pen, and the will to use them--never mind the fact that while under fire in the Chamber one day he did feel constrained to deny flatly that he had "any power whatever."[51] If he could persuade or frighten a ministry into doing what he thought necessary, he was not unhappy to remain outside. As he explained once to Wythe Williams, "You see, during the greater part of my life I have been identified with political office-- the affairs of government. But I would rather be a journalist than anything....It is simply that as a newspaper columnist, I felt power--power without the annoyance of holding a political job."[52] He found freedom outside the restraints of ministerial solidarity sweeter than the perquisites of office: "I have a newspaper so that I can say the things I should enjoy reading if I had not written them."[53] Some charged that consequently he was arrogant and irresponsible. Jean Martet probed him:

> *Martet.* Sir, you are a man of action. Men of action do not err on the side of excessive humility.

> *Clemenceau.* I observe what these men do. I see that it is criminal and imbecilic. I say so. That's all.

> *Martet.* Yes, but you are certainly persuaded that there is only one good solution: yours.

> *Clemenceau.* I am of the opinion that there is only one bad solution: theirs. They have chosen the worst. As for me, I propose nothing extraordinary....[54]

Perhaps consciously, he was paraphrasing Demosthenes, the subject of a book he had published recently: "There are some who think they confute a speaker by asking, 'What must we do?' I can give them a perfectly just and true answer: 'Not what you are doing now.'"[55] His characteristically blunt replies to Martet do more justice to his feelings than to his judgment of himself. His obvious self-assurance, relentless will and, as an intimate observed, "a certain innate taste for domination,"[56] bespoke a man who thought himself equal to any challenge. He admitted to a streak of arrogance: "Following the example of my noble father, I have no taste for submission."[57] He was, nevertheless, free of one of the most common blemishes of men in politics, personal vanity. He respected the traditions of Parliament and the dignity attending affairs of state, but he did not care a fig for the "grandeurs" of public life--ceremonial trappings, ranks, and privileges. Proud though he was--at bottom, indeed, a very proud man--his near-total lack of pomposity helped more than any other of his virtues to win back affections he lost through abrasiveness.

A devastating, often wounding, frankness and an utterly irrepressible wit which spilled over into flippancies that appalled friend and foe alike contributed to judgments that he was irresponsible. It was a pardonable misunderstanding. He meant what he seriously said and was prepared to act if given the opportunity. He turned the accusation against his accusers: "[The] fear of responsibilities is the capital vice of our times. A weakness in private individuals, the evil becomes cowardice in men of government, whose first duty is to put their initiative at the service of the public interest."[58] André Maurel once asked him what he was thinking when he went to the rostrum; he answered, "I thought of taking their [the ministers'] places in order to try to do better."[59] As he told a correspondent for *The Times* of London in 1885:

> Surely I cannot say "take me," but I have always declared my readiness to accept office. A politician in opposition who is not ready to accept office, if offered it, is not a serious man. I do not refuse, for my cabinet would be speedily formed; but my programme, which is no secret, would of course have to be accepted with me.[60]

VIII

Until 1906 that opportunity was denied him. A year earlier he had made one of his rare references to his exclusion: "It is probably a piece of luck for which I should thank Heaven that they have never given me a trial, for I should probably have done no better than the others. They should at least leave me the benefit of this part of my virginity."[61] Yet while the power and pleasure of operation outside the walls were undeniable, he knew full well that a position inside offers the maximum opportunity for effective public action. He answered the problem posed by his refusal to chase after office by taking seriously the hoary maxim that the office seeks the man. High office was to him something that presents itself spontaneously at the doorstep of the man who has prepared himself and, like the Kingdom of God, at an hour no one can predict. As one of his friends put it, "He wanted glory to come to him as if from Heaven."[62] If he were to be called, it should be because of what he *was* and because the interests of the country commanded it.

Hence a constant theme in his writings and speeches: that *character* is the most important quality required of men in high position. Lacking it they cannot act--and action was in his view the master key to life itself. Policy disagreements can be resolved somehow, but deficiencies of character are irremediable. A fight against strong men with bad policies invigorated him. It was the struggles with weak men which drove him to exasperation, for the merit of their policies was bound to become irrelevant. He made a striking statement of this theme while in retirement (and profiting from hindsight):

> When you have before you a magnificent political career, as is the case with him [André Tardieu], you must not waver and always seek to humor [*ménager*] certain personalities. The first quality of a man in politics who aspires to govern his country some day is character, and when it is a question of the interests of the state, you must not spare [*ménager*] anyone...even your friends, when they deceive you....No doubt you make enemies for yourself, and on that score I have paid the price of instruction, but at difficult moments, when the country needs men, sooner or later it will turn to you. In politics, more than in any other career, you must know how to wait ....[63]

Character, then, but patience too. A patient Clemenceau? In all ordinary matters, it is true, he was "the soul of impatience" described by General Mordacq.[64] But a prolonged acquaintance with the man tended to uncover an impressive ability in him, developed from hard experience, to bide his time, to choose the hour. Certainly as far as his own career was concerned, he learned to wait out his opponents until they caved in or came to him.

What led him to link office so closely to character? Again, answers may be sought in psychological considerations. One might take a clue from the role he assigned in human affairs, for whatever deeper reasons, to rewards and punishments. He believed that people must learn that their actions have consequences and that reward or retribution should follow swiftly and cleanly. (One of his grandsons told of a game the old man would play with him and his cousins. Grandpa would clear the table after supper and then perch on top of it with a pitcher of water while one of the youngsters would crouch underneath. At a signal the boy would try to scramble out. If he made it, a one-franc reward; if not, a cold dousing.[65]) He was exceedingly tolerant of private moral faults, but he had no sympathy for persons who brought hurt to others through cowardice, malevolence, or stupidity. As noted earlier, nothing caused him deeper pain than instances of undeserved suffering. No problem of principle here: personal feelings and duty coincided perfectly when the most elementary standard of justice had been violated. Toward errant public servants in particular he could be harsh to the point of inhumanity. He thought they had, so to speak, a duty to be competent. Honest incompetents, not to mention dishonest ones and even "serviceable mediocrities," should be shown the gate.

In the matter of rewards he showed some ambivalence. He was capable of exquisite small attentions, which surprised people who knew him only as a tigerish public figure, and he could do favors without showing condescension, an important virtue for politicians. But when he gave rewards he wanted nothing back except a polite acknowledgement. He detested effusive gratitude as an indignity to both parties.

His discomfort at being thanked reflected his attitude toward the reception of rewards. Should one expect reward? He answered with a categorical no. He found inspiration in a stoicism which "expects nothing either of gods or men": "Never has there been anyone who had the power to confer a reward upon me. There is strength in looking to no one but oneself for anything."[66] Misdeeds are usually punished, and should be. But virtue is not necessarily rewarded for it is not always discernable, and acts of duty have no claim for reward. "Men should not hope for recompense. What would heroism be reduced to if it were a fine piece of business?...The recompense comes, and should come, from a place we should never expect it to come from: ourselves."[67] He set out to believe, again with a disarming simplicity, that virtue is its own reward. A kind of moral syllogism, then, expressed the attitude he adopted toward seeking high office: Since office is a species of reward, it must not be the object of one's action.

Behind these beliefs, these patterns of conduct, surely loomed the figure of Benjamin Clemenceau. He dwelt with his ideals, where the air was clean and cold. His standards were exacting. He punished without hesitation. Such rewards as he conferred most often came in quiet, unspoken ways, and to anticipate them would only mute the high call of duty. "If you would avenge me, work." That was all ye knew, and all ye needed to know.

When Georges Clemenceau turned to view the men on the heights, he found most of them insensitive to such purities. A myopic selfishness infected them. No doubt he was unjust to many worthy persons. Could he be so sure, after all, that he was not infected too? Beyond doubt he could not. But of one thing he *could* be certain: his will was a match for any. "All my life," he told Martet near the end, "I played politics with men who didn't know what they wanted."[68]

NOTES
CHAPTER V

1   See the letter to Mme. Jourdan, 7 April 1870, in Wormser, *Clemenceau vu de près*, pp. 55-56.

2   Martet, *Clemenceau*, p. 124 (edited).

3   Wormser, *Clemenceau vu de près*, p. 62, a lost letter quoted from Michel Clemenceau's unpublished memoirs.

4   Quoted by Jean Jaurès in "Préface aux Discours parlementaires: Le socialisme et le radicalisme en 1885," présentation de Madeleine Rebérioux (Geneva: Slatkine Reprints, 1980), p. 65.

5   See *Le Temps*, 5 Oct. 1872, for the trial; Jean Martet, *Le Tigre* (Albin Michel, 1930), p. 95; and Duroselle, *Clemenceau*, p. 130.

6   There is no detailed study of his years on the council (Aug. 1871-Feb. 1876). The best accounts are in Ellis, *The Early Life of Georges Clemenceau*, pp. 60-63, and Duroselle, *Clemenceau*, pp. 114-122; but see also Geffroy, *Georges Clemenceau*, pp. 37-40; Jeanne Gaillard, "Le conseil municipal et municipalisme parisien (1871-1890)," *Société d'histoire moderne: Bulletin* 81 (1982), no. 3, pp. 7-16, *passim*; and Allan Mitchell, "Crucible of French Anticlericalism: The Conseil Municipal de Paris, 1871-1885," *Francia* 8 (1980):395-405, *passim*.

7   See GC, *La mêlée sociale*, pp. 48-50; and Geffroy, *Georges Clemenceau*, p. 40. See also "Clemenceau et les enfants assistés," *L'hôpital et l'aide sociale à Paris* 6 (1965):641-643.

8   As quoted by Mitchell, "Crucible of French Anticlericalism," p. 397.

9   See Duroselle, *Clemenceau*, p. 129. In 1880 he started *La Justice*, which was supposed to pay him 30,000 francs per year. See p. 85 below.

10   From Camille Ducray, *Clemenceau* (Payot, 1918), pp. 32-34, dated 1879. Post-office anecdote in GC, *Le grand Pan*, p. 230. See also GC, *Au fil des jours*, pp. 86-93.

11   GC, *Le grand Pan*, p. 231.

12   *Ibid.*, pp. 231-236. See Madeleine [Mme. Michel] Clemenceau and Juliette Goublet, *Georges Clemenceau: Sa vie racontée à la Jeunesse de France*, récit de Madeleine Clemenceau présenté et commenté par Juliette Goublet (Éditions du Centre, 1966), p. 23.

13 GC, *At the Foot of Sinai*, trans. E. V. Earle, Introd. by Dr. A. Coralnik (New York: Bernard G. Richards, 1922), pp. 15-16.

14 Results in JORF, 10 March 1876, pp. 1710-1711: Clemenceau, 15,204; Arrault, 3,772. Elections to the Chamber now were from single-member constituencies (*scrutin d'arrondissement*). Due to the pressures of his new post, he resigned from the Paris Council on 25 April.

15 *Ibid.*, 16 May 1876, pp. 3332-3341.

16 See Ellis, *The Early Life of Georges Clemenceau*, pp. 69-77, 137, a psychological dissection; diagnosis in Duroselle, *Clemenceau*, pp. 131-132.

17 See Clemenceau-Jacquemaire, *Le pot de basilic*, pp. 83-85, 224; and Wormser, *Clemenceau vu de près*, p. 37n. The Clemenceaus moved to 6, rue Clément-Marot nearby in 1887.

18 See JU, 12, 20, 26 Feb. 1884 for comments by Clemenceau.

19 See Martet, *Clemenceau*, pp. 310-311; Ellis, *The Early Life of Georges Clemenceau*, pp. 68-69; and Duroselle, *Clemenceau*, p. 137.

20 Results in JORF, 8 Nov. 1877, p. 7270: Clemenceau, 18,617; others, 1,585.

21 See Nicolet, *L'idée républicaine en France*, pp. 156-161, 185. The anecdote was related to me by Hélène Keniger (the daughter), proprietress of the Hôtel Marignan in Paris.

22 See Chamber sittings of 21 Feb. (amnesty), 27, 3 June (Blanqui), and 16 Dec. 1879 (amnesty renewed).

23 See Chamber sittings of 3 March 1879; John P. T. Bury, *Gambetta's Final Years: 'The Era of Difficulties,' 1877-1882* (New York: Longman's, 1982), pp. 145-146; and Allan Mitchell, *The German Influence in France After 1870: The Formation of the French Republic* (Chapel Hill, NC: University of North Carolina Press, 1979), p. 247n. But see also Duroselle, *Clemenceau*, pp. 140-141, who places his break with Gambetta and his circle at the Marcère affair.

24 A laudatory letter by Blanqui, dated 18 March 1879, was never sent, but they met in June. See Gustave Geffroy, *L'enfermé*, rev. ed., 2 vols. (Éditions G. Crès, 1926), 2:188-198; Watson, "Clemenceau and Blanqui," pp. 387-388; and Alain Decaux, *Blanqui l'insurgé* (Librairie Académique Perrin, 1976), pp. 610-611. On Michel's letter of 29 May 1879, in Alexandre Zévaès [Bourson], *Louise Michel* (1936), p. 21, see Edith Thomas, *Louise Michel, ou la Villéda de l'anarchie* (Gallimard, 1971), pp. 168, 178. At the same juncture a Dr. Séméré, a Positivist friend of Clemenceau, published a pamphlet, *La politique républicaine: à propos de l'article 7. Lettre à M. Clemenceau* (1879). It called for him to establish a "young, progressive dictatorship" which would

combine order with the idea of progress. See Claude Nicolet, "Jules Ferry et la tradition positiviste," in Furet, ed., *Jules Ferry, fondateur de la République*, pp. 29-30; and *idem, L'idée républicaine en France*, pp. 232-233.

25   The letter is reprinted in Jules Ferry, *Lettres de Jules Ferry, 1846-1893* (Calmann-Lévy, 1914), pp. 274-276. See Pierre Chevalier, *La séparation de l'Église et de l'École: Jules Ferry et Léon XIII* (Fayard, 1982), pp. 128-129. Watson, *Georges Clemenceau*, p. 67, rightly notes, however, that in the 1880s he in fact did not give the religious question "a very prominent place" in his attacks on the moderates as it would have had little tactical appeal at a time when the latter were under fire from an "almost hysterical" Catholic opinion.

26   See Francine Amaury, *Histoire du plus grand quotidien de la IIIe république: Le Petit Parisien, 1876-1944*, 2 vols. (Presses Universitaires de France, 1972), 2:782, 790n.

27   Michael Burns, *Rural Society and French Politics: Boulangism and the Dreyfus Affair, 1886-1900* (Princeton, NJ: Princeton University Press, 1984), p. 168. More precisely, after the Boulanger Affair (1886-1889), the last stand of the *images d'Épinal*.

28   See Duroselle, *Clemenceau*, pp. 146-48, 794-95, on the founding of *La Justice*. (The Dr. Louis Fraix he mentions is probably the Dr. Fiaux cited in Ch. IV, n. 28, above.) Watson, *Georges Clemenceau*, p. 68, mentions 300,000 francs provided initially by his father. Duroselle thinks it more likely that his father and his sister Emma Jacquet helped to "plug holes" later on. He notes (p. 349) that his father had sold some lands to liquidate certain *La Justice* debts and for this reason--and probably in view of other support he had provided to him over the years, one could add--he left l'Aubraie in 1897 to his wife, who at her death in 1903 left it *not* to Georges but to his brother Paul. Paul died in 1946, childless. Subsequently, Michel's son Georges Clemenceau II purchased it from his (Georges') brother Pierre and refurbished it. After his death in 1979 it went to his wife, Jeanne, and upon her death to their daughter Marie Phelipon, the present owner, whose invalided sister Françoise lives there year round. These details are from a letter to me from Pierre Clemenceau, 14 Aug. 1986, for which I am most grateful.

29   On 21 Aug. 1880 *La Justice* printed 12,847 copies, placing it 29th of 60 papers and 20th of 34 Republican papers. On 17 June 1884 it printed 8,000 copies. From about 1900 to the War it was a "morgue" paper owned by a syndicate which kept the name legally alive via irregular printings of 300 to 4,000 copies. See Albert, Feyel, and Picard, *Documents pour l'histoire de la presse*, pp. 38-62, *passim*.

30   The phrase is from the American journalist James Reston.

31   See Jean Ajalbert, *Clemenceau* (Gallimard, 1931), p. 29. Ajalbert was at *La Justice* and close to him personally.

32   Marquis [Henri] de Breteuil, *La haute société, journal secret, 1886-1889* (Atelier Marcel Jullian, 1979), p. 86. The best description of his Chamber oratory is in Camille Pelletan *et al.*, *Célébrités contemporaines* (A. Quantin, 1884), pp. 5-7.

33   Alexis Wicart, "Clemenceau, orateur," *Annales politiques et littéraires* 106 (1935):130-131.

34   "The Clemenceau Case," *New York World*, 14 March 1892.

35   Note 32 above. See Nicolet, *L'idée républicaine en France*, pp. 156, 238-239, for interesting remarks on the classical rhetorical mode of Clemenceau, Gambetta, and Ferry, with content governing form. Their speeches were "structured" and rich in content.

36   GC, *Vers la réparation*, 2nd ed. (P.-V. Stock, 1899), p. 36. See also AU, 20 Dec. 1904.

37   GC, *Demosthenes*, trans. Charles Miner Thompson (Boston: Houghton Mifflin, 1926), p. 56. Reference is to Mirabeau's speech on 23 June 1789.

38   David Lloyd George, *War Memoirs of David Lloyd George,*, new ed., 2 vols. (London: Oldhams Press, n.d.), 2:1604; Earl of Oxford and Asquith [Herbert Henry Asquith], *Memories and Reflections, 1852-1927*, 2 vols. (Boston: Little, Brown, 1928), 2:195.

39   Léon Abensour, *Dans la cage du Tigre: Clemenceau intime. Souvenirs d'un ancien secrétaire* (Éditions Radot, 1928), p. 75.

40   JOC, 29 Jan. 1891, pp. 155-156 (see p. 150 below); *ibid.*, 8 March 1918, pp. 355-358 (see pp. 377-378 below).

41   John Grigg writes in *Lloyd George: From Peace to War, 1912-1916* (Berkeley and Los Angeles: University of California Press, 1985), pp. 246-248, *passim*:

> Lloyd George was a disturbing colleague mainly because he was so dynamic, and because his zeal for public business was so tireless. These characteristics made him seem more self-servingly ambitious than he really was, and caused every impatient outburst of his to be interpreted as calculated subversion or conspiracy....
> [He said in a conversation with Lord Riddell in 1915]: "I have never intrigued for place or office. I have intrigued to carry through my schemes, but this is a different matter."...
> In intriguing for his schemes he could not help intriguing to some extent for himself, because he believed that he was best qualified to carry them through. His motives, therefore, were less pure than he claimed, though purer than his critics supposed.

42   The origins of this famous nickname are disputed. Gohier claimed he (Gohier) first used it in an article in *Fantasio* in 1908 which was reprinted in *L'Oeuvre*, 6 Jan. 1910. Chichet claimed to have used it to describe him to Alfred Gérault-Richard during the first ministry (1906-1909) and that Gérault popularized it. Brulat said Émile Buré invented it. Madeleine Clemenceau says Buré did this at *La Justice*, while Wormser says Buré "reinvented" it on the eve of the War, following Gohier's lead. And Dr. A. Raiga-Clemenceau says that Wormser, however, related that Buré told him (Wormser) that as a member of Clemenceau's personal cabinet in 1906 he witnessed a scene in which Clemenceau, angered by a reply from a prefect, "positively bounded toward the man" and threw him out of the office. Buré told his friends, "I thought I saw a tiger," and the label made the rounds. It was not widely used until the War, however. Clemenceau rather liked it. See Urbain Gohier, *La vraie figure de Clemenceau* (Éditions Baudinière, 1932), p. 45; Étienne Chichet, *Feuilles volantes: Quarante ans de journalisme* (Nouvelles Éditions Latines, 1935), pp. 217-218; Paul Brulat, *Lumières et grandes ombres: Souvenirs et confidences* (Bernard Grasset, 1930), p. 126; M. Clemenceau and J. Goublet, *Georges Clemenceau*, p. 23; Wormser, *La république de Clemenceau*, p. 9n.; and Dr. A. Raiga-Clemenceau, "Le vrai caractère de Clemenceau," *Nouvelles archives hospitalières*, 1973, no. 4, p. 96.

43   Général [Jean-Jules-Henri] Mordacq, *Clemenceau* (Éditions de France, 1939), p. 234.

44   GC, *Sur la démocratie. Neuf conférences de Clemenceau rapportées par Maurice Ségard* (Librairie Larousses, 1930), p. 90.

45   Pierre Drieu la Rochelle, "Paroles d'outre-tombe," *Revue hebdomadaire*, 7 Dec. 1929, p. 7 (dated 1923). Clemenceau forbade publication of this interview during his lifetime.

46   GC, *In the Evening of My Thought*, 2:414.

47   GC, *The Strongest* (Garden City, NY: Doubleday, Page, 1919), pp. 155-157. It was widely believed that Paul Deschanel was the model.

48   GC, *Vers la réparation*, p. 351; GC, *Injustice militaire* (P.-V. Stock, 1902), p. 368.

49   Ellis, *The Early Life of Georges Clemenceau*, p. 137.

50   See, e.g., Harold Lasswell, *Power and Personality* (New York: Viking Press, 1962), pp. 38, 44, 98, and *passim*; and Robert E. Lane, *Political Thinking and Consciousness: The Private Life of the Political Mind* (Chicago: Markham, 1969), pp. 156,161-163, 265, 293, and *passim*.

51   JOC, 10 April 1886, p. 740, as noted by Duroselle, *Clemenceau*, pp. 176-177.

52   Williams, *The Tiger of France*, pp. 95-96.

53   Letter, 7 Jan. 1914, in Georg Brandes, *Correspondance de Georg Brandès: Lettres choisies et annotées* par Paul Krüger, 2 vols. (Copenhagen: Rosenkilde og Bagger, 1952-1966), 1:308.

54   Martet, *Le Tigre*, p. 281.

55   Demosthenes, *On the Chersonese* 38; my rendering from translations by J. H. Vince (The Loeb Classical Library, 1954 ed.) and Charles Rana Kennedy (Everyman's Library, no. 546, 1923 ed.).

56   Wormser, *La république de Clemenceau*, p. 19.

57   AU, 7 Aug. 1905 (edited).

58   GC, *L'iniquité*, 3rd ed. (P.-V. Stock, 1899), p. 64.

59   André Maurel, *Les écrivains de la Guerre* (La Renaissance du Livre, 1917), p. 9. Maurel knew him well from the *La Justice* days.

60   *The Times* (London), 6 April 1885, as quoted in Ellis, *The Early Life of Georges Clemenceau,,* p. 142.

61   AU, 7 Aug. 1905. As noted (p. 95), this editorial explicitly mentioned his father.

62   Jean Lefranc, "Clemenceau, souvenirs et portrait," *Revue politique et parlementaire* 141 (1929):351.

63   Mordacq, *Clemenceau au soir de sa vie*, 1:217.

64   Mordacq, *Clemenceau*, pp. 218-219.

65   Gatineau-Clemenceau, *Des pattes du Tigre*, p. 64.

66   GC, *In the Evening of My Thought*, 2:478; GC, *Grandeur and Misery of Victory*, trans. F. M. Atkinson (New York: Harcourt, Brace, 1930), p. 10.

67   GC, *Sur la démocratie*, p. 185. See also GC, *La France devant l'Allemagne*, p. 9n..

68   Martet, *Clemenceau*, p. 312.

CHAPTER VI

Radical Leader
(1880-1885)

Clemenceau came to political maturity in the 1880s. It was not a fortunate coincidence. The decade, in many respects among the least attractive of modern times, lacked the confident, creative vigor of the High Victorian mid-century or the dynamism of the industrial surge beginning by the mid-nineties. The tone of its public life was set in the ostentatious, overstuffed parlors of power-brokers whose wealth called the tune during the Gilded Age.

In France, the Republicans were torn between desires to show what they could accomplish or else to settle back and enjoy the fruits of their newly won power. Since a majority of the deputies were elected by peasants and their small-town neighbors--persons of modest and traditional expectations--the latter disposition tended to prevail, particularly when they were faced with proposals involving social issues or a reduction of the highly centralized powers of the state they now controlled. To be sure, they did some significant legislative work in the areas of civil rights, public works, and above all in education with laws making elementary education compulsory, public elementary schools free and accessible to all, and secondary schools open to girls. But otherwise the majority of deputies were tending to find favor-seeking in ministerial antechambers and the making and breaking of cabinets more absorbing occupations. When an agricultural and business slump, which had begun in 1873 but had eased after 1878, returned again soon after the elections of 1881, the mood in some quarters began to change. The movement which coalesced around General Boulanger after 1885 drew much of its impetus from a mounting disgust with the sterility and greed permeating politics at all levels.

Such was the environment in which Clemenceau operated during the few short years it took him to become one of the half-dozen or so most visible men in public life. In view of his rapid ascent, it seems paradoxical to speak of frustrated ambitions. But as the real, if unofficial, leader of a group at one of the extremities of the Chamber, a representative of a city constituency, and an advocate of swift action on a vast spectrum of reforms, he stood little chance of winning recognition as the leader of a parliamentary majority. So he set his sights on the elections of 1885 and tried in print and pulpit to build a national Radical Republican movement. The effort made him a chief, and an important one, but of an operation which increasingly looked like a relentless guerrilla war against the men in office resulting only in "a perpetual immolation of a sawdust brigade."[1]

II

Clemenceau lived to see most of what he advocated in the seventies and eighties enacted into law. He never won much thanks for playing the prophet. The charge that he was a mere wrecker, a sterile, even dangerous, man was hung on him in the eighties, and it stuck, partly from inertia, but partly from his continuation of habits acquired in this formative period. The petty hypocrisies and disloyalties he witnessed in a milieu where pure politics, backstage power-plays, and influence-peddling were becoming the norm engendered in him a visceral distrust of most politicians and confirmed a disabused view of human nature which he had first contracted from his father. No doubt he drew some satisfaction now and then from proving to his opponents that he could be as tough and clever as they, all the more since he had a dread of being made to look foolish. But when some serious misjudgments led him to an exposed position in the late eighties and early nineties, their savagely vengeful assault on him confirmed every negative opinion he had formed about their tribe and calloused his sensitive spirit with a baked-leather hide.

His political programs mingled proto-socialist and democratic-liberal elements with a freedom his contemporaries thought daring but which in the main merely typified late-Victorian radicalism. He was no truly original thinker in politics and certainly no system-builder. His distrust of systems, which at bottom probably owed more to personality traits than to strictly philosophical considerations, helps to explain why he found Marxian socialism indigestible even though in legislative matters he often agreed with the Socialists and to their annoyance sometimes liked to call himself one. When added to the fact that he never acquired a serious interest in economics, it may account for the singular circumstance that his large library, still housed at the rue Franklin apartment, contains not a single work by Marx or Engels or their French disciples Jules Guesde and Paul Lafargue, although it does boast some sixteen books and brochures by the free-spirited anarcho-socialist Proudhon.[2] His prejudice against doctrinaire socialism, however, in no wise prevented his inviting its adherents to join forces against the dogmatists of unrestrained laissez-faire capitalism, who seemed to him in effect to sanction oppression of the weak by the strong. (His only novel, *The Strongest*, would center on this theme.) "There can be a struggle for the development of material well-being," he told the Chamber in 1884, "but I do not concede that the fight for existence can be allowed."[3] But when it came to doctrines of class warfare and revolution, that was something else again. At the Cirque-Fernando on 25 May 1884 he explained his differences with the Socialists at some length:

> In the case of humanity, progress is accomplished by groups. To the degree that men become enlightened, they gather together following their interests and thus create in all societies a succession of small oligarchies which defend what they believe to be their immediate interests as best their means permit....
> I maintain that the entire policy of a democracy is to effect the emancipation of the less enlightened group, with the shortest delay possible, by the group which has the advantage of enlightenment and education....
> Look around you--we see a striking example--look to the other side of the Vosges [Germany]. There you see hierarchical classes not mixed together as we have here. You know that, of course, because I continually find middle-class men [*des bourgeois*] in your [the Socialists'] ranks. I don't

reproach them; they obey the law I just evoked, but don't you see that their presence among you shows what is artificial in an organization of a political party on a purely manual-work basis, as if manual work doesn't necessarily involve [*entraîner*] mental work? Far from separating muscular activity from mental activity, we would unite them, and the distinction which you claim to institute is a distinction from the past against which all modern civilization protests.

Earlier, at Marseille on 28 October 1880, he had sounded a similar note:

...intellectual emancipation is the true foundation of emancipation and the true foundation of economic emancipation. It is inevitable that the two reforms should proceed together. The true tool of emancipation is not violence, as some insufficiently "demonarchized" Republicans claim: it is science. It alone furnishes to those involved, to the degree that the progress of national education increases their number, the means of creating the milieu necessary to the useful exercise of their faculties.[4]

His faith in the emancipatory power of education and science differed not a whit from Jules Ferry's, for example, nor from the bulk of Republican opinion. The Socialists, meanwhile, as they grew in number and confidence through the eighties, grew also less inclined to answer his invitation. Their dismissal of him in time as just another bourgeois moderate masquerading as a radical reformer bothered him more than he cared to admit.[5]

His program during these years in essence amounted to a point-by-point repetition or elaboration (in social matters) of Gambetta's famous "Belleville Program" of 1869. Its most distinctive element was the strong admixture of social demands with the political. As he put it, "The political emancipation of the citizen will be only a deception [*leurre*] without the social emancipation of man. To the degree that the Republic is established and strengthened, the questions of social reformation will inevitably outweigh political questions."[6]

In brief, from a seemingly endless list, the program included separation of church and state and suppression of the monastic orders (congregations); civil divorce; free, obligatory, and secular primary schools and expansion of education at all levels; expanded freedoms of assembly, association, and the press; popular election of judges; abolition of the death penalty; administrative decentralization and full municipal rights for Paris; list-voting and multi-member constituencies (*scrutin de liste*) to replace single-member constituencies (*scrutin a'arrondissement*); full freedom of organization and affiliation for labor unions; increased rights and power for employees versus employers; limitations on hours of work; forbidding of child labor in factories and mines; encouragement of producer and consumer cooperatives; provision for credit and insurance for workers; an income tax and increased inheritance taxes to replace the traditional indirect taxes; liquidation of the large railway, canal, and mining concession companies, with the workers to run them; short-term, universal military service instead of reliance on a long-term professional standing-army; opposition to imperialism; and--for awhile first in emphasis because of its potential aid to the enactment of "truly Republican" reforms--a revision of the constitution featuring abolition of the presidency and especially of the Senate.

One striking omission was voting rights for women. He favored full civil and educational equality for them, which was more than many men of his day were ready to grant, but he never concluded that the time was ripe in France to give them the ballot. While in America (and preparing to marry) he had made notes for a book to refute Mill's feminist theories, for example, advancing biological arguments proving female subordination. But despite these and other dubious reasons, his real objection, shared by most Frenchmen down to World War II, was that women in Catholic countries listened too much to the priests. Such was not the case in the Protestant states and North America, he pointed out, and he expressed sympathy in 1913 for the English Suffragettes' cause, if not altogether for their methods.[7]

Clemenceau's radicalism stemmed not just from his program but also from his tactic, which was to demand the earliest possible passage of the whole agenda--"Tout et vite!" He got little help, however, from the current economic situation. The economy was in the doldrums much of the time until the mid-nineties, and industrialization in France was advancing at only a leisurely pace. The governments of the day consequently felt no great pressure from a rapidly swelling urban working-class as was the case in Germany, and moreover they could argue persuasively that, since the budget was suffering from stagnating tax receipts, there was no money available for ambitious social schemes.

The balance of political forces was also against him. The Senate was a trough of moderation and could veto or interminably delay any reform measure. In the Chamber, the "socialist" Radicals around Clemenceau numbered some 20 to 40 of the 560-odd members; other left-wing Radicals brought the figure up to 65 to 80, to which old-line Radicals and maverick Gambettists added between 50 and 100.[8] But the governing majority ordinarily was found in Gambetta's Republican Union and Ferry's Republican Left, with reinforcements from a small but influential group of conservative "Center Left" Republicans recently converted from Orleanism. This amalgam, dubbed "the Opportunists" after Gambetta had said reforms would be enacted "when opportune," could be pressured into concessions, but frequently the Left had to join forces with it to forestall a monarchist Right bent on embarrassing the government by voting with the Radicals--the famous *politique du pire*, or "make-a-mess" policy.

Clemenceau denied *he* played the *politique du pire*; usually he held his nose and voted for measures he considered mere stopgaps after failing to get them amended to his taste. But sometimes he charged ahead anyway, arguing that it wasn't his fault if his ballot was found in the same urn with those of monarchists making mischief or voting *their* consciences:

> ...the principal vice of the parliamentary regime [he later wrote] is the mixing of two votes in one. In each instance you must declare yourself both on the issue being debated and the very existence of the government. What can you do when the issue has in its favor only its intrinsic merit?[9]

The angered Opportunists accused him of systematic overbidding. He replied that he wanted action: "We do not demand that you apply our program. We simply demand that you apply your own."[10] If good for a debating point, his retort was disingenuous, for the Opportunists, once in power, had decided that they no longer agreed with some of the planks of the old Republican program to which the Radicals still adhered. In resisting calls, for example, for a decentralization of the Napoleonic administrative apparatus, for separation of church and state, or for bold social legislation, they *were* carrying out their program.[11] But while appearances often favored them when they charged that the Radicals were behaving irresponsibly, they undermined their case with stodginess, an unseemly haste to protect vested interests, and a complacent belief that the administration of duly enacted laws could be left to gentlemen whose republicanism would not bear close scrutiny.

III

It was his opposition to imperialism which thrust Clemenceau into the limelight most dramatically. The occupation of Tunisia in 1881 inaugurated French participation in the great drive by the West for outright control over the non-Western world. Conquest overseas helped to soothe the pride wounded in 1871 and furnish tangible proof that France was still a Great Power, a point the Republicans were eager to make: it was, in fact, the preeminent motive behind French expansion. Popular support of imperialism fluctuated nevertheless. If empire could be had on the cheap, well and good. But French farmers didn't want *their* sons to be sent to die in some African desert or Asian swamp, and any momentary enthusiasm for dominion on the Mekong could quickly shrivel at mention of the menace on the Meuse. Opinion in Parliament generally was more favorable, though far from consistent. The members understood international politics better than did their constituents; and, besides, they certainly were closer in so many ways to those good patriots who expected the empire's growth to swell their bank balances.[12] Opponents of imperialism consequently needed more than arguments from principle.

Clemenceau opposed imperialism on three main grounds.[13] First, while he would not condemn all imperialism root-and-branch, he found little good to say for it. His Darwinian views were sophisticated enough to resist simplistic justifications for conquests of ancient civilizations whose sole disadvantage, he asserted, lay in military technology.[14] If the imperialists went out as true empire-builders and civilizers, if colonists flocked to the colonies, he was prepared--in theory, anyhow--to see some use in it all As he exclaimed once, to the amusement of the Chamber, "Since you are great colonizers, since you want to colonize, well--colonize!...But up to the present [1890] you have exported only bureaucrats who cost you very dearly and seem to have no other job than to impede everything."[15] France's "civilizing mission" mostly looked to him like the age-old game of conquest dressed up to pander to a mass public barely a generation removed from illiteracy while sharpsters made killings on the Bourse.

Secondly, if France bled herself of men and money overseas, how could she face German power in Europe? What could soldiers guarding oases in the Sahara do for the defense of Paris or the liberation of Alsace-Lorraine? Would the nation be strengthened by pouring into Africa and Asia funds which could be used for industrial and educational development at home? His opponents replied that *he* was obsessed by "the blue line of the Vosges." Certainly no one was more frank than he in pointing to Bismarck's suspicious sympathy for French involvement outside Europe. Ferry did go so far as to admit, privately, that he was obsessed by the possibility of exchanging a colony for Alsace-Lorraine, but Clemenceau never took the idea seriously.[16] France could not successfully resist Germany unaided, he observed, yet by continuing in the scramble, France was alienating potential allies--Great Britain, Italy, Russia. The argument was telling, but after an alliance with Russia was locked up in 1894, it began to lose its force.[17]

Nothing, however, aroused more anger in debate or did more to encourage formation of hostile coalitions in Parliament than the methods that ministries used to win approval of actions overseas: equivocations, secrecy, manipulations of parliamentary procedure, invocations of "reasons of state"--the familiar panoply of executive arrogance. So in the third place, because he was the principal figure in the imperial drive and a persistent user of sharp practice with Parliament, Jules Ferry became an issue. Courageous, self-confident, dour, and possessing a will as unyielding as the iron of his native Lorraine--"a general who takes no prisoners," as Charles de Freycinet described him[18]--he made enemies easily. And not just in Parliament: mayor of Paris and prefect of the Seine in 1870-71, "Ferry-Famine," "Ferry-la-Guerre" was the bête noire of the Parisian masses.

Clemenceau came to detest him almost as much as he had Thiers. Even in retirement he was heard to snarl that "if they made him [Ferry] president of the Council [premier], it was precisely because he was of no use for anything."[19] (Yet when Émile Buré once called Paul Deschanel an

Opportunist, he had exploded, "The Opportunist...was Gambetta, it was Jules Ferry, it was Spuller; they were men, I tell you!"[20]) Ferry responded with icy disdain, when he responded at all. As already noted, he thought Clemenceau was an irresponsible demagogue; he viewed his neo-Jacobin radicalism as precisely the kind of thing Republicans had to wean themselves from if they were to avoid alienating the fundamentally conservative masses who still harbored fears that the Republic would mean disorder and a threat to property.[21] Clemenceau showed no resentment at being counterattacked; he expected it and enjoyed the clash. Rather, it was Ferry's unconcealed contempt that cut into his gut. Between the two it was war to the knife.

IV

Ferry's methods in the Tunisian venture (1879-81) served warning of what would come later in Indochina (1883-85): intervention on a pretext in order to jump the claims of another (Italy); extortion of a treaty from a helpless native government; massive intervention and undeclared war to put down a resultant native uprising; patriotic appeals to Parliament to support an army already in the field; requests for insufficient funds so as to force Parliament to ex post facto expenditure; siphoning of troops from metropolitan garrisons; a last-moment change of date for a general election, thus buying time to finish the "war" without Parliament's "interference"; and peculiar gyrations on the Bourse benefitting speculators with interests in the conquered territories.

Clemenceau at first confined himself to pointed questions about the effect of the affair on France's international position, and he was the only speaker to risk open mention of Bismarck's "surprising" friendliness toward French successes; but he went no further than an abstention in the vote on the Treaty of Bardo (23 May 1881).[22] Succeeding developments brought him into full opposition. He attacked Ferry hammer-and-tongs during the summer election campaign and in the session opening in November.[23] The voters, except in Paris, refused to get worked up about Tunisia, even when it was charged (wrongly, it turned out) that Ferry's family stood to gain from the shenanigans on the Bourse. But the election results signalled trouble for Ferry, who prudently announced that he would resign once he had obtained funds to cover past expenditures. He got the money after several days of angry and utterly confused debate (4-9 November), and the way was now open for an event which had been anticipated for months: Gambetta would become premier.

Léon Gambetta was the leader of the Republican majority, but partly through his own choice, abetted by President Grévy's hostility, he thus far had avoided the premiership. President of the Chamber since 1879, he had exercised a powerful, semi-concealed influence on the majority which prompted complaints of an "occult dictatorship," especially from Clemenceau's Radicals, who thought this situation distorted proper parliamentary government: ministries could come and go, but Gambetta, the Master, was beyond reach. Clemenceau also had a more serious objection, namely, that he had become an opportunist in more than label, a likeable fellow still, but a leader who had betrayed his mandate.[24] The Republic would stagnate until Gambetta changed his ways or was dethroned. Differences deepened, relations became embittered. Nonetheless, both Gambettists and Radicals did well in the elections of 1881. Clemenceau won in both districts of the XVIIIth--it had been divided because of its size--and in the South at Arles, where the Radicals saw a chance to pick up a seat. He opted for Montmartre-Clignancourt and joined the twenty-two other victorious candidates of the thirty-two that *La Justice* had backed in Paris, among them Tony Révillon, who had beaten Gambetta himself in one of his old fiefs after a rough-and-tumble fight.[25]

Gambetta's "Great Ministry" lasted only eleven weeks. He and Parliament knew what the country did not know, that it was doomed virtually from the outset. Exasperated by the attacks on him, his health failing (although he was only forty-three), he resolved to challenge his tormentors with a fistful of proposals topped by a project to revise the constitution. The Chamber recoiled before "the Dictator" and sent the project to a commission which returned an unfavorable report. Clemenceau and Pelletan, both of whom were members, registered objections to the report and to the choice of a talented mischief-maker, Louis Andrieux, as *rapporteur*,* but this was only

---

* In French practice, the *rapporteur* of a commission (committee) is often more important than the president (chairman). He writes the report on a bill and leads the defense of the commission's version on the floor.

window-dressing. Clemenceau favored *scrutin de liste*, the heart of Gambetta's proposal, believing it would foster the growth of large, organized parties and thus facilitate enactment of reforms. Although it cannot be proved outright, it seems probable that he worked with Andrieux to finesse the affair so partisans of *scrutin de liste* could vote against Gambetta.[26] When the vote was taken (27 January 1882), those who wanted more sweeping changes--Clemenceau's target was the Senate--joined with those who wanted none to bring him down, 218 to 268.

Gambetta's fall brought nobody any credit. Pelletan's editorial rang no peals of joy, affecting instead a note of unconcern: "What tomorrow will bring we do not know. It is no business of ours. The tiller remains in the hands of the Moderate majority that M. Gambetta pushed to the limit."[27] Nobody dreamed that Gambetta had but a few months to live. He died near midnight on the last day of 1882, worn in body and spirit. The heroic days of the Republic's founding were truly over. Clemenceau never expressed regret at his fall, but he mourned the man and to the end of his life treasured a deathmask of him. As premier twenty-seven years later, he dedicated the statue at his birthplace in Nice, and in 1918 he welcomed the return of Alsace-Lorraine in the name of the tribune of the early Republic who had fought on in 1870 when all seemed lost.

V

The tribulations of the New Imperialism returned to the agendas of Gambetta's successors. A revolt by xenophobic Egyptian army officers led by Colonel Arabi (1882) prompted an invitation to France by Britain to intervene jointly to protect their mutual interests at Suez. Freycinet sought parliamentary sanction in advance, an improvement on Ferry's methods, but his request was denied (30 July 1882) by a resounding 75-416 vote when he could offer no ironclad assurances of neutrality from the other Powers. The diplomatic situation in the Middle East, murky at its best, had clouded considerably during the two days preceding the climactic debate, which made Clemenceau's warnings appear all the more pertinent. He played upon suspicions of Bismarck--unduly, it is clear in retrospect--which he had expressed during the Tunisian expedition:

> In truth it appears there is somewhere a sinister hand preparing a terrible explosion in Europe. Who will dare to take responsibility for what is being prepared?...
> Europe is covered with soldiers; everyone is waiting, all the Powers are reserving their freedom of action for the future; reserve the liberty of action of France.[28]

The "double salvo" of applause he won reflected the sentiments of the public at large, which wanted no talk of war, and the victory gained him a national reputation as a top "tombeur" (ministry-breaker). It also added to the international attention he had earned in the Tunisian affair. Years later, when André Maurel asked him what had been one of his greatest satisfactions in his public life, he replied that after a speech on Tunisia, Henry de Blowitz, the famed correspondent of *The Times*, was told by Bismarck, "That's a man to watch." "The day Blowitz told me that," he said, "I was happy."[29]

The full truth of Freycinet's fall, however, was more complex than popular perceptions of it. Ferry (one of Freycinet's ministers) and Gambetta had worked behind the scene and played more crucial roles in the ministry's fall than Clemenceau. Also, the huge negative vote was doubly misleading. It covered a coalition of discontents, those who thought Freycinet too bold voting with those who thought him too timid. And the recorded vote included many who had clambered aboard the bandwagon after a preliminary show of hands had already revealed the ministry's defeat.[30]

The next day Freycinet received Bismarck's reply to his sounding about an intervention. It was favorable, but its tardiness did nothing to allay suspicions about the sender's intentions. The British pressed on and intervened unilaterally, therewith opening a generation of wrangles with France which helped frustrate chances of an alliance. Ironically, this alliance was one of Clemenceau's most persistent dreams, but it could not materialize so long as France was bent upon expansion and Britain was not fully aroused over the growth of German power. Clemenceau would have preferred to avoid this detour but had no power to prevent it.[31]

Some Gambettists appeared ready to swing behind Clemenceau after their leader's death, but President Grévy, who exercised a great deal of covert influence, was flatly hostile to the idea of him in a ministry, much less a premier. Nor does it appear that Clemenceau himself took the prospect very seriously at this juncture. In any event, Ferry stifled the threat, such as it was, and after the short-lived ministries of Eugène Duclerc and Armand Fallières, he returned to power in February 1883. For the next twenty-five months Clemenceau pummeled his ministry's policies. Ferry accepted battle and even warned darkly that the Republic had as much to fear from the "extravagances" of the Left as it did from the Right.[32] Bank failures in 1882 and the outbreak of phylloxera in the vineyards had shoved the economy into a recession. A grand debate on economic policy, partly instigated to expose the alleged hollowness of Clemenceau's and others' solutions, led to a predictably barren official inquiry in which Clemenceau participated. The government did push through a law sanctioning labor unions, but with features the Radicals thought invidious. Clemenceau's famous report (1884) on the Anzin coal mines showed how many obstacles labor confronted. A government, however, which could find little reason to take action in a cholera epidemic (1884) could hardly be expected to answer calls to ease the sufferings of miners. Clemenceau rode constitutional revision hard, too, helping to organize a national league to promote it. Even granting the unicameral tradition of the Republicans, which dated back to the Great Revolution, one wonders how he thought he could make headway on a proposal as divisive as abolition of the Senate. Ferry shrewdly answered with a modest revision abolishing life-senatorships for the future and somewhat reducing the Senate's malapportionment, leaving the Left and Right to flail about in impotent rage.[33] His majority seemed secure but for approaching elections in 1885 and the imbroglio in Indochina.

VI

Southeast Asia was vastly more complicated than Tunisia. Ferry never clearly explained his intentions there (assuming he had clear intentions), and to many it appeared that he again was forcing Parliament's hand. Like his American counterparts eighty years later, he knew little about that distant world and plunged on in confident hope that success was just around the corner. A treaty with China, which claimed nominal sovereignty over the area, had given France a protectorate in Cochin China (Saigon) in 1874, but from the start it was flouted by both sides. French activities in

Annam (Hué) and Tonkin (Hanoi) at length provoked an insurrection, more intervention, and a new treaty (1883) extending the protectorate to the disputed areas. But Chinese-supported guerrillas fought on. Ferry responded with an undeclared naval war on China accompanied by attempts to negotiate. In June 1885 a treaty reconfirmed the protectorates, but by that time Ferry was no longer in office. Some of his opponents usually supported him on Indochina, which helped him considerably since no issue was more likely to unite the Extreme Left and the Right. Indochina did nothing, however, to help his frail popularity: "Ferry-Tonkin" joined "Ferry-Famine." Small wonder that with the elections in view his supporters had left him when a momentary defeat at Lang-Son gave them a pretext.

Clemenceau's first major intervention on Indochina came in late 1883. His forbearance in the wake of Henri Rivière's defeat at Hué (May 1883) had implied no promise of support for an aggressive policy certain to involve hostilities with China, and he repeated the familiar litany of arguments against imperialism.[34] The undeclared war of 1884-85 confirmed his prophecies. The knowledge, too, that Ferry was negotiating with Bismarck drew fire: "It is clear in all this that Bismarck commands and France obeys!" cried *La Justice*.[35] A setback at Bac-Lé and an apparent missing of a chance to make peace touched off an even more acrimonious debate in November 1884. Ferry's ranks wavered but held. Through the winter, however, his support leached away.[36]

The sudden arrival, beginning on 24 March, of a succession of ominous reports from the field started to turn the trickle into a torrent. Ferry had a treaty with China in his grasp, but he could say nothing for fear of jeopardizing negotiations. And who would have believed him by now? The dam cracked in an interpellation* on 28 March. Clemenceau tore into him:

---

* A formal question put to a minister which he must answer. The exchange is concluded by a motion to proceed to "the order of the day" (the agenda). Motions are framed to express support or rejection of the minister's (and hence, as a rule, the ministry's) position. Adoption of a hostile motion forces the minister or ministry to resign for "lack of [the Chamber's or Senate's] confidence" if the question is regarded as sufficiently important.

> No, I do not judge you because of a defeat; I most certainly
> would avoid that! I judge you on a set of circumstances, on
> what you have said, on what you have done....There always
> comes a time when the reckoning can no longer be put off, a
> moment when the whole country finally opens its eyes and
> recognizes it has been deceived. That moment has come....By
> your lack of foresight and by your infatuation you have put in
> peril the vital interests of France.

He warned the deputies, who needed no reminders, that they would soon be facing the voters: "Who can say what the situation in Europe will be at that moment?"[37] Ferry's margin sank to an anemic twenty-nine votes.

That night (28-29 March) the most alarming dispatch to date came in: a reverse at Lang-Son, the commanding general wounded, the survivors in full retreat. A cable in the morning attenuated it, but by then crowds were in the streets calling for Ferry's head. A meeting of Gambettist leaders that evening and of delegates from the other parliamentary groups on the morning of the 30th sealed his fate. He promised to resign after presenting a request for further credits--a proud stance, but one which looked like another ploy.

The sitting of 30 March was short and starkly dramatic. While crowds howled outside, Ferry's "execution" proceeded. He sat smiling with disdain: China had verbally confirmed she would sign, and he would have it in writing the next day. Clemenceau delivered a coldly furious masterpiece of invective. He declared he would vote funds, but only after a new ministry had fully informed the country of its intentions:

> Yes, all debate between us is over; we no longer want to listen
> to you, we can no longer discuss with you the great interests of
> the country. We no longer know you, we no longer want to
> know you....
>   These men stand accused of high treason...[men] on
> whom, if there is still a principle of responsibility and justice
> left in France, the hand of the law will descend without
> hesitation.[38]

Clemenceau's speech remained in the memory of all who heard it, becoming a veritable legend. But the true crusher that day was delivered by a key figure of the Center Left, Alexandre Ribot, who followed him at the rostrum. Only a week before, the Chamber had voted to institute *scrutin de liste* for the approaching elections. The effect was to make the deputies supporting Ferry highly sensitive to the opinions of potential running-mates on the departmental lists and thus to give the Radicals (with Clemenceau in the lead) great leverage when it had suddenly come to a question as volatile as "war or peace." The Radicals were for "peace" now--and nobody could forget the losses the Republicans had suffered in 1871 when they had been dubbed "the war party." Ribot did not need to spell this out in detail to Ferry's panicked supporters. When his short speech was finished, so was Ferry, by 149 votes to 306.[39]

VII

Indochina remained on the agenda of Ferry's successor, Henri Brisson. Clemenceau did vote the emergency credits on 31 March, but he refused Brisson's next request, voted again (a demand on 31 March having failed) to indict the Ferry cabinet, replied to Ferry's retrospective defense of his policies in July with a long speech of his own, and in December imperiled Brisson, whom he mostly supported, with another denial of funds for Indochina. Privately, he was quoted as saying he found the Indochina situation to be "inextricable," with the government "always at the mercy of a futile incident and unable to concern itself with our internal affairs or the reorganization of the army."[40]

But what would he have done if perchance he had been called to succeed Ferry? When Georges Périn, his closest lieutenant in foreign policy, answered "Pull out," he shot back, "No, it's impossible!"[41] The honor of the flag was too deeply engaged for him to sanction a flat withdrawal *if he were in the government*. He drew a distinction between the duties of ministers and of deputies: a deputy should register his opinion, a government should govern. He never missed a chance to criticize ministers for doing the opposite of what they had advocated as private members, and later he was to find himself accused all the more enthusiastically on the same count. Yet if a bare majority of deputies registered a contrary opinion, a government could not govern. And when such occasions became frequent, the resultant ministerial instability rendered firm, far-sighted executive action all but impossible. The "mixing of two votes in one," which he had noted as being intrinsic to parliamentary systems of government, lay at the root of the difficulty.

Circumstances both inside and outside the parliamentary arena should have counselled him to show some restraint in 1885. He had grown during the past decade, but not enough, and too much in one direction. For while he had mastered the necessary art of putting fear into his opponents, he had not inspired either at home or in Europe an overarching confidence in his judgment, the *sine qua non* of anyone staking a claim to the premiership. His rash use of the word "treason" at the rostrum proved to be an unwitting contribution to the opening of an unexpected, dangerous passage for the young republic--the strange adventure of General Boulanger.

NOTES
CHAPTER VI

1   Henry M. Hyndman, *Clemenceau, the Man and His Time* (New York: Frederick A. Stokes, 1919), p. 86.

2   See Duroselle, *Clemenceau*, p. 183. He met Marx in London in May 1880 and perhaps again in 1883. Charles Longuet, one of Marx's sons-in-law, was a staffer on *La Justice* and a close friend. For discussions of his relations with socialism in these years, see especially Jaurès, "Socialisme et radicalisme en 1885," *passim*; Alexandre Zévaès [Bourson], *Clemenceau* (René Julliard, 1949), pp. 93-120; and Watson, *Georges Clemenceau*, pp. 84-88.

3   JOC, 1 Feb. 1884, p. 250.

4   JU, 27 May 1884; 1 Nov. 1880.

5   It should be borne in mind, however, that until at least the mid-nineties the term "socialist" was employed very loosely, covering "all those concerned with the 'social question,' with the lot of the working class, or with the reorganization of society." Stephen Wilson, *Ideology and Experience: Antisemitism in France at the Time of the Dreyfus Affair* (Rutherford, NJ: Fairleigh Dickinson University Press, 1982), p. 730.

6   Speech at Marseille, 28 Oct. 1880, in JU, 1 Nov. See especially Leo Loubère, "French Left-Wing Radicals: Their Economic and Social Program Since 1870," *American Journal of Economics and Sociology* 26 (1967):189-203.

7   Jean Martet, *M. Clemenceau peint par lui-même* (Albin Michel, 1929), pp. 257-264 (notes for a book); HL, 13 May 1913, repr. in GC, *Dans les champs du pouvoir* (Payot, 1913), pp. 48-55 (Suffragettes). For other remarks see GC, *In the Evening of My Thought*, 2:441-444; GC, *Sur la démocratie*, pp. 38, 162; and Geneviève Tabouis, *The Life of Jules Cambon*, trans. C. F. Atkinson, Jr. (London: Jonathan Cape, 1938), p. 238.

8   The Extreme Left (Radical-Socialist) in turn split into factions behind Clemenceau and Madier de Montjau, the former refusing to allow members to join other groups. Clemenceau refused to assume the presidency of the Extreme Left proffered him. See JU, 18 Dec. 1881; and Ellis, *The Early Life of Georges Clemenceau*, pp. 125-126. Figures on groups vary considerably from source to source. Those given here are from Leo A. Loubère, "The French Left-Wing Radicals: Their Views on Trade-Unionism, 1870-1898," *International Review of Social History* (Netherlands) 7 (1962):203-204. But see also Antoine Prost and Christian Rosenzweig, "La Chambre des députés (1881-1885): Analyse factorelle des scrutins," *Revue française des*

sciences politiques 21 (1971):5-49; and Jean-Thomas Nordmann, *Histoire des radicaux, 1820-1973* (La Table rond, 1974), pp. 74, 84.

9   GC, *La mêlée sociale*, p. 5.

10   JOC, 9 March 1882, p. 275.

11   See Douglas Wayne Ellingson, "The Politics of the French Chamber of Deputies, 1881-1889" (Ph.D. diss., University of Minnesota, 1977), pp. 85, 106-107, and *passim*; and Susan A. Ashley, with Comment by Jolyon Howorth, "The Radical Left in Parliament, 1879-1902," *Proceedings of the Annual Meeting of the Western Society for French History* 11 (1983):308-309, 328-329.

12   In practice, however, expansion owed much more to political than economic motives. See, e.g., Jean Ganiage, *L'expansion coloniale de la France sous la IIIe république, 1871-1914* (Payot, 1968), pp. 20-26, 415-418, and Pierre Guillen, *L'expansion, 1881-1898* (Imprimerie Nationale, 1984), p. 111.

13   See JOC, 30 July 1885, pp. 1677-1686, his most complete exposé.

14   JOC, 31 Jan. 1884, p. 250. See also GC, *Injustice militaire*, pp. 295-296.

15   JOC, 27 Nov. 1890, p. 2302. See also JOC, 3 July 1883, p. 1571.

16   See Fresnette Pisani-Ferry, *Jules Ferry et le partage du monde* (Bernard Grasset, 1962), pp. 76-77; and Martet, *Clemenceau*, p. 275.

17   On Ferry's policies, see especially the essays by Claude-Robert Ageron, pp. 191-206, and Raymond Poidevin, pp. 207-222, in Furet, ed., *Jules Ferry, fondateur de la République*. On Clemenceau's, see Ageron's essay in *Clemenceau et la justice*, pp. 69-84.

18   Charles de Freycinet, *Souvenirs, 1848-1893*, 2 vols. (Charles Delagrave, 1912-1913), 2:167.

19   Martet, *Clemenceau*, p. 274.

20   Paul Strauss, "Souvenirs: Gambetta et Clemenceau," *Le Temps*, 9 Nov. 1930, rpt. in Strauss, *Les fondateurs de la République* (La Renaissance du Livre, 1934), p. 67

21   Clemenceau's behavior during the 31 Oct. 1870 uprising probably began Ferry's alienation, and at the Commission of Inquiry's hearings in 1872 Ferry had harshly criticized his actions regarding the 18 March 1871 affair. See Odile Rudelle's essay in *Clemenceau et la justice*, pp. 48-50 and *passim*; and François Furet's essay in Furet, ed., *Jules Ferry, fondateur de la République*, pp. 21-22.

22   JOC, 23 May 1881, p. 982. Alfred Talandier cast the sole negative vote, not Clemenceau as is often asserted. On 7 April Clemenceau had voted money for "operations on the Tunisian frontier."

23   See Chamber speeches of 26 July, 8, 9 Nov. 1881.

24   See JU, 8 Aug. 1881, commenting on his "drunken slaves" outburst against his opponents in Belleville (the XXth Arrondissement).

25   See JOC, 31 Oct. (pp. 1896, 1907), 17 Nov. (p. 2044), and 24 Nov. (p. 2077) 1881. In XVIII-1, Clemenceau, 11,436, others (incl. Dereure, 977), 2,778; XVIII-2, Clemenceau, 5,958, others (incl. Vauthier, 2,098), 3,296; Arles, Clemenceau, 5,735, Granet, 5,667, De Cadilliau, 3,979; in the Arles run-off, Clemenceau, 7,977, others, 142. He opted for XVIII-2 on the advice of the Radical committees of Paris (JU, 27 Nov.) and supported his friend Jean Lafont's successful bid in the by-election in XVIII-1. Félix Granet, an Opportunist, may have agreed to join the Extreme Left if Clemenceau opted for Paris. Granet won the ensuing by-election at Arles and subsequently became minister of posts and telegraphs under Freycinet in 1886 with Clemenceau's endorsement. See JU, 8, 11, 12 Dec. 1881; and Ellis, *The Early Life of Georges Clemenceau*, p. 127.

26   See JOC, 15 Nov. 1881, pp. 2030-2032; JU, 15-18 Nov. 1881, 23-25 Jan. 1882; and Strauss, *Les fondateurs de la République*, pp. 64, 233-237 (Andrieux letter denying Strauss' charge that Clemenceau was acting in cahoots with Grévy and Daniel Wilson).

27   JU, 28 Jan. 1882.

28   JOC, 29 July 1882, p. 1509. Scheurer-Kestner claimed his whole speech was written by Nubar Pasha, a moderate opposed to Arabi; see Watson, *Georges Clemenceau*, p. 80; and Duroselle, *Clemenceau*, p. 209. See also Chamber speeches of 1 June, 19 July 1882.

29   André Maurel, *Clemenceau* (Éditions de la Nouvelle revue nationale, 1919), pp. 25-26.

30   See Freycinet, *Souvenirs*, 2:234-239; Bernard Lavergne, *Les deux présidences de Jules Grévy* (Librairie Fischbacher, 1966), pp. 76-82; Bury, *Gambetta's Final Years*, p. 337; J. Dietz, "Jules Ferry: Sa première présidence du conseil," *Revue politique et parlementaire*, 10 Oct. 1935, p. 107.

31   See JOC, 19 July 1882, p. 1327; 27 Nov. 1884, p. 2500.

32   His words in a speech at Le Havre, 14 Oct. 1883, were simplified by the left-wing press as a cry, "The peril is on the Left!" and accordingly denounced *ad infinitum*.

33   See Clemenceau's speeches of 1883, 6 March (revision), 19 March (miners' rights); of 1884, 31 Jan. (economic policy), 13 March

(unions), 8 April (Anzin mines), 24 July and 2 Aug. (cholera); National Assembly speech, 13 Aug. 1884 (revision). The Anzin mines report is in *Annales de la Chambre des Députés. Documents parlementaires*, 1884, no. 2695 (2e annexe), annexe du procès-verbal du 11 mars 1884. See also retrospective comments in JU, 31 Aug. 1893, and GC, *La mêlée sociale*, pp. 219, 280-282. Ellis, *The Early Life of Georges Clemenceau*, pp. 128-129, cites his tactics on constitutional revision as especially illustrative of a tendency toward self-defeating behavior.

34   See his Chamber speeches of 31 Oct. 1883.

35   JU, 28 Sept. 1884.

36   See his Chamber speeches of 17, 21, 27 Nov. 1884. The closest margin was eighty-two votes.

37   JOC, 28 March 1885, pp. 693, 695.

38   JOC, 30 March 1885, p. 704.

39   See the analysis in Odile Rudelle, *La République absolue: Aux origines de l'instabilité constitutionelle de la France républicaine, 1870-1889* (Publications de la Sorbonne, 1982), pp. 107ff., 283. See also Pisani-Ferry, *Jules Ferry et le partage du monde*, pp. 284-289; and Lavergne, *Les deux présidences de Jules Grévy*, pp. 269-276.

40   Paul Cambon, *Correspondance, 1870-1924*, 3 vols. (Bernard Grasset, 1940-46), 1:272 (dated 13 Dec. 1885).

41   Jaurès, "Socialisme et radicalisme en 1885," p. 22.

CHAPTER VII

Boulanger
(1885-1889)

General Boulanger's emergence into national prominence was an unforeseen by-product of the agitated and confused elections of 1885. The economy was in the third year of a recession, and the voters were in a mood. The new election law compounded difficulties. All of a department's deputies would be elected at large--meaning that in Paris, for example, the voter had to choose no fewer than thirty-eight--but (unlike the case in 1871) election required an absolute majority of votes cast, failing which a run-off would be held with only a plurality needed. To assist the voter, so to speak, ad hoc committees representing every shade of opinion circulated "lists" of candidates which they hoped the voters would then elect *en bloc*. Consequently, the voters were puzzled more than ever about how to express their views, a puzzlement which extended to the politicians (and historians later) trying to decipher the "real" meaning of the results.

For four years Clemenceau had worked in hopes that the 1885 elections would inaugurate something resembling the two-party regime, now the norm in England, in which a strong Radical bloc would face an Opportunist Right, the retreating monarchists having been driven from the field. A working majority might then be formed by combining Radicals with left-leaning Opportunists.[1] This pleasing scenario collapsed in the first round of the elections (4 October), however, when monarchists and Bonapartists, running on lists labeled "Conservative," captured 179 seats outright while Republicans of all stripes were winning only 129. This shocking result probably owed much to protest voting by anti-Ferryists favoring "peace" but also to a return to the polls by large numbers of conservative-minded voters who had stayed home in 1881. A strategy of "Republican unity," i.e., a rallying behind whichever Republican list had scored highest, averted disaster in the 18 October run-off round. The Republicans pushed their total to 372 while holding the Conservatives to 205. They then used their strength to nullify the elections of a number of Conservatives, and after the subsequent by-elections in February 1886 to fill these seats and the seats vacated by those who had run in more than one constituency, the final tally stood at 183 Conservatives (119 real or presumed monarchists and 64 Bonapartists) and 401 Republicans (279 moderates, largely Gambettist Opportunists, 110 assorted Radicals, of which about 79 were left-wingers around Clemenceau, and 12 sundry Socialists).[2]

Clemenceau played a large role in promoting and enforcing the "Republican unity" strategy. Aside from its intrinsic value as a means to save the Republican cause, it fortuitously helped the Radicals, whose lists had run first in many departments where their Republican opponents had presented more than one list or had lost anti-Ferryist protest voters to them. If the complexion of the Chamber, then, was not what he had anticipated before the first round, the final result, oddly, gave him a position resembling what he had sought from the outset. In a three-sided legislature--Conservatives, Opportunists, and Radicals--he would have powerful leverage. The Opportunists, whose axis had shifted leftward because of the virtual elimination of the Center Left and large losses among the Ferryists, could continue to govern, but only with significant Radical aid. (It was unthinkable that they would turn to the Conservatives.) More than that, enough Opportunists might tilt left to make a Radical-led ministry possible.

In Clemenceau's view, "Republican unity" should amount to something more than an election-time expedient. It should lead to action, for that was what the electorate really wanted--or so he read the polls.[3] Probably he was correct. What is more debatable, however, is just what kind of "action" the voters wanted. Domestic reform, more than likely, and an end to the recession, but according to the Radicals' prescriptions and under M. Clemenceau's leadership? Many voters thought the Opportunists in fact had not done so badly, except perhaps for Ferry's risking war with an aggressive colonial policy, and would do better if the Radicals would leave off being "obstructive." Others were souring on parliamentary government altogether, with its endless factional quarrelling, and looking for strong executive leadership to give the state "a head and a brain."[4]

That Clemenceau himself had some doubts about a widespread desire for Radical rule may be inferred from the fact that during the legislature of 1885-89 he opposed a dissolution and new elections. At the rostrum and in *La Justice*, however, he prescribed a forward line of march. The 100-plus votes on the Left at least would keep the Opportunists moving. When Parliament convened he lost no time in signalling his intentions. To Brisson's appeal for support on Tonkin, he tartly replied, "I never look back, always ahead."[5]

He had cleared the ground to play a larger personal role when, to some surprise, he had opted for a seat representing the Mediterranean port of Toulon and its agricultural hinterland, the department of the Var. He had run on lists which won, albeit on the second round, there and in Paris.[6] His first contacts in the Var may have come when he spoke at Hyères in January 1881 while on a visit to the coast "for personal reasons."[7] He returned again in the summer of 1884 on a parliamentary inspection tour of the Midi in connection with the cholera epidemic, and on this occasion, if not the previous one, met the mayor of Toulon and publisher of the Radical Republican *Le Petit Var*, Henri Dutasta, whose measures he singled out for praise in a speech in the Chamber on 2 August. As the campaign of 1885 warmed up, Dutasta began to put his name forward as a means of strengthening the "advanced" Radicals against backsliding "governmentals." Clemenceau, who had been making speaking tours around the country during the late spring and summer, finally accepted an offer from a union of Varois Republicans on 16 August and from 12 to 20 September ranged through the department in an intensive campaign.

Discomfort over the progress of socialism, as was alleged then and later, probably had something to do with his decision to abandon a still quite secure seat in Paris. From 1881 to 1885 Simon Dereure, his ex-ajunct mayor and now an amnestied former Communard and Marxian socialist, and especially Jules Joffrin, a "Possibilist" socialist, had waged an unrelenting campaign to destroy his position as the symbolic chief of the city's Far Left and to undermine his hold in Montmartre.[8] At the same time, divisions among the Radicals were proliferating. He doubtless saw advantages in the Var's extreme distance from Paris: he could make himself less accessible to favor-seekers and be embroiled less personally in the quarrels of the city's Radical satrapies. (Once elected, in fact, he was said to have remarked, "I'm not the Var's deputy; I'm the representative of the nation...[and] if you have questions about railways, schools and other trifles [*bagatelles*], address yourself to Maurel and to Daumas."[9])

The Var, for its part, had a long Republican tradition, being one of the few departments which had revolted against Louis-Napoléon's coup in 1851. It viewed itself as a standard-bearer of advanced republicanism, and Dutasta made Clemenceau's candidacy attractive to stalwarts there by emphasizing the symbolic value of having the national leader of the Radical Republicans as their personal chief.[10] Of special interest to Clemenceau in 1885, moreover, was the presence there of a former *La Justice* staffer, Jules Roche, a deputy of national repute from Draguignan (1881-85) who had had a falling-out with him and gone over to the Opportunists at a time when the Radicals were beginning to be challenged by a Socialist movement in the department. Hence the Var was a constituency where a Radical victory could appear to have some national significance.[11]

From 1885 to 1889--more than at any period before or after--Clemenceau's attention centered on cabinet politics. As if to deliberately make himself appear more "responsible" and less likely to be brushed off as a gadfly, he dramatically cut back on his interruptions and speechmaking in Parliament--from 144 interruptions and 60 authorized interventions and speeches in the 1881-85 legislature to only 38 and 17 respectively between 1885 and 1889.[12] While professing indifference to his own prospects for office and all but certain, moreover, that neither President Grévy nor the Opportunists would invite him in, he strove to get the levers of power into friendly hands.[13] When Brisson gave up in January 1886, he found Freycinet ("the White Mouse") ready to conciliate him by putting a couple of Radicals (Lockroy and Granet) in the cabinet and Gen. Georges Boulanger at the ministry of war.

II

From the outset of his career Boulanger had made a reputation as a brave, able, and lucky field commander, swiftly rising to become at age forty-three (1880) the army's youngest general. He had attracted only passing public notice, however, until he served a two-year stint in the ministry of war as a reform-minded inspector of infantry (1882-84). A tour as commander in Tunisia (1884-85) further increased his visibility when he locked horns with the resident-general, Paul Cambon, an Opportunist of note. Their dispute, which (personalities aside) revolved around the question of the subordination of military authority to civil control, played in the press for months and won Boulanger friends in some Radical circles, where few generals were held in much esteem. Cambon won his point, and Boulanger was forbidden to return to Tunisia (August 1885). Only nominally commander there now, he was morosely awaiting reassignment when the Brisson ministry resigned. Enter Freycinet and the offer of the ministry of war, next to chief of staff the most cherished object of his ambition.

Although he was arguably a leading candidate once generals Saussier and Campenon (the retiring minister) had removed themselves from consideration, Boulanger was perceived as owing his elevation to Clemenceau. The truth was less simple. They had long known each other, having been at least briefly (for Boulanger was four years older than Clemenceau) schoolmates at the Nantes lycée. Clemenceau had kept an eye on him over the years, and when he came to town as inspector of infantry they were sometimes seen together. Correspondence which came to light in 1979 shows their relations, while not quite as intimate as rumor had it at the time, were closer than Clemenceau and his partisans later cared to admit.[14]

What is most difficult to decipher is Clemenceau's real opinion of the man. He seems to have found him an engaging fellow personally, though no intellectual heavyweight, and he most decidedly supported his reforming activity in the army, which was attentive to the well-being of the rank-and-file and boosted morale. But he had been rather put off when he talked of resigning if he were not named chief of staff (no less) after his inspectorship; and his quarrel with Cambon, while it made trouble for the Opportunists, struck him as petty in its origins, the act of a "farceur," as he acidly put it.[15] In sum, while he had no exalted opinion of Boulanger's capacities and was uneasy about the man's ambition and his taste for noisy notoreity, he nevertheless regarded him as the equal of most generals who had been minister of war. "Boulboul," as he half-playfully, half-mockingly called him, could, if properly guided, administer a good dose of Republican tonic to a hidebound military establishment.

Freycinet, who coincidentally had an inordinate fear of Clemenceau, especially of his tongue, said nothing in his memoirs about a recommendation from the Radical leader. According to him it was General Campenon, the outgoing minister and an unimpeachably Republican senator besides, who suggested Boulanger's name.[16] In fact, Freycinet's offer was not the first Boulanger had received, for Ernest Constans had sounded him while trying to form a ministry after Ferry's fall in March 1885. It seems unlikely that Constans had done so at Clemenceau's behest since they were enemies.[17] Yet the general perception that Boulanger was "Clemenceau's man," while not strictly true, was not far off the mark. Freycinet knew the appointment would go down well with the Radical leader, and he wanted no trouble from that side. Clemenceau's version, delivered in later years, was that he had "concurred" in the appointment and that he had, "as part sponsor at least," introduced him to the political scene.[18] Overmodest as these admissions were, they basically accord with what can be securely known about a step which had momentous consequences for him personally and for the country.

III

The new war minister set to work with a will and soon churned up a flurry of reforms ranging from adoption of the Lebel rifle to painting sentry boxes in the national colors, all of them carried out--and here lay the rub-- with a maximum of publicity that displayed to the nation at large a trait he had long exercised in less exalted theaters, namely, an uncanny talent for self-advertisement. It was in the Bastille Day parade of 1886 that he fully burst upon the public consciousness. Mounted on a magnificent black charger, the vigorous, handsome, blond-bearded general pranced up the boulevards, putting the drab civilian dignitaries completely in the shade. The common people of Paris, who had had little to cheer for since the Commune, found a hero, a leader who would restore French pride and send the hated Prussians scampering from Alsace-Lorraine. Song-writers enlisted on the instant, and the music halls rang with ditties in honor of "not' brav' général."

In six months Boulanger had become an annoyance to the government; six more and he was a problem, an incipient force. When the colorless and undulating Freycinet fell in December 1886 after disappointing the Radicals by declining to embrace an income tax, the crisis lasted a full week. Freycinet recommended Clemenceau or Floquet, currently president of the Chamber, but René Goblet, an Opportunist converting to Radicalism, won Grévy's designation. Boulanger would stay on, but under close watch. Both Clemenceau and the Opportunists figured that a few months would "use up" Goblet and then all bets would be off. Had Boulanger been gracefully dropped at this moment, he might have been just a summer day's infatuation. But Clemenceau and many others still held to him despite an uneasiness caused by his having been caught in a public lie some months ago and by rumors that he had sent feelers to the Right.[19] Clemenceau continued--much too long, without a doubt--to dismiss most criticisms of him as the politically motivated grumblings of Opportunists anxious to check the Radicals, and he also continued to exchange confidences and advice with him.

A banal frontier incident in late April 1887 involving an illegal arrest of a French spy, Guillaume Schnaebele, by German authorities who had framed him probably marked the onset of Clemenceau's break with the general. Or so it was perceived. Grévy and Bismarck soon settled the affair sensibly, but Boulanger's noisier supporters claimed Bismarck's moderation proved that France had a man the terrible chancellor feared. Clemenceau may have been put on guard by loose talk from a Radical senator, Naquet, of a coup d'état with Boulanger's help. In any case, while advocating, as were Boulanger and Goblet in cabinet discussions, a defiant stance toward any provocations from Germany. La Justice had noticeably declined to bang the patriotic drum in the style of Rochefort and other Boulanger enthusiasts. Recovery of pride and reform of the army were all well and good, but war with Germany over a captured spy? Word began to spread that Clemenceau was ready to see Boulanger eased out.

Goblet fell in mid-May, a victim of harassment by impatient Radicals which the Opportunists, led by Maurice Rouvier and Ferry, astutely exploited to move against Boulanger. Floquet, Clemenceau's candidate, was presumed to want Boulanger kept on. *La Justice* maintained that the issue was reform, "not a question of persons," and scarcely mentioned Boulanger.[20] Translation: Clemenceau was for Floquet even if it meant keeping Boulanger--which was not exactly to say that he *wanted* Boulanger, or wanted him, anyhow, in the same way or for the same reasons as a disturbingly large number of Paris left-wingers now wanted him. Put another way, Clemenceau apparently calculated that whether Boulanger stayed or went, his popularity in the last analysis could only strengthen the Radicals' pressure on the Opportunists.

His equivocation cost him. Georges Clemenceau was conspicuously absent from the parade of consultants and aspirants invited to the Élysée during the two-week crisis, a snub he never forgot. Worse followed when Grévy sanctioned a deal the Radicals had discounted to the end: an Opportunist link-up with the Right. On a promise of no further action against Catholic schools (the "Pacte Mackau"), Rouvier became premier, and Boulanger was out.

IV

Almost a year to the day after the triumphant review of 1886, the Gare de Lyon was invaded by shrieking thousands seeking to prevent Boulanger's departure for a command at Clermont-Ferrand. He managed to get out of town, but this alarming event marked the birth of Boulangism as a serious political movement and the opening, too, of a fissure among the Radicals. Amidst boos and cheers Clemenceau excoriated Rouvier for the Pacte Mackau, calling it a stupid, if unintentional, aggravation of all the discontents massing behind the general. He attributed his popularity to attacks on him by the Right and the German press, and he rejected inferences that the rioters really wanted a dictatorship: "We must win back public opinion which has gone astray...: it must be won back by action." He confessed he found the speech difficult because of his friendship with

Boulanger, but he could not deny the general had erred: "Well, yes! This popularity has come too fast to someone who has loved acclaim too much, or to be just, who did not flee it enough...."[21]

The speech did not mark a definitive break with Boulanger, although the general thought so and made known his disgust at "this kick in the ass."[22] Through the autumn of 1887 Clemenceau continued saying that Boulangism was rooted in popular frustrations with the sterility of Opportunist rule. Studies have since confirmed his thesis,[23] but it sounded hollow coming from one to whom the general owed so much and who was often to be heard showering his name with sarcasms.

The Boulangist din mounted steadily through 1888 to a fortissimo climax at the Place de la Madeleine on the night of 27 January 1889, a rousing celebration of yet another triumph by the general in Chamber by-elections, this one in the capital itself. Clemenceau spoke for many that night when he wryly asked a former Communard what life was like in New Caledonia.[24] But such apprehensions were largely groundless. Boulanger almost certainly was counting on a plebiscitary victory by exploiting the list-voting and multiple-candidacy rules in the upcoming general elections, not a coup d'état from the streets. That night he merely bade his excited followers farewell and drove off to visit his mistress. The cheering faded, the crowd drifted away, and within a week the wave began to subside. Two months later, on April Fools' Day, the "brav' général," in the words of a disillusioned follower, "slipped out like an enema." Fearing imminent arrest, he took flight to Belgium, and Boulangism wheezed to collapse like a punctured blimp. When he shot himself at the grave of his mistress in 1891, most of the country could accept Clemenceau's cruel verdict: "He died as he had lived, like a second lieutenant."[25]

V

That Boulangism--a farrago of left-wing exasperation, jingoist histrionics, high ideals, base calculation, royalist intrigue, and public-relations flapdoodle--had come within even shouting distance of victory was due to the opening presented by the fall of President Grévy in late 1887. A compound presidential-ministerial crisis lasting a paralyzing month had ignited the hopes of every element.

Grévy foundered in a messy little scandal implicating his son-in-law, Daniel Wilson, a deputy who had peddled influence from the Élysée. Eight years as president had won him enough enemies to make his removal a temptation. On 17 November a conclave including Ferry, Brisson, Ribot, Goblet, and Clemenceau decided to provoke his resignation by toppling Rouvier. Clemenceau charged ahead after the others had gotten cold feet, and in a short speech on the 19th he so convincingly exposed the ministry's weakness (and by implication Grévy's) that to general surprise, including perhaps his own, it resigned.[26]

But Grévy refused to budge. The depth of his desperation was revealed when on the 21st he asked Clemenceau to form a ministry. Clemenceau declined, stating that the crisis was presidential, not ministerial.[27] Later that day he returned with Freycinet, Floquet, and Goblet to listen to the pathetic old man's evasions, a painful scene punctuated by nervous taps of Clemenceau's riding crop on his boot. Two days later, however, Clemenceau and the Radicals suddenly woke up to an awful prospect: Grévy's successor could be Jules Ferry.[28] His unpopularity might be irrelevant since he still had numerous supporters in Parliament, especially the Senate. The Right, too, might vote for him hoping that an unpopular president succeeding a ridiculous one might bring down the Republic itself. Perhaps the only way to stop Ferry-Tonkin, and a possible revolt in Paris, would be to buy time for Grévy's retirement by putting into a ministry someone whose popularity in Paris would overmatch Grévy's unpopularity. Someone like Boulanger.

On the 27th Charles Laisant, a mutual friend, brought Clemenceau and the general together to attempt a reconciliation. The grandiloquently named "Historic Nights" followed on 28-29 and 29-30 November, palavers attended by Clemenceau, Boulanger, Laisant, Rochefort, Paul Déroulède, Georges Laguerre, and others, most of them future participants in the Boulangist adventure.[29] The air of urgency only increased as news arrived of the triumphant reelection on the 27th of three Ferryists in by-elections in the populous departments (a half-million voters) of the Nord and the Pas-de-Calais. Foggy schemes drifted up to dissipate with the cigar smoke. At the end of every solution lay a resort to force if Parliament or the public could not be brought to heel.

Clemenceau said little. He lent himself to a stillborn attempt to get Floquet or Freycinet to head a combination with himself and Boulanger aboard, but he would not consider a simple Clemenceau-Boulanger solution because his pride rebelled at being a mere cover for a discredited president and a popularity-gathering general and because of grave suspicions about the man. (A justified distrust: During one meeting Boulanger slipped away to lend an ear to a royalist proposal to support him for minister of war as a prelude to a crisis which would bring back the monarchy.) Clemenceau recognized--finally--the absurd pass to which everything had come when he absently remarked that he could "see Augereau"[*] but wondered what the army would do if there were riots. Boulanger, hitherto silent, replied, "You don't have to use the army, just confine it to barracks." Clemenceau turned, stared at him for a long, cold moment, then murmured as he walked off with Madame Laguerre for some refreshments, "To think that a general of the French army has been listening to all this."[30]

The Historic Nights only delayed Grévy's decision. Clemenceau discussed the situation with Rochefort on the night of the 30th and passed on an interesting idea he had picked up: run an outsider--Sadi Carnot, for example. "Carnot is not strong and in addition is a perfect reactionary," he admitted, "but he has a good Republican name, and besides, we don't have anything better." Rochefort offered to contact the Blanquist chiefs to threaten the National Assembly with a riot if Carnot were defeated, but Clemenceau later swore he had resisted such a notion.[31] Whatever the case, huge, ugly crowds of working-class folk began to swarm the squares and boulevards near the Palais-Bourbon, reviling Ferry's name and cheering Boulanger's.

Grévy at last resigned on 2 December. In Republican caucuses before the election the next afternoon, Clemenceau supported Floquet, then swung to Freycinet because Floquet had little Senate support, and finally dropped the stalled Freycinet for fear that Carnot's small bloc might turn to Ferry.

---

[*] A general used by the Republican Directors in the coup d'état of Fructidor 1797.

Unless a unity candidate were found in time, the Right might go for Ferry. The word went out: Vote for Carnot--or, as Clemenceau's flippancies were translated, "Vote for the stupidest."[32] On the first official ballot Carnot comfortably passed Ferry, who promptly withdrew on the second to assure the election of a Republican. The Caudine Forks had been passed.

VI

Clemenceau in pressing his relentless war on Ferry and Ferryism had won what proved to be a Pyrrhic victory. Carnot, though a fine man, notwithstanding his patron's sarcasms, and well suited by reputation and temperament to his new post, was barely a whit more sympathetic to the Radicals than was Grévy. It was Pierre Tirard, an Opportunist senator, who emerged after ten days of negotiations as premier. Boulanger had tried to slip back into office, but finding himself shut out he then cut loose altogether, and soon his name began to appear in by-elections with "constitutional revision" the theme of his promoters. The government replied by expelling him from the army--a great blunder because now he could run for office legally. Clemenceau, who had dropped him for good after the Historic Nights, wrung a repudiation of him from the left-wing Radicals and then set out to forestall the revisionist campaign by backing a government-sponsored revision, a very risky maneuver. He got the friendly ministry he needed when he pushed on to defeat Tirard at the end of March 1888 by combining forces with the Conservatives. Floquet got the succession--at long last, the first Radical premier.[33]

An incredibly ill-timed practical joke cost Clemenceau the single vote he needed to break a 169-169 tie with Méline to succeed Floquet as president of the Chamber. On returning to his seat after voting, Clemenceau saw Casimir Michou--whose habit of hiding food on his person to eat during sittings had begun to irritate him--munching on a piece of chicken. He went off to the buffet and returned to sit behind Michou. Leaning forward he asked, "Say there, Michou, aren't you thirsty?" "Yes indeed!" To general laughter, Clemenceau poured a glass of wine down his neck: "There, that'll moisten up your chicken." Michou voted for Méline when his turn came.[34]

More fundamentally, his defeat owed much to the fact that the vote was secret, which encouraged desertions by deputies (including a fair number of Radicals) who were unhappy with his leadership but had felt obliged to support him in public ballots because of electoral considerations in their districts. His failure turned out, in fact, to mark the end of the Radicals' prospects for further power before the 1889 elections.

Floquet favored revision and reform, but his eleven months in office were consumed in the conflict with Boulangism. As the general's by-election victories mounted, Clemenceau tried to pull the Republicans together. With Jules Joffrin, his erstwhile foe who now needed Radical support to be elected deputy, and Arthur Ranc, an Opportunist, he founded the Society of the Rights of Man and Citizen, a civil-rights protective association.[35] When Boulanger showed up in Parliament and set off a tumult with a revision proposal, Clemenceau backed Floquet with a fighting speech in defense of parliamentary government, now threatened by Boulanger's demagogic campaign.[36] He momentarily thought laughter would finish the "brav' général" when the near-sighted Floquet ran him through in the duel which followed, but for once ridicule did not kill in France.[37] Money poured into Boulanger's campaign, a tide from royalist coffers, and the ballyhoo went on while time and again large numbers of protest voters from the Left joined forces with the Right. Clemenceau even heard rumblings from the Var.

Paris, however, would be the test supreme. *La Justice* confidently challenged Boulanger to run in a by-election occasioned by an incumbent's death.[38] But a weak opponent (André Jacques, a drab Radical of pre-1848 vintage), high bread prices, the collapse of the Panama Canal Company, and a wave of strikes rolled an avalanche of votes to the general. The Republican leadership was stunned, Floquet condemned. Urged on by Clemenceau, who was playing for time in hopes that the Radicals would be the ones to profit once the voters had seen through Boulanger, he had continued to espouse reform and revision. After the Paris fiasco the Opportunists and provincial Radicals would hear no more of it; they abolished *scrutin de liste*, postponed revision indefinitely, and dumped Floquet.

Tirard returned (22 February), this time with an interior minister, Ernest Constans, as unscrupulous as any Boulangist operative. A sham threat of arrest backed by a bold use of police powers, decrees, and outdated laws sufficed to bring the general to flight and his movement to paralysis. *La Justice* righteously condemned such tactics, although Clemenceau's raking fire on Boulangism after the Paris election had helped prepare the counterattack.[39] He also declined on principle to testify on the events of 1887 at the ensuing Senate trial of the Boulangist leaders. Even so, he did depart from accepted Republican doctrine to the extent of sponsoring a bill forbidding multiple candidacies.[40]

VII

The elections of 1889 registered a clear victory (366 to 210) for the Republicans over a Conservative-Boulangist opposition, but it also marked a setback for Clemenceau's left-wing Radical faction, which declined from 79 seats to 66, only one more than it had held in 1877.[41] For himself, in agreement with his fellow deputies, he took the precaution of avoiding Toulon to run in his strongest constituency in 1885, rural Draguignan, and on a watered-down platform, even supporting a questionable railway project there.[42] He campaigned vigorously against the local Boulangists, however, and stubbornly kept revision in his platform, albeit a "Republican revision" which might "if necessary" retain a Senate shorn of its veto. "Republican unity" again figured prominently, all the more because of the unpredictable effects of a quarrel (which had led to a duel) with Auguste Maurel, a deputy from the Var who had resigned in 1888 thinking he would receive a colonial governorship and who subsequently had blamed him when the appointment fell through. He also wanted to get Louis Martin's Radical votes in the run-off if the Boulangist, Achille Ballière, a former Communard who had been parachuted from Paris into the race by Baron Mackau, had not been beaten.

As was the rule in the Var, many voters abstained, with only 15,286 of the 26,294 on the registers going to the polls. Boulangism had had only a modest appeal there, but the waverings of the Radicals in the face of it had caused a growth of cynicism and thus even more abstentions. Clemenceau fell 276 votes short on 22 September, but Maurel stayed out, Martin made the sacrifice, and Ballière then gave up a now-hopeless contest.[43]

The victory of 6 October was welcome. Once again the Republic had been saved, and Gustave Eiffel's new marvel could stand proud guard over the centennial celebration of the Revolution. Still, there was no denying that the hopes of the Left--and the career of Georges Clemenceau--had been badly damaged by the clattering passage of a Man on Horseback.

NOTES
CHAPTER VII

1   Watson, *Georges Clemenceau*, pp. 67-68, 71-72, makes a persuasive case.

2   Again, figures vary. See Loubère, "The French Left-Wing Radicals: Their Views on Trade-Unionism," pp. 203-204; Guy Chapman, *The Third Republic of France: The First Phase, 1871-1894* (London: Macmillan, 1962), pp. 260-264; and Jacques Chastenet, *Histoire de la troisième république*, vol. 2 *La république des républicains, 1879-1893* (Librairie Hachette, 1954), p. 176.

3   JU, 7 Oct. 1885, from an interview in *Le Matin*.

4   Zeev Sternhell, *Maurice Barrès et le nationalisme français* (Éditions Complexe, 1985), p. 363. See Rudelle, *La République absolue*, pp. 157, 206-207; and *idem.*, "Clemenceau et le souvenir de l'Année terrible," pp. 64-65.

5   Jaurès, "Le socialisme et le radicalisme en 1885," p. 21. Jaurès called the continuation of the Tonkin dispute with the Opportunists "the capital error" of Clemenceau's life, since it paved the way for Boulangism. The opinion has merit; see p. 524 below.

6   See JOC, 13 Nov. 1885, pp. 19-22. In Seine: 4 Oct., placed 6th (4 won) with 202,543 votes of 215,383 needed; 18 Oct., 284,844, 22nd of 34 (Allain-Targé 1st with 289,866). Var: 4 Oct., 1st with 24,858 of 26,126 needed; 18 Oct., 34,060, 2nd of 4 (Maurel 1st, 34,103).

7   On this and following contacts and his campaign, see Duroselle, *Clemenceau*, pp. 229-235.

8   See *ibid.*, pp. 184-187.

9   J.-J. Letrait, "Clemenceau et le Var," *Société d'études scientifiques et archéologiques de Draguignan, Bulletin*, n. ser., 9 (1964):47.

10   See Yves Rinaudo, "Clemenceau vu d'en bas: l'air et la chanson," *Revue d'histoire moderne et contemporaine* 32 (1985):324-328.

11   See JU, 23, 24 Jan. 1883, 13-22 Sept. 1885; on Roche's career see Lavergne, *Les deux présidences de Jules Grévy*, pp. 249-250, 518. The Radical and Conservative lists trounced Roche's list on 4 Oct., and he withdrew before the run-off.

12   By Duroselle's count, in *Clemenceau*, pp. 195, 238.

13   For a contrasting view see Ellis, *The Early Life of Georges Clemenceau*, pp. 137-138, 139-185 *passim*. He finds him noticeably less active than he had been in 1881-1885 and attributes it to a "withdrawal," as in 1865-1867 and 1877-1879, due to a "psychological reaction against his role as the defender of his father's ideals." He courted failure, his "unconscious aim" being "self-punishment." This explanation of his failures in this period is interesting and to a degree persuasive, but "withdrawal" seems difficult to support.

14   Wormser, *Clemenceau vu de près*, pp. 73-89 *passim*. See also his article in *Georges Clemenceau*, par Jacques Chastenet *et al.*, Collection Génies et Réalités (Librairie Hachette, 1974), p. 103 and *passim*.

15   Wormser, *Clemenceau vu de près*, p. 79. Breteuil says Clemenceau had been on the lookout for a general to patronize, finally favoring Boulanger over Carey de Bellemare, another "farceur." Breteuil, *La haute société*, pp. 24-25.

16   Freycinet, *Souvenirs*, 2:329-331.

17   Wormser, *Clemenceau vu de près*, pp. 77-78. But see also James Harding, *The Astonishing Adventure of General Boulanger* (New York: Charles Scribner's Sons, 1971), pp. 59-60.

18   Speech at Salernes (Var), 8 Aug. 1893, in JU, 10 Aug.; Stephen Bonsal, *Heyday in a Vanished World* (New York: W. W. Norton, 1937), pp. 120-21. Berta Zuckerkandl wrote on 17 Nov. 1885: "Georges is rather fond of Boulanger....If, as Georges expects, Freycinet comes to power soon, he [Georges] would like Boulanger to become minister of war...." Berta Szeps Zuckerkandl, *My Life and History*, trans. John S. Sommerfield (New York: Alfred A. Knopf, 1939), p. 119.

19   The day before the Bastille Day parade, Boulanger, pursuant to a Radical-inspired law exiling members of previous ruling houses from the country, expelled the duc d'Aumale from the army. Boulanger at the same time falsely denied having solicited a promotion from him some years ago. Clemenceau seconded him in a duel before the truth emerged in August.

20   JU, 24, 27, 28 May 1887.

21   JOC, 11 July 1887, pp. 1658-1664, 1668. *La Justice* (29, 30 June, 7 July) had warned of trouble before the riot. Clemenceau's refusal to shake hands with General Férron, who had replaced Boulanger, is usually described as a pro-Boulanger gesture. The context of his alleged remarks shows he resented Férron's breaking a promise not to join the "Tonkinois." Also, Férron may have been made a major general by Boulanger on Clemenceau's recommendation. See Mermeix [Gabriel Terrail], *Les coulisses du boulangisme* (Chez Léopold Cerf, 1890), pp. 34-35; and Alexandre Zévaès [Bourson], *Au temps du boulangisme* (Gallimard, 1930), pp. 62-64.

22   Telegram to Charles Laisant, in Adrien Dansette, *Le boulangisme* (Librairie Arthème Fayard, 1946), p. 104.

23   See especially Frederick H. Seager, *The Boulanger Affair: Political Crossroads of France, 1886-1889* (Ithaca, NY: Cornell University Press, 1969); Jacques Néré, *Le boulangisme et la presse* (Librairie Armand Colin, 1964); and Philip G. Nord, *Paris Shopkeepers and the Politics of Resentment* (Princeton, NJ: Princeton University Press, 1986), pp. 305-307.

24   Dansette, *Le boulangisme*, p. 251.

25   Like so many of his reputed quips, its authenticity eludes verification. JU, 28, 29 Jan. 1889 confirms Seager, *The Boulanger Affair*, pp. 203-210, on the legend of the *coup manqué*. He de-emphasizes the flight's effect on Boulanger's polls in 1889; the ending of *scrutin de liste* and multiple candidacies (pp. 141-142 below) were more damaging.

26   JOC, 19 Nov. 1887, pp. 2066-2067. On the 18th Rouvier had invited Clemenceau to go ahead, perhaps hoping to return stronger under a Ferry presidency.

27   Pelletan's curious remarks on the 21st (in Lavergne, *Les deux présidences de Jules Grévy*, p. 470) hint at an idea of a quick resignation to be followed by a return after the Wilson affair had been settled.

28   *La Justice* hinted at it on 24 November and denounced it on the 26th. Back in June the canny Grévy had wondered if Clemenceau saw the danger. See Adrien Dansette, *L'affaire Wilson et la chute du président Grévy*, 2nd ed. (Perrin, 1936), p. 157.

29   Boulanger providentially was in town on army business. The meetings were held at the Grand-Orient Masonic headquarters on 28-29 November (Boulanger was absent but later dined with Clemenceau, Déroulède, and Rochefort) and on 29-30 November at the home of Georges Laguerre and his new wife, the actress and later feminist leader Marguerite Durand. Laguerre, a brilliant, ambitious young lawyer, was currently one of Clemenceau's closest lieutenants until they broke up over Boulangism, which destroyed Laguerre's political career. Clemenceau, Laisant, Rochefort, and Radical journalist Eugène Mayer attended both meetings. *La Justice* (30 Nov.-2 Dec.) issued oblique denials. Pelletan, who had advised against the enterprise, covered Clemenceau while taking private digs at him.

30   Mermeix, *Les coulisses du boulangisme*, pp. 223-224. According to another version, Clemenceau confronted Boulanger: "You've agreed, it appears, with M. de Mackau. Is that so?" Boulanger said it was but that he had been trying to gather support for their candidate (Floquet or Freycinet?) against Ferry. Clemenceau retorted, "Ah! that's that!" and walked away. Wormser, *Clemenceau vu de près*, pp. 97-98. On Boulanger's first contacts with the Royalists see William D. Irvine, *The Boulanger Affair Reconsidered: Royalism, Boulangism, and the Origins of the Radical Right in France* (New York: Oxford University Press, 1989), pp. 75-76.

31 Carnot was a grandson of Lazare Carnot, "the Organizer of Victory" of the Revolution, and son of a minister of the Second Republic. See Henri Rochefort, *Les aventures de ma vie*, 5 vols. (Paul Dupont, 1896), 5:108-109. In JU, 6 Sept. 1890, Clemenceau denied assenting to "revolutionary proposals" which "you [Rochefort] and your friends spent a whole night making to me." Duroselle, *Clemenceau*, p. 249, cites a report he had contacted (at some point) the Blanquist militant Émile Eudes.

32 See JU, 4 Dec. 1887, 5 Sept. 1890.

33 See JOC, 20 March 1888, pp. 1100-1101, 30 March, pp. 1230-1231; JU, 20 March ("Manifeste de l'Extrême-Gauche" condemning Boulanger), 28 March-2 April. Goblet thought his brusque tactics hampered Republican unity; Rudelle, *La République absolue*, pp. 207-209, sharply criticizes him on the same score. As late as 16 March Pelletan was still trying to separate Boulanger's person from his sponsors. On 19 April the Extreme Left voted to expel members of the Boulangist national committee from its ranks.

34 On 3, 4 April 1888. Méline was declared the winner by virtue of age. See Gatineau-Clemenceau, *Des pattes du Tigre aux griffes du destin*, p. 127. Variant versions in Louis Andrieux, *A travers la république* (Payot, 1926), pp. 349-50; Ajalbert, *Clemenceau*, p. 71; Treich, *L'esprit de Clemenceau*, p. 40; and Gilbert Prouteau, *Le denier défi de Georges Clemenceau* (France-Empire, 1979), p. 39 (memoirs of Albert Boulin, Clemenceau's valet).

35 See JU, 24, 25 May 1888. Dissolved by 1889, it was revived, permanently, in 1898 during the Dreyfus Affair as the League (etc.).

36 JOC, 4 June 1888, pp. 1637-1638.

37 He seconded Floquet. See Stephen Bonsal, *Unfinished Business* (Garden City, NY: Doubleday, Doran, 1944), p. 73.

38 See JU, 6 Jan. 1889 and following issues.

39 See JU, 31 Jan., 10 Feb., 8, 12 March, 5 April 1889; JOC, 31 Jan. 1889, pp. 265-267. Goblet charged Clemenceau reneged on a promise to support an exceptional law against Boulanger; René Goblet, "Souvenirs de ma vie politique," *Revue politique et parlementaire* 149 (1931):193-194. For bitter remarks against Clemenceau by Boulanger in exile, see Joseph O. Baylen, "An Unpublished Note on Général Georges Boulanger in Britain, June 1889," *French Historical Studies* 4 (1966):344-347.

40 On 13 July 1889. He voted for *scrutin de liste* (11 Feb.), against ajournment of revision (14 Feb.), and for prosecuting Boulanger (4 April), which he defended in the *Thermidor* speech, 29 Jan. 1891.

[41] See Loubère, "The French Left-Wing Radicals: Their Views on Trade-Unionism," p. 204.

[42] See JOC, 6 July 1889, pp. 1850-1851; JU, 6 Sept. 1889. The defeat of his candidate in an 1888 by-election by Gustave Cluseret and then Cluseret's decision to run in Toulon in 1889 perhaps helped persuade him to opt for Draguignan. See Tony Judt, *Socialism in Provence, 1871-1914: A Study in the Origins of the French Left* (Cambridge: Cambridge University Press, 1979), pp. .70-71, 223-224. On Ballière see Irvine, *The Boulanger Affair Reconsidered*, p. 137.

[43] See JOC, 14 Nov. 1889, pp. 48-49. On 22 Sept., Clemenceau, 7,367, Martin, 3,592, Brémond, 751, Ballière, 3,576; 6 Oct., Clemenceau, 9,495, Ballière, 267, Brémond, 16. See also Judt, *Socialism in Provence*, pp. 66, 224.

CHAPTER VIII

Defeat
(1889-1893)

Scheurer-Kestner wrote of Clemenceau in 1889, "His role is finished; he belongs henceforth to the tribe of replacements who never replace any but themselves." A prominent Opportunist thought him "used up."[1] They proved to be poor prophets, but it was undeniable that his fortunes had declined. His diminished Radicals sat glumly between the revived Opportunists-- "républicains de gouvernement" they now called themselves--and the dozen Socialists and three-dozen Boulangists comprising a new Far Left. He was not a happy man.

He still had important leverage, but it looked more formidable than it really was. Some Radicals had been lost to Boulangism or lost altogether, while a large and growing number on the right flank either were new men, less committed to the old battle cries, or veterans growing tired of waiting and increasingly disposed to go along with the Opportunists in return for modest concessions. Clemenceau recognized how things stood and seemed subdued. Boulangism had altered the familiar terrain of his battlefield by linking up authoritarianism, traditionally assigned to the Right, with universal suffrage, social reform, and nationalism, hitherto staple themes of the Left. And his tackings and weavings to contain it during the past four years had damaged his public image. When he intervened in debate now, sometimes after months of silence (he made only five prepared speeches from 1889 to 1893), he often appeared to do so either in a burst of impatience or from a desire to speak "for the record," his attention more focused on distant political vistas than on the fate of the current occupants of the *banc des ministres*.[2]

The Tirard ministry weathered the elections but slowly sank once the new legislature got fully underway. Freycinet--the inevitable, indispensable M. de Freycinet--returned to the helm in March 1890 resolved to soothe the animosities of the Boulangist era, a task well suited to his smooth talents. The Parliament turned to a new agenda featuring a weekly debate on labor questions (a portent), reforms in the military and financial spheres, and tariff legislation, while the cabinet took up the interesting matter of a possible alliance with Russia. A brief uproar interrupted these agreeable occupations in January 1891 when the government banned Victorien Sardou's *Thermidor* from performance at the state-run Comédie-Française because of the play's criticism of the Jacobins. Clemenceau's fiery intervention signalled his waxing impatience after a year of marching to and fro. He supported the ban with a short, impassioned speech justifying the Jacobins' defense of the Republic during the Terror and extended it to a justification of the Republicans' measures against Boulangism. While in full flight he coined a famous phrase, "The Revolution is a bloc," which was to suffer no end of misinterpretation. As he later explained (1898), he meant that it is the *principles* of the Revolution, not all the actions of the revolutionaries, which are a bloc, principles which must be defended if necessary by force or other measures justified by raison d'état.[3]

Four months later a tragic fusillade by troops sent to keep order in a strike at Fourmies underscored how far France still stood from fulfilling the promises of the Revolution he had celebrated. The Republic had yet to find a place for the laboring masses, "the Fourth Estate," as he called them in another eloquent outburst:

> Yes, I grant they have not always made the best use of these rights and liberties. Alas! who is without reproach in this respect? Men are what the social state has made of them....Take care! the dead are great converters. We must pay heed to the dead![4]

The long-bruited "social question," notably the plight of industrial workers, whose condition had scarcely improved in a decade, was penetrating the gap left by the decline of imperialism and constitutional revision as issues. Freycinet himself had taken note of this development in his ministerial declaration, but his, and Parliament's, failure to fathom the urgency of the question left Clemenceau feeling frustrated and depressed:

> For a hundred years [he wrote to the comte d'Aunay] we've been told ridiculous stories of the French Revolution, progress, the necessary liberties, social justice. Is there anything in this other than the flute solos of the Freycinets present and past and future? I have no idea. All these fellows mock us naïve types, and the facts seem to bear them out. As for me, I feel myself becoming revolutionary, and the opinions I'm preparing to take frighten me.[5]

It was not some new question, however, but an old warhorse, withal in new trappings, which finally brought Freycinet to earth. The religious question had reared its head when a Catholic republican movement, the *Ralliement*, took form after 1890. The alarm went out from the Left that Rome was now boring from within more insidiously than ever. Hostility to the Church was bred in Clemenceau's bones. His whole political experience convinced him that separation of church and state was mandatory if France were to progress in the modern world. Hence, when Freycinet tried to skirt the issue by proposing a bill on "associations" which would strike a glancing blow at the monastic orders, a standard move, while nevertheless refusing to come out in favor of separation, he responded (18 February 1892) in the standard way, with a denunciation of the Roman menace. A solid bloc of Radicals and other anticlericals joined with the Right to embarrass the ministry, and the next day Freycinet, who had tired of trying to humor the Radicals without handing them the game, concluded it was time to resign.[6] The sequel, too, was predictable: another combination little different from the one Clemenceau had overthrown. No doubt he would have been astonished to have been told he would not cut down another ministry for two decades and even more that he had won his last such victory ever from the benches of the Palais-Bourbon.

II

About two weeks afterward, early in March 1892, he divorced his wife. If the account of an erratic grandson is to be believed, Clemenceau discovered her with a younger man, their children's tutor, went on a destructive rampage in his home, and had her tried for adultery and deported to America.[7] At some point in the affair and while in an obviously anguished state, he sought out Scheurer-Kestner. (They had long ago separated politically.) Scheurer's remarks in his diary suggest that the breakup was more truly tragic than the grandson's version might imply: "I told myself after listening to his recital of this drama that one must never rely on rumors in matters of quarrels between husband and wife."[8] In 1894 Clemenceau would write to young Violet Maxse (the future Lady Milner) on the occasion of her first marriage, "Absorb all the happiness you can. Take *too much* if you can. It will not be enough, even then, for the great cost of life."[9] Although "sadly battered," as he described himself to her, he in time regained his equilibrium, and his later writings expressed a deep compassion for men and women floundering amid conflicting emotions.[10] Mary eventually returned to France, probably c.1900, but he refused a reconciliation attempted by his daughters, saying he was temperamentally unfit to live with any woman, which was hard to deny. She lived in Paris until her death in 1922, a mildly eccentric semi-recluse running a small guide service in museums and keeping a "shrine room" in her apartment devoted to mementos and scrapbooks of her former husband's career.

Whatever Mary had done could have been an act of revenge for humiliations and emotional neglect he had inflicted on her. "The American," as he slightingly called her, had soon come to bore him. He was a good father and she a devoted mother, but he held to the idea, conventional enough to his milieu but alien to her sheltered upbringing, that a man's activities outside the home are his own concern. By the eighties he had become a figure in "Tout Paris," a sought-after guest in the salons of the elites of politics, business, and the arts, including three of the most coveted: the Ménard-Dorians's, Mme. de Loynes' (until the Boulanger affair), and Mme. Arman de Caillavet's. Stories of his mordant wit, refined tastes, gallantries, duels, and after-theater suppers in high-class restaurants lost nothing in the telling. (One notes, for example, that Jean Ajalbert, who was at *La Justice* in those days and close to him for many years, later asserted that such tales were quite overblown.[11]) A contemporary who had often encountered him in the early 1890s while riding in the Bois de Boulogne at daybreak long before the fashionable crowd would arrive, recalled the striking impression he had received:

> His gaiters, his riding vest, his battered felt hat reminded one of the notary-hunter, the countryside. He had a fierce air; his brutal physiognomy reflected the intense application of his intelligence to the act in which he was engaged: the dressage of a high-bred beast.[12]

His name was linked, too, with women, though how truly seriously he was involved with them is impossible to say since there is no record that he was ever "caught" with anyone and besides was ordinarily very reserved in talking about such matters. The ones whose names found their way into print were the fiftyish but still vibrant Léonide Leblanc, a famed courtesan dating back to the Second Empire and called for good and sundry reasons "Mademoiselle Maximum," whose attentions he was said to have shared with the duc d'Aumale; Rose Caron, a famous singer at the Opéra; Suzanne Reichenberg and Suzanne Devoyod of the Comédie-Française; Selma Everdon, an American model for Rodin, with whom he competed for her favor; Violet Maxse, for whose favor he apparently competed at some point with Sir Alfred Milner; the comtesse d'Aunay, the American-born wife of a diplomat and senator; and an unidentifiable "comtesse V." Everything indicates that none, except perhaps for a time the comtesse d'Aunay, with whom he carried on a correspondence into the 1920s, were more than diversions for him, and at no time after his divorce did he cohabit with a woman. More to the point here, none of them exercised the remotest influence on his politics--or was ever reputed to have done so except, again, the comtesse d'Aunay, briefly, in connection with his break with Delcassé, as will appear.[13]

The evidence, scanty and allusive at best, would appear to indicate that companionship and feminine admiration were as much, if not more, his object than carnal pleasure, and that anticipation was often sweeter than fulfillment. Some stray remarks, in any case, seem suggestive:

> The most beautiful moment of love is when you go up the stairs.[14]

> All the great pleasures of life are silent.[15]

> I am forced to admit that the birth of a baby impels man toward polygamy and woman toward monogamy. There can be, it seems, no improvement except through reform of the husband.[16]

> I have never been particularly occupied with women during my life.[17]

> Woman is at once the mother we venerate and the whore we despise. How many nuances between the two![18]

> [After reading of Châteaubriand's many loves]: But what did he have...which made him so loved?[19]

> [To Tardieu]: I have always been betrayed.[20]

> Women are real 'phenoms.' My loves with Y. of the Française, I have never told you [Martet] about that?...I was in love with Y. I never knew the carnal act with Y.: the heart alone was the story.[21]

Some people said he enjoyed off-color stories and gossip about sexual matters and even that he had boasted of having made love to eight hundred women during his life. Others testified that he seldom spoke of such things and that when he did he showed himself to be fundamentally an old-fashioned Victorian in his attitudes toward women. The most sensible conclusion, and the most obvious, would seem to be that this component of his life and personality contained contradictions or complexities like those found in the others. The best proof of their existence is the fact that nobody, even if they had known him for many years, seems to have come away convinced that they fully understood him: they were always finding something new to wonder about.

To return, Clemenceau's mode of life in this period helped destroy his marriage. And it was dangerous. It lent credence to the charges of corruption levied against him when the stench of the Panama Affair wafted up in the autumn of 1892.

III

Ironically, persistent under-capitalization lay at the root of the failure of Ferdinand de Lesseps' grand project of a sea-level canal across the Isthmus and the ruin of tens of thousands of investors.[22] The reputation of the conqueror of Suez, "the Great Frenchman," and his soaring confidence lulled him and a trusting public into belief that each new obstacle was the last. The company had appealed for money on ever more onerous terms until, with the failure of the lottery loan of 1888, it had gone to the well once too often. The directors had had to resort to progressively dangerous expedients. Their offices had become a mother lode of subventions to newspapers, bond sellers had gotten fatter commissions with each new issue, and when they had finally resorted to a lottery-loan scheme, which needed parliamentary sanction, a vicious circle of appeals, payoffs, and blackmail had closed shut.

An investigation, begun in 1891 in response to cries from outraged investors, was moving gingerly toward indictments in the autumn of 1892 when opposition newspapers--Édouard Drumont's new, anti-Semitic *Libre Parole* and the Boulangist *La Cocarde*--began naming bribed politicians. Baron Jacques de Reinach, a respected banker and chief agent of the company, was hinted to be the orchestrator of corruption. The government hesitated amid the swirling fogs of suspicion but at length decided to prosecute the company's directors. The indictments caught the headlines on 20 November, but the real shocker was in an accompanying dispatch: the star witness was a corpse. Baron Reinach had been found dead at his mansion, a victim of "cerebral congestion."

Sensation followed sensation. Jules Delahaye, a Boulangist, hurling undocumented charges that Parliament contained 175 bribetakers, extorted the naming of a commission of inquiry from a wildly excited Chamber. A banker named Thierrée produced twenty-six cancelled checks totalling 3.4 million francs dating from July 1888 which Reinach had paid to a clutch of deputies, senators, and some intriguingly illegible endorsers. Two checks for a million each had been cashed by one Cornelius Herz, who had left for

London the day of Reinach's death. On 16 December three directors and a former deputy were arrested, and on the 20th Parliament lifted the prosecutorial immunities of five senators and five deputies, among them the current minister of finance, Maurice Rouvier.

Deputies and gallery visitors were departing for supper that evening when a Boulangist suddenly appeared at the rostrum to put a question. The crowd hastily returned to pack the hall as Paul Déroulède, president of the League of Patriots and a writer of Kiplingesque verse, began to speak into a tension-ladened silence: every day since revelations in *Le Figaro* on the 12th, this moment had been anticipated. Déroulède's question concerned Herz, a Grand Officer in the Legion of Honor. How had he advanced so far and so fast?

> ...a Frenchman was needed, a powerful Frenchman, influential, audacious, who was at one and the same time his client, his protegé, his patron, and his supporter.
> Without patronage or patron the little German Jew would not have made such strides on the route to honors....He needed the most compliant and the most devoted of friends so that he could rub shoulders as a peer and companion, now with the ministers, now with the publishers of newspapers, now even, I know for a fact, with General Boulanger. *(Ah! ah! from the center.)*
> Well, this compliant, this devoted, this indefatigable intermediary, so active, so dangerous, you, all of you, know him, his name is on all your lips; yet not one of you, still, will name him, for he has three things you fear: his épée, his pistol, his tongue. So be it; as for me, I brave all three and I name him: it is M. Clemenceau. *(Movement.)*

All eyes turned toward him. Arms folded, legs crossed, his dark eyes drilling the speaker, he sat expressionless, calm, and very pale.

Déroulède's talent, which was not inconsiderable, fell miles short of his ambition, but in those twenty minutes he was superb. Clemenceau, he thundered, had pushed favors for Herz and accepted upward of two million francs from sums Herz had extorted through Reinach from the Panama Canal Company. Herz had lost 200,000 francs on *La Justice* shares when Clemenceau had bought them back, as Clemenceau had told the inquiry? But when a Herz "loses" in public he expects to gain back in private. Then came a truly sensational charge, one he had hinted at a week before: Herz was a foreign agent.

> One must ask oneself if what he expected was not precisely all these topplings of ministries, all these aggressions against all the men in power, all this trouble brought on by you through your great talent in all the affairs of this country and the Parliament.
>
> For it is to destruction that you have consecrated your efforts. How many things, how many men you have broken! Your career is made of ruins. Here Gambetta, there another, and then another, and always another, always devoured by you....
>
> How Cornelius must have rejoiced at this ever-renewed spectacle![23]

Déroulède's terrible indictment won only scattered applause, mostly from Boulangists. The large majority in the Chamber half-believed barely half the charges, but few sought to conceal their pleasure at seeing their tormentor brought low.

Clemenceau's reply matched Déroulède's *tour de force*. Although he had known an attack in open session was likely after the hearings and newspaper polemics of the preceding days, and although he had that very morning shown a serene disposition while treating a sick family friend, the full force of the assault must have shaken him. Nevertheless, he spoke calmly, his arms folded. He glided through explanations he had made about Herz, especially singling out his and Herz's opposition to Boulangism.[24] This predictable defense having fallen somewhat flat, his debater's instinct came to the rescue when he grasped that Déroulède had erred in introducing a charge of treason without a shred of proof. So he hastened on to a moving denunciation of the accusation, at the conclusion of which he turned and coldly called his accuser a liar, an unheard-of-act from the rostrum of Parliament. Accompanied by polite applause from many and cheers from a few, he returned to his seat. Altogether it was an amazing performance under nerve-bending pressure.[25]

Clemenceau was not "out," but he was down. At one point he had called for his friends to register their support; a few voices broke an awful moment of silence, among them, boldly, Stephen Pichon's--who at that instant unwittingly took a giant step toward assuring his future.* Déroulède's "error," it has been noted, was a master stroke. Corruption charges needed facts and figures, boring impedimentia. But a charge of treason, by nature a monstrous thing and seldom susceptible of clear proof, would drip poison into the public mind.[26]

IV

The inquiries spawned by the scandal produced no actions against Clemenceau nor incontrovertible evidence to disprove his statements. If he received any Panama money through Herz--although no trace of it has ever been found--the story of extorted millions seems altogether incompatible both with the testimony of his intimates about his indifference and carelessness in money matters and with the fact that he was many years in paying off *La Justice*'s debts, which he insisted upon doing even though he was not wholly liable for them under the law. So what became of the famous millions? An exhaustive study of his resources and mode of life has shown that, so far as any records indicate, he depended entirely on his 9,000-franc salary as a deputy plus a fraction at best (when he took anything at all) of the 30,000 francs he was put down for as the publisher of *La Justice*.[27]

As for expenses, these sums went virtually untaxed since there was no income tax until after 1917. He apparently owned no bonds or stocks save for a 500-franc share in a hunting club, and no real property save for a country retreat at Bernouville (Eure) from 1908 to 1923. The meaning of such figures becomes clearer when one takes into account that it has been estimated that 5,000 francs was about the minimum needed in those days to support a "bourgeois" style of living. For example, his spacious fifth-floor apartment (about ten rooms) at 6, rue Clémont-Marot, to which he moved in 1887, cost him 2,800 francs annually, the same as his previous rue Montaigne place nearby, and the valet and cook probably cost no more than 1,000 francs plus board and room. His household effects were insured at the same time for 140,000 (a tidy sum, although no "millions" here), but at a very low premium for both apartment and furnishings of 166.65 francs. Furthermore,

---

* Clemenceau made him minister of foreign affairs in both his cabinets (1906-1909, 1917-1920).

there are no records of clandestine expenditures, e.g., gambling losses (he was not a known gambler), mistresses, or lavish parties and such. It is more than likely, too, that as a publisher and the close friend of Gustave Geffroy, a well-known critic, he got free tickets for his frequent attendance at theaters and concerts. He also received several paintings as gifts from artist friends and a Poussin from Madame Jourdan (which he had to sell in 1921).

As for what might be termed extraordinary expenditures, he bought a horse for 2,100 francs in 1891 and paid 5 francs a day for nine months for the upkeep of this or (perhaps) another horse; he spent 7,402 francs on his daughter Madeleine's wedding in 1889, the bulk of it for her trousseau, but he gave her no dowry; and from the 1880s on he collected Japanese incense boxes (*kogos*), eventually some 3,500 of them worth roughly 50,000 francs, which he left to his son. (Michel sold them in 1938-39 to a collector who bequeathed them to the Musée des Beaux-Arts in Montreal.)

So what is one to say? It seems clear enough: the evidence which has been unearthed and which by now is all that is ever likely to come to light shows that he was living quite comfortably in the 1880s and early '90s--but no more than that and certainly not lavishly notwithstanding his well-remarked minglings with the elites of "Tout Paris." The charges of extorted and squandered millions, in short, were an utter travesty of the truth.

V

Judging from his correspondence, Clemenceau's demeanor in private in 1892-93 was as calm as it was self-possessed in public--hardly the picture of the ravaged beast who stalks the pages of Maurice Barrès's *Leurs figures*, a monument of artful distortion.[28] On the other hand, nobody has fully penetrated the Panama morass or likely ever will. Beyond opening *La Justice*'s books and carefully answering questions, Clemenceau said nothing. Reinach died, probably a suicide, before he could be called to testify, and his papers were tampered with before sealing. And Herz, a proven swindler, for his part issued self-serving statements from time to time while protected by a rigid English extradition law (and the English government, some believed) until his death in 1898.

Herz (or Hertz) was the nub of Clemenceau's problem. He was a naturalized American citizen born in 1845 in Besançon of German-Jewish parents who had emigrated shortly afterward. He had returned to Europe to study medicine, served as an assistant surgeon in the French army during the Franco-Prussian War, and then had become a quack in San Francisco using electricity for cures. In 1877 he had absconded with a hoard of cash siphoned from associates and patients and surfaced again in Paris, where he used a facile understanding of the new technology of electricity to become in record time a company promoter, an associate of the distinguished physicist Marcel Deprez, the publisher of a respected technical review, an expediter of contracts for the Lebel rifle, a dabbler in diplomacy, an art collector, a figure well known in the highest political circles, and (in 1886) the first American ever awarded the Grand Cross of the Legion of Honor.

His Panama connection was simple in outline but mysterious in detail. He offered to use his influence in favor of a lottery-loan bill in return for ten million francs if it passed. The bill failed, but he managed to pry 600,000 francs from the company before the contract was torn up. He then persuaded Reinach--blackmailed him, probably, but nobody really knows--to renew the contract personally, the balance to be paid off from proceeds of a new lottery loan. This second bill passed the Chamber on 28 April 1888; Reinach confirmed the "contract" in writing on 11 May, the bill passed the Senate on 4 June, and on 17 July Reinach got five million francs on which he drew the Thierrée checks, including Herz's for two million. Herz, however, continued to squeeze him, ostensibly for the balance of his promised ten million. How much he got altogether is unknown; the highest estimates run to twelve million, reputedly over nine million of it from the Panama Canal Company.

Senator Adrien Hébrard, the respected publisher of *Le Temps*, had introduced Herz to Clemenceau in 1880 or 1881. Clemenceau tended to overrate technical experts, which Herz was, after a fashion, and like many others he was impressed by this ordinary-looking man with extraordinary persuasive powers. From 31 March 1881 to 16 June 1883 Herz made loans to *La Justice*, as he had to other papers. Clemenceau's brother Paul joined Herz's *La Lumière Électrique*, and Clemenceau for a time had even named Herz the legal guardian of his children in the event of his death. Unable to repay the loans in cash, he gave Herz half his personal shares, a paper value of 250,000 francs, on 26 February 1883. On his father's advice and perhaps because of some uneasiness about the man, he bought back the shares on 15 April 1885 with 50,000 francs raised by his brother Albert among reliable acquaintances. Herz remained treasurer of the paper until September 1886, after which business relations ceased, although personal contacts continued sporadically. For the rest, Clemenceau denied everything: he never recommended Herz for anything and did not further his enterprises (e.g., he voted in committee against Herz's telephone concession project); he knew Reinach personally, knew he owed Herz large sums, but said he knew nothing of a connection between the debt and the Panama company. He had supported the Panama project, voted for the lottery loan of 1888, and gotten nothing for it. (Déroulède had implied that Herz's two million went to him.) Twice the company offered him financial assistance, twice he had refused; and he testified that he even forbade *La Justice* agents to mention his name when visiting the company's offices to obtain advertisements--under the circumstances a peculiarly fussy precaution.[29]

The suspicion that Clemenceau had gotten a Herz payoff stemmed mainly from an approach he and Arthur Ranc had made to Freycinet, who was a member of Floquet's cabinet and a friend of Lesseps' son Charles, executive head of the company. Clemenceau testified that early in July 1888 Ranc, who had recently helped him found the Society of the Rights of Man to combat Boulangism, had expressed concern over possible political repercussions of a lawsuit threatened by Reinach against the company. Clemenceau recalled that Reinach had mentioned this suit a month or so before and had hinted that a scandal might result. Since Ranc was to see Freycinet on other business, Clemenceau suggested it might be "useful to call his attention to the question." They went off together, called Freycinet out of a cabinet meeting, and gained the impression he would express concern to Charles de Lesseps about the impending suit. Clemenceau testified that neither Herz nor sums of money were mentioned, nor had Herz spoken to him about the suit: "It was simply a question of a suit which M. Reinach affirmed would be scandalous, without saying precisely why; and because we did not know anything more, we could not be more specific."[30] Freycinet did confer with Lesseps, on 12 July. The latter expressed anger about Reinach but said he feared no suit. Freycinet relayed this intelligence back to Ranc. On 15 July, however, Lesseps paid Reinach five million francs, believing, as he testified later, that this was what Freycinet had wanted done.

There was a sequel. In late September or October 1888 Charles de Lesseps came to Clemenceau (they were personally acquainted) to discuss the company's difficulties. When Clemenceau casually asked what he thought of Reinach's threats, Lesseps hotly accused the banker of extortion. Clemenceau replied, "Do what you want," and quickly changed the subject. Testimony on this visit conflicted at several points. Clemenceau denied that he had sent Reinach to Lesseps to suggest a meeting, that Herz's name had been mentioned, and that his words had been, as Lesseps testified, "Do what you can."

Under questioning, Lesseps abandoned his attempt to place the meetings with Freycinet and Clemenceau during the period (April-June 1888) when the lottery bill had been before Parliament. Clemenceau also got supporting testimony from a company official that Sadi Carnot, not Herz (as Lesseps claimed), had arranged a meeting with Lesseps in 1885. Even so, Lesseps can hardly be blamed for interpreting Freycinet's inquiry as political pressure, however exaggerated his response to it. And the puzzlement expressed by Clemenceau, Ranc, and Freycinet at Reinach's hints of scandal seems, to say the least, disingenuous.[31]

VI

Clemenceau's acquaintance with Herz figured in the murkiest of all the murky chapters of the affair: the events on the eve of Reinach's death. Le Figaro broke the story on 12 December 1892. Reinach, it said, had spent most of the day before his death with Herz, Rouvier, and Clemenceau.

Clemenceau (in the press) and Rouvier (in the Chamber) gave the following account. On 19 November, four days after the government had decided to indict the company's officers but before the indictments had been published, Baron Reinach, who did not know he was to be cited, tried to halt the press campaign against him by begging Rouvier to ask Herz to "put into play certain influences," saying that it was "a matter of life or death." Rouvier agreed out of "humane concern" for Reinach, but on condition that there be a witness. They agreed on Clemenceau since he could not be suspected of partiality toward Rouvier and knew both Reinach and Herz. Rouvier found Clemenceau, who consented. Clemenceau arrived at Herz's at 7:00 P.M. and Rouvier and Reinach likewise "at almost the same time" (Clemenceau). Herz at once denied he had the means of rendering such a service. Reinach, crestfallen, then asked Clemenceau to go with him to see Ernest Constans, who was rumored to be feeding *La Cocarde*. (The erstwhile "slayer" of Boulanger was said to be disappointed with the rewards he had gotten for this service, especially when Émile Loubet, not he, had been picked to succeed Freycinet as premier.[32]) Clemenceau agreed, while Rouvier departed. A gloom-ladened half-hour ride across town brought them to Constans' home. He seemed surprised at the visit and roundly denied he had the influence attributed to him. The two then withdrew after five painful minutes and separated, Reinach murmuring that he was "lost."[33] (Apparently he went home, learned from his nephew, Deputy Joseph Reinach, that he was to be indicted, spent some time with two sisters he kept, and then retired. The next morning a servant discovered him dead in bed.)

On 22 December, enter Louis Andrieux. Acting as Herz' attorney (Herz having meanwhile decamped to London), he brought to the parliamentary inquiry,[34] appointed in response to Delahaye's charges, a photograph of a list in Herz's possession naming persons whom Reinach had paid off. Andrieux had snipped out a name he claimed to be honor-bound to protect, a fine bit of mischief which unloosed floods of speculation about "Monsieur X." The list confirmed the stubs of the Thierrée checks but added a general reference to a total of 104 corrupt persons. In January, the inquiry heard a bank clerk, Paul Stéphane, testify that Reinach had dictated the now-famous list to him back in 1890 and told him to take it to Clemenceau. He had left it with a servant at Clemenceau's apartment. Andrieux returned to the inquiry to assert that he had shown the list to Clemenceau just before he (Andrieux) had testified in December. All this implied that Clemenceau was the one who had given the list to Herz, had known of it during his visits with Reinach to Herz and Constans, and that he and Andrieux may have been preparing some kind of maneuver--most of the names were those of Opportunists--which Déroulède had forestalled by his attack on 20 December.

Clemenceau denied having seen the list before Andrieux had shown it to him in January at the inquiry or known of its existence before Andrieux had returned from London with it. He said he had met with Andrieux and Emmanuel Arène, who was on the list, as a mediator to prevent a duel. Andrieux had only *told* him some names, including that of "Monsieur X," when he (Clemenceau) had asked about it after Andrieux mentioned having cut out a name.

Stéphane's evidence was crucial to Clemenceau. The list apparently was in Stéphane's hand. His credibility suffered, however, when he made serious mistakes describing the hallway entry of Clemenceau's apartment, falsely denied having spoken about his testimony before appearing at the inquiry--he had introduced Clemenceau's name there casually but had tipped off others that he was going to "shake up" Clemenceau--and was found to be the vice-president of a Boulangist shooting club sponsored by Déroulède. And neither he nor anyone else could decipher Reinach's motives. As Clemenceau put it, why did Reinach "feel the need to expose the leaders of his party [Opportunist] to me?"

> To this end he dictated to a young bank clerk--who was not even in his employ--a note in which he formulated against his best friends accusations of the highest gravity, with supporting figures. After which he sent the said clerk...on a jaunt across town without having commanded secrecy, without having given orders to deliver it to me personally.[35]

Andrieux supported Clemenceau by testifying that Herz told him he had gotten the list from Reinach. He also confirmed Clemenceau's account of the December meeting and obliquely admitted an obvious discrepancy: If Clemenceau had ever seen the list, he would have had no reason to ask the identity of "Monsieur X" and would have expressed some surprise when Andrieux gave him a false name (as Andrieux later testified).[36]

Contradictory testimony only fed endless speculation about the last hours of the unhappy baron. Did Reinach want the list back from Herz? Why would Clemenceau have wanted to retrieve a document so damaging to his enemies or to help a political foe (Rouvier) if his purpose in giving it to Herz (if he had done so) had been to hurt his opponents? Would not Herz,

Clemenceau, and Reinach have kept copies anyhow? Was not Reinach's real concern Constans? Had Clemenceau arrived early at Herz's in order to warn him of something? Would he have consented to visit Herz if he had had anything to conceal about their relations? Or did he go in order to keep some control over the situation? Could he and Rouvier, especially the latter, have been as innocent of suspicion that Reinach would be indicted as they later asserted?

Clemenceau's imprudence--at the very least--had put him in a desperate fix. He had participated in attempts to cover up the scandal, and he had good reason to fear embarrassment if his connections with Herz were broadcast. Many contemporaries suspected the worst, and decisive disproof of it was not, and cannot now be, produced. Georges Wormser has suggested, however, that the simplest assumption--that he told the truth--may be closest to the facts.[37] He knew the Boulangists hated both himself and the Opportunists and were exploiting the scandal to the detriment of the Republic. So he answered a request from Rouvier, an opponent but a loyal Republican, to serve as a witness in an eleventh-hour attempt to stave off an explosion, an act analogous to his interventions in 1888. If this were the case, one might conclude that he responded in good faith but, considering the situation, with highly questionable judgment. Certainly he should--indeed must--have known that if his actions came to light, his former relations with Herz would effectively nullify any claim by him that he had acted from disinterested motives. And it must be added, too, that if he told the truth and nothing but the truth, he never did tell the whole truth.

VII

Reinach's pitiful appeals failed, his death blew open the scandal, but the Republic weathered the storm with surprising ease. The elections of 1893 registered the collapse, not of the regime, but of any future for Boulangism as such. This outcome owed much to the stupidity its leaders exhibited in the Norton Papers affair. Forgetting the grander aims of their movement, they hared off into a campaign to ruin Clemenceau, a man they had thought could be used but whom they had come to believe was the prime author of the country's troubles and of their failure to sweep to victory in 1889.[38]

Through the winter and spring of 1893 Clemenceau's stock was very low. A duel at the Saint-Ouën racetrack had followed Déroulède's attack. Several hundred spectators saw him miss three shots. Although the distance was extreme and the umpire's count unusually long, Déroulède could boast that he had not killed M. Clemenceau but had "killed his pistol."[39] (He refused Clemenceau's challenge to a rematch, however.) In January a technical expert treated him contemptuously in a Chamber debate, behavior unthinkable a few months before.[40] Deputies ostentatiously ignored him. On 19 June, when he attempted a speech on an elections bill, Déroulède and Lucien Millevoye savagely mocked him while the rest of the Chamber let the Boulangists turn the place into a bear garden. Millevoye promised a showdown at the next sitting, to which Clemenceau retorted with shouts that they were "charlatans of patriotism," "liars," and "cowards."[41]

In the interim Édouard Ducret, editor of *La Cocarde*, foretold "revelations of an extraordinary gravity" from British embassy papers in Millevoye's possession which had been turned over by an embassy employee named Norton. Millevoye and Déroulède meanwhile consulted with the premier, Charles Dupuy, and the minister of foreign affairs, Jules Develle. They agreed that Millevoye would read only a few selected passages, because there were indications of forgery, and then demand an investigation--a repetition of Delahaye's tactic. The documents mentioned several persons and newspapers as recipients of English secret funds--Rochefort, a Boulangist and notorious Anglophobe, was inexplicably on the list--but only Clemenceau would be implicated. The government played a double game, however, by insisting that Millevoye take full responsibility while, in the meantime, informing Clemenceau, unbeknown to Millevoye, that it thought the papers were forged.[42]

The Chamber, oppressively hot, was jammed to the eaves while hundreds of perspiring Boulangist militants stood outside when Millevoye went to the rostrum on the 22nd. As planned, he turned a *pro forma* question about Herz into a rambling recital of Clemenceau's English-inspired machinations and closed with a call for an investigation. But Clemenceau, who had warned that he would permit no such escape, dared Millevoye to show his proofs, and the expectant assemblage took up the cry. Millevoye evaded, but Clemenceau shouted "Liar!" at him until he took the bait.

The dossier contained fourteen letters (two mentioned Clemenceau) and a list, all purportedly exchanged between Sir Thomas V. Lister of the Foreign Office and H. Austin Lee of the Paris embassy. As the reading proceeded incongruities began to accumulate. Murmurs arose, then snickers, and finally laughter. Develle intervened to clear the government and told Millevoye that in its opinion he was the victim of "an abominable mystification." Millevoye tried to stop, but the president, urged by a crowd around the rostrum, ruled that he must continue. The reading and the laughter rolled on, Clemenceau rocking back and forth in helpless hilarity. Déroulède announced he was resigning "in disgust" and stomped out, but Millevoye marched his lonely way as if in a trance. At last came the list: Rochefort's name brought down the house.[43] Millevoye, by now a pitiful figure, closed his folio and resigned amid ironical applause, and the Chamber adopted, 384 to 2, a motion by Adolphe Maujan expressing regret for wasting its time on "odious and ridiculous calumnies." The crowd outside dispersed quietly.[44]

The affair achieved part of its purpose, however, for it forced Clemenceau to use up six precious pre-election weeks in press battles and investigations. A trial (5 August) resulted in convictions of one Louis-Alfred Véron, alias Norton, for forgery--he was a forty-three-year-old mulatto, a British subject born on the island of Mauritius but long a resident in France, where he had a record of convictions for fraud--and of Ducret for use of forgery. Both were fined one hundred francs, Norton was sentenced to three years in jail, Ducret to one year, and Clemenceau, as a civil party, received the one franc he had asked for damages. Millevoye, who had received the papers from Ducret and had interested others in them, escaped prosecution because of his parliamentary immunity, as did Déroulède. Others also escaped, apparently because of conflicting testimony. Among them were Hippolyte Marinoni, millionaire inventor of the rotary press and owner of *Le Petit Journal*, France's largest newspaper; Ernest Judet, its editor-in-chief and a bitter opponent of Clemenceau since the elections of 1885;[45] the marquis de Morès, a scapegrace adventurer newly embarked in anti-Semitic politics;

and Lionel de Cesti, a former army officer living by his wits in the underworld of journalism. Marinoni apparently put up the money to pay Norton but had backed out at the last moment. Norton mostly maintained that he had translated papers given to him by Ducret, a story which left the jury unconvinced but which some circumstantial evidence supported.[46] (The affair acquired an ironical footnote: the conspirators' crucial meeting had been held at a café at the Rond-Pointe Champs-Élysées, where Clemenceau's statue now stands.)

The whole business remained a puzzle. The government never explained its devious conduct. Millevoye and the others went forward apparently because they saw, or doubtless wanted to see, some truth in the forgeries and calculated that an inquiry would cripple Clemenceau, their chief target, whatever the outcome. The conspirators' naïveté was so grossly demonstrated that some observers even hinted that Clemenceau had masterminded the whole thing. But Sir Thomas Lister probably got it about right: "A band of swindlers exploited a band of imbeciles."[47]

At the trial Clemenceau appeared to be in high spirits, going over to sit on the lawyers' bench and joining in loud laughter with them while throwing friendly waves to the journalists, very obviously enjoying his vindication. But at the end, in his appeal to the jury, he had spoken movingly of the tribulations of a life in politics and of the use and abuse of patriotism:

> The most odious suspicions, the daily attacks, the insults and outrages, these are nowadays what compose the life of political men whom you do the honor of holding in fear. I do not recriminate; political life is not a prison; you can leave the day disgust sickens your heart; until then you must submit; it is our law....
>
> Men appear who claim to sit as judges of the patriotism of all, and if I dare to have an opinion on any question whatsoever which is not precisely that of M. Déroulède, I am a bad patriot and a traitor; if I oppose squandering the blood and gold of France at every corner of the horizon, if I look to the banks of the Rhine rather than the banks of the Mekong, I am an enemy of the country! At all times, in all places, if M. Déroulède should speak, I must bow, and if the cut of my coat does not conform precisely with the patriotic garb of M. Déroulède, I am a traitor.
>
> Gentlemen, it is time to finish with all this playacting....

As for me, I have the right to say these things. I have attacked my adversaries in political struggles, but never--do you hear me, never--have I held them in suspicion, attacked their patriotism. To me the Fatherland is not only the soil we tread, where we build our homes, where we raise our families, where we make the France of tomorrow after that of today. It is the community of ideas, of passions and, if I may be permitted to say this in a vanquished, dismembered land, it is the community of hopes.[48]

Noble words from a heart tried by bitter experience. Yet one wonders--did he ever if only for a fleeting moment, think back to a day in March eight years ago when he had hurled a treason charge against Jules Ferry. And if he did, were his words, spoken five months after Ferry's death, intended to convey in passing an oblique apology?[49]

VIII

Clemenceau reached Draguignan barely two weeks before the 20 August election. The opposition had formed a "League of Local Candidacies" and adopted the standard strategy: a first-round free-for-all to force a runoff, then a rally behind their first-round leader as a union candidate.[50] Three candidates (Arthur Engelfred, Félix Antelme, and Fortuné Rouvier) were mere nuisances, but three others were threats: Maurel, the ex-deputy Clemenceau had offended in 1888 and who thought that Clemenceau had not expressed his gratitude to him sufficiently for withdrawing during the runoff in 1889; Gustave Vincent, the mayor of Flayosc and a leader of the district's growing Socialist movement; and Joseph Jourdan. Nearly unknown in the district, Jourdan was an obscure lawyer-politician in Marseille whom Draguignan conservatives--"clerico-monarchists," according to Clemenceau--invited in at the last moment. He ran as a "Radical Republican" but carefully wrapped his pronouncements in gauzy generalizations.

Clemenceau's Anglophilia, the Herz-Norton charges, memories of the Egyptian affair of 1882, stirred up again in July when the most serious crisis in Anglo-French relations since Egypt occurred as the result of a dispute over Siam,[51] and his scepticism about the imminent Franco-Russian alliance, currently being promoted by a projected visit of a Russian fleet to Toulon in October--all hurt him in a district hard by that traditionally Anglophobic naval base. Its sizeable Corsican settlements were duly reminded of a petition he had forwarded to the National Assembly in 1871 on behalf of the Paris Positivist Club calling for the return of the Bonapartes' homeland to Italy.[52] (He claimed he had merely done the club a service.) But the most effective weapon was the cry of "Var for the Varois!" Clemenceau was an outsider who was laggard in tending to his constituents. In a district as remote as Draguignan, and moreover one badly in need of assistance because of the phylloxera epidemic devastating the vineyards, the argument scored. He was, however, by no means defenseless. Clemencist committees abounded, many mayors supported him, the prefect was presumed to be on his side, although this cut both ways, and his personal prestige helped among voters who liked having a prominent man represent them.[53]

The first confrontation came on 8 August at a public debate in Salernes attended by most of the candidates. Clemenceau overwhelmed them with a magnificent fighting speech. He challenged every charge large and small which had been made against him, repeating again and again, "Where are the millions?"[54] He spoke eloquently about the Republic's past and laid down his program for the future: constitutional revision, separation of church and state, social insurance laws, and an income tax. Widely circulated, the speech badly shook his opponents, but they presently got massive help from Paris.

The double campaign which followed, one by the official opposition, the other led by Ernest Judet and the marquis de Morès, won lasting fame as a classic of roughhouse politics. (A brand by no means alien to the Var. Back in 1856, an exasperated prefect there had noted about the region: "People stay at home and don't associate with others except to harm their enemies. They don't kill enemies, as in Corsica, but denounce them, destroy them by every means. There is something of the Italian and the Arab in the character of the inhabitants...and war has long been, more than elsewhere, the normal state of the country."[55]) The candidates kept the Judet-Morès onslaught at arm's length, at least in public, but the invasion drew even international attention. Morès, enraged by Clemenceau's slyly casual revelation at the Norton trial that Herz had loaned him money, brought in fifty tough Parisian newsvendors and some Corsican and Piedmontese brawlers from Marseille to disrupt Clemenceau's meetings with fistfights and shouts in English of "Oh yes!" and "Cornelius Herz!" and "Roast beef!" Railroad cars disgorged bales of leaflets, placards, and free copies of *Le Petit Journal* stuffed with diatribes against "Sir Georges." Toiling through villages baking in a Provençal summer sun, Clemenceau time and again had to surrender use of his best weapon, oratory. His angered partisans meanwhile struck back with a news sheet whose rantings were nearly as uncontrolled as the opposition's and with groups at Jourdan's meetings waving prayer books and crucifixes.

Oddly enough, election day passed quietly. As usual in this district, many voters abstained (41%), so many that even if Clemenceau had won a majority, which he missed by fewer than a thousand votes, a runoff would have been mandatory. His 6,634 votes fell only 874 short of his first-round total in 1889; Jourdan got 4,686, Vincent 1,702, Maurel 1,018, and the others shared 900. The Clemencists crowed victory, certain that Vincent would not support Jourdan, who had swept up the conservatives while letting the others divide the middle and left-wing vote.

But Clemenceau had made two bad mistakes. He had done little to soothe Maurel and continued to ignore him after the first round. And, secondly, he had indiscriminately characterized his opposition as "reactionary," "Boulangist," and "monarchist." Vincent, angrily declaring that a worker's word was worth at least as much as that of "the friend of Cornelius Herz," withdrew in favor of Jourdan, as had all the others. Jean Jaurès, the emerging leader of French socialism, and the Socialist miners of Carmaux, whom Clemenceau had visited during a bitter strike in 1892, pleaded with their Varois comrades not to vote for a "reactionary," but the Socialist mayor of Marseille, Siméon Flaissières, for reasons of his own, countered with an endorsement of Jourdan.[56]

Vincent's decision sounded the knell. Judet, Morès, and their bands closed for the kill. Clemenceau's meetings were broken up, his carriage stoned. He fell ill and stayed at a hotel in Draguignan, virtually under seige. Even so, he kept his sense of humor. A young man, so a story went, found his room to ask him face-to-face if he were sold to the English. Clemenceau solemnly told him it was true and then suddenly threw aside the bedclothes.

"See that jewel there?" he rasped. "Queen Victoria is mad about it!" The fellow stumbled out, trailed by hoots of laughter.[57]

On 3 September came the day of reckoning. Abstentions fell to thirty percent, and Clemenceau pushed his total to 8,610. But Jourdan got 9,503.[58] A shift to Clemenceau of 447 votes, less than seventeen percent of Vincent's and Maurel's first-round totals and only fractionally more than a quarter of Vincent's, would have made the difference.

Clemenceau's lieutenants and his children, who seemed quite crushed, waited for word at *La Justice*, silently gazing now and then at a one-word sign hung from a building across the street: HERZ. Down the way *Le Gaulois* posted a bulletin. Cheers rolled up into the night. Moments later a telegram came in: "Beaten. My name takes its place among the others. Until tomorrow. G. Clemenceau."[59]

IX

The prefect advised a swift departure from Draguignan to avoid trouble. He refused. The next morning he left as planned, accompanied by some supporters to prevent a beating, or worse. As the train moved out he looked back at the gesticulating crowd through windows streaked with spittle.

Thirty-five years later Martet evoked some memories. "I must say that Cornelius Herz was a thoroughly bad lot," mused Clemenceau. "Unfortunately, it wasn't written all over his face."[60]

NOTES
CHAPTER VIII

1   From Scheurer-Kestner's unpublished *Journal*, as quoted in Krebs, "Le secret de Clemenceau," p. 83; and Henri Lavertujon, quoted in Cambon, *Correspondance*, 1:336.

2   See especially Watson, *Georges Clemenceau*, pp. 120-121; and Duroselle, *Clemenceau*, p. 262.

3   JOC, 29 Jan. 1891, pp. 155-156; GC, *L'iniquité*, pp. 233-236. Some phrases strikingly echoed Blanqui; see Maurice Dommanget, *Les idées politiques et sociales d'Auguste Blanqui* (Marcel Rivière, 1957), p. 307.

4   JOC, 8 May 1891, pp. 814-816.

5   Dated 23 Dec. 1891; from Wormser, *La république de Clemenceau*, p. 8.

6   JOC, 18 Feb. 1892, pp. 136-138; and Freycinet, *Souvenirs*, 2:453-454, 495. See also his speeches against "theocracy," 27 May, 8 June 1889.

7   Gatineau-Clemenceau, *Des pattes du Tigre*, pp. 27-28. See also Edmond and Jules de Goncourt, *Journal des Goncourt--Mémoires de la vie littéraire*, 4 vols. (É. Fasquelle, 1891-1907), 4:528-529. The *New York World*, 18 March 1892, p. 5, carried a version, probably Mary's, saying that she had obtained the divorce quietly after discovering him *in flagrante delicto* with the comtesse d'Aunay but had returned to America before the verdict rendered three weeks ago (*sic*). Duroselle, *Clemenceau*, p. 358, cites a notice in the *Petit Var*, 21 March 1892, that contrary to the allegations of certain journalists (*sic*), Clemenceau had brought the action.

8   Scheurer-Kestner's *Journal*, as quoted in Watson, *Georges Clemenceau*, p. 118.

9   Violet Georgianne (Viscountess) Milner, *My Picture Gallery, 1886-1901* (London: John Murray, 1951), pp. 59-61. Violet Maxse (Lady Edward Cecil, later Lady Alfred Milner), with whom he carried on a long correspondence as well as one with her sister Olive, was a daughter of Adm. Frederick Maxse and sister of Leo Maxse, editor of the *National Review*, likewise close friends. See Duroselle, *Clemenceau*, pp. 375-377.

10   See GC, *Aux embuscades de la vie: dans la foi, dans l'ordre établi, dans l'amour* (É. Fasquelle, 1903), part III; GC, *Au fil des jours*, pp. 303, 311; and *Le Bloc*, no. 35 (22 Sept. 1901).

11   Ajalbert, *Clemenceau*, p. 45.

12   Jacques-Émile Blanche, "Clemenceau écuyer de haute école et écrivain hippique," *Les Nouvelles littéraires*, 14 Dec. 1929, p. 4. James Fillis, an unlettered British horseman, dictated and dedicated to Clemenceau a treatise, *Principes de dressage et d'équitution*, published by Flammarion and translated into English, German, Spanish, and Russian. He became the director of the Cavalry School at the Russian court. See Duroselle, *Clemenceau*, p. 419. Blanche says he was also *Hofstallmeister* to Emperor Franz Josef.

13   See p. 229 below. Duroselle, *Clemenceau*, pp. 367-386, discusses in detail his relations with women, e.g., Violet Maxse (pp. 375-376). See also Gatineau-Clemenceau, *Des pattes du Tigre*, pp. 27-28, 65; on Léonide Leblanc see Joanna Richardson, *The Courtesans: The Demi-Monde in Nineteenth Century France* (Cleveland: World Publishing Co., 1967), pp. 102-103, 123, and *passim*; on Rose Caron, Pierre-Benjamin Gheusi, *Cinquante ans de Paris: Mémoires d'un témoin*, 3 vols. (Librairie Plon, 1939-41), 2:120, 136-137; on Selma Everdon, Williams, *The Tiger of France*, pp. 88-90, 255, and Georges Suarez, *La vie orgueilleuse de Clemenceau* (Éditions de France, 1930), pp. 143-157; and on the comtesse d'Aunay, David S. Newhall, "Georges Clemenceau, 1902-1906: 'An Old Beginner'" (Ph.D. diss., Harvard University, 1963), 1:289-94, 2:143-152, *passim*.

14   GC, *Les plus forts*, p. 125.

15   Frances Stevenson [Louise, Countess Lloyd George], *Lloyd George: A Diary of Frances Stevenson*, ed. A. J. P. Taylor (New York: Harper & Row, 1971), p. 174.

16   GC, *In the Evening of My Thought*, 2:444n.

17   Adam de Villiers, *Clemenceau parle*, pp. 23-24.

18   *Ibid.*, p. 29.

19   Lefranc, "Clemenceau, souvenirs et portrait," p. 332.

20   *Ibid.*, p. 338, quoted at second hand.

21   Martet, *Le Tigre*, p. 271.

22   On this complicated affair, see especially Bruno Weill, *Panama*, trans. Albert Lehman (Bernard Graset, 1934); Adrien Dansette, *Les affaires de Panama*, 2nd ed. (Librairie Académique Perrin, 1934); Jean Bouvier, *Les deux scandales de Panama* (René Julliard, 1964); and Maron J. Simon, *The Panama Affair* (New York: Charles Scribner's Sons, 1971).

23   JOC, 20 Dec. 1892, pp. 1886-1889. See also the sittings of 13, 15 December.

24   Herz had been very close to Boulanger in 1886-87 but had broken with him, hence the Boulangists' anger. See *Le Figaro*, 20 Jan. 1893.

Duroselle, *Clemenceau*, p. 998, cites evidence which may indicate that Déroulède received information from one Nourrit, a police agent with Boulangist sympathies.

25 JOC, 20 Dec. 1892, pp. 1889-1890. See also JU, 21 Dec.; and Maurice Barrès, *Leurs figures* (Émile-Paul, [1902]), pp. 143-149.

26 Dansette, *Les affaires de Panama*, p. 177.

27 The study, a hugely valuable contribution which is the source of the information in this section, is Duroselle, *Clemenceau*, pp. 299-302, 359-360 (Madeleine's marriage), 387-388, 390-393 (salons). See also Wormser, *Clemenceau vu de près*, pp. 26, 27, 31; and JU, 10 Aug. 1893, his famous justificatory speech on 8 Aug. at Salernes (Var).

28 See letters to the comte d'Aunay in Wormser, *La république de Clemenceau*, p. 171. Barrès later expressed regret that he wrote the book, though not to Clemenceau. See Martet, *Clemenceau*, p. 131; and Duroselle, *Clemenceau*, pp. 395-396. He is said to have played a role in getting Clemenceau elected to the Académie Française in 1918.

29 See JU, 2 Dec. 1886, 13, 15, 20 Dec. 1892, 12, 21, 26 Jan., 4, 6 Feb., 2, 11, 12 March 1893; and Martet, *Clemenceau*, p. 125.

30 JU, 2 March 1893, from testimony leaked to *Le Figaro*.

31 See JU, 26 Jan., 28 Feb., 2, 3, 9, 11, 12, 24 March 1893, transcripts of testimony plus reports from other papers.

32 According to Fulton, Constans and Clemenceau were friends for a time in this period. Constans was angling for the presidency. See L. B. Fulton, "Ernest Constans and the Presidency of the French Republic, 1889-92," *Australian Journal of Politics and History* 30 (1984):32-33, 40-41.

33 See JU, 13-15 Dec. 1892, 22 Jan. 1893; and JOC, 13 Dec. 1892, pp. 1809-1810.

34 Pelletan was a member. Clemenceau consistently voted for an inquiry with the widest possible powers. *La Justice* maintained that the company was trying to divert attention from its misdeeds by indicting Parliament. Pelletan thought wholesale corruption in Parliament was a myth. I am inclined to agree; about three dozen bribe-takers seems a reasonable estimate.

35 JU, 20 Jan. 1893.

36 See JU, 19-22, 24, 25, 28, 30 Jan., 11, 12, 22, 29 March 1893.

37 Wormser, *La république de Clemenceau*, pp. 168-169.

38   See C. Stewart Doty, "Parliamentary Boulangism After 1889," *The Historian* 32 (1970):268 and *passim*.

39   It seems unlikely he would have wanted to kill Déroulède, i.e., murder him, but only wound him--which demanded very careful aim. His seconds, Gaston Thomson and Paul Ménard-Dorian, protested the 25-meter distance and the count. The crowd was ugly; it might have lynched him had he succeeded. See JU, 22, 23 Dec. 1892; *New York World*, 22, 23 Dec. 1892; and Goncourt, *Journal des Goncourt*, 4:342.

40   JOC, 28 Jan. 1893, pp. 292-297. See also sittings of 6, 16 Feb., 23 March 1893 for similar incidents.

41   JOC, 19 June 1893, pp. 1764-1768.

42   See JU, 6 Aug. 1893. He was suspicious of the government's motives; see GC, *L'inquité*, p. 121.

43   The list (dated 10 June 1893 and signed "Thomas W. [*sic*] Lister"):*Le Temps*, £800; Charles Laurent, £600; Clemenceau "in London," £20,000; and Rochefort "in London," £3,600. Norton (?) had listed Rochefort, and Déroulède let it remain, perhaps because of his well-known jealousy of him.

44   JOC, 22 June 1893, pp. 1787-1794; JU, 24 June; and Barrès, *Leurs figures*, pp. 232-244.

45   See JU, 27 July 1893. Judet was on a losing Radical list endorsed by Clemenceau. The election was voided. In February 1886 four Republicans won, but Susini was forced into a runoff. Judet wanted to run, but Clemenceau stuck by Susini. Judet ran anyway, as a Boulangist, and lost. Thereafter he carried on a lifelong vendetta against Clemenceau.

46   See JU, 20 June-16 Aug. 1893, *passim*. Lord Rosebery, the Prime Minister, denounced the affair in the House of Lords on 23 June 1893. Norton never was employed by the embassy. Gaston Calmette (*Le Figaro*) and Arthur Meyer (*Le Gaulois*) testified he had tried to sell them papers. There were hints that the Russian ambassador, Baron Mohrenheim, had had a hand in the affair; he had been tainted by Panama and disliked Clemenceau's scepticism about the pending Franco-Russian alliance, completed in 1894. See, e.g., Friedrich Engels and Paul and Laura Lafargue, *Correspondance (1868-1895)*, 3 vols. (Éditions Sociales, 1956-59), 3:288. Clemenceau later wrote (*L'iniquité*, p. 121) that a man at the Quai d'Orsay had helped compile the Norton Papers. Cesti surfaced again, in 1894, swindling the Dreyfus family out of 2,000 francs while posing as an informant and investigator; see Mathieu Dreyfus, *L'Affaire: Telle que je l'ai vécue* (Bernard Grasset, 1978), pp. 28-30.

47   JU, 8 Aug. 1893, from *L'Intransigeant*, Rochefort's paper.

48   JU, 7 Aug. 1893. On his conduct, Maurice Talmeyr, "Clemenceau, Degas et Cie," *Le Figaro*, 17 Dec. 1930, an eyewitness.

49   In any event, he tended Ferry's wounds when he was shot in 1887 and voted for a national funeral for him in 1893.

50   Offspring of a Boulangist society for Varois Parisians begun in 1888. On this election see especially Yves Malartic, "Comment Clemenceau fût battu aux élections législatives à Draguignan en 1893," *Provence historique* 12 (1962), no. 47, pp. 112-138; Francisque Varenne, "La défait de Georges Clemenceau à Draguignan en 1893," *Revue politique et parlementaire* 215(1955):255-259; and Yves Rinaudo, *Les vendanges de la République: Les paysans du Var à la fin du XIXe siècle* (Lyon: Presses Universitaire de Lyon, 1982), pp. 183-186.

51   On its gravity see William L. Langer, *The Franco-Russian Alliance, 1890-1894* (Cambridge, MA: Harvard University Press, 1929), p. 332.

52   See *Annales de l'Assemblée Nationale*, 4 March 1871, pp. 152-155.

53   JU, 7 Sept. 1893, said the prefect, Chadenier, did not work against him, an interesting way of putting it, but many *fonctionnaires* did. A prefect, Fernand Bret, sympathetic to Jourdan was named prefect after the election. He was a son-in-law of René Brice, a centrist deputy, and a brother-in-law of Paul Deschanel. See Christophe Charle, *Les élites de la république, 1880-1900* (Librairie Arthème Fayard, 1987), pp. 298-300, 492.

54   See JU, 10 Aug. 1893. As Watson notes (*Georges Clemenceau*, p. 129), he refuted accusations but did not go on to explain *La Justice*'s sources of income.

55   Le Clère and Wright, *Les préfets du Second Empire*, p. 132.

56   See JU, 31 Aug., 1 Sept. 1893; and *La Petite République*, 1 Sept. 1893. Henry Hyndman, in *Clemenceau, the Man and His Time*, p. 130, says Clemenceau laughed off his (Hyndman's) warning that the Socialists might desert. Most of the Socialists returned to support him after 1902 until his first ministry (1906-9) alienated them; Vincent offered him a banquet in 1904. See Judt, *Socialism in Provence*, pp. 81-84.

57   Treich, *L'ésprit de Clemenceau*, pp. 47-48.

58   See JOC, 16 Nov. 1893, p. 56. Clemenceau filed no protest, and there was no discussion.

59   See Ajalbert, *Clemenceau*, pp. 92-94, an eyewitness. "Others" included Floquet, Pichon, Maujan, Déroulède, Millevoye, Drumont,

Delahaye, Andrieux, and Rouvier.   Pelletan survived, but he and Clemenceau were drifting apart.

60   Martet, *Clemenceau*, p. 125.

CHAPTER IX

Crusading Journalist
(1893-1899)

Three weeks after his defeat at Draguignan, Georges Clemenceau turned fifty-two--a washed-up politician. Even the Radicals shed few tears over his fall: most of the surviving veterans scarcely stifled an "Ouf!" of relief, while the newcomers soon showed themselves more than content to leave to the Socialists the unrewarding role of perpetual opponents. In less time than it took to tell, Attila the Hun, the Scourge of the Palais-Bourbon and Terror of the Ministries had become yesterday's breakfast, passé.

Clemenceau was given to rapid, unpredictable changes of mood, reflections of his internal conflicts and extreme sensitivities. His abounding energy and willpower were at constant grips with an unfeeling, crushing cosmos wholly indifferent to his strugglings. As he remarked in 1914 to a friend, the Danish critic Georg Brandes:

> When a little bubble of foam breaks the surface of the ocean, this is no great matter. Are we only this? My pessimism replies that it is not a great matter, while my optimism wills absolutely, before the little bubble bursts [sic], that it be made into a Zeppelin.[1]

Hence it is no surprise to find that his acquaintances recorded varying impressions of his state of mind following his defeat. To Charles Edmond, the Senate librarian, he wrote:

> I have been misunderstood in my home, betrayed in my friendships, deserted by my party, ignored by my constituents, suspected by my country. *La Justice* has closed its offices, its creditors clamor at my door. I am loaded with debts, and I have nothing, nothing more....[2]

And words to his brother Paul's sister-in-law, Berthe Szeps: "I had faith in man. Nothing remains of all that. There is a void opened in me which can never be filled."[3] Commiserations from the English socialist Henry Hyndman brought a reply expressing bitterness toward the Var's Socialists who had deserted.[4] Maurice Sarraut, publisher of the *Dépêche de Toulouse*, later asserted that he had spoken of suicide or emigration to America, but he claimed to have persuaded him to become a full-time journalist instead.[5]

Yet to others he seemed still the robust warrior of happier times. Three days after his defeat he dismissed it in a letter as one of "these little accidents found in all times and places."[6] That same day he wrote to the comte d'Aunay disclaiming any desire to recriminate:

> Materials would not be lacking, but what good would it do? What I most vividly feel, on the contrary, is a profound admiration for the eight thousand brave fellows [in the Var] who had the heroism to resist everything. They truly performed prodigies. I shall never forget it.[7]

And the novelist Octave Mirbeau, who spent a day with him and Gustave Geffroy some time in 1893 after the defeat, recalled that he had observed no change whatever in him, no sign of discouragement, of disgust, ill humor, or flagging enthusiasm.[8]

In truth, an absence of alternating moods during this supremely testing passage in his life would have been more remarkable than their presence. In the long run, however, the most profound effect of his defeat was to confirm him in a disabused view of human nature and a love of independence. His hide grew tougher still. On 3 October 1893, a month to the day after the debacle at Draguignan, his debut article in *La Justice* as a professional journalist bore a title which distilled the lesson he had drawn: "En avant" (Forward). He had determined once again not to look back, but always ahead.

II

Rather than try to find another constituency and scramble back to Parliament, he set about over the next several years to make a new life for himself. As part of this program he moved, in 1895, to what turned out to be his home for the rest of his life: a modest ground-floor apartment at No. 8, rue Franklin, in the Passy quarter, the fashionable XVIth Arrondissement which borders the Bois de Boulogne across the Seine from the Eiffel Tower. Because this apartment became so much a part of his life and was eventually so associated with him in the public mind, it deserves a word.[9]

Located a block west of the Metro's Trocadero station by the Palais de Chaillot, the apartment is shielded from the bustling rue Franklin (which carried a streetcar line in Clemenceau's day) by being set at the far end of an entirely enclosed courtyard which one enters through a door in the building at No. 8. It has been preserved exactly as it was the day he died there in 1929, and together with a set of rooms on the floor above which house exhibits and a small library, it is a museum maintained by a private foundation, the Society of the Friends of Georges Clemenceau, begun in 1930.

As one enters, to the right of the vestibule is a kitchen and to the left a fairly commodious dining room with windows on the courtyard. Straight ahead the vestibule leads to a library lined with bookshelves to the ceiling and dominated by a richly carved, eight-legged, unequally U-shaped walnut desk, a reproduction of an early eighteenth-century piece made for the abbot of the Abbey of Sainte-Geneviève in Paris. Here, seated in a swivel chair facing a sofa, two easy chairs, and a reproduction of a Daumier watercolor, *Don Quichotte et Sancho*, Clemenceau received visitors and wrote. Between the library and the bedroom is a book-lined gallery leading to the garden, with entrances to it from the library, bedroom, vestibule, and (via a short passageway past the bathroom) the dining room. Like the library, the bedroom has a window on the garden. The bed, whose headboard is decorated with a Chinese dragon's head, holds only a mattress laid flat on a plank frame. In addition to two chests of drawers, a wardrobe, and two easy chairs, there is a small walnut treadle writing-desk in an ornate pseudo-Renaissance style. The garden--about sixty feet deep by twenty-five feet wide, bounded on the left by a high cement wall separating it from the yard of a Jesuit lycée and on the right by an apartment building--overlooks the boulevard Delessert below and (to Clemenceau's distaste--"a monstrosity") toward the Eiffel Tower across the river. Here he cultivated roses and sometimes was known to keep a few chickens.

Aside from its modesty as the dwelling of a world-famous figure, what most impresses visitors (of whom about a thousand per year come by nowadays) are the ambience created by its extraordinary contents and the intimate introduction they furnish to the man who assembled them. Some five thousand books range the walls, predominantly Greek, religious, and contemporary political histories; archeology; histories of art, especially Greek and Oriental; geography and travel books; natural science; philosophy; sociology; and French, English, and Classical literature. The remaining wall space is crowded with pictures, most of them photographs, mainly of Greek buildings, statues, and bas-reliefs, especially in the dining room, but also of Italian Renaissance and Dutch School art and architecture. Originals, paintings or engravings, are few, however, the only ones worth mentioning being a watercolor by Forain, a dry-point engraving of his daughter Madeleine by Paul Helleu, three paintings--two of his seaside cottage (after 1920) at Saint-Vincent-sur-Jard and one of Monet's garden at Giverny--by Blanche Hoschedé, step-daughter of Claude Monet, and the only true prize, Monet's *Le Bloc (Creuse)*, dated 1889, a gift of the artist.[10]

Everywhere tables, shelves, desks, and mantelpieces are cluttered with small photographs of art work and with mementos and *objets d'art*-- mouldings, terra cottas, vases, figurines, incense holders--mostly Japanese but also Hindu and Greek. Among them are three original plasters given him by Rodin and, on his library desk, a set of seven *kogos* (wooden Japanese figurines used as incense boxes) which he liked to fondle while talking or reading. Literally any place he might have cast an eye or rested a hand there is something beautiful or curious to contemplate.

Oddly, save for the engraving of Madeleine, a photograph of his mother, and a photograph of a painting of her kept at l'Aubraie, one finds no pictures of his family and exceedingly few family souvenirs. But one notices, by contrast, a photograph of an otherwise unknown friend, "Lambert (1865)," and of a favorite dog, "Dunley (1900-1909)."

Finally, there is no clearer testimony to the astonishing range of his interests than what one finds was on his bedroom desk when he died: a French translation of Polybius' histories of Rome; Pierre Lanfrey's *Histoire politique des Papes* (1862), open to page 79; Eugène Carré's translation of *The Poetry of Giacomo Leopardi* (1887); *The Book of Tea*, an English translation of Okakura Kakuzo's description of the Japanese tea ceremony; René Grousset's recently published *Sur les traces du Bouddha* (1929); a catalog from the Ventes de l'Hôtel Drouot of a coming sale of pre-Columbian Peruvian art and primitive Asian art from Oceania; and an unfinished manuscript page of his last work, *Grandeur et misères d'une victoire* (1930).

III

Clemenceau's bachelor existence at the rue Franklin presently settled into a pattern which he would follow with minor variations for the rest of his life. To handle household chores he took on a valet and a cook--from 1919 young Albert Boulin and his wife assumed the roles--and in 1906 hired a chauffeur, Alfred Brabant, who, like Boulin, remained with him to the end. Because of recurrent health problems, including bouts of insomnia which plagued him throughout his life, he took to breaking up his day into blocks of work and rest. He would retire early most evenings after stopping by his newspaper office and then rise between 2 and 3:00 A.M. to do his stint with the goose-quill pens he persisted in using to the despair of the typesetters. After that he would nap, then take breakfast and spend the rest of the morning with correspondence and reading and visitors. After lunch he would always take another, shorter, nap and then read for an hour or two, especially favoring Greek or Roman classics. (In the 1880s and '90s he was a close friend of the Hellenist savant Louis Menard, with whom he liked to discuss them and receive suggestions.) Rounds at Parliament and the ministries usually followed from mid-afternoon to early evening, after which he would dine, usually at home and not infrequently with guests. Then it would be back to the newspaper to begin another day.

It was about 1890 that his health had begun to cause concern.[11] Thus far he had been almost excessively thin, though muscular, but now he started to take on weight rapidly. A long-time addiction to cigarettes and cigars, which had caused a severe throat irritation in the late 1880s, aggravated a chronic bronchitis, and he began to suffer episodes of asthma, heart palpitations, colic, and uremia, culminating in the appearance of symptoms of diabetes around 1900. At that point his doctor told him he should stop smoking. He promptly handed him his package of cigarettes and quit on the spot. (He continued, however, to keep a box of cigars on his desk for guests-- and to test his will.) A few years later, possibly as a side-effect of his diabetes, he also developed a chronic circulation problem in his fingers resulting in a blueness of the skin and an eczema, which he treated, unsuccessfully, with sundry rays and ointment. To cover it he usually wore cloth gloves--those "eternal gray gloves" which an unknowing public tended to interpret as an affectation of elegance or mystery. In his last years the circulation problem also affected his feet to the point of preventing him from going down stairs without a cane.

To counter his accumulating ailments he tried to watch his diet, but he dearly loved to eat and had trouble resisting sweets. On the other hand, fortunately, he had no problem with alcohol, although he was reputed to favor an after-dinner dose of laudanum, a mixture (tincture) of alcohol and opium widely used at the time for insomnia, diarrhea, or pain.[12] Family tradition had made him a virtual teetotaler. He would have a glass of wine after a major speech, but otherwise he drank only at meals, a small glass at most, preferring instead English tea or bottled springwater sent up from the Vendée. From 1891, also, at the recommendation of Moritz Szeps, the publisher of the *Wiener Tageblatt* and father-in-law of his brother Paul, he began to take an annual "cure" at the spa at Karlsbad in Bohemia.

He went there for two or three weeks every summer until 1913, religiously downing the ritual three daily glasses of sulfur water "for the liver" to be followed by a hike through the forests, and then whiling away the rest of the time with fellow cosmopolites on the hotel verandas and at the Elephant Café. (He could converse in German in this largely central European society but rather preferred not to.) His smoking ended and the onset of diabetes having made him more careful, his system became more stable after 1900 and his weight leveled off, the latter result doubtless an effect of a vigorous daily exercise period he instituted about this time with a professional masseur-trainer who would come by each morning. He continued this directed exercise, in fact, to the very end of his life, to the respectful awe of his family and friends.

Now that he was out of active politics, he turned more than ever to the world of the arts--painting, sculpture, the theater, music, and literature-- for friendship and stimulation. His financial straits and the pressures of newspaper work caused him to trim back his attendance at the salons, theaters, and concerts, but he still was to be seen here and there, notably at the Opéra, where he and the painter Degas frequently kept company in the wings offstage.[13] In music his special favorites were Mozart, Wagner, and modern French works, but he was not nearly as much of a connoisseur as his brother Paul, who was a close friend of Maurice Ravel.[14] In the theater he particularly patronized contemporary works, French and foreign, and the experimental productions of André Antoine's Théâtre-Libre and Lugné-Poë's L'Oeuvre. But painting, above all that of the Impressionists, and the art of Japan were his passions.

His love of Japanese art, which his apartment reveals so strikingly, may have taken root as a result of contact with a fervent admirer of it, Claude Monet, with whom he began to keep company after 1887. On 13 May that year Octave Mirbeau published a famous piece in *Gil Blas* praising Monet to the skies, so Clemenceau assigned his friend Gustave Geffroy, *La Justice*'s art critic, to cover the Salon of 1887.[15] Geffroy in due course became Monet's leading proponent among the critics, and through him Clemenceau and Monet began a friendship which deepened over the years, ending only with the latter's death in 1926. The most important early landmark of this friendship was a long article by Clemenceau in *La Justice* on 20 May 1895 on the Rouen cathedral series. "Révolution de Cathédrales," which singularly impressed Monet. This series prefigured the *Décorations des Nymphéas* (Walter Lilies) series, and Clemenceau's proposal to his "sovereign of the day," President Félix Faure, to buy the cathedral series for the state, while fruitless, was probably the germ of his (Clemenceau's) later project to have the State commission the *Décorations* and display them at the Orangerie gallery in thc Tuilcrics gardens.[16]   Hence the reason why the Orangérie contains two busts (by Rodin):   Claude Monet, of course, and Georges Clemenceau.

IV

It seems reasonable to suppose that Clemenceau had to fight off temptations to wallow in misanthropy and self-pity, at least for awhile. His high-strung interior sensitivity which made him "vibrate at everything," as Georges Wormser recalled, plus a view of the universe and mankind which fed the tendency toward pessimism that he admitted to Brandes in the letter quoted above conceivably could have been strong enough to push him over the edge into a depression from which, one imagines, he might have sought release from time to time by febrile attempts to clamber back to political eminence. But his tireless, fathomless energy and that streak of optimism he also admitted to withstood the test, and his debut article in *La Justice* announced it. In old age he congratulated himself on his "luck": "One day I was not re-elected. I returned to solitude: it was the happiest period of my life. Ah! I loved my books more than deputies. I worked for nine years."[17]

He worked indeed. To help meet his debts he sold some personal effects and a collection of paintings (Raffaëlli, Pissarro, Manet) and Japanese art objects, while *La Justice* was kept afloat by ever more heroic economies and a succession of (presumably forced) displacements--from 10, rue Faubourg-Montmartre, where it had been housed since its founding, to 24, rue Chauchat, on 27 October 1894, and finally to 27, rue Faubourg-Montmartre, on 13 November 1896.[18] In addition to writing almost daily for *La Justice* until December 1897, he sought to place articles with other publishers.

His ambitions at first amused them, and they thought that in any case he would soon "write himself out." But in time he won some contracts and proved he was no flash in the pan: four to eight articles a month from 1894 to 1906 for the *Dépêche de Toulouse* (he later showed his gratitude to Maurice and Albert Sarraut for this opportunity); eighty-four in 1895-1897 for *Le Journal*; sixteen in 1897 for the *Écho de Paris*; occasional work for *L'Illustration*, *Le Français*, and (in 1902-1905) the Vienna *Neue Freie Presse* (read by many Paris Jews); daily articles for *L'Aurore* from October 1897 to December 1899 and (as editor-in-chief) from June 1903 to March 1906; and sixty issues of a weekly paper, *Le Bloc*, which he wrote almost entirely by himself from January 1901 to March 1902. These articles, moreover, were formidable pieces whose length (usually 200-300 lines) would put today's syndicated columnists to shame. Between 1895 and 1903 he also published some thirteen collections in book form, seven devoted exclusively to the Dreyfus Case, plus a novel, *Les plus forts* (The Strongest, 1898), and a one-act play, *Le voile du bonheur* (The Veil of Happiness), first performed on 4 November 1901 at the Théâtre de la Renaissance (Théâtre Gémier) with stage music by Gabriel Fauré.

His range of interests and information surprised the general public, which until now had had no reason to think of him as anything but a politician. Here were essays on political affairs, of course, but as many or more on social problems, art, and literature, all of them enriched by an extraordinarily wide-ranging, if at times oddly selected, reading. He also produced sketches of city and village life, peasant tales, stories of life among the East European Jews (culled during his annual visits to Austria-Hungary), and reminiscences of the Vendée of his youth. Although he selected and arranged these writings for the bound collections, he did little polishing. After the War he wrote books and consequently worked them over more, with mixed results.

The style of his writing varied.[19] The prefaces to *La mêlée sociale* and *Le grand Pan*, long discourses in a self-consciously literary-philosophical vein, contrasted sharply with the Vendée tales, for example, or with political articles, especially when written under the stir of cold passion. His writing, particularly in the books he wrote after the War, often mixed incisiveness with an over-ladened, allusive discursiveness almost never found in his oratory. Perhaps in defense he affected an unconcern about it. As he remarked to Martet:

> ...the question of style is an arabesque; what difference do one, two, or ten words make? It is merely a matter of cumulative effect and general construction.[20]

> Sentences too nicely done are like women who are too beautiful: you aren't moved--you admire them, and have no desire to kiss them.[21]

One suspects that those empty columns stretching out before him in the night tempted him unconsciously toward prolix constructions and wordy digressions--a temptation all the harder to resist despite the danger to his style because, far from running a risk of writing himself out, he never lacked for things he wanted to say. As Émile Faguet once said of Voltaire's, his writings were "a chaos of clear ideas."[22] In spite of his efforts he neither deserved nor won literary laurels; it was to his wartime services that he owed his election in 1918 to the Académie Française, an honor he accepted but also ignored by refusing to make the ritual personal appearance there.[23] He was, however, undeniably entertaining in an original way, which he needed to be in order to win and hold a steady readership, an exceedingly shrewd commentator on the passing scene, and, when aroused by a cause, one of the greatest crusading journalists ever.

The mood of his writing was as versatile as his personality and as difficult to capture in a phrase. *La mêlée sociale*, for example, was thought by most commentators to be the work of a pessimist, while he thanked Jean Ajalbert for drawing the opposite conclusion.[24] But in the preface to *Le grand Pan*, which followed, he seems to have sought to answer again by denying either conclusion:

> Optimism, pessimism: What sense can there be in these words which suppose the world to be made with a view to our imaginings and our claim to judge it according to whether it adapts itself to us or opposes us? Isn't the whole effort of cultivated reason one of substituting for the caprices of imagination these two terms: verified, or contracted, law?
> The world is. We discover its law if we can. Why, if not to accommodate ourselves to it given its refusal to accommodate itself to us?
> No doubt we can combat a law by means of others--that is in fact our life's whole effort--but what are we doing if not affirming thus our dependence? There is neither optimism nor pessimism in recognizing the ineluctable fact.[25]

Critics were much impressed by his stern emphasis on a Darwinian struggle in which all life feeds on life, a theme not especially popular in France, where

Social Darwinism never won the acceptance it enjoyed in England and America.[26] He never tired of reminding his readers how slowly and at what cost humanity makes its way.

Yet he tempered the harshness of this tableau by a belief in progress through science and through the growth of a social "solidarité" stemming from the idea of justice.[27] Like his beloved Greeks, he found inspiration in life itself, its manifold variety, beauties, and cruelties. In the preface to *Le grand Pan* he wrote of how they had vested the joy of life in the god Pan, whom Christianity had killed. Science, however, was bringing man back from the "illusion" of religion and into contact again with nature:

> Pan commands us. We must act. Action is the principle, action is the means, action is the goal. The obstinate action of the whole man for the profit of all, disinterested action, superior to puerile vainglory, to the renumerations of dreams of eternity as to the hopelessness of lost battles or ineluctable death; action in evolution toward the ideal, the sole force and total virtue.[28]

Beyond the consolations to be found in a Marcus Aurelius or a Spinoza, nothing in the universe, he believed, promises any personal happiness. In his play, he devised a lugubrious scenario to propose that happiness is best guaranteed by illusions. A blind but contented Chinese mandarin receives back his sight only to discover that all those dear to him had deceived him. His best friend is his wife's lover:

> One hundred bamboo strokes for adultery; will that return my happiness to me? The punishment itself is the last lie. There is no punishment. There is no virtue. There is no crime. There is only sadness, sadness.[29]

In his novel, *Les plus forts*, the characters mostly are driven, unhappy, amoral idolators of wealth who corrupt the innocent:

> Money isn't everything [observes the hero, representative of a fading aristocracy of birth]; but the whole human race is its votary. There is no counterbalance;...all the other social powers crowd around wealth; even those who pretend to protect mankind are swept up. They say it has displaced brute force; but it only expresses brute force in other

words. Someone has said that in the old days there was God against the world's oppressions. But I have always found that God is on the side of the strongest. Jesus himself tenderly reproached Him from the cross.[30]

Darwinism and scientific materialism might draw him toward pessimism or even nihilism, but he lived too intensely ultimately to embrace a life-denying philosophy. Three qualities which strongly marked his writing--independence, compassion, and irony--show where he found a refuge. He said what he thought, ranging where his spirit led, unconstrained by the presumptive dictates of any ideology or school or party. The fact that he was (after 1893) both a politician and a journalist set him apart from all but a very few of his contemporaries (Jaurès comes to mind), who were either politicians who occasionally wrote for the press or journalists who had gravitated into politics. By combining the roles he increased his opportunities to be independent in thought and action. Secondly, the quality of compassion, so much in evidence in his articles on social conditions and the daily lives of ordinary folk, gave voice to his interior sensitivity. There was nothing maudlin about it; it was a militant compassion which demanded justice for all, even for the strong, for unlike many advocates of reform he did not fall prey to the sentimental belief that the weak are right just because they are weak.

The third note, irony, was the most important, for it threaded through almost all he said and how he said it. He sounded it in all its notes: mocking, pitying, accusing, self-deprecating. It saved him from mere aimless raging, self-pity, and despair. It allowed him to exercise his wit and yet remain deadly serious, to believe and assert that he had no illusions while giving full rein to his compassion for life's victims and his hatred for their oppressors. Whether pillorying the stupidities and callousness of politicians and bureaucrats or recounting, with obvious affection but no cloying sentimentality, the humble annals of Vendée peasants or Parisian workers or Polish ghetto Jews, it enabled him to contend with the dramatic turns of his own life by reminding himself and the world at large that all men and women, rich and poor, powerful and weak, wise and foolish, struggle on through life against forces they scarcely comprehend.

V

An after-dinner address to the Académie Goncourt in March 1895, an opportunity tendered to him through the intervention of Gustave Geffroy, marked his first public appearance since his defeat. He was a trifle nervous, the object of some cool curiosity, and won mixed reviews from the assembled luminaries for a speech on the inspirational role of writers in society.[31] Neither then nor for years afterward did he show signs of a desire to return to office. In 1898 he politely but firmly rejected invitations from the Socialists of the IIIrd Arrondissement of Paris and from Draguignan. He said he cherished his independence after seventeen years in the Palais-Bourbon and was content to write. A private reason accompanied the refusal of a Paris seat: only a success in the Var would bring true reparation. Without saying so, he may have feared that memories in Draguignan were still too fresh, and a second defeat might prove irreparable. (The Radicals there were in fact in deep trouble and went on to lose the election to a revolutionary Socialist, Maurice Allard.) Moreover, Ernest Vaughan, the editor of *L'Aurore*, had made non-candidacy a condition of his hiring when he had joined the paper a few months ago.[32] And his interlocutors certainly needed no reminder that he was now wholly absorbed there in a magnificent fight, the furious struggle unloosed by the greatest court case in modern history.

Capt. Alfred Dreyfus, a hard-working, colorless, mildly unpopular Jew on temporary duty with the General Staff, was convicted of espionage in December 1894 and sent to rot on Devil's Island in the Guiana prison colony. An epic drama thereafter slowly unfolded: the discovery of the real traitor, a Maj. Charles Walsin-Esterhazy, by Lt. Col. Georges Picquart and Dreyfus' brother Mathieu; the trial and acquittal of Esterhazy; Émile Zola's sensational denunciation of the cover-up, "J'accuse...!, and his trial for libel; the revelation of Maj. (now Lt. Col.) Hubert Henry's forgeries of evidence against Dreyfus and Picquart; a nine-months' reinvestigation of the Dreyfus case by the Court of Cassation held amid lawsuits, duels, and raging political passions; a second trial and conviction of Dreyfus in 1899; his acceptance of a pardon pressed upon him by an embarrassed government; and ultimately, in

1906, the proclamation of his innocence by the Court of Cassation after years of reexamination of evidence on appeal.

Clemenceau's entry into the case came early, but also late. He turned to it on 1 November 1897 when serious rumblings in Parliament and the press were first beginning to sound and two weeks before Esterhazy was publicly implicated. Given the long history of the Affair, this was an early debut. (His opening line--"Is it really impossible to finish once and for all with this story?"--proved to be a monumental inadvertent irony!) On the other hand, ever since the autumn of 1896--when *L'Éclair* had revealed (14 September) that a secret file of evidence against Dreyfus had been communicated to his judges before their verdict, when *Le Matin* had published (10 November) a photograph of the *bordereau*[*] which raised some doubts about its being in Dreyfus' handwriting, and when André Castelin had interpellated the government (18 November) about its "lenient" treatment of Dreyfus--it had been public knowledge that Dreyfus might well have been illegally, and just possibly even wrongly, convicted. Such, indeed, was the thesis of a brochure published in Brussels at this moment by a well-known but eccentric young literary critic, Bernard Lazare. He sent copies to the Paris press (7-8 November). *La Justice*, for whom Lazare had written occasionally, commented on it "with all reserves."[33] But through all this flurry of interest (which presently faded, however), Clemenceau had stayed silent.

Some months later the pot had begun to bubble again. On 13 July 1897, Picquart's lawyer, Louis Leblois, revealed to Scheurer-Kestner, currently a vice-president of the Senate, the discoveries the colonel had made respecting Dreyfus and Esterhazy and the ensuing efforts of the army chiefs to silence him. Scheurer promptly told several senators he was convinced Dreyfus was innocent. Clemenceau may not have gotten immediate word of

---

[*]   The original incriminating piece: an unsigned list of documents the sender proposed to give to the German military attaché, Colonel von Schwartzkoppen. A cleaning woman in the employ of the army's intelligence service retrieved it from the attaché's wastebasket. In March 1896 Picquart discovered an incriminating pneumatic-post letter card (the *petit bleu*) from Schwartzkoppen to Esterhazy. After reexamining the *bordereau*, he concluded in late August that its handwriting was that of Esterhazy, not Dreyfus.

all this--his father died on 23 July, and he spent August in Karlsbad--but in any event he again said nothing publicly.[34] The case simmered from July until November while Scheurer tried to persuade the government and the army to act before he would feel obliged to make a public statement.

The first issue of *L'Aurore* appeared on 19 October. Its publisher, Ernest Vaughan, long associated with Rochefort, had gathered an impressive staff for this venture. He found Clemenceau, with whom he shared memories of Blanqui, prepared to give up the struggle at *La Justice*. Whether *L'Aurore* was founded with the intent to pursue the Dreyfus case is a moot point.[35] According to Clemenceau, when Vaughan asked him about bringing Lazare aboard, he agreed on condition that the young man discontinue his campaign in favor of Dreyfus. A few days after *L'Aurore*'s debut, he met Arthur Ranc by chance, and when Ranc mentioned Lazare he complained about his tiresome Dreyfus talk. Ranc expressed surprise that he did not know that Dreyfus was innocent and told him to look up Scheurer, who had proofs. "If that's how things are," exclaimed Clemenceau, "this is the greatest crime of the century!" Two days later he met with Scheurer, and more visits followed:

> ...finally finding myself convinced, not of the innocence of the condemned (it was the Zola trial which was to open my eyes definitively in that respect) but of the irregularity of the conviction [in the 1894 trial], I vigorously enjoined my friend to undertake a campaign for a judicial review of the case. He had no need of my counsel. He had resolved upon it.[36]

Clemenceau's writings lend credence to this account as regards his belief in Dreyfus' innocence. In 1894 he wrote two articles before the trial-- one somewhat tangential to the case ("Les attachés militaires," 4 December), the other ("Haute trahison," 4 November) calling Dreyfus a "wretch" (*misérable*) and his crime "abominable"--and a harsh one afterward ("Le traître," 25 December), the only one of the three he reprinted in *L'iniquité*, in which he took consolation from the thought that imprisonment for life is a more severe punishment than execution.[37] From then until 1 November 1897, as already noted, he did not devote a line to the case, while *La Justice* merely followed it in its news columns and expressed no sympathy toward attempts to reopen it. The day after Zola's "J'accuse...!," with the Affair now in full cry, he wrote (14 January 1898):

> It is not at all for tactical reasons that I have refused from the outset to let myself be drawn to proclaim the innocence of Dreyfus. I cannot believe [admettre] that they agreed to condemn this man if there was nothing beyond the *bordereau* and the grotesque expertise of [Alphonse] Bertillon.[38]

And in his speech to the jury at Zola's trial, he confined himself to a denunciation of the illegal methods used in the 1894 trial.[39]

Other evidence, however, raises a question as to how "definitive" the Zola trial was in his conversion. In an article on 3 November 1901 he mentioned "grands combats intérieurs" preceding it which he linked to conversations with Picquart *after* the trial.[40] Mathieu Dreyfus lends indirect support to this version. He noted that for quite some time after the trial he (Clemenceau) appeared reserved toward him and about the guilt question but that he melted toward the summer of 1898, and not until then did they begin meeting frequently.[41] In any event, Clemenceau was not "drawn" to affirm a belief in Dreyfus' innocence publicly for many months, and no doubt tactical reasons in due course played a role. It was only after the Court of Cassation's investigator issued a report containing what he (Clemenceau) now asserted were "irrefutable" proofs of innocence did he publish his belief in it, on 29 October 1898,[42] a full two months after Colonel Henry's arrest and suicide had blown the government's case against revision to smithereens.

It is difficult to believe, nevertheless, that he needed several talks with Scheurer (who mentions only one[43]) to bring him merely to recognize the patent irregularities of the 1894 trial. More likely, before charging into a case so potentially explosive, he wanted assurance there was a reasonable chance that Dreyfus was innocent. Scheurer, bound by a promise to Leblois not to reveal Esterhazy's name without Picquart's permission, could only show him bits of evidence, but the rock-like certainty of his old friend surely impressed him. And he did need assurance. For it had not been just a belief in Dreyfus' guilt that had kept him silent about the case for so long. It had also been his respect for the army as an institution, whatever the failings of some of its leaders, and its close symbolic link to a sentiment which ran deeper in him than any other: his patriotism.[44] Any attack on the army's handling of the case would inevitably unleash attacks on the army itself, with all the distress and dangers for the nation they would certainly bring.

One of the most striking proofs that he feared such a reaction is found in the fact that his true first article on the Dreyfus Case, "Haute trahison" (4 November 1894, mentioned above), went straight to a point he would later hammer on relentlessly and help make one of the central issues of the whole Affair, namely, that a particular person's lack of "honor" must not be imputed to the institution he serves. Criticizing the minister of war for issuing vague statements in answer to all the rumors about a treason investigation in progress, he said that the only way to reassure public opinion is from the outset to tell the whole truth as far as possible and not play games. He went on:

> There is no honor of the army, an honor of the judiciary or the Council of State any more than an honor of farmers or cigar sellers. There are personal faults whose consequences should fall only on the guilty....The army is composed of civilians, clothed in a certain fashion and subordinated to a special regime for a certain purpose. Men are neither better nor worse if they wear red pants or gray, a kepi or a bowler hat.[45]

Perhaps he had only alighted on this theme by chance. But probably not. In its very infancy the case had struck a nerve, and he had "vibrated."

One is left to guess what, if anything, Clemenceau and Scheurer decided about tactics. Whatever the case, Clemenceau opened his campaign on 1 November by stoking his readers' curiosity with impatient calls for Scheurer to produce his rumored proofs of Dreyfus' innocence. After two weeks of hints, summonings, maneuverings, and mounting suspense, Mathieu Dreyfus--who in the interim at last had met Scheurer and compared conclusions--publicly accused Major Esterhazy on 15 November of being the true author of the *bordereau*. Picquart filed the same day a libel complaint against Esterhazy with the minister of war. The next afternoon the minister informed the Chamber that care for the army's "honor" was compelling the government to demand that Esterhazy's accusers show their proofs.[46]

With that the floodgates swung open.

VI

For more than two years Clemenceau lived and breathed the Dreyfus Case. Some 666 articles collected in seven volumes numbering 3,305 pages[47]--one of the monuments of journalism--stand as mute witnesses to a prodigious mental energy disciplined to the ringing of a thousand turns on a limited number of themes. The liberation of a man unjustly convicted of a terrible crime and sent in chains to a living death on a tropic isle was an undertaking which appealed powerfully to the heirs of Michelet and Victor Hugo. The Dreyfus Affair was the last battle of the journalists who had passed their youth in the twilight years of Romanticism.[48] Clemenceau's involvement was in some measure, too, a posthumous offering to his father (who had died only three months before he joined *L'Aurore*), proof that in the son the cause of liberty still lived. To defend Dreyfus was to defend the inheritance of the Revolution: that governments are answerable to the people, and that the state cannot use its power to trample down truth, justice, and human dignity. The attack on Dreyfus by vested authority stirred up the deep-running anarchistic strain in him. He was quite conscious of its presence: all authority took the shape of a potential menace which must be watched, tracked, and, if necessary, attacked.[49] Unlike the tiger, he hunted in daylight, but it was an apt comparison nonetheless.

The legacy had to be defended on more than one front. Like Déroulède, Rochefort, or Barrès, ex-Boulangists now dubbed Nationalists, Clemenceau derided corrupt financiers, bourgeois politicians, pettifogging bureaucrats, and the new oligarchs of commerce and industry. As one of his subordinates recalled, he "held in horror" the merchants of the Temple, as to the same measure beggers and thieves.[50] But while he spared no irony at the expense of the idealistic dreams of his youth, he consistently defended political liberalism and parliamentary rule. Like his opponents on the right, he too admired heroism, energy, and the will to action. Yet while praising the Revolution for exhibiting these virtues, he did not empty it of its universalist, libertarian content.[51] His definition of *la patrie*, as the speech at the Norton trial witnessed, underscored the common ties of family, land, history, and especially ideals but left scant room for "blood and soil" doctrines, much less racism. *Fin de siècle* conservatives were trumpeting the "bankruptcy" of science and "arid rationalism." But Clemenceau, who was much impressed by Ernest Renan's *L'avenir de la science* (1890), clung stubbornly to the tradition of the philosophes and the Positivists and refused to repudiate the gospel of progress and the modern world of industrialism, urbanism, and technology.[52] He loved Old France and was never happier than when among the pious folk of the Vendée, but he did not permit his feelings to color his judgment in such matters. Prophets of the *pays réel* and nascent fascism were to be repeatedly disappointed in him.

He combined a commitment to democracy, however, with an elitist conception of leadership. By birth and allegiance a democrat, he had acquired (probably during the Boulanger Affair if the Commune had not sufficed) a low opinion of the views of the masses, whose naïveté and fickleness he both scorned and feared. (Eugène Lautier recalled going with him during the Affair to see Ibsen's *An Enemy of the People* and his loud applause for the lines, "The majority is never right. The majority is made up of imbeciles." When Lautier chided him at the intermission about the Convention and about the Revolution's being a "bloc," he retorted, "The Convention! An assemblage of cowards who killed each other out of fear."[53]) Yet he had no truck with ideas of rule by an aristocracy of birth or wealth, nor even with "Tory democracy" in the usual sense. Rather, he believed that the masses needed guidance and instruction by mobile, ever-renewing elites recruited among those with the requisite talent and experience. "Finding the best means of forming elites," he concluded while looking back on the Affair, "is the essential problem posed to democracy." The Affair was an example of an elite coming together from all points of the horizon because their consciences were moved: "They fought, they triumphed. Their role is finished...and they must give way to another elite which will fight for another idea."[54]

Self-confident, even imperious, he took for granted his own candidacy for the elites, and the long development of the Affair presented him, without his having to seek it, an opportunity to prove that 1893 had not finished him as a power in the state. In this respect he (and Jaurès) occupied a special place among the combatants. He was both a politician and an "intellectual," a term he helped to popularize--though he did not invent it, as has often been said.[55] Unlike the latter, he understood the pressures under which the politicians labored and subsequently was to some degree insulated from the disillusionment the intellectuals contracted when *mystique* turned into *politique*.[56] On the other hand, he was out of office, showed no strong desire to return, and hence was freer to follow his own leadings than were the politicians.

Journalism answered his strong needs for self-expression and constructive activity, whatever might be said about his imputed taste for destruction. Camille Mauclair left a precious sketch of him at work at *L'Aurore* during the Affair:

> Clemenceau arrived, briskly, his hat tipped slightly on one ear, with the rapid step of a doctor going up to see his patient, rubbed his hands, leafed through the newspapers, tossed off a terrible witticism with a strident laugh, said something very subtle on Claude Monet or [Katsushika] Hokusai, sat down, took out of a drawer some papers and chocolate tablets, exchanged some earthy humorous remarks with a new arrival, gave me a bit of information, angrily wadded his half-begun page into a ball and threw it, went to the window, teased Geffroy or [the painter Eugène] Carrière sitting silent in a corner, sat down again, whistled to himself, broke a pen, turned himself backward on his chair, chewed some more chocolate--and suddenly called the office boy and tossed him his article finished in the noise and agitation, an article which was concise and as polished and cold as steel, exposing a lie, refuting an argument, implacably reestablishing the logic of the daily events, a marvel of clarity, recommenced every day.[57]

He thrived on challenge, the reagent which unlocked his vast energies, and the Dreyfus Case was one worthy of the grandest dreams of any journalist. Early in the Affair in reply to an inquiry on the role of the press, he spoke of "the double resistance of the many [*du nombre*], who do not know, and the oligarchies, who do not want to know." The struggle against "the syndicates of ignorance [and] the syndicates of egoism" is "the highest kind of human calling."[58] Much later, while the Affair ground on month after weary month, he reflected on his labors:

> "If the people knew," we now exclaim. It seems the eternal problem is to enlighten the sovereign. The king never knows.

The king cannot know. All the avenues to enlightenment are barred. The people can learn. Yet what an arduous labor to teach thousands of ignorances! But we must bend to the task nevertheless....[59]

He once compared his *métier* to a carpenter's, whose art is to hit the nail always on the head until it is driven home.[60] The unstinting exercise of his critical faculties soothed him:

> I can err as much as anyone, but I believe I can judge men and events with an entirely free spirit. My heart is not at war with anyone whomsoever, and I see the faults in my camp all too well for me to feel obliged to be indulgent toward the adversaries' camp.[61]

One catches here an interesting glimpse into his psychology. Unlike those whose consciousness of fault leads them to excuse others, his made him more aware of the faults of others and encouraged him to say what he pleased about them: no quarter asked, none given.

In his memoirs about the Affair, Léon Blum speculated that Clemenceau may have been moved by reminders of the Norton case.[62] He guessed correctly. As early as his third article (8 November 1897), he mentioned the possibility of a "Nortonesque" machination in the evidence against Dreyfus, and on 10 January 1898 he admitted outright that the Norton affair was feeding his suspicions. He repeated the comparison on several other occasions, particularly underlining the "naïveté" (to say no more) of Dupuy and Develle when first confronted with Norton's forgeries.[63] Blum also thought that in avenging Dreyfus Clemenceau was to an extent avenging himself. That he again found the likes of Barrès, Déroulède, Millevoye, Judet, and Drumont across his path lends weight to this supposition. It is true, moreover, that his return to Parliament in 1902 and his advancement to the premiership in 1906 owed much to the Affair.

Yet it is impossible to judge the extent to which he purposely used the Affair to effect a personal rehabilitation. Blum, who judged his later career harshly, observed that men like him and Joseph Reinach whom Panama had tarnished had made themselves easy targets when they took up a fight for a convicted Jewish traitor.[64] Characteristically, too, a few days or weeks of intense interest in the case would be followed by long stretches when it would fade from the public's attention and into the back pages. *L'Aurore* was the only paper, in fact, to keep it front-and-center from start to finish. Not until the revelation of Henry's forgeries (30 August 1898) did the Dreyfusards' ranks swell at all dramatically; and even so, to the very end a majority of the press never did become truly "Dreyfusard."[65] If popularity and refurbished reputations were the goals of men like Reinach and Clemenceau, they certainly chose a tortuous path, even if, as has been argued, they had nothing to lose. The power to prolong the Affair, furthermore, rested not nearly so much with the Dreyfusards as with the government and the army: the case could never have ballooned into "the Affair" but for their ineptitude, foot-dragging, myopia, and corporate defensiveness and the brutality of their supporters in the press and in the streets.

VII

No more than an outline of Clemenceau's role can be undertaken here. In the opening phase (November 1897 to mid-January 1898), after Mathieu Dreyfus accused Esterhazy of being the author of the *bordereau*, it presently became clear that a Colonel Picquart was being harassed by the army for having discovered evidence against him. The "Uhlan Letters,"* confiscated from one of Esterhazy's mistresses, shocked Clemenceau profoundly. It appeared indisputable now that the man was a scoundrel and probably a traitor--which did not mean, he hastened to add, that Dreyfus hence was innocent.

From the start, however, Esterhazy's villainy was less important to him than another question, which he pounded on day after day: "Who is protecting Esterhazy?" He confessed himself utterly at a loss to understand why the government would neither prosecute Esterhazy nor declare plainly whether Dreyfus had been properly tried. The authorities' hostility toward Picquart, their kid-glove treatment of Esterhazy, their invocations of secrecy and "reasons of state," their charges against critics that they were unpatriotic

---

* Esterhazy had written in 1884 that he would be "perfectly happy" as a uhlan (lancer) captain "stabbing Frenchmen to death" or seeing Paris "abandoned to the pillaging of 100,000 drunken soldiers."

denigrators of the army--all fed his suspicions. He mocked the *raison d'état* argument as "quite simply worthless," a transparent cover-up, arguing that there are legitimate state secrets which justify trial in camera but that a "double in camera," i.e., keeping evidence from the accused, is both illegal and unjust.[66]   As for the accusations of anti-patriotism, he reiterated arguments he had advanced back in 1894: the honor (so to speak) of the army and of the minister of war (to say nothing of Esterhazy's) are not the same thing. Surely, he cried, this was a point even the feeblest intelligence could grasp! On the eve of the trial Esterhazy had demanded to clear his name, he summed up the moral confusion of the country in a moving litany of contradictions (prefiguring the form to be used by Zola) which was one of the finest articles he ever wrote: "C'est dommage" (It's a Pity).[67]

Esterhazy's triumphant acquittal after a two-day trial surprised nobody. The next day (12 January) Clemenceau predicted that if the government did not dare to prosecute "the Syndicate," as its critics were being labeled, it might be forced to defend itself against a move to haul the minister of war, General Billot, before a jury.[68] That afternoon Émile Zola, who had published several articles on the case, the most recent in *L'Aurore* on 4 January, brought around an "Open Letter to the President of the Republic." Its broadside charges of obstruction of justice went beyond what Clemenceau and many others on the staff were prepared to assert. Would such a provocation at this moment be wise? Vaughan finally gave way, as did the others. And since the bridge was to be crossed, it was decided to go the whole route, with a massive printing of 300,000 copies, placards posted citywide to announce it in advance, and all staff and pressmen to remain at the office to keep the text secret until the vendors hit the streets. Caught up in the drama of the moment, Clemenceau suggested that the prosaic "Open Letter" headline be changed to the words used in its litany of charges: "J'accuse...!"[69]

The government could not ignore the world-famous novelist, but it carefully confined its libel action to only a few statements in the Letter. Thirsting for battle, gaily saluting demonstrators who lobbed rocks through *L'Aurore*'s windows, crying "Bravo!" when the government arrested Picquart, calling for more arrests and more trials to get all the heroes and villains before the bar,[70] Clemenceau was infuriated by the government's tactic, which permitted the judge at Zola's trial (7-23 February) time and again to shut off questions germane to Dreyfus but outside the narrowly drawn indictment. Relentless questioning by Fernand Labori[71] and Albert Clemenceau (inserted when the judge forbade Clemenceau to conduct the newspaper's defense) brought revelations, nevertheless, which months later led to the crucial break in the case, the discovery that the secret dossier used against Dreyfus contained forgeries. The judge did permit Clemenceau to address a final plea to the jury. His eloquent moral appeal (too moderate, thought Reinach) was repeatedly interrupted by howls of a mob led by Déroulède. When he pointed dramatically to the crucifix on the courtroom wall as an example of justice denied, his gesture only set off hoots of laughter.[72]

Zola and Alexandre Perrenx, the paper's manager, fortunately were convicted and drew jail terms and fines. Clemenceau later said they probably would have been lynched if they had been acquitted.[73] The Court of Cassation ordered a new trial on procedural grounds, but on Labori's and Clemenceau's advice Zola fled to England (19 July) before sentencing in order to take advantage of a legal technicality which would make the threat of his return a standing menace to the authorities. A clever maneuver, perhaps, but to many it looked like Zola was saving his skin.[74]

VIII

The fevered weeks of the Zola trial unloosed the demons. Some sixty-six anti-Semitic riots flashed through the country and were very serious in Algeria. Death threats rained from the streets and through the mail. Polemics and duels abounded. Clemenceau fought with Drumont (26 February 1898) and was nearly killed when an anarchist fired a pistol (possibly accidentally) in the office next to his.[75] Zealot monks and priests abetted the hysteria being whipped up by Jew-baiters like Jules Guérin and the marquis de Morès. How deeply all this touched the masses, especially the peasants in the provinces, is debatable, but to Clemenceau it came as a shock. His articles began to reflect the most somber apprehensions about the future of France and even of modern civilization, bending before "the wind of madness" and "mental anarchy."[76] His anticlericalism, muffled until the riots, burst forth in full cry. He linked the Church with the army chiefs, something he had not done explicitly heretofore. As he wrote after the Affair had subsided (6 May 1900), their connection had surprised him:

> There is no doubt that before the Dreyfus affair nobody suspected the abominable state of mind of certain military chiefs nor the disastrous esprit de corps of an excessive number of officers in the service of the [monastic] congregations.[77]

The abuses perpetrated by the Church of the Inquisition and the "praetorians" of the General Staff had brought disaster in 1870, and this alliance of "sabre et goupillon" [holy-water sprinkler], a phrase he popularized,[78] would do so again:

> The Church, mistress of France, is preparing a renewal of the Wars of Religion with the complicity of certain army chiefs-- who are not the army, as they claim to be. And if you want to know what will become of us, look at what the Roman Church has made of the noble people of Spain.[79]

"Twenty years of sterile battles"[80] against the ancient forces of *la Réaction* had not reduced them:

> Do you believe that the Church and the Caesarian band would have joined in a dance of such fanatic fury for so small a matter as one Jew more or less in the army if behind the screen of the trial were not joined together the eternal party of human domination?[81]

Was Clemenceau himself anti-Semitic? From what has been said thus far, this must seem an odd question. He associated easily and frequently with Jews throughout his life and because of it was a target of crass aspersions by anti-Semites. He abhorred religious persecution more than any other kind and thus felt the plight of the Jews very keenly, not least of all because most of their mistreatment had come at the hands of Christians, for whose doctrines and especially their churches, above all the Roman Catholic, he had no use. That Christians should persecute the people who had produced their own Savior was a phenomenon he found utterly revolting, in some measure mystifying, and yet at bottom so sadly typical of human beings as they are, "a mixture of St. Francis of Assisi and Attila the Hun."[82]

On the other hand, he made free with remarks about Jews which must be called anti-Semitic.[83] They ran the gamut of physical and characterological stereotypes--long noses, grasping fingers, intelligence, cleverness, unscrupulousness, greed, and so on. The Jews' survival in spite of all that had befallen them fascinated him: "There is no more astonishing history in the world."[84] Yet in the next breath he could employ stereotypes to praise them for it: "Oh race, reviled by the whole world, what Aryan could ever compete with you?"[85] He readily used the word "race" about them. But it should be noted that theorizing about race had become a vogue in those days, and the term was used with much less embarrassment than nowadays. That despite the stereotyping and jibes in questionable taste at their expense his Jewish friends remained loyal probably should be laid to the fact that they had learned that he made no distinction between persons or peoples of any kind or degree: he put all humanity on the same level--and all took their lumps. In short, there was nothing truly malicious or hateful here. When it came to the crux--How are Jews to be treated?--they knew where he stood:

> Instead of condemning a race whose luck or unlucky faculties have made it a factor in present society, instead of crying cowardly that it must be annihilated to give us room to live--why do we not try, simply and more justly, to frame a more equitable, a more disinterested social code, in which the power of selfish appropriation--be it Jewish or Christian--is rendered less harmful and its tyranny less crushing for the great mass of humanity?[86]

IX

During the twenty months from the first Zola trial to the retrial, conviction, and pardon of Dreyfus (February 1898-September 1899), Clemenceau's writings showed continual alternations of hope and frustration. Some of his reactions probably mirrored his physical state, in which dramatic recoveries followed sudden invasions of exhaustion and depression. Time and again it seemed the decisive break, *the* victory, was at hand, victory which would inspire the country to some new level of achievement: "All Europe is traversing a marked period of reaction. The great recoil, perhaps, before the decisive spring into a better social organization."[87] The issues posed by the case and the world-wide attention it was drawing were giving to France, as if by some divine election, he thought, a supreme opportunity to demonstrate what a civilized society could accomplish: an act of justice, simple yet sublime, to an ordinary man of a despised race wrongfully convicted of the worst of crimes against that society. Such high hopes, he suspected, were destined to be frustrated, men being what they are, but this suspicion did not spare him genuine pain when the chances were missed.

The aftermath of the Zola trial was an uphill fight against official obstruction, confusion, and simple incompetence. The unmasking of Henry's forgeries, which permitted the Court of Cassation to accept Lucie Dreyfus' appeal, brought a momentary elation, but it evaporated as the delays, twisting, lying, shuffling, and buck-passing continued. The unedifying death of President Félix Faure (16 February 1899), whom Clemenceau utterly despised ("a fat Tartuffe") and strongly suspected of masterminding the cover-up,[88] earned another of his tart obituaries ("There is not one man the less in France") and a proposal ("I vote for Loubet") which even at this late date probably hurt the candidate by making his Dreyfusard sympathies an issue.[89] An attempt by the ineffable Déroulède and others to persuade the troops at Faure's funeral to march on the Élysée to "save" the country,[90] the assault on Émile Loubet, the new president, by Baron Christiani at the Auteuil racetrack, and Parliament's scandalous intervention in the Court of Cassation's proceedings through a law altering its membership,[91] were to Clemenceau evidences of rot in the nation's morale and leadership.

The court's verdict (3 June) heralded both triumph and defeat. For while it meant a retrial, thus giving the army a chance at last to undo the wrong of 1894, it effectively prevented (or so the Chamber of Deputies concluded) the prosecution of General Mercier, the man who as minister of war had been the one most responsible for the original miscarriage of justice. When Dreyfus was brought back to face the new court-martial, convened at Rennes (7 August-9 September), his judges knew that if they found him innocent they were saying that Mercier--and through him the army--was guilty. Clemenceau did not go to Rennes because he had returned from Karlsbad with "a terrible bronchitis which tears at my chest day and night" and because it was decided that his presence might be inflammatory.[92] For the same reason Reinach and Zola also stayed in Paris, but they kept in close touch with the defense, lending advice.

Clemenceau's hopes for an acquittal waxed and waned but were never strong. He at first advised against allowing the fiery and nervous Labori to assist Dreyfus' attorney, Edgar Demange. But when Labori went anyway, he reversed course and summoned him to "march against all the criminals" and confront them with everything in the entire (by now mountainous) dossier: "Our objective is to be conquerors in the eyes of the public." A majority of the Dreyfusard inner circle and their supporters in the government, however, judged that such a tactic would only corner and alienate the unhappy officers conscripted to sit on the court.[93] Probably they were right. Frustrated, he watched the chances (as he saw them) for a crushing blow against Mercier and his band go by the boards and on the eve of the verdict found himself reduced to writing an appeal to Colonel Jouast, the court's president, to search his conscience:

> It is a fine thing to be a soldier in order to defend something; but first of all it is necessary to have something to defend. And that is exactly what we have, we French; we have the traditions of justice and rights which are the beauty of our fatherland.
> ...There is more heroism in conquering oneself all alone, in private, face-to-face with one's thoughts, than in sabering down the enemy in a drunken murderous fury.[94]

X

Dreyfus's second conviction, a well-meant but ludicrous finding of "treason with extenuating circumstances," did not persuade Clemenceau to give up. Much as he sympathized with the man's sufferings, the person of the captain had never been for him paramount:

> What I see beyond Dreyfus is the salvation of France: the collapse of arbitrary rule, the reconstitution in the French mentality of the notion of justice as the unique sanction of liberty.[95]
> What are the Jews to me, and an innocent Dreyfus whom I do not know, and Picquart who offers himself in sacrifice and whom I love? All that is nothing to me when set beside my country which is dying. If there is no more justice, if there is no more law, then where is our country?[96]

He was quite prepared to press for trial after trial until the job had been done right: "...there has never been perhaps a more beautiful [*beau*] living drama, with a whole people for an actor."[97] Reinach thought such dreams of triumph, at this hour and oblivious to mundane realities, among them the likelihood that Dreyfus could not physically survive such an ordeal, were expressions of a personality whose rough exterior enclosed the soul of an artist.[98]

Chagrined by the Rennes verdict, anxious to still the world-wide condemnation of it on the eve of the International Exposition set to open soon in Paris, and convinced that to prolong the Affair would be politically sterile or even dangerous, the government, at Reinach's suggestion, offered to pardon Dreyfus immediately--thus making it a plain rebuke to the court-martial--if he would withdraw his new appeal. For those who had fought so long, the decision was agonizing. Assurances were given that a pardon would not foreclose an appeal later if new evidence were found. Exhausted, Dreyfus left the question to the inner circle who had worked with Mathieu.

Clemenceau was the last holdout. In his unpublished *Journal*, Reinach observed his reactions:

> To pardon Dreyfus is to remove, to snatch, the bread from Clemenceau's mouth. The daily bread of beautiful articles, the beautiful rhetoric. In vain he polishes up the most brilliant arguments: the basic cause of his bitter, violent opposition is there, not elsewhere. At times he realizes it and blushes at it [*en a quelque pudeur*]. But he comes back, always with more force, less embarrassment, and more cynicism.[99]

Mathieu gave him the deciding vote saying he would not go ahead without his approval, a gesture at once intrinsically cruel and the highest compliment he could bestow. Clemenceau admired Mathieu profoundly--"the greatest heart, the most valiant man I have ever been privileged to know"[100]--even more than he did Picquart, of whom he had once written, "Dreyfus is a victim, but Picquart is a hero."[101] Facing Mathieu, who was convinced his brother would die if an end could not be made soon, he had to answer the call of humanity and let the dream go. He consoled himself with the thought, too, that a pardon might help restore France's good name.

Reinach recorded the surrender, which came at a meeting on 11 September at the office of Alexandre Millerand, formerly of *La Justice* and now minister of commerce:

> Now we are four [Jaurès, Alfred Gérault-Richard, Millerand, Reinach] against Clemenceau, for Mathieu confines himself to saying, "I won't do anything without Clemenceau!" Millerand restates the thesis, with admirable clarity. Clemenceau turns to me, personally, accuses me of having derailed the greatest affair of the century, of making it a question of private interests. I riposte, accusing him directly, this time, of making a living creature into a battering-ram against military and political institutions. He protests that this morning, as Mathieu has told, he cried, broke down in sobs. I respond with a *boutade*: "That you can't cry twice in a day proves you are very tired." And this *boutade*, which disarms everybody, finishes the fight. "So be it," says Clemenceau, "let Mathieu go ahead!" [*Soit, que Mathieu marche!*][102]

As Mathieu left the meeting for Rennes to see his brother, Clemenceau told him, "In your place I'd do as you're doing!"[103] So it was no flat capitulation after all. But more he just could not do.

After some last-moment hesitations by the government, the pardon came down on 19 September, and Alfred Dreyfus walked free.

XI

Two months afterward, on 15 December 1899, Clemenceau walked out of *L'Aurore*. He said he did not wish to engage in polemics with a colleague, Urbain Gohier, whose strident anti-militarism and some disparaging remarks about his fellow Dreyfusards had grated his nerves. The explanation was not convincing. Was it his response to the letdown after the pardon? his fluctuating health? simple restlessness? a proposed cut in salaries? a desire to be chief editor? Vaughan probably got closest to the truth when he concluded that Clemenceau himself did not really know why he quit.[104]

Out of office, no longer regularly employed, still tracked by debts,[105] his health uncertain, divorced, his children long grown, his father dead, and his mother soon to follow (1903), Georges Clemenceau was never to be more alone than he was at the dawning of the new century.

NOTES
CHAPTER IX

1   Brandes, *Correspondance*, 1:no. 201.

2   In Zévaès, *Clemenceau*, p. 153. The reference to *La Justice* is misleading. The paper did not fold, but on 27 Oct. 1894 it moved to 24, rue Chauchat. See below, p. 186.

3   Berthe [Berta] Szeps Zukerkandl, *Clemenceau, tel que je l'ai connu* (Algiers: Éditions de la Revue Fontaine, 1944), p. 107.

4   Hyndman, *Clemenceau, the Man and His Time*, p. 137.

5   Maurice Martin du Gard, *Les mémorables, 1918-1923* (Flamarion, 1947), pp. 9-10n.

6   To Mlle. Marie André, 6 Sept. 1893, in Wormser, *La république de Clemenceau*, p. 175.

7   *Ibid.*, pp. 175-176.

8   Octave Mirbeau, *Les écrivains*, Deuxième série (E. Flammarion, [1925-27]), pp. 24-30. He wrote this piece in 1895.

9   The description below is from personal observations and François Monod, *Musée Clemenceau: Guide descriptif* (Librairie Larousse, n.d.).

10   The Musée piece may be a copy, for Wildenstein says this painting, given to Clemenceau in 1899, is in the British royal collection. See Daniel Wildenstein, *Claude Monet*, 4 vols. (Lausanne and Paris: La Bibliothèque des Arts, 1974-1985), 3:124, 300-301 (letter, 23 Dec. 1899, Clemenceau to Monet).

11   See especially Dr. Louis Robert, "Un médecin politicien, le docteur Georges Clemenceau," *Berry médical*, no. 63 (1953), p. 79; Dr. J.-L Pierre, quoted in HL, 21 May 1936; and Gatineau-Clemenceau, *Des pattes du Tigre*, p. 113.

12   See Eugen Weber, *France, Fin de Siècle* (Cambridge, MA: Harvard University Press, 1986), p. 31, from Émile Goudeau, *Paris qui consomme* (1893), p. 34. On his visits to Karlsbad below, see the account by

Dr. J.-L. Pierre in HL, 21 May 1936; and Duroselle, *Clemenceau*, pp. 549-554.

13   See Talmeyr, "Clemenceau, Degas and Cie."

14   Letter to me from Pierre Clemenceau (grandson), 14 Aug. 1986.

15   See Wildenstein, *Claude Monet*, 3:3. Wildenstein's work contains extensive references to Monet's correspondence. The private archive at the Musée Clemenceau, dossier no. 6, contains letters from Clemenceau to Monet, including 133 from 11 April 1920 to 21 Sept. 1926, some of which Wormser quoted in *Clemenceau vu de près* and Duroselle in *Clemenceau*.

16   See Wildenstein, *Claude Monet*, 3:68. The article was reprinted, with variations, in GC, *Le grand Pan* (1896), pp. 427-437, and GC, *Claude Monet: Les Nymphéas* (Librairie Plon, 1928), pp. 81-89. Wildenstein shows (3:33), contrary to some assertions, that Clemenceau took no active part in the private subscription campaign in 1890 to acquire Manet's *Olympia* for the state. He speculates that he was too absorbed in political affairs at the time.

17   Drieu la Rochelle, "Paroles d'outre tômbe," p. 7.

18   The rue Chauchat no longer exists under that name. Presumably it was near the rue Faubourg-Montmartre in this former newspaper district north of the Montmartre Metro station, which is now a somewhat shabby tourist area a couple of blocks from the Folies-Bergéres.

19   For comments below on his writing, see especially Applebaum, *Clemenceau, Thinker and Writer*, *passim*; Jules Bertaut, *Figures contemporaines: Chroniqueurs et polémistes* (E. Sansot, 1906), pp. 96-111; André Billy, *Les écrivains de combat* (Les Oeuvres représentatives, 1931), p. 94 and *passim*; Alfred Capus, "M. Georges Clemenceau," *Revue hebdomadaire*, 22 Feb. 1919, p. 427 and *passim*; Ernest Dimnet, "Georges Clemenceau, Writer and Philosopher," *Nineteenth Century* 61 (April, 1907):616-617; Edmund Gosse, "The Writings of M. Clemenceau," *Edinburgh Review* 229 (April, 1919):253-270, *passim*; F. de Homem Christo, *Les porte-flambeaux* (Éditions Fast, [1918], pp. 1-33, *passim*; Maurice Martin du Gard, "Clemenceau," *Les Nouvelles littéraires*, 30 Nov. 1929, p. 1; Marcel Théaux, "Les idées philosophiques de M. Clemenceau," *Mercure de France*, 1 April 1906, pp. 354-366, *passim*; and the essays by Jacques Julliard and Pierre Guiral in *Clemenceau et la justice*, pp. 93-112, *passim*.

20   Martet, *Clemenceau*, p. 68.

21   Martet, *Le silence de M. Clemenceau*, p. 190.

22   From Homem Christo, *Les porte-flambeaux*, p. 23.

23   The Académie elected him without his having requested it, an exception to its rules. He inherited the seat of a fellow Vendean, the savant and critic Émile Faguet. Aside from his dislike of the Académie's snobbish air and general conservatism, he may have been put off somewhat by the prospect of having to eulogize Faguet, who had written *L'anticléricalisme* (1906), a trenchant criticism. Probably more to the point was another consideration. According to Dr. Louis Robert, Dr. Charles Coutéla said Clemenceau had written (when? to whom?) that Poincaré, in his speech receiving Foch on 5 Feb. 1920, had "bellowed off about me [*m'a engueulé*] when I couldn't defend myself." If he had made a speech, he went on, he would have made an even stronger reply. But why write a speech he should be obliged to change or not give? "And I wouldn't have changed a word. So leave me alone about all that crap." [*Donc, que l'on me fiche la paix.*] Robert, "Un médecin politicien," p. 100.

24   Letter, 10 May 1895, in Ajalbert, *Clemenceau*, p. 113. See Maurice Agulhon's essay in *Clemenceau et la justice*, pp. 85-92, on this work.

25   GC, *Le grand Pan*, p. lxviii.

26   See Clark, *Social Darwinism in France*, pp. 60-61.

27   On his relationship to the Radicals' semi-official philosophy of *Solidarisme*, see Watson, *Georges Clemenceau*, pp. 140-141.

28   GC, *Le grand Pan*, p. lxxxi. His principal visit to Greece came in May 1896; see Duroselle, *Clemenceau*, pp. 776-777.

29   GC, *Le voile du bonheur*, pièce en un acte (É. Fasquelle, 1901), rpt. in *La Petite Illustration*, 4 Jan. 1930, p. 13.

30   GC, *The Strongest*, p. 80. The hero, the marquis de Puymaufray, resembles Clemenceau. Changing mores and the consequent overthrow of fortunes were favorite themes of Second Empire literature. See André Bellesort, *La société française sous Napoléon III* (Librairie Académique Perrin, 1932), p. 260.

31   In GC, *Le grand Pan*, pp. 405-13. See Goncourt, *Journal des Goncourt*, 4:755-756; Ajalbert, *Clemenceau*, pp. 127-128; and Duroselle, *Clemenceau*, pp. 319-323.

32   Maurice Allard, a revolutionary Socialist, won the Draguignan seat from Jourdan in 1898. See *Le Petit Var* (Toulon), 5 March, 5, 7 April 1902; Zévaès, *Clemenceau*, p. 175; Leo A. Loubère, *Radicalism in Mediterranean France: Its Rise and Decline, 1848-1914* (Albany, NY: State University of New York Press, 1974), pp. 162, 186, 203, 208; and Ernest Vaughan, *Souvenirs sans regrets* (Félix Juven, 1902), p. 19.

33   JU, 10 Nov. 1896, on Bernard Lazare's *La vérité sur l'affaire Dreyfus* (Brussels: Imprimerie Monnom, 1896).

34   Berta Zuckerkandl says he was aware of Picquart's discoveries at that time, but her chronology is unreliable. Zuckerkandl, *My Life and History*, pp. 185-86.

35   Georges Michon, *Clemenceau* (Marcel Rivière, 1931), p. 77n., makes a strong case that it was. But Vaughan denied it; *Souvenirs sans regrets*, pp. 44, 60-69.

36   GC, *L'iniquité*, p. v; see also p. 189. Wormser, *La république de Clemenceau*, p. 185, says it was Mathieu Dreyfus who convinced him of the illegality of the 1894 trial. This seems unlikely as Mathieu did not meet him until the Zola trial; see Mathieu Dreyfus, *L'Affaire: Telle que je l'ai vécue* (Bernard Grasset, 1978), p. 196.

37   GC, *L'iniquité*, pp. 1-4.

38   *Ibid.*, pp. 129-130. See also GC, *La honte*, pp. 131, 342.

39   GC, *L'iniquité*, pp. 190-216.

40   GC, *La honte*, p. 342.

41   M. Dreyfus, *L'Affaire*, p. 196.

42   GC, *Vers la réparation*, pp. 355-363.

43   On 30 Oct. 1897; see Watson, *Georges Clemenceau*, p. 146n.

44   See, for example, Joseph Reinach, *Histoire de l'Affaire Dreyfus*, 7 vols. (La Revue blanche, 1901-11), 2:638; and Paul Desachy, *Une grande figure de l'Affaire Dreyfus: Louis Leblois* (Éditions Rieder, 1934), p. 174.

[45] JU, 4 Nov. 1894. I have come across no references to this remarkably prescient article in the literature, doubtless because for some reason he did not reprint it.

[46] See Jean-Denis Bredin, *The Affair: The Case of Alfred Dreyfus*, trans. Jeffrey Mehlman (New York: George Braziller, 1986 [Julliard, 1983]), pp. 203-212. His account raises serious doubt that Clemenceau and Scheurer had reached an agreement on tactics.

[47] Julliard's figures in *Clemenceau et la justice*, p. 167. His friends Étienne Winter and Henri Leyret collected and published them while the Affair was in progress as part of the campaign. As Julliard notes, they do not include all his articles on the case.

[48] See René Mazédier, *Histoire de la presse parisienne de Théophraste Renaudot à la IVe république, 1631-1945* (Éditions du Pavois, 1945), p. 246.

[49] See GC, *Injustice militaire*, p. 320; also *La mêlée sociale*, pp. 349-461, on the anarchist wave of the early 1890s.

[50] Pierre Godin, "Qu'eut fait Clemenceau," HL, 15 June 1951. Godin was once his *Directeur du cabinet civil*.

[51] See Zeev Sternhell, *Maurice Barrès et le nationalisme français*, pp. 362-364.

[52] See Harry W. Paul, "The Debate Over the Bankruptcy of Science in 1895," *French Historical Studies* 5, no. 3 (Spring, 1968), p. 323.

[53] Eugène Lautier, "Clemenceau," HL, 25 Nov. 1929.

[54] Abensour, *Dans la cage du Tigre*, p. 44.

[55] The "Manifeste des Intellectuels," in AU, 14 Jan. 1898, the day after "J'accuse...!" appeared, gave the term currency. See Bredin, *The Affair*, p. 276; Julliard, in *Clemenceau et la justice*, pp. 101-102; and W. M. Johnston, "The Origin of the Term 'Intellectuels' in French Novels and Essays of the 1890s," *Journal of European Studies* 4 (1974):43-56.

[56] See Alain Silvera, *Daniel Halévy and His Times: A Gentleman-Commoner in the Third Republic* (Ithaca, NY: Cornell University Press, 1966), pp. 87-89; and Julliard in *Clemenceau et la justice*, pp. 170-172.

57   Camille Mauclair, *Servitude et grandeur littéraires*, 6th ed. (Librairie Ollendorff, n.d.), p. 131.

58   GC, "Reponse à l'enquête sur les responsabilités de la presse," *Revue politique et littéraire (Revue bleue)*, 11 Dec. 1897, p. 741.

59   GC, *Contre la justice* (P.-V. Stock, 1900), pp. v-viii.

60   HE, 26 Oct. 1917.

61   GC, *Injustice militaire*, pp. 479-480.

62   Léon Blum, *Souvenirs sur l'Affaire* (Gallimard, 1935), pp. 83-84.

63   See GC, *L'iniquité*, pp. 10, 34, 89, 121, 358; *Vers la réparation*, p. 128; and *Contre la justice*, p. 35.

64   Blum, *Souvenirs sur l'Affaire*, pp. 68, 71.

65   See Sorlin, *Waldeck-Rousseau*, pp. 410, 418-19; and Janine Ponty, "La presse quotidienne et l'affaire Dreyfus en 1898-1899," *Revue d'histoire moderne et contemporaine* 21 (April-June, 1974):200-201 and *passim*.

66   GC, *L'iniquité*, pp. 32-33, 36-41. Contrary to some assertions, neither then nor in his attack on the Censorship during the War did he deny the legitimacy of *raison d'état*, only its abuse.

67   *Ibid.*, pp. 110-112 (7 Jan. 1898); see Appendix I below. He later used a phrase--"la France, d'abord soldat de Dieu, plus tard soldat de l'homme"--revised, in his speech on the Armistice in 1918.

68   *Ibid.*, p. 128.

69   See *ibid.*, pp. 273-274; GC, *Vers la réparation*, p. 515; Reinach, *Histoire de l'Affaire Dreyfus*, 3:229; Mauclair, *Servitude et grandeur littéraires*, p. 135. But Vaughan says Zola *sent* it in and is silent on hesitations; *Souvenirs sans regrets*, pp. 71-72.

70   He later revealed (17 Aug. 1898) that Billot had sent a colonel around to persuade him of Dreyfus' guilt, the danger of war, and the need to fight the Jews. GC, *Vers la réparation*, pp. 76, 202; and GC, *Des juges* (P.-V. Stock, 1900), p. 409.

71   See his obituary tribute to Labori in HE, 15 March 1917.

[72]   In GC, *L'iniquité*, pp. 190-261. See GC, *Le grand Pan*, p. 289, for a previous use of the crucifix analogy.

[73]   JOS, 11 Dec. 1906, p. 1110.

[74]   See GC, *L'iniquité*, pp. 492-495; M. Dreyfus, *L'Affaire*, p. 166; and F. W. J. Hemmings, *Emile Zola*, 2nd ed. (Oxford: The Clarendon Press, 1966), p. 169. Perrenx went to Belgium. Zola let himself be condemned *in absentia* at the second trial (18 July, adjourned from 23 May). Not having been officially informed of his sentence, he could still appeal. They were also buying time in a parallel case against Esterhazy (arrested 12 July).

[75]   See GC, *Injustice militaire*, p. 347, on the duel. On the shooting, following Henry's death on 31 Aug. 1898, see Émile Buré (who was present with Octave Mirbeau), "M. Georges Clemenceau, homme de lettres," *L'Éclair*, 23 June 1924.

[76]   GC, *L'iniquité*, pp. 145-148 (19 Jan. 1898). This was his first article clearly sounding the theme that the Church was behind the anti-Semitic outcry. See also an unpublished article in Wormser, *La république de Clemenceau*, pp. 484-486. For a linking of the Affair to Boulangism, see *L'iniquité*, p. 218, and *Vers la réparation*, p. 67. On the failure of either side to reach the countryside effectively, see Burns, *Rural Society and French Politics*, pp. 169-170. On public opinion generally, see Jean-Pierre Peter, "Dimensions de l'Affaire Dreyfus,: *Annales: Économies, Sociétés, Civilisations* 16 (1961):1149-1167.

[77]   GC, *La honte*, p. 131.

[78]   See René Rémond, *L'anticléricalisme en France de 1815 à nos jours* (Fayard, 1976), pp. 174, 206.

[79]   GC, *L'iniquité* (26 Feb. 1898), p. 222. The Spanish-American War (April-Aug.) furnished more ammunition for this theme.

[80]   GC, *Vers la réparation*, p. 66. An unconscious judgment on his life in politics thus far?

[81]   GC, *Justice militaire* (P.-V. Stock, 1901), p. 334 (7 Aug. 1899)--a succinct statement of his view of the political implications of the Affair.

[82]   *Ibid.*, p. 238.

83   See especially Wilson, *Ideology and Experience*, pp. 236, 305, 480, and *passim*.

84   GC, *At the Foot of Sinai*, p. 133.

85   *Ibid.*, p. 89, at the end of a humorous story ("How I Became Farsighted") about how he had been conned by a clever Jew into buying glasses and at a high price.

86   *Ibid.*, p. 135.

87   GC, *Justice militaire*, p. 12 (22 May 1899).

88   See GC, *Vers la réparation*, pp. 166-167, 184-194, and *Contre la justice*, pp. 278-81. Faure died at his office while in the company of (rumors said being fellated by) Mme. Steinheil. But see Dr. Germain Galérant, "L'odieuse légende de la mort du président Félix Faure," *Histoire des sciences médicales* 19 (1985):175-182.

89   GC, *Contre la justice*, pp. 287-288. See Reinach, *Histoire de l'Affaire Dreyfus*, 4:554.

90   Nothing Déroulède did surprised him, but he found General Roget's "curious reticences" suspicious; GC, *Contre la justice*, pp. 314-327. His suspicions were misplaced; it was Gen. Georges de Pellieux whose role was open to doubt. Larkin concludes, however, that "the contemporary cries of 'la République en danger' were unnecessarily alarmist." Maurice Larkin, "'La République en danger'? The Pretenders, the Army and Déroulède," *English Historical Review* 100 (1985):100-101, 104.

91   Cautiously optimistic in December 1898, he was outraged by the Dessaisessement Law. He had it repealed (4 March 1909) during his first ministry.

92   Letter to Labori, 11 Aug. 1899, in Robert Gauthier, ed., *Dreyfusards! Souvenirs de Mathieu Dreyfus et autres inédits* (Julliard, 1965), pp. 221-222; GC, *Justice militaire*, p. 261; and Reinach, *Histoire de l'Affaire Dreyfus*, 5:267.

93   Letter to Labori, note 92 above; M. Dreyfus, *L'Affaire*, pp. 222, 234; and Reinach, *Histoire de l'Affaire Dreyfus*, 5:332-333. The affair heightened tensions in the Dreyfusard camp.

94   GC, *Injustice militaire*, pp. 210-211.

95   GC, *Contre la justice*, p. 93 (1 Jan. 1899).

96   *Ibid.*, p. 209 (31 Jan. 1899). On Dreyfus' sufferings see GC, *Justice militaire*, pp. 196-200, 216-219, 241-248.

97   GC, *La Honte*, p. 332 (7 April 1901).

98   Reinach, *Histoire de l'Affaire Dreyfus*, 5:556.

99   Pierre Vidal-Naquet, "Joseph Reinach: vers la grâce de Dreyfus," *Passé Présent* (Paris), 1983, no. 2, p. 116.

100   GC, *Justice militaire*, p. 245 (9 July 1899). Mathieu met with him and Jaurès almost daily at *L'Aurore* from the summer of 1898.

101   GC, *Vers la réparation*, p. 396 (6 Nov. 1898).

102   Vidal-Naquet, "Joseph Reinach," p. 125.

103   *Ibid.*, p. 128, from the *Journal*. As he points out, in Reinach's *Histoire de l'Affaire Dreyfus*, 5:558, the words became, "Eh bien, si j'étais le frère, j'accepterais," the same words M. Dreyfus recalled in *L'Affaire*, p. 242. On the pardon see also Alfred and Pierre Dreyfus, *The Dreyfus Case*, trans. and ed. Donald C. McKay (New Haven, CT: Yale University Press, 1937), pp. 142, 177-178, 272-276.

104   Vaughan, *Souvenirs sans regrets*, pp. 277-292. He had defended Gohier in print when he was prosecuted for defaming the army. (Gohier would later end as a Vichyite.) See GC, *Vers la réparation*, pp. 297-302; *Contre la justice*, pp. 396-400; and *Injustice militaire*, pp. 333-338, 346-350. Also Urbain Gohier, *La vraie figure de Clemenceau*, pp. 33-37; and Brandes, *Correspondance*, 1: no. 190.

105   But see below, p. 219.

CHAPTER X

Toward the Heights--Again
(1900-1906)

The years 1900 and 1901 were difficult for Clemenceau. As in 1893, he fought through bouts of black depression, feeling he was "deserted by everyone" and confessing later that "bitter disgust" and a decline in his will power had left him thinking he was "dead."[1] His newspaper collaborations had ameliorated his financial condition in the latter nineties, when he was possibly taking in something like 30,000 francs yearly (although probably nothing from *La Justice*); at any rate, on 24 January 1899, perhaps as a result of his contracts with Pierre-Victor Stock to publish the collections of Dreyfus articles, he at long last had liquidated the 25,000-franc debt assumed in 1869 and renewed in 1874. But now that he had left *L'Aurore*, his only remaining outlets were *Le Français* (very occasional) and the *Dépêche de Toulouse*, and there were still the debts from the defunct *La Justice*. He tried without success to found a daily paper, but finally, in January 1901, with help from Camille Cerf, a friend of Stephen Pichon, he launched *Le Bloc*, a weekly he wrote and managed by himself with passing assistance from Gustave Geffroy, his secretary Étienne Winter, and his brother Albert. It did not prosper, and the unremitting toil of producing up to forty manuscript pages a week sapped his health.[2]

His spirits and fortunes especially suffered as a result of the swift decline of interest in the Dreyfus Case after the Rennes trial and the pardon. In a labored defense of the pardon while still at *L'Aurore* (24 September

1899), he gratuitously included a cutting reference to Dreyfus. The captain's letter of thanks for his past services tactfully ignored the wound, and he in turn managed to write a gracious reply.[3] Besides fraying his nerves, however, the negotiations surrounding the pardon damaged his confidence in the intentions of René Waldeck-Rousseau, whom he had personally urged back in June to accept the premiership.[4]

The ink on the pardon had barely dried when rumors of an amnesty bill confirmed his worst suspicions, sending him into a fury which probably contributed to his decision to leave *L'Aurore*. The bill was introduced in December with the intention of quieting down the country and protecting the army by quashing all sentences and preventing further prosecutions, notably of General Mercier--who promptly got himself elected to the Senate. Through 1900 Clemenceau excoriated the bill's authors for their whitewashing of a decade of villainy. He found almost no support, however; Reinach and Francis de Pressensé were the only considerable figures to join his protest. Even Mathieu Dreyfus saw no use in trying to fight the measure, while Jaurès stayed quiet because (Mathieu suspected) he wanted to keep Millerand, Europe's first socialist minister, in the government.[5] Predictably, the bill turned into a legal quagmire before finally going into effect in December 1900. When Clemenceau reprinted these last articles on the Affair, he entitled the book *La honte* (The Shame).

Ironically, by the time it appeared (1903), Jaurès and others had found a legal foothold permitting Dreyfus to seek an annulment of the Rennes verdict by the Court of Cassation. Clemenceau coldly declined Dreyfus' invitation to rejoin the inner councils on a continuing basis, although he allowed himself to be convinced to support the appeal and occasionally offered advice.[6] He put in a word with the Combes government, generally supported the movement in the press, and raised embarrassing questions about the army's administration through an interpellation in the Senate.[7] But he continued to advocate retrial by a court-martial rather than allow the Court to close the case by a decree: "Soldiers have erred. It is up to soldiers to repair the error of other soldiers."[8] He still wanted complete victory: "Our task here is less the saving of a man, who has already made himself secure, than to achieve the laborious evolution of minds from which will surge forth a better future for all."[9]

A long article he selected to close *La honte* underscored a major lesson he had drawn from the Affair. In June 1901 a national congress had formally organized the "Parti républicain radical et radical-socialiste." He had taken part in discussions of the future party's program and tactics but had soon soured on the enterprise and in the end was not even invited to attend the congress--though it is doubtful he would have gone in any case. Angered by this public snub, he struck back by lofting acid-tipped shafts at the congress from the sidelines.[10] (He became a member of the party later, in January 1909, but quit in less than a year.) He would not say that parties have no function, for "progress itself is only the universal *consensus* of men in groups." But they are mere "agents of diffusion," not initiators, and in time they invariably become vehicles furthering the selfish interests of the members. Social progress, he wrote,

> ...can only be the result of the progress of individuals: from which I conclude that the work which dominates all others is individual education first of all....When all the parties, magnificently organized for action...refused the call, Zola, all alone, acted--and by the spontaneous help which came from all quarters, set France and Europe in motion.[11]

II

Clemenceau had begun a second year of *Le Bloc* when, in late February 1902, emissaries from the Var asked him to stand for a Senate seat awarded to the department by lot upon the death of a life-senator, Louis Denormandie. He politely declined, but the next day they were invited back to receive good news. The arguments of his intimates--Gustave Geffroy, Étienne Winter (his secretary since 1880), his daughter Madeleine, above all his brother Albert and, on this occasion, Pierre-Victor Stock--had for once prevailed. His optimistic assertions about his finances were demonstrably hollow: *Le Bloc*'s future was bleak, the *Dépêche* collaboration uncertain, and the current negotiations about production of a stage version of his novel unlikely to come to anything. At sixty he could not wait much longer if he expected to return. Maurice Allard, a Socialist, had defeated Jourdan in 1898 with help from Clemencist Radicals on the run-off ballot. If he were to stand for a Chamber seat in the upcoming 1902 elections, he would risk splitting Draguignan's Radicals even more--if that were possible, for their disarray had become chronic. So a successful Chamber race in his old bailiwick was looking more and more like a forlorn hope. On the other hand, his name still awakened echoes throughout the department as a whole despite the memories of 1893, still symbolizing the stout, left-oriented republicanism on which it had long prided itself with all the verve of true Provençals.[12]

The Senate, with its indirect mode of election, department-wide constituency, and nine-year term would at the same time confer a relative freedom from local political chores. And his election, too, would be a fitting reply to General Mercier's, which had outraged all good Dreyfusards.[13] He would almost certainly regain his former eminence; publisher's doors would open, and new contracts plus a senator's salary (9,000 francs) would help pay his debts, which he surely did not wish to leave to his heirs. (Also, his daughters' marriages were breaking up about this time, leaving them temporarily more dependent on him.[14]) Politics "disgusted" him? But was this any reason to stay out of Parliament while continuing to write on political subjects--he, the apostle of action? Could he--an argument that especially shook him--refuse to reenter the arena when those pleading for it had stood by him even in the darkest days of '93?[15]

All this, however convincing, skirted a most sensitive point. Senator Clemenceau? He could hear the hoots of derision. Yet he had frankly confided to the delegation that he had changed his mind about the Senate. Boulangism had killed revision while the Senate had stood as a bulwark against demagoguery. During the Affair he had even praised it--faintly.[16] "Events have taught me," he was to say later (1910), "that one must give the people time for reflection," and the Senate furnishes the means.[17] If he had changed his mind, then why not admit it openly?

His announcement (5 March) stirred less criticism than he probably expected. Jaurès' warm welcome more than offset Rochefort's jibes about retired whores becoming concierges.[18] The election was never in doubt. His oratory and a program of "the peril on the Right," anticlericalism, an income tax, workers' pensions, two years of military service instead of three, aid to agriculture, and "a more humane social organization," though not the "despotic centralization" of orthodox socialism, swept aside the lackluster candidate of an opposition reduced to rumor-mongering and cries of "Var for the Varois!" A 344 to 122 victory (6 April), if not the reparation a Chamber election would have brought, was sweet enough.[19]

Clemenceau assumed Victor Hugo's old seat on the left in the elegant hall of the Palais-Luxembourg. Plush armchairs, short sittings, and sober debates among the three-hundred graying luminaries of the political, administrative, and academic *haut monde* offered a soothing contrast to the hurly-burly of the Chamber. The senatorial gerontocracy was a perennial butt of jokes, but while the Chamber got the headlines, the canny veterans of the Upper House accumulated quiet power, especially through their commissions. Many colleagues of his years as a deputy had gravitated there with him--familiar faces, familiar ideas. He was a power in the place from the day he arrived.

He lengthened his reach when he returned to *L'Aurore* on 2 June 1903, this time as editor-in-chief. Louis Leblois, Picquart's attorney, facilitated the move, buying control of the paper and even helping him to liquidate many of *La Justice*'s debts. (Such generosity made him uncomfortable--or so one might infer from some mordant remarks in old age at Leblois' death. Leblois was anxious to play a role in politics.[20]) Ignoring advice not to hurt his career by resuming the daily battle in the press, Clemenceau rolled ahead full tilt. The pace left little time for repose: "At my age," he wrote Brandes, "it's probably the last shot."[21] His spirits revived. By reelecting him, he told some constituents in 1904, they had made him "a better man."[22]

III

In accordance with his long-established habit, in the evening Clemenceau would arrive in a gust at *L'Aurore*'s offices. (They were on the third floor of a building, smelling of paper and dust, which was shared with *Le Radical* at 147, rue de Montmartre. A couple of blocks up the street from the present locale of *Le Figaro* and *L'Aurore*, the place has since been torn down.) If he had not already done so, he would swiftly write his daily leader and then leave in another gust after tossing off a few remarks, humorous or stinging as the spirit moved. A former staffer, Jean Philip, later remarked that he doubted Clemenceau had ever bothered to read the paper through: as far as he (Clemenceau) was concerned, his article *was* the paper. The job of putting together each edition and making something out of the chaos consequently fell to the staff's harried general secretary. Nevertheless, he admitted, he and other young beginners in journalism in those days prized the chance to work for M. Clemenceau, such was his prestige. And from reading his work they learned the art of composing an article and of paring away from an idea all superfluous trappings and seductive phraseology: "At *L'Aurore*, one thought and wrote French."[23]

Clemenceau's disdain for the mundane routines of administration was not the sole reason he gave only minimal attention to his paper's operation. Once again, politics had become a daily preoccupation. His return to Parliament had coincided with the advent of Senator Émile Combes, to whom Waldeck-Rousseau bequeathed the premiership and the application of the Associations Law of 1901. Waldeck had intended the law as little more than a curb on the more obstreperous monastic orders and as a means to spare the army from the wrath of the Bloc des Gauches, which had assumed control of the Chamber in the wake of the Affair. But the white-bearded, stumpy ex-seminarian set about to forge it into a weapon of war against the Church. To Clemenceau and other deep-dyed anticlericals, Combes' almost monomaniacal concentration on the religious question rekindled hopes they hadn't felt since Ferry's heyday. He confessed he had long since reconciled himself to leaving to posterity "only the possibility of Republican institutions," but a merciful Providence had spared him: "All the lands bent under Catholic clericalism are gasping for life," he cried to his constituents in 1904. "It is France alone who fights."[24]

As president (no less, already) of the Senate's Commission on Congregations, he was well-placed to aid Combes. When Waldeck-Rousseau, mortally ill from cancer, roused Senate moderates with tardy complaints (20 November 1903) that his Associations Law had been abused, Clemenceau sabered him down with arguments as cruel as they were just.[25] As vice-president and then president of a board of inquiry, he shielded Combes' odd choice for navy minister, former comrade Camille Pelletan.

(He had more or less let Clemenceau hang out to dry during the Panama and Norton affairs, had left *La Justice* in October 1893 when Clemenceau had begun to write full time, and in the latter's opinion had stayed neutral too long during the Dreyfus affair.) The inquiry focused on technical questions until the opposition, led by an ambitious maverick Radical, Paul Doumer, lost interest.[26] (His role in this aborted investigation would return to haunt him during his first ministry.) Despite angry passages with the minister of war, General André, over shocking neglect in the medical service, he bore with him until scandals involving Masonic influence in promotions forced him out.[27] And when the Socialist *blocards* showed signs of restlessness, he defended Combes from charges by Alexandre Millerand, from whom he had parted because of the pardon and amnesty questions during the Affair, that anticlericalism had sidetracked social reform. He agreed that Millerand had a point, but he thought (or hoped, anyhow) that Combes might move on both fronts. Besides, he feared Combes' successor would be a moderate who would neglect both.[28]

His support of Combes bought him a license to criticize, and needless to say he used it freely. A proper solution to the religious question, he contended, would be found only in a separation of church and state. Successive monarchies, empires, and republics had chased the monks and wrangled with bishops without daring to sacrifice the controls embodied in Napoleon's Concordat. The invariable result had been stalemate and exasperation which had turned Catholics against the Republic and anticlericals toward proposals to curb the clergy's civil liberties or to abolish private schools. He regarded the monastic orders as "instruments of a foreign power" (the Vatican) and as violators of the principle forbidding voluntary "slavery." He detested Rome, but he also detested petty persecution of Catholics by tunnel-visioned libertarians. In speeches he confessed he would not have made in his earlier years, he opposed a state monopoly of education, defending the rights of private education, even that conducted by the Church (though not by the monks), providing the State retained appropriate oversight.[29] And he used his commission presidency to bury a bill, the "Loi Massé," which would have put niggling restrictions on the teaching rights of former monks.[30] He was, as he archly reminded Waldeck-

Rousseau, en route to a separation of church and state: "And who put me on the road? M. Waldeck-Rousseau, one fine day," with his misconceived Associations Law.[31]

Combes hesitated, while his majority decayed. Only after more squabbling with the Vatican did he start work on a separation bill, which he defended in a speech at Auxerre. Clemenceau, past patience, lathered him and his proposal with sarcasms: "He spoke as if he considered Napoleon to be a Combes on horseback."[32] Revelations of political spying in the army and in Parliament brought on the last agonies. Clemenceau cast votes for Combes--against their mutual enemies--but slashed the government in print, scorned André ("a plumed mollusc"), and worked the lobbies to force the ministry's resignation at the first suitable opportunity.[33] In January 1905 Combes finally bowed out rather than face a ritual execution.

IV

Not since 1887 had Clemenceau stood so close to the top. A loyal *blocard*, yet showing independence and a liberal spirit which a corps of rising men both in and out of Parliament found attractive, he would be certain to press a separation bill, therewith revitalizing the faltering Bloc. He wanted the succession and may have expected it.[34] Instead, he again watched outside the gates, not even formally consulted. With elections due in a year, separation frightened many. A man with more links to the Center than Clemenceau would be safer. Besides, President Loubet would not have him. He still resented the implication that he owed him something for his "vote" in 1899, and it was no secret that he disliked the anticlerical campaign: Clemenceau would mean Combism sans Combes. Madame Loubet, who detested Clemenceau, agreed.[35]

The call went to another survivor of the Panama wreck, Senator Maurice Rouvier, the man who had won out in 1887. Clemenceau masked his disappointment with comic mockery of the scramble for portfolios, quips-- "It's not a ministry, it's a board of directors" (business interests were heavily represented)--and a refusal to support protests from the Radicals over their modest share of the spoils. But he left no doubt that he thought the man of the Pacte Mackau would bury reforms with flowers.[36]

If such was Rouvier's intention, he soon found the current favoring separation was too strong to stem. The Socialists' calls for workers' pensions and an income tax alarmed moderates more than a separation administered by the moderate Rouvier. The government bowed to an ultimatum from the Radicals and, to Clemenceau's happy amazement, promptly brought in a bill stronger than Combes' which won an initial endorsement by 150 votes. A 108-vote majority finally carried it in the Chamber on 3 July.

Prospects appeared good in the Senate, the ancient graveyard of separatist hopes, but Clemenceau's attitude fueled anxiety. His vehement objections to an amendment inserted to assure Chamber passage threatened to upset *blocard* strategy designed to finish with the bill before the elections of 1906--in effect, Senate passage without change and before January 1st. The amendment, to Article IV,, obliquely recognized the Catholic hierarchy's authority as an "organizational rule" which parish associations (*associations cultuelles*) claiming to be Catholic must observe to receive church properties. Without the amendment schismatic *cultuelles* might be formed. Clemenceau argued heatedly that a law assuring liberty had no business protecting churches from schism. It is true, he admitted, that religions, contrary to what the *philosophes* had thought, are "a natural phenomenon of the human spirit" even though they are "magical constructions," "displacements of hope" doomed by the advance of science. But schisms there have been, and schisms there will be: all the more reason for a law of liberty to escape the "concordatist mentality" still infecting both the Left and Right.[37]

Stung by summonses from leading *blocards* to prove he was no longer a "wrecker," he finally promised (7 August) not to jeopardize the January deadline.[38] Taking no chances, Rouvier convoked Parliament much later than usual. Clemenceau raged, but he kept his pledge. He settled for a major speech raking the bill's deficiencies, warning that the "privileges" awarded the hierarchy might be withdrawn later "if events impose upon us the obligation to do so....I do not hide from you that it is with this hope that I shall vote for the bill."[39] The *Journal Officiel* noted "agitation"; many were wondering how much longer he would be kept out of a ministry.

Clemenceau could savor nuances, but he loved the blacks and whites. On the religious question he framed logical theses supported by beliefs held from his youth: Catholicism, condemned by science, was dying, and most Catholics really wanted to be "liberated" from the hierarchy's grip. Briand, *rapporteur* of the bill, and Jaurès made a more realistic assessment. Events confirmed their judgment, not Clemenceau's, when Catholics obeyed the hierarchy despite grave difficulties created by the pope's subsequent condemnation of the law.[40]

V

Absorbing as he found domestic questions, Clemenceau owed much of his influence toward 1906 to his role in the controversies surrounding the reign of Théophile Delcassé at the foreign ministry.

It was Delcassé who reaped the credit for concluding the Anglo-French Entente (8 April 1904). Clemenceau of course welcomed the signing. He had, after all, made his name a byword for the English connection. He had even sought, in 1891, to forestall a looming Russian alliance by sounding out Joseph Chamberlain for terms,[41] and in 1898 he had raged at the foolish attempt to preempt England's claims to the headwaters of the Nile at Fashoda: "The brutal fact is that France cannot think of throwing herself into a war for the possession of some African marshes when the German is camped at Metz and Strasbourg."[42] Delcassé had squirmed out of the Fashoda affair in the first months of his seven-year tenure and then patiently proceeded to construct the Entente's agreements. They turned on an exchange of France's nuisance rights in Egypt for recognition of her special interests in Morocco. Clemenceau, however, was uneasy over the "gift" of Morocco and Delcassé's intentions there. The Russo-Japanese War, which erupted two months before the Entente was signed, heightened his anxiety. The play of alliances (Franco-Russian, Anglo-Japanese) would threaten the Entente, presenting inviting opportunities to Germany and severely testing Delcassé's judgment--unhappily not a commodity in which Clemenceau put great stock.

It was Delcassé's confidence in Russian strength which concerned him most. From the onset of the war, Clemenceau steadily predicted defeat for France's giant ally, to the high indignation of most of the press. His opinions, though, did not lead him to refuse *L'Aurore*'s small share of the largesse distributed by the Russian embassy.[43] If they were so stupid as to think their *petits paquets* would change his tune, it only proved what he was saying about them. In the absence of stronger assurances than Britain seemed ready to make, he regarded the Russian alliance as the riposte to German power in *Mitteleuropa*, expensive disaster insurance written by a shaky company but the only one doing business in the area. He thought France should keep Russia's attention focused on Europe, but the tsar had fed Delcassé's vanity, he charged, and won him to a blind support of adventurism in Asia. Result: a disastrous war, revolutionary upheaval, and a grave weakening of French security.

Clemenceau's rough handling of Delcassé had other, less public, stimulants. Unadmitted envy of his laurels as the architect of the Entente may well have given edge to his criticism. As he was quite prone to make judgments about people on the basis of quick impressions, a dislike could have germinated from little more than a vibration set up by Delcassé's appearance and manner: a moon-faced, neatly mustachioed little man, glittery eyes staring through a pince-nez, the brisk, self-assured air of a professor lecturing Parliament as if it were a congregation of schoolboys. "Our small-bore Metternich," Clemenceau sniffed.[44] But more specifically, and for both of them, the Aunay affair had blighted their modest chances of agreeable relations.

Sometime in the 1880s Clemenceau had succumbed to the lively charms of the strikingly beautiful, American-born wife of a diplomat, the comte d'Aunay. Thus began a friendship, perhaps more than platonic at first, which was to last into old age. Aunay's career flowered while the comtesse kept Clemenceau *au courant* in diplomatic circles. During the final negotiations of the Franco-Russian Alliance in 1894, however, Aunay was held responsible for press leaks embarrassing to the tsar and relieved of his post as minister to Denmark. Clemenceau, smelling a reprisal connected with the Norton affair, tried without success to get him reinstated. He tried again when Delcassé, a Radical, became foreign minister. Delcassé, however, cooly informed him that he could find nothing in the record to warrant reversing the decision. Clemenceau exploded in a towering rage. Henceforth the two men went their separate ways.[45]

VI

In January 1905 Delcassé's situation, heretofore unshakable, began to deteriorate rapidly. He dispatched Saint-René Taillandier to Fez to hasten a "peaceful penetration" of Morocco. Clemenceau growled warnings about the "wasps' nest" there: "Peaceful penetration is an idyll fit to bring tears to the eyes of all the little lambs of the Quai d'Orsay."[46] Later that month, on the 22nd, "Bloody Sunday" in St. Petersburg heralded a revolution to answer the slaughter on the plains of Manchuria. Clemenceau, who thought he saw a Russian 1789 in the making, reacted violently to Delcassé's attempt to excuse the tsarist regime's brutalities. Strikes and savage repressions roiled through Russia, and in March came crushing defeat at Mukden at the hands of the Japanese. Delcassé must face facts and urge Russia to sue for peace at once, he warned. What could Russia do tomorrow if the alliance had to be invoked? In effect, nothing.[47]

Such was the grim prospect when Wilhelm II stepped from his yacht at Tangier (31 March) to proclaim his brotherly concern for the independence of the sultan of Morocco.

Inexplicable as it seems in retrospect, for the ensuing crisis lasted a year and was followed by a train of others down to 1914, Clemenceau evidently was the only considerable public figure in France to take early alarm.[48] At the first announcement of the impending visit, a week before Wilhelm landed, he exposed Germany's game. Even though she was a party to the Madrid Convention of 1880 on Morocco, Delcassé had failed to notify her officially of his accords with Britain, Italy, and Spain concerning Morocco; Germany, thus, could exploit this capital blunder by converting a right to negotiate about Morocco into a device to split the new Entente.[49]

Events swiftly confirmed his prediction. Germany demanded an international conference to examine the status of the Madrid Convention. Instead of negotiating about this, Delcassé refused to budge. Bolstered by private assurances from Britain, he believed the kaiser would not risk losing his fleet, ports, and colonies to the British navy in a quarrel over Morocco. Clemenceau quite agreed that Germany was probably bluffing, but any conference would find France well supported if it were carefully prepared. So why play Double or Quits on it? If Wilhelm were left no honorable way out, that unstable man might well decide that, with Russia temporarily impotent, the hegemony of Europe could be won by sending his legions west. Germany and Britain would terminate *their* quarrel somehow--over the prostrate body of France.

Was such a game worth the skin of M. Delcassé? By mid-May Clemenceau did not think so, nor did Rouvier and his ministers.[50] A veiled threat from Germany to answer in kind any use of force in Morocco brought Delcassé to a bitter resignation on 6 June.

His departure should have signalled the beginning of the end of the crisis. Instead, the kaiser, true to form, overbid his hand by trying to haul France to a conference without prior agreement on an agenda, while the German press trumpeted victory. Clemenceau both reflected and stimulated a sharp reaction in French opinion against such behavior. On 18 June a ringing article, "To Be or Not to Be," answered threats from across the Rhine to hold France "hostage" for Britain's actions:

> I have always thought that an implacable fatality from which we cannot escape will some day force use of the military weapon which the Germans forged when they founded their empire on the battlefield....
> It is nothing less than the fate of France which would be the stake of the battles. *To be or not to be*: this is the issue which is put to us for the first time since the Hundred Years War by an implacable will to supremacy....
> We owe it to ourselves, we owe it to our fathers and to our children to give all we have to save the treasure of French life we have received from those who have gone before and for which we will stand accountable to those who will follow us.[51]

At a British embassy reception a week later, he was seen standing a few feet from the German ambassador, eyes sparkling and hand on hip, audible (as usual) above the chatter: "From here on we can no longer give way....If Germany wants war, well--we'll fight!" The comte d'Haussonville remarked to Maurice Paléologue, "I've just heard Clemenceau holding forth. That Jacobin all of a sudden appeals to me. Danton must have talked like that."[52]

He mingled tough talk to Germany, however, with attacks on those who still viewed acceptance of a conference as an humiliation. The important thing, he contended, was to return from a conference with the

Entente intact. Moreover, some internationalization of Moroccan affairs would curb the kaiser's "caprices" and France's own "temptations" to "warlike adventures" there.[53] Rouvier finally embraced the conference idea but held firm for a prior accord on an agenda. Germany backed off, and a conference was announced (6 July). But while negotiations went forward on the agenda, the head of the German mission in Fez, Count Tattenbach, began getting all the concessions he could from the sultan. Clemenceau reacted to this move in the strongest terms, as did the rest of the Paris press in his wake, and summoned Rouvier to tell Germany politely but absolutely firmly that there would be no conference unless Germany respected the status quo during the current negotiations.[54] So outspoken did he become--for he viewed the agenda question as crucial to the matter of whether France would be able to thwart Germany's attempt to break her English and Russian connection--that Jaurès accused him of being provocative toward Germany. His charge in turn ignited a running debate between them in the press about pacifism, the unification of the Socialist parties in France, and the unified party's endorsement of the Second International Working Men's Association's policy of a general strike in case of war--exchanges which proved to be a curtain-raiser for their debates in 1906-9 during Clemenceau's ministry.[55]

Rouvier and Chancellor Bülow eventually managed to sidestep a direct confrontation. An agenda agreement was signed on 28 September, but three more months of tortuous negotiations ensued before the conference finally met on 16 January, in Spain at Algeciras, and then another three were consumed in hagglings and confrontations before an accord was signed (7 April). Clemenceau followed the affair step by step, seeking the fine line between sensible compromises and defense of French honor and security. Aside from President Roosevelt's mediation of a peace between Russia and Japan, he found little to cheer about and had come to take a dim view of the impending conference's prospects of achieving anything very lasting:

> What is called the peace of Europe is an equilibrium of violence accomplished and in preparation. Over this collection of crude banalities, the "statesmen" try to spread the soothing poison of a verbalism of equity.[56]

In the quiet of his apartment, he wrote to Brandes at the dawn of the new year:

> Dear friend, No. Germany will not declare war on us. But in my opinion the situation in Europe is such that a great armed conflict appears to me inevitable at some date which I can in no way predict, and our duty is to prepare for the worst.[57]

Russia's situation continued critical. Peace with Japan brought no quick peace at home. Clemenceau distrusted the tsar's promises of constitutional government. The arrest of the St. Petersburg soviet and the brutal repression of an uprising in Moscow in late December sickened him. The opening of negotiations in Paris for a new Russian loan found him in the blackest of moods. The Alliance, he wrote, is "a sonorous word...which cannot stand for any objective reality under present circumstances." Financially, it amounts to "the right for us to provide for all the follies of an absolutism in delirium." Unless reforms are forthcoming, let the kaiser support barbarism![58]

He had never gone this far since the signing of the Alliance, nor was he to do so in the future. It was one of the ironies of his life that a few months later he found himself obliged, as a minister, to approve the loan he had denounced. The price of Russia's cooperation at Algeciras was the money which allowed the tsar to dismiss the Duma and continue for another decade a policy which he (and the Left generally) considered disgusting and doomed.

VII

Domestic troubles, not foreign policy, brought down Rouvier's government. Due to a coincidence in the constitutional terms of office, elections would be held in 1906 for the Senate (partial renewal), the Chamber, and the presidency. While Clemenceau was uninvolved in the first, none of the Var's seats being at stake, he was a major factor in Armand Fallières' election as Loubet's successor. Although Fallières, the genial and respected president of the Senate, was a Waldeck-Rousseau moderate, Clemenceau infinitely preferred him to the president of the Chamber, Paul Doumer, a driving, self-made man who was seeking to put together a coalition of anti-Combist Radicals and ambitious young deputies while, to curry favor with the Center and Right, preaching patriotism and homely virtues. In a finely paced campaign, Clemenceau followed up several weeks of low-key warnings about Doumer's activities with a devastating flood of sarcasms against an incipient Strong Man, "the new-style Boulanger," *"le grand chef d'arrivisme à tout prix."*[59] When Léon Bourgeois declined to run and Brisson and Rouvier faded, he announced for Fallières (29 December) and helped him through to victory on 18 January.

Rouvier's government was expected to resign after the close of the Algeciras Conference and the Chamber elections in the spring. Its premature fall resulted from uncertain handling of a crisis of over-production in the vineyards and of violent incidents arising from the first attempts to apply the Separation Law's provisions for an inventory of properties prior to their devolution to the *associations cultuelles*. The inventory was intended as a protection against confiscations or theft, but in a number of localities the government's agents were met by barricaded church doors and angry crowds determined to prevent "spoliation" and "desecration." Right-wing politicians and clergy exploited the troubles to discredit the law, moderates groaned in dismay when the pope seized upon the troubles to issue a bull condemning separation in principle, while anticlericals, Clemenceau in the lead, called for no compromise with insurrection. The government could please nobody and went down to defeat on 7 March after extraordinarily confused debates.

A week to the day after Rouvier's fall, a ministry crowded with formidable figures but headed by a colorless Radical veteran, Jean Sarrien, won a vote of confidence. The sensation of the hour was M. Clemenceau's appearance in the preeminent election-year post of minister of the interior.

He had been eliminated early from consideration for the premiership.[60] After refusals from Bourgeois and Poincaré, Fallières decided to yoke together a large number of "name" politicians in his first government, and for this he needed a broker. Sarrien, currently president of the Délégation des Gauches, the Bloc's steering committee, filled the bill nicely. But would Clemenceau be a minister in another man's cabinet? The assumption had long held sway that he would not, but it had never been put to a serious test. Nobody could deny that he had earned his chance. Also, for what it was worth, in February he had organized, though he declined its presidency, the Groupe Radical-Socialiste, fifty-three fellow senators from the Gauche Démocratique (an unwieldy amalgam of Radicals and Radical-Socialists) who had pledged themselves to push for all "socialist" legislation short of "collectivized" private property. How seriously he took group memberships, though, may be judged from a statement in *L'Aurore* back in December that he belonged to no group.[61] It remains doubtful, nevertheless, that Sarrien would have made him an offer but for the insistence of Aristide Briand.

The Separation Law was bound to be a major preoccupation. Briand had had more to do with its passage than anyone else, and Sarrien was determined to put him in charge of its implementation. But Briand made Clemenceau's entry the condition of his own. He had two reasons: 1) the most dangerous critic of the law would be muzzled by ministerial solidarity, and 2) he had agreed with him that French politics needed stronger orientation toward social reform and had accepted a proposal from him (in a letter, 1 May 1903) that neither would enter a ministry without the other. When Sarrien made his offer, Briand kept his pledge. The moderates in the proposed combination, especially Poincaré, made known their displeasure, but in the end they wanted Briand badly enough to choke down his partner.[62]

It was not just Clemenceau's inclusion which caused misgivings. It was putting him at the ministry of the interior in an election year. A story made the rounds that at a meeting discussing portfolios Sarrien had approached him with some refreshments. "What'll you have?" "Interior," came the crisp reply--and it was done. The truth was more prosaic. This celebrated exchange may well have occurred; certainly it is in character. The error is to suppose, however, that he got Interior on the spot or without much discussion.[63] The Radicals, the largest party, were insisting on Interior for one of theirs, and Clemenceau would not settle for a minor post. Justice? He was not a lawyer. Finance? He frankly admitted his incompetence there and got no argument. Foreign Affairs? Perhaps, but the Algeciras Conference was at a critical stage, and someone less involved in debate on the subject--and more acceptable to the Russians--would be preferable. Education? For it to be a major post, the under-secretaryship of religion would have to be retained there, but Religion was Briand's promised preserve. War? Possibly, but Clemenceau...Dreyfus? It would be Interior or nothing, and nothing meant no Briand. When it was all over, the moderates were left to console themselves that the government would contain no fewer than five former interior ministers who could keep an eye on this unsettling presence.[64]

VIII

On 14 March 1906 the new government filed into the Chamber and took its place on the front-row *banc des ministres*. Thirteen years ago Clemenceau had been hounded from this hall, covered with epithets, ruined. Some of those who had cheered Déroulède and Millevoye were still there. But they were behind him now. Reporters noted that he sat very quietly, seeming lost in thought.

NOTES
CHAPTER X

[1]   Letter to Geffroy, 21 Dec. 1901, in Duroselle, *Clemenceau*, p. 458; and J. H. Rosny *aîné* [J. H. H. Boëx], *Torches et lumignons, souvenirs de la vie littéraire* ("La Force française," 1921), pp. 239-240.

[2]   On his finances see Duroselle, *Clemenceau*, pp. 315, 440-441. On *Le Bloc* see Brandes, *Correspondance*, 1: nos. 191, 193; Gabriel Astruc, *Le pavillon des fantômes, souvenirs* (B. Grasset, 1929), pp. 99-100; Claude Lévy, "Un journal de Clemenceau: *Le Bloc* (janvier 1901-mars 1902)," *Revue d'histoire moderne et contemporaine* 10 (1963):105-120; and Duroselle, *Clemenceau*, pp. 456-464.

[3]   GC, *La honte*, pp. 1-5; letter, 15 Oct. 1899, in A. and P. Dreyfus, *The Dreyfus Case*, pp. 275-276.

[4]   Along with Louis Leblois; see AU, 13 Aug. 1904.

[5]   See M. Dreyfus, *L'Affaire*, pp. 264-265.

[6]   See A. and P. Dreyfus, *The Dreyfus Case*, pp. 177-179, 198; and Bredin, *The Affair*, pp. 458-461, *passim*.

[7]   On the medical service; see his Senate speeches of 12 March and 18 June 1903.

[8]   AU, 1 Dec. 1903.

[9]   AU, 30 Dec. 1903.

[10]   See *La Dépêche de Toulouse*, 15 May 1901; and *Le Bloc*, 9, 16 June. Many Radicals had thought for a long time that he was going too far during the Affair and hurting the army's prestige. When they saw how much influence the monastic orders were getting at the highest levels, they supported Waldeck-Rousseau, but Clemenceau meanwhile had alienated a considerable number of them for good. See François Albert, "Les paradoxes d'une carrière: L'homme libre et son parti," *L'Ère Nouvelle*, 24 Nov. 1929.

[11]   GC, *La honte*, pp. 352-354, from *Le Bloc*, 3 Nov. 1901.

[12]   See Yves Rinaudo, *Les vendanges de la République*, p. 148; and *idem*, "Une sensibilité politique de gauche: le Var rural au début de XXe siècle," *Provence historique* 32 (1982):370-371 and *passim*.

13   See his letter to Lady Cecil (Violet Maxse, later Lady Milner), 10 Dec. 1899, in Wormser, *La république de Clemenceau*, p. 189, in which he hoped that Mercier's imminent election would short-circuit the rumored amnesty bill.

14   Numa Jacquemaire, Madeleine's husband, shot himself in 1902 after discovering her with Maurice Bernard, a prominent lawyer, and Thérèse separated from an alcoholic official, Louis Gatineau. See Gatineau-Clemenceau, *Les pattes du Tigre*, pp. 28-30, 34-35.

15   See Pierre-Victor Stock, *Mémorandum d'un éditeur, 3e série: L'Affaire Dreyfus anecdotique* (Éditions Stock, Delmas & Boutelleau, 1938), pp. 40-44; Wormser's essay in *Georges Clemenceau* (Collection Génies et Réalités), p. 11; and Francisque Varenne, *Mon patron Georges Mandel* (Editions Défense de la France, [1947]), pp. 16-20.

16   See GC, *Contre la justice*, pp. 327, 331 (28 Feb. 1899). As late as 1896 he had supported Bourgeois on revision, however; see JU, 27 Feb., 30 April.

17   GC, *Sur la démocratie*, pp. 64-65, 82. See also HE, 20 Jan. 1916.

18   *La Dépêche de Toulouse*, 14 March 1902; *L'Intransigeant*, 6 March.

19   His opponent was a Dr. Louis Trotobas, a member of the Var's general council. See *Le Petit Var* and *La République du Var* (7Toulon), 5 March-8 April 1902; and JOS, 10 June 1902, p. 807. On this election and his career to 1906, see Newhall, "Georges Clemenceau, 1902-1906: 'An Old Beginner.'"

20   See Martet, *Clemenceau*, pp. 124-125, 144; and Desachy, *Une grande figure de l'Affaire Dreyfus*, pp. 174-180. Mathieu Dreyfus probably was the source of the warning about Leblois Clemenceau referred to in Martet; see M. Dreyfus, *L'Affaire*, pp. 292, 298-300. Interestingly, Leblois left Clemenceau's name off his list of heroes of the Affair; Louis Leblois, *L'Affaire Dreyfus: L'iniquité, la réparation; les principaux faits et les principaux documents* (Librairie Aristide Quillet, 1929), p. 73. Sen. Jean Dupuy, *Le Petit Parisien*'s publisher, was another benefactor at this time and a permanent friend. It is not clear from Duroselle, *Clemenceau*, pp. 794-795, if the Belgians supporting Vaughan were part of this operation. In 1920 Clemenceau repaid a 20,000 fr. debt from *L'Aurore* to the widow of a Belgian senator, Lambiotte.

21   Brandes, *Correspondence*, 1: no. 195 (7 Jan. 1904).

22   AU, 30 Sept. 1904.

23   Jean Philip, "Souvenirs d'un parlementaire désabusé," *La France active*, no. 150 (July-Aug. 1935), p. 28 and *passim*. See also

recollections by another young staffer, Gérard Bauër, "Lorsque Clemenceau dirigeait 'L'Aurore,'" *Nouvelles littéraires, artistiques, et scientifiques*, 30 Nov. 1929. Philip says (p. 29) Clemenceau got 2,000 francs per month but ordinary staffers only 200 francs.

24 AU, 21 Oct. 1903; and a speech at Brignoles, in AU, 20 Sept. 1904.

25 JOS, 20 Nov. 1903, pp. 1404-1405. The press thought he had saved Combes.

26 See JOC, 27, 28 March 1907, *passim*; and Newhall, "Georges Clemenceau, 1902-1906," 1:175-189, 2:92-98. On Pelletan in 1893 see Duroselle, *Clemenceau*, pp. 315-316. The inquiry was voted on 30 March 1904 with Pelletan as president ex officio and Clemenceau and Gaston Thomson vice-presidents. When Rouvier named Thomson navy minister in Jan. 1905, Clemenceau was left in charge. He called no meetings after 18 March. Delcassé used the naval question to bring him down in 1909; see pp. 292-293 below.

27 See n. 7 above. He supported the Two Years' Service Law and restrained army budgets, 1902-1905; see a summary in *La Dépêche de Toulouse*, 26 Aug. 1904.

28 See AU, 19, 20 March, 25, 29 May, 12 June, 11 July 1904; and *La Dépêche de Toulouse*, 19 March 1904, 20 June 1905. On their earlier split at *La Justice* in 1889 over Boulangism, see Leslie Derfler, *Alexandre Millerand: The Socialist Years* (The Hague: Mouton, 1977), pp. 43-45. Georges Laguerre, a Boulangist later, had brought him to Clemenceau in 1882.

29 See Senate sittings of 30 Oct. 1902 and 17 Nov. 1903. He had signalled his opposition to a state monopoly in *Le grand Pan*, pp. 438-447; *Injustice militaire*, p. 275; *Justice militaire*, pp. 12-13; and *La honte*, pp. 43-48. See *L'iniquité*, p. 398 (8 June 1898) against parental choice of education (the *droit du père*); he reversed his position on this in 1902.

30 See AU, 15, 18, 20 June; and *La Dépêche de Toulouse*, 28 June 1903.

31 JOS, 20 Nov. 1903, p. 1404.

32 AU, 6 Sept. 1904.

33 See AU and *La Dépêche de Toulouse*, 29 Oct. 1904-16 Jan. 1905, *passim*; Émile Combes, *Mon ministère: Mémoires, 1902-1905*, ed. Maurice Sorre (Librairie Plon, 1956), pp. 203-204, 251-256; Madame Bernain de Ravisi, *Sous la dictature de Clemenceau: Un forfait judiciaire: Le procès Paul-Meunier, Judet-Brossard* (André Delpeuch, 1926), pp. 42-43; and Wormser, *La république de Clemenceau*, p. 202n. In a letter to me (12 March

1962), M. Wormser said the disputed appointment mentioned by Combes concerned a former deputy, not Étienne Winter.

34   See AU, 11, 16 Jan.; and *La Dépêche de Toulouse*, 20, 23 Jan. 1905. On the "Viel dinner" group, which included such future ministerial colleagues as Ruau, Cruppi, Clémentel, and Jeanneney, see Général [Adolphe] Messimy, *Mes souvenirs* (Librairie Plon, 1937), pp. 30-31.

35   See Abel Combarieu, *Sept ans à l'Élysée avec le président Émile Loubet* (Librairie Hachette, 1932), pp. 21-22, 209, 249. Clemenceau nevertheless said later that Loubet was the best president France had had in his lifetime; Martet, *Le Tigre*, p. 34.

36   See AU, 23, 25, 26 Jan.; and *La Dépêche de Toulouse*, 27 Jan. 1905.

37   GC, *Contre la justice*, pp. 5-6, 199; *La mêlée sociale*, p. 375; and GC, "Quelques considérations sur la séparation des églises et de l'État," *La Grande Revue*, 1 May 1903, p. 264.

38   AU, 7 Aug. 1905. The quotation on p. 95 above referring to his father shows the pain it cost him.

39   JOS, 23 Nov. 1905, p. 1484. He voted for Art. IV, which passed, 252 to 6.

40   Briand also regarded Art. IV as necessary to help keep France from falling into a religious "war" at the very time the Tangier crisis (below) was in full swing. See Raymond Escholier, *Souvenirs parlés par Briand* (Librairie Hachette, 1932), pp. 86-88.

41   See especially Joseph Chamberlain, *A Political Memoir, 1880-1892*, ed. C. D. H. Howard (London: Batchworth Press, 1953), pp. 295-297; Baron Boris Nolde, *L'alliance franco-russe: Les origines du système diplomatique d'avante-guerre* (Librairie Droz, 1936), pp. 609-612; Wormser, *La république de Clemenceau*, pp. 487-489, 491, letters to Aunay and from Chamberlain; JU, 5, 12, 13 Sept. 1892, a charge by Morès that he was working against the Franco-Russian alliance, and letters exchanged with the Russian ambassador, Baron Mohrenheim, denying it; and Newhall, "Georges Clemenceau,1902-1906," 1:311, 2:161-162, a discussion of his views of the alliance.

42   AU, 25 Oct. 1898.

43   See A. Raffalovich, *L'abominable vénalité de la presse, d'après les documents des archives russes, 1897-1917* (Librairie du Travail, 1931), pp. 42, 75, 81, 90, 97, 122; and James W. Long, "Russian Manipulation of the French Press, 1904-1906," *Slavic Review* (Seattle) 3 (1972):343-354. Several subsidies, apparently of a standard amount for smaller papers (1,500 fr. the maximum) were received from Sept. 1904 to Feb. 1906. The French government insisted on having bribes paid in order to avert a financial panic.

An emigré at *L'Aurore*, Alexander Ular (an alias), published a violent attack on the regime, *Inside Russia Today* (London: W. Heinemann, 1905), including charges of press corruption in France.

44   AU, 19 Oct. 1903.

45   Aunay served in the Senate, 1898-1918. On the comtesse d'Aunay (née Sarita Burdan) and the Aunay affair see Gatineau-Clemenceau, *Des pattes du Tigre*, pp. 27-28, 65; and Newhall, "Georges Clemenceau, 1902-1906," 1:289-294, 2:143-152. Gatineau implies they had a child together. Georges Clemenceau II, who spoke to me frankly on several subjects in 1959, considered the relationship to be no more than a close friendship. Neton, who was close to Delcassé, denied that Delcassé and Clemenceau were wholly estranged; Albéric Neton, *Delcassé* (Académie diplomatique internationale, 1952), pp. 386-387. On the correspondence with the comtesse d'Aunay and her daughter Mary, see Duroselle, *Clemenceau*, pp. 484-485.

46   AU, 23 Dec. 1904.

47   AU, 7, 12, 13 March; and *La Dépêche de Toulouse*, 12, 19 March 1905.

48   See Eugen Weber, *The Nationalist Revival in France, 1905-1914* (Berkeley, CA: University of California Press, 1959), pp. 30-31.

49   See AU, 23, 25 March; and *La Dépêche de Toulouse*, 27 March 1905.

50   Clemenceau broached resignation on 20 April but found it "distasteful." From 9 May on he hammered Delcassé hard but did not publicly demand resignation until the day he in fact resigned. Rouvier had told him and several others on 5 June that Delcassé would go. If he knew of Rouvier's private negotiations with Germany, he said nothing in print.

51   AU, 18 June 1905. He admitted in 1908 that, while he believed war was inevitable, it was "perhaps unnecessary" to have said so in print. Georges Louis, *Les carnets de Georges Louis*, 2 vols. (Éditions Rieder, 1926), 1:21.

52   Maurice Paléologue, *Un grand tournant de la politique mondiale, 1904-1906* (Librairie Plon, 1934), p. 373. It has since become clear that Germany did not intend war at this time. For a convenient summary see David E. Kaiser, "Germany and the Origins of the First World War," *Journal of Modern History* 55 (1983):452-453.

53   *La Dépêche de Toulouse*, 25 June; and AU, 28 June 1905. He had regarded a conference as a solution; on 10 June (AU) he declared it the best.

54 See, especially, AU, 1 ("Pas de duperie!"), 5 ("Non"), 6, 12, 15 ("C'est trop!"), 22, 27 Aug; *La Dépêche de Toulouse*, 6, 10, 20 Aug.; and the *Wiener Neue Freie Presse*, 13 Aug., 1905. Contrary to some accounts, he did no about-face on the desirability of a conference *if* it were properly and fairly prepared.

55 They summarized their debate over pacifism in *La Dépêche de Toulouse*, 18 Sept., and AU, 22 Sept. 1905. Jaurès's resumé is reprinted in Jean Jaurès, *Oeuvres: Textes rassemblés, présentés par Max Bonnafous*, 9 vols. (Éditions Rieder, 1931-1939), 2:276-296. For Clemenceau at this time on Socialist unification, see especially AU, 2, 5, 9, 13, 20 Oct.; and *La Dépêche de Toulouse*, 26 Aug., 8 Oct. 1905. For a detailed discussion, see Newhall, "Georges Clemenceau, 1902-1906," 1:407-432, 2:209-220.

56 AU, 26 Nov. 1905.

57 Brandes, *Correspondance*, 1: no. 197 (9 Jan. 1906).

58 AU, 30 Jan. 1906.

59 AU, 20 Nov.; and *La Dépêche de Toulouse*, 29 Dec. 1905. He had turned against Doumer originally for accepting the governor-generalship of Indochina (1897-1902) from Méline.

60 See *Le Radical*, 10 March 1906; and Louis Andrieux, "Georges Clemenceau," *North American Review* 184 (Feb. 1907):379. Jaurès denied he had "vetoed" him; *L'Humanité*, 10 March.

61 See AU, 21 Dec. 1905, 26 Jan., 15 Feb.; and *La Dépêche de Toulouse*, 21 Feb. 1906. Forty-two, including Clemenceau, continued membership in the Gauche Démocratique.

62 Letter in Zévaès, *Clemenceau*, pp. 182-183. See *Le Temps* and *Le Radical*, 11, 12 March 1906.

63 Wormser, in *La république de Clemenceau*, p. 14, says Fallières and Sarrien had agreed in advance on it, though contemporary accounts cast doubt on this.

64 Sarrien (Justice), Louis Barthou (Public Works), Georges Leygues (Colonies), Bourgeois (Foreign Affairs), and Eugène Étienne (War). For the cabinet's membership see Appendix IV.

CHAPTER XI

On the Heights
(1906-1909)

The colorful minister of the interior assumed first place in the government from its inception. When Sarrien resigned seven months later, citing not wholly fictitious reasons of health, he won the succession virtually uncontested.[1] He swiftly formed a cabinet and for the next thirty-three months dominated the political scene as had no premier since Jules Ferry.* During the Third Republic's seventy-year reign, only Waldeck-Rousseau's thirty-six month ministry outlasted Clemenceau's first. Afterward he seldom mentioned these years, probably because the War had come to bulk so large in his thoughts, but also because he undeniably had achieved less than he had hoped. He contented himself with saying he had done his duty as he had seen it and at least was no worse than many others.[2] In retrospect it seems fair to say, however, that he did a better job than he got credit for at the time or later.

A tranquil Clemenceau government would be impossible to conceive, but circumstances conspired to ensure that these particular years would rank among the Third Republic's most agitated. Labor relations were especially troubled. The phenomenon was not confined to France: Great Britain, Spain, Italy, Germany, Austria-Hungary, Russia, and the United States all

---

* See Appendix III for a chronology of this period and Appendix IV for a list of the cabinet membership.

experienced waves of unrest as industrialism and urbanization flooded agrarian regions or societies. By 1910 parliamentary government everywhere in Europe was in trouble.[3] In France the change had become clearly perceptible by the 1880s, when it helped to fuel the Boulangist agitation, and was even more in evidence in the nineties, as Clemenceau's speeches and articles witness, but the Dreyfus Affair, the religious struggle, and the Moroccan crisis had deflected the politicians' attention. By 1906, however, working-class patience had worn to a crust. The crisis operated in tandem with a declining unemployment rate, a reduced fear of prolonged depressions, a growth of literacy, and an erosion of provincial attitudes and habits. But levels of unemployment remained high (9% in 1906) while real wages were continuing to stagnate or fall, a state that would continue until at least 1910.[4] Such improvements as there were, in short, seemed precisely calibrated to raise hopes for a fairer sharing of the heralded benefits of industrialism while furnishing little tangible evidence of their fulfillment.

In response, anarcho-syndicalism, espousing doctrines of "direct action" and the General Strike, had waxed steadily since the 1890s and in the Clemenceau years reached its apogee. Socialism likewise gained ground. In 1905 its adherents, save for a few Independents, had united into a "revolutionary" party, the French Section of the Workers' International (SFIO), claiming to speak for the laboring masses--who in turn were sternly being warned by the syndicalists that all politicians, Socialists included, deserved loathing or worse. The Socialists continued nonetheless to vote for reforms, but they sought to prove their *bona fides* as foes of bourgeois rule by criticizing the bills as mere palliatives and interpellating ministries at every turn. Providentially, they found Clemenceau, paladin of the Old Left and scourge of past ministries, a heaven-sent target and in *La mêlée sociale* and *Le grand Pan* a wonderfully convenient store of ammunition.

II

In 1906 the Republic seemed ready for reform, or at least reforms. Clemenceau announced an ambitious program. In addition to proposals advanced by Sarrien's ministry--abrogation of the Falloux Law in order to remove the Church's privileges in secondary education, modification of the Separation Law, measures to define and strengthen the status of civil servants and of unions, and steps to ensure the spread of a "democratic spirit" in the military through reform of its promotion and judicial systems--he called for increased powers for regional authorities and an enlargement of voting districts, a law providing stronger guarantees of civil rights, creation of a ministry of labor, passage of the workers' pensions and ten-hour-day bills, a collective bargaining law, extension of the industrial accidents law to cover agricultural workers, tightening of the state's rights over mining concessions, nationalization of the troubled Western Railway Company, rigorous application of the laws against wine frauds, reform of departmental and municipal finances, and an income tax plus "if necessary" a tax on capital. Given such a comprehensive list, the absence of any mention of women's issues is only the more noticeable. His ministry saw passage of the Schmahl Law (1907) giving married women control of their earnings. But the struggling movement for female suffrage got nowhere with him, and its adherents were glad when he fell.[5]

Obviously, cooking and eating such a feast would take time. In fact, as early as June 1906, during the Sarrien ministry, he had told the Chamber that if only half the government's program were enacted he would be proud.[6] The inescapable complexity of the bills and the unattractiveness of social questions as compared with time-honored political and religious issues were more important, if less glaring, reasons for the ensuing delay than were the vast amounts of time consumed in coping with an unrelenting rain of interpellations. By 1908 calls for electoral reform, featuring *scrutin de liste* and proportional representation, were being sounded to meet a purported "crisis" in the parliamentary regime; and Clemenceau had retreated to a "fundamental program" of an income tax, workers' pensions, the Western Railway bill, and reform of the military justice system.[7] Before the Popular Front of 1936, no government had proposed to do more than Clemenceau's first, but it lacked the lash of the Great Depression. The French New Deal, like the American, came thirty years after Clemenceau and Theodore Roosevelt. In 1906 hopes were high, if ill-defined, and the ministry's accomplishments were to fall well short of fulfilling them. The outcome seems predictable in hindsight, but at the time it engendered a pervasive sense of frustration.

Passage of even a respectable fraction of the program required the presence of a committed, reasonably disciplined majority in Parliament. In effect, this meant cooperation between the large Radical delegation and the Socialists--a delicate business. Clemenceau brought to the task a fund of good intentions but also the impediments of past differences with them. When he interrupted labor minister Viviani once in 1906 to assert that he *too* was a socialist, he was at least half-serious despite his bantering tone.[8] In May 1907 he told the Chamber he intended to govern "in a socialist spirit."[9] Socialism, he had written in *La mêlée sociale*, is "social benevolence [*bonté*] in action," adding that to complain that collective action diminishes liberty "is to speak in favor of the strongest, whose name is oppression."[10] Indeed, insofar as he repudiated untrammeled laissez-faire, scored off the sins of capitalism, and advocated social insurance, labor unions, employee stockholding, an income tax, and nationalization of selected industries, he *was* one, at least in the sense understood by the Left in his youth or the Right in any age. Marx, in fact, in the late 1870s had briefly thought him a possible recruit as had, later on, Lucien Herr, the converter of Jaurès.[11]

But in the end Clemenceau had remained unconvinced: "If you're not a revolutionary at twenty, you have no heart; if you're still one at fifty, you have no head."[12] His socialism, whatever its ilk, bore more resemblance to the humanitarianism of 1848 than to what socialism proper had become by the turn of the century. There is probably some truth in the suggestion that he remained personally more familiar with, and hence more responsive to, the miseries of the street--abandoned children, prostitutes, thieves, poor artisans, unemployed day-laborers--than of the factory.[13] Economic theory bored him, as the lack of books on the subject in his library suggests. He scorned the dogmatism of an "anonymous, collective absolutism."[14] Collectivized property was a myth: "France, above all rural France, which is the real France, constituting the bulk of Frenchmen," he had confided to Henry Hyndman in the 1880s, "is and always will remain steadfastly individualist--founded on property, property, property!"[15] He never tired of asking Jaurès to embody collectivism in a bill, a ploy which invariably provoked applause and ironic laughter. Cloud-castle rhetoric about rising proletariats and bliss-to-come in a classless society dissolved in his sceptical presence. "Do you know how to recognize an article by Jaurès?" he once asked André Maurel. "All the verbs are in the future tense."[16] Nothing was more predictable than his deflating response to Jaurès's most famous speech on the theme--that he, Clemenceau, was a humble worker in the plain, a mason who contributes his stone to a cathedral he will never see. And in point of fact, not until a discussion of workers' pensions at the Nîmes party congress in 1910 did the Socialists descend from doctrinal generalities.[17] The Socialists' "interesting prophecies" aside, he found the Radical and Socialist proposals for the immediate future indistinguishable: "My program," he chided Jaurès, "is in your pocket; you took it from me."[18] For the life of him he could not understand why the Socialists had left the Bloc at the behest of the Second International (1904). Loner that he was, individualist to the core, personal abnegation and party discipline of that magnitude was beyond his ken and even smacked of intellectual dishonesty.

III

Without the cement supplied by the Socialists, Jaurès, and the religious question, the Bloc crumbled, and attempts to revive it came to nothing. Whatever its chances, it would have been impossible to cast Clemenceau in the role of a Combes following the lead of a steering committee. He wryly mocked men like Pelletan and Ferdinand Buisson whose "watches had stopped" when Combes left office.[19] Shortly before he had been called to power in 1906, he had confided to Lady Cecil (Violet Maxse):

> The strength of my situation derives from the fact that I prefer not to be a minister. If I enter the government, it will be only under certain conditions. I tell you this in all frankness at the risk of seeming very presumptuous in your eyes: I do not want to be the head of a coalition; I want to be the true head [*chef*] of the government. In my cabinet I want to have only my own men. If I fail, it will be because of my own fault and not that of others. I won't stay on a minute longer than necessary once the job is done.[20]

The hard fact of the moment, however, was that the majorities found to settle questions of authoritarian government versus democracy or to define the role of Catholicism in French society could not be transferred intact to questions spawned by the growth of modern industry. To all appearances, Clemenceau's problem seemed simple because of the presence of 250 Radicals and Radical-Socialists, only about 40 votes shy of an outright majority. But the Parti républicain radical et radical-socialiste was no more than a confederation of local committees. Many deputies used the label only to position themselves in run-off elections and paid no party dues. As already noted, Clemenceau himself joined only for a few months. Radicalism was fast becoming little more than a tag and an attitude, a transformation which the Clemenceau experience accelerated; and one largely defensive: defense of the sacred principles of 1789, defense of the small man against *les grands*, the small town against the city. This stance, however, left its leaders stranded with reform policies they could not implement when its most important constituency, small property-owners, began to drift rightward because of divisions over the best way to deal with working-class demands and violence.[21] Anticlericalism, moreover, had always been the party's strongest glue, but the Clemenceau-Briand policy of evading confrontations with the Church acted as a solvent.

In short, those 250 votes were no bloc: Clemenceau was a non-party leader of a non-party.[22] Furthermore, the other 40 votes (more likely 100) had to be coaxed from Socialists, Independent Socialists, and more moderate Républicains de Gauche, the descendants of the Opportunists. A tilt to one side risked losses on the other, if not on the bill at hand then at the next interpellation. The quarrelsome household extending from Jules Guesde, "the Marxist Pope," to Raymond Poincaré, the soul of "sound" Liberalism, reminded Clemenceau of one where somebody is always threatening to go home to mother.[23] All in all, his ministry's longevity is more of a puzzle than its relative failure as a great engine of reform.

It survived partly because the Radicals for the moment had no suitable replacement for him. He knew it and hence felt free to hold his resignation over their heads. He was closing his career. He had not sought office (a proposition many critics by now were prepared to concede) and would gladly return to the pleasures of his daily article. The deputies knew him too well to dismiss such attitudes outright as the stock "humility" of men in high places, even though he obviously enjoyed giving orders and "astonishing the bourgeoisie." His authoritarian temperament and Parisian sophistication clashed with the typical Radical's nonchalance and provincialism, but he seemed to feel no need to spare their sensibilities. Under fire because of his stiff policy toward union agitation among teachers and postal workers, he told Radical intriguers in language they never forgot nor quite forgave that he would not be "strangled by the mutes of the seraglio."[24] He jerked discussions down to realities and spoke his mind with a candor as blunt as it was unconventional. His unpredictability, his "incoherence" (one of several casual verbal gifts he handed his critics), kept opponents off balance. And he entertained--and found a perfect foil in Jaurès, likewise a master entertainer.

He also intimidated. Murmurs arose about the activities of his staff, particularly about a solemn, prematurely stooped, black-garbed young Jew with a card-index mind, Georges Mandel (1885-1944), who had come to *L'Aurore* in 1903 and made himself indispensable to the Patron. Mandel's carefully cultivated air of mystery and his thirst to know everything that was going on in politics coupled to a memory phenomenal enough to regurgitate it faultlessly on command vastly intrigued Clemenceau and amused him, too, although the fellow's doglike devotion sometimes got on his nerves. It was the beginning of an association which would last until Clemenceau's death and of a career for Mandel which would end heroically in death at the hands of the Gestapo.

But Mandel was much less important to Clemenceau in these years than he was to be during the War. At all events, the reports of spying and intrigue by the premier's office, although not without foundation, were overblown.[25] If anything, Clemenceau seemed careless about staying in touch with the lobbies, especially in the ministry's last months. Instead, believing that most deputies dearly wish to avoid decisions, he cornered them by not hesitating to put votes of confidence, thus playing to their desire to "go along." And for thirty-three months a majority of them did just that.

IV

At least two others factors made for longevity: the abilities of his ministers, and the opposition's lack of a rallying issue. A cabinet containing five future premiers offers some proof that he had an eye for talent and suitability, although the presence of Gaston Thomson (Navy), Raphaël Milliès-Lacroix (Colonies), General Picquart (War), and Julien Simyan (under-secretary at Posts, Telegraphs, and Telephones) can be cited to the contrary.[26] Stephen Pichon (Foreign Affairs), one of Clemenceau's satellites since *La Justice*'s inception, has often been numbered among the latter and dismissed as "letterbox" who owed his elevation to cronyism.[27] He had no "presence," looking like a remote but kindly professor, endured without complaint the most cavalier treatment by his patron, and lacked the force and administrative skill to put checkreins on a band of ambitious, hard-nosed young men who were entrenching themselves in the foreign ministry's bureaus, a deficiency which did not help an important modernization of its operations (1907-21) which he inaugurated.[28] On the other hand, he had served in important diplomatic posts, notably as minister in Peking during the Boxer Rebellion and as resident-general in Tunisia (1901-1906), and was respected enough for his tact and diplomatic judgment by many insiders at the Quai d'Orsay, including Jules Cambon and Philippe Berthelot, for Briand to keep him on in the next ministry and Barthou to choose him again in 1913. He also was skillful with words, an important talent in this post, and had a beautiful voice. (When Sir Maurice Hankey heard him speak in 1919 at the Peace Conference, he thought he at last understood why this unprepossessing man had "gotten on."[29]) Clemenceau unquestionably called the shots, but in Pichon he had a very knowledgeable lieutenant and a veteran parliamentary hand whose personal loyalty had met every test for a quarter-century and who knew how to temper his vagaries and bluntness with finesse and a quiet courage.[30]

The future premiers, still comparative youngsters--Aristide Briand and Louis Barthou, both forty-four, and René Viviani, Joseph Caillaux, and Gaston Doumergue, all forty-three--comprised a firm, vigorous core for his cabinet while as individuals not being strong enough yet to threaten his leadership. The genial Doumergue (Commerce, later Education) helped keep Radical feathers smoothed. Briand (Education and Religion, later Justice), whose golden baritone could soothe the most fevered assembly, was a virtuoso of conciliation with contacts everywhere. Viviani, a prodigious orator, found favor with the Left as an Independent Socialist charged with the new ministry of labor and social security, whose creation met a demand going back to 1848. He was heavily engaged in shaping the complex regulations for the Old Age Assistance and Weekly Rest laws--the myriad small businesses wanted exception which usually drew left-wing criticism-- and in byzantine negotiations with Caillaux (Finance) and the Senate over funding of the proposed Workers' Pensions Law, not a point which the Chamber had liked to think about. Barthou (Public Works), a superb debater, tough and adroit, found himself well tested by the Western Railway bill. The company even stooped to bribery and blackmail threats to defeat it and in the Senate (25 June 1908) came within three votes of toppling the ministry. He also had to contend with the question of civil service unions and the troubles of his under-secretary, Simyan, with striking postal workers. As a Left Center moderate he was in tune with the basic majorities in both houses on these issues.

Caillaux, whose skill in finance was almost as high as his own opinion of it, served as the indispensable expert in the area which was Clemenceau's weakest suit. (A corporation executive, Nicolas Pietri, one of his closest friends, was once heard to exclaim, "M. Clemenceau is a child in business, a child!"[31]) He carried the marathon struggle over the income tax to victory in the Chamber. Writing after his wartime prosecution by Clemenceau, he asserted that his chief had left the whole battle to him and had let him down.[32] Evidence on the latter point is sketchy at best. When he threatened to resign once (31 January 1909), it was because of his dissatisfaction with the 1909 budget, and Clemenceau hastened to calm him down. All in all, they got along with each other with a minimum of friction. Nothing suggests that Caillaux had wanted to share the spotlight, and both men knew who understood the bill's intricacies. Clemenceau's role was to ram through confidence votes, which he did without obvious hesitation, while Caillaux in turn respectfully deferred to him in general policy matters.[33] Ultimately Caillaux justly got the credit (and the blame) for the most important tax reform since the Revolution.

A joke made the rounds that the second worst job in the world was being a prefect under Clemenceau--the worst, a minister. When a deputy reminded him later that he had been in the opposition during his first ministry, Clemenceau shot back, "Me too!"--asserting that he had opposed all his ministers. Certainly he tried their mettle. He disliked memoranda, preferring to confer face-to-face. These encounters could be unnerving, given his daunting presence and extreme impatience with rambling explanations. Two minutes of chatter was the outside limit, a friend observed, after which no power on earth could hold him still.[34] Despite an utter freedom of expression and a cocky air, signalled by the trademark jaunty tilt of his hat, he had a high sense of responsibility--perhaps excessively so, which might account for his prickly sensitivity to points touching the government's authority or dignity and his tendency at times to take more drastic action than was warranted.

He held his ministers to strict account in following policy lines. While in this regard authoritarian, he was no busybody and avoided undue interference in their work, although he did keep Picquart and Pichon on short leads. (Even in relations with servants he respected delegated responsibilities. Having announced a destination, he would leave routes and other details entirely to the chauffeur, although anything less than top speed would usually bring an impatient tap on the shutter from his cane.) He was, in fact, occasionally criticized for leaving too much to his ministers and being uninformed on legislative details. The charge has some truth in it. Despite decades in lawmaking bodies, he was not fundamentally a legislator but a critic and *animateur*. As such, he was in talents and temperament miscast as the chief of a cabinet framing large quantities of complicated legislation. Apart from his duties as minister of the interior, far more a political than legislative post, he involved himself most in foreign affairs, a non-legislative field par excellence, where he was on the whole successful.

By and large his minsters expressed few regrets at having served with him. Occasional "scenes" and sarcastic swipes--"Oh go, and take your forty hairs with you!," he snapped once when the shiny-domed Caillaux asked to leave[35]--were relieved by good-natured bantering, paternal airs, use of nicknames (which he coined habitually), and the pleasure of being led to the fray by a man who loved a fight. In time and not without some pain they learned how to get along with him. Years later Barthou recorded an amusing and wholly typical instance. In the course of a meeting, the eminent prefect of the Seine, De Selves, was startled by Clemenceau's sudden scowling displeasure over something he had said. During a recess Barthou drew him aside and told him he had used a non-standard verb, *solutionner* (analogous to "finalize"), instead of *régler* or *résoudre*. When they reconvened De Selves presently used a correct word, to the beaming approval of the Old Man and the relief of everyone else.[36]

V

The fact that the ministry's eventual resignation came unexpectedly as the result of a personal incident in the Chamber underscored the failure of the opposition to find a suitable issue. Compromises on the religious question to satisfy the Pope were sweetened for the Combists by high-handed treatment of the Vatican's agent, Monsignor Montagnini, expulsions of bishops from their residences, and stern measures protecting the state's rights over church properties. Careful handling of the Moroccan question left Jaurès and the *Colonialistes* to cancel each other out. The former's almost obsessive fear that Germany might take umbrage made him sound as if he were searching for arguments to put in Chancellor Bülow's mouth, while grumblings in the latter camp about alleged failures to support the army or Sultan Abd al-Aziz raised the ghosts of 1905.

Senate stalling on reforms frustrated the Chamber and ministers alike, but who wanted a constitutional crisis? Besides, there were always deputies willing to blame senators for killing bills they had passed but secretly disliked. Even *Le Temps*, the most prestigious organ of the big interests, tired of the Senate's dawdling on workers' pensions. Both employers and the unions resisted the bill, the former because they feared increased expenses, the latter because state-subsidized benefits might make union membership less attractive. The obligatory features of the bill also gave trouble; Clemenceau himself had opposed obligatory social insurance in his earlier years.[37] To the relief of many politicians, the complex financing of the scheme handed the Senate's commission an excuse to spend months in actuarial computations, abetted by the fact that Viviani's and Caillaux's own estimates conflicted. Caillaux, not surprisingly, had the last word: expectations would have to be curbed.

The expense of the new social legislation, when added to the budgetary effects of military expenses deferred from 1905, the Midi winegrowers' revolt, and a business slump from latter 1907 into 1909, were proving that a petrified tax system could not meet modern demands. Hence the income tax. The bill was a minefield, but in the end many deputies found themselves against a wall of past promises. Many there were, too, for whom the thought of the Senate graveyard brought unexpressible comfort. Pelletan himself admitted in 1909 that a secret ballot on the bill would have garnered only two-hundred votes--leaving one to puzzle over his thesis that the government was lagging behind its "real" majority.[38]

Labor troubles aroused passions and gave the ministry its worst moments, but contending views again cancelled each other. The backwardness, confusion, and erratic enforcement of labor legislation were both cause and effect of troubles in the unions. While strong enough to make a stir, their small memberships, scattered locals, miniscule treasuries, and feuding leaders left them too weak to hold out for long in strikes and thus drawn to compensate through inflated rhetoric and violence. Violent strikes were six times more frequent before the War than after. Only 8.6 percent of labor was unionized, 3 percent in unions belonging to the General Confederation of Labor (CGT),[39] whose rotten-borough organization (allowing one vote in its congress to each union regardless of size) favored the smaller, and generally less responsible, unions at the expense of the large ones. On the other hand, although by 1906 fifty percent of the labor force was employed by only one percent of all industrial firms, tens of thousands of employers--more numerous than ever before or since--often as not opposed unions root-and-branch.[40] The whole tradition of French working-class life, from the failed *journées* of the Great Revolution through the June Days and the Commune, fed a sense of alienation. Hence the appeal of apolitical doctrines preaching that the workers must free themselves by their own efforts--a vicious circle, because freedom could be won only through the kind of large-scale organization which such a milieu stymied at every turn.

The Socialists claimed to speak for labor, but they lacked solid backing among the workers and gazed wistfully toward Great Britain and Germany where huge, well-financed unions supported the Labour Party and the Social Democrats. Jaurès, despite his tireless efforts, often brought to mind Ledru-Rollin in 1849, following the crowd down the street because he was their leader. The government was in similar straits. There was nobody to negotiate with; or what amounted to the same thing, there were too many, both unions and employers. Absent collective bargaining laws and strong, responsible unions, troubles with scabs were inevitable. The Radicals, Clemenceau included, not to mention groups to their right, could never fully come to grips with this problem because of their allegiance to individual liberty. The right to life, Clemenceau told Jaurès, had to take precedence over the right to improve one's lot.[41] His point was indisputable, but he was framing the question like a philosophe defining the State of Nature. When troubles arose, the government had to act. In the great debate of June 1906, with an eloquence in portraying harsh realities which Viviani once compared to hail hitting a roof,[42] he levelled Jaurès with a question:

> But you, I ask you--it's not a question of Jules Ferry but of you and me--in my place what will you do if your prefect telegraphs: "They are pillaging a miner's home"?
> Have the courage to reply, since you interrupt, and say yes or no if you will act to protect order!
> I'm waiting for your reply. (*Lively applause on the left and center.*)
> You have no reply?
> By not replying you have replied. (*Lively applause on the left.*)[43]

In 1909 he was still asking Jaurès for an answer. There could be none--none, that is, short of finding ways to resolve disputes before miners' homes were pillaged.

The ministry ran its greatest risks when dealing with unionism among minor *fonctionnaires*, especially postal workers and teachers, where patronage questions intruded, a particular preoccupation of the Radicals. In 1909, having promised privately (not in so many words, but clearly enough) that Simyan would be replaced, Clemenceau exploded when the postal workers publicly announced that they no longer "recognized" Simyan. The Chamber backed Clemenceau, grudgingly, when he stated he would not rehire men fired during the ensuing strike. The affair indirectly hastened his fall. Briand, his successor, was famous for never saying never. Briand's experience proved, however, that the problem of labor unrest was fundamentally systemic rather than due much to the personality of the premier of the moment. Unlike Clemenceau, who was principled, rigid, and rather out of touch with the current labor movement, he was opportunistic, flexible, and quite knowledgeable about it, having begun his career as a Socialist lawyer defending anarcho-syndicalists. Yet Briand's relations with militant labor were in the main similar to Clemenceau's.[44] When the railwaymen struck in 1910, for example, he replied by drafting them into the army, no less. Yet for all that it was not he, but Clemenceau, who found himself labeled for posterity as a "strikebreaker." Personality, it seems, often has more to do with the conferring of labels than do actions.

To sum up, the government could count on overwhelming support in both Parliament and the country when it acted to protect public order, but although it repeatedly tried conciliation and mediation, it was hampered by the rudimentary state of laws, concepts, and organizations relating to labor. So it temporized, falling back on traditional methods when pressed while fending off calls to break up the CGT in the hope, which began to materialize late in 1908, that it would modify its statutes so as to give a greater voice to the larger, more moderate unions.

VI

However much Clemenceau's fame ultimately centered on his role in the War and the Peace Conference, his tenure at the interior ministry in 1906-9 strongly affected his reputation among his own countrymen. His first three months--marked by the horrendous Courrières mine disaster (1,200 deaths), a great wave of strikes and demonstrations, national elections, and repeated interpellations--made for a rude introduction to responsibility. On the evening he accepted Sarrien's offer of a portfolio, he rode home with Émile Buré, a veteran of *La Justice* and *L'Aurore* who had joined his ministerial staff. The thunder of the Courrières explosion (10 March) had scarcely died away before a roar of anguished rage from the Black Country miners had come rolling in. Buré sensed his torment. Clemenceau finally broke the silence:

Mon petit, you are a Socialist; I assure you that at the Place-Beauvau I shall try to apply what I preached in the paper. I am and remain against preventive sending of soldiers into strikes. I hope the Socialists will find it in their hearts to facilitate my task of peacemaking.[45]

It was not to be. Tracing a scenario he had once imagined in print, he went to the scene, "hands in pockets" and at considerable personal risk, to talk to the miners and managers, promising not to call in troops if they would discipline themselves.[46] The dramatic gesture failed. Opposing camps accused him of taking sides, incitement, and grandstanding. Violence welled up, miners against the companies, but also miners against miners--the old moderate union versus a new anarcho-syndicalist one and both against scabs. After passing "some of the abominable hours of my life,"[47] he sent troops but ordered them to stay in the background. When trouble continued he brought them out in force, although with strict instructions to endure to the limit before using their weapons. The orders cost a young lieutenant his life, but the rifles did not crack in reply. Hunger and discouragement eventually drove the miners back to the pits. Clemenceau caught it from all sides, the Left accusing him of denying his past by using troops to "break" a strike, the Right charging he had provoked trouble with dilatory methods.

The May Day affair completed the tableau. The occasion had been preached up for more than a year, not merely as the traditional demonstration in favor of the eight-hour day, but as the opening of the Final Struggle against capitalism. Respectable bourgeois householders panicked and rushed to lay in supplies against the dread Day. Clemenceau decided to take no chances. He called in some CGT leaders on 24 April for a friendly chat in which he couched a warning that if there were trouble he would do his duty: "You are behind a barricade and I am in front of it; your means of action is disorder; my duty is to keep order. My role, therefore, is contrary to your efforts."[48] On the strength of police reports of influence and infiltration by right-wing elements in the CGT, reports which had been accumulating since 1903 but whose multiplication during the miners' strike had impressed the Sûreté Générale, he ordered searches and the arrest of several right-wing activists and CGT leaders on May Day eve. Meanwhile, he brought nearly 50,000 troops into Paris for posting near potential hotspots. The Day passed with some fights and stone-throwing resulting in 28 hospitalizations and 665 arrests (492 of them "cool-offs"), but again he took heavy fire.[49] The "plot" smelled too much like pre-election scaremongering, for the cases were soon dismissed, and since violence had been sporadic it was argued, after the fact, that the Day never had posed a threat commensurate with the measures taken.

Despite the notoreity Clemenceau earned for his use of the military in strikes during his first ministry, the instances have not to date been systematically cataloged or analyzed. All things considered, those which at least drew attention in Parliament appear to have involved clearly dangerous situations or, arguably, an overriding public interest: the Nantes dockers' strike (1907), after a striker was killed; the vast Midi upheaval in 1907, obviously beyond containment by available police; subsequent May days in Paris (1907 was a small-scale 1906, while 1908 and 1909 were untroubled); the Draveil strike (1908), when dragoons were sent to patrol a fourteen-mile stretch along the Seine after clashes between scabs and strikers; mail shipments by the navy during the seamen's strike (1909); use of soldiers to replace striking Paris postal workers, the small minority who finally did walk out, and deployment of armed patrols after some telegraph lines were sabotaged (1909); and threats to use army engineers to restore power during the Paris electricity stoppages in 1907 and 1908.

The events of the spring of 1906, nevertheless, sufficed to brand him early as "the man on the other side of the barricade" and to read into this a denial of his past. Later that same year at a meeting of policemen to which he had been invited by the famed prefect of police Louis Lépine, he warned against abuse of their authority. The Republic's police, he said, are "servants of the law, not the instruments of despotism." In the course of his remarks he jokingly observed that his own post made him in effect the "Top Cop" (*le premier des flics*) in the country.[50] The press picked up the quip, and the tag stuck. Its connotation underlay the Socialists' visceral opposition to his accession during the War and the readiness of the workers to forget that it was he who in 1919 got the Eight-Hour Day Law passed--shades of May Day, 1906.

The smoke of battle tended to obscure his position. He was a man of the Left but not of the Commune. (René Benjamin found him late in life still moved by a memory. An old man and his grandson had hailed him from behind a barricade where they were awaiting certain death, asking him at least to cry, "Vive la Commune!" He did.[51]) The Revolution of 1870 had returned sovereign power to the people; and in a republic, change may be sought only through peaceful exercise of civil liberties. The French, he thought, having spent a millenium acquiring habits appropriate to life in a despotism, were still learning the disciplines of self-government.[52] When they sought change with guns, pickhandles, and paving stones they were expressing atavistic impulses. He never forgot that democracies are historical rarities and mostly of recent vintage--a thought quite natural to a man who, had he been born only ten months earlier, would have qualified as a contemporary of a member of the Jacobins' Committee of Public Safety.[53]

The latent power of the Right had always seemed to him greater than that of the Left, a theme he stressed frequently during this ministry. As he put it once to Léon Abensour, "...the whole history of the Revolution demonstrates this great truth: violence exercised by the party of Liberty always rebounds against the party of Liberty."[54] It is more than doubtful, for example, that he believed the "plot" of 1906 amounted to much by itself. But he *was* concerned that the labor movement might abandon the Republican camp if the revolutionary syndicalists should prevail. As did most people at the time, he overestimated the syndicalists' strength in the movement. Determined though he was to protect moderate unionists from subversion by the radicals, his deepest concern was to see that the Right reaped no benefits from the disarray in labor's ranks. Violence would in the long run, he believed, most likely drive the masses--the bulk of them conservative at heart, devoted to family and property--into the arms of the Church and the army. The Bonapartes had known this and profited accordingly. Thiers and the Moral Order had battened on the Commune. The masses had cheered Boulanger. Had they ever been truly Dreyfusard? He would have been among the last to be surprised at the Vichy regime or, for that matter, the success of Gaullism.

In 1906 the inventory riots and papal intransigence over the regime of the *associations cultuelles*, moreover, were raising the specter of endless religious conflict to which labor violence would contribute a Red Scare. He permitted himself some ill-timed mockery of Briand over the debacle of Article IV--"We are in the midst of incoherence because we've been put here. *J'y suis, j'y reste.*"*--but he vowed to make no martyrs for the Right even if it meant revising laws to meet each papal veto.[55] Combists cried that because of his [sic] "incoherence" he had "capitulated to Rome." Instead, the Right had had ground cut from under it by an outspoken anticlerical who nevertheless hated persecution and was anything but stupid.

VII

Calling in the army to preserve order was at best distasteful and at worst downright dangerous. France, as did most countries then, lacked sufficient and competent police. Paris and Lyon were reasonably well served by nationally run forces, and Clemenceau extended this regime in 1908 to Marseille. But in general, police manifestly lacked numbers and training to deal with very large or especially violent movements. The Gendarmerie, a specialized branch of the army constituting a national rural police and scattered in small units in some 3,600 localities, was used in preference to the army, as a rule. But it was undertrained in crowd control, undermanned, and paid less than the Paris street sweepers. In 1906 and 1907 the government proposed creation of a *gendarmerie mobile* which could be dispatched to troubled areas, but the idea was a political nettle. The Right feared its use by anticlericals against religious protestors, the Socialists feared it as a strike-breaking organization, and the Radicals, caught in the middle and traditionally worried about civil control of the military, let it drop with the silent complicity of the government.[56] Clemenceau did improve the Sûreté Générale, putting it under a remarkable police official, Céleste Hennion, its only head before or since who was not a member of the prefectorial corps, and created (1907) the Brigades mobiles de police judiciaire (which later came to be called the "Tiger Brigades"), especially to counter a crime wave

---

* "I am here, and here I stay," General MacMahon's famous Crimean War dispatch.

by gangs using automobiles to elude local police. But the Sûreté and Brigades mobiles, despite their titles, were investigative and coordinating, not protective, services.[57]

Lacking, thus, a proper riot police, such as the later Garde Républicaine Mobile (1921) and Compagnies Républicaines de Sécurité (CRS) which furnish current interior ministers with the bulk of some 30,000 trained operatives, Clemenceau had to resort, as had his predecessors, far more quickly and often than today's governments to that bluntest of instruments, the army. Although he had often criticized use of troops in strikes, contrary to some assertions he had never vetoed it absolutely. A statement in 1882 regarding a miners' strike in the Gard typified his attitude: "I say that you have sent in the army without there having been a true conflict, without your having to reestablish an order which [in any case] had not been troubled."[58] So saying, he tried to depart from the practice of using troops at the beginning of a strike and in a "preventive" role, i.e., to discourage non-strikers from joining the strike by their presence. But after 1906 he never waited as long as he had during the miners' strike before sending in soldiers. He became impressed, too, by the other, more conventional, meaning of prevention: that is, the presence of troops might indeed inflame tempers and undermine the strikers' appeals for support, but their absence for very long can encourage the growth of large crowds and correspondingly large, rather than minor, levels of violence.

He also showed an undeniable taste for dramatic and rapid measures when persuaded that he must make a move. (In 1899, one notes, he had given evidence of this propensity when he had roundly criticized Waldeck-Rousseau for his wait-them-out handling of Jules Guérin and his comic-opera insurrectionaries during the "siege of Fort Chabrol."[59]) Nevertheless, if by 1909 he had gradually moved back toward the old strategy of "prevention through saturation," he left in force his circular of 16 April 1906 admonishing prefects to avoid provoking strikers by using troops too hastily, and he issued (via Picquart, 18 October 1907) a detailed Instruction which prescribed limits on the army's methods and increased the civil authorities' powers over the troops used in strikes.[60]

That he would keep a tight rein on the military was a foregone conclusion. His attitude toward the army was rooted in a suspicion of the officer corps stemming from his experiences during the Second Empire and the war of 1870-71, a suspicion which the Boulanger and above all the Dreyfus affairs did nothing to abate. Like most of the Left, he had come to think that the corps was shot through with clericalism and anti-republicanism. He had refused to countenance the crasser methods of surveillance used by Combes and André, but neither he nor his successors ceased compiling political dossiers.[61] That such suspicions were largely mistaken has become clear in hindsight. The vast majority of officers, even at the highest levels, were non-clerical and apolitical in attitude, wanting only to be left alone to pursue their profession and hotly resenting doubts expressed about their loyalty to the legally constituted regime, whatever it might be. Ironically, in pursuit of a largely phantom political threat, the Left sought to politicize to its own tastes an army that preferred to have as little as possible to do with politicians of any hue.

Its morale already low in the wake of the Dreyfus and André scandals, miserably underpaid, its training and equipment starved by an unsympathetic Parliament, and intensely uncomfortable when called to perform domestic police duty, the army found Clemenceau's regime a trial. Morale hit bottom and recovered hardly at all before the War. The appointment of Picquart, newly promoted to general, as minister of war amused Clemenceau and sent a message, but it was not what the army needed. Reduction of the traditional protocol rankings of officers (1907), whose thin pay-envelopes had since the Revolution been partly augmented by marks of public esteem, gratuitously injured their self-respect and was not worth the pleasures some politicians, including Clemenceau, may have felt at seeing a mere sub-prefect occupy a finer seat at a banquet than a colonel twice his age and vastly senior in service. Sending several hundred members of the 17th Infantry off to disciplinary battalions in southern Tunisia for mutinous acts when called out during the Midi winegrowers' revolt could perhaps be justified. But the real culprits were the steady erosion of the authority of officers and non-commissioned officers (which the well-intentioned Courts-Martial Reform Bill could only abet) and the system of regional recruitment--which resulted in reservists having to level their weapons at their relatives and neighbors, as had happened in the Midi.

Some parade was made of the creation of a Conseil Supérieur de Guerre, an upgrading of the Reserve's training periods, and a filling of the Two Years' Service Law's deficiencies, but the latter measures' financial inadequacies were such that the Generalissimo,* General Hagron, resigned in protest (20 July 1907). And when Admiral Germinet, commander of the Mediterranean fleet, criticized in a press interview the navy's sorry supply situation, Clemenceau promptly sacked him (5 December 1908) for insubordination. But the deficits continued. It is small wonder that his appointment (24 September 1908) of one General Foch to direct the War College despite his having a Jesuit brother has always seemed worth special notice.[62]

VIII

On the other hand, whatever his attitudes toward the military establishment, Clemenceau was indubitably a patriot, espousing sentiments that would sound quaint and at times even hollow to generations raised in the wake of two world wars--a bedrock, tricolor patriot of the Old Left, which put him out of step with the growing internationalist pacifism of the newer Left at the same moment that the Right was abandoning an aristocratic cosmopolitanism for nationalist themes. By remaining part of the old, however, he stayed in communion with the large majority of his countrymen, who were wary of internationalism, revolted by Gustave Hervé's "Let's put the flag on a dunghill" brand of pacifism, mistrustful of Rightist chauvinism, and bemused by Barrèsist lyricism about "blood and soil" but who were still resolved to defend *la patrie* without a backward look if the call should come. A simple faith, really, whose clean beauty would trickle into the mud of Verdun and the Aisne, never to be quite the same again.

Hervéism, though distinctly a minority opinion among the Socialists, became a millstone around their necks as a result of its currency among the anarcho-syndicalists and the debates it sparked inside the Second

---

* The vice-president of the Conseil Supérieur de Guerre and ex officio the designated general-in-chief in case of war. The Chief of Staff was charged with day-to-day operation of the army.

International, a dead weight which not even Jaurès' feats of verbal legerdemain could lighten. No single issue did more to sour relations with the Radicals,[63] hinder reform legislation, tar the union movement with a big black brush, and stir up the public to no constructive end. Many good Dreyfusards, even, took alarm, renounced the Bloc, and fell to accusing Clemenceau of taking too soft a line toward a looming threat of leftist anarchy, which they feared would bring back *la Réaction* to strangle the Third Republic as it had the Second. In their eyes, especially after the hitherto "reliable" winegrowers and *fonctionnaires* were infected, Jaurès had become an arsonist, while Clemenceau was an incompetent, "incoherent" fireman.[64]

Contrariwise, from the Socialists' perspective, Clemenceau was using Hervéism as a red herring to assure himself of easy triumphs in public opinion and the Palais-Bourbon. But his denunciations of it were not merely tactical even if they did help him to recoup in the Center what he lost on the Far Left. He had paid his dues in the fight against right-wing nationalism, and charges that he was toadying to reactionaries to get their votes were both stupid--he did not want or need them--and personally offensive. He put the case in a nutshell once when the Socialists protested that an attack on Hervéism was winning applause from the Right: "They love me against you." *"Socialisme, voilà l'ennemi!"** cried Édouard Vaillant, a noble old Blanquist survivor of the Commune. "It's impossible to understand less what I've said," he replied, to general laughter.[65] He had debated the issue in the press before he came to office, most recently (as noted) in 1905 with Jaurès, and he understood his opponents' arguments. His deep feelings on the subject, however, made calm discussion difficult. The spectacle of a school teacher, for example, advocating insurrection as the answer to *la patrie en danger* appalled him. As an issue, in short, Hervéism was a distraction he was emotionally unable to ignore.

But that was not the whole reason. Hervéism and anarcho-syndicalism had become bedfellows. All governments in the prewar decade worried about the effect of violent strikes on their countries' social fabric and morale at a time when international storm-clouds were gathering. Above all

---

* Recalling Gambetta's war cry in 1877, "Clericalisme, there is the enemy!"

they worried about possible strikes in key industries, utilities, and transport during a mobilization. Hence they were highly sensitive to any inroads syndicalism and Hervéism might make among state employees. Clemenceau's unbending response to the postal strike in 1909 was his reply to a growth of syndicalism among some postal employees and was meant to show the CGT that the government would draw a line when it came to vital public services. To underscore the point, and to cover his political flanks, he concurrently showed himself more conciliatory toward the railway workers and merchant seamen, who were little affected by syndicalism. His move paid a dividend by easing passage of the Railway Pensions Law in July, which (for the time being) averted a dangerous strike.[66]

The ministry's problem with the long-festering issue of the rights of civil servants, in particular the right to organize, would have been troublesome enough without the distracting intrusions of Hervéism and anarcho-syndicalism. How distinguish private civil rights, for example, from the rights of the state to exact obedience from its agents? Who are *fonctionnaires*? Employees in shipyards? in tobacco works? postal clerks? teachers? May *fonctionnaires* form unions? (Unofficial unions, "associations," had long been tolerated.) May they strike? Is a union truly a union if it cannot strike? May civil service unions affiliate with the CGT? The issue was a basket of crabs, especially for the Radicals because of their large clientele among minor state employees. The controversy, in fact, was a harbinger of the future movement of unionism, for it was among state employees that it would experience its greatest growth after the War. Pressured by the postal and electrical strikes, the ministry, reflecting the general confusion, proposed, withdrew, revised, and resubmitted a *statut de fonctionnaires*, but to no avail. About all that a wearisome train of interpellations proved was that Parliament would not countenance strikes in "essential" services or affiliations by employee "associations" with the CGT and would support the government *in extremis* whenever it decided some *fonctionnaires* had crossed the still-undefined line dividing the exercise of civil rights from obedience to state authority.

IX

Meanwhile, the machinery of state rumbled on. At the ministry of the interior, Clemenceau gave bureaucrats and routines a dust-raising pummeling. (He had once compared the bureaucracy to a giant capstan harnessed to the task of lifting a fly.[67]) The central offices were reorganized, its administrative inspectors markedly improved, and its budget increased by twenty-five percent. But more ambitious plans came to nothing. Administrative decentralization, for example, part of the government's formal program, would wait another sixty years before making perceptible headway against Napoleon's legacy. When the dust settled the routines continued much as before. Failure to achieve a major reform of the bureaucracy, he confessed later, was one of his greatest disappointments.[68]

His term at Interior not surprisingly earned him a reputation as a "fist." The personnel there shuddered at the memory. Such popularity as he enjoyed with the public in these years often was distilled from tales of hard-bitten prefects emerging ashen-faced from his office, of snap inspection and sign-in sheets to catch malingerers, and favors granted or withheld for quixotic reasons. The pestiferous applicant for a decoration, for example, who is at last "authorized" to wear the Grand Cordon...but only in his bedroom.[69] Or the story of the prefect who had taken to spending most of his time in Paris. M. Clemenceau calls him in for a mortal five minutes, tells him his train leaves in thirty minutes and that he'd better be on it. The shaken fellow dashes to the station, jumps aboard and rides home. As he comes in the door, the phone rings:

"Ah! *c'est vous?*"

"*Oui, monsieur le ministre.*"

"You didn't miss your train? *Bonsoir, mon cher.*"[70]

Firmly believing that public servants owe a day's work for a day's pay, exasperated with red tape, and detesting favoritism or petty tyrannizing by bureaucrats, he cracked the whip with a will, a lion tamer at the Place-Buveau as in the Palais-Bourbon.

His ministerial staff found life a great trial. Jean Philip, who had been with him at *L'Aurore* and was a senator after the War, served for awhile at the beginning until he thankfully escaped. In his memoirs he served up several pages of caustic recollection of the experience which leave the impression that Clemenceau's long years in the nonchalant ambience of newspaper offices had not comprised a proper apprenticeship for running a great department of state. He seemed well suited, Philip thought, to rule from afar and on high (the editor-in-chief and his lead article) but out of his element in daily administrative routines. As a first-timer, unlike most major ministers, he arrived without an entourage of experienced assistants and proceeded to throw a staff together as if he were still at *La Justice* or *L'Aurore*, i.e., according to his mood or whimsy and with only the vaguest definitions of people's duties. He seemed to expect them to be able to turn their hand to anything at a moment's notice at any hour. Long stretches of silence and inactivity would be shattered by the dreaded impatient ringing of his bell and a volcanic eruption about something or other, important or trivial. Occasionally, it was true, he might call one in and sit quitely, munching his habitual chocolate or patting his dog, saying, "I'm listening"; but one got out of there as soon as possible. Nobody knew what to expect, and morale suffered in consequence. To young Philip he seemed to be a mass of nerve endings, "a tormented soul." Only once, and to his amazement, did he "catch a glimpse of the depths." Early one morning, Clemenceau came out of his office and said to him in a poignant, agonized tone, "Philip, I'm disgusted with others and with myself." But then the cry stopped brusquely and he said no more.[71]

He showed scant respect for the rules of administrative procedure and delighted, for example, in ignoring seniority tables in promotions, notably when it came to the prefectorial corps. One memoir-writer went so far as to say that prefectorial transfers were his "grand preoccupation."[72] It might be noted, however, that a student of the subject has concluded that while there was a fairly large number of transfers, it was rare for a prefect to be dropped, and those who were got other positions in the *grands corps* or the finance ministry.[73] He seemed, indeed, to carry something like a grudge toward this key service--perhaps a kind of subconscious desire to avenge the sufferings his generation had experienced at having been, or seeing their fathers, bundled into prison coaches. The anecdote related above tells something about what prefects experienced at his hand in turn. Philip related a more painful instance. Accompanied by the prefect of the Var, whom he had recently promoted, Clemenceau visited a school. Entering a classroom, he told the pupils, "You don't know, my children, what a prefect is and what he's good for? For this!"--and with an insulting gesture he tossed his coat across the prefect's arm as if he were a valet. Whatever embarrassed giggles he got were surely not worth it. Did he think such acts were funny and assume they would be taken in a light spirit? Or didn't he care one way or another? Or what? In any case, the man remained a friend, but he never forgot the scene. When Philip voted against Clemenceau for the presidency in 1920, the prefect remarked, "I understand that."[74]

Perhaps the transition to a position of authority was too abrupt for one who had spent a lifetime on the outside. On the one hand, it was exhilarating to be able to give orders and see things happen pronto. He *liked* to have things happen pronto. When Claude Monet told him in 1907 that Manet's *Olympia* should be sent to the Louvre--a controversial move--he had it there in three days: no need for wheedling letters, petitions, articles, and comings and goings.[75] The exhilaration probably accounts in good measure for the note of stridency which marked a significant amount of his behavior during these years. On the other hand, his past and persona made him an irresistible target if he should fall the least bit short of brilliance in anything he did. The Great Critic, the Wrecker, was fair game for the press and all the men who had suffered for forty years from his pen, tongue, and pistols. There is every reason to think he was highly aware of this and that it put his system on edge. Since he was the last kind of a man to run from a fight-- fights, too, exhilarated him--it put him in a habitually confrontational mode. And not just against "others" but also himself. It is worth noting, however, that when he arrived in power a second time, in 1917, he appeared to be in markedly better control of himself--he knew he *had* to be because of his age and health, if for no other reason--and in better control of his role as an administrator.

X

While demanding of others, he kept a rigorous regime for himself. He continued to live at the rue Franklin apartment, to rise early, and put in hours that belied his years, although keeping sacred the early afternoon reading and nap. For weekend relaxation he leased (1908) and later bought a run-down hunting lodge with a small farm attached at Bernouville (Eure), about fifty miles from Paris, the Vendée being too far away. (He kept it until 1922.) At work his attention to detail varied according to interest or mood. He was no clean-desk man and relied heavily on an excellent memory. His judgment was extraordinarily rapid: he routinely answered 100-200 letters a day, dictating responses instantly. Sometimes it ran to impetuousness, though it was generally sure, and in crises he could stay cool; but small impediments irritated him inordinately. He could bide his time, but when he acted he could be too impatient for results. He was a good listener despite his outbursts, could take advice, and his ego was strong enough to tolerate reversing a decision or admitting a mistake without mulish resistance.

Some other characteristics, nevertheless, did not always serve him well. He showed a prickly sensitivity about his privacy and a penchant for secrecy. An odd symptom of this was his preference for old-fashioned sanding instead of using paper blotters, which he thought were indiscreet. Surprisingly, perhaps--but perhaps not--his relations with the press left something to be desired. Charles Morice, a prominent journalist who dealt with every premier from 1902 to 1940, found him the most resistant of all to being interviewed by the press. At the beginning he regularly called them in, but one day a young reporter wrote an item which prominently mentioned the bottles of medicine on his desk. Angered by this (rather mundane) violation of his privacy, he refused to admit anybody and gave out news only through his under-secretary of state. Eventually he relented, but only to the extent of choosing five or six reporters to see him in his office on important days.[76]

In a like mode, possibly because of what a journalist friend described as "a fear of the unknown and the unforeseen consequences entailed,"[77] he paid too much attention to raw police reports. It was said that unlike Waldeck-Rousseau, who had grandly swept them into a basket every morning, Clemenceau (ever the journalist) would pour over the stuff. He seemed to savor the air of intrigue, the underside of police activity--a Blanquist legacy. He felt genuine sympathy, for example, for Marcelin Albert, who had gotten in over his head as leader of the Midi winegrowers' revolt. But immediately telling the press about Albert's secret interview with him, that Albert had shed tears and expressed repentence for the trouble he had caused--things which could only tend to discredit him in the eyes of his followers--could not help but feed suspicions of Machiavellianism. When the Métivier affair came to light in 1911, such suspicions seemed more than amply confirmed. Since it has remained the most controversial single episode of his ministry, the affair deserves a word.

It occurred in connection with a long, bitter strike (2 June-4 August 1908) of the Draveil (Seine-et-Oise) sandpit workers which cost six lives in clashes with police on 1 June and 30 July. The latter affray took place during demonstrations protesting arrests on 27 July of several persons for incitement, one of the more outspoken of whom was Lucien Métivier, secretary of the pastrymen's union. Métivier was later (1911) revealed to have been a paid informer who had visited Clemenceau at the ministry on 20 May. The 30 July bloodshed in turn forced the CGT leadership to make good on a long-standing threat to call a general strike, an action it privately had come to fear would fail. The fear was well founded. The general strike on 3 August flopped dismally. Anarcho-syndicalism, long in trouble, declined slowly from this point on, while the CGT was rent by quarrels from which a new, basically reformist and non-revolutionary, leadership emerged in early 1909.

In light of what had followed Métivier's arrest, had Clemenceau used him not merely as an informer but as an *agent provocateur* to call the CGT's hand? So the question runs, but no conclusive proof has turned up, nor is it likely to. Métivier, it must be said, would have been a poor choice as a *provocateur* since he had no strong following or influence and already was under some suspicion among the CGT chiefs. Moreover, his supposed service was hardly necessary, for the Draveil strike had long attracted a buzzing, multi-hued swarm of idealists and troublemakers pretty clearly bent on provocation. The weight of supposition, however, has usually fallen against Clemenceau. The chain of circumstances is too nicely linked not to have aroused suspicion. That he had wanted bloodshed is more than doubtful, but there is no disputing that throughout the strike he showed more readiness to confront than to conciliate and that he ruthlessly exploited his advantages in the conflict, even to the rash--and cynical--extent of invoking Métivier's name in debates as an example of union extremism.[78]

To conclude, Clemenceau was quite capable of exercising tact, patience, and finesse. But open challenges were something he had the greatest difficulty in brushing off. Once in a fight, he played to win, and he enjoyed it. This combativeness also reflected itself now and again in brutality and bullying in personal relations. Labeling issues with the names of persons as he was wont to do--a habit picked up from Blanqui?[79]--can be a useful mental shorthand but is liable to mislead when prejudicial opinions enter in. Admittedly, a natural peremptoriness can often leave an impression of insensitivity where none is intended. Nevertheless, a species of sadism can be detected in him, a counterpart to his very high level of interior sensitiveness. "I cannot love someone without ragging [*engueuler*] him," he once remarked. "Ragging is my safety valve. As soon as I've finished I feel calm and in a better frame of mind."[80] He felt he needed to take strong precautions against any play on his sympathies lest he fail his duty. If he were to err in action, he preferred that it be on the side of over-forcefulness. (On one occasion, having become irritated by the delicate strokes of a billiards partner, he proceeded to slam the balls around the table. Emphasizing his words with the butt of his cue, he growled, "You'll never get anywhere with your goodness, Granet. In life you have to be bad! bad! bad!"[81]) As a fellow journalist once wryly observed, "M. Clemenceau can be terrible when you prevent him from being kind."[82] His personality, in short, abounded in defiant complexities. Léon Abensour, his secretary for several years, could not recall having been the object of a single harsh word from him, although sometimes he would be silent for days on end.[83] Many others testified quite differently. An old acquaintance perhaps put it best when he concluded that one had to be around the man for a very long time before one truly began to understand him.[84] Such knowledge necessarily was forbidden to all but a few. The rest coped with him as best they could.

XI

In foreign affairs, Clemenceau's reputation for outspokenness and as a *protestaire* of 1871 and an advocate of the English connection preceded him into office. It aroused some misgivings at home and abroad, but he soon showed he was no wild man. When still only interior minister he played a role in seeing to it that France would emerge from the Algeciras Conference with her alliances intact and German political hopes in Morocco foreclosed. As premier, after settling some scores at the Quai d'Orsay--Aunay was reinstated and sent to Berne, Philippe Crozier replaced a "réactionnaire" at Vienna, Paléologue was sent away to Sofia[85]--he conducted affairs with a caution but firmness which won him genuine respect in the chancelleries. The delicate balances among the Powers mandated a policy of prudent brokering.   Agreements with Britain and Spain on the western Mediterranean (16 May 1907) and with the North Sea border-states (23 April 1908) to maintain the status quo in these areas, sponsorship of a Russo-Japanese pendant (30 July 1907) to a Franco-Japanese accord respecting the "integrity" of China (10 June 1907), and a discreet encouragement of an Anglo-Russian entente (31 August 1907) marked new steps in the march back from the near-isolation of 1905.

To the surprise of many, Franco-German relations in general were never better between 1871 and 1914 than they were during his ministry. Morocco might have spoiled them and did brush by disaster once when the Casablanca Deserters affair suddenly turned grave. The muddy formulae of the Algeciras Convention gave little guidance through the feudal anarchy there.   Failure to protect the lives of foreign nationals who were being subjected to outbursts of xenophobia would have compromised France's hard-won rights, but every action risked a German reaction and scenes in Parliament. Germany had to be kept informed--no repetition of Delcassé's blunder--but without handing her a veto power.   Jules Cambon, a highly skilled diplomat and advocate of a conciliatory policy toward Germany in colonial questions, was transferred from Madrid to Berlin in the spring of 1907 at the moment incidents in Morocco had begun to accumulate. He and Clemenceau and Pichon walked on eggs.   Clemenceau wanted no protectorate over Morocco and did not want to intervene there militarily if he could avoid it; but neither did he want German influence on the Algerian border.   He had always thought, he was to say in 1912 in the Senate, that because of Algeria, Morocco was an exceptional case in the colonial sphere.[86] Pichon, a founder of the Groupe Colonial in Parliament and more responsive than his chief to imperial concerns, likewise resisted being hustled by the *Colonialistes* and their allies among the Algerian generals, although Cambon and Clemenceau sometimes felt a need to buck him up about it.[87]

The expedition sent in 1907-8 despite Clemenceau's considerable misgivings to pacify the coastal region after anti-foreign outbreaks was controlled from Paris as far as spotty communications permitted. But field commanders needed latitude to cope with hit-and-run raiding and complained bitterly about orders reflecting "governmental anarchy" in Paris, or what they viewed as such.[88] General Drude was over-cautious, or over-controlled, and fell ill. General Lyautey, whose proconsular airs both irritated and impressed Clemenceau, was delegated to watch over d'Amade, Drude's almost-too-vigorous successor. Clemenceau nearly went too far in tying French fortunes to Abd al-Aziz, who was being challenged by his brother. The feeble young sultan was the fragile link to the Algeciras accord, whose unimplemented police regime for the ports (with Spain) gave France such legal standing as she had for the intervention. But contacts were established with the victorious Mawlay Abd al-Hafid in time to prevent his falling into a waiting German embrace.

The Casablanca Deserters incident (25 September 1908), in which French authorities seized several Foreign Legion deserters from German consular officials aiding their escape, occurred after the expeditionary force had begun to leave. It took on menacing tones mostly because Chancellor Bülow saw opportunities to score a cheap diplomatic victory, pressure the Entente in the early stages of the Bosnian crisis, and divert domestic attention from his gaffe in approving the kaiser's embarrassing interview in the *London Daily Telegraph*. More than once Clemenceau flared up hotly at Bülow's erratic proceedings, but Cambon and Pichon were quick with appeals to his good sense. Together they waited out an investigation which produced a report on the incident at variance with the sketchy German version, and they got timely assistance from Vienna, where efforts had been made early during the ministry to establish friendly relations.

The contradictory reports gave Bülow a graceful excuse to retreat to his initial proposal, which had been to send the case to the Hague Tribunal. Clemenceau had accepted this solution but then had had to hold firm when

Bülow abruptly set conditions which included apologies in advance for the actions of the French arresting agents. Clemenceau later toned down a famous story that said he had pulled out his watch and told the German ambassador, Prince Radolin, who had asked for his passports if the condition were not met, that he had better hurry if he didn't want to miss his train. Such treatment of ambassadors, he said, was not his "style."[89] (Prefects were different.) Diplomatic files in fact mention no Clemenceau-Radolin interview.[90]

The affair, nevertheless, came closer to precipitating a war than was generally known then or later. Its gravity may be judged from entries Lord Esher made in his journal:

> I have never known a more anxious day [5 November]. I was at the Defence Committee for many hours....
> On Saturday last [7 November] it looked like war....The French have behaved perfectly and with great distinction....They never asked or attempted to enquire whether we were going to their assistance. In point of fact, Asquith, Grey and Haldane had decided to do so.[91]

As Clemenceau told Barthou afterward, "*Mon petit*, until you've dealt with the Germans, you'll never know what those words, *querelles d'Allemagne*,* can mean."[92]

This close call if anything appears to have hastened completion three months later (9 February 1909) of a treaty with Germany--the only such bilateral accord between 1871 and 1914--which recognized French political concerns in Morocco in return for encouragement of mutual economic operations there. Caillaux later claimed that Pichon had sprung it on Clemenceau, an intrinsically unbelievable story.[93] Both sides reaped some domestic political credit for it, especially Bülow, who also was anxious to put the English off balance. But the advantage lay with France, which had traded hypothetical future benefits for written confirmation of a presently strong position. The treaty seemed a hopeful augury, but nothing much came of it before it died in the Agadir crisis of 1911-12.

---

* "German quarrels," a popular term for petty disputes.

XII

Close ties with Britain and Russia were a condition of success in dealing with the Germans, who Clemenceau believed respected strength alone. Barely two days in office in March 1906, with the Algeciras Conference at a crisis point, he officially reassured the Russian ambassador that he could not regard Russia with anything except "sympathy and confidence" and that he wished to help conclude the pending loan.[94] Thereafter he tried to protect Russia's credit on the Bourse and keep her from indiscretions while she was still recovering from the Far East disaster. More particularly, he put on pressure to use the loan money to build strategic railways to ensure a rapid westward concentration of their army. Relations tended to be uneasy, with neither partner regarding the other's intentions or military power as altogether reliable.

The great test arrived in the crisis over Austria-Hungary's annexation (6 October 1908) of Bosnia-Herzegovina from the Ottoman Empire. It trailed on until the end of March 1909 and proved to be a dress rehearsal for the crisis of July 1914.[95] Count Izvol'skii, the Russian foreign minister, had met with his Austrian counterpart, Count Aehrenthal, at Buchlau in Bohemia on 16 September and agreed not to protest an annexation of this region (which Austria had administered since the Congress of Berlin in 1878) in return for support in opening the Straits to free navigation by all the states bordering the Black Sea. But Aehrenthal had then stolen a march and announced the annexation much sooner than Izvol'skii had been led to believe (or so he claimed) and before he had been able to finish contacting the other Powers about the Straits. When Serbia exploded in indignation, having come to regard Bosnia as her destined outlet to the sea, and Russian opinion rallied behind their South Slav brethren, the stage was set for a highly dangerous Austro-Russian confrontation.

Throughout the crisis France held close to a line of preventing a conflagration at any cost except a ditching of the Russian alliance. At bottom, Clemenceau, the Quai d'Orsay, and informed French opinion generally viewed it as a Balkan, not a European, quarrel. They did not think especially highly of Izvol'skii, didn't think that Russian interests in the question were primordial, took a reserved view of the Serbs' objections,[96] and not unnaturally regarded Morocco as a more vital issue for France and European peace, hence something worth the risk of war, than the fate of a region they had long come to think of as Austrian. Great Britain's attitude, which was stiffer than France's on the whole, also concerned them, for if war broke out France would be more vulnerable to attack than the British behind their sea rampart. Consequently, French policy remained reserved, willing to support Britain and Russia in a crunch but taking only limited initiatives.

Through the winter of 1908-1909, Great Britain and France tried to guard an exit for Izvol'skii via a proposal to recognize the annexation only in a formal conference and with some kind of compensation (probably economic rather than political) for Serbia. It failed. Austria firmly opposed having an issue of such importance to her decided by others, even for appearances' sake (which is about all the conference would have come to), and Germany only drew closer to her in the face of what looked like an Entente "gang-up." Moreover, France had benefited from Austria's good offices in settling the Casablanca Deserters affair--which largely accounts for a sudden shift by France in mid-October until latter November toward an almost pro-Austrian stance on the annexation--and did not want to jeopardize the new Morocco treaty's chances with Germany. As for the English, they had never been keen on opening the Straits to Russian warships and thus were anything but enthusiastic about Izvol'skii's bargain at Buchlau.

The crisis finally deflated with unexpected speed when Germany sent (21 March) a thinly disguised ultimatum to Russia to drop support of Serbia's protests. Since the Turks by now had long accepted the annexation (12 January), the protests had become rather an embarrassment.[97] Izvol'skii, his nerves cracking, was privately relieved by the ultimatum, which gave him a convenient excuse to drop the affair despite renewed assurances of loyalty from Britain and France. Nevertheless, he and Russia came out of it all feeling they had been let down by their partners. France subsequently got paid back when Russia signed a secret agreement with Italy in October 1909 to maintain the status quo in the Balkans without informing France, made an agreement with Germany on Persia and the Baghdad railway in November

1910, and refused to be of much help during the Moroccan crisis of 1911-12.[98]

XIII

Measured by friendly visits and mutual expressions of esteem, the Anglo-French Entente looked to be in the best of health. But Clemenceau wanted more--for example, a strong expeditionary force ticketed for the Continent in case of a German attack. While in London in mid-December 1905, three months before he joined Sarrien's ministry, in fact, he raised the subject privately with Lord Esher (13 December) in anticipation of troubles which might arise at the forthcoming Algeciras Conference. His initiative, however, appears to have had at most an indirect influence in starting up the military staff consultations, which began to be discussed on 16 or 18 December and not undertaken seriously until January.[99] The case was critical because the Russians were reluctant to renew assurances of offensive action against Germany in case of war. Unsupported French regiments could not hope to withstand the full weight of the kaiser's hosts. He also insistently urged British leaders to adopt conscription: it was not Trafalgar but Waterloo that finally had brought Napoleon down, he reminded Edward VII at Marienbad in 1908 during his annual Karlsbad cure.[100] But a parliament which later would resist a draft until two years into a world war could scarcely be expected to heed a French premier who appeared to be dealing with the Germans quite capably.

It is easy to forget, moreover, that the Entente was still very new while Anglo-French rivalry was very old. The French did not cease overnight to be "frogs" for masses of Englishmen nor the English "perfidious" to like numbers of Frenchmen. The Mediterranean agreement in 1907, for example, was directed against German pressures there, but the form the accords took partly reflected suspicions the partners held of each other.[101] It remained true that Britain, not Germany, was still France's principal imperial rival, and consequently the *Colonialistes* in particular (and their friends at the Quai d'Orsay) tended to anticipate more long-term profit from a cooperation with Germany overseas at Britain's expense. At the same time, Britain's strong support during the 1905-1906 crisis could be offered as assurance that France need not worry so much about any threats from the Germans, at least for now. Clemenceau, however, was not so sanguine. He genuinely admired the English for their free institutions and got along well with them in personal relations. But he was no sentimental Anglophile, and he had no illusions about their motives in foreign policy--and for cause: their imperial interests in turn made the need to support France something of an embarrassment, the more so since their military means were lacking, as he was always reminding them.[102] He had long since concluded that it was imperative for both countries, for their own good, to stand together against the present and potential menace of Germany's military and economic power so long as she did not change her authoritarian ways.

All things considered, it would not be hard to argue that at the end of the Clemenceau ministry the position of Britain, Russia, and France vis-à-vis Germany and Austria was not as strong as it had been in 1906. The Anglo-French staff conversations had pursued a fitful course. Not until the end of 1908 did the Admiralty, with no help whatever from Admiral Fisher, begin to evince much interest in parallel naval arrangements.[103] Meanwhile, the unreformed regime of the tsar was stumbling on. Clemenceau left office shrouded in gloom about the future.

Nevertheless, he had shown he was someone to be reckoned with in diplomacy. Paul Cambon, heretofore no particular friend, was impressed: "He understands, he gets roused up, but he listens, providing you know very well what you want to say and get to the point."[104] Prince Radolin, after early misgivings, soon reported to Berlin that with him "you know exactly where you are."[105] In a different forum, a distinguished German editor who interviewed him was struck by his ability to combine candor with the impenetrability of "a Dalai Lama."[106] French pride grew. A leader who could unself-consciously trot off to visit the museums of London, Vienna, Munich, and Berlin, or send unciphered telegrams to the Quai d'Orsay from Karlsbad as a way of informing the Germans that his policy regarding Morocco was what he had *told* them it was, or dedicate monuments to Goblet, Scheurer-Kestner, and Gambetta with moving yet unprovocative evocations of the wrong done to Alsace-Lorraine,[107] something no premier had risked before: a man of this stamp was one to keep in mind.

Even so, for Clemenceau personally, the frustrations of office seemed to bulk larger than the satisfactions. Conscientious public service is never easy. Addressing his constituents at Draguignan after only seven months in harness, he reflected on his responsibilities in words which were among the wisest he ever spoke: "You'll never appreciate us enough for the evil we *don't* do."[108]

NOTES
CHAPTER XI

1   It was said that Sarrien recommended Bourgeois but did not insist.   Bourgeois declined a more-or-less *pro forma* invitation from Clemenceau to continue at Foreign Affairs.

2   See JOC, 12 July 1909, p. 2017; and HE, 4 Feb. 1916. Significantly, the conversations with Martet are almost devoid of references.

3   See especially Norman Stone, *Europe Transformed, 1878-1919* (Cambridge, MA: Harvard University Press, 1984), pp. 11, 107-128 (a section entitled "1905: the Ghost of 1848").

4   See Thelma Liesner, *Key Economic Statistics, 1900-83: Main Industrial Countries, United Kingdom, United States, France, Germany, Italy, Japan* (New York: Facts on File Publications, 1985), Table F.6; and Peter N. Stearns, *Revolutionary Syndicalism and French Labor: A Cause Without Rebels* (New Brunswick, NJ: Rutgers University Pres, 1971), pp. 18, 111-120, a revision of the usual claim that real wages had risen since 1900.

5   JOC, 5 Nov. 1906, pp. 2386-2387; and Steven C. Hause, with Anne R. Kenney, *Women's Suffrage and Social Politics in the Third Republic* (Princeton, NJ: Princeton University Press, 1984), pp. 16, 94, 98, 129, and *passim*.   Hause cites a 1907 pamphlet by Clemenceau, *La "Justice" du sexe fort*, previously unknown to me, which stated the need to institute equal rights for women, but not the suffrage until the distant day "when they are rid of their atavistic prejudices," i.e., Catholicism.   On his lack of support for the suffrage in 1919, which the Radicals and the Senate also opposed, see *ibid.*, pp. 222-247, *passim*, 280-281.

6   JOC, 19 June 1906, p. 2009.

7   JOC, 27 Feb. 1908, p. 457.   Nevertheless, the Third Republic down to 1914 has never been given sufficient credit for laying the foundations of the welfare state.   See William Logue, *From Philosophy to Sociology: The Evolution of French Liberalism, 1870-1914* (De Kalb, IL: Northern Illinois University Press, 1983), pp. 10, 221-222.

8   JOS, 16 Nov. 1906, p. 911.

9   JOC, 14 May 1907, p. 1000.

10   GC, *La mêlée sociale*, p. xxiv.

[11] On Marx and Engels see Zévaès, *Clemenceau*, pp. 111-114; and Watson, *Georges Clemenceau*, pp. 85-86. On Herr see Charles Andler, *Vie de Lucien Herr (1864-1926)* (Éditions Rieder, 1932), p. 95; and Julliard's essay in *Clemenceau et la justice*, p. 112, citing a thesis I have not been able to consult: Daniel Lindenberg, "Les écrits posthumes de Lucien Herr," Thesis, 3rd cycle, University of Paris V, 1979), ch. 8, "Herr et Clemenceau," pp. 160-176.

[12] Often attributed to him, but derivation is uncertain.

[13] Agulhon, in *Clemenceau et la justice*, p. 89.

[14] JOC, 19 June 1906, p. 2008.

[15] Hyndman, *Clemenceau, the Man and His Time*, p. 130, indirect quote except for "founded...." As late as 1911 the rural population (locales of less than 2,000 inhabitants) numbered c.56% of the whole; see Jean-Marie Mayeur and Madeleine Rebérioux, *The Third Republic from Its Origins to the Great War, 1871-1914*, trans. J. R. Foster (Cambridge: Cambridge University Press, 1984), p. 333.

[16] Maurel, *Clemenceau*, p. 29.

[17] See JOC, 18 June 1906, pp. 1994, 1998; and Georges Lefranc, *Le mouvement socialiste sous la troisième république*, 2 vols., 2nd ed., rev. (Payot, 1977), 1:172.

[18] JOC, 19 June 1906, p. 2007.

[19] JOC, 12 July 1909, p. 2016.

[20] Lady Milner [Violet Maxse, formerly Lady Cecil], "Clemenceau intime," *Revue des deux mondes*, 15 Feb. 1953, pp. 615-616. The remainder of the statement indicates that he had the religious question especially in mind. Lady Milner says it is difficult to convey the modesty and simplicity of his declaration. He wished, she said, to serve not the cause of a party, but the country.

[21] Judith F. Stone, *The Search for Social Peace: Reform Legislation in France, 1890-1914* (Albany, NY: The State University of New York Press, 1985), p. 89. See also Susan Rovi Mach, "French Radical Ideology, 1906-1914: The Audience, the Medium, the Message" (Ph.D. diss., Bryn Mawr College, 1980), from *Dissertation Abstracts International: History, Europe*, vol. 41/08-A, p. 3691.

[22] Theodore Zeldin, *France, 1848-1945*, 2 vols. (Oxford: Oxford University Press, 1973-77), 1:722. See also Paul Warwick, "Ideology, Culture, and Gamesmanship in French Politics," *Journal of Modern History* 50 (1978):638-639.

[23] JOC, 19 June 1906, p. 2011.

24   JOC, 14 May 1907, p. 1007. On the clash of temperaments see Nordmann, *Histoire des radicaux*, pp. 162-165.

25   See JOC, 24 June 1909, pp. 1630-1637, on the use of police notes.

26   He respected Picquart but found him a poor leader. Simyan (a personal friend) and Thomson, respectively too stiff-necked and too lenient, could not master notoriously wasteful and inefficient ministries, while Milliès-Lacroix's ignorance of colonial affairs became a subject of jokes.

27   He was named only after Bourgeois, Poincaré, and De Selves had declined. Millerand wanted it and declined Justice.

28   See John F. V. Keiger, *France and the Origins of the First World War* (New York: St. Martin's Press, 1983), pp. 24-39, *passim*, very critical of him.

29   Lord [Maurice, 1st Baron] Hankey, *The Supreme Command, 1914-1918*, 2 vols. (London: George Allen & Unwin, 1961), 2:821-822.

30   See *Le Radical*, 24 Oct. 1906; *Le Temps*, 26 May 1908; Jules Laroche, *Au Quai d'Orsay avec Briand et Poincaré, 1913-1926* (Librairie Hachette, 1957), p. 96; Pierre-Antoine Perrod, "Autour d'une correspondance inédite: Stephen Pichon et ses amis," *Revue des sciences morales et politiques* 139 (1984):43-62; and D. J. Miller, "Stephen Pichon (1857-1933) and the Making of French Foreign Policy, 1906-1911" (D.Phil. diss., Cambridge University, 1977), unpublished, which I have not been able to consult.

31   Chichet, *Feuilles volantes*, p. 252. On Pietri see Louis Altieri, *Nicolas Pietri, l'ami de Clemenceau* (Albin Michel, 1965).

32   Joseph Caillaux, *Mes mémoires*, 3 vols. (Librairie Plon, 1942-1947), 1:255-257, 266.

33   See Chamber debates of 16 Jan., 27 Feb., 25 May, 9 July 1908, 2 March, 12 July 1909; Jean-Claude Allain, *Joseph Caillaux*, vol. 1: *Le défi victorieux, 1863-1914* (Imprimerie Nationale, 1978), pp. 93-95, 349-352, and *passim*; and Rudolf von Albertini, "Die Diskussion um die französische Steurreform, 1907-1909," *Schweizer Beitrage zur Allgemeinen Geschichte* 13 (1955):183-201.

34   Georges Lecomte, *Georges Clemenceau: The Tiger of France*, trans. Donald Clive Stuart (New York: D. Appleton, 1919), p. 108; anecdotes in Treich, *L'esprit de Clemenceau*, pp. 20-21, 37.

35   Stevenson, *Lloyd George*, p. 28.

36   Louis Barthou, "Sous les griffes du Tigre," *Les Annales*, 15 Dec. 1929, p. 544.

37   See, e.g., JOC, 31 Jan. 1884, p. 257.

38   Camille Pelletan, "La crise du parti radical," *La Revue (Ancienne Revue des Revues)*, 15 May 1909, pp. 145-164. But see also Judith F. Stone, "Political Culture in the Third Republic: The Case of Camille Pelletan," *Proceedings of the Western Society for French History* 13 (1986):225-226.

39   Viviani's figures, in JOC, 23 Oct. 1908, p. 1882.

40   There were some 3,927,000 enterprises or self-employed persons. See Sanford Elwitt, *The Third Republic Defended: Bourgeois Reform in France, 1880-1914* (Baton Rouge, LA: Louisiana State University Press, 1986), p. 4; and L.-H. Parias, ed., *Histoire du peuple français* (Nouvelle Librairie de France, 1953), vol. 4: *De 1848 à nos jours*, by Georges Duveau, p. 175.

41   JOC, 19 June 1906, p. 2006. See also AU, 6, 12 July, 20 Aug. 1904.

42   Martin du Gard, "Clemenceau."

43   JOC, 18 June 1906, p. 2001.

44   See Arthur Fryar Calhoun, "The Politics of Internal Order: French Government and Revolutionary Labor, 1898-1914" (Ph.D. diss., Princeton University, 1973), pp. 304-306; J. Stone, *The Search for Social Peace*, p. 97; and Madeleine Rebérioux, "Jaurès devant les radicaux et le radicalisme," *Société d'études jaurèsiennes, Bulletin*, no. 94 (1984):29.

45   Émile Buré, "Clemenceau et la classe ouvrière: Réponse à R. de Marmande de 'Syndicats,'" *L'Ordre*, 14 Aug. 1938.

46   See GC, *La mêlée sociale*, pp. 319-320. He visited twice, on 17 March and 18-19 April.

47   Speech at Solliès-Pont (Var), in *Le Temps*, 10 Oct. 1908.

48   Nicholas Papayanis, *Alphonse Merrheim: The Emergence of Reformism in Revolutionary Syndicalism, 1871-1925* (Boston: M. Nijhoff, 1985), pp. 22-23. See also *Le Temps*, 25, 26 April 1906.

49   See Calhoun, "The Politics of Internal Order," pp. 304-306; and Georges Carrot, *Le maintien de l'ordre en France*, 2 vols., Thèse Droit, Nice, 1982 (Toulouse: Presses de l'Institut d'études politiques, 1984), 2:685.

50   See *Le Temps*, 3, 4 Dec. 1906.

51   Benjamin, *Clemenceau dans la retraite*, pp. 220-221.

52   See GC, *Injustice militaire*, pp. 479-483.

53   Bertrand de Barère died on 13 Jan. 1841. The reputed last Girondin, Doulcet de Pontécoulant, died in 1853.

54   Abensour, *Dans la cage du Tigre*, p. 70.

55   JOC, 30 Jan. 1907, p. 355. Briand walked out, but Clemenceau apologized, heading off a resignation and a possible cabinet crisis. He resisted, however, Briand's suggestion that a veto over appointments to bishoprics be established: "We must remain in the logic of separation....That is none of our business." Maurice Larkin, *Church and State After the Dreyfus Affair: The Separation Issue in France* (New York: Harper & Row, 1973), pp. 167-168.

56   See especially Jean-Claude Jauffret, "Armée et pouvoir politique: La question des troupes spéciales chargées du maintien de l'ordre en France de 1871 à 1914," *Revue historique* 270, no. 547 (July-Sept. 1983), pp. 127, 144, and *passim*.

57   See Philip John Stead, *The Police of France* (New York: Macmillan, 1983), pp. 4-7, 70-76; Georges-André Euloge, *Histoire de la police et de la gendarmerie: Des origines à 1940* (Librairie Plon, 1985), pp. 269-273; and Carrot, *Le maintien de l'ordre en France*, 2:652-659. On Hennion see Duroselle, *Clemenceau*, pp. 506-509.

58   JOC, 9 March 1882, p. 272. See also Leo Loubère, "Left-Wing Radicals, Strikes, and the Military, 1880-1907," *French Historical Studies* 3 (1963):93-105.

59   See GC, *Justice militaire*, pp. 394-398, 457-469.

60   An Instruction (20 Aug. 1907) issued in the wake of the Midi troubles, reinforced the Circular of 23 Sept. 1905 which gave the government wide latitude in requisitioning troops for internal security. See Calhoun, "The Politics of Internal Order," pp. 15-16, 86-87, 291-292, 317-319, 327-330, 379-381, and *passim*.

61   See Pierre Rocolle, *L'hecatombe des généraux* (Éditions Lavauzelle, 1980), p. 357. On other matters below see especially Douglas Porch, *The March to the Marne: The French Army, 1871-1914* (New York: Cambridge University Press, 1981), pp. 87-88, 180, 202-212, and *passim*.

62   He confirmed the famous story--"I have a brother, a Jesuit." "I don't give a damn." [*Je m'en fiche.*]--in *Grandeur and Misery of a Victory*, pp. 15-16, and in Martet, *Le Tigre*, p. 104. But see also Wormser, *La république de Clemenceau*, pp. 41-43; Charles Le Goffic, *Mes entretiens avec Foch, suivis d'un entretien avec le général Weygand* (Éditions Spec, 1929), pp. 92-103; and

J. Ruinant, "Autour de Clemenceau (d'après de recentes publications)," *Revue des questions historiques*, 1 July 1930, pp. 80-81, 85.

63   As Ferdinand Buisson moaned, "What finally determined the retreat of the Radical spirit--in spite of its resistance to anarchism--was the debatable anti-patriotic propaganda of Hervé." Buisson, *La politique radicale* (Brière, 1908), p. 81, as quoted in J. Stone, *The Search for Social Peace*, p. 221n.

64   See Gérard Baal, "Un salon dreyfusard, des lendemains de l'Affaire à la Grande Guerre: La marquise Arconti-Visconti et ses amis," *Revue d'histoire moderne et contemporaine* 28 (1981):446-447; and *idem*, "Jaurès vu par les radicaux," *Société d'études jaurèsiennes, Bulletin*, no. 94 (1984), pp. 35-36.

65   JOC, 6 April 1908, p. 893.

66   See Calhoun, "The Politics of Internal Order," pp. 172-174, 379-385.

67   Scheurer-Kestner, *Souvenirs de jeunesse*, p. 11.

68   Geffroy, *Georges Clemenceau*, p. 100.

69   Octave Homberg, *Les coulisses de l'histoire: Souvenirs, 1898-1928* (Arthème Fayard, 1938), p. 81.

70   Treich, *L'esprit de Clemenceau*, pp. 19-20.

71   Philip, "Souvenirs d'un parlementaire désabusé," no. 151, p. 25; see also pp. 18-30, *passim*.

72   Henry Maunoury, *Police de guerre, 1914-1919* (Éditions de la Nouvelle revue critique, 1937), p. 13, writing about his first ministry.

73   Jeanne Siwek-Pouydesseau, *Le corps préfectoral sous la troisième et la quatrième république* (Presses de la Fondation nationale des sciences politiques, 1969), p. 79.

74   Philip, "Souvenirs d'un parlementaire désabusé," no. 151, p. 28.

75   But he had to intervene again in 1917 to get the Louvre to display it. See Wildenstein, *Claude Monet*, 4:52-53, 371; and Weber, *France, Fin de Siècle*, p. 157. At the end of Oct. 1907 he participated in the negotiations for state purchase of Monet's *Cathédrales de Rouen* for the Luxembourg museum.

76   Charles Morice, *Quarante ans de journalisme, presse, et parlement: Souvenirs et anecdotes*, 2 vols. (Bibliothèque Nationale, unpub., n.d.), 1:67. See also Maurel, *Clemenceau*, pp. 62-63.

[77]   Paul Brulat in *Le Radical*, 28 Oct. 1906.

[78]   See JOC, 11 Feb. 1909, p. 357, and 12 July, p. 2007. For the 1911 revelations, probably instigated by Caillaux, see *L'Humanité*, 21-23 July; *La Bataille syndicaliste*, 22 July, 19 Nov.; *Le Temps*, 25 Nov. (Clemenceau's reply). Jacques Julliard, *Clemenceau, briseur de grèves: L'affaire de Draveil-Villeneuve-Saint-Georges*, présentée par Jacques Julliard (Collection Archives Julliard, 1965), is the most complete study, very critical but more balanced than R. de Marmande, *L'intrigue florentine*, 2nd ed. (Éditions de la Sirène, 1922). Worth consulting to compare conclusions are Watson, *Georges Clemenceau*, pp. 200-205; Calhoun, "The Politics of Internal Order," pp. 351-369, *passim*; Richard W. Sanders, "The Labor Policies of the French Radical Party, 1901-1909" (Ph.D. diss., Duke University, 1971), pp. 235-236 and *passim*; Allain, *Joseph Caillaux*, 1:366-369, *passim*; and Paul Mazgaj, *The Action Française and Revolutionary Syndicalism* (Chapel Hill, NC: University of North Carolina Press, 1979), pp. 62-72.

The chain of events has tended to encourage *post hoc ergo propter hoc* reasoning. More thought might be given to the question of why Clemenceau would have decided to risk direct provocation, assuming he wanted a showdown--which is likely but cannot be proved. A confrontation of some kind which could force the frustrated, hard-pressed syndicalist leaders to call a general strike--an issue on which they had painted themselves into a corner--was not unlikely to occur sooner or later. He had the stronger hand, and public opinion was behind him. The nearly two-month gap between the two clashes might suggest that his patience finally ran out, thus leading him to risk provocation. But it also might suggest that he was playing a waiting game, or even that he had no "game" in mind and was responding to events as they occurred. One other problem meriting thought: The fact that Métivier was an informer inevitably affects judgments about Clemenceau's silence on him and his failure to release him so as to avoid a now-likely violent confrontation. Clemenceau, for whatever reasons, chose not to violate the rule that governments do not expose their own agents. In this case four men may have died as a result. When such tragedies occur, where does guilt lie and how do we measure it? Hard questions indeed.

[79]   See Paz, "Clemenceau, Blanqui's Heir," p. 607.

[80]   Martet, *M. Clemenceau peint par lui-même*, p. 51. See also Gatineau-Clemenceau, *Des pattes du Tigre*, p. 115.

[81]   Stephane Lauzanne, *Great Men and Great Days*, trans. L. B. Williams (New York: D. Appleton, 1921), pp. 226-227.

[82]   J.-J. Cornély in *Le Siècle*, as quoted in *Le Radical*, 22 Dec. 1906.

[83]   Abensour, *Dans la cage du Tigre*, pp. 89-92, *passim*.

[84]   André Maurel, "Souvenirs intimes sur Clemenceau," *Revue de France*, 15 Dec. 1929, p. 709.

85   Aunay had been rumored to be posted to Berlin or Vienna. At Berne he lived in a villa named "La Favorita," which amused insiders. Paléologue was close to the Dreyfus Case and Delcassé. Erlanger says that Reverseaux told him he was not returned to Vienna when he refused to invite the Aunays to a dinner; Philippe Erlanger, *Clemenceau* (Grasset, Paris-Match, 1968), p. 365.

86   JOS, 10 Feb. 1912, p. 273.

87   On Pichon see, e.g., Christopher M. Andrew and A. S. Kanya-Forstner, *The Climax of French Imperial Expansion, 1914-1924* (Stanford, CA: Stanford University Press, 1981), p. 28.

88   General Lyautey to Jacques Silhol, 28 July 1907, in Hubert Lyautey, *Un Lyautey inconnu: Correspondance et journal inédits, 1874-1934*, ed. André Le Révérand (Librairie Perrin, 1979), p. 235. On d'Amade (below) see Jacques Augarde, "Le général d'Amade, pacificateur de la Chaouia," *Revue historique des Armées*, 1987, no. 1, pp. 24-32.

89   Martet, *Clemenceau*, pp. 233-234.

90   See Watson, *Georges Clemenceau*, p. 229; and especially Gerard E. Silberstein, "Germany, France, and the Casablanca Incident, 1908-1909: An Investigation of a Forgotten Crisis," *Canadian Journal of History* 11 (1976):331-354. Michel Clemenceau emphatically confirmed two interviews and says preliminary measures for a military alert were taken. He claimed to have been close to the scene and to have accompanied his father home after the second, at which Radolin had given way. Michel Clemenceau, "La vie ardente de Georges Clemenceau," Conférence faite aux anciens combattants de la Seine-Maritime le 11 novembre 1957" (MS, Musée Clemenceau).

91   Reginald Baliol Brett, 2nd Viscount Esher, *Journals and Letters of Reginald, Viscount Esher*, ed. Maurice V. Brett and Oliver, Viscount Esher, 2 vols. (London: I. Nicholson & Watson, 1934-1938), 2:356, 359.

92   Barthou,"Sous les griffes du Tigre," p. 544.

93   Caillaux, *Mes mémoires*, 1:277-279. See David R. Watson, "The Making of French Foreign Policy During the First Clemenceau Ministry, 1906-1909," *English Historical Review* 86 (1971):774-782. On the accord see especially Raymond Poidevin, *Les relations économiques et financières entre la France et l'Allemagne de 1898 à 1914* (A Colin, 1969), pp. 458-480, *passim*. On unofficial earlier probing see Peter Grupp, "Eugène Étienne et la tentative de rapprochement franco-allemand en 1907," *Cahiers d'études africaines* 15 (1975):303-311.

94   René Marchand, ed., *Un livre noir: Diplomatie d'avant-guerre d'après les documents des archives russes, novembre 1910-juillet 1914* [vol. 3 to 1917], 3 vols. (Librairie du travail, 1922-1934), 1:15. See also Count V. M. Kokovtsov, *Out of My Past: The Memoirs of Count Kokovtsov*, trans. L. Matveev, ed. H. H. Fisher (Stanford, CA: Stanford University Press, 1935),

pp. 115-117; and Olga Crisp. "The Russian Liberals and the 1906 Anglo-French Loan to Russia," *Slavonic and East European Review* 39 (1961): 496, 504-505.

95   The standard monographs remain Bernadotte Schmitt's *The Annexation of Bosnia, 1908-1909* (London: Cambridge University Press, 1937); and Momtchilo Nintchitch, *La crise bosniaque (1908-1909) et les Puissances européennes*, 2 vols. (Alfred Costes, 1937). The latter contains a convenient summary of French policy, 2:310-317.

96   See Ljiljana Aleksić-Pejkovič, "La Serbie et les rapports entre les puissances de l'Entente (1908-1913)," *Balkan Studies* [Thessalonika] 6 (1965):305-318, *passim*.

97   On the decline of France's influence at Constantinople, due in considerable measure to the peculiar operations of ambassador Ernest Constans, who seemed to profit from Clemenceau's indulgence, see L. Bruce Fulton, "France and the End of the Ottoman Empire," in Marion Kent, ed., *The Great Powers and the End of the Ottoman Empire* (Winchester, MA: Allen & Unwin, 1984), pp. 153-157, 166. One must wonder if Clemenceau knew of Constans' consorting with royalists (!) in 1898. See Larkin, "'La République en danger,'" p. 91.

98   See Keiger, *France and the Origins of the First World War*, pp. 88-89.

99   See George Monger, *The End of Isolation: British Foreign Policy, 1900-1907* (London: Thomas Nelson & Sons, 1963), p. 239.

100   On 26 Aug. 1908.   See France, Ministère des Affaires étrangères, Commission de publication des documents relatifs aux origines de la guerre de 1914, *Documents diplomatiques français, 1871-1914*, 3 series (Imprimerie Nationale, 1929-59), 2nd ser., vol. 11, no. 434. See also Great Britain, Foreign Office, *British Documents on the Origins of the War, 1898-1914*, ed. G. P. Gooch and Harold Temperley, 11 vols. (London: His Majesty's Stationery Office, 1926-38), 6: nos. 9-11; and Henry Wickham Steed, *Through Thirty Years, 1892-1922: A Personal Narrative*, 2 vols. (Garden City, NY: Doubleday & Page, 1925), 1:284-288.

101   See K. A. Hamilton, "Great Britain, France, and the Origins of the Mediterranean Agreements of 16 May 1907," in *Shadow and Substance in British Foreign Policy, 1895-1939: Memorial Essays Honouring C. J. Lowe*, eds. B. J. C. McKercher and D. J. Moss (Edmonton, Alberta: University of Alberta Press, 1984), p. 143.

102   See Watson, *Georges Clemenceau*, p. 388; and Keith M. Wilson, *The Policy of the Entente: Essays on the Determinants of British Foreign Policy, 1904-1914* (Cambridge: Cambridge University Press, 1985), pp. 2-3.

103   See Samuel R. Williamson, Jr., *The Politics of Grand Strategy: Britain and France Prepare for War, 1904-1914* (Cambridge, MA: Harvard

University Press, 1969), pp. 112-113, and *passim*; and Paul Halpern, *The Mediterranean Naval Situation, 1908-1914* (Cambridge, MA: Harvard University Press, 1971), p. 8.

104 P. Cambon, *Correspondance*, 2:260 (26 Nov. 1908). He was ambassador to Britain, 1898-1920.

105 Dispatch to Bülow, 13 Jan. 1907, as quoted in Duroselle, *Clemenceau*, p. 528.

106 Theodor Wolff, *Through Two Decades*, trans. E. W. Dickes (London: Heinemann, 1936), p. 264.

107 Speeches of 6 Oct. 1907 (Goblet); 11 Feb. 1908 (Scheurer-Kestner), in GC, *La France devant l'Allemagne*, pp. 26-29, 79; and 25 April 1909 (Gambetta).

108 *Le Temps*, 15 Oct. 1906 (italics added).

CHAPTER XII

Tiger in Waiting
(1909-1914)

On 20 July, only five days after it had emerged victorious from a month-long siege by interpellators, the Clemenceau ministry lost a confidence motion by 176 votes to 212 and resigned. No fewer than 175 deputies had left early for the summer recess, a large number on a jaunt to Scandinavia, among them some 79 who had supported the ministry in the closest vote (284 to 177) on 15 July and who evidently had concluded that the government was home free until the autumn session. They had decamped, moreover, despite a new Chamber rule which made voting by proxy impossible, thus leaving the ministry to the mercy of those actually present in the hall.

In reality, however, it was less the ministry which was overthrown on the 20th than its chief. The government's general policy still commanded a majority, as a 333-151 vote on the first part of the 15 July motion had shown. But the 284-177 margin on the second part, which had supported Clemenceau's rejection of amnesty for dismissed civil service strikers, could be read as a verdict on his personal leadership, and it boded him no good.

The number of deputies scouting a suitable occasion to drop him had in fact been growing for months. His handling of the Draveil and postal strikes had refueled charges of "incoherence," and his truculent replies reminiscent of newspaper polemics had too often soured debate. Three years of enforced association had eroded the patience and loyalty of his ministers, some of whom, most noticeably Briand and Caillaux, had ambitions of their own for the top spot. Especially dangerous to him was the Radicals' mounting dread of facing the voters in 1910 without assurance of Socialist support in run-off elections, a near certainty if he should stay on until then.

A less obvious factor at work, and by no means least in importance, was the state of his health. Throughout his ministry colds and bronchitis had plagued him intermittently. In 1909 he was down with grippe in the latter part of March during the tense final days of the Bosnian crisis and the start of the postal strike, and it hung on fitfully until past mid-May. Then in the middle of June the death from appendicitis of a beloved grandchild (Colette Gatineau, Thérèse's twelve-year-old daughter) had hit him quite hard and depressed him noticeably. His diabetes was now well established, too, and in addition to the cares of watching his diet, it subjected him to bouts of high irritability, its victims' fate before the introduction of insulin injections in the mid-1920s. Hence it is no surprise to find him a few days after his fall writing to General Lyautey that he was "in the greatest need" of rest.[1]

The "suitable occasion" had materialized suddenly when, on the eve of the summer recess, Delcassé had risen to speak on the report on the condition of the navy submitted (1 July) by a commission of inquiry which had been established with the government's grudging consent on 25 March. The naval question had festered since the spring of 1907. The explosion of the battleship *Iéna* on 12 March with the loss of 118 men had prompted a first inquiry. Thomson had had to resign as navy minister on 19 October 1908 as a result of a string of further accidents and charges of slipshod administration, and in 1909 his able successor, Alfred Picard, a professional engineer, had been obliged by Caillaux to reduce his request for supplemental appropriations, a reduction which had prompted the new inquiry. But the naval question had threatened the ministry less than several other issues, and it was assumed that Clemenceau would get off by accepting some criticism and a pallid confidence motion.

Delcassé, however, had set a lure. Caillaux, Jean Cruppi, Briand, and Viviani probably were *au courant*. He cunningly baited him with a charge (not without some merit) that he had been negligent in the 1904 investigation. Clemenceau at first feigned an insulting indifference, facetiously asking his neighbors in a very audible voice, "What's that gentleman's name?" But when Delcassé finished he went for the hook. Furiously accusing him of having once led the Republic to "the greatest humiliation we have endured," he thrashed on into a shocking violation of confidentiality by disclosing cabinet discussions in 1905 about the country's military unpreparedness. Delcassé, angry in turn in spite of himself, responded effectively in a tone of patriotic injured-innocence. In a din of shouts and banging desk-lids, the question was called and the vote taken. As the defeated ministers filed out, a voice cried above the tumult, "His name is Delcassé!"[2]

II

A friend recalled never having witnessed an explosion of happiness so sincere as Clemenceau's when he signed the decree naming his successor (Briand). "I'm in the full joy of deliverance," he wrote to another on the 21st. "No more people to see. No more demands. Nothing more but freedom."[3] On the 25th he set off for his annual cure at Karlsbad, savoring with the cream of Europe the delights of one of those last summers in the mountains before the farewell of '14. Edward VII courteously invited him down to Marienbad to share somber reflections on the Balkans and the feeble state of the British army.[4]

The vacation inaugurated five years of a freer, less frenetic existence than he had known in four decades. His debts largely liquidated, a handsome honorarium for lectures in South America in 1910 even conferring a relative affluence, he could invoke the prerogatives of age and eminence to work when he pleased, receive distinguished callers (e.g., Theodore Roosevelt in 1910), enjoy more than ever the company of writers and artists, attend the coronation of George V, and oversee production of a musical version of *Le voile du bonheur*. Produced by Paul Ferrier with music by Charles Pons, it opened at the Opéra-Comique on 20 April 1911 and ran for fifty performances. (The play was also filmed in 1910 and 1923.) The friendship with Claude Monet now became very close, helped by the coincidence that the artist's home at Giverny was only a dozen miles from Bernouville. During weekends there Clemenceau periodically would go over for lunch, a walk in the famed garden, and quiet contemplation of the great artist at work. In Monet's company his spirit seemed to expand and quiet down. Monet, who treasured calm and privacy, appears never to have complained about his presence--quite the contrary.

The Bernouville place proved to be a healthy diversion even though he usually spent only a couple of days at a time there and never stayed more than a week. The lodge was simply furnished and tranquil. He saw to the grounds with an ambitious planting program including some trees transplanted from his rue Franklin apartment (carried on the roof of his car), stocked the stream, and on the attached farm raised a couple of cows, a dozen hens, some swans, and several pigs, one of which to his great joy won a prize at a local fair. He also got in some hunting, always one of his greatest pleasures. And in May 1912, continuing in the spirit of the thing, he agreed to be elected to the town council. He resigned after only a year, however, when the mayor changed a decision on a swamp-drainage project without consulting the council.[5]

Family concerns also occupied him off and on, although not always happily. Michel had been educated in Switzerland as an agronomist. Energetic and headstrong, he had married a Hungarian while working in Austria, returned to France in 1905, and then gotten involved in some ill-advised business ventures while his father was premier, one of them with the army's supply services. As a result of the embarrassment and the financial burden his father assumed, their relations were badly strained until the outbreak of the War brought a tearful (and permanent) reconciliation. Madeleine, fortyish and widowed, a talented bluestocking with rather proud airs, wrote articles and novels and presided over a salon which the likes of Madame de Caillavet, Julien Benda, and sometimes Marcel Proust were known to frequent. Thérèse, involved in a contested divorce action which dragged on until 1911, for lack of money had had to move with her two children (one of whom, Colette, later died in 1909, as noted above) into the rue Franklin apartment for at least several months--exactly when is unclear but possibly during his first ministry: an uncomfortable situation for all concerned. On the other hand, meanwhile, his brothers prospered: Albert as a leading attorney with high business and political connections, and Paul as an engineer with Schneider-Creusot (the great metallurgical and arms concern) and ultimately as chairman of the board of the Compagnie Française de Dynamite, an affiliate of the Nobel cartel. Georges remained exceedingly close with Albert, but his relations with Paul had become rather distant after the deaths of their parents.[6]

III

Writing was what Clemenceau enjoyed most of all, especially in newspapers where, as he joked after his fall, "I can amuse myself with the idiocies of others instead of committing them myself."[7] After an abortive attempt to get control of *Le Petit Var* upon Dutasta's death, he founded *Le Journal du Var* (Toulon), which started up on 16 April 1910 with Mandel as its Paris director. The young man had continued to ingratiate himself after Alfred Roth, Clemenceau's right arm at Interior, and Étienne Winter, his long-time secretary, had decided to continue in the civil service. Clemenceau intended to write for the paper but presently was invited by the Alliance Française to deliver a series of lectures in Argentina, Uruguay, and Brazil.

The South American tour (28 June-27 October 1910) lifted his spirits and filled his pockets with a princely honorarium reported as coming to 300,000 francs--probably a considerable exaggeration.[8] He gave a set of eight lectures, on democracy, in Buenos Aires and repeated them (or portions) at Rosario, Tucumán (where he laid the cornerstone of an "École Georges Clemenceau"), Montevideo, São Paulo, and Rio de Janiero. In opera houses packed with high-paying subscribers, he captivated audiences who discovered him to be not only an eminent political figure but a highly cultured man. He was welcomed officially by the governments of Argentina and Brazil, undertook a busy round of visits to schools, museums, prisons, asylums, factories, and plantations, and in Brazil was even honored with a big army review. He noted that Marshal von der Goltz had raised Germany's prestige during a recent visit to these parts and was happy to do what he could to raise France's accordingly. True to form, he did not avoid controversy altogether. He refused to give permission to a theater director to stage a performance of *Le voile du bonheur* because Argentina had not adhered to the international convention on copyrights. The performance was given anyhow and was a great success, but he denounced it in a public letter.

As a result, an embarrassed Argentine senate signed the convention. In Rio de Janiero he agitated again, and Brazil soon followed suit with its own "Ley Clemenceau."[9]

"Gentlemen, Brazil is the land of the future," he announced to the press at dockside on his return, and then after a pause added, "In fact, Brazil will *always* be the land of the future."[10] In 1911 he published a collection of articles containing observations on the societies he had visited,[11] but renewed political activity permanently sidetracked a seven-volume (!) study of democracy for which he had begun gathering material before the trip. Léon Abensour had been put to work on this project. How formidable an affair Clemenceau had had in mind came home to him when he outlined the results of his researches into deepest antiquity only to be told, "That's fine, but the ants! the bees!"[12]

As for the lectures, although he had prepared the texts in advance with the assistance of Abensour, Mandel, and François Ichon, a member of his private cabinet during his ministry, he delivered them *ex tempore* after his accustomed fashion, departing freely from them as the spirit moved. Fortunately, notes were taken down by a traveling companion, Dr. Maurice Ségard, whom he invited along to watch over his increasing prostate problems. These notes along with jottings by Abensour were destined to comprise his most concentrated published discussion of political philosophy. The rubric, however, begs a liberal interpretation because, typically, he served up reflections and pointed observations rather than systematic constructions--the eternal critic-in-action.

He reaffirmed a belief in democracy and its eventual world-wide triumph, but his experience as premier and his uneasiness over threats to the peace markedly diluted any optimism about the near future. He accented the Darwinian note sounded in *La mêlee sociale*. Yet, with an insistence that hinted at private doubts, he clung to his idealism, trying to hold a middle ground between "might makes right" doctrines, especially those in vogue across the Rhine, and the (to him) unrealistic belief of pacifists in the power of "the will to peace." Force rules. It is an inescapable necessity in social relations, but--here an affirmation of faith, for who could prove it?--ultimate victory rests with force put at the service of justice.[13] Although his confidence in the triumph of civilized values sometimes wavered, he could still find solace in the memory of a tiny band of courageous men who had defied the brute power of ignorance and bigotry to win freedom for a humble soldier.

He thought democracy's greatest virtues to be its openness to change and its encouragement of individual self-improvement, the prerequisites of Evolution itself. But the almost magical powers he and his generation had once vested in it had plainly faded:

> [Men have] a marked tendency to abuse their liberty....
> When the people are enlightened, when they know their rights,
> are they able to use them? Often not, because they are
> insufficiently prepared. At the same time you modify the laws,
> you must modify men's minds....Sometimes they decide on a
> revolution, and when it succeeds they don't know what to do
> with it.[14]

He admitted that self-government had come a measureable distance in France since the Bourbons and Bonapartes and that life had in truth become less harsh for most men; but in all too many instances the Republic had only changed the name of abuses. Without a lively sense of common interests, a willingness to sacrifice for the public good--in short, without enlightened patriotism--democracies die. Parliaments reflect the state of public virtue. Despite their faults, which he knew intimately, he remained their partisan, quoting with approval Cavour's "The worst Chamber is worth more than the best antechamber."[15] But if civic virtue withers, stable, far-sighted, reforming government becomes impossible. Even in the best of circumstances reform is difficult to carry out: "Democracy should leave the field to authority, which should exercise itself freely in the domain granted to it, subject to parliamentary oversight."[16] Jules Ferry might have permitted himself a sour smile at this; in any event, ex-premier Clemenceau expected precious little reforming initiative from Parliament or the public. Repeating a warning he had sounded during the Dreyfus Affair, he observed that leadership readily degenerates into manipulation: "The people are like kings. They do not know the truth, dislike having it unveiled, and adore flattery."[17] He could see the end all too clearly: the fate of Athens. In 1918 he would confess to

Poincaré that on the eve of the War, "everything led me to believe in our decadence."[18] Would France, a similar miracle of civilization, perish at the hand of a modern Sparta?

In a preface (generally overlooked) which he wrote in 1911 for a translation of Lord Byron's letters, he provided some further evidence of a jaundiced view of public opinion he had acquired as a result of the Affair and his experience as premier. Byron clearly appealed to his imagination and temperament. "The most imperiously proud" man of his time "including Napoleon himself," with obvious weaknesses, errors of conduct, and faults "such as you find in any 'hero' it pleases you to choose," he held the advantage over Napoleon because he sacrificed his life at Missolonghi for "a cause which was beautiful." He had lived his life disdaining alike the adulation or the hatred of a "'public opinion' prompt to express a feigned puritanism [which had] hastened to take against the idol...the revenge of coalesced impotences."[19] One is reminded of his verdict on Blanqui, likewise a man with great defects but at the core loyal to his own vision.

This preface seems to have been written as if he were reminding himself that he must continue to guard against feeling too keenly the pains of unpopularity among a fickle public and to take inspiration from examples of unrewarded faithfulness. The years soon to come would prove the worth of such reminders.

IV

Out of office, Clemenceau again could choose in politics when and where to intervene. He had won reelection to the Senate in January 1909 in a sharp fight with the Socialists which further split the confused Varois Left and led to his resignation (January 1910) from the Radical party only a little more than a year after he had joined.[20] Although he scoffed at rumors he wanted to be premier again or even president, he privately nourished some hopes of a call. Not until December 1913, however, during the formation of the Doumergue ministry, was he formally consulted in a cabinet crisis.[21] In 1912 he apparently believed Poincaré would offer him Foreign Affairs or War, but nothing was tendered, a snub which probably contributed to his opposition to Poincaré's presidential ambitions later that year. As president, Poincaré did use a meeting with him on 23 May 1913 about the Three Years'

Service Law as a warning to others that he had a card in hand;[22] but with this foe at the Élysée, Clemenceau gave up hopes of a return...unless war should come. In that eventuality he expected he would be called--a startling assumption in a man entering his eighth decade.[23]

His opponents sought to ensure his absence. Such, at any rate, was one of the motives behind an inquiry initiated by Jaurès in 1910 into the Rochette scandal. Back on 20 March 1908 Clemenceau had become angered by rumors that he was shielding Henri Rochette, a rascal involved in complicated stock-jobbing schemes. Perhaps heeding an appeal from Senator Prevet, *rapporteur* of the troubled Western Railway bill, although this allegation was never proved, he had ordered Prefect of Police Lépine to go and find a plaintiff so that the swindler could be brought to book. While not unprecedented, the action was rather high-handed, and it involved, moreover, the prefect using powers whose abolition Clemenceau himself had proposed in a private-member bill in 1904 and which the Senate passed on 9 February 1909.[24] Briand, at Justice in 1908, was also, though less conspicuously, one of Jaurès' targets. Probably by design, he waited until Clemenceau had left for South America before launching the inquiry. On his return, however, Clemenceau testified with such disarming candor that the operation to discredit him fizzled. The Chamber contented itself with a motion (1 December 1910) rebuking "irregular, imprudent, and abusive practices" in judicial matters by the executive branch.[25]

The Rochette inquiries (for the affair resurfaced in 1912 and 1914) illustrate a striking feature of the political scene from 1910 to the War, namely, an increase in the tendency of policy questions to become questions of persons. The election of 1910, which returned some 230 neophyte deputies and left party lines incredibly tangled, handed the masters of the lobbies almost limitless opportunities to maneuver. Eleven ministries came and went in five years. For good reason, reports of Clemenceau's activities in this interval often emphasize his relations with other personages.

Briand, for example. Clemenceau had recommended him rather than Caillaux for the succession in 1909 believing that Caillaux would be hampered in the Senate by his association with the income tax.[26] But he had reservations about Briand which steadily deepened into distrust. As early as

1910 he was heard comparing the effects of Briand's maneuverings to the optical illusions produced by the wheelings of a seagull.[27] Barthou left on him a similar impression, though to a less marked degree. He appreciated his wit and ability but came to regard him as unreliable, too clever by half.[28] As for Caillaux, he frankly admired his brains, energy, and feisty courage. He supported him on the income tax, which had made him the bogy of the *possédants*, and was indulgent toward his efforts to stir some reforming zeal into the Radical-Socialist Party, whose leadership he assumed after 1910. But he disagreed with his estimate of Germany's intentions, and on 9 January 1912, in his first major stroke since his fall, he did not hesitate to force his resignation as premier by deftly calling him to account when he made an egregious error while testifying before the Senate foreign affairs commission.

Caillaux foolishly stated that he had not used unofficial channels to negotiate with Germany during the Agadir crisis in 1911 even though by now many persons knew otherwise. Clemenceau instantly asked De Selves, the foreign minister, to confirm Caillaux's statement. He could not, of course, and resigned. After trying to get Delcassé to replace him, a move Clemenceau not surprisingly opposed, and then encountering a "strike" by other eligibles, Caillaux quit two days later. Nevertheless, in 1913-14 the two observed a kind of benevolent neutrality toward each other because they opposed Poincaré, notably on the issue of proportional representation.[29]

His toppling of Caillaux did not prevent ratification of the treaty Caillaux had concluded, which surrendered part of the Congo territory in return for a free hand in Morocco; but it underlined his opposition to the treaty and, as matters turned out, brought the premiership to Raymond Poincaré. To considerable surprise around the Senate because of his known personal antipathy toward Poincaré, he came out in favor of his accession. He respected the patriotism of this Lorrainer, whose views more nearly jibed with his own when it came to dealing with the Germans, and he answered his call to support an extension of conscription from two years to three. But when Poincaré went back on his word (or so he asserted) by supporting proportional representation and, furthermore, in defiance of his "veto" accepted support from the Catholic Right in order to become president (17 January 1913), he never forgave him.

For once, he had failed to "make" a president. His own candidate, Sen. Jules Pams, an intelligent, congenial, but not excessively distinguished Radical, had fallen only one vote shy of winning the endorsement of the Republican caucus, but Poincaré had refused to withdraw in Pams' favor even when summoned by a delegation of Radical brass hats led by Clemenceau and Combes. Clemenceau and the Radicals then considered substituting Ribot for Pams, but Ribot was persuaded to reject the idea, and Poincaré had then gone on to win the official election. The affair in the end only confirmed in spades a dislike he had harbored ever since the Dreyfus days for that dour, precise, ambitious little man.[30]

V

Intriguing as such considerations can be--contemporaries found them endlessly so--they disguise the fact that to Clemenceau persons were secondary. Not that he underestimated their importance: if anything, he had a tendency to overestimate their ability to affect events. Nor is it untrue that too often personal antipathies could color his reactions. But fundamentally he took positions on the big issues before the War because of his conclusions on their merits.

In foreign affairs, for example, his apprehensions about Germany had grown into something akin to an obsession. He regarded the 1912 Moroccan treaty as a product and breeder of delusions. While as premier he had sought to protect France's political and economic rights in Morocco under the Algeciras accords. He had never favored conquering Morocco and saw no merit in making territorial concessions to Germany to do so, least of all after Germany had backed up her (not unjustified) objection to the French move on Fez in 1911 by sending a warship to a Moroccan port (Agadir), thus forcing France to negotiate under a gun. In opposing the treaty, which sanctioned now a French protectorate, he used a long speech on 10 February 1912 (which he nevertheless had had to cut in half because of pain from a prostate ailment) both to warn the country about Germany's ambitions and to send a message to Germany that she should not believe that the logic of her victory in 1870 meant "domination" by her nor that France would accept that the logic of her defeat meant "vassalage": "We are pacifists--pacific, to use the precise word--but we are not submissive."[31] He said he favored renegotiation of the treaty--under the circumstances not a very viable alternative--and affirmed his confidence in Poincaré, not wanting a cabinet crisis at this juncture. He voted against the treaty, which passed on a 212-42 vote, but given the situation at the moment he probably would have voted in favor if he had thought its passage doubtful.[32] Afterward, he continued his fight against the pacifist Left, plumped for patriotism, supported increased armaments, the Three Years Law (after some hesitation), and closer ties with Britain, while continuing to resist adopting the Poincaré-Delcassé school's high opinion of Russia's power.[33]

At home he held firm to the old Radical motto, "Neither Revolution nor Reaction," which in practice meant defense of the lay laws, no truckling to "clericalism" (even if the Right *was* patriotic), enactment of the income tax and workers' pensions bills--he vied with Combes to sponsor a stronger Senate motion for passage of the latter[34]--and consolidation of "the Radical Republic" by opposing the fragmentation implicit in schemes of proportional representation so attractive to the Far Left and Right. This last-named idea had considerable appeal as a reform which would avoid the question of constitutional revision, the Boulanger affair having rendered it moot, while presumably permitting a desirable reclassification and solidification of parties which the current confusion made desirable. Beyond the imminent dangers that it posed to the Radicals, nevertheless, Clemenceau saw in the complex modalities of the proposal a threat to the achievement of the overriding purpose of elections, viz., the forming of majorities which could make decisions and hence govern. Proportional representation, no matter how attractive it looked because of its evident fairness in producing a Chamber which would be a mirror of the political opinions of the country. would in practice inhibit the forming of working majorities, thus making the present situation worse. His Senate speech of 18 March 1913 on the issue delivered the *coup de grâce* to Briand's fourth (already!) ministry.[35]

His faithfulness to Radical traditions in all this had the ironic effect of making him look like a dated maverick. "I know I'm old-fashioned," he wrote, "I boast in it, for I need neither criticism nor praise to hold me to my chosen path."[36] In truth, it was not he who was inconsistent, but the Radicals--divided and squabbling, scouring votes in all directions. He could not deny, however, that his cavalier attitude toward party affairs over the years had contributed to their predicament. When had he, their inspirer and greatest spokesman, ever troubled himself overmuch to employ in their behalf the arts of conciliation? They knew the answer and loved him all the less for it.

VI

In sum, Clemenceau occupied a unique, undefinable place in French political life by the summer of 1914. He commanded no group, much less a party. Poincaré's election had shown that he was no longer the Warwick who had made presidents since Jules Grévy. There was literally nobody in the upper reaches of politics he had not crossed at one time or another. The most he could count on was momentary allies, none of whom seriously wanted or expected him to return to office. The Moderates quailed before his immoderacy, the Right gagged on his unrepentant anti-clericalism, while the Socialists and left-wing Radicals shuddered at memories of his ministry and gladly welcomed the chance to write him off as a *réactionnaire* when he joined the likes of General Mercier, the Catholic spokesman Lamarzelle, and Action Française's Dominique Delahaye in the votes on the 1912 treaty and the Three Years Law.

On the other hand he had assets, not for the moment compelling, but real nonetheless. He was again in reasonably good health despite his diabetes. On 2 May 1912 his prostate trouble, probably due to a cancer, was taken care of by an ablation, a highly risky procedure in those days--whence his famous quip that he knew of "two useless organs, my prostate and the presidency of the French Republic"--and he had regained much of his old bounce. Quite in character, he had it done at a Catholic infirmary--it was more convenient for his doctor--which caused a lot of wry comment; he gave his family no advance warning, twitted them afterward on their "disappointment" that they would not inherit yet, and conducted a friendly running debate with the nuns by trying to convert them to atheism. One of them, a Sister Théoneste, would stay with him at his insistence through all his remaining illnesses until his death.

He was a senior member of the Senate, in most ways its most visible representative. He still had a brain, a tongue, and an undiminished will to exercise them without let or hindrance. The general public, for its part, had long come to relish in him what the English had relished in a Lord Palmerston or the Americans in a "Teddy" Roosevelt and later a Harry Truman--his "be-damnedness."[37]

And he again had a newspaper. In May 1913, after preparations which may have begun as early as 1911, he launched the aptly titled *L'Homme Libre* (The Free Man).[38] Alphonse Lenoir, a newspaper agent with connections in the ministry of finance, probably played a role,[39] but Mandel was the one most responsible for the arrangements after the sale of the *Journal du Var* at the end of 1912, and it was from this time that his intimate association with Clemenceau began. Four-page *journaux d'opinion* were in full decline, but it was the form he knew and loved. The paper reincarnated *La Justice* and *L'Aurore*: the genial Auguste Bernier, who had directed the administration of *L'Aurore* in the Dreyfus days and enjoyed Clemenceau's absolute trust (they were friends for forty years), back in his accustomed job of scraping up money;[40] the staff of talented, underpaid writers--among them, Gustave Geffroy, François-Albert, Étienne Chichet, Roland Dorgelès, Francis Carco, Gérard Bauër, Émile Buré, Mandel, André Billy,[41] and guest columnists Paul Painlevé, Séverine, Anatole France, Alphonse Aulard; and all captained by the Terrible Monsieur Clemenceau, whose daily editorial would be required reading for the political elite, whatever they thought of him.

VII

Georges Clemenceau had been executed in 1893, was dead again in 1900, and to all appearances buried in 1909. Talent, pile-driving energy, an unbreakable will, and journalism had thrice resurrected him. A remarkable career. If he had died in his seventy-third year, it would have assured him a respectable, even notable, place in his country's long history. No one, not even the Tiger himself, would have predicted that all he had done thus far could some day appear but a prelude. For this singular twist of fortune he could thank a young Bosnian patriot-turned-assassin and an indubitably dead heir to the crowns of the Habsburgs.

NOTES
CHAPTER XII

1   In Georges Wormser, *Le septennat de Poincaré* (Arthème Fayard, 1977), p. 76.

2   The "humiliation" was Delcassé's resignation at Germany's behest in 1905, not the Fashoda affair, as is sometimes asserted. See JOC, 20 July 1909, pp. 2222-2243; and Charles Bénoist, *Souvenirs de Charles Bénoist*, 3 vols. (Librairie Plon, 1932-1934), 3:155. Also Georges Suarez, *Briand: Sa vie, son oeuvre, avec son journal et de nombreux documents inédites*, 6 vols. (Librairie Plon, 1938-52), 3:214; Robert Dreux, "Clemenceau et Viviani," *L'Ordre*, 23 Nov. 1938; and "Le 'tombeur' de Clemenceau," *Le Journal du Peuple*, 26 Jan. 1920.

3   Maurel, *Les écrivains de la Guerre*, p. 21; and a letter (recipient unnamed) in Wormser, *La république de Clemenceau*, pp. 213-214.

4   See France, Ministère des Affaires étrangères, *Documents diplomatiques françaises, 1871-1914*, 2nd ser., vol. 12, no. 289.

5   See Geffroy, *Georges Clemenceau*, p. 108; Maurel, "Souvenirs sur Clemenceau," p. 733; and Duroselle, *Clemenceau*, p. 548.

6   See p. 222 above; and Gatineau-Clemenceau, *Des pattes du Tigre*, pp. 20-40, *passim*, 51-58, 384-385. The Clemenceau's marital lives certainly were not dull: in 1890 sister Sophie shot her philandering husband, Ferdinand Bryndza, a journalist of Jewish-Polish-Austrian extraction, but was not prosecuted, having been certified as temporarily insane. She never remarried. Emma was married--apparently happily, however--to a marine engineer, Léon Jacquet; Adrienne, crippled, never married.

7   Zukerkandl, *Clemenceau, tel que je l'ai connu*, pp. 182-183.

8   See "Les projets de M. Clemenceau," *Le Cri de Paris*, 19e année, no. 677 (Musée Clemenceau, Folio "Articles de journaux sans reférence"); Abensour, *Dans la cage du Tigre*, pp. 79-80; and Allan Nevins, *Henry White: Thirty Years of American Diplomacy* (New York: Harper & Bros., 1930), p. 310. Duroselle, *Clemenceau*, pp. 554, 895, says he invested 100,000 francs in Argentina, which he got back in 1920-21 at a good profit. Some of it also may have paid for the Bernouville place; see p. 490 below.

9   On this episode see GC, *Sur la démocratie*, pp. 69-71. Incidentally, the caption on a photograph of this trip at the Musée Clemenceau is mistaken. Elihu Root could not have accompanied him on a visit to a coffee plantation on 29 Sept. 1910 because he was in Saratoga, NY,

at the Republican State Convention. See Philip C. Jessup, *Elihu Root*, 2 vols. (New York: Dodd, Mead, 1938), 2:162-163.

10   Related to me by Marcel Wormser at the Musée Clemenceau in May 1987.

11   GC, *Notes de voyage dans l'Amérique du Sud: Argentine, Uruguay, Brésil* (Librairie Hachette, 1911), from *L'Illustration*. See a review by Paul Groussac, *Revue politique et littéraire (La Revue bleue)*, 11 Nov. 1911, pp. 621-627.

12   Buré, "M. Georges Clemenceau."

13   Léon Abensour, "Un grand projet de Georges Clemenceau," *La Grande revue*, Feb. 1930, p. 549.

14   GC, *Sur la démocratie*, pp. 42-43.

15   *Ibid.*, p. 67.

16   Abensour, "Un grand projet de Georges Clemenceau," p. 541.

17   GC, *Sur la démocratie*, p. 43. See GC, *L'iniquité*, pp. 255-256.

18   Raymond Poincaré, *Au service de la France: Neuf années de souvenirs*, 11 vols. (Plon-Nourrit, 1926-33; Librairie Plon, 1974), 10:121.

19   Lord George Gordon Byron, *Lettres de Lord Byron*, traduisées par Jean Delachaume, Préface de G. Clemenceau (Calmann-Lévy, 1911), pp. ii, iv, xi.

20   See JOS, 15 Jan. 1909, p. 9; and *Le Temps*, 31 Dec. 1909, 1, 19, 27 Jan. 1910. Results: Clemenceau, 390 (elected); Louis Martin, a former deputy, 377 (elected); Victor Reymonencq, a Toulon arsenal worker, 320 (elected); Louis Sigallas, incumbent, 145; Victor Méric, incumbent, 119; others, 19.   Méric's son was a Hervéist journalist convicted in 1908 of defaming the army. See Victor Méric [the Younger], *A travers la jungle politique et littéraire*, 1st ser. (Librairie Valois, 1930), pp. 240-263; Judt, *Socialism in Provence*, pp. 81-84 and *passim*; Rinaudo, "Clemenceau vu d'en bas," pp. 330-335; *idem, Les vendanges de la République*, pp. 208-215; Calixte de Rieux, "Clemenceau et le parti radical," *Les Cahiers de la République* 2 no. 8 (July-Aug. 1957), pp. 93-108; and Jacques Kayser, "Note sur Clemenceau et le parti radical," *Les Cahiers de la République* 2, no. 9 (Sept.-Oct. 1957), p. 100.

21   See *Le Temps*, 4 Dec. 1913. He later denied he was formally consulted about the succession; JOS, 16 Dec. 1913, p. 168. In 1911 Caillaux had consulted him about cabinet appointments. If he recommended De Selves for Foreign Affairs (a poor choice), as Caillaux asserted, one notes that the meticulous Allain is silent about it. Joseph Caillaux, *Agadir, ma*

politique extérieure (A. Michel, 1919), p. 106; and Allain, *Le défi victorieux*, pp. 365-366.

22   See Maurice Paléologue, *Au Quai d'Orsay à la veille de la tourmente: Journal, 1913-1914* (Librairie Plon, 1947), pp. 139-40. Keiger says he once offered him the ambassadorship to Great Britain, "much to Jules Cambon's distress"; in *France and the Origins of the First World War*, p. 136.

23   See Wormser, *La république de Clemenceau*, pp. 274-275. Fallières told Klotz during the Agadir crisis (1911) that if war came he would ask Clemenceau and Déroulède (!) to head a *Union sacrée* government; Louis-Lucien Klotz, *De la guerre à la paix: Souvenirs et documents* (Payot, 1924), pp. 73-74.

24   A bill abrogating Art. 10 of the Criminal Code, a rarely used provision giving prefects certain broad police powers when swift action was needed; see *Journal Officiel. Sénat. Documents Parlementaires* 1904, Annexe no. 344. Clemenceau's father's arrest in 1853 may have come under this article. Final passage of a revised bill came on 30 Dec. 1932, but it in turn was largely abrogated in 1935 and 1939. See Le Clère and Wright, *Les préfets du Second Empire*, pp. 73-74; and Gaston Pontal, *L'article 10 du Code d'instruction criminelle* (Carcassone: L. Bonnafous et Fils, 1941), pp. 50-53.

25   Clemenceau later said he had acted himself because he distrusted Briand; see Martet, *Clemenceau*, p. 281. A delay in Rochette's prosecution in 1911 resulted in a new inquiry in 1914 with Caillaux now the main target. For Clemenceau's and Lépine's involvement and testimony, see *Le Matin*, 8 July 1910; and *Le Temps*, 13, 16, 26 July, 23 Sept., 16 Nov.-2 Dec. 1910, *passim*. The hearings are in Rapport Daniel de Folleville, *Journal Officiel. Chambre des Députés. Documents Parlementaires*, 1911, no. 814, annexe au procès-verbal de la séance du 10 mars 1911. See also Louis Lépine, *Mes souvenirs* (Payot, 1929), pp. 255-262; Joseph Caillaux, *Mes mémoires*, 2:139-146; Jean-Noël Jeanneney, *L'argent caché: Milieux d'affaires et pouvoirs publiques dans la France du XXᵉ siècle* (Arthème Fayard, 1981), pp. 93 120; and Jeanneney's essay in *Clemenceau et la justice*, pp. 153-159.

26   See a letter (recipient unnamed) in Wormser, *La république de Clemenceau*, p. 213; also Allain, *Le défi victorieux*, p. 353.

27   Caillaux, *Mes mémoires*, 2:39.

28   See, for example, HL, 17 May 1913, in GC, *Dans les champs du pouvoir*, p. 71.

29   See especially Allain, *Le défi victorieux*, pp. 390-391, 397-400, 403-407; and comments in Martet, *Clemenceau*, p. 79n.

30   Citing the parable of the paralytic needing a blind man to carry him, he said he would settle for a one-eyed man to carry Poincaré; GC, *Justice militaire*, p. 143 (15 June 1899). See *Le Bloc*, 15 March 1902, "Le Poincarisme." He was infuriated when he learned that Madeleine's husband,

a suicide (p. 238 above), had named Poincaré as guardian of their son, René Jacquemaire. Madeleine's paramour at that time, Maurice Bernard, was a friend of Poincaré and later one of Rochette's attorneys. See Gatineau-Clemenceau, *Des pattes du Tigre*, pp. 28-29; and Jean-Denis Bredin, *Joseph Caillaux* (Librairie Hachette, 1980), p. 88.

31   JOS, 10 Feb. 1912, p. 232. See pp. 227-234, *passim*; and HE, 18 Oct. 1914.

32   See, e.g., Varenne, *Mon patron Georges Mandel*, p. 46.

33   In 1911 he joined Lord Roberts' National Service League, which was pushing for conscription in Britain; see Martet, *Le Tigre*, pp. 258-260. As regards Poincaré, he was suspicious of his relations with Izvol'skii,, currently ambassador in Paris.

34   See JOS, 2 June 1911, pp. 528-529.

35   JOS, 18 March 1913, pp. 298-301.

36   HL, 4 July 1913.

37   See Barbara Tuchman, *The Proud Tower* (New York: Macmillan, 1966), p. 141.

38   Clemenceau revived a title Rochefort and Vaughan had once used. He left the paper in Nov. 1917 when he became premier, but it survived until 1939.

39   See Joseph Caillaux, *Devant l'histoire: Mes prisons*, 2nd ed. (Éditions de la Sirène, 1920), pp. 275-277.

40   See his obituary in HL, 7 Dec. 1937. Charles Morice claimed that Bernier, like many administrators, got substantial amounts from the state's secret funds; *Quarante ans de journalisme*, 1:6.

41   Billy, the eminent critic, soon left with unhappy memories; see André Billy, "Clemenceau, homme de lettres," *Le Figaro littéraire*, 23 Feb. 1970, p. 25.

CHAPTER XIII

Tiger in the Night
(1914-1917)

Georges Clemenceau was made for drama--a survivor into the twentieth century of a generation whose fathers had known Stendhal, Byron, and Victor Hugo in the flesh; a Victorian gentleman in dress and manners but one confessing he would have preferred to live in the sixteenth century, when men discovered the world and forthrightly sent their enemies to the stake;[1] a creature of fine-tuned sensitivity, elevated taste, earthy humor, explosive energy, patience, cunning, furious will, sentimentality, and playfulness whom an admiring English general (Sir Edward Spears) uniquely acquainted with leaders of both world wars would remember withal as "the toughest, the hardest, and perhaps the most cruel" man he had ever met.[2] Through some sort of alchemy these clashing traits combined to form a character which would find its natural habitat in the tempests of a world war. At the end of the struggle, Clemenceau was the triumphant leader of a mighty coalition, a world-famous figure acclaimed by millions as "Père-la-Victoire," his name inscribed on plaques in every school and town hall in France to remind future generations that he had earned the nation's gratitude.

Hence it is all the more striking that until the last year of the war he was not a member of the government, much less its leader. Whether he really was France's last hope for victory before a patched-up peace or stark defeat, most Frenchmen by the war's end had come to think so, a belief which became the cornerstone of his already burgeoning legend. Most importantly, President Poincaré held this view of him. Or so he wrote afterward. According to his memoirs, he had regarded him from the outset as a great risk but also as the one man who might save everything if all seemed lost.[3] As things turned out he looked (or made himself to look) like a prophet. If he had called him earlier, would victory have come sooner and at less cost? Clemenceau's whole career, indeed, so marked by long postponements and exclusions, invites such speculations. As for his own view of it at the time, while he knew quite well that he was out of the running for a peacetime ministry after 1909, he apparently had thought, as has been said, that he would be a (probably *the*) logical candidate in case of war. But when war came, the call did not. For thirty-nine long months he prowled the forests outside the gates.

II

Part of the reason for his absence lay in the premium French democracy put on "going along in order to get along," the price of government by coalition. The natural answer to the war emergency was the "Sacred Union," which was embodied symbolically in cabinets containing representatives of all shades of opinion. The result, easy to predict and hard to avoid, was mushy compromise and an attrition of leaders matching the attrition at the front. Clemenceau four times received more-or-less serious invitations to join cabinets, by Viviani twice (4, 24 August 1914), Briand (27 October 1915), and Paul Painlevé (early September 1917). He refused because, at bottom and despite disclaimers, he disagreed with the Sacred Union device and would not risk depleting his aging energies in struggles inside a government of which he was not the uncontested chief.[4] Poincaré in turn would not make him chief because *he* wanted to conduct the orchestra-- the *Union sacrée* conformed with his desire to increase the power of the presidency--and because to call him almost certainly would provoke a revolt by labor leaders and the Socialists.

Whatever Clemenceau may have thought of his chances, they depended on his ability to persuade Poincaré. Instead, his behavior only confirmed the prudent president's worst fears.

The outbreak of the war in August 1914 had climaxed for Clemenceau a long period of mounting anxiety. By 1913 he had become so convinced that the peace would not last that he had swung over to support of the Three Years' Service Law with a flat declaration that he would vote whatever any government asked for national defense.[5] Although his articles immediately following the assassination of Archduke Franz Ferdinand (28 June 1914) were measured, he was among the very few commentators who at the first reports sensed the full gravity of the danger, being especially impressed by the wild charges sounded in the semi-official press in Berlin and Vienna that the Serbian government had instigated the murder.[6] Grim consultations at his *L'Homme Libre* office on the rue Taitbout[7] filled the tense weeks of July. With questionable timing he provoked revelations by Senator Charles Humbert of France's military unpreparedness, notably in heavy artillery, delivering anguished speeches on the subject himself on 13 and 14 July and on the 15th a particularly fierce article, "Neither Defended Nor Governed."[8] A week later Austria's sudden dispatch of an ultimatum to Serbia (23 July) shoved Europe to the precipice. In his editorial on the ultimatum (25 July), he asserted that it was impossible to believe that Austria had acted in anything but "full accord" with Germany, that the conflict in the Balkans was "the inevitable consequence" of the German action against Russia in the Bosnian annexation affair, and that the chances of saving the peace or confining the hostilities to the Balkans were small "if not impossible"--which within a week proved to be the case.

The hurricane roared in--declarations of war by Austria on Serbia, Germany on Russia, France, and Belgium, and England on Germany; the wretched assassination of Jaurès (31 July) by a nationalist fanatic;[9] the fever of mobilization; the swift advance of the German armies into Belgium and northeastern France while a great French offensive was being massacred in Lorraine. Clemenceau was blown from pole to pole, patriotic firmness and exaltation, unwavering in print, struggling against awful private visions of a repetition of the debacle of 1870 which he did not conceal from his intimates. Years later after the war he publicly admitted that in 1914 he had indeed believed that France was doomed and that he had wanted to die rather than witness the end.[10] Harried ministers scarcely knew what to expect from him.

Poincaré's nobly worded proclamation of war had brought him to the Élysée (possibly at the president's invitation) for a tearful patriotic embrace. The next day he returned with a friend, the Italian commercial attaché Count Sabini, to begin an attempt, which muddled on until early October, to draw Italy into the war on the side of the Entente.[11] On the other hand, when the young minister of the interior, Jean Malvy, paid him a visit, he all but called him a traitor for deferring a roundup of suspects on *Carnet B*, a list of 2,501 persons, mostly aliens and antimilitarist labor figures, marked for preventive detention in case of war.[12] And when Viviani asked him to join the government, his refusal mixed expressions of personal sympathy with brutal questionings of Viviani's competence, a treatment not likely to soothe that high-strung man's nerves.[13]

The last turn came on 27 August. The dimensions of the retreat in the northeast had become clear enough to prompt formation of the *Union sacrée* government on the 26th, but word was running through Paris that the situation was far more grave than the communiqués had even suggested. (On the 29th would come shocking confirmation--Clemenceau said he was "completely bowled over"--when the communiqué casually mentioned a stabilization of the front on the Somme, a penetration far deeper than anything hinted at up to now.) Beside himself with anxiety and wracked by frustration at the authorities' refusal to tell the country the full truth of what was happening, he stormed to the Élysée to rage at the president like a man gone mad. Poincaré, appalled, showed him the door. Only once in the next three years was he to cross the president's threshold.[14]

Following this scene Clemenceau tried to get Parliament reconvened, an ill-considered enterprise which aroused suspicions about his intentions, before reluctantly joining the governmental exodus to Bordeaux.[15] His last articles before the departure nevertheless were clear-headed and resolute. Most remarkably, in the last of them (31 August-3 September) he discerned the tactical implications of the use of aerial observation, the overextension of the German lines, the rumored (and true, it turned out) sudden dispatch of important German forces eastward to meet the Russian advance, and the possibility of hurling the large and mobile Paris garrison against the German right flank in combination with an Anglo-French counteroffensive--all of which were to lead a week later to the eleventh-hour victory at the Marne. "How does he get that way?" a reporter later wondered aloud. "Well, he's damned smart, you know," replied Frederic Villiers, the famous English correspondent, "just about the wisest of them all."[16]

III

Until he returned to Paris in early December, Clemenceau lived and worked in a couple of rooms in Bordeaux, with a grandson (Thérèse's boy) running copy to Toulouse for printing by the *Dépêche*. It was at Bordeaux that he first seriously ran afoul of the Censorship. At the outset of the war he had strongly supported instituting a censorship--"The tale of '70 must not begin again," he told his staff[17]--and had participated in the creation of a liaison body between the directors of the Paris press and the government.[18] But after 19 September the regime was extended even to a censoring of outspoken political opinion, so it was all but inevitable that sooner or later he would become the Censorship's most celebrated victim. He made it sooner. On 24 September he denounced the abominable conditions on trains transporting wounded soldiers.[19] The article went through, but Mandel warned him that his license, which he had been using with increasing liberality, was running out. So he decided to provoke a showdown. On 29 September--relying in part on information supplied by his son Michel, an infantry lieutenant recuperating from a leg wound received in Belgium, and daughter Madeleine, a nurse now and living with him in Bordeaux--he revealed in scathing anger that wounded soldiers were getting tetanus from being transported in cars also used for horses. For good measure he doubled the usual printing of 50,000 copies. The government promptly ordered the paper suspended for a week, but the Censorship's various authorities got badly confused, and thousands of uncensored copies reached the stands in the provinces. To the public's amusement, the wily veteran of the Second Empire's press battles riposted the next day with a "new" paper, *L'Homme Enchaîné* (The Chained Man).[20] It too was suspended, however, when a printer unfortunately left a *L'Homme Libre* heading on the back pages, thus proving the connection.[21]

After the suspension expired on 8 October, the new name remained, going on to acquire a considerable fame--or, in the eyes of a considerable fraction of the public, infamy. Until 8 December, when he returned with the government to Paris, the paper was published in both Paris and Bordeaux, but after that the latter edition was ended for reasons of economy. In any event, for the next three years at the Censorship, the arrival of "le Clemenceau" was to be a daily "event" met with mingled curiosity and apprehension. And doubtless with some feelings of frustration, too, for the author was known to be mailing uncensored copies to members of Parliament and the 1,500-or-so paid subscribers.

Skirmishes with the censors were only part of what presently became a running fight with the government. The invasion emergency over, military activity congealed into a gigantic siege, and Parliament reconvened in Paris (December 1914), the whole problem of how to wage a protracted war had to be faced. All the belligerents were slow to understand the novel requirements. French democracy, boasting an ancestry dating from 1789 but in continuous operation for less than forty years, faced a particularly stern test, for the traditions of the French State--administrative centralization and authoritarian methods and mentality--reached back through more than eight centuries and persisted still as a powerful subsurface current. Even the democratic tradition made room (if grudgingly) for Robespierre and the Committee of Public Safety. The laws put in force in August 1914 at first gave to Army General Headquarters (GQG) nearly absolute power over every public activity. The ministers felt disarmed by the military--the war was seven months old before General Joffre deigned to give them casualty figures--but at the same time they tended to view Parliament as a time-wasting, potentially dangerous nuisance. Parliament in turn groped to find a role, afraid to hurt public confidence by criticizing, but resenting its exclusion from all action save the levying of men and money to be pitched into the furnace.

Clemenceau vigorously upheld the right of Parliament and the public to be informed and to judge. He did so from tactical necessity, certainly, having no seat on the inner councils, but fundamentally from conviction. He never had trusted others in power very far, and he was convinced that the secrecy mania now gripping the government and the military was dangerous. There are bonafide military secrets, he readily admitted, but not very many.

The government should publish a daily bulletin, "absolutely true for the good and for the bad," and allow freedom of opinion about everything, even military operations.[22] In principle and practice alike, a democracy's government can wage war effectively only if it takes the people into its confidence. To do otherwise is to court disaster when the truth gets out. The frightful spectacle of civil disintegration in 1870-71 haunted him; the scene with Poincaré was largely prompted by his belief that the government, by waiting too long before telling the truth about the retreat, was risking turning a defeat into a panicky collapse and a revolution.[23] The British government, he liked to point out, had long made a virtue of the necessity to answer to Parliament. He even thought for a time that the Russian government did and heaped praise on the Duma as a way of shaming his own.[24] Because no other avenue to frank discussion seemed open, and because the device would extend the commissions' influence in the chambers, thus bringing further pressure on the ministry, he converted to the idea of secret sittings of Parliament to discuss especially delicate questions. But after the first round of these (June-July 1916) failed to put Briand to the wall, he gradually soured on the practice, asserting that the sessions seldom revealed information that had not already circulated in the lobbies. None were held after he became premier.[25]

IV

The commissions, which worked behind closed doors, naturally assumed increased importance. In this arena Clemenceau was singularly well placed. On 19 December 1914 he was elected a vice-president of the Army Commission, on 5 February 1915 was named to the Foreign Affairs Commission and made a vice-president, and on 4-5 November 1915 assumed the presidency of both these prestigious bodies when Freycinet, who had hitherto held these posts, was made a minister of state (at age 87) in Briand's government. His responsibilities and convictions happily coincided to make him a leader in Parliament's fight to gain direct access to information and to conduct inspections in the battle zone--the famous *contrôle* issue.[*] The

---

[*] This word which means "oversight," not "control," caused some confusion at the Paris Peace Conference.

question was complex and delicate. The main accusations of the Army Commission against the War ministry, where the dispute tended to focus, centered on disparities between what *had* been done and what it was *necessary* to do. It was hard to decide what was indeed necessary and who was to make the decision. The GQG would send requests, and the minister of war would carry them out, but under the supervision of the GQG. The Army Commission was charged with exercising Parliament's oversight in what was done and wanted power to carry out its mission, but it could not call officers to testify, and in addition it confronted a mare's nest of constitutional questions involving the powers of ministers and of the Chamber of Deputies and *its* commissions. Moreover, the GQG, with a good deal of support from the public, could muster a powerful case based on the theme that politicians should not "interfere" in military matters during a desperate war.[26]

Clemenceau pressed hard to get answers and answerability, but he knew that prudence set limits on the commissions' power: "We must be moderate to have the Senate and the country with us, but at the same time we must be active because the higher interests of the country require it."[27] Viviani's government, with Millerand as minister of war adamantly defending Joffre and the GQG, conceded virtually nothing, but the commissions' drumfire criticism of Millerand weakened Viviani and helped persuade him to resign (October 1915). Millerand's successors did not dare to imitate his intransigence, but Briand, who followed Viviani, characteristically promised more cooperation than he delivered. Joffre's fall (December 1916) and Briand's resignation (March 1917) brought in Painlevé. As minister of war under Ribot (March-September) and then as premier (September-November 1917), he gave Parliament most of what it could reasonably expect. Clemenceau had no trouble with the issue while premier until it revived, in a different guise, during the peace negotiations in 1919.

Commission work gave Clemenceau a formidable knowledge of the myriad questions entailed in running a war by the time he became premier and helped him to surmount the disadvantages of his exclusion from cabinet posts. The Army Commission alone averaged nearly ten plenary meetings per moth through March 1916, after which, having won many of its major contentions, it moderated its pace to about six per month. It rendered excellent service on the whole, notably on questions of munitions and heavy artillery (major worries in 1915), aviation, manpower allocation, and medical services. From the outset it put great emphasis on the war's economic dimension, which it thought the ministry of war and the GQG consistently underestimated, and pressed for hitherto unimagined levels of production in all war-related sectors. Not until the battle of Verdun in 1916 could it be said to have won its point with a full range of production programs now in operation.

Clemenceau's powers as a commission president were distinctly fewer than those of a chairman of a United States Senate committee, for example, but his informal influence was considerable. Both the foreign affairs and army commissions contained a raft of political heavyweights, and he slowly but fairly steadily built solid working-majorities behind him which also had links to like-minded blocs in the Chamber commissions, majorities which over the long haul proved more stable than those on which the ministries could rely--a covert reason for his rise to the premiership. He presided over hearings vigorously but with courtesy. He seldom spoke at length but was influential in mediating final decisions. One gains the impression that he drew a significant distinction between the behavior he permitted himself in commission meetings, where his strong sense of the responsibilities of power--of his own as president and of the ministers in theirs--counseled restraint, and that in which he indulged as an editorialist, where he spoke his mind and relieved his frustrations with an abandon (circumstances and censorship permitting) which everyone, however painful they found it, had long since come to expect from him on the printed page.

Despite his reputation as an old "Jacobin," he rejected proposals to resurrect the Revolution's Committee of Public Safety and its representatives-on-mission exercising carte-blanche authority. His spirit was Jacobin in its fiery patriotism and penchant for brook-no-obstacle decisiveness, but in political principles he was a nineteenth-century leftish liberal who thought that governments should be up and doing but checked safely short of "despotism" by vigilant parliaments. He saw no pressing need to alter constitutional practice; except for tinkering with the electoral system, he had long since given up revision. Nor did he propose novel administrative schemes, a subject which, besides, he found boring. Agencies concerned with the economy and inter-Allied cooperation would proliferate in 1917-18, but otherwise his own regime's main machinery was already in place when he became premier.

Instead, it was the moral factor, broadly speaking, which preoccupied him. France was fighting for her life. He had no desire to see her soldiers die in imperishable glory: he wanted them to win. And they would not win unless the politicians discarded their old habit of sacrificing action on the altar of accommodation. Government-by-palaver, clever balancings of Monsieur X with Monsieur Y, preoccupations with appearances, attempts to manipulate opinion rather than meet problems, postponements of decisions in the Micawberish hope that something would turn up[28]--all this he counted as a prescription for defeat. The country was fundamentally sound, with reserves of courage and intelligence he frankly admitted he had underestimated at first. But it needed direction and inspiration. Month in, month out he called for leaders who knew what they wanted and were willing above all to act without counting the cost to their persons or reputations.

Not infrequently his charges were overblown or sometimes downright unjust. With good reason the *Gazette des Ardennes*, the Germans' French-language propaganda paper, quoted him lavishly, and *L'Homme Enchaîné* was alleged to be the only French paper permitted in some POW camps. He spared no one, and he drew blood--as he was often heard to say, "I'll get them, right down to the stump!"[29] "I had a wife," he once remarked to General Spears, "she abandoned me; I had children, they turned against me; I had friends, they betrayed me. I have only my claws, and I use them."[30] His adversaries charged that he was vindictive. Not altogether convincingly, he denied it: "To hell with grudges! I've never known what they mean by that. I have disdained, or scorned. I have never hated [!]. Besides, I certainly have other things on my mind with the Germans at Noyon."[31] The government tapped his telephone,[32] and almost every day his mail brought threatening letters, but he disdained hiring a bodyguard and walked about alone, even when choosing to make the long hike home to Passy at night. In a reflective mood he once penned two lines which went to the heart of the matter and which could have comprised a fitting epitaph for his life in journalism:

> It is a noble thing to love one's country. It is even nobler to serve it, at the risk of being misunderstood, by warning it of its errors.[33]

He wrote under deadlines, and to blame those in charge when things went wrong was sometimes to take the path of least resistance. War is par excellence the domain of chance and the unexpected. France's leaders probably made no more mistakes than one should expect in such trying circumstances, but time was against them. Joffre suffered no outright defeat, but he won no victories after the Marne and finally had to go. To their credit the Poincarés, Vivianis, Briands, Ribots, and Painlevés likewise avoided defeat. But none seemed able to touch the soldier and civilian masses or make things move; and to continue with them into a fourth grinding year was to ask more than the country any longer wanted to give. It was time for an "outsider." By the summer of 1917 Clemenceau, unwanted by many and dreaded by many others who were beginning to be heard saying that they wanted him nonetheless, was coming on inexorably. In June he told a young intimate, Georges Wormser, that he would be called before the year was out.[34]

V

Besides the moral theme, which was central, others bearing more directly on policy furnished clues to what he might do if he were put in charge. First and foremost, he was a "bitter-ender." At the very beginning of the war he had stated that the stake was "the destiny of all European civilization," its independence and diversity versus a unity by a "mechanical Germanization under an iron claw"[35]--which would make it hard to regard anything short of complete victory as a tolerable outcome. "Can anyone conceive of anything more perfectly nonsensical [*fou*] than to ask a man whose land has been invaded what his *war aims* are?"[36] The German Empire, he wrote, had criminally and stupidly resorted to force to seize an economic and political preeminence it soon would have won without a war.[37] (Unfortunately, Germany's leaders in 1914 had concluded the opposite.)

Even its intellectual elite had applauded this choice and the barbaric methods used to carry it out, which meant that the issue as he saw it-- Germany's prostitution of modern science and civilization to atavistic ideals of brute force--would be settled only on the battlefield. Germany neither expected nor intended any other outcome.[38]

The case of Austria-Hungary, "a formless assemblage of mutilated parts," as he termed it,[39] was less clear with him. Vacations at Karlsbad and family connections by marriage to citizens of the Dual Monarchy perhaps tempered his opinions to some degree, although one could easily argue the reverse.[40] Back in 1886 he had told Archduke Rudolf (in a meeting arranged by a mutual friend, Moritz Szeps, editor of the *Wiener Tageblatt*) that Austria's independence was "an absolutely vital necessity for France in order to counterbalance Bismarck."[41] Nevertheless, he held a low opinion of the Habsburg aristocracy. A ferocious passage in a letter from America in 1867 on the execution of Maximilian in Mexico--"...all these emperors, kings, archdukes, and princes are grand, sublime, generous, and superb; their princesses are everything you could want. But I hate them, with a merciless hatred like they hated in the old days, in '93...."[42]--expressed sentiments which time mellowed not at all; and he put heavy blame on them for starting the war because "they only know how to intrigue wretchedly in the service of German hegemony."[43] "It was not at Sadowa [1866] that Austria succumbed," he wrote in 1915, "but at the signature of the Triple Alliance [1882]. The supreme convulsions of her end have only a dramatic value...."[44] Still, while he sympathized warmly with the plight of the subject nationalities, especially the Poles and Czechs, he left the door open in October and November 1918 to some kind of a confederation, even under a Habsburg figurehead, until events in the last days slammed it shut.[45]

Everybody in the Allied camp saw in Austria's weakness a possible avenue to peace. What he knew at the time, if anything, of conversations in Switzerland between his brother Paul's Austrian-born wife, Sophie Szeps (Moritz' daughter), her sister, Berta Szeps Zuckerkandl, and German and Austrian authorities is impossible to say. He disliked Sophie, who conducted a Germanophile salon, but long was in very cordial relations with Berta. At some point during the war but probably very early, he wrote to his brother

Albert that he wanted nothing more to do with either of them, and such evidence as has been turned up confirms his alienation from them. After he became premier he was said to have contemplated having Sophie arrested. The whole imbroglio not surprisingly led to a permanent estrangement from his brother Paul after 1918. At all events, the talks in Switzerland, like a dozen other soundings, led nowhere.[46]

It is certain, anyhow, that he remained very sceptical about the usefulness of all such attempts to negotiate a separate peace with Austria. As premier, his "listen but don't talk" instructions for the renewed Armand-Revertera meetings (February 1918) and his drastic action in the Czernin affair (in April, related below) reflected views he had held for a long time. By mid-1916 Austria did want peace, but she was not strong enough to split the Entente from Italy and defy Germany to get it, at least on terms which could keep her from falling to pieces; and if she were *that* strong, she didn't need to make peace.[47] In the last analysis, his conclusion was that her fate would be settled by what happened to Germany in the one place where Germany could *win* the war or the Entente *lose* it--on the Western Front.

To the end of the war he was a convinced "Westerner." He did at first support the naval move at the Dardanelles to break through to Constantinople (February-March 1915), although he suspected (rightly) that it was ill-prepared. When troops, mainly British, were sent in at Gallipoli (25 April) in the wake of its failure, he again raised questions about "improvisations."[48] The strategic benefits of a seizure of the Straits were undeniable, but Gallipoli soon turned into a hellhole. Toward October, meanwhile, Bulgaria joined with Germany and Austria in order to crush the Serbs. To save them and win over Greece and Romania to the Allies' side, an Anglo-French expedition was sent to Salonika (Greece) and was later reinforced when the suffering Gallipoli force was withdrawn (December 1915-January 1916). Clemenceau could see the merits of helping the Serbs and winning the Balkans away from the Central Powers, and so could the Army Commission. Aware of the commission majority's opinion and doubtless feeling bound by his presidency to exercise restraint, he confined himself in hearings to asking pointed questions of the ministers. But in the press he was altogether outspoken, and for weeks on end in the latter part of

1915 and early 1916 he returned almost daily to "the mess" in the Balkans. His questions at bottom were simple: Do we have the means to do what everyone grants would be a good thing to do? And have we prepared? Joffre had sacrificed hundreds of thousands of infantry in 1915 in a series of offensives in Champagne and Artois, yet the Germans had hardly been budged. If, because of the threat in the West, enough men could not be sent to take the *offensive* in the East, then why send them at all?[49]

He predicted the worst for the Salonika force as it fell back on that port following the Serbs' defeat (December 1915), but disaster was averted-- which damaged his political stock.[50] Reinforcements were sent to this "gala of insanities" early in 1916, but not enough to accomplish anything important.[51] Yet the Salonika army stayed on to become a disease-ridden encampment of half-a-million men, large enough to draw fire from Westerners as a waste but too small to do anything but feed a Great Dismal Swamp of military-diplomatic complications in which successive ministries wallowed, Briand's in particular. As far as Clemenceau was concerned, the best that can be said of this dreary scene was that it at least saved him from worry over what to write about on slow days.

The titanic struggle in the West mesmerized Clemenceau and most of his countrymen. With "the Germans at Noyon" it could hardly do otherwise. (He made the phrase a byword after the Censorship cut his 28 August 1915 editorial, "The Germans Are at Noyon," title and all.) In commission meetings and the press he scrupulously, even ostentatiously, refrained from seriously playing the armchair strategist, although his questions often seemed cunningly framed to allow himself the luxury of saying later, "I told you so!" As he somewhat archly put it in the first days of the war:

> My perfect incompetence in the art of war, sustained by this idea that no science escapes the superior laws of good sense, leads me to experience no hesitation in freely offering opinions which can bind nobody but myself but in which the reader may encounter elements suitable for meditation.[52]

This statement was already proving to be disingenuous, for in fact from beginning to end he was continually torn by agonizing choices between his desire--as he saw it, his duty--to warn and his desire to bolster confidence and courage.

His comments on operations and tactics, which as a rule had to be swathed in Delphic allusions to escape the censors' shears, exhibited a certain ambivalence in that while his taste for action chimed with the doctrine in vogue at the GQG which emphasized attack and the superiority of will and sheer guts over barbed wire and high explosive, his mind registered the vital importance of matériel, planning, and inter-Allied cooperation. Early in the war, with offensives all the rage, he sometimes wrote romanticized gush--troops in joyful charges à la baïonnette against cowardly, stupid Boches--which sadly showed the vulnerability of even the finest minds to war hysteria.[53] His confidence in General Joffre, however, never ran very deep. During the discussion of the Humbert revelations on the eve of the war, he had written, "In my eyes this excellent man is totally destitute of character," arguing that he must have known of the deficiencies but had done nothing to rock the boat.[54] Interestingly, he also had risked expressing clear reservations about the wisdom of Joffre's offensive in the opening days, reservations which events bore out all too sadly.[55]

Joffre's magnificent recovery at the Marne naturally earned his praise, but the sanguinary check of the spring offensive in 1915 inevitably began to bring his doubts about him to the surface again, though not in print. He briefly entertained some high hopes during the big September push when he at last was allowed to visit the front,[56] and certainly he did not altogether abandon faith in offensives. In fact, in 1916, the year of Verdun, whose appalling toll rendered problematical any future grand offensives by the French, he began to think of none other than Foch, the high priest of attack, as his man for the top command.[57] But all in all he had no real confidence in the capacity of the current civil and military chiefs to conduct such operations.

Joffre stayed on and on, an untouchable deity. Rather than sack him, Briand put General Gallieni, whom Clemenceau greatly admired, at the War ministry (October 1915) to keep watch over him. But Gallieni's health gave out by March 1916 (he died in May), and his replacement, General Roques, was a Joffre man. When Briand at long last eased Joffre out, a year too late

(December 1916), he installed General Nivelle, the Radicals' latest darling (a Protestant), who had won a deserved renown defending Verdun. Nivelle convinced himself, most of the politicians, and the army that he had the secret to The Breakthrough. Clemenceau, although he liked him, did not conceal his anxiety. General Pétain, for one, had remained sceptical and, when Clemenceau had come by for a visit in January 1917, had advised staying on the defensive until the Americans, as now seemed likely, should join the Allies.[58] The heartbreaking failure at the Chemin des Dames (16-20 April) confirmed their worst forebodings and opened a six-months crisis which brought Pétain to the head of the army and himself to the premiership. No more bloodbaths, Pétain again advised; hold fast and wait for the Americans. Clemenceau agreed.[59]

It was not enough to find a commander. The government, he insisted, must set grand strategy and hold him accountable for its execution. He believed the famous line attributed to him, "War is too important to be left to generals," even if he didn't coin it.[60] Strategy in a world war means planning with one's allies. He suspected even before the Marne that the war would be long, fought until "the deep resources" were exhausted, and said it would be won by the side which could last "a quarter-hour" longer.[61] Hence his emphasis upon France's need to recognize that she could neither wage war nor make peace without allies. Hence the importance he attached to unifying command on the Western Front, a project which made modest headway under Painlevé (September-November 1917) and to which he devoted some of his last articles before becoming premier.[62] Hence, too, the importance of the United States.

Clemenceau regarded American intervention as a near-certain guarantee of victory and of a peace (he assured the Socialists) which would not be abused by the victors.[63] Having some knowledge of the United States, he sought to interpret that distant land to his readers, particularly the president's problems in leading a huge, ethnically diverse country much less centralized than France. Woodrow Wilson attracted him by the elevation of his mind and repelled him by a lofty moralizing which he likened to the pope's. (He once portrayed him as a professor on a riverbank lecturing a drowning child on how to avoid floods.[64]) Despite recurrent disappointments, especially when outrage over the loss of American lives on the *Lusitania* did not bring a declaration of war, he never lost hope that the United States would come in.   When the final German-American crisis boiled up--the Zimmermann Note,[*] he said, surpassed even *his* low estimate of German intelligence[65]--he sponged away his often bitter criticism of Wilson by explaining that the president had acted with statesmanlike patience in order to get opinion solidly behind him when the time came to intervene.[66] "A world safe for democracy" won his warm approval. "The American avalanche" was on its way.[67]

VI

In the meantime he worked and waited for his hour. Disclaimers then and later notwithstanding, he did want it. Without succumbing to illusions of infallibility, he believed he had the ideas and *caractère* needed to pull the country to victory. His only doubt, a very real one, was whether he could bring it off physically--his age, diabetes, bronchitis, and bouts of insomnia and lassitude. He concluded he could give it a year.[68]

His decision to accept nothing in effect but the premiership meant that the others, above all Poincaré, would have to come to him. Nor would he go out of his way to meet them, for that might undercut the authority he wanted and believed he needed. Long after the war Martet set down a conversation typical of those endless months in waiting:

> "In your today's article [said Martet] you take a line against M. Poincaré. You reproach him with not wanting to know and not knowing what he wants...."
> "Yes, because it's true. Oughtn't it to be said?"
> "I don't know if it ought to be said or not. But I do know that in saying it you take away from M. Poincaré all desire to entrust you with power...."
> "Well?"
> "The war will end without you, and I am afraid that in consequence it will end very badly...."

---

 * A coded message (19 Jan. 1917) from Foreign Secretary Zimmermann to the minister in Mexico ordering him to promise Mexico the return of the Mexican Cession if she would fight the United States as Germany's ally. British Intelligence intercepted it and passed it to Wilson, who published it on 1 March.

"It will end as it is being prosecuted...."

"Exactly! I am sure that M. Poincaré is only waiting for a sign from you in order to appeal for your co-operation. For the love of God, make that sign!"

Clemenceau stopped joking and looked at me with sardonic eyes:

"No, Martet," he said to me, "I shan't make that sign-- you can do what you like. I shan't do it, for this reason: that, far from seeking power like all these worthy people, I'm afraid of it. I am terribly afraid of it. I would give anything to escape from it! You have merely to look at me and see clearly that I'm a goner: seventy-six years old, rotten with diabetes....How do you expect me to pull it off? Secondly, I'm not at all sure that we could pull it off in the pass to which we've come."

"You think that Germany can't be beaten?"

"I think it's a job, a difficult one...not because Germany is Germany; German strength has its limits: the Boche is stupid, narrow. But because France is France. My unhappy country frightens me. I look about on all sides: I see nothing. I see...Parliament bewildered and enslaved, a press...preposterous, a public opinion unbalanced, distracted...and beyond all that just words. Ah! those magnificent words. Never have such beautiful speeches been heard! A pity that it isn't enough for victory!"

"But, nevertheless, if M. Poincaré tendered you office?"

"But do you really mean that he will offer it to me? Despite everything, alas! Despite everything!"

"What shall you do?"

"I shall accept. One cannot refuse office. But I shall not have sought it. There will be nothing to reproach me with: not the wink of an eye, not the shuffle of a foot. Then the power that will be offered me will have this new and special quality about it, that it will be real power."[69]

In truth, the Poincaré problem stymied him. He wanted "Raymond I" out, but how to force his hand? He belabored him mercilessly in 1915, but in 1916 he slackened this sterile exercise somewhat and by 1917 was taking only occasional, if still stinging, swipes. Another way around might be to blow up a cabinet from the inside somehow, since public votes of confidence were nearly automatic, and then get all potential premiers to go on strike, thus forcing Poincaré to resign so that a new president...but all that seemed impossibly complicated, typical of the advice one sometimes got from Georges Mandel.[70] Political realities and good sense led him to the only practical course: wait, let the others use themselves up, attack their weak points, and then trust Poincaré's prudence and patriotism to persuade him to heed the message on the wall and give in or get out.

Rumors that he was "plotting" trailed him around as they had for decades. His article in *L'Homme Enchaîné* on 15 December 1916 once set tongues wagging, for example, when three days after his sole meeting with Poincaré, during a severe crisis in the Briand ministry, he called on the people to make known to the government, but without violence, that they would maintain their right (*droit*) and will. The anti-parliamentary tone of this outburst echoed the *Thermidor* speech back in 1891, where he had warned that if the government did not do its duty, the people would do theirs.[71] But in the days following, "like those sons who do not want to know anything about their mother's error,"[72] he defended Parliament as the link between the people and the government. Such assurances did not sufficiently impress the British ambassador, Lord Bertie, for one, who told his government after Clemenceau came to power that he thought him quite capable of calling in the army if he were defeated in the Chamber.[73]

At all events, his name continued to float through transoms, especially when things went worse than usual. But not until September 1917, when Painlevé replaced Ribot, was it heard distinctly. As already noted, he had advanced somewhat in the autumn of 1915 only to fade when the Salonika army stayed intact. He rode with the assault on Briand and Joffre over Verdun and policy in the Balkans in June-July 1916, struggling through a long speech during the Senate's secret sessions of 4-9 July while in the throes of a diabetic crisis. In the public roll call Briand swept up 251 votes to a derisory 6 for Clemenceau's "forces." He took his humiliation philosophically, invoking for his readers the hero of his favorite play, Ibsen's *An Enemy of the People*, and hung in his office a Forain cartoon, "The Death of Shere Khan," depicting Briand as a buffalo trampling on a tigerskin rug.[74] He had been down before: it was 1900 again, but he was seventy-five and sick. "Well, Monsieur le Président, what will you do now?" asked Paul-Boncour. "Rest a bit...let them blow...and then resume the struggle...."[75]

Briand had triumphed, but after that it was slowly downhill for him. A "rested" Clemenceau was telling General Haig in October, "I'm seventy-five...and the whole future is before me."[76] By late November the ministry's troubles were grave (Joffre, Greece, Romania, the economy), and Clemenceau was again, quite obviously now, setting his sights. The Chamber's opposition now numbered between 160 and 200, while the Senate's climbed dramatically from July's 6 to 56. Hoarse with bronchitis and in pain from a complication of his 1912 surgery, he hammered away during the secret sessions of 19-23 December, but his ideas and vehemence frightened the growing flocks of fence-sitters. They fluttered back to Briand, who bought time with virtuoso oratory and, adroitly on the eve of the Senate sessions, a cabinet reshuffle and a "promotion" for Joffre from field command to "senior military councillor" to the government. (He resigned after three weeks of inactivity.) Clemenceau's pale star faded once again. But General Lyautey, the new minister of war, presently stepped up political censorship, which Briand had eased significantly during his tenure, got at loggerheads with Parliament on the *contrôle* question, and suddenly resigned in a huff. When Briand found he had to throw in his hand as a result (17 March 1917), it was Alexandre Ribot, highly intelligent and vastly experienced but aging (75) and something of a ditherer, who got the call. With him the Furies descended.

VII

The slaughtered offensive on the Chemin des Dames in April and May brutally exposed every weakness, every doubt and illusion. At the very moment the Russian Revolution (begun in early March) was showing signs of precipitating a general collapse of the Eastern Front, a wave of mutinies swept through the French armies, a few of them violent but most amounting to refusals to go up to the lines on reliefs or to attack when ordered. Fed by disillusionment over pointless bloodbaths, by miserable food, a bungling medical service, lack of leave, a harsh, unfeeling discipline, and fueled, too, by ample cheap wine, oratory inspired by the Russian Revolution, anti-war literature, a strike wave, rumors of peace, and agitation about a proposed conference of Socialist pacifists in Stockholm--the mutinies deeply shook the commanders and the government. In early June it was reported that there were only two reliable divisions immediately covering Paris. Amazingly, pure luck and a ferocious censorship managed to keep the Germans in the dark. (Clemenceau got away with a surprisingly broad hint of trouble in print on 9

June, though he framed it as if it were an occasion to assert his confidence.) As for the public, by late spring postal inspection reports for the first time in the war indicated that a majority appeared resigned to settling for something less than complete victory and were holding firm only against outright defeat. In response to this alarming wave of discouragement, an epithet, "defeatist," surged to popularity in the "patriotic" press.[77]

Pétain took over from the discredited Nivelle, and by mixing a handful of executions with some sensible measures regarding food, rest, and offensives, he managed to restore a barely sufficient cohesion by mid-July. He partly covered the GQG, however, by blaming the government for failing to crack down on "defeatist" propaganda, labor agitators, slackers, and deserters. His principal target was the Radicals' longtime key cabinet member at Interior, Jean Malvy. Clemenceau, whose stock was rising again as it always did in a bear market, resolved on a showdown. On 22 July, after biding his time through three days of secret sessions he had helped to provoke in order to soften up the government, he went to the rostrum in open session and for two mortal hours turned Malvy on a spit.

The 22 July attack on Malvy had begun to be expected by the political world as far back as early May, although Clemenceau had said almost nothing about him in print until 2 June during the mutinies crisis. Nor, in fact, was this their first confrontation: in the secret sessions of 19-23 December 1916 he had pressed him vigorously about sabotage and pacifist-inspired disorders in defense industries.[78] This and related themes concerning the circulation of subversive literature among the troops had been taken up subsequently by Nivelle and, as already noted, by Pétain after Nivelle's fall. In the Army Commission from May onward and in articles on the eve of the July secret sessions, Clemenceau harried Malvy relentlessly, with Ribot and Painlevé also drawing fire when they tried to defend their colleague.[79] The 22 July speech burst the boil. From then until he became premier four months later, he took a leading role in a campaign against defeatists and defeatism which gained great momentum from a succession of scandals bursting like a row of wired land-mines--German money; venal, naïve, or intrigue-prone journalists and politicians; treason and quasi-treason of every hue.

Because the attack on Malvy proved to be the turning point in Clemenceau's fortunes, questions have arisen as to his motives and methods. Usually they imply that since he had failed on other issues he turned to crying "Spies and traitors!"--cries which the Chemin des Dames fiasco and the ensuing mutinies providentially made all the more believable. Malvy's indulgent handling of potentially dangerous elements (with his colleagues' approval, it must be granted) and his general continuance of peacetime methods during a war were arguably worth the risk so long as morale held firm--as it had. But when a deepening malaise at home, apparent by late 1916, was suddenly compounded by mutiny at the front, Clemenceau drew the rather obvious conclusion that this crisis was truly grave, perhaps the beginning of a slide to the abyss which (he once told General Haig back in May 1916) could gain speed quickly among a people as volatile as the French.[80] Malvy stubbornly defended his methods, but his homeopathic cures certainly needed time, and in Clemenceau's view time had become the least expendable of commodities.[81]

It seems clear, too, that Clemenceau took his charges against the defeatists seriously, although some were flimsy because he wrote on the wing and from information supplied by others from, for example, such dubious sources as raw police reports. Yet events kept bearing him out. He did know many things about many people--Malvy and the Senate were greatly surprised at the wealth of his "inside" documentation in his 22 July speech[82]-- and was shrewd enough not to tell all, nor all at once. He had not spent a half-century in politics without learning how to put fear into foes. Having measured Malvy in December 1916, he sensed the moment to level him. But he roundly denied he was on a witch hunt.[83] No more than a quarter of his articles after 22 July were directed chiefly to the treason scandals. Moreover, just as he had not advised a wholesale application of *Carnet B* in 1914, so in 1917 he held that only a limited number of persons posed a danger. And since they were loosely connected, "a nest," they could be dealt with expeditiously: take the ringleaders out of circulation and the small fry would come to heel. The crux of the matter was not so much the danger presented by a few traitors or renegades as the moral effect of action against them. The slide would continue unless the common soldier and civilian believed his sacrifices were not in vain and could *see* that his leaders meant business.[84] To Clemenceau this seemed little enough to ask from gentlemen who *every day* were in effect calling upon nearly *nine hundred* men to lay down their lives.

Finally, while he could hardly have been unmindful of political calculations--that Malvy's fall would likely bring on a cabinet crisis, that the defeatist issue could make him a live option by bringing him support from hitherto hostile Rightists and Moderates while driving the Socialists out of the *Union sacrée*, that Pétain's quarrel with Malvy presented an opportunity to win favor at the GQG, where he had long been regarded with suspicion or worse--it is hard to prove that they ruled his conduct more than they had in the past.[85] He had always gone his own way and was as indifferent to his fellow travelers as a politician could be. So "royalist" demagogues at Action Française were attacking the defeatists? But their campaign was nothing new--and besides, even fools are right once in awhile. (The paper in fact did not support him until after he came to power.) In the same vein, the Socialists. While he tilted with them over things like their prewar pacifism or the Stockholm Conference, he thought, and repeatedly affirmed, that most of them were good patriots. He respected their influence with labor and made serious overtures to them on the eve of his ministry--in particular to Albert Thomas, an able minister of armaments under Briand and Ribot, despite having roundly criticized him back in June for a statement favoring retrocession of Alsace-Lorraine to France only after a plebiscite. More, however, he would not do. His train was leaving and he hoped they would climb aboard, but the choice was theirs.[86]

The Radicals got the same treatment. Back in December 1916--would he have changed so much in six months?--André Maginot had scolded him: "Really, you are impossible! You want to be premier and you get at loggerheads with a man [Malvy] who has 150 deputies at his beck and call." "What did he say?" asked Abel Ferry. "Nothing. He looked at me."[87] Indeed, the Malvy and (presently) the Caillaux cases acutely embarrassed and divided the party, and at its congress in late October they gave the presidency to Senator Debierre rather than Senator Couyba, whom Clemenceau was known to want. But he forged on, and three weeks later the

Radicals caved in, voted for his ministry, and raised no official protest over his actions against Malvy and Caillaux.[88]

VIII

Clemenceau's speech on the 22nd, although impressive in general statement and tone, trailed off into readings of police reports whose importance Malvy could minimize. But his retorts during Malvy's explanations drew blood: "I charge you with having betrayed the interest of France!" he burst out at one point. Ribot intervened to help his minister through. A clause obliquely blaming Malvy was added to the confidence motion after Clemenceau had astutely promised to vote for the ministry "if it gives me the means." For the moment he apparently would have been satisfied with having Malvy out, if not Ribot--yet.[89] The *grande presse* soft-pedaled the affair, while the public paid only passing attention at first even though *L'Homme Enchaîné* printed thousands of extra copies of the speech. Not so the political world. Malvy could answer on particulars, but the cumulative record damned him beyond the saving power of a labored motion of confidence. The fact that it was nearly identical to one passed a few days earlier by the Chamber hinted that parliamentary opinion was solidifying. A few days later the arrest and prison "suicide" of Miguel Almereyda, the mysterious, well-connected director of the pacifistic (and lately German subsidized) *Le Bonnet Rouge*, broke the scandals full open. Malvy languished through the dog days of August while Ribot subtly plied his old arts to undermine him. On the 31st he resigned. Ribot's subsequent attempt to reshuffle the ministry failed, however, and with that he had to give up too.

An unusually confused cabinet crisis lasting a week set the tone for Paul Painlevé's short run as premier. His was the first war cabinet without the Socialists. Ironically, Ribot's reshuffle had been designed to exclude them and had unravelled when Painlevé had refused to join in a combination without them. But when Painlevé then formed his own ministry, they had declined to participate because he had decided to keep Ribot on as foreign minister. Improbable as it seems in light of the events of the next three months, the Socialists (notably Albert Thomas) thought they were on the road to full power in the near future[90]--this even despite their own mounting ideological quarrels, exacerbated by the Russian Revolution, which would have needed all the skill and personal ascendance of a Jaurès to master. The consequences for them, and the country, of his assassination would only grow in the months--indeed, the years--ahead.

IX

Despite the disarray at the top, the country's morale had revived somewhat from July to September. The British were pounding at Ypres, and doing the bleeding, while Pétain, who put more faith in big guns than bayonets, was bracing up his shaky divisions with well-planned modest successes won at minimal cost. Clemenceau returned from a tour of the front in mid-September publicly radiating confidence in the *poilus* and their chiefs.[91] Privately, however, he was still deeply concerned about the army's morale, so much so that on about 2 September he had gone so far as to enlist a nonplused top commander, General Castelnau, in a bizarre attempt to persuade the American First Division's commander, General Sibert, to agree to an immediate entry of his unit into the line. The embarrassed Sibert, having no such authority in General Pershing's absence, politely declined.[92]

Even before Clemenceau's subsequent tour of the front, in fact, the barometer had begun to fall again, and all through the autumn it showed no signs of stopping. The Americans still had but a single division in the battle zone, while the British, dying by tens of thousands in a sea of mud at Passchendaele, were going nowhere. On 24 October Italy's armies were sent reeling by a huge Austro-German breakthrough at Caporetto, and on 7 November Lenin's Bolsheviks seized what passed for power in Petrograd, ending the Kerenskii government's lingering agony. With Romania also standing inches from capitulation, the Eastern Front looked all but hopeless. At home another winter was looming, decked with coal shortages and the promise of longer lines at the bakeries, while in Parliament the government, beset by quarrels which the public either could not comprehend or scorned when it did, was living from day to day, squeezing votes of confidence from men who had become convinced almost from the hour it was formed that it was at the end of its tether.

The signs were everywhere. On 2 November during yet another tour at the front, Clemenceau stopped by unannounced to see Gen. Henri Mordacq, a top-rated division commander, with whom he had had contacts since at least 1913, and told him to prepare for duty as his personal assistant (*chef de cabinet militaire*) at the War ministry.[93]

Painlevé had masked the *Union sacrée*'s demise by making his cabinet the largest to date. He had even invited Clemenceau--a straw in the wind-- but the latter had long since soured on him after some early hopes.[94] (Did he know of his reputed leanings toward a negotiated peace?[95]) Painlevé, a mathematician of high repute, was a well-meaning, hard-working, overly sensitive man who listened too much to advice from his intimates and always saw too many sides to a question. And he was unlucky. The scandals roared on. He ordered investigations and some arrests; but his fear that his own secret correspondence with General Sarrail (at Salonika) when they had been intriguing against Briand and Joffre in 1916 might come to light led him to act with a too obvious reluctance.[96] As an Independent (Republican) Socialist, he knew he was vulnerable in the Center and Right and hence felt impelled to conciliate the Socialists and those Radical-Socialists with allegiances to Caillaux. Nothing worked very well. When Malvy made public (4 October) an outrageous letter from *Action Française*'s Léon Daudet to Poincaré accusing him (Malvy) of treason in connection with the Chemin des Dames disaster, he went after the paper with a suspension but also with a proposal to stiffen the libel law which aroused protests from the Socialists and many others, Clemenceau among them. Clemenceau called Daudet "an anachronism," another "Norton," and his charges against Malvy grossly exaggerated and unjust. But he also accused Malvy, Painlevé, and Poincaré of confecting a whitewash instead of simply suing Daudet for libel.[97] Painlevé's clumsy and, as further details became known, somewhat devious handling of the affair finally prompted the Socialists to vote against the ministry (rather than abstain, as had been their custom) on a roll call which the ministry carried by only 246 to 189 (16 October).

Another, concurrent, attempt to mollify the Left also damaged Painlevé when he unwisely tried to get General Brugère, chairman of a board investigating the Chemin des Dames affair, to expunge altogether from his report an already watered-down version of the charges of parliamentary interference and pacifist intrigue. Brugère indignantly informed the Senate

Army Commission, where Clemenceau lost no time in rousing opposition in both houses against political interference of this sort.[98]

In the meantime, the peace issue continued to churn. To the sensitivities of the Socialists about it were being added those of the Radical-Socialists sympathetic to Caillaux. At Mamers on 22 July (a piquant coincidence) he had made his first major speech since 1914, calling for a war to establish democracy in Europe as the foundation of a stable peace, one based on justice, not on a crushing of the opponent, and ensured by a world organization of the nations. Contrary to later, widespread belief, he did not want "peace now at any price," but he stood prepared to negotiate fair terms once the Germans had been persuaded by a victorious Allied offensive that they must give up their dreams of conquest. Unfortunately for him, and certainly for others identified with the peace issue, in the weeks following the speech his name began to surface in the *Bonnet Rouge* investigations as someone who had had contacts over the years with a striking number of persons now suspected of trafficking with the Germans.[99]

The damage to the peace party had worsened when a pointed question from Clemenceau in *L'Homme Enchaîné* on 15 October led to a secret session of the Chamber on the 16th in which Ribot and Briand were forced to confront each other over the latter's recently aborted project to comply with an invitation from a German diplomat, Baron von der Lancken, to meet in Switzerland to discuss possible bases of a separate peace between France and Germany. Ribot and the government had advised Briand against walking into a possible trap, and Briand had, with some reluctance, backed out.[100] The secret session led to the shelving of both Ribot and Briand, very important men, for the rest of the war--Briand because he had been made to look like either a naïf or a closet defeatist, and Ribot because the peace party thought he had again wasted an opportunity to explore an avenue to a settlement. A week later Painlevé dropped him as foreign minister, thus pleasing the Socialists, only to replace him with Barthou, a good choice per se but as "the Man of the Three Years Law" no more acceptable to them and some of their Radical-Socialist sympathizers than Ribot had been. The ministry won a 288-137 vote of confidence, with the Socialists again voting in opposition.

Once more Painlevé sought to recoup on the Left. Prompted by Caillaux--who was seeking to rally the Left behind himself by striking at *Action Française*, where Daudet had added his name to Malvy's on the roll of traitors, and by splitting *Action Française*'s anti-defeatist campaign from its informal alliance with that launched by Clemenceau on 22 July--Painlevé acted (28 October) on a tip from a disgruntled former *Action Française* adherent and ordered a search of the paper's offices. It turned up a quantity of mostly ancient small arms and some plans for a coup in case of certain eventualities. The government's (and Caillaux's) counter-coup, so to speak, misfired, however, when the judicial authorities, unsympathetic to the ministry's policies, refused (5 November) to return an indictment. Failure in an operation of this nature only made the government look impotent. Years later Clemenceau remarked to a Socialist deputy that if *he* had run that operation instead of Painlevé, *Action Française* wouldn't have gotten off so lightly.[101]

X

The denouement was swift yet in its actual arrival a surprise. A crisis atmosphere pervaded the first days of November. The Caporetto disaster in Italy brought Lloyd George over for a conference at Rapallo on the 6th and 7th and the creation of a Permanent Military Committee to be based at Versailles--the germ of a unified command--while Foch and some reinforcements entrained for Italy to set up a new line on the Piave. On the 8th came news of the Bolshevik coup in Petrograd. Feeling the rising wind, the Socialists met on the 9th and formally vetoed in advance (an unprecedented act) any Clemenceau ministry as "an insult to the working class and a danger to the national defense"[102]--an affront which Clemenceau never wholly forgave. Two days later, on his return from Italy, Lloyd George, who needed no more than a zephyr to sense a coming wind, dropped by his apartment for a chat with Monsieur Clemenceau and a try at getting him to back the Versailles scheme. But he found the old man still outspokenly sceptical about "military parliamentarianism" when what was needed in his view was a commander-in-chief.[103]

That was how matters stood when on the 13th a mistake, a mere slip of the foot, suddenly sprang the gate. Painlevé reported on the Rapallo conference to a testy Chamber. Despite some harsh criticism and expressions of no confidence from some leading members, he won a watery endorsement, 250 to 192. But then, for no discernable reason, he let himself get involved in supporting a maverick Radical-Socialist during an emotional set-to with a right-winger, at the end of which he asked for a postponement of interpellations on current cases in the courts. Protests rained down, whereupon he put a confidence question on it. The hour was late, the Right, which heretofore had voted for him out of "patriotic duty," was in a mood, the Socialists were not thinking clearly, and the tally showed 186 to 277. For the first time ever in the war a ministry had been defeated on the floor. Noise and confusion swept the hall. From the Socialist benches--a Day of Dupes for them--came cries of "Down with Clemenceau!"[104]

But it was too late for that.

NOTES
CHAPTER XIII

Note: Chapter title from Jacques Barzun in *New Republic*, 6 Dec. 1943, p. 824, recalling William Blake's famous lines in "The Tyger."

1   Martet, *Le Tigre*, pp. 36-39.

2   Sir Edward L. Spears, *Assignment to Catastrophe*, 2 vols. (London: Heinemann, 1954), 2:238.

3   Poincaré, *Au service de la France*, 5:189.

4   See HL, 29 Aug. 1914, where, because *Le Temps* had revealed it, he felt obliged to his "infinite regret" to explain his refusal to join Viviani's new *Union sacrée* government. He said he was willing to join a ministry in a subordinate capacity but not one which was not "in my eyes a sufficient instrument of action" and not headed by "a chief who was a chief in the sense required by the [present] situation." He declined to name any prospective chiefs.

5   HL, 21 May 1913. See also his Senate speech of 6 Aug. 1913.

6   See HL, 1 ("En route vers l'inconnu"), 3 July 1914. For a contrasting view see Duroselle, *Clemenceau*, pp. 577-578.

7   Nos. 13-15, rue Taitbout, a nicer locale than that of his previous papers, is just off the boulevard Haussmann about five minutes' walk from the Opéra (Metro, Chausée d'Antin) and is presently used in some of *Le Monde*'s operations.

8   Messimy, the minister of war, later wrote that Clemenceau had prompted Humbert, with Poincaré, not himself, as the real target. Messimy, *Mes souvenirs*, p. 127n. See also HL, 16-18, 23, 24 July 1914. Clemenceau defended his own ministry's record as best he could; the heavy-artillery deficiency had first become an issue during its tenure.

9   See HL, 2 Aug. 1914, for his obituary tribute to this man "who honored his country by his talent, put to the service of a high ideal, and by the noble elevation of his views....It was Jaurès' fate to preach the fraternity of peoples and to have so firm a faith in this grand idea that it could not even be discouraged by the brutal evidence of facts. He fell at the very hour when his idealism would have had to descend from the serene heights of thought in order to call all his friends to the fight for the Fatherland which is, at the same time, the fight for the idea. A great force has been taken from us at the moment it was making ready for supreme efforts...."

10   See an excerpt from his speech at the Lycée Clemenceau (Nantes), 27 [*sic*] May 1922, in Mordacq, *Clemenceau*, p. 75. See also Lautier, "Clemenceau," for recollections of remarks in 1914; Drieu de La Rochelle,"Paroles d'outre-tombe," p. 8; and Fernand Neuray, *Entretiens avec Clemenceau* (Éditions Prométhée, 1930), p. 49.

11   See Duroselle, *Clemenceau*, pp. 583-586, on this strange affair.

12   See Louis-Jean Malvy, *Mon crime* (E. Flammarion, 1921), pp. 36-37. Clemenceau later said he believed a handful of arrests would have sufficed and that he had never seen *Carnet B* personally; JOS, 22 July 1917, p. 754. In 1909 he had ordered the list expanded to include not just potential spies but anyone who might sabotage mobilization. Apparently no master list was kept until late 1912; hence he arguably could not have "seen" (all of?) it "personally." See Jean-Jacques Becker, *Le Carnet B: Les pouvoirs publics et l'anti-militarisme avant la guerre de 1914* (Klencksieck, 1973), pp. 111-113 and *passim*.

13   See HL, 29 Aug. 1914; and HE, 18 Feb. 1915; and Poincaré, *Au service de la France*, 5:171.

14   See HL, 30 Aug. 1914; and Poincaré, *Au service de la France*, 5:186-89. On 12 Dec. 1916 he called him in to consult on a peace offer from Germany after her victory over Romania; see Wormser, *Le septennat de Poincaré*, pp. 76-77.

15   See HE, 30 April 1915; and Poincaré, *Au service de la France*, 5:198, 216.

16   Williams, *The Tiger of France*, pp. 126-127.

17   Georges Gombault in *L'Oeuvre*, 13 Oct. 1919.

18   See HL, 3, 21 Aug. 1914; and Jean-Claude Devos and Jean Nicot, "La censure de la presse pendant la guerre de 1914-1918," *Actes du 105ᵉ Congrès national des Société savantes, Caen, 1980* vol. 1: *La diffusion du savoir de 1610 à nos jours. Questions diverses* (Comité des travaux historiques et scientifiques, 1983), pp. 344-345.

19   He had written previously on deficiencies in the medical service; see HL, 17, 19, 20 September 1914.

20   A ploy already used by Emmanuel Brosse at *L'Indépendant* which Clemenceau had noted with approval in HL, 21 Sept. 1914.

21   The Musée Clemenceau contains both the censored and uncensored copies of HL and HE in their entirety. See HE, 8 Oct. (Bordeaux), 8 Dec. 1914; Gatineau-Clemenceau [the grandson], *Des pattes du Tigre*, pp. 147-149; Georges Wormser, *Georges Mandel, l'homme politique* (Librairie Plon, 1967), pp. 42, 45; John M. Sherwood, *Georges Mandel and the*

Third Republic (Stanford, CA: Stanford University Press, 1970), p. 307n; Marcel Berger and Paul Allard, *Les secrets de la Censure pendant la Guerre* (Éditions des Portiques, 1932), pp. 68-73, 79; and Jean-Jacques Becker, *The Great War and the French People*, trans. Arnold Pomerans (New York: St. Martin's Press, 1986), pp. 44-45, 52-53.

22   HL, 3 Aug. 1914.

23   See HL, 21, 24-26 Aug., 3 Sept. 1914.

24   See HE, 5 Aug., 2-10, 14 Sept. 1914; repr. in GC, *La leçon de la Russie* (Floury, 1915). Ironically, the Kadet paper *Rech'*, 14 Aug. 1915, praised the *Union sacrée* as a "lesson" for Russia.

25   E.g., HE, 24 Aug. 1915, 24 Jan., 18 March, 23 April, 25 May, 6, 14, 24-27 June, 1, 12, 13 July, 29 Nov. 1916, 22 Jan., 22 May 1917. A secret session proposal was debated once (Chamber, 4 June 1918) during his ministry after another Chemin des Dames disaster. But by then the device, principally promoted by the commissions in order to use the Senate and Chamber plenums as sounding boards, had lost meaning due to the power the commissions had acquired. See Inge Saatmann, *Parlament, Rüstung und Armee in Frankreich 1914/18* (Düsseldorf: Droste Verlag, 1978), pp. 329-332, 403, 408-409.

26   See Saatmann, *Parlament, Rüstung und Armee*, pp. 189, 192. See also Jere Clemens King, *Generals and Politicians: Conflicts Between France's High Command, Parliament, and Government, 1914-18* (Berkeley, CA: University of California Press, 1951), *passim*. Saatmann's study, despite an occasionally intrusive Marxian interpretation, is an indispensable guide to the commissions' work.

27   Saatmann, *Parlament, Rüstung und Armee*, p. 192 (23 June 1915?).

28   See HE, 20 May 1916, on Briand as "Mr. Micawber."

29   Maunoury, *Police de guerre*, p. 148.

30   Spears, *Assignment to Catastrophe*, 1:57.

31   HE, 26 Jan. 1916.

32   See HE, 17 Sept. 1915.

33   HE, 20 Aug. 1915.

34   See Wormser, *Le septennat de Poincaré*, p. 102n. On the "outsider" role in French politics see Stanley Hoffmann, *Decline or Renewal? France Since the 1930s* (New York: The Viking Press, 1974), p. 82.

35   HL, 4 Aug. 1914.

36   HE, 30 June 1917. See also 7 May 1915, 27 Oct. 1917.

37   HE, 26 April 1915. See also HL, 11 March, 5 Aug. 1914; and GC, *Discours de guerre*, recueillis et publiés par la Société des Amis de Georges Clemenceau, new ed. (Presses Universitaires de France, 1968), pp. 57-58, repr. of GC, Preface to *Notre avenir*, by Gen. Friedrich von Bernhardi, trans. Emile Simonnot (Louis Conrad, 1915).

38   E.g., HL, 8 Aug. 1914; HE, 1 Oct. 1914, 20 Jan., 16 Feb., 24 April, 20 Oct. 1917; and articles occasioned by his bitter break with Georg Brandes, HE, 11, 29 March, 25 May 1915, 5 July 1916.

39   HL, 18 Sept. 1914.

40   See René Pinon, "Clemenceau et l'Autriche," *Revue politique et parlementaire* 194 (1948):154-162. Sophie and Paul married Polish-Austrian Jews, son Michel a Hungarian.

41   Zuckerkandl, *My Life and History*, p. 133. The meeting, on 22-23 Dec., occurred in connection with Paul's wedding.

42   Of 6 Sept. to Mme. Jourdan, quoted from Zévaès, *Clemenceau*, pp. 22-23. See p. 55 above.

43   HL, 18 Sept. 1914.

44   HE, 31 March 1915.

45   On the negotiations in Berne see Bogdan Krizman, "Austro-Hungarian Diplomacy Before the Collapse of the Empire," *Journal of Contemporary History* 4 (April 1969):97-115.

46   A tangled, obscure affair. See Zuckerkandl, *My Life and History*, pp. 223-248; Duroselle, *Clemenceau*, pp. 349, 590, 701-702, 810-811; André Scherer and Jacques Grunewald, eds. *L'Allemagne et les problèmes de la paix pendant la première guerre mondiale: Documents extraits des archives de l'Office allemande des Affaires Étrangères*, 2 vols. (Presses Universitaires de France, 1962-1966), 2: nos. 18, 298; Leo Valiani, *The End of Austria-Hungary* (New York: Alfred A. Knopf, 1973), pp. 260-262; and Friedrich Engel-Janosi, "Die Friedensaktion der Frau Hofrat Szeps-Zuckerkandl im Fröhjahr 1917," *Archiv für Österreichische Geschichte* 125 (1966):257-268.

47   See Alan J. P. Taylor, *The Struggle for Mastery in Europe, 1848-1918* (New York: Oxford University Press, 1954), p. 560.

48   E.g., HE, 23 Feb., 3, 8, 10, 12, 19, 22 March, 29 April, 30 May 1915.

49   In the Army Commission on 15 Jan. 1916 he asked, "What good will it do us to stay at this place [Salonika]? One should at least be in a

position to take the offensive." Saatmann, *Parlament, Rüstung und Armee*, p. 324n. She cites this as evidence that he favored staying and sending large reinforcements. But his actual meaning was the opposite. That same day in HE he called the Salonika situation "a gala of insanities."

Space forbids a proper discussion of Saatmann's contention (pp. 307-308, 317-318) that in the light of Clemenceau's generally moderate and occasionally approving remarks in commission sessions his reputed opposition to the Eastern operations is a "legend." Saatmann's discovery that his conduct was as restrained as it was is very interesting. Set against this, however, is the unanimous impression of his contemporaries and the plain meaning of some 128 articles (at rough count) devoted wholly or largely to Eastern questions in 1915-1916 alone. Rereading the articles in the light of Saatmann's research does cause one to catch shadings or reservations. But if he was no opponent of Eastern "sideshows," then what he said in his paper was an exercise in mystification which deceived everybody, even his intimates, from that day to this. And to what end?

50 E.g., 27 Sept. 5, 10 ("a delirium of incoherence"), 11, 21 Oct., 4, 16, 20, 23, 30 Nov., 2, 4, 10, 13, 15, 20, 25 Dec. 1915. Kitchener wrote Asquith on 10 Dec. 1915 that keeping British troops at Salonika had helped defuse a crisis that would have brought Clemenceau in, "which would be difficult to deal with since he hates [Poincaré]." Paul Guinn, *British Strategy and Politics, 1914 to 1918* (Oxford: The Clarendon Press, 1965), p. 115. See also Lord [Francis L.] Bertie, *The Diary of Lord Bertie*, ed. Lady Algernon Gordon Lennox, 2 vols. (New York: George H. Doran, 1924), 1:278-279.

51 See HE, 15 ("gala of insanities"), 16, 19, 28 Jan. 1916.

52 HL, 13 Aug. 1914.

53 E.g., HL, 19 Aug. 1914; HE, 9 Oct. 1914, 14 March 1915.

54 HL, 23 July 1914.

55 See HL, 13, 15, 19 Aug. 1914. But elsewhere, in "buck-up" articles, he praised Joffre, e.g., 6, 23, 26, 27 Aug.

56 See HE, 1-6 Oct. 1915. He made eight visits in 1915-1917.

57 See GC, *Grandeur and Misery of Victory*, pp. 13-20; Charles Meunier-Surcouf, "Notes personnelles, 1916-1917," MS (Musée Clemenceau); and Maj.-Gen. Sir Charles E. Callwell, *Field-Marshal Sir Henry Wilson: His Life and Diaries*, 2 vols. (London: Cassell, 1927), 1:285. He corresponded with Foch via, among others, his brother Albert, a captain on Foch's staff for a time.

58 See a Pétain letter in Jacques Isorni, *Philippe Pétain*, 2 vols. (La Table rond, 1972-1973), 1:10. See also HE, 14 Dec. 1916, 22, 24 Feb., 20, 22, 25 March, 19, 22, 24, 27 April, 16 May 1917; and Colonel [Émile]

Herbillon, *Le général Alfred Micheler, d'après sa correspondance et ses notes* (Librairie Plon, 1934), p. 110.

59   See HE, 25 April, 1, 16 May, 28 June, 20 Aug., 15 Nov. 1917; and Callwell, *Field-Marshal Sir Henry Wilson*, 1:364.

60   It has also been attributed to Talleyrand. I have never found the literal phrase in his writings or speeches. Corday quoted it on 4 June 1916 from "J. M." (Jean Martet?). Stevenson said Lloyd George heard it from Briand, and Vercors says Briand ascribed it to Philippe Berthelot. See Michel Corday, *L'envers de la guerre: Journal inédit, 1914-1918*, 2 vols. (Flammarion, 1931), 1:257; Stevenson, *Lloyd George*, p. 118; and Vercors [Jean Bouiller], *Cent ans d'histoire de France*, vol. 1: *L'apogée de la Republique ou Moi, Aristide Briand, 1862-1932: Essai d'auto-portrait* (Librairie Plon, 1981), p. 157.

61   HL, 16 ("quarter-hour"), 20 ("resources") Aug. 1914. He often repeated the "quarter-hour" phrase--ascribed to a Japanese general, Nogi, during the Russo-Japanese War--notably in the Chamber on 8 March 1918 (see pp. 377-378 below).

62   E.g., HE, 12 Nov. 1915, 22 Sept. 1916, 11, 14, 17 (Dumont-Wilden) Nov. 1917.

63   See HE, 6 April, 8 June 1917.

64   HE, 25 Jan. 1917. On 16 Feb. 1916, e.g., the Censorship cut a long passage on Wilson's submarine policy which was particularly outspoken, calling him "undulating and fleeing [*fuyant*]...the fish-man of diplomacy."

65   HE, 3 March 1917.

66   See HE, 6, 13 Feb., 1, 3, 5, 7, 15 March 1917. Before the Chemin des Dames offensive he warned not to count on American troops--"they have none." When the attack failed he flatly said they were needed. See HE, 8, 13 Feb., 25 April 1917.

67   HE, 26 March ("avalanche"), 7 April 1917. On 28 May he published an Open Letter to Wilson in favor of giving Theodore Roosevelt, whom he hugely admired, an AEF command. See also Gaston Monnerville, *Clemenceau* (Fayard, 1968), pp. 532-552, which attributes to him more influence on American opinion than seems warranted.

68   See Callwell, *Field-Marshal Sir Henry Wilson*, 1:267; and Alfred Capus, "M. Georges Clemenceau," p. 434.

69   Martet, *Clemenceau*, pp. 13-14.

70   See Gordon Wright, *Raymond Poincaré and the French Presidency* (Palo Alto, CA: Stanford University Press, 1942), pp. 166-167, Wormser, *Georges Mandel*, pp. 53-55; and n. 95 below.

71   See JOC, 29 Jan. 1891, p. 156, and a rectification, 31 Jan. pp. 163-164.

72   HE, 19 Dec. 1916.

73   Report of 14 Nov. 1917, quoted in Watson, *Georges Clemenceau*, p. 269. On plotting see also n. 95 below; Suarez, *Clemenceau*, 2:178-180; and Philip C. F. Bankwitz, *Maxime Weygand and Civil-Military Relations in Modern France* (Cambridge, MA: Harvard University Press, 1967), pp. 16-17.

74   The six: Clemenceau, Pichon, Reymonencq (Var), Guingand, Murat, and Debierre. See Martet, *Le Tigre*, pp. 204-206, for comments on them. For Ibsen see HE, 12 July 1916; for the Shere Khan story, Kipling's *Jungle Book*.

75   Joseph Paul-Boncour, *Recollections of the Third Republic*, trans. George Marion, Jr., 3 vols. (New York: Robert Speller & Sons, 1957), 1:252. He confuses July 1916 with 22 July 1917, a common error.

76   Esher, *Journals and Letters of Reginald, Viscount Esher*, 4:57.

77   See Guy Pedroncini, *Les mutineries de 1917* (Presses Universitaires de France, 1967), *passim*; Catherine Slater, *Defeatists and Their Enemies: Political Invective in France, 1914-1918* (New York: Oxford University Press, 1981), p. 2; and on opinion here and below, Becker, *The Great War and the French People*, p. 225 and *passim*; and *idem*, "L'opinion publique française en 1917," *Historiens-Géographes*, no. 315 (1987), p. 1505 and *passim*.

78   Monnerville, in *Clemenceau*, pp. 436-523, published the first extensive account of the Senate's secret sessions based on the Senate's records, which are in deplorable condition. The decipherable fragments were then published as an annex to JOS, 29 Sept. 1968. Saatmann shows that editorial errors have resulted in assigning Clemenceau's first attack on Malvy to the 4-9 July 1916 session instead of the 19-23 December 1916 session; see *Parlament, Rüstung und Armee*, pp. 334-336, 412-414; and JOS, 29 Sept. 1968, pp. 712-13 (the misdated fragment, Clemenceau vs. Malvy). But see also Martet, in *Le Tigre*, p. 200, citing 4 July 1916 as the first attack.

79   On Malvy see HL, 25, 27 Aug. 1914; and HE, 2, 10 Nov., 19 Dec. 1914, 1 Nov. 1915, 2, 21 June, 7, 10-12, 15-18 July 1917; and retrospective comment in, e.g., GC, *Grandeur and Misery of Victory*, pp. 370-377. See also Saatmann, *Parlament, Rüstung und Armee*, pp. 402-405, 411-434, *passim*; Poincaré, *Au service de la France*, 9:167, 207; Alexandre Ribot, *Journal d'Alexandre Ribot et correspondances inédites, 1914-1922* (Librairie Plon, 1936), pp. 155-157; Bertie, *The Diary of Lord Bertie*, 2:140, 142-143; and Watson, *Georges Clemenceau*, pp. 260-263.

80   Douglas Haig, *The Private Papers of Douglas Haig, 1914-1919,* ed. Robert Blake (London: Eyre & Spottiswoode, 1952), pp. 141-142 (4 May 1916)--a rather striking forecast. But on the indifference and dull resignation of the public through most of the war see Gabriel Perreux, André Ducasse, and Jacques Meyer, *Vie et mort dès français 1914-18* (Hachette, 1962), pp. 256-258.

81   See HE, 5 Sept. 1917.

82   The sources remain obscure. He and Léon Daudet apparently had the same ones, but Daudet never flatly said he (Daudet) had fed him. Maunoury says he had an important source in the Sûreté générale. See Alfred Kupferman, "Le rôle de Léon Daudete et de *L'Action Française* dans la contre-offensive morale: 1915-1918," 2e *Colloque Maurras, Aix-en-Provence 1970, Études maurrassiennes,* 1973, 2:131-132; and Maunoury, *Police de guerre,* p. 49. A picquant sidelight: Alphonse Daudet loved Clemenceau and on his deathbed told him to look after Léon. See Buré, "M. Georges Clemenceau."

83   HE, 2 Oct. 1917, replying to *Le Temps.* For evidence supporting his charge that Almereyda influenced Malvy not to apply *Carnet B,* see Jean-Jacques Becker, *1914: Comment les Français sont entrés dans la guerre* (Presses de la Fondaton nationale des sciences politiques, 1977), pp. 385-387.

84   See HE, 23 June, 7 July, 4, 10, 16 Oct. 1917.

85   Saatmann's book is to date the most elaborate of the (mainly) socialist criticisms of his actions. In sum, she holds that the mutinies gave credence to a stab-in-the-back legend which he and his supporters had been pushing in December 1916. Having radicalized strategic perceptions and war production (in which they had financial interests), they turned to a psychological offensive by attacking peace advocates, whom they equated with "socialism." In this fashion prewar liberalism, which was tending rightward, completed an evolution which, in cooperation with Pétain and Action Française, gave it predominant power henceforth through the 1920s to the detriment of socialism. Saatmann, *Parlament, Rüstung und Armee,* pp. 433-434, 451-452, 453, and *passim.* Georges Michon's *Clemenceau* (1931) is a classic earlier version from this perspective.

86   E.g., HE, 21 June 1915, 28 Dec. 1916, 3, 27 Aug., 10-13 Sept., 12, 25 Oct., 11 Nov. 1917; for criticism of Thomas, 29, 30 June, 3, 5 July 1917. See also Aristide Jobert, *Souvenirs d'un ex-parlementaire, 1914-1919* (Éditions Eugène Figuière, 1933), p. 155; Steed, *Through Thirty Years,* 2:157-159; Geoffrey Warner, *Pierre Laval and the Eclipse of France* (New York: Macmillan, 1968), pp. 13-14; Wormser, "Au sein du cabinet de guerre de Clemenceau," *Histoire de notre temps,* 1967, no. 1, pp. 115-116; Wormser, *Georges Mandel,* p. 57; and Andler, *Vie de Lucien Herr,* 245-246.

87   Abel Ferry, *Les carnets secrets (1914-1918) d'Abel Ferry* (Bernard Grasset, 1957), p. 206.

[88]   See Serge Berstein, *Histoire du Parti Radical*, vol. 1: *La recherche de l'âge d'or, 1919-1926* (Presses de la Fondation nationale des sciences politiques, 1980), pp. 94-95.

[89]   See JOS, 22 July 1917, pp. 751-769; and Martet, *Le Tigre*, pp. 209-229. On his intentions see a conversation in Bertie, *The Diary of Lord Bertie*, 2:172.

[90]   See Bertus Willem Schaper, *Albert Thomas: Trente ans de reformisme social* (Assen, Neth.: Van Gorcum, 1959), pp. 167-168.

[91]   See HE, 20 (trans. of *New York Herald* text), 22 Sept. 1917.

[92]   See George C. Marshall, *Memoirs of My Service in the World War, 1917-18* (Boston: Houghton Mifflin, 1976), pp. 36-38. The division later entered the line on 20 Oct.; Sibert, who was more at home as an engineer, was relieved of command on 14 Dec. 1917.

[93]   See HE, 5, 6, 9 Nov. 1917; Général [Jean-Jules-Henri] Mordacq, *Le ministère Clemenceau: Journal d'un témoin*, 4 vols. (Librairie Plon, 1930-31), 1:1-17; and Duroselle, *Clemenceau*, p. 595.

[94]   See HE, 29 March, 22-24 April, 18 May 1917.

[95]   See n. 46 above; and Scherer and Grunewald, *L'Allemagne et les problèmes de la paix*, 2:vi and no. 180. Berta Zuckerkandl reported Sophie (Paul Clemenceau's wife) as saying Painlevé was seriously interested in making a colonial deal in return for Alsace-Lorraine and that he intended to make Clemenceau foreign minister when he became premier. She attributed the latter's attack on Malvy to an intrigue to get Poincaré out by means of papers about Mme. Poincaré in Malvy's possession. Gatineau-Clemenceau says Sophie was Painlevé's mistress; *Des pattes du Tigre*, p. 27. It is hard to take these assertions very seriously, however.

[96]   See David Dutton, "Paul Painlevé and the End of the Sacred Union in Wartime France," *Journal of Strategic Studies* 4 (1981): 46-50 and *passim*.

[97]   See HE, 6 ("Une Affaire Norton:), 7, 21, 31 Oct. 1917. The scandals shot *Action Française*'s circulation up from 48,000 to 156,000 in Oct.; it fell to 78,000 as of 1 May 1918. By way of comparison, HE's printing on 1 July 1917 was 44,000; it slipped to 37,000 by 1 Oct. because the price doubled to ten centimes but reached 45,000 on 1 Nov. It ranked 24th of 58 papers for which figures have been published. *L'Humanité* rose from 60,000 to 66,000 in Oct.; *Le Bonnet Rouge* printed 24,000 on 1 July 1917 and *Le Pays* (another "peace" paper), 78,000. See Albert, Feyel, and Picard, *Documents pour l'histoire de la presse*, pp. 60-61.

[98]   See Saatmann, *Parlament, Rüstung und Armee*, pp. 441-448.

99   See Jean-Claude Allain, *Joseph Caillaux*, vol 2: *L'oracle, 1914-44* (Imprimerie Nationale, 1981), pp. 85-91.   Clemenceau first mentioned Caillaux in print on 9 Oct.

100   Ribot, too clever or too trusting, had informed Clemenceau of the details of Briand's project.   See HE, 15, 18 Oct. 1917; Wormser, *La république de Clemenceau*, pp. 294-296, 492-497; Saatmann, *Parlament, Rüstung und Armee*, pp. 406-407; and Henri Castex, *Les comité secrets*, vol. 2, *1917, la paix refusée, un million de morts inutiles* (Gedalge, 1972), pp. 103-152, 192-196.

101   Jobert, *Souvenirs d'un ex-parlementaire*, p. 200.   See Allain, *L'oracle*, pp. 127-129.

102   The motion (see HE, 10 Nov.) did not specify Clemenceau by name, only "a ministerial combination which would appear to be," etc.); but everybody knew what was meant.

103   See HE, 11, 14 (quoted) Nov. 1917; and Hankey, *The Supreme Command*, 2:725.

104   See Georges Bonnefous, *Histoire politique de la troisième république*, vol. 2: *La Grance Guerre, 1914-1918*, 2nd ed. (Presses Universitaires de France, 1967), pp. 341-343.   Allain, *L'oracle*, p. 531n., corrects Bonnefous's faulty vote analysis as follows:

	For	Ag.	Abst.	Abs.
Action Libérale(20)	0	17	0	3
Indépendants non inscrits (39)	3	31	1	4
Droites (13)	0	11	1	1
Fédération républicaine (33)	5	24	2	2
Gauche démocratique (30)	5	17	3	5
Gauche radicale (57)	21	30	3	3
Républicains de gauche (51)	25	17	7	2
Union républicaine radicale et socialiste (17)	9	5	2	1
Radicaux socialistes (166)	103	32	21	10
Républicains socialistes (26)	8	13	2	3
Socialistes (96)	4	76	10	6
Hors groupe (7)	3	4	0	0
Totals	186	277	52	40

At age ten, reputedly painted by his father. (The Bettmann Archive.)

At age 16, a year before his father's arrest. (*L'Illustration.*)

As a medical student in 1862. (Photograph by Henri Manuel.)

In 1870, the year he became mayor of Montmartre.
Daguerrotype by Nadar, a Latin Quarter friend. (Musée Clemenceau).

By Edouard Manet in 1879 on the eve of the founding of *La Justice*.
(Musée du Louvre.)

At the Cirque-Fernando in Montmartre in the 1880s, by Jean-François Raffaëlli. Gustave Geffroy is at the far left with his hand on a balustrade; Stephen Pichon, in glasses, is above his right shoulder.
(The Bettman Archive.)

Around 1890 (?). (Musée Clemenceau.)

Arriving at the Chamber of Deputies as Premier, probably during
his first ministry (1906-9). (Photograph by Rol.)

Addressing the Chamber of Deputies on November 20, 1917, at the inauguration of his ministry, Paul Deschanel presiding. At the right center Georges Mandel, arms folded, watches. (Musée Clemenceau.)

Visiting the Western Front in 1918.
(Keystone Press Agency.)

The Big Four of 1919 -- Orlando, Lloyd George, Clemenceau, and Wilson -- in Wilson's apartment.
(*L'Illustration.*)

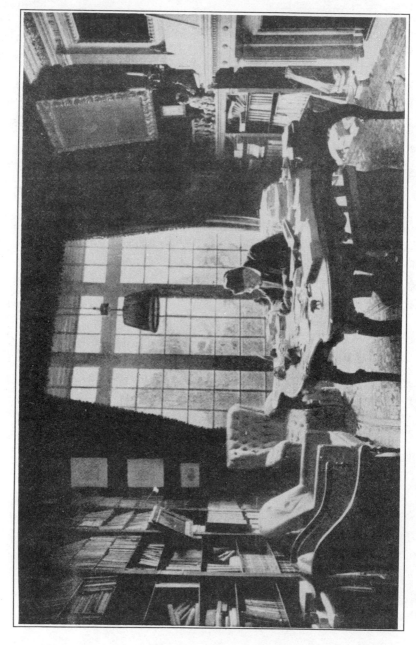

At the horseshoe desk in his library at the rue Franklin apartment in the 1920s. (Photograph by Henri Manuel.)

In New York in 1922.
(Musée Clemenceau.)

At the statue by François Sicard in Sainte-Hermine (Vendée).
(Photograph by Commandant Tourassoul, *L'Illustration*.)

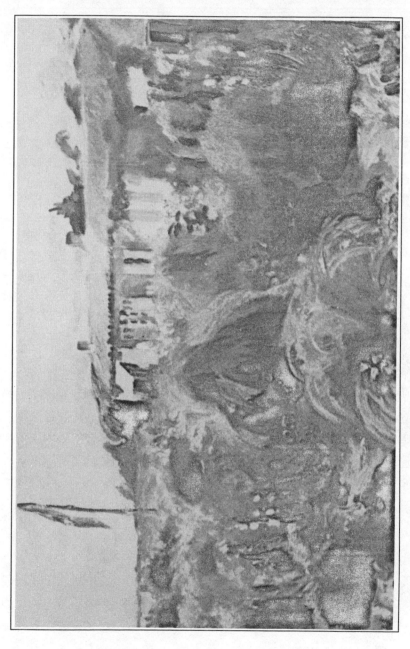

"Belébat," his seaside retirement cottage near Saint-Vincent-sur-Jard (Vendée), by MacAvoy.
(Musée Clemenceau.)

At Claude Monet's burial in 1926.
(Musée Clemenceau.)

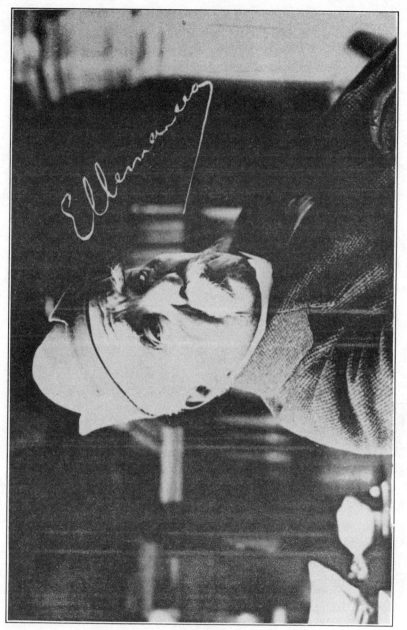

At the rue Franklin in retirement.
(Photograph by Henri Manuel.)

Statue by François Cogné at the Ronde-Pointe Champs Elysées.

CHAPTER XIV

A Famous Victory
(1917-1918)

When President Poincaré called Clemenceau to the premiership, he proved he would put the interests of the nation ahead of his personal feelings--and he reminded the world of it in his memoirs. The unvarnished truth of the matter was that in his eyes he had no other option except to take the post himself, a move charged with grave political and constitutional risks.

Conceivably, Joseph Caillaux could construct a majority based on the Left by winning the Socialists back into the government with a domestic program more to their tastes and an active exploration of avenues toward peace which would not be premised upon a total military defeat of Germany.[1] But a Caillaux combination would be virtually hostage to the quarrelling Socialists and terribly vulnerable in the Senate. Worse, Caillaux's moral authority at this moment was low at best because of accusations that he had trafficked with traitors. Moreover, Poincaré, besides truly hating the man (which in spite of everything was not exactly how he felt about Clemenceau), disagreed with his policies and believed that in the main the country did too.

With Caillaux eliminated, that left, at the end, Viviani, Briand, Louis Barthou, and Clemenceau. Viviani was politically and psychologically frayed, and Poincaré thought besides that he would serve as little more than a shield for Caillaux. Briand was "used up" and, as a result of the Lancken affair, was suspected in many quarters of "defeatism." Barthou--despite the esteem he enjoyed among impressive numbers of his colleagues and notwithstanding his own confident belief that he was the inevitable choice even if a Clemenceau experiment should be attempted for (as he expected) a short time[2]--was, as Painlevé and Poincaré had recently learned, hardly more acceptable to the Socialists and left-wing Radicals than Clemenceau. Furthermore, he lacked something which Clemenceau undeniably had, something of special importance at this moment of the war: a sharply etched national and even international notoriety. In Clemenceau's case, as everybody knew, such a notoriety might well be dangerously divisive. If labor should indeed revolt against choosing him, a "peace now" surge carrying the gravest implications for the conduct of the war could very likely be unloosed. On the other hand, his reputation could make him a national rallying point. Barthou's repute, in contrast, did not clearly reach much beyond the precincts of the Palais-Bourbon and the Luxembourg. With him the risk was greater that he could be "strangled" more easily by "the mutes of the seraglio."

So it had come down to Clemenceau. Poincaré had sensed this for quite some time. On 16 September, only four days after Painlevé had taken over, he had invited Clemenceau to drop by for consultation on a matter of palpably modest importance. (It is not known, however, if Clemenceau responded to this subtle signal of a desire for a rapprochement.[3]) At some point, perhaps before but probably after this overture, Poincaré was approached by Albert Favre of the Chamber's Army Commission, who asked on behalf of a collection of deputies drawn from all parties that he install a forceful government under Clemenceau. He declined this proposal, but when Favre returned bearing a list of members of the group which included the names of two deputies (Saumande and Babaud-Lacroze) ordinarily charged with casting the proxy votes of the huge Radical and Radical-Socialist blocs, he was reported to have replied without comment that he would call Clemenceau.[4]

Whether Favre's demarche was as decisive as this report alleges cannot be known, although it seems rather doubtful. Whatever the case, on 2 November Alfred Capus, reportedly inspired by Poincaré, published an article in *Le Figaro* which floated Clemenceau's name. He posed a choice between him and Caillaux and followed it with a series of articles on the same theme.[5] Poincaré, ever careful, made a point of consulting widely both before and after Painlevé's fall. If the move to Clemenceau were to result in disaster, *he* at least would be "covered." The only figure of note he did not consult even as a courtesy was Caillaux, an almost unbelievable snub and ironically akin to what Clemenceau had experienced more than once himself.

As for the principal in all this, Clemenceau, not surprisingly, saw Poincaré's predicament in stark relief. He believed that any choice but himself would shortly stir talk of peace, an eventuality which would thrust the president into terribly difficult straits. As he put it later, "He protected himself by calling me, and he knew it full well."[6]

II

On 16 November, twenty-four hours after Poincaré formally commissioned him, Clemenceau presented his ministry at the Élysée. What the press called a speed record owed much to Georges Mandel, who by stages had made himself indispensable as an observer, buffer, and trouble-shooter. Since 1916 he had worked especially hard among the newer deputies, to whom Clemenceau was mostly a legend, for less than a third of the current Chamber had served during his first ministry. Through Pierre Laval and others he had even sounded the Socialists despite their veto, variously offering Finances to Albert Thomas, Agriculture to Compère-Morel, Labor to Arthur Groussier, Merchant Marine to Fernand Bouisson, and an under-secretaryship at Interior to Laval himself. But in the end all felt obliged to honor the boycott. Clemenceau choked down his resentment enough in due course to persuade two to accept sub-cabinet posts (18 February 1918) as commissioners of Food Supply (Compère-Morel) and Merchant Marine (Bouisson). But the party, as Laval had warned at the time, had made a grave mistake in sticking to the boycott of cabinet posts, for as it turned out it had therewith excluded itself from the inner councils during the rest of the war and the Peace Conference.[7]

"The Capitol wasn't saved by eagles,"* Clemenceau quipped when chided about the dearth of *grands ténors* in his cabinet. Georges Leygues,

---

* Recalling the geese who allegedly saved the Roman Capitol from the Gauls in the fourth century B.C. by waking a sleeping garrison with their honking.

who now embarked on his first tenure at the navy ministry, where he was to gain repute between the wars as the modern "father" of the French fleet, was arguably the only bonafide "name" in the lot--a moderate Radical chieftain and president of the Chamber's commission on foreign affairs who had served under Waldeck-Rousseau and had known Clemenceau well since the Dreyfus days. Clearly, Clemenceau would dominate utterly: the ministry of war for himself as a proclamation of both its real and symbolic importance, with a close friend, Sen. Jules Jeanneney, as under-secretary at War but "attached to the Presidency of the Council," thereby emphasizing the link between War and the cabinet-coordinating functions of the Presidency (which had its own administrative autonomy) and underscoring again the importance of the conduct of the war;[8] Stephen Pichon, "a faithful dog,"[9] again at Foreign Affairs, his prewar associations with Briand, Poincaré, and Barthou excused and his recent refusal to accept the post from Painlevé rewarded; Jules Pams, his candidate against Poincaré in 1913, at Interior but little more than an expediter of Mandel's orders; Louis Nail, an honest nonentity, at Justice, stiffened by Édouard Ignace, relentless and absolutely loyal (being a longtime friend of Clemenceau's) as under-secretary of military justice to handle the treason cases; and Louis Loucheur at Armaments and Albert Claveille at Public Works, able non-parliamentary "technicians." Only Claveille, Loucheur, Louis Klotz (Finance), and Étienne Clémentel (Commerce), carryovers from Painlevé's cabinet, had been wartime ministers. But the others had more experience and contacts than comment then or later usually credited, e.g., Pierre Colliard (Labor), an Independent Socialist, and Albert Favre (under-secretary at Interior) were on the Chamber's Army Commission, Louis Lafferre (Education) was a Masonic mogul, Henry Simon (Colonies) a Briandist, and Klotz an ally of Poincaré.

All of them took orders, worked hard, intrigued only in a low key, and contrived at least to get the big jobs done. Remarkably, of the twenty-four ministers and under-secretaries, all but two lasted out the war.[10] Clemenceau treated them like high-rung clerks, infrequently asking their advice, unceremoniously ignoring them to deal directly with their service chiefs, and in general leaving them to know or find out no more than his judgment or whim of the moment dictated. After the Armistice they presented him with a bronze plaque and a Daumier portrayal of Don Quixote and Sancho Panza--an apt choice. Confessing himself "very touched, very moved," he told them he could have done "nothing" without them and said they deserved "the greatest part" of the credit; but in 1927 he admitted to Martet that he could barely remember most of them: "Nice fellows! They had one fault: they were too decent. They weren't made for war: things are different when you're looking into the jaws of the Boche."[11]

In his lifetime-last editorial, "Wanted: A Government," published on 15 November, the day of his call, he had set down what he expected of them and of Parliament:

> I believe in the sincerity of all the parties--without that one would despair of politics, which is not at all the case with me.
> ...This or that group may have made mistakes. Who has not? It is up to the representative assemblies, sole firm expression of the national conscience and sole authorized organ of the French will, to rise above all secondary considerations....
> Those days [of the French Revolution], those great days have returned, in blood, in tears, and the men of the Marne and the men of Verdun have shown that they have not degenerated from those of Valmy. Well then, we have the soldiers. What more do we need? Is it really conceivable that fifty years of the Republic, during which we have governed ourselves freely, have deprived us of the means of constituting an authority capable of conducting our war for survival [*salut*]? What a condemnation of ourselves if we were reduced to this admission!
> ...isn't the problem for us simply one of a concentration of usefully apportioned forces until the crushing blow of the American avalanche?
> ...[We need] *a team of workers, of workers ready to work,* who won't sermonize [*commenteront*] about their *work* until they've done it.[12]

On 20 November he entered a tense, almost silent Chamber, its galleries packed to the eaves, while outside a huge crowd pressed against the grilles. More than two-thirds of the deputies, as has been noted, had never before witnessed him at their rostrum. The issue was the war itself, and the man. Could his seventy-six years bear the burden--and could the nation's representatives bear him? From the gallery Winston Churchill, Britain's forty-three-year-old minister of munitions, watched a scene reborn from the Convention of 1793. Many years later he described it: Clemenceau, ranging "from one side of the tribune to the other, without a note...barking out sharp, staccato sentences...a wild animal pacing to and fro behind bars, growling and glaring"; and an assembly, "which would have done anything to avoid having him there," sitting obediently, disciplined by "dire perils close and drawing nearer, awful lassitude, and deep foreboding," resolved to play "the last desperate stake...to unbar the cage and let [France's] tiger loose upon all foes, beyond the trenches or in her midst."[13]

He straightaway turned their thoughts to the men dying at the front: "...they have claims on us....A single duty, plain: dwell with the soldier, live, suffer, fight with him." His phrases, clearly audible to the farthest reaches, came down like a blade:

> Mistakes have been made. Think of them only to repair them.
> Alas! there are also crimes, crimes against France which call for prompt punishment. (*Lively applause.*) Before you, before the country, which demands justice, we promise that justice will be done according to the rigors of the laws. (*Hear! Hear!*) Neither considerations of persons nor impulses of political passions (*Lively applause on the left, the center, and right.--Interruptions from the seats of the Socialist party*) will divert us from this duty nor make us exceed it. (*Hear! Hear!*)...No more pacifist campaigns, no more German intrigues. Neither treason nor semi-treason: war. (*Applause.*) Nothing but war. Our armies will not be caught between two fires. Justice takes its course. The country will know that it is defended. (*More applause.*)[14]

An electric moment occurred when someone cried, "And Caillaux?" Sitting only a few rows away, Caillaux flushed and three times nearly stood while Clemenceau silently withered him with a long, terrible gaze.

In the ensuing debate he refused to be drawn into particulars but otherwise spoke candidly, appealing to the assembly to bury old quarrels. Once or twice he lapsed into a dangerous flippancy--e.g., for the "beauty" of it they should censure him when the victory was won--but Leygues murmured cautions. The sitting ended with a few cheers and a 418-65 vote of confidence, a surprisingly stout margin. Some 25 Socialists abstained, not voting against him, with the curious result that fewer (63) had voted against him than against Painlevé (76). If the "peace party" had ever come as close to the 200 votes Poincaré was estimating it contained when Painlevé fell, that must have been a momentary peak, for nobody could have any doubt about where Clemenceau stood.[15] By the same token, however, his own figures were misleading. Perhaps half his support was firm, and most of that was in the Right and Center, not his accustomed corral.[16] Duty or fear held the rest--and that could change overnight. Many of them, in fact, were thinking he probably would not last long.

The press before and after the ministry was formed appeared to believe that the spy and treason scandals were uppermost in the public's mind. Whatever the case with Parliament, the great bulk of the populace and the army was perceived to be favorable toward calling in Clemenceau. The expectant crowd waiting quietly outside the Palais-Bourbon might have brought to mind the public's silent siege of 1-2 June 1793 when the Convention voted to expel the Girondin leaders and bring the Jacobins to power. As a correspondent for the Lisbon paper *O Seculo* observed, his appointment was not the product of an intrigue at the end of which the people would be wondering why *he* was there: "For once, they know. The present ministry is its work: it exists because they wanted it."[17]

III

Three problems dominated Clemenceau's activity: morale, manpower, and command. It was to the first that he made his most personal and striking contribution to the victory of 1918. France was the Allies' linchpin, her soil the decisive battleground, her army the largest (now that Russia's had broken up). But she was drawn and battered, answering the bell from instinct. Clemenceau was summoned to wring out all her remaining energy, save her from defeat, and ensure her continuance as a Great Power. He achieved the first two, but the last was beyond full reach except in appearances, which he did all he could to conserve. The assignment was truly daunting--so much so that Martet detected a tremor beneath his confident exterior when he saw him at the War ministry on the first evening after the full, true situation (men, arms, supplies, money) had been spread before him: "He shook his head as if to say, 'I expected everything...but not this!'"[18] Henry Lémery, one of the under-secretaries, recalled him saying a few days later, "If you knew, my dear friend, what France expects of us, you would be appalled."[19]

Contrary to legend, his arrival brought no immediate surge in morale, only a calming effect for the most part which cast a wan glow in the general atmosphere of "patriotic gloom."[20] Significantly, a much ballyhooed new National Defense Loan went undersubscribed in December. In the fighting units morale had edged slowly upward since October, but it was estimated that by itself the advent of Clemenceau made an important difference to only four percent of the men at the front, the mass continuing to give their trust to Pétain, if to anybody, rather than to any politician. Not until some time in January, when the last mutinous outbreak was recorded, could it be said that the crisis begun in April 1917 had ended altogether.[21] Civilian morale, however, after a modest rise in late December, sagged again in February and March under the weight of winter shortages and the collapse of Romanian and Russian resistance. An outburst of pacifist propaganda and strikes followed, notably in the vital metallurgical industries of the Loire valley. The test came during the great German onslaughts of late March and April and the final crisis, truly critical at its peak, in late May and early June when they broke through at the ill-starred Chemin des Dames. Mid-July marked the turn. The army, meanwhile, like the nation, never did recover the *élan* of 1914-15; Verdun and Nivelle's failure had seen to that. But it doggedly fought on against the field-grey German masses and its own grinding fatigue, as grimly resolved as the old man at the War ministry to pay the price to win.[22]

Clemenceau affected morale by what he did and fully as much by how he did it. The task he faced was appalling, as he had said; but, as Martet observed, he had always tended to think that even the largest problems are only human and thus not beyond his capacity to meet them. Having described the pang of discouragement when he got his first look from the inside at how things were, Martet went on to add:

> Not for a moment did he tremble before the war, which to each of us appeared like a monstrous thing and beyond our scale--like a cataclysm. From the first days he disentangled the

elements and understood--and deeply felt--that each one of these elements in itself was a thing both simple and solvable.[23]

The note of stridency, the uncontrolled raging and other behavioral excesses, while not absent altogether, were markedly less in evidence during his wartime ministry than they had been during his first.

To be sure, the Tiger was a tiger still. "He tolerates contradiction badly," Georges Leygues noted in his diary, "all the while in good faith believing the contrary. There are days when he is ready to pounce on everybody and when you have to use a great deal of patience to avoid incidents."[24] But he knew the country needed discipline and iron self-control, and he seems deliberately to have sought as best he could to set an example. Georges Wormser, who worked daily with him on his staff, recalled that no matter how preoccupied he was, even in the worst moments, he kept his sang-froid and did not give way to "nerves": "Impatient by temperament, he always controlled himself and showed (perhaps not without effort!) the most impressive calm. He had always been the man for difficult hours; in the most delicate circumstances of the war he showed himself impassive."[25]

The contradictions in such testimonies about his behavior may be more apparent than real. The impediments and annoyances attending ordinary days or situations could, as always, suddenly trigger an explosive release of pressure. But when things were truly serious, the stakes high, the prospects grim, he may well have experienced something like a settling calm at finding himself again in the climate he understood best: the storm.

His energy and natural vigor appeared still undiminished and were contagious. Lord Ridell remarked that one even seemed to think faster in his presence.[26] If when necessary he could set a killing pace which amazed much younger men, he tried, not always successfully, to avoid overtaxing himself. He continued to eat and sleep (insomnia permitting) at his rue Franklin apartment, not at the War ministry's facilities, and shunned telephones, which he abominated; his aides religiously refrained from calling him at night. From long habit he rose early, returned home by mid-evening to prepare for the next day's agenda (no longer to write his editorial), and attended only the most strictly necessary banquets and ceremonies. The morning ritual of massage and fencing exercises, an hour after lunch for his garden and reading in the classics, and a quarter-hour in the evening for a romp with his grandsons were his only relaxations. He fussed over his health as usual, keeping close watch on his sugar level, which his craving for sweets made all the more necessary, and mostly ate moderately (stews, boiled eggs, and water) because otherwise he tended to gain weight easily.

He left speaking in most parliamentary sittings to his ministers, and the daily crowd of petitioners to his aides. For speed and to force decisions he called few cabinet meetings and kept them short, dealing instead face-to-face as he had always preferred, listening intently and deciding cases on the spot with a joke or a growl. But in highly important cases, especially those dealing with persons, he required that they be dealt with in writing and with a full day's delay before dispatching to give time for reflection. As during his first ministry, once policy was set he left the details to others, rarely intervening as long as they held his confidence. He still liked to have people on instant call, and he was reported to have kept all his ministers under surveillance by police agents, whose morning reports told him where they had spent the night.[27] His methods worked in the main. As Leygues jotted down in his diary, "Makes war after his manner and does it well....Shakes up the hesitant, heats up the tepid, threatens the sleepers. Infuses his spirit everywhere."[28] The other side of the coin was that while important decisions could be made rapidly once he dealt with them, they would have to wait until he could find the time--the Achilles heel of "dictatorship." The not infrequent result was a friction in the gears caused by a certain lack of coordination. Ministers grumbled that too often they didn't know what was going on or that their chief had made a decision without their knowledge or on the basis of insufficient information or, worse, because of one of his celebrated whims.

His disdain for meetings and memoranda persistently nettled the punctilious Poincaré. (And his facetiousness. Alone at last together before the first cabinet meeting, he quipped, "Well, Raymond old boy, are we going to make love?" Such talk was hardly to the president's taste.[29]) Their relations stayed coolly correct for the first six months, but almost from the start he began--whether deliberately or not is hard to say--to cut Poincaré out of the circuit and to reduce to a nullity the president's long-established right to a voice in judicial and foreign policy matters. Disagreements about the handling of the Chemin des Dames crisis in June, when Poincaré wanted sanctions taken against Pétain (whom he disliked besides), brought on strains which in October burst into personal recriminations and threats to resign over Poincaré's questioning of the wisdom of granting Germany's request for an armistice. Henceforth, Poincaré, who by now had seen himself become more than any of his predecessors "the prisoner of the Élysée," was reduced to sending long letters of unwanted advice through third persons, especially Pichon. "Every time I saw his dainty little handwriting," Clemenceau recalled, "it threw me into a fury."[30]

He believed intensely that leaders should set an example. To dismiss this as a cliché would be to overlook the problem created by the distance trench warfare had put between the men under fire and their chiefs, to say nothing of their separation from the masses in the hinterlands before the age of giant air raids. The gap spawned most of the Great War's best literature and, as noted, was the theme of his first speech as premier.[31] As a result, he made visits to the front his trademark. Of all his roles during his long life, this one lodged deepest in popular memory.

IV

His most obvious purpose in these visits, which began with a trip to the Champagne and Lorraine fronts on 19-20 January, was to avoid blind dependence on subordinates, many of whom had "made a home" in the war and needed stirring up. Half the trips were undertaken mainly to confer with the chiefs (Foch, Pétain, Haig, Pershing) and their key army, corps, and division commanders. The telephone could have saved time, and Poincaré and others understandably complained of his absences--some sixty-four in a year.[32] But personal confrontation was his element, where he could catch the mood behind the words, elicit an opinion that would never be spoken over a wire, or offer counsels that on paper or from third parties might sound like commands. He could also brush aside formalities impeding communication between generals, among whom the morale factor was important too, especially in crises. With lines straining and wires cut, what lonely *divisionnaire* wouldn't believe that someone Up There cared when the premier himself wheels in through the smoke to hear his tale, wring a chuckle from him, and tell him help is on the way? Later on, mental notes taken, he could give Pétain or Foch a reading on the situation and the man. And what served them also served Parliament. The ex-commission president sometimes complained about the time demanded by commission hearings, but the visits to the front lent credence to his testimony, all the more so when he invited a flattered commission president or two along. During dark days he also sometimes went to the lobbies to scotch rumors. All in all, he counted his travel time as well spent, with the automobile's privacy a welcome bonus.

Visits also served to knit relations with the Allies. His patriotism made him sound like a deep-dyed chauvinist, but nobody warned the French more emphatically that they could neither beat the Germans nor make peace unaided. And he meant it unequivocally. Back in 1916 as president of the French Section of the Anglo-French Interparliamentary Committee, he had welcomed a visiting delegation from the British parliament with a moving tribute to Allied solidarity that came from the heart.[33] Allied contingents and commanders saw him frequently, especially Douglas Haig, for whom he had a sincere affection even if, ironically, Haig was notorious for the infrequency of *his* frontline visits. His fluent (if heavily accented) English gave him a precious advantage among the British and Americans as did his earthy, unpretentious style. British generals fairly doted on "the Old Boy," an attitude he cultivated and knew how to turn to account. That Lloyd George, because of his revulsion at blood and death, positively shrank from going into the lines hurt his (Clemenceau's) case not at all.[34] His popularity with the British and Americans, indeed, put him in a class by himself when compared with any other French public figure of his day.

All this traveling about the front, useful as it was, nonetheless ran some high risks. For one, it made it all the more necessary for him to take great care to control his feelings and give an appearance of coolness and calm when things were going badly--as they often did well into the summer. Any sign of panic or impulsive display of exasperation over the failings of subordinates could have had disastrous consequences in the tension-filled atmosphere of a headquarters in the midst of a critical battle. He recognized the danger and fortunately was able to give an impression of calm or even of smiling ease at the worst moments.

For another, he had to tread very carefully in the matter of giving advice on military operations. Strictly speaking, operations were not his domain, and the generals--who certainly at the outset regarded him with a great deal of well-grounded suspicion and even resentment in view of his past (Boulanger, the Dreyfus Case, and during his first ministry his use of the army in strikes and his decree on the honors of precedence, which he adamantly refused to alter even now despite Mordacq's pleas[35])--would have been swift to resent any interference in their professional sphere. Fundamentally, his object was to give moral and psychological reinforcement to their authority. Such advice as he gave had to be clearly rendered as such and offered only after careful listening. He was not there to give commands. Wormser later testified that he knew of only one such instance: on 30 March, after conferring with Haig and Churchill, he gave orders to support the Canadians at the Avre River without consulting Pétain. The situation was urgent, and Pétain, in Wormser's view, would not have acted differently in light of the circumstances.[36] In this object of supporting his commanders he largely succeeded, a result due in no small measure to his practice of always taking along General Mordacq, a sensible man of great tact and much respected by his fellow generals. Mordacq's presence reassured them that he was getting the professionals' views, and in truth he had rapidly acquired a profound trust in his aide's expertise, judgment, and character. Mordacq spoke candidly on all matters but was meticulously careful not to intrude during conversations with the chiefs except sometimes when with Pétain, whom he knew very well.

A third risk on these visits was to his personal safety. Clemenceau was the last of an ancient line: the leader of a great nation personally present in battle. Churchill in the Second World War brought him to mind, but they differed in ambience. Their sculptors sensed it: Churchill (at Westminster) in his greatcoat, hunched and glowering, but withal the statesman still; Clemenceau (on the Champs-Élysées and at Sainte-Hermine, Vendée) striding into the storm or ringed by adoring soldiers. He mingled the arts of infantry captain and politician, talking easily with the men, listening, prodding, cracking jokes, poking into dugouts, sampling food, slogging down trenches--once on impulse taking a path under enemy observation to the last outpost on the Swiss frontier at Pfetterhausen, barely two hundred meters from a German post, to bring *la Patrie*'s thanks to a pair of startled *poilus*. He ran risks beyond the call of duty, surely, but even of good sense, careening down shell-swept roads, moving about within machine-gun range, going up among attacking units, once (at Fère-en-Tardenois, 29 May) even narrowly escaping capture. On another occasion (near Rouvrel, 1 April) he wandered off and was spotted by German observers. Mordacq knew registering rounds when he saw them and raced to shove him under an embankment, where they spent a long quarter-hour. Needless to say, when they emerged they got a rousing welcome from the troops.[37]

Why did he do this? Poincaré, by no means a coward, sensibly invited the Élysée's sentries inside during an air raid. Clemenceau was dumbfounded: "Such things call for mute contemplation. Any commentary would weaken the comic bitterness of this breed of bourgeois."[38] He knew the potency of symbols, above all how to create an "image" without seeming to by simply being himself. In the field he disdained military dress or (Heaven forbid!) something like Poincaré's self-designed uniform which had earned him derision as "Our National Chauffeur." He remained the undisguised civilian ("War is too important..."), brandishing his familiar cane and garbed in his customary white shirt and black bow-tie, but complemented by a sturdy old suit, a greatcoat for the cold, hobnails and buckled leather gaiters, and a shapeless fedora or hunting hat bashed on his head. No platoons of bodyguards or scurrying swarms of aides, reporters, and photographers. He underplayed as a rule, at most allowing an occasional notice in the papers or a clip in the newsreel, and let word of mouth, the seedbed of legend, do its work. No doubt it was a simpler day.

Something else also led him out: himself. War sanctioned, as peace never had, the aggression stored in him since childhood. "Besides," he cracked, "if there were an accident it would please so many."[39] War is an intoxication his devastating sanity understood. He admired Pétain's acerbic good sense, but he did not give him the supreme command in part because, unlike Foch, he lacked "a grain of madness."[40] His character contained a streak of nihilism, a species of death-wish. "There is no higher emotion than the mastering of danger," he wrote later,[41] reminding one of Churchill's remark that there is no finer thrill than being shot at--and missed. The thunder of the guns, the energy of men and machines in movement, the rumble of mighty events, life and death in the balance, "the frontiers of Chaos"--a paradigm of existence: it acted on his aged self like a resurrecting drug. "War life rejuvenated me," he later told Stephen Bonsal.[42] Churchill, in an article in 1926, recorded a priceless vignette. On 30 March, while with an Anglo-French party on a tour of a very dangerous sector near Amiens, a visit which he (Clemenceau) claimed as "my reward" for helping the Canadians at the Avre, their departure was interrupted:

> As we reached the road a shell burst among a group of led horses at no great distance. The group was scattered. A wounded and riderless horse came in a staggering trot along the road toward us. The poor animal was streaming with blood. The "Tiger"...advanced towards it and with great quickness seized its bridle, bringing it to a standstill. The blood accumulated in a pool upon the road. The French General expostulated with him, and he turned reluctantly towards his car. As he did so, he gave me a sidelong glance and observed in an undertone, "*Quel moment délicieux!*"

They got back to Paris at one o'clock in the morning, Clemenceau "alert and fresh as when we started."[43] In a letter to his wife later that day he went on:

> He is an extraordinary character. Every word he says--particularly general observations on life and morals--is worth listening to. His spirit & energy are indomitable. 15 hours [actually 17] yesterday over rough roads at high speed in motor cars. I was tired out--& he is 76![44]

What stirred him most profoundly, overthrowing his defenses, was the mute appeal of the *poilus*, nameless heroes of the ethic of unrewarded virtue he had learned from his father. In 1916, to Léon Martin, a former personal secretary and *L'Homme Libre* staffer at the front:

> Thanks for your little note, my dear friend. I found it on returning from a visit to the front which procured for me the pleasures of a night at Fort Douaumont [Verdun]. A voyage in icy mud. I saw there poor devils who are sublime

beings. How sad to return to the rear. I envy you with all my heart.[45]

His ingrained scepticism and will to dominate dissolved in their presence, and they returned the love they sensed. What it meant to him can perhaps be caught from his reply to a young American who asked him just before his death what he thought really mattered in life. Intellectual honesty, he answered, but first of all "to love and be loved."[46] Had he fully known it before those voyages in icy mud? The memory went with him to his grave. On 6 July, a week before the last German offensive and the dawn of victory, he had toured the forward positions near Épernay in Champagne. The men there were to remain behind as a screen so that the main force could mount a crushing counter-attack from reserve lines. He knew as well as they that they were marked for sacrifice. Making his way down a trench he came upon a small delegation. A man stepped forward and offered him a bouquet of wild flowers. Overcome, he finally stammered some thanks and told them their flowers would never leave him.[47] He kept his word. A few desiccated stalks still repose on the mantel at the rue Franklin. The rest, according to his will, were laid beside him in his coffin.

V

Other, less dramatic, measures were taken to lift the army's morale. When Painlevé suggested retaining some of his assistants at the War ministry, Clemenceau snapped, "I'm burning everything, even the furniture."[48] No such holocaust swept the offices on the rue Saint-Dominique. Personnel shifts and a considerable reorganization in the bureaus were effected in the early months, but experience had to count for something. "Recommendations" from politicians got short shrift, and great emphasis was put upon speed in decision and communication. Promotions and decorations, long-standing causes of bitterness among frontline soldiers because of favoritism often shown toward rear-echelon "operators," got close attention. Months of pressure were needed, nonetheless, to overcome Pétain's natural reluctance to replace worthy but aging comrades in generalships with deserving younger officers who could meet the demands of the more open warfare of 1918.

At lower levels unremitting war was waged meanwhile against the hordes who had found shelter in deferments, in swollen support services, or in field hospitals "recuperating" at leisure. The *embusqués* (skulkers) had been the subject of repeated investigations and decrees since 1914. Clemenceau, who may have invented the word (in *L'Homme Libre*, 3, 19, 24 August 1914), had written many articles on the scandal, and his paper since the early weeks had run a column, "Embusqué Notes," publicizing outrageous cases of favoritism.[49] The key was enforcement. His vigor, which sometimes could manifest itself in an unfeeling harshness, and his peremptory treatment of recommendations stiffened the enforcers' spines. "Briand," it was said, "tells you, 'Yes, but...,' Poincaré, 'No, because...,' Clemenceau, 'No.'"[50]

New men and methods could not fully undo the habits of three years. But within a few weeks the troops' deportment and appearance were showing dramatic improvement. When the Germans launched their great offensive in the spring, they met an army that Clemenceau, with signal help from Pétain and Mordacq, had purged of the smell of defeat which had hung about it in 1917. It was again an instrument to be reckoned with, bone-tired still, but toughened by adversity and led by men it believed in.

VI

Civilian morale was almost as worrisome as the army's and in most respects harder to grapple with. Some quarters feigned surprise when the late editor of *L'Homme Enchaîné* confirmed that censorship would remain in force. "Get rid of the Censorship?" he told its chief. "Never! I'm not a total fool! You are my best policemen! Only, as a matter of fact, I have my little ideas on the question."[51] What they amounted to in practice was an abolition of the despised censoring of harsh political criticism. Otherwise, military and diplomatic news plus information "susceptible of troubling civil order"--in particular, news of strikes or meetings promoting them--got close scrutiny. Feeling somewhat sensitive, nevertheless, about this whole subject, he delegated broad powers over news management to Mandel, whose brutal finesse in using them diverted wrath from his chief. Clemenceau appreciated the service: "When I fart, he stinks."[52] On the whole, Clemenceau's censorship was the least restrictive employed by the wartime governments. Needless to say, it was impossible to satisfy everybody. Pétain, Poincaré, and the Right, for example, grumbled that he gave too much rein to the "defeatist" papers he had once denounced. Both here and in his indulgent handling of labor leaders like Alphonse Merrheim whom he had denounced Malvy for coddling, he showed that he suffered from no lack of self-confidence: so long as he, not a Malvy, was in charge, they wouldn't dare make real trouble.

Fears of what labor might do had haunted many minds on the eve of his arrival in the premiership. In retirement he made light of them:

> It's ideas that give men courage, and your revolutionaries are as gifted with ideas as my boot. They have spite, bitterness--but that doesn't get one very far. I saw them during the war; I have talked with them and tried to find something in them! It was pathetic. I've never had the least trouble with any of those specimens. When M. Malvy said to the Senate, "Don't meddle with those fellows! There will be a Revolution," he was pulling our legs. I didn't even have to engage in a struggle with them. They melted away like pale shadows.
> I've had far less trouble with the anarchists than with Poincaré and Foch.[53]

Perhaps it seemed so in hindsight, for the labor troubles that did occur never came close to setting off a general disintegration of the home front. Whether they ever had had any chance at all is a moot point. What is certain is that a clumsy handling of the situation would have entailed grave consequences. And he knew it, otherwise his actions likely would not have exhibited such a careful blending of persuasion, tact, force, and cunning.

On the one hand, he had to give the impression that the government would tolerate no disorder. "I simply drew a line," he related, "which I never would let them cross....They knew it!"[54] When scattered acts of sabotage greeted his new ministry, he reportedly told the CGT leaders that he had taken measures preliminary to bringing masses of troops into Paris--something he dearly wanted not to have to do if for no other reason than that he could not yet be sure of their steadiness.[55] The incidents subsided, although a tension remained and began to mount sharply in January. On the other hand--and reversing the pattern of previous governments, which had seemed accommodating in public while frequently repressive in private--he stayed in contact with the leaders and even went so far as to offer Merrheim, secretary of the critically important Federation of Metal Workers and a long-time syndicalist and outspoken critic of the war, a post in his government as chief of liaison with labor. Merrheim declined this proposal and also an assignment as an agent to contact Lenin and Trotsky to urge them to keep Russia in the war. But he remained in touch with the government behind the scenes in the interests of protecting the workers.[56] Clemenceau and some of the labor leadership, in short, were playing both sides of the street.

Tension slackened once again in March but then mounted in April and climaxed in a wave of strikes in May and early June which mainly struck the war industries, particularly metallurgy, in the Paris region and the Loire and Allier valleys (Bourges, Nevers, Clermont-Ferrand). Unlike the wave in the spring of 1917, the strikes were political rather than economic in motive (governments since then having pressured employers into economic concessions) and featured calls for an end to the war and to opposition to the Russian Revolution. The great German offensives of the spring were not a cause, but the strikes' coincidence with them greatly heightened anxiety in official quarters. The movement peaked on 23-24 May, when the government took a determined stand, and then fairly swiftly faded. As it did the government got tougher, probably more so than was strictly necessary, and jailed, transferred, or sent to the army several hundred leaders and activists. Resentment over these measures threatened to prolong the troubles, but it too died away in June.

The government in effect had gambled and won. Whether Clemenceau had deliberately encouraged the strike wave in order to have a pretext to crush the movement, as some have speculated, probably never will be known.[57] The risks of this policy were such as to make it doubtful that he did, but it cannot be ruled out altogether. At all events, the strikes had been promoted by the left wing of the CGT, whose leadership was at best lukewarm to the idea, while the workers, apart from small, hard-core elements, showed little desire to push matters vigorously. The agitators stopped short of saying that German peace terms should be accepted, which would have branded them as "defeatists." But what, then, did it mean to call for peace? The practical question of how and on what terms to make peace eluded answers which were clear enough to inspire workers to get bloodied up like good "revolutionaries." And as for invoking the example of Russia, the place was far away, and nobody, even the government, really knew what was going on there anyhow.[58]

Most significantly, the general public had showed the strikes no sympathy whatever. Through the winter and spring its mood was mainly a mixture of pessimism and resignation which the peace movement had proved unable to turn to account. People seemed to have quietly reaffirmed after the waverings of 1917 that at least the war must not be *lost*. But the end now seemed years away, not mere months as it always had before that anguished year. Preoccupied with getting along despite scarcities (which, though serious and in the case of coal critical, never approached the depths touched in World War II), they were not yet ready to cheer Clemenceau. Mostly they just hoped that maybe he, after all the others, could take charge, put things right, set people in their places, and get on down the tunnel toward daylight. The best he was able to do during these months--and it was no mean accomplishment--was progressively to convince them he was indeed doing what they had all along wanted done.

VII

Nothing was more critical to Clemenceau in fostering this conviction than his handling of the treason cases. Contrary to most accounts which later grew up around him and those dark days, all the major cases save one (unless one must count Loustalot's) had been opened before he became premier. To him fell the prosecution. The one remaining was that of Joseph Caillaux.[59] His name had oozed up repeatedly in the investigations, particularly those concerning *Le Bonnet Rouge*, but he still walked free under his parliamentary immunity. Compared to him, a former premier, late president of the Radical-Socialist Party, and lodestar of the "peace party," a Bolo, Duval, Marion, Goldsky, Landau, or Lenoir, a Senator Humbert or a deputy like a Turmel or Loustalot was a nobody. Only Malvy was arguably in the same class, and he had soon removed himself from immediate concern by requesting (22 November) a trial by the Senate as High Court to clear his name. If nothing were done about Caillaux, the ringing promises of the Ministerial Declaration would sound hollow. Even so, it was widely believed that Clemenceau, having waited so long to reach the top, would find such high personal satisfaction in his ascension that he would retract his claws.

There is no good reason to think that he needed prompting from the British to prosecute Caillaux, as some darkly hinted, or from Poincaré, who sent him a letter calling for Caillaux to be shot, no less.[60] Unlike Poincaré, he at bottom did not hate Caillaux: "He impressed me," he later remarked to Martet, "as having a sort of go, a courage about him which I liked."[61] As he was to tell the Chamber commission examining the immunity question, Caillaux was probably the only man with whom he had never exchanged polemics: "It's unusual, but that's the way it is."[62] What cautioned him was the political risk, for it was universally assumed that his ministry would fall if Caillaux should win an acquittal. The man might or might not be a traitor, but he was indubitably a symbol, and he wanted no martyr on his hands. The decision weighted on him more than many may have suspected: shortly before the Armistice he observed to a friend that in hindsight the only "difficult" thing he had done during that tumultuous year had been to arrest Caillaux.[63]

Late in November, having decided to proceed after a full-dress cabinet meeting, he ordered General Dubail, in charge of security cases as military governor of Paris, to open a preliminary inquiry, the results of which were laid before a Chamber commission on 11 December as justification for the lifting of Caillaux's immunity in order to permit his arrest should the following full investigation yield sufficient grounds. Testifying before the commission, Clemenceau adopted a moderate but very firm tone, emphasizing his determination to meet his responsibilities and coolly noting (what was undeniable) that allegations like those being leveled againstt Caillaux would long since have brought any ordinary citizen to book:

> Do you believe that it is a good state of mind for the *poilus* to be in, knowing these things vaguely, but feeling them all the same, to think that while they are fighting there are behind them people who betray them? Anything but that! I could cite you numberless examples of men whom I have seen, whom I do not know, who come out of their trenches to tell me these things and even to say to me things so violent that I would not repeat them here. You should think of the fact that the morale of the soldiers has never been better [*sic*], in the

gravest of circumstances, and you would remove the certitude of knowing that he is defended! I said it in my [Ministerial] Declaration: he will know that he is defended; but you don't defend him with speeches, but with acts, and the first of all, since there are laws and justice, is to submit all citizens, including senators and deputies, to justice and the laws. That is my principle, and I hold to it.[64]

On the 22nd the commission's report recommending that the immunity be lifted was debated by the Chamber before packed galleries. Caillaux held the floor for two hours with an impassioned defense featuring poignant reminders to Clemenceau of Déroulède and Herz and Dreyfus and closing with a quotation from his speech to the jury at the Norton trial. Clemenceau knew better than to risk a rebuttal. He evaded by answering, amid protests, that as head of the military justice system he ought not to comment. The result had become a foregone conclusion anyhow once Caillaux, deciding that he should not let himself be shown up by Malvy, had asked in his speech that the immunity be removed so he could clear his name in court. It was so ordered, 418 to 2, with 76 Socialists and 29 other leftists thankful that they had only to abstain in order to keep a good conscience.

The government's request to lift the immunity caused an immense stir. Caillaux's arrest on 14 January, just in time to foreclose a libel suit he had brought to discredit the government's case, was almost anticlimactic because, given the political situation, it was inevitable. In the weeks preceding the arrest, Clemenceau had pushed the investigation hard in hopes of finding conclusive proof of treason. No such evidence was found, but papers Caillaux had stashed in a bank box in Florence contained enough damning material, including sketches for a coup d'état, to justify an arrest, an indictment before a military court, and imprisonment without bail.

Clemenceau was in no hurry to try him. Caillaux languished in a common felon's cell--an almost ostentatiously severe treatment calculated to impress the public, which nevertheless soon lost interest--while agents slowly heaped together more evidence from sources in France, Italy, the United States, and Latin America. But no "smoking gun" ever turned up. In the absence of irrefutable proof of outright treason, an acquittal still loomed. So the government, to the great chagrin of the Chamber's *Clemencistes*, finally

·decided to remove the case from the military's hands and send it instead (15 October) to the Senate as High Court, a political forum, in the meantime granting the prisoner the amenities of the *régime politique*. The Senate then dawdled along for a year on its own investigations and did not begin debate on a verdict until February 1920, a month after Clemenceau had left office. On 23 April Caillaux was convicted under Article 78 of the Penal Code (which had never figured in the indictments) for causing "damage to the external security of the State" through "correspondence with subjects of an enemy power," but with extenuating circumstances, and sentenced him to time already served, ten years' deprivation of civic rights, and 53,000 francs in costs. (In December 1924 he was amnestied, and four months later Painlevé made him his minister of finance.)

When all had been said--interminably said--and done, what had really mattered was the decision to prosecute. In the mid-1920s Clemenceau himself privately observed that he did not think that Caillaux had "positively" committed treason.[65] But the public, among whom Caillaux enjoyed little sympathy and less popularity, had taken comfort from the thought that the Tiger still had claws, the *poilus* had cheered, while peace advocates and real or would-be revolutionaries had caught a chill from which they never recovered. Nor was the signal missed elsewhere: "His proceedings against Caillaux," wrote General Ludendorff in his memoirs, "showed clearly what we were to expect of him."[66] The "rot" slowed to a stop. In the end, Joseph Caillaux had served the war effort well, if not quite in the manner he had intended.

VIII

Malvy's case, if less important, was analogous to Caillaux's. Clemenceau, who roundly despised him, intended to see that he too should be made an example. On 21 January, a week after Caillaux's arrest, the Senate as High Court received the indictment which Malvy had requested the Chamber to bring. Because the charges were confined to the highly doubtful ones made by Daudet that he had informed the Germans about the attack on the Chemin des Dames and had provoked military mutinies, the government smelled an acquittal in the offing-which doubtless was what a majority of the deputies wanted. So it persuaded the much-more-conservative Senate to conduct its own investigation of a broader set of charges, focused around those Clemenceau had made on 22 July 1917, of complicity in treason by failing to act against security risks and traitors.

Even so, despite all the pressure the government could muster by way of largesse from secret funds and promises of favors, and notwithstanding the disgust for him felt by the army and much of the public, Malvy nearly escaped, for in his trial (16 July-6 August 1918) the Senate voted to acquit him of all treason accusations. Wanting no Malvyist triumph even though the military tide had turned, Clemenceau persuaded Sen. Étienne Flandin (who presently was named resident-general in Tunisia) to move a conviction for dereliction of duty, a charge not in the original bill of particulars.[67] The Senate grasped the proffered branch and condemned him (by an uncomfortably close 101-81 margin, nonetheless) to five years' exile for "criminal neglect of duty"--not an unreasonable verdict whatever its legal frailties.

Clemenceau then washed his hands of the affair and left it up to the Chamber to take the appropriate parliamentary action: "In so doing, the Chamber will have the pleasure of judging Malvy itself, and it will judge itself at the same time."[68] (After the war the Radical-Socialist Party, embarrassed to be tarred as the party of Caillaux and Malvy, refused to condemn those members who had voted to convict. Like Caillaux, Malvy was later amnestied. He returned to the Chamber in 1925, briefly became minister of the interior again under Briand in 1926, and remained a prominent deputy until 1940. He didn't change his ways: the chagrined Radicals finally expelled him from the party after World War II for consorting with the collaborationist Vichy regime.)

The trials of the smaller fry, less than a dozen of note, went forward in the meantime. Three resulted in executions by firing squads in the moat of the Château de Vincennes: Paul Bolo (or Bolo Pasha, 17 April), Émile Duval (17 July), and in 1919 Pierre Lenoir (24 October), all for accepting German money to influence or buy into the press. The rest earned jail terms and fines, while Senator Humbert, whose super-patriotic *Le Journal* had been an object of Bolo's machinations, was acquitted (9 May 1919) on a split vote. Clemenceau's old nemesis, the half-mad Ernest Judet, meanwhile had fled to Switzerland to avoid prosecution for intelligence with the enemy but was acquitted following his return long after the war. Such, along with draconian comb-outs of *embusqués* and arrests, prosecutions, and some jailings of perhaps 1700 sundry pacifists and anarchists--among them Hélène Brion, the feminist and anti-war Socialist secretary of the teachers' federation, whose much-publicized trial in March 1918 resulted in a three-years' suspended sentence--comprised Clemenceau's "reign of terror."[69]

When measured against the strains and horrors of that war, and worse to come, it would appear almost derisible. He retained the ordinary forms of justice and instituted no special tribunals or procedures beyond a liberal resort to a use of military rather than civil courts or the High Court. Public meetings continued to be forbidden as before, but he conserved the right of petition and permitted "private" political protest meetings by allowing resort to a legal subterfuge which even Malvy had refused to approve.[70] Police forces were beefed up, their visibility and heavy-handedness became more pronounced, and a Commissariat général à la Sûreté nationale was created (12 February 1918) which centralized the various security and surveillance services in an office reporting directly to the premier. Some excesses of zeal in digging up evidence or applying pressure to reluctant deputies and senators got a blind eye, but no flagrant illegalities were encouraged or condoned in order to "get" Caillaux and the others. The Censorship was manipulated to the government's advantage, of course, and it was known that the authorities were not above reminding reporters now and then that the draft awaited them if it might be concluded that they could serve the national interest better at the front. But self-censorship was encouraged in preference to official suppression more than it had been heretofore, and the CGT, for example, was not prevented from circulating pamphlets blaming France for the war despite objections from numerous political and army figures. Even in Caillaux's case, while the prosecution used leaks to help persuade the public, the defense was tacitly permitted to do the same despite the known (and feared) presence of a respectable amount of sympathy in favor of a negotiated peace.[71]

In hindsight, what is perhaps most striking about the crackdown is that it never degenerated into a raging witch hunt. Given the conditions and climate of the time, it could well have done so with little more than a firm shove from the top. Justice pure and undefiled nevertheless had taken troubling turns at the hand of a man who once upon a time had baptized his newspaper with its name and had so eloquently pilloried *raison d'état* in the Norton and Dreyfus cases. Even though he had never quite gone so far as to rule out political trials for political offenses, his critics feasted.[72] A lifelong opponent of the death penalty, he had to live with painful memories of eleventh-hour appeals for mercy, of telling the weeping mother of young Pierre Lenoir, the son of an acquaintance who had helped him launch *L'Homme Libre*, that he could not in conscience grant a reprieve when so many innocents had died at their posts. "Who wills war," he had written on the eve of his ministry, "wills the means of war."[73] What had he thought, Martet asked him, when Caillaux had raised the specter of another Dreyfus and appealed to his magnanimity? "I was thinking there was France, that's all."[74] It had to suffice, for beyond it he stared into the void.

IX

The arrest of Caillaux was Clemenceau's most pointed answer to the peace offensive of 1917. Peace, however, was altogether too sensitive, too important to the whole morale problem for him to dare think that he could dispose of it with a grand gesture and some arrests of the more notorious agitators. Within days of his coming to office, the Bolsheviks launched their own peace offensive, featuring revelations of the contents of the secret agreements made with the Allies by the defunct tsarist regime and calls for the Allies to join the negotiations they were opening for an armistice with the Central Powers. At the same moment, America's growing diplomatic weight was being advertised by the arrival of President Wilson's confidante, Edward M. ("Colonel") House, to conduct a reconnaissance mission and participate as an "observer" at the first session, at Versailles (29 November-3 December), of the Supreme War Council (SWC) created at Rapallo to ensure closer Allied coordination.*

---

* The SWC consisted of the premiers of France, Great Britain, and Italy plus an observer from the United States and was to meet monthly. A permanent military advisory committee composed of the chiefs of staff or their deputies sat at Versailles. Technically, the United States at Wilson's insistence was an Associated Power. The term "Allies" usually included the United States, but not always, with context governing the meaning.

Thus, pressure was building on the Allies to state their war aims, not just to counter the Bolsheviks but to woo opinion in enemy and occupied lands. Above all, they had to steel their own populations to further sacrifices. They could not leave them to wonder if what they were fighting for were really worth the hideous cost, nor by the same token could they risk giving credence to charges they had missed any good chance to end the slaughter.

Clemenceau certainly was not unmindful of these reasons to speak out on war aims. But there were other considerations that made his need less acute than that of his partners or that at least argued for caution. His problem was much simpler than Lloyd George's or Wilson's or even Orlando's in two respect. France had been invaded, but Great Britain, the United States, and Italy (initially) had not. The latter governments thus stood more in need of ideological appeals--to "make the world safe for democracy," for example. Moreover, they would find it harder to justify any territorial claims than would France in calling for the return of Alsace-Lorraine. At the same time, the peace movement posed more of a threat to France than to Britain or the United States (though not to Italy) because she had had to make greater sacrifices of every kind and would have to continue to do so.

The strain on France being so intense, it was more important to Clemenceau than to the others that his people not be distracted or lulled by talk of peace, for the bow might snap. As far as he was concerned, really, the less peace talk there was in France, the better. He had long held that circumstances at the moment of Germany's surrender would largely shape specific terms, and hence pronouncements in advance, especially if they should make French aims appear too ambitious, would only stir up quarrels with allies and open the mouths of "defeatists."[75] To the very end of the war he had the Censorship riding herd on all news, bad *or* good, which might divert the country's attention from achieving military victory.

Talk of peace was a two-edged sword. Although Clemenceau recognized its possible value (if handled with care) and understood how profoundly important it was to France to stay in harmony with the Allies on a question touching such vital interests, he feared its effects in France. On the other hand, he underestimated its potential impact in Germany and Austria.

Consequently, it was not he but Wilson (with Lloyd George a distant second) who delivered the capital propaganda stroke of the war.

At the SWC meeting Colonel House had broached the idea of a joint declaration of war aims. But the others held back, with the result, intended or not, that the door was now open to unilateral action. Ironically, Clemenceau was the first to walk through. He did so because Lloyd George's and Wilson's recent evasions of a firm commitment to the return of Alsace-Lorraine both worried and angered him, because he suspected that Lloyd George might be flirting with the idea of a negotiated peace,[76] and because he was moving against Caillaux and the peace party and so had a reason to say something on the subject himself to reassure the public. His manner, nevertheless, was instructive, for he left the assignment to Pichon and framed the statement (on 27 December in answer to an interpellation about the Bolsheviks' offensive) in very general and conventional terms: the return of Alsace-Lorraine, a united and independent Poland, evacuation of all conquered territory, reparations, "guarantees" of security from German aggression, and a league to preserve peace.[77] Lloyd George followed on 5 January with a major statement, but almost immediately it was thrust into the shade when Wilson delivered his Fourteen Points address to Congress on 8 January. In no time his words sped around the world.

Wilson's program won nearly universal applause in France. Clemenceau himself told Mordacq that he thought it would be best, "in view of the Allies' situation," to accept it "purely and simply" since, despite some rather "utopian" articles, it gave France satisfaction on all "vital questions."[78] In the Chamber on 11 January, Pichon, with Clemenceau present, turned aside (377 to 113) a Socialist proposal to press for a joint declaration by the Allies by saying that they were basically in accord and that the essential thing was to gain the victory "without which all our war claims will be meaningless."[79]

Before the month was out, however, Clemenceau began to have second thoughts about some of the Points--e.g., "open" diplomacy, disarmament, adjustment of colonial claims, freedom of the seas, and reduction of trade barriers--and to feel uneasy over Wilson's growing dominance.[80] At the second SWC meeting (31 January-2 February), he tried to persuade Lloyd George and Italy's foreign minister, Baron Sonnino, to join him in a declaration to rival Wilson's. They declined, and following sharp exchanges with Wilson in late February and early March after the President had rather high-handedly expressed resentment over the mild show of independence which the Allies had mustered in the SWC communiqué, he apparently decided the game was not worth the candle.[81]

His cards were poor besides: at bottom France needed America more than America needed France, and he was finding, too, that the British were tending to lean more now toward Wilson than to him on many questions. Henceforth until the Armistice negotiations began in October and despite recurrent complaints from some of his ministers, he contented himself with pressing forward particular concerns via diplomatic channels, especially in regard to eastern Europe. In the interim he put to work a reformed and greatly expanded Propaganda Service (of the army), which he was astonished to learn had been thus far a largely phantom organization. One of its more important tasks was to scatter bales of the Fourteen Points in enemy lines.[82]

For the French, however, he wanted no more distractions. On 8 March, expecting the Germans' win-the-war offensive to burst soon, he seized the chance offered by an interpellation to make a statement which, as it turned out, also ran around the world and became inseparably bonded to his name in popular memory:

> *The president of the Council.* Ah! I too, I desire peace as soon as possible, and everyone desires it. Anyone who thinks otherwise would be a great criminal; but you must know what you want. It's not by bleating peace that you're going to silence Prussian militarism. (*Lively applause on the left, center and the right.*)
>
> A moment ago M. Constant sent a shaft my way about my silence on foreign policy. My foreign policy and my domestic policy are one. Domestic policy, I make war; foreign policy, I make war. Always, I make war. (*Applause from the same seats. Divers movements.*)
>
> *M. Pierre Renaudel.* That's simple enough!
>
> *M. Charles Benoist.* Yes, but you have to keep it in mind.
>
> *M. Paul Poncet.* Red képis for the officers! (*Noise.*)
>
> *The president of the Council.* I seek to maintain close relations with our allies. Russia betrays us, I continue to make war. Unfortunate Romania is obliged to capitulate: I continue to make war, and I shall continue to the last quarter of an hour,

for the last quarter of an hour will be ours. (*Lively applause on the left, center and right.--Interruptions from the Socialist party's seats.*)[83]

Finally, it was the morale factor, once again, which underlay his action during the Czernin affair, the most serious diplomatic crisis of the last year of the war.[84] The Germans' first offensive (21-29 March) had stalled near Amiens after desperate fighting, but another blow was imminent. The Austrian foreign minister, Count Czernin, chose this moment to strongly reaffirm the alliance with Germany, to strike at his domestic opponents, especially the peace advocates at court, and probably at the same time to shake Clemenceau's hold in France (although this motive was later disputed) by asserting in a speech (2 April) that France had recently sought to negotiate, that her claims to Alsace-Lorraine had caused the project to fail, and that Austria besides had never contemplated a separate peace. Informed by telephone while at Foch's headquarters, Clemenceau exploded, "But this count is an infamous liar!"--and ordered Mandel to tell it to the world.[85]

Sensational exchanges followed during which Clemenceau, after a veiled warning which young Emperor Karl rashly ignored, published on 14 April a letter (of 24 March 1917) supporting France's claims to Alsace-Lorraine which Karl had sent to Poincaré during negotiations mediated by Prince Sixte of Bourbon-Parma. Czernin finally had to resign (another trophy for the Tiger), while poor Karl, his confidence violated and word discredited, had to go to Germany and proffer an explanation which nobody believed. With that the last wisps of hope for a negotiated peace drifted away: henceforth Austria was locked to Germany and in the event doomed to military defeat and internal disintegration.

Clemenceau's ruthless conduct appalled diplomatic circles. Wilson, still trying to sound Austria, thought it "a great blunder" and Secretary of State Lansing "a piece of the most astounding stupidity."[86] Reactions in London and Rome were scarcely less severe. In France shock waves ran through Parliament, the public, and even the army. Had he deceived the nation by secretly asking for terms while proclaiming war to the end? Or, on the other hand, had he thrown away bonafide chances for peace? He denied both charges. Czernin had revealed the Armand-Revertera meetings (of 1 and 23 February 1918), but these soundings had first begun during Ribot's premiership and at Austria's request. To portray as a serious peace initiative Clemenceau's very reluctant agreement to renew them but to offer no proposals was to perpetrate a distortion which put him in a terribly delicate position.[87] Labored explanations would not do.

But Czernin was foolish to play games with such an experienced and well-armed foe. Instantly and with lethal cunning, Clemenceau had diverted attention to the Sixte negotiations of 1917, believed by the French government to have been a plain bid for a separate peace, thus making Czernin a liar. Czernin and Karl blundered on. Karl had gambled that Clemenceau would not reveal the letter even if pressed. Czernin, for his part, probably did not know its precise contents. Clemenceau put them to the wall and by shrewdness, vigor, and some luck--for a "Congress of Oppressed Nationalities of Austria-Hungary" acclaiming Wilson's gospel of self-determination had convened in Rome (8-9 April) during the fracas--had managed to face down the parliamentary commissions, avoid an interpellation, and ride out the storm.

As for bonafide chances of peace in the spring of 1918, he thought them a mirage. Whatever the truth, it seems clear enough in retrospect that in the Czernin affair he only nailed shut a door which Austria on her own had already closed a fortnight earlier.[88] His behavior, though open to justifiable criticisms that it exceeded the requirements of the situation and violated the accepted norms of diplomacy, nevertheless served to remind his partners (especially Wilson, who of late seemed waxing high-handed and toplofty) that he still had to be reckoned with and, above all, his people that he meant business. Surely by now this war was going to be settled only on the battlefield, so they had best leave off thinking there might be an easier way out and just get on with the bloody job.

X

Vital as morale was, it was not a subject readily dealt with by councils of war. Manpower--"l'éternelle question des effectifs," in Mordacq's weary words--usually headed agendas, and for France the figures were deeply troubling. If fighting were heavy in 1918 (a certainty), the army could only decline in size. From September to December 1917 Pétain had had to disband fifty-five infantry battalions, and from April 1918 on he expected to lose a division a week from the ninety-nine on line in March. Losses through battle or the release of overaged classes from combat (men aged thirty-three to fifty-one filled half the ranks) could be made good only by more rigorous comb-outs, early drafting of the class of 1919, and the extension of conscription to Muslim natives of Algeria and blacks in West Africa. The last-named measure netted 50,000 Algerians and 72,000 West Africans in 1918 at the price of concessions regarding naturalization, voting rights, and local powers of government, concessions which Clemenceau took all the more pleasure in granting because the *Colonialistes* wailed about them.[89] Rejecting Parliament's customary request to release the older men, he warned in December in a very frank and vigorous intervention that in fact he might even recall some to the colors for trench digging. He defeated a counter-proposal by a 62 to 388 margin but subsequently managed to obtain 70,000 Italian laborers after some delicate negotiations with Rome.[90]

His position was decidedly uncomfortable in several respects. Others had the men and the ships to carry them, ships France also needed for fuel and steel. This circumstance alone largely explains the French government's enthusiasm for the creation of inter-Allied boards, such as the Allied Maritime Transport Council, and why Clemenceau straightaway overhauled the whole machinery of coordination when he came into office and charged one of his closest friends, Under-Secretary Jeanneney, with supervising the job.[91] America was the great reservoir of men (as of everything else), but only if they could be trained and transported in time. Once in France, a common language might draw them to the British, who were holding only a quarter of the front, albeit the most active sectors of late, and resisting appeals for extensions of their lines while still keeping hundreds of thousands in the Isles, in over-manned support services in France, and in the Eastern theaters. Eight French divisions, it was true, were vegetating at Salonika, mostly to maintain France's "presence" in the East, but if he pulled them out, Lloyd George, a fervent "Easterner," would surely try to replace them with troops he wanted kept in France.

He did, however, enjoy certain advantages. Since France was the main theater and had sacrificed the most, no one could ask *him* for more. Wilson was far away and Lloyd George roundly distrusted by most of the British generals. Moreover, the top post in any unified command almost certainly would go to a Frenchman. The Allies would feel obliged to defer to this commander, while Clemenceau could remind him when necessary that French generals, whatever their assignments, must answer to the minister of war. Lastly, and not least of all, he could exploit his own personality to get his way, whether with the Allied generals or their political chiefs. "You like me," he once slyly twitted Lloyd George, "you can't help yourself!"[92] And it was true.

The manpower problem, broadly construed, thus largely governed his relations with Britain, Italy, the United States, and the Russians. By mid-December a simple, harsh reality had come to dominate all calculations: The Americans would not arrive in time to prevent Germany's achieving temporary superiority in the West through massive transfers of troops from the moribund Russian front. Several responses were deduced. The British and French must cooperate more closely than ever before, prompt to shift reserves to threatened sectors. Formation of a full-dress American field army might have to wait so that infantry units could be rushed over and inserted into or between Allied divisions. And action should be continued against Germany in the East: support the Romanian remnants still in the field; persuade the Bolsheviks not to sign a peace; help them or their domestic opponents to keep a front in being; at the very least keep the Germans' hands off the veritable mountains of supplies stacked up in Russian ports.

The Allies botched policy toward Bolshevik Russia from start to finish.[93] The German victory in the East inspired horrific visions of the kaiser sending millions of indentured Russian soldiers and workers against them; of hordes of released German and Austrian POWs seizing control of Siberia; of the 650,000 tons of supplies in Vladivostok alone being shipped west on the Trans-Siberian while dismantled German submarines went east to be reassembled for operations in the Pacific; of Siberia and the Ukraine eventually becoming gigantic "colonies," threatening India and assuring

Germany domination of the rest of Eurasia--hence victory in the war--if outright victory could not be won in the West. The source of such fantasies was fear inspired by overestimates of German military might and domestic solidity and by the madhouse state of Russia, where what remained of a central government now belonged to a tiny party of revolutionaries led by an exile whose passage home had been expedited by the Germans. Clemenceau, Lloyd George, and the rest peered into the chaos, agreed that something ought to be done, but never adopted a consistent line or escaped being led on by events, ill-informed counsel, or people with axes to grind.

Clemenceau had greeted the Russian Revolution with hosannas.[94] He lucidly explained the tsar's fall, but never, then or later, did he comprehend the depth of Russia's disorganization and war-weariness. With his British counterparts he shared illusions that somehow "the healthy elements" could be rallied by outside support to continue the war on Germany. Dismayed by Kerenskii's decline in the autumn of 1917, he had suggested dispatch of a French military mission and refloated a misty idea he had advocated back in 1914-15, viz., massive intervention by Japan, this time not in the West but through Siberia to rebuild the Eastern front.[95]

The advent of Lenin, whom he had denounced as "a criminal or a madman" back in June, and whose German connections were reported to him in detail as premier, greatly complicated affairs.[96] Over the objections of his representatives in Russia and without consulting the Allies, he broke off formal relations (22 November) when Lenin sued for peace, but when Lenin began to resist German demands, he quickly resumed unofficial contact and support. To the eve of the signing of the Treaty of Brest-Litovsk (3 March), he, and the British, clung to hopes that the Bolsheviks would reject a German-dictated peace. The treaty's coincidence with the German offensive in the West, however, helped brand it on his mind as a "betrayal."

Intervention beckoned, for the moment to forbid Germany access to the Trans-Siberian railway, the ports, Ukrainian wheat, and Causasian oil, but more fundamentally to forestall a German economic and political penetration which could alter the European balance of power for years to come. Intervention would reestablish an Eastern front, which would then induce the Germans to keep large forces there while at the same time ensuring that those forces would not reap, now *or* later, the fruits of their recent victory. It was a formula which before long would bring to mind the famous recipe for bear stew: First, catch a bear.

XI

From his first days in office Clemenceau had urged intervention by the Japanese.[97] Urging was about all he could do, having neither men nor ships to spare. This lack of means thoroughly undermined his bargaining position in all the debates among the Allies over the next two years about what to do. For that matter, while others were not nearly so strapped for men, the severe shortage of shipping played a role in all plans for action in Russia which has often been underappreciated.[98] In hopes of keeping what was left of the Romanian army in the field but even more to keep the Ukraine's resources out of Germany's grasp, he did find money and some officers to assist a break-away Ukrainian regime and an anti-Bolshevik force under General Alekseev on the Don.

It being obviously desirable, meanwhile, to coordinate policies, the British sent Lord Milner and Lord Robert Cecil over to Paris for a conference (22-23 December 1917) from which emerged an agreement dividing southern Russia into "spheres of action," with France to take responsibility for the Ukraine, Bessarabia, the Crimea, and provisionally the Don basin, and the British for the Caucasus, Georgia, Armenia, and Kurdestan. Although it dealt with expenses only, the agreement was interpreted by the French, not unmindful of their large investments in the Don area, as conferring a privilege of influence, with the result that it became the cause of repeated misunderstandings between Paris and London and eventually of accusations that the whole arrangement was little more than a plot to partition Russia for future imperialistic exploitation.[99] In Clemenceau's case, to the extent that he devoted time to policy toward Russia, which he gave an impression of doing only when compelled by force of circumstances, he showed himself not particularly interested in its economic dimensions. It was military-political considerations which dominated his thinking, not some of the other interests which were impressing the bureaus at the Quai d'Orsay.

By February the hopes put in the Romanians and Ukrainians had crumbled. Furthermore, the contacts retained with the Bolsheviks and the encouragement given them in hopes they would stay embroiled with the Germans, peace or no peace, had come in the meantime to seem to the Quai d'Orsay (above all to Philippe Berthelot, the Political Director, who steadily garnered influence when Pichon's health and willpower declined) to be a dangerously passive policy and contradictory to boot. Prospects of continuing and even increasing France's long-standing influence in a (one could hope) unified Russia would be better served by open aid to the anti-Bolsheviks (the "Whites"), the more so since virtually all analyses assumed it to be self-evident--and persisted in so assuming well through 1919--that the Bolsheviks could not hold out for long, much less gain control of the whole country. This view of the matter finally won Clemenceau over sometime between 5 and 16 April.[100] Since he nevertheless wanted no British or American forces diverted from France, the Japanese alone remained. But they would not move without Wilson's approval, which he was refusing, and made no secret of their intention to confine their operations to Vladivostok and northern Manchuria--far from the most promising centers of White resistance and thousands of miles from any Germans.

Intervention thus hung fire for weeks on end. As late as June the only one, aside from an abortive Japanese move on Vladivostok in April, was a landing at Murmansk by a contingent of British marines. It was the Czechoslovak Legion which turned the balance. At the moment, it was the most formidable single armed force in the country, even coveted by the Bolsheviks. Numbering, it was thought, some 70,000 (in reality more like 42-50,000) deserters from the Austro-Hungarian army who had fought under Russian auspices, the Legion after Brest-Litovsk was strung over thousands of miles of the Trans-Siberian in some eighty trains crawling to Vladivostok, there to take ship for France in response to Clemenceau's urgent pleas.

The plight of the Czechs and their national movement had for some time, in fact, drawn his attention. Back in 1916 he had signed a declaration calling for recognition of the Czecho-Slovak government-in-exile. On 16 December 1917 he had followed up with a decree recognizing a Czecho-Slovak autonomous army under French military authority and the political authority of the Czecho-Slovak National Council, and in April 1918 he had promised a delegation from the Rome Congress of Oppressed Nationalities his support for full independence. Bringing the Legion to France thus was to him a project which had considerable appeal.

British planners, however, began to view the Czechs as a force to be used in Russia to support pro-Allied elements, protect the ports, and as a lever to win Wilson's consent to a Japanese intervention. So when French planners suggested (16 April) diverting a majority of the Czechs up to Archangel for quicker evacuation, they unwittingly handed the British an opportunity to "reinterpret" the Legion's mission. Clemenceau approved the split at an SWC meeting on 2 May because American shipping was not available for Vladivostok for the present, but he was still thinking evacuation was the goal when news arrived that the Czechs had clashed (26 May) with the Bolsheviks, who had been watching them suspiciously, and were rapidly gaining control of the Trans-Siberian.

A renewed plea (2 July) featuring the need to "rescue" deserving Czechs at last won over Wilson, who saw in it a rationale for limiting the intervention being pressed upon him.[101] In August large Japanese and token American, British, and French (one battalion) forces landed in Vladivostok. By then Clemenceau had suspended Czech evacuation (12 July), although when General Janin was subsequently dispatched to Siberia to take command of the Legion and organize a new anti-Bolshevik Russian army, his orders (7 August) still contemplated eventual removal of some of the Czechs. The merits of using them, however (as he had noted in a memorandum of 7 July), to help "all elements of order favorable to our cause," to "bar the route to German expansion toward the east," and form "a veritable advance guard" for the Vladivostok landings had grown increasingly persuasive now that action was the note.[102] His arm was in the wringer.

XII

By the end of October the principal body of Czechs, under attack from a revived Red Army, was in full retreat from a front they had been told to establish against the Germans at the Volga while awaiting Allied help. Neither the Germans nor the Allies had appeared there. Yet intervention plans and operations continued to go forward. Ironically, intervention in the

East, conceived when the Allies' cause was in dire peril, got underway at the very moment Germany began to confront disaster in the West. Far away, across endless plains and forests, the Allies were now involved with forces fighting not the Germans but the Bolsheviks, and henceforth seemed utterly unable to do anything but salvage bad ideas with worse. The British were the most active in creating the imbroglio, but Clemenceau from haste, ignorance, and inattention reaped a full share of blame for a tragedy which would cost the world dearly.

Irony abounded. In hindsight, Germany should have stayed on the defensive in 1918. The war had shown that a well-prepared defense (a German specialty) usually could master the offense. Germany arguably could have continued the war long enough to obtain a negotiated peace which would have saved for her more than she was able to save in November 1918. Ludendorff, however, decided to gamble on winning, which meant breaking the Allies in the West--a gamble whose odds, ironically, both he and the Allies underestimated. A lover of paradoxes hence could argue that the Allies' failure to keep the Eastern front in being served their cause better than a success might have done, for in the latter case Ludendorff might have been persuaded to stay on the defensive.

That despite his Western offensive he still kept more than thirty-eight divisions in Russia to reap the rewards of Brest-Litovsk was something for which the Allies could offer up thanks, especially since his rewards, notably in badly needed grain supplies, proved largely unobtainable--a bitter disappointment. It was one of the more signal ironies, however, that the Allies' activities in Russia had no discernable effect on this decision. Nevertheless, the large German forces tied down in Russia should not be invoked, as they often have, to fault Ludendorff's military dispositions seriously. The truth is that he did precisely what the Allies all along feared he would do: he moved all *battle-worthy* units in Russia to France. Moreover, he combed out even those divisions which stayed behind, leaving them with men and equipment fit only for limited duty, not for the rigors of the West.

Some 34 divisions rolled west between 1 November 1917 and 21 March 1918, with 12 more following in April and May, bringing Germany's total in the West to 204, their highest during the war and one giving them a peak advantage of 13 over the Allies. The advantage, however, was all but nullified by the grave logistical problems the Germans were experiencing, worse than the Allies suspected, and by the tactical realities of Western front fighting, which required a much larger superiority for attacking forces than those 13 divisions conferred.[103] As already noted, Ludendorff took a high-stakes, long-odds gamble.

But war by nature is always a gamble, and such was the impression produced by his early successes that both he and his opponents could see a clear chance of his winning. The first offensive (21 March) came agonizingly close to breaking the Allies asunder, raising the specter of a general rout, while the April onslaught in Flanders compelled even the phlegmatic Haig to summon his sagging army to die to the last man where they stood. With a third offensive (27 May) straining the line of the Marne after having swept over the Chemin des Dames and the unblown Aisne bridges in a matter of hours, Foch told Clemenceau on 31 May that he was losing men faster than the Americans were arriving, "which could mean losing the war."[104] Such words from one usually so confident confirmed a fear which long had gnawed at Clemenceau. Back in January Gen. Sir Henry Wilson had heard him, tired and morose, muttering that the Americans would come too late.[105] It helps explain the fevered tones of debates that spring over American reinforcements which culminated in a request (2 June) for 100 divisions to win the war--maybe in 1919 or 1920.

XIII

Questions of how and where to use the Americans frayed Anglo-French relations, with each side rightly suspecting the other of angling for advantages. In light of the fact that at the end of 1917 there were only 175,000 American troops in France, including no more than four divisions* in various stages of training, it is not surprising that proposals regularly began to emerge calling for integrating American into Allied units. The German

---

* U.S. divisions, however, numbered c.27,000 men, up to three times more than the depleted French and British units.

offensives from March on brought hurry-up pleas to rush American infantry to France as soon as possible and delay for the time being their normal support units. Under siege, General Pershing, without consulting Washington, agreed with Lord Milner on a May shipment of 100-120,000 combat troops, mostly infantry, which would train in British units. When Clemenceau got wind of this, he hotly demanded reciprocity for June. Pointing his cane at a carcass in a butcher's window while on his way to a meeting, he exploded to Sir William Wiseman, "Pershing is getting all of the meat. I want some of the meat!"[106] But then it was Lloyd George's turn to complain when Clemenceau and Pershing revised a shipping schedule without consulting him.[107] Clemenceau's main advantage in these arguments was that the quietest sector, hence the one most suitable for easing the Americans into battle, lay on the French right, far from the British. Vendean stubbornness, however, met its match in a mule from Missouri when Pershing utterly refused simply to amalgamate his troops with the Allies for combat unless an emergency should compel it: Americans would fight in American divisions under American commanders.

Later, in mid-August after the crisis had passed its peak, Clemenceau admitted to Pershing that he had changed his mind about amalgamation and that he (Pershing) had been right all along.[108] But he continued to conserve his long-standing doubts that Pershing and his staff had the experience necessary to cope with Ludendorff (no Pancho Villa, after all). He could do nothing, however, but go on trying to press French advisers on them. Much later, when the Meuse-Argonne offensive (26 September-15 October) stalled in a tangled mess after the first few days, he did not pass up the chance to proffer some unwelcome I-told-you-soes. But in fairness to Pershing, it must be said that some of the blame had to attach to repeated scheduling revisions he had had to make to accommodate others.[109]

Ironically, once again, virtually none of the 950,537 men rushed to France from April through July fought in the critical battles. Furthermore, with the tide turning in August, Lloyd George and Clemenceau began to trim previous troop requests dramatically in order to reduce Wilson's leverage when peace should come.[110] The Americans' presence, nevertheless, did permit a bold use of Anglo-French reserves before August and severely affected German morale. Their ultimate contribution thereafter was to ensure a victory before another awful winter--far sooner than anyone had dared hope during the dark days of spring.

XIV

Anglo-French cooperation, vital to success, was persistently bedeviled by questions of manpower, strategy, and command, no one of which could be addressed without leading to instant effects on the others. The feud between Lloyd George and his strongly "Western" generals Robertson (chief of staff) and Haig complicated Clemenceau's efforts. Haig did fulfill, though not until February, a promise to extend his line sixteen miles to Barisis (Aisne), but farther he would not go, partly because Lloyd George, with Passchendaele fresh in mind, was keeping a lid on recruitment. As the prime minister candidly stated, "I don't trust Haig with men."[111] Clemenceau, however, impressed by Haig's and Pétain's overly gloomy assessments, tore into Lloyd George's cherished idea of a crushing offensive against the Turks with sarcasms about the futility of "looking for *la victoire* on the Euphrates" and got him at least to agree (2 February) to divert no men from France to pursue Eastern schemes.[112]

When the German drives in the spring made *effectifs* an agonizing question, Clemenceau was more than happy to find that Lloyd George, who was under heavy fire for alleged failures to keep Haig supplied with men, was agreeable to having a French expert, Colonel Roure, go to London to look around and offer advice. The War Office received him coolly, to say the least. Roure concluded that 2,300,000 more combatants could be combed from men already in uniform, and Lloyd George agreed because he opposed drafting more men and did not like the way the army was using the ones they had. What the Roure missions (in May and June) mainly achieved, however, was to dissolve Clemenceau's belief, widely shared in France, that the British still had a reserve army in the Isles chock-full of men fit for the front, for the general reserve, retained in Britain with Haig's consent heretofore, had already been sent over during the first month of the German offensive.[113] Yet he remained convinced that Britain, following France's (not altogether relevant) example, could draft a far larger number of men from occupations Lloyd George insisted were vital and use them plus the "B-category" soldiers (fit for overseas but not "general," i.e., fighting, service) to keep combat divisions steady in size and number. Lloyd George had a good case as regards occupational deferments, though less good as regards "B" men, a categorization Clemenceau dismissed as "a mere sailor's notion."[114] and castigated Clemenceau's and Foch's eventual support of Pershing's building of an American army on the French, rather than the British, right flank as an attempt "to put the screw upon us" in order to keep the number of divisions at a fixed number "regardless of the effect upon our industries and national life generally."[115]

The whole problem really, was just too shot through with clashing figures, judgments, and emotions to be resolved without repeated noisy rows. Everybody wanted more American "meat" (on their own terms, of course), and Clemenceau, Foch, and Haig could never have too many men from Britain in France. On the other hand, both Haig and the British government were haunted by fears, acute in June, that the French army was about to go belly-up. So while feeling obliged to respond favorably to French entreaties, they also worried about getting sucked down to defeat with them. As for Lloyd George himself, while having to fend off critics who were crying that he was "starving" Haig, he was convinced, as were the French to some extent (though they tended to cite swollen service units), that Haig wasted the men he *did* have in murderous, pointless offensives. Moreover, to his dying day he never really believed, whatever Clemenceau said, that the Somme was superior to "the Euphrates" as the avenue to victory.

XV

Command was a question whose subtleties forced Clemenceau into temporizations and detours. The SWC's military advisory committee at Versailles left him cold. He favored a single commander for the Western Front. But in November he told Colonel House he had "nothing in mind," in House's words, and did not dare to "formulate a plan because it might be looked upon with suspicion"; he suggested, however, that the United States might take the initiative and that he would support "any reasonable suggestion that we make."[116] When Milner came over for the 22-23 December meeting on Russian affairs, he lobbied for an Anglo-French strategic reserve "under a single direction," which seemed to point to a generalissimo.[117] Nothing came of it, but he began to see possibilities for the advisory committee when the SWC on Lloyd George's initiative decided (2 February) to make it into the Executive Military Committee, thus allowing the top chiefs to be part of it, and give it control of an Inter-Allied General Reserve, with Foch (the French chief of staff) to chair the committee: "As we [cannot] have a single Commander-in-Chief, such as a Hannibal or a Charlemagne," Clemenceau quipped, "we might at least have a Commander of Reserves."[118] Yet only six days before the Germans struck in March, the SWC shelved the idea; and when Foch protested, Clemenceau peremptorily shut him up.

Why? Because he had given up on Foch or a unified command? Although decisive proof is lacking, it appears most unlikely. At bottom, a single condition governed. Since the supreme commander would be French, a premise never seriously contested, the British--in effect Haig or, if Lloyd George could have done as he pleased, his successor--would have to *ask* for one, and Haig, it was plain, was as yet not at all disposed to do so. While it may be dismissed as an ex post facto attempt to color the truth, Clemenceau long afterward told Martet that he had only pretended to oppose a unified command: "My game was to lead the English to the idea without imposing it on them."[119]

The Repington affair showed how complicated and dangerous this game could be. Following the 30 January-2 February SWC meeting, Colonel Repington, the *Morning Post*'s noted military commentator and a known good-acquaintance of Clemenceau, criticized Lloyd George's Eastern plans but also leaked word of the new General Reserve scheme. Repington later asserted that Clemenceau was his source, although a recent, quite thorough investigation of the matter has cast considerable doubt on it.[120] Repington's reports (8, 11 February) were intended to support General Robertson, a diehard Westerner, in his struggle with Lloyd George over grand strategy and thus, wittingly or not, played into Clemenceau's hands--as Lloyd George could not fail to appreciate. But Repington, with Robertson's support, was also at loggerheads with Lloyd George over the role of the Versailles military committee, whose control of the General Reserve appeared to be opening the road to Foch's becoming generalissimo. Repington's leak brought on the final showdown between Lloyd George and Robertson. The prime minister at last got up the courage to fire him (19 February); but he replaced him with Sir Henry Wilson, who could leave him freer than had Robertson to pursue the Eastern plans Clemenceau opposed, although Wilson, it was known, *was* more open than Robertson to the unified command idea. The affair thus ended, as far as Clemenceau was concerned, in something resembling a stand-off but promising further complications.

Lloyd George, however, did not dare to touch the popular Haig, whose price for staying quiet about Robertson's removal presently proved to be the abandonment of the General Reserve. And there it rested. Neither Haig nor Pétain had wanted to give up their local reserves to Foch's committee because 1) they were crying for men anyhow, 2) they objected to placing such a responsibility in the hands of a committee rather than with a supreme commander, and 3) because they disagreed with Foch's defensive doctrine, which called for powerful early counterattacks. When asked what means existed to carry out such attacks, Foch had no answer.

This dispute over tactics already had found its way to Clemenceau's door in the first weeks of his ministry. Pétain's novel defense-in-depth plan, which placed more emphasis on the second than the first line of defense, worried him. To answer his doubts, to affirm his authority over Pétain, and incidentally to support Foch, who was somewhat miffed because he (Clemenceau) had seemed to be getting along better with Pétain than with him that winter, he pressed Pétain hard on technical points--a sensitive business for a civilian minister of war--and even used reports by General Roques, a former minister of war, to bolster his case. But Pétain's arguments were sound, the man stubborn. Sacking him was out of the question. In the meantime, Pétain reached agreement with Haig on measures of mutual support in case of need.[121] The Reserve--and Foch--would have to await a better day. Or a worse.

XVI

It came in a rush. At 4:40 A.M. on 21 March a six-thousand-gun thunderclap announced the long-expected German drive for victory. Within forty-eight hours the offensive, which slammed into the British Fifty Army north of the Oise River near the juncture with the French, was threatening to separate the two armies. On 24 March at 12:50 P.M., even before receipt of Haig's call for help, Lord Milner entrained for Paris. A series of high-level meetings culminated on 26 March at the *mairie* of the village of Doullens with the naming of Foch to "coordinate the actions of the Allied armies on the western front."

Clemenceau had gotten his first impression of the full gravity of the crisis when he visited Pétain on the 23rd: "I saw Gough's [Fifth] army spreading like an eggwhite."[122] While returning to Paris he remarked to Mordacq, "After an interview like that you need an iron-bound spirit to retain your confidence."[123] A second visit, on the 24th, moderated this impression, but on neither occasion did he take serious issue with Pétain's operations, although he did express to his ministers afterward some scorn for Pétain's persisting fear of a possible attack in Champagne.[124] Pétain was sending reinforcements on a massive scale toward the British, but it was understood that if--and only if--the hole could not be plugged, then the defense of Paris must take precedence. Meanwhile, several super-long-range guns ("Big Berthas") had begun dropping shells every quarter hour in Paris. Measures already were underway there to remove vital records, though no decision had yet been made about transferring the government, and the train stations were reported to be as jammed as in 1914 with refugees from the north and persons trying to leave. Despite some bad scenes, however, in the main they were still orderly.

That same day (the 24th) Foch proposed a unified command, but Clemenceau abruptly dismissed it. Since he gave no reasons beyond citing his own good relations with Haig and Pétain, one can only speculate--an undiplomatic approach by Foch; aftereffects of the scene with him at the last SWC meeting; momentary satisfaction with Pétain's plans; old habits of disguising his intentions about appointments and of saying little when he inwardly agreed with a suggestion; the necessity of being discreet until he had cleared it with Pétain (who was long known to have some hopes of his own for the job[125]); ignorance as yet of Milner's journey and that the British might be coming around?

After the second visit to Pétain and a night of reflection, he had decided by the morning of the 25th (when Milner arrived) that Foch's view of what *must* be done, not Pétain's, was correct, and that the time for the unified command was now and Foch the man. Foch's insistence on the need to concentrate everything possible on plugging the breach and defending the key railway center of Amiens, the hinge of the Paris-Channel ports line, in order to preserve the link between the two armies without changing their present fronts had impressed him and answered the British anxiety; whereas, behind Pétain's orders and somber remarks there persistently appeared a disposition to give his highest priority to keeping the French forces united and covering Paris.[126] Moreover--and arguably of equal weight during the two days of tense meetings which climaxed at Doullens--Foch's blazing spirit stood in stark contrast to the coldness and pessimism emanating from Pétain, who on the morning of the 25th had gone so far as to remark to Louis Loucheur that Clemenceau should be pressed to ask for peace.[127] The surging psychological lift given to all parties in these meetings by Foch's fire and clarity of purpose was of the highest importance at this critical moment when confusion and panic could have swept the field. Clemenceau commented after Doullens, "Foch and Haig have been very good. I will not say as much about another. Happily, Foch will be there to shake him up."[128]

During the meetings of the 25th and 26th Clemenceau was tact incarnate. At the critical instant, on the 26th at Doullens, he gave Milner the opening to suggest Foch's name. And when he composed the agreement, he restricted Foch's powers to "coordinating action in front of Amiens," the most modest draft possible, leaving it to Haig to ask for their extension to "the western front"--something which he (Clemenceau) not only wanted and knew to be sounder but which responded to the understandable desire of the British to disguise a defeat by invoking the needs of the whole front and putting Pétain on the same footing as Haig. The only sour note he struck was a parting jibe to Foch: "Well, you finally got what you wanted!"[129] How typical, this swipe of the paw to conceal a deeply felt gratitude.

XVII

Foch once in place, Clemenceau felt no compunction about pressing for extensions of powers and titles. Having soothed Haig by persuading Foch to send him a reserve division he had been asking for, he won Lloyd George's agreement (3 April at Beauvais), over General Wilson's objections, to giving

Foch "strategic direction" of operations providing only that the national commanders retained a right to appeal to their governments if they believed he was imperiling their armies. The title of General-in-Chief (later, in usage, Commander) followed fairly easily (14 April) after Haig was hit by another offensive, while the Americans in full and the Italians and Belgians to lesser degrees were gradually brought under the tent.

After the war, memoir writers and historians often fastened on the Doullens meeting as an epochal event and attributed great importance to Foch's role in the final victory. Time has tempered both judgments. The impact of his appointment on the course of the fighting immediately following Doullens is debatable. On the one hand, the German drive was already passing its peak on the 26th because of stiffening Allied resistance but even more because logistical problems and fatigue were taking their usual toll on any attempt to break through decisively. On the other hand, General Byng (commander of the British Third Army on Gough's northern flank) later stated that on the 25th Haig had "made it quite clear...that no help could be expected from the South," i.e., the French, and that "any further withdrawal must be in a North West direction and the Third Army must safeguard the right flank of the BEF [British Expeditionary Force] by swinging its own right flank back," taking for granted that "no help was to be expected from the remains of the Fifth Army [Gough]." Foch's appointment, by resolving Anglo-French differences on strategy, had the effect of cancelling further consideration of such a movement.[130]

As for Foch's general contribution, his status wanted definition which later agreements never fully supplied, and he found his every decision the subject of wary scrutiny in all quarters, especially Lloyd George's, because he was suspected of being the tool by which the redoubtable premier of France intended to "run" the war--a suspicion not wholly off the mark. (In a dispatch to Foreign Secretary Balfour in April, Lord Derby complained from Paris, "What amuses me is Clemenceau's open contempt of our P[rime] M[inister]. He evidently thinks he can do what he wants with him."[131]) The truth was that Foch (and hence Clemenceau) never had a realistic chance to pursue any such grandiose project. With neither the authority nor a staff at all comparable to that of the Eisenhowers or Mountbattens of World War II, he was truly more a coordinator than commander. As with the American effort, so with Foch: his contribution was to hasten and ensure a victory which in its essentials was saved and won by others. One must nevertheless add a qualifier. If he had been removed during the June crisis, as it had momentarily seemed might happen because of his questionable judgments about where to commit his reserves, the unified command probably would have foundered, for who could have been put in his place? And if the command had collapsed, the Allies might well have begun to fall apart, with everyone looking out for their own skins.[132]

In light of what has been said about Foch's authority, it almost goes without saying that the unified command never functioned to Clemenceau's entire satisfaction. Foch, he thought, whatever titles he claimed he needed, never used the powers he *did* have to full effect.[133] His impatience about this imputed failure kept surfacing to the end of the war. The March offensive was contained and another in Flanders in April, but on 27 May a massive breakthrough at the Chemin des Dames dealt the French their first outright defeat since 1914,[134] with responsibility for it lying heavily on the high commanders. The tide was stemmed at the Marne after desperate fighting, which incidentally saw the Americans get their first serious baptism of fire at Château-Thierry and Belleau Wood, but for several days Paris was very tense and the railway stations again were packed.

For Clemenceau it was the most critical moment of the war. Terribly worn from non-stop exertions in dangerous trips to the front, he defended Foch and Pétain before a nervous and disorderly Parliament on 4 June. He didn't hesitate to pull out all emotional stops, picturing a dead-tired general in "the hardest battle of the war" being summoned by politicians to answer niggling questions: "Drive me from the rostrum if that's what you're demanding, because I won't do it!"[135] A 377-110 vote of confidence proved his hold was more secure than some had thought; Briand watched from the sidelines but did not intervene. "I had to hold both of them [Foch and Pétain] by the scruff of their necks," he sighed on his return home, adding sourly, "I've saved them, but they don't deserve it."[136]

Fortunately, he didn't have to play this scene again. Similar failures were avoided in the subsequent tide-turning battles. Then, with victory in sight at last in early October, he suddenly took Foch to task for not "commanding" Pershing when the difficult Meuse-Argonne operation faltered, and threatened to lay the matter before President Wilson and ask for Pershing's head. He had his reasons. He saw French soldiers dying because of American mistakes; he saw an opportunity slipping away to endanger the entire German defense at the moment they were asking for terms; and he certainly spied a chance to increase his leverage before a peace conference by humbling Wilson, his big American army, and its stiff-necked commander. In this instance, however, as in his threat to resign during his quarrel with Poincaré over the desirability of granting an armistice, the fever of fatigue, exaltation, impatience, and worry in which he passed the last six weeks of the war must be held largely responsible for a patent and embarrassing overreaction. Foch could not simply "command" Pershing (or Haig, or Diaz of Italy, whose government had adhered only to the Doullens formula of "coordination"), and Clemenceau's pressing of a moot point fatefully damaged their relationship.[137]

About his authority as premier and minister of war, however, he was clear and very sound. Foch held an inter-Allied command, but he was still a French general:

> "Do you know," the Marshal said to me one day, "that I am not your subordinate?"
> "No, I don't," I replied with a laugh. "I don't even want to know who put that notion into your head. You know that I am your friend. I strongly advise you not to try to act on this idea, for it would never do."[138]

Behind his firm grasp of the principle of the supremacy of civil authority, there did lurk, however, a long-standing wariness of military men. "Ah! Monsieur Martet! I saw what they did during the Dreyfus Affair! They did everything!" He had written in those days that the minister of war needs "a hand of iron," and that if the generals were made to feel it, "all those ferocious lions" would behave like "lambs."[139] The war mitigated these views, but it never expunged them. On the other hand, his quarrels with Foch after the war tended to obscure the fact that, all things considered, he got along well with the generals, even with Foch. An iron hand held them to close account, and Foch and Pétain grumbled now and then about the frequency of his visits, but rumors that he interfered in operations were without serious foundation. Certainly he--and Mordacq--did great service in composing the inevitable differences among generals of diverse nationalities and ample egos commanding gigantic forces in the greatest war the world had ever seen.

XVIII

The Chemin des Dames affair had led to the last important command shake-up. Parliament wanted heads. Poincaré called in Briand (30 May) and criticized Pétain. Briand's friends spread it about that the president meant it as an anti-Clemenceau signal, with the result that Clemenceau, infuriated, threatened to resign if there were a repetition of this sort of thing.[140] From then on they were hardly on speaking terms. After a suitable interval, Clemenceau authorized a joint Army-Parliament inquiry, a striking departure from previous practice. In a painful interview at Provins on 10 June, Pétain defended General Duchêne (Fifth Army), the one most at fault, and offered to resign. Moved by his sincerity and caught off balance, Clemenceau refused: "We are at war. We have no choice to make. You will obey."[141]

Yet in truth he had lost confidence in him. The day after defending him in Parliament, he had recalled General Guillaumat from Salonika, where back in December he had been sent to replace General Sarrail, whose ties to Caillaux and the *Bonnet Rouge* circle plus his strained relations with the British had put him at the top of Clemenceau's transfer list.[142] Nobody could mistake the meaning of Guillaumat's return. Pétain's noble frankness at Provins, however, impressed him. On the way back to Paris, Mordacq defended Pétain warmly and said that he, Mordacq, would in honor have to resign if he were fired because of all he owed to him. Clemenceau said nothing, but that may well have clinched it, for not even Mandel had become so important to him as Henri Mordacq. Still, he did continue to wonder for some time if he had done the right thing.[143]

In the end, Duchêne, Franchet d'Esperey, Micheler, and several others were relieved, Guillaumat was kept close by as military governor of Paris just in case, and a compromise was arranged to settle disagreements between Pétain and Foch.[144] The tiring Germans granted the respite their opponents desperately needed. Had they put in another big offensive in mid-

June, General Buat (Pétain's new chief of staff) admitted later, "nobody can say what would have happened."[145] When Ludendorff finally shot his bolt, on 15 July in Champagne around Rheims, Pétain's defense-in-depth passed the test, and the first large-scale counterattack (18 July)--led by Charles Mangin, a fire-eater in the Patton mold whom Clemenceau reinstated in his old command after he had been shelved during the troubles of 1917-- heralded the opening of the drive to victory.

XIX

August and September passed in a rolling barrage of Allied offensives. The Germans fought on with stubborn bravery and skill, inflicting heavy losses on their foes, who kept crunching forward at a pace averaging a mile per day. But the edifice of German power was crumbling. On 15 September the "gardeners" of Salonika--under Franchet d'Ésperey, ("Desperate Frankie," the English called him), whose somewhat unjust firing Clemenceau had rectified by appointment to a command for which he was eminently qualified but without clearing the matter with Lloyd George, a blunder[146]--at long last got their chance and smashed into the Bulgarians, who sued for terms on the 28th. Six days later Germany and Austria, smelling catastrophe, suddenly asked President Wilson for a ceasefire. Clemenceau was overcome at the news: "At the first armistice requests, I almost went mad...mad with joy!"[147]

It was a joy mixed with profound surprise, which was nearly universal. The way the armistice was negotiated was highly peculiar and thus the source of important difficulties and misunderstandings among all parties.[148] The armistice request went to Wilson, not to the Allies collectively. This did not seem to bother Clemenceau very much at first. For one thing, perhaps because he had been favorably impressed by Wilson's tough handling of the exchanges with Germany leading to America's entry into the war,[149] he did not share the fears felt in some quarters that the American president would be too soft. For another, when Wilson replied, as he had anticipated, with some very hard questions for the Germans, he suspected they would back off and continue fighting, with Wilson, not he this time, becoming the target of the public's inevitable disappointment over another "lost chance" for peace.

But Germany did not back off, and information reaching him from intelligence sources by mid-October confirmed that the situation there was so grave that they probably would accept almost any terms short of outright capitulation. From this point on he held quite steadily to a belief that after the usual protesting and stalling Germany would sign. He gave little credence to talk in both camps about the need to grant liberal terms so as to prevent Germany and subsequently even France and Italy from being swept by Bolshevism--a German bluff, he thought--and even objected (ultimately unsuccessfully) to granting Germany's request to let troops stay on temporarily in her Russian conquests after the armistice in order to protect the local populace from the Bolsheviks. His only real worry, which became most acute at the last moment with the fall of the kaiser (9 November), was whether Germany's negotiators were agents of a credible government--the same worry Bismarck had had about France in 1871.[150]

The question of what terms to grant was bound inextricably with that of the wisdom of granting a ceasefire at all. On the latter point, Clemenceau soon learned to his satisfaction that the public wanted the fighting to stop but only under terms which would prevent Germany from improving her position during the ceasefire and guarantee the possibility of France achieving her war aims as regards her future security from aggression. This was his view, too. At the outset, however, until he got a better feel for public opinion, which during much of October wavered between hope for a rapid end and a desire to see the Boche kicked out of France before granting them any terms at all,[151] he was almost excessively cautious from fear of being accused of asking terms which would impede negotiations and thus prolong the bloodshed. He even momentarily agreed, for example, that while the Germans should be required to evacuate Alsace-Lorraine, the Allies would not yet occupy it.

Moreover, for reasons nobody has deciphered but which conceivably might have had some connection with a severe diabetic crisis he experienced in October and November,[152] he was uncharacteristically slow to grasp what Lloyd George and Foch in particular had understood almost immediately: that any armistice terms would have critical bearing on what could be gotten later at a peace conference. Foch, much disturbed by this fuzziness, finally spelled it out to him in a memorandum (16 October) asking for guidance in preparing military terms. Clemenceau, embarrassed and also concurrently embroiled with him over the Pershing-Argonne affair, reacted by reading him a lesson on proper civil-military relations in matters political. But Foch's lesson to him struck home, and henceforth, with the seriousness of Germany's situation and intentions meanwhile having become clearer, he began to pay much closer attention to proposed terms.

He was forced, nevertheless, to cross one final bridge. On 23 October Wilson and Germany concluded their dialogue with an agreement that Germany, understanding that the following peace would be based on the Fourteen Points, would have its request for an armistice passed on to the Allies. This understanding left Clemenceau "very much annoyed," and likewise the British and Italians.[153] Wilson ("Jupiter," Clemenceau called him) had them in a box, for it would be all but impossible to renege on the Points even though, as Clemenceau growled, nobody had asked *him* about them. At the inter-Allied conference of 29 October-4 November, Colonel House finally responded to their objections by threatening America's withdrawal from the war. It was Lloyd George (again, not Clemenceau) who found a way around by entering "reservations" regarding freedom of the seas and compensation for damages which House proved willing to accept. Clemenceau joined in without further ado.[154] No doubt he could not afford to be odd man out, the more so since he took it as axiomatic that future French security would depend on having close ties with Britain and the United States, but also because he was seeing in House's concession evidence that there would be ample opportunity to "interpret" the Points in the give-and-take of the peace conference and that armistice terms, once again, could be used as leverage there.

Indeed, it was time to finish. Quarrels with Foch and the Americans about the Argonne operation and with the British about the eastern Mediterranean and whether it would be a French or British admiral (the British, it turned out) who would accept the Turks' surrender; Poincaré's missive warning that a premature armistice would "hamstring" a victorious French army, which provoked him into another threat to resign;[155] the great influenza epidemic, which by now was carrying off twelve hundred lives a week in Paris alone, among them Thérèse's new second husband, Jules Iung, a lawyer and front-line soldier[156]--they all flayed his nerves and taxed his strength to the limit. But when the Turks gave up (30 October), when the Italians had at last taken the bit and launched an offensive which compelled the Austrians to conclude a separate armistice (3 November), and when the Germans had showed themselves prepared to accept terms far more severe than anything imaginable a month ago, the answer was clear. Could he condemn to death another hundred thousand *poilus* (at the least) because of an hypothesis that Germany would never learn unless she were invaded and forced to her knees without conditions?

XX

At the eleventh hour of the eleventh day of November the guns fell silent. The old man's hands trembled as he read out the terms at four o'clock to a Chamber in delirium. The "Marseillaise"...Alsace-Lorraine...he the sole survivor of the 107 *protestaires* of 1871--it was almost too much.

Afterward, he went over to the war ministry, where he appeared once at a window to accept the cheers of a crowd gathered there. A touchingly strange moment occurred when the sister of Paul Déroulède (who had died in June 1914) appeared and presented him with the musket her brother had carried in 1870.[157] Before long a car was summoned, and he was sped back to his apartment, where he disconnected his phone and sent his valet away.

In the evening his sister Sophie came by and discovered him sitting in his study in the dark. After fixing him something to eat, she managed to persuade him to go out for a walk and see the celebrations. They wandered unaccompanied for miles until they were recognized in the boulevard des Capucines. The police came to their rescue and bundled them into the Grand Hotel, overlooking the Place de l'Opéra, where his daughter Madeleine and some others soon joined them. Chants of "Cle-men-ceau!" brought him out on a balcony for a few words, but nobody could hear them above the roar. Finally, during a lull he shouted, "Do not cry 'Vive Clemenceau,' cry 'Vive la France'--and always 'Vive la France!'"[158] He turned and sank into a sofa, quiet and morose. Conversation in the room dwindled to whispers. Outside, the din went on. Sophie suggested they should go home, but he paid no attention. Madeleine finally spoke up:

"Papa, tell me that you're happy." "I can't tell you that because I am not," he replied. And then he betrayed his thoughts: "It will not have done any good!"[159]

It was the greatest night of his life, but already "the miseries of a victory" were descending.

NOTES
CHAPTER XIV

1   See Allain, *L'oracle*, pp. 132-137.

2   See Schaper, *Albert Thomas*, p. 167. Barthou unaccountably lacks a satisfactory biography. Clemenceau had considered keeping him, but not at Foreign Affairs, which he insisted on. Early in 1918 Clemenceau (to rid himself of a critic or rival?) tried to persuade Barthou to accept the ambassadorship to Switzerland. He declined when it became apparent it would be only a sinecure. See Duroselle, *Clemenceau*, p. 633; and Henri Allizé, *Ma mission à Vienne (mars 1919, août 1920)* (Librairie Plon, 1933), pp. 34-35.

3   See Wormser, *Le septennat de Poincaré*, pp. 101-102. Poincaré's memoirs are silent on this demarche. Watson, in *Georges Clemenceau*, p. 258, cites a dispatch from Lord Bertie to the Foreign Office on 21 Feb. 1917 mentioning unsuccessful "advances" by Poincaré for a "reconciliation," but their time and nature are unstated. Perhaps Bertie was alluding to the 12 Dec. 1916 meeting noted above (p. 339).

4   See Henri Castex, *Les comités secrets*, vol 3: *La "Grande Guerre" pour rien?* (Éditions Roblot, 1974), p. 41n., quoting memoirs by Paul Lacave-Laplagne, a deputy. Maunoury, in *Police de guerre*, p. 149, says Léon Bourgeois worked to bring Poincaré and Clemenceau together. Poincaré's memoirs are silent on the Favre *démarche*.

5   See Pierre Miquel, *Poincaré* (Éditions Arthème Fayard, 1916), p. 366.

6   Wormser, *Le septennat de Poincaré*, p. 31.

7   See pp. 331, 336, above; and Fred Kupferman, *Laval, 1883-1945* (Balland, 1987), pp. 39-40. Blaise Diagne, a Senegalese Ind. Soc., was concurrently named commissioner for native recruitment. As noted below, Colliard (Labor) also was an Ind. Soc.

8   See Marie-José Domestici-Met, "Le deuxième gouvernement de Clemenceau, 1917-1920: contribution à l'étude du chef de gouvernement en régime parlementaire," *Revue du droit public et de la science politique en France et à l'etranger* 102 (1986):127-128.

9   Clemenceau in Steed, *Through Thirty Years*, 2:157.

10   See Appendix IV for the cabinet's roll. Charles Jonnart (Blockade and Liberated Territories) resigned after a week for health reasons but was later named governor-general of Algeria. Justin Godart

(under-sec., Medical Services) resigned under parliamentary fire in Feb. 1918. Only one other, Boret (Agriculture), resigned under fire, in July 1919.

11   Martet, *Clemenceau*, pp. 32-33. See Jacques Raphaël-Leygues, *Georges Leygues, le "père" de la marine (Ses carnets secrets de 1914 à 1920)* (Éditions France-Empire, 1983), pp. 192-193.

12   "On demande un gouvernement," HE, 15 Nov. 1917 (his italics).

13   Winston S. Churchill, *Great Contemporaries* (New York: G. P. Putnam's Sons, 1937), pp. 271-272. Churchill had tarried on the return from the Rapallo conference.

14   JOC, 20 Nov. 1917, pp. 2962-2963. "La justice passe" is not readily translatable.

15   Poincaré, *Au service de la France,* 9:365. See Georges Soutou, "La France et les Marches de l'Est, 1914-1919," *Revue historique* 260 (1978):372-373.

16   Allain, *L'oracle*, p. 53n., gives the following analysis:

	For	Ag.	Abst.	Abs.
Action Libérale (20)	16	0	0	4
Indépendants non inscrits (39)	37	0	0	2
Droites (13)	12	0	0	1
Fédération républicaine (33)	32	0	0	1
Gauche démocratique (30)	27	0	0	3
Gauche radicale (57)	53	0	1	3
Républicains de gauche (51)	48	0	1	2
Union républicaine radicale et socialiste (17)	16	0	0	1
Radicaux socialistes (166)	149	1	12	4
Républicains socialistes (26)	22	0	1	3
Socialistes (96)	1	63	25	7
Hors groupe (7)	5	1	1	0
Totals	418	65	41	31

17   HL, 21 Nov. 1917. (The paper's name had reverted to *L'Homme Libre* after his accession.) An usher at the Palais-Bourbon said he had never seen such a crowd at the grilles.

18   Jean Martet, "Clemenceau," *L'Illustration*, 30 Nov. 1929, p. 603.

19   Henry Lémery, "Clemenceau comme je l'ai vu," *Histoire de notre temps*, no. 6 (1968), p. 175.

20   Becker, *The Great War and the French People*, p. 248

21   See Pedroncini, *Les mutineries de 1917*, pp. 60, 255-256.

22   On morale here see especially Becker, *The Great War and the French People*, pp. 242-248; *idem*, "L'opinion publique française en 1917," pp. 1505-1507; Poincaré, *Au service de la France*, 10:4-5, 30; Georges Liens, "L'opinion à Marseille en 1917," and Georges Rufin, "L'opinion publique en 1917 dans l'arrondissement de Tournon," *Revue d'histoire moderne et contemporaine* 15 (1968):54-78, 79-96, *passim*; Pierre Renouvin, "L'opinion publique en France pendant la guerre, 1914-1918," *Revue d'histoire diplomatique* 84 (1970), no. 4, pp. 324-326; Jean Nicot, "Psychologie du combattant français de 1918," *Revue historique de l'Armée* 28 (1972), no. 2, pp. 61-74; and R.-G. Nobécourt, *L'année de 11 novembre 1918* (Robert Laffont, 1968), p. 59.

23   Martet, "Clemenceau," p. 603.

24   Raphaël-Leygues, *Georges Leygues*, p. 128 (5 May 1918).

25   Wormser, *Clemenceau vu de près*, p. 198.

26   Lord Riddell [George Allardyce Riddell], *Lord Riddell's Intimate Diary of the Peace Conference and After, 1918-1923* (New York: Reynal & Hitchcock, 1934), p. 99.

27   See Stevenson, *Lloyd George*, p. 286, quoting Louis Loucheur at second hand.

28   Raphaël-Leygues, *Georges Leygues*, p. 144 (26 June 1918).

29   Miquel, *Poincaré*, p. 374.

30   Martet, *Clemenceau*, p. 153. On the "hamstringing" affair in Oct., see pp. 401, 421 below.

31   See especially Paul Fussell, *The Great War and Modern Memory* (New York: Oxford University Press, 1975), pp. 64-79, 82-90.

32   By count from Mordacq, *Le ministère Clemenceau*, vols. 1, 2. Elapsed time amounted to roughly 64 days, counting as half-days trips of several hours to Bombon (Foch) or Provins (Pétain), and including the 13-17 March trip to London.

33   See HE, 23 Feb. 1916, repr. in GC, *Discours de guerre*, pp. 61-64.

34   See Grigg, *Lloyd George*, p. 386.

35   See Mordacq, *Le ministère Clemenceau*, 2:287-290.

36   Wormser, *Clemenceau vu de près*, p. 200; see also pp. 198-214, *passim*. Mordacq's *Le ministère Clemenceau* does not mention this order. Churchill gave an account of the incident; see Martin Gilbert, *Winston S. Churchill*, vol. 4: *The Stricken World, 1916-1922* (Boston: Houghton Mifflin, 1975), p. 95.

37 See Mordacq, *Le ministère Clemenceau*, 1:160, 261-263, 2:46-47.

38 Benjamin, *Clemenceau dans la retraite*, pp. 124-125.

39 Corday, *L'envers de la guerre*, 1:241.

40 Martet, *Clemenceau*, p. 138. "In order to act you must be somewhat insane. A reasonably sensible man is satisfied with thinking." *Ibid.*, p. 76.

41 Letter to Marguerite Baldensperger, 20 July 1924, in GC, *Lettres à une amie, 1923-1929*, ed. Pierre Brive (Gallimard, 1970), p. 32.

42 Bonsal, *Unfinished Business*, p. 72. "Chaos" from Amos Wilder, "At the Nethermost Piers of History. World War I, A View from the Ranks for Jules Deschamps," in *Promise of Greatness: The War of 1914-1918*, ed. George Panichas (New York: John Day, 1968), p. 351. See impressions in HE, 4 Oct. 1915, 17 Oct. 1916, 9 Nov. 1917.

43 Gilbert, *The Stricken World*, pp. 97-98. The account of this tour also appears in Winston S. Churchill, *Amid These Storms: Thoughts and Adventures* (New York: Charles Scribner's Sons, 1932). pp. 165-178.

44 Gilbert, *The Stricken World*, p. 99.

45 Dated 9 Jan. 1916, in GC, *Discours de Guerre*, p. 51. Martin (in 1913-1914) succeeded Étienne Winter and Abensour and preceded Martet (1915-1929).

46 Lewis W. Douglas, "Clemenceau," in *The History Makers: Leaders and Statesmen of the 20th Century*, eds. Lord Longford and Sir John Wheeler-Bennett (New York: St. Martin's Press, 1973), pp. 31-32. Lewis, son of Clemenceau's great friend, copper magnate James Stuart Douglas, became the American ambassador to England (1947-1950).

47 See GC, *Discours prononcé à Sainte-Hermine le 2 Octobre 1921*; passage repr. in Mordacq, *Le ministère Clemenceau*, 2:105-107.

48 Suarez, *Clemenceau*, 2:212.

49 See especially HE, 5-24 April 1915.

50 Wladimir d'Ormesson, *Qu'est-ce qu'un Français? Essai de psychologie politique: Clemenceau, Poincaré, Briand* (Éditions Spes, 1934), p. 169.

51 Berger and Allard, *Les secrets de la Censure*, p. 236. On his regime see especially Wormser, "Au sein du cabinet de guerre de Clemenceau," pp. 126-128; Sherwood, *Georges Mandel and the Third Republic*, pp. 26-27; and Saatmann, *Parlament, Rüstung und Armee*, 173-174n.

52 Treich, *L'esprit de Clemenceau*, p. 74.

53   Martet, *Clemenceau*, p. 194.

54   Alfred Capus, "Une visite à M. Clemenceau," *Le Gaulois*, 26 May 1920.

55   See Bertie, *The Diary of Lord Bertie*, 2:215; and Becker, *The Great War and the French People*, p. 273. For details of the strike movement, especially in the Loire valley, see Kathryn Amdur, *Syndicalist Legacy: Trade Unionism and Politics in Two French Cities in the Era of World War I* (Champaign, IL: University of Illinois Press, 1986), pp. 77-107.

56   See Papayanis, *Alphonse Merrheim*, pp. 105-110. He doubtless recalled that Merrheim had helped to woo the CGT away from extreme anti-militarist positions in 1908. See *idem.*, "Alphonse Merrheim, and the Strike of Hennebont: The Struggle for the Eight-Hour Day in France," *International Review of Social History* [Netherlands] 16 (1971):176-177, 183; and Jacques Julliard, "La CGT devant la guerre (1900-1914)," *Le Mouvement social*, no. 49 (Oct.-Dec. 1965), pp. 51-52.

57   See Bernard Georges and Denise Tintant, *Léon Jouhaux, cinquante ans de syndicalisme* (Presses Universitaires de France, 1962), pp. 307-308.

58   See Becker, *The Great War and the French People*, pp. 111, 251-301, *passim*; and Max Gallo, "Quelques aspects de la mentalité et du comportement ouvrier dans les usines de la guerre 1914-18," *Le Mouvement social*, no. 56 (July-Sept. 1966), pp. 3-33, *passim*.

59   For Caillaux's accounts see *Mes mémoires*, vol. 3, and *Devant l'histoire: Mes prisons* , 2nd ed. (Éditions de la Sirène, 1920).

60   Repr. in Emile Roche, *Caillaux que j'ai connu* (Librairie Plon, 1949), p. 156. See also Caillaux, *Mes mémoires*, 3:204-206; Poincaré, *Au service de la France*, 9:282; and Allain, *L'oracle*, pp. 143-145.

61   Martet, *Clemenceau*, p. 78.

62   Jean-Claude Allain, in *Clemenceau et la justice*, p. 130n., quoting from the Rapport Paisant de la Commission de la Chambre des députés, chargée d'examiner la demande de levée d'immunité parlementaire de Caillaux, décembre 1917. As he points out, Martet quotes it, undocumented, in *Clemenceau*, p. 79n.

63   To Maurice Winter, 24 Oct. 1918, in Wormser, *Clemenceau vu de près*, p. 243.

64   From GC, *Discours de guerre*, pp. 151-152. The date given (21 Dec.) is in error; the government testified on 14-16 Dec.

65   François Charles-Roux, *Souvenirs diplomatiques. Rome-Quirinal. Février 1916-février 1919* (A. Fayard, 1958), p. 166. Charles-Roux agreed but added that Caillaux had been used by an enemy agent, the Italian deputy Filippo Cavallini, in a German propaganda effort in Dec. 1916. See Rudolph Binion, *Defeated*

Leaders: The Political Fate of Caillaux, Jouvenel, and Tardieu (New York: Columbia University Press, 1960), p. 77.

66   General [Erich] Ludendorff, *My War Memories, 1914-1918*, 2 vols., 2nd ed. (London: Hutchinson, [1919]), 2:513.

67   See Malvy, *Mon crime*, pp. 272-278; Maunoury, *Police de guerre*, pp. 155-157; and Lémery, "Clemenceau comme je l'ai connu," p. 169.

68   *Le Cri de Paris*, 18 Aug. 1918.

69   Absent a solid study of the 1917-1918 crackdown, figures are approximative at best; see John Terraine, "The Aftermath of Nivelle," *History Today* 27 (1977):433. On Brion see H. Dubief, R. Garmy, and A. Kriegel, "Legs Hélène Brion," *Le Mouvement social* 44 (1963):93-100; and Hause, *Women's Suffrage and Social Politics*, pp. 126, 193.

70   See Domestici-Met, "Le deuxième gouvernement de Clemenceau," pp. 145-146.

71   See Allain, *L'oracle*, pp. 186, 208, 211-212; and Becker, *The Great War and the French People*, pp. 309-310.

72   See GC, *Injustice militaire*, pp. 374-375; and the *Thermidor* speech, JOC, 29 Jan. 1891, pp. 155-156.

73   HE, 11 Nov. 1917.

74   Martet, *Clemenceau*, p. 78: "Je pensais qu'il y avait la France, tout simplement." The article "la," which creates an emotional ambience around the country's name, renders translation imperfect, as the translator admits.

75   E.g., HL, 15, 18 Sept. 1914; and HE, 25 April 1915, 16 July, 21 Aug., 27 Dec. 1916, 25, 26 May 1917.

76   See David R. Woodward, "The Origins and Intent of Lloyd George's January 5 War Aims Speech," *The Historian* 343 (1971):32.

77   JOC, 27 Dec. 1917, pp. 3626-3631. An independent Poland would make any negotiated peace in eastern Europe very difficult to come by. For an extensive treatment of war aims negotiations at this time, see especially David Stevenson, *French War Aims Against Germany, 1914-1919* (Oxford: The Clarendon Press, 1982), pp. 94-103.

78   Mordacq, *Le ministère Clemenceau*, 1:123.

79   JOC, 11 Jan. 1918, pp. 39-44. Clemenceau (p. 42): "All the allies are basically in accord. It is questions of timeliness [*opportunité*] which are posed."

80   E.g., see letter, Poincaré to Clemenceau, 28 Jan. 1918, in Perrod, "Autour d'une correspondance inédite," p. 55.

81   See Woodrow Wilson, *The Papers of Woodrow Wilson*, Arthur S. Link, ed., 60+ vols. (Princeton, NJ: Princeton University Press, 1966-), 46:233-235, 360-361, 415, 438, 444; and A. Pingaud, *Histoire diplomatique de la France pendant la grande guerre*, 3 vols. (Editions "Alsatia," 1938-1940), 3:352-354.

82   See Raphaël-Leygues, *Georges Leygues*, pp. 103, 105, 142, and *passim*; Mordacq, *Le ministère Clemenceau*, 1:180; George C. Buntz, *Allied Propaganda and the Collapse of the German Empire, 1918* (Stanford, CA: Stanford University Press, 1938), pp. 15-18; and Nobécourt, *l'année du 11 novembre*, p. 62.

83   JOC, 8 March 1918, p. 857. On the "last quarter-hour" phrase, see p. 343, above. "I wage war" might be a more apt translation, but "make" has become entrenched. The speech made an "enormous" impression in Rome, where peace rumors had been circulating; Charles-Roux, *Souvenirs diplomatiques*, p. 277.

84   Literature on the affair is abundant. For what follows here see especially Allizé, *Ma mission à Vienne*, pp. 179-92; David Sylvester Payne, "The Foreign Policy of Georges Clemenceau: 1917-1920" (Ph.D. diss., Duke University, 1970), pp. 86-112, an exceptionally complete account; Arthur J. May, *The Passing of the Hapsburg Monarchy, 1914-1918*, 2 vols. (Philadelphia: University of Pennsylvania Press, 1966), 1:486-491, 2:630-636; and Gary W. Shanafelt, *The Secret Enemy: Austria-Hungary and the German Alliance, 1914-1918* (Boulder, CO: East European Monographs, 1985), pp. 182-191.

85   Mordacq, *Le ministère Clemenceau*, 1:272-273. Interestingly, in 1916, anticipating a weak reply to Bethmann-Hollweg's Peace Note, he wrote (HE, 27 Dec.), "It will lack the lift of a sharp riposte which would enable the non-combattants themselves to avoid being impressed by it "[the Note].

86   Lansing's desk diary, 22 April 1918, from Victor S. Mamety, *The United States and East Central Europe, 1914-1918: A Study in Wilsonian Diplomacy and Propaganda* (Princeton, NJ: Princeton University Press, 1957; repr. ed., Port Washington, NY: Kennekat Press, 1972), p. 238; and Robert Lansing, *War Memoirs of Robert Lansing, Secretary of State* (London: Rich & Cowan, 1935), p. 265.

87   See p. 320 above. On the 18 Nov. 1917 decision, see Poincaré, *Au service de la France*, 9:427. Capt. Count Armand and Count Revertera had met on 7, 22 Aug. and 1, 23 Dec. 1917. See especially *L'Opinion*, 10 July 1920, pp. 31-37, 24 July, pp. 87-94, 31 July, pp. 115-121; and Leo Valiani, *The End of Austria-Hungary*, pp. 219-220, 261, 414-415, 440.

88   In Rothwell's judgment the *volte-face* by Austria in the Kerr-Skrzyński talks in Berne in mid-March, not the Czernin affair,"marked the end of negotiations between the allies and Austria...." Victor H. Rothwell, *British War Aims and Peace Diplomacy, 1914-1918* (New York: Oxford University Press, 1971), p. 170.

89   On his attempts to help the Algerian Muslims during his two ministries and otherwise, see Ageron's essay in *Clemenceau et la justice*, pp. 79-81; Raphaël-Leygues, *Georges Leygues*, pp. 285, 291-292; Andrew and Kanya-Forstner,

The Climax of French Imperial Expansion, pp. 138-140; and Domestici-Met, "Le deuxième gouvernement de Clemenceau," pp. 1143-1144.

90   Orlando had promised 100,000 in Dec. 1917. After a renewed plea on 13 Feb., 70,000 (some sources say 90,000) arrived by the end of March. In May Italy sent a 48,000-man army corps to show that not just laborers would come from Italy; France left one corps in Italy but had to withdraw the rest in March. See JOC, 28 Dec. 1917, pp. 3662-3663, repr. in GC, *Discours de guerre*, pp. 152-157; Mordacq, *Le ministère Clemenceau*, 1:165-166; Guy Pedroncini, *Pétain, général en chef, 1917-1918* (Presses Universitaires de France, 1974), pp. 185-190; and Charles-Roux, *Souvenirs diplomatiques*, pp. 269-270, 281-282.

91   See especially André Kaspi, *Les temps des américains: Le concours américain à la France en 1917-1918* (Publications de la Sorbonne, 1976), pp. 154-224, *passim*.

92   At the SWC meeting of 30 Jan.-2 Feb. 1918, in Hankey, *The Supreme Command*, 2:773.

93   The literature is enormous. For 1917-1918 see especially George A. Brinkley, *The Volunteer Army and Allied Intervention in South Russia, 1917-1921* (Notre Dame, IN: University of Notre Dame Press, 1966), pp. 3-70; Michael Jabara Carley, *Revolution and Intervention: The French Government and the Russian Civil War, 1917-1919* (Kingston and Montreal: McGill-Queen's University Press, 1983), pp. 24-110; Richard L. Debo, *Revolution and Survival: The Foreign Policy of Soviet Russia, 1917-18* (Toronto: University of Toronto Press, 1979); Anna Hogenhuis-Seliverstoff, *Les relations franco-soviétiques, 1917-1924* (Publications de la Sorbonne, 1981), pp. 4-107; Kalervo Hovi, *Cordon sanitaire ou barrière de l'Est? The Emergence of the New French Eastern European Policy, 1917-1919* (Turku: Turin Yliopisto, 1975), pp. 67-149; Josef Kalvoda, *The Genesis of Czechoslovakia* (New York: Columbia University Press, 1986) on the Czech Legion; Wolodymyr Kosyk, *La politique de la France à l'égard de l'Ukraine, mars 1917-février 1918* (Publications de la Sorbonne, 1981); Thomas Rhca Peake, "The Impact of the Russian Revolution Upon French Attitudes and Policies Toward Russia, 1917-1918" (Ph.D. diss., University of North Carolina, 1974); and Richard H. Ullman, *Anglo-Soviet Relations, 1917-1921*, 3 vols. (Princeton, NJ: Princeton University Press, 1961-1973), vol. 1.

94   See HE, 18, 19, 21, 24, 27 March, 2, 8 April 1917.

95   See HE, 26, 27 Sept., 24 Oct. 1917; and Senate Foreign Affairs Commission, 3 Oct. 1917, in Watson, *Georges Clemenceau*, p. 318. For 1914-1915 ideas on use of Japanese troops see GC, *Discours de guerre*, pp. 43, 50, letters to Violet Cecil (later Lady Milner); and HE, 16 Aug., 25, 27, 29 Dec. 1914, 2, 21 Jan., 12, 15 Feb. 1915. Such ideas enjoyed strong support in the highest circles for a time; see Pingaud, *Histoire diplomatique de la France pendant la grande guerre*, 1:142-150.

96   HE, 26 June 1917. See J. F. N. Bradley, "France, Lenin and the Bolsheviks in 1917-1918," *English Historical Review* 86 (1971):73-89.

97 Beginning at the SWC meeting of 29 Nov.-3 Dec. 197. Given Japan's reluctance to fight in Europe, the proposal contemplated seizing control of the Trans-Siberian.

98 See, e.g., Kalvoda, *The Genesis of Czechoslovakia*, pp. 275, 286, regarding what to do with the Czech Legion.

99 See Carley, *Revolution and Intervention*, pp. 27-28; Hogenhuis-Seliverstoff, *Les relations franco-soviétiques, 1917-1924*, pp. 48-50; Ullman, *Anglo-Soviet Relations*, 1:53-56, Kosyk, *La politique de la France à l'égard de l'Ukraine*, pp. 186-189; and Philippe Schillinger, "Un projet français d'intervention économique en Russe (1918)," *Relations internationales*, 1974, no. 1 (May), pp. 115-122.

100 See Carley, *Revolution and Intervention*, pp. 42-44.

101 See Eugene P. Trani, "Woodrow Wilson and the Decision to Intervene in Russia: A Reconsideration," *Journal of Modern History* 48 (1976):440-461.

102 On Janin's orders see Watson, *Georges Clemenceau*, p. 324; for the 7 July memorandum, see Hovi, *Cordon sanitaire ou barrière de l'Est?*, p. 130.

103 See Richard S. Cromwell, "Russia's Collapse in World War I: The Military and Economic Impact on the Central Powers," *East European Quarterly* 7 (1973):265-284.

104 Pedroncini, *Pétain, général en chef*, p. 400.

105 Callwell, *Field-Marshal Sir Henry Wilson*, 2:51.

106 Edward M. Coffman, *The War to End All Wars: The American Military Experience in World War I* (New York: Oxford University Press, 1968), p. 173. See GC, *Grandeur and Misery of Victory*, pp. 65-66; and W. B. Fowler, *British-American Relations, 1917-1918: The Role of Sir William Wiseman* (Princeton, NJ: Princeton University Press, 1969), pp. 144-146, 152-153.

107 On 23 June. See Mordacq, *Le ministère Clemenceau*, 2:90-92; Callwell, *Field-Marshal Sir Henry Wilson*, 2:112-114; and Stephen Roskill, *Hankey, Man of Secrets*, 3 vols. (New York: St. Martin's Press, 1970-1974), 1:581, 583.

108 See Donald Smythe, *Pershing: General of the Armies* (Bloomington, IN: Indiana University Press, 1986), p. 169.

109 See especially Mordacq, *Le ministère Clemenceau*, 2:8, 13, 37; and Kaspi, *Le temps des américains*, pp. 227-252, 352-353.

110 Nine divisions (1st, 2nd, 3rd, 4th, 26th, 28, 32nd, 33rd, 42nd) saw varying amounts of action in March-July; some elements of three of these (4th, 28th, 33rd) came over in May. On leverage maneuvers, including Wilson's, see Edward B. Parsons, *Wilson's Diplomacy: Allied-American Rivalries in War and Peace* (St. Louis: The Forum Press, 1978), pp. 137-163.

111   David R. Woodward, *Lloyd George and the Generals* (Newark, DE: University of Delaware Press, 1983), p. 238. Woodward separates recruiting policy from "one of the most enduring myths of the war: that Lloyd George starved Haig's army by holding back among the 449,000 category 'A' men in the home forces who were available for drafts overseas" (p. 236). See also *idem*, "Did Lloyd George Starve the British of Men Prior to the German Offensive of 21 March 1918?," *Historical Journal* 27 (1984):249, 251-252.

112   Pedroncini, *Pétain, général en chef*, p. 237. On one occasion Clemenceau did appear to abandon a strictly Western strategy. In Dec. 1917 he presented a plan by General Micheler to beat Germany by attacking the Austrians in Italy. After Lloyd George objected that this would divert shipping from Salonika and Palestine, he dropped the idea. See *idem*, "Le Haut Commandement français et le front italien (1917-1918)," in *La France et l'Italie pendant la Première guerre mondiale*. Actes du Colloque tenu à l'université des Sciences sociales de Grenoble...28, 29 et 30 septembre 1973 (Grenoble: Presses Universitaires de Grenoble, 1976), p. 570.

113   See Woodward, *Lloyd George and the Generals*, pp. 238, 310, 313, 338n, 340n.

114   GC, *Grandeur and Misery of Victory*, p. 104.

115   On 26 July; in Woodward, *Lloyd George and the Generals*, p. 323.

116   Wilson, *The Papers of Woodrow Wilson*, 45:112-113 (23 Nov. 1917). Did he subsequently have André Tardieu, high commissioner to the United States, say that America desired a generalissimo? See *ibid.*, 45:312, 322 (15, 18 Dec. 1917).

117   See Woodward, *Lloyd George and the Generals*, p. 255.

118   Guinn, *British Strategy and Politics, 1914 to 1918*, p. 290n. See Pingaud, *Histoire diplomatique de la France pendant la grande guerre*, 2:158.

119   Martet, *Le Tigre*, p. 105. Mordacq, whose knowledge of Clemenceau's thinking during this time was unrivaled, is categorical as to his aim and need to maneuver; see Mordacq, *La verité sur le commandement unique*, pp. 56-58. For a contrasting view see Général [André] Laffargue, *Foch et la bataille de 1918* (Arthaud, 1975), p. 94 and *passim*. On the unreliability of Lloyd George's version (in *War Memoirs of David Lloyd George*, 2:1716-1717), see Watson, *Georges Clemenceau*,pp. 299-300.

120   In Lieut.-Col. Charles à Court Repington, *The First World War, 1914-1918* (London: Constable, 1920), 2:207-210. See W. Michael Ryan, "Lieutenant-Colonel Charles à Court Repington: A Study in the Interaction of Personality, the Press, and Power" (Ph.D. diss., University of Cincinnati, 1976), pp. 329-351. Ryan thinks Gen. Sir Frederick Maurice was "most likely" the leaker but admits there is no certain proof. Lloyd George blamed the high command. On Robertson's firing (below) see Woodward, *Lloyd George and the Generals*, pp. 262-278.

121   See Pedroncini, *Pétain, général en chef*, pp. 222-276, *passim*; *idem*, essay in *Clemenceau et la justice*, pp. 162-167; and Wormser, *Clemenceau vu de près*, p. 204.

122   Wormser, *Clemenceau vu de près*, p. 199.

123   Mordacq, *Le ministère Clemenceau*, 1:228.

124   Poincaré, *Au service de la France*, 10:86. These fears lasted at GQG until at least the 27th.

125   Pétain several times offered himself for the job in Oct. and Nov. 1917 and had support in army circles, but evidence lacks that Clemenceau ever preferred him to Foch. Certainly the British did not.

126   Pedroncini, in *Pétain, général en chef*, pp. 300-335, and *idem*, "Trois maréchaux, trois stratégies," *Guerres mondiales et conflits contemporains* 37 (1987), no. 145, pp. 56-58, offer a stout defense of Pétain's analyses and actions. Duroselle, *Clemenceau*, pp. 682-689, takes sharp issue with it. See also the critical comments on both Pétain's and Foch's directives by the immediate field commander involved in Maréchal [Marie-Émile] Fayolle, *Cahiers secrets de la Grande Guerre*, Henry Contamine, ed. (Plon, 1964), p. 264.

127   Archives, Hoover Institution of War, Revolution and Peace, Louis Loucheur Papers, B12.F10, Diary, 25 March 1918. See also Watson, *Georges Clemenceau*, p. 302, quoting from a police report on Pétain's attitude. Jacques Isorni, in *Philippe Pétain*, 1:150-151, claims that Pétain wanted Foch appointed and deliberately spoke pessimistically to ensure it. If so, he certainly put on a good act.

128   Wormser, *Clemenceau vu de près*, p. 199. See also GC, *Grandeur and Misery of Victory*, pp. 35-39.

129   Maréchal [Ferdinand] Foch, *Mémoires pour servir à l'histoire de la guerre de 1914-18*, 2 vols. (Librairie plon, 1931), 2:24. Incidentally, when Clemenceau reported to the cabinet, he praised Poincaré highly for his help. See Raphaël-Leygues, *Georges Leygues*, pp. 119-120 (27 March 1918). At one point General Wilson had seriously proposed making Clemenceau "Grand Chef de la Guerre" with Foch as his chief of staff, but Foch objected. When Clemenceau heard of it afterward, he thought it a comical idea.
    Doullens has a large literature. See especially the Archives, Hoover Institution, Louis Loucheur Papers, B2.F3 and B12.F10, Diary; Louis Loucheur, *Carnets secrets, 1908-1932*, presentés et annoté par Jacques de Launay (Brussels: Brepola, 1962), pp. 50-61; *idem*, "Le commandement unique," *L'Illustration*, 24 March 1928, pp. 272-276; Lord [Alfred] Milner, "Memorandum to the Cabinet by Lord Milner on His Visit to France, Including the Conference at Doullens, March 26th, 1918," *New Statesman*, 23 April 1921, pp. i-iv; W. Basil Worsfold, "Lord Milner and the Unified Command: A Chapter in the History of the Great War," *United Empire* [London], May, June 1929, pp. 237-244, 316-324; and General [Jean-Jules-

Henri] Mordacq, *La verité sur le commandement unique*, new and rev. ed. (Éditions Albert, [1934]).

130 Tim Travers, *The Killing Ground: The British Army, the Western Front and the Emergence of Modern Warfare, 1900-1918* (London: Allen & Unwin, 1987), p. 237.

131 Lord Derby Papers, 25 April 1918, in John Toland, *No Man's Land: 1918, the Last Year of the Great War* (Garden City, NY: Doubleday, 1980), pp. 203-204. Derby had replaced Bertie at the British embassy.

132 See, e.g., Martet, "Clemenceau," p. 603.

133 See GC, *Grandeur and Misery of Victory*, pp. 44-46.

134 The April 1917 affair was a failed offensive, like the others in 1915-1916 except for its consequences. See Pedroncini, *Pétain, général en chef*, p. 364.

135 JOC, 4 June 1918, p. 1615.

136 Wormser, *Clemenceau vu de près*, pp. 209-210. See also GC, *Grandeur and Misery of Victory*, pp. 47-62; and King, *Generals and Politicians*, pp. 225-231.

137 See especially GC, *Grandeur and Misery of Victory*, pp. 63-95; Mordacq, *Le ministère Clemenceau*, 2:244-286, *passim*; and Frank E. Vandiver, *Black Jack The Life and Times of John J. Pershing*, 2 vols. (College Station, TX: Texas A. & M. University Press, 1977), 2:972-976.

138 GC, *Grandeur and Misery of Victory*, p. 124. Poincaré had been forging links with Foch.

139 Martet, *Le Tigre*, p. 121 (23 April 1929); and GC, *Contre la justice* pp. 65, 409.

140 See, e.g., Raphaël-Leygues, *Georges Leygues*, p. 135. Duroselle doubts Poincaré was behind it; *Clemenceau*, p. 693.

141 Pedroncini, *Pétain, général en chef*, p. 364.

142 Clemenceau released the news of Sarrail's removal the same day (11 Dec.) he asked the Chamber to lift Caillaux's immunity. The deputies were too preoccupied with Caillaux to trouble about Sarrail. In April he offered Sarrail the military governorship of Paris so that he would be the one to sign the indictments against Caillaux, but Sarrail refused it and stayed on the shelf. See Jan Karl Tanenbaum, *General Maurice Sarrail, 1856-1929: The French Army and Left-Wing Politics* (Chapel Hill, NC: University of North Carolina Press, 1974), pp. 181-183; Dutton, "Paul Painlevé and the End of the Sacred Union in Wartime France," *passim*; and *idem*, "The Balkan

Campaign and French War Aims in the Great War," *English Historical Review* 94 (1979):97-113, *passim*.

143   See Wormser, *Clemenceau vu de près*, pp. 211-212. On p. 215 see a postwar assessment by Clemenceau of Pétain's strengths and weaknesses, well-balanced and shrewd.

144   General Buat, friendlier to Foch, replaced Anthoine as Pétain's chief of staff, and Pétain lost his right under the 3 April formula to appeal over Foch's head.   But Pétain's strategic analysis, with which Clemenceau agreed, was adopted by Foch. See Pedroncini, *Pétain, général en chef*, pp. 384-387; and Duroselle, *Clemenceau*, pp. 663-665.

145   Gen. Fernand Gambiez, "Allocution d'ouverture," *Les fronts invisibles: Nourrir-fournir-soigner*. Actes du Colloque international sur la logistique des armées au combat pendant la première guerre mondiale, organisé à Verdun les 6, 7, 8 juin, organisé par le Comités national du Souvenir de Verdun, Université de Nancy II, communications resumés par Gérard Canini (Nancy: Presses Universitaires de Nancy, 1984), p. 17.

146   Lloyd George later tried to go behind Franchet's back to put General Milne under Allenby's Palestine command. See GC, *Grandeur and Misery of Victory*, pp. 127-130; and Alan W. Palmer, *The Gardeners of Salonika* (New York: Simon & Schuster, 1965), pp. 167-168, 183.

147   Martet, *Le Tigre*, p. 152.

148   For full accounts see Harry R. Rudin, *Armistice 1918* (New Haven, CT: Yale University Press, 1944) and Pierre Renouvin, *L'armistice de Rethondes, 11 novembre 1918* (Gallimard, 1968). For the discussion here see especially Stevenson, *French War Aims Against Germany*, pp.115-132.

149   See HE, 1, 3, 7, 15 March, 5-7 April 1917.

150   See Henning Köhler, "La révolution allemande 1918/19 et la France: Problèmes et perspectives politiques en France entre l'armistice de Rethondes et la paix de Versailles," *Francia* 8 (1980):457-458.

151   See Becker, *The Great War and the French People*, pp. 316-320.

152   See Robert, "Un médecin politicien, le docteur Georges Clemenceau," p. 81. His blood sugar climbed from a usual 40 gr. per day to 150.

153   Lord Derby to Balfour, 24 Oct. 1918, in Stevenson, *French War Aims Against Germany*, p. 124.

154   House's rather self-congratulatory account of his ultimatum and its effect (Wilson, *The Papers of Woodrow Wilson*, 51:511-513, 515-517) appears misleading. All parties concerned were testing each other's limits, and Lloyd George and Clemenceau, veteran politicians, were quick to

understand when they had reached them, although they both replied by affirming their willingness to continue the war alone. See Lloyd George's account in Lord Riddell [George Allardyce Riddell], *Lord Riddell's War Diary 1914-1918* (London: Ivor Nicholson & Watson, 1933), p. 380 (10 Nov. 1918).

155   See GC, *Grandeur and Misery of Victory*, pp. 112-114; Poincaré, *Au service de la France*, 10:379-385; Loucheur, *Carnets secrets, 1908-1932*, pp. 62-64; Raphaël-Leygues, *Georges Leygues*, pp.170-173 (Leygues acted as a mediator); and Wormser, *Le septennat de Poincaré*, pp. 142-177. But when Clemenceau and Foch showed him the terms, he thought Germany would refuse to sign. See Général [Maxime] Weygand, "Le maréchal Foch et l'armistice," *Revue des deux mondes*, 1 Nov. 1938, p. 29.

156   A grand-nephew (grandson of his sister Emma) died of wounds after the Armistice. Son Michel recovered from his 1914 wounds and served with distinction, notably as a captain in the first French unit to enter St.-Mihiel in Sept. 1918.

157   *L'Ère nouvelle*, 25 Nov. 1929. He told Paul Mantoux later, "I have not changed my mind on his politics. But he was a man of heart, and who loved his country."

158   Williams, *The Tiger of France*, p. 173. Williams was present; see pp. 170-175.

159   Wormser, *La république de Clemenceau*, p. 341: "Cela ne servira à rien." The reference obviously was to the sufferings of the war; see p. 421 below.

CHAPTER XV

Peacemaking
(1918-1920)

The Paris Peace Conference of 1919-1920 was the greatest gathering of its kind in history. No such comprehensive conference followed the Second World War, and in every respect it dwarfed its nearest rival, the Congress of Vienna, which had closed the Napoleonic Wars a century ago. Nobody among the thousands who thronged the hotels and palaces by the Seine--ranks of dignitaries and delegates, companies of high officials, battalions of experts, regiments of staffers and clerks--could fully grasp the consequences of the fifty-two month binge of blood and destruction begun in 1914 nor expect to find a well-marked path through the rubble of the German, Austrian, Russian, and Ottoman empires, where bands of every imaginable political and ethnic hue had begun to brawl over squatters' rights even before the armistices had written *finis* to official hostilities.

Yet the world expected the leaders of the victor nations to try and, more than that, to succeed. They had bought their victory at an appalling price, one so out of proportion to anything known to history that well before the end they had felt compelled to justify the sacrifices they were demanding by going so far as to promise that this war would be the last. The world would have to be put right--and for all time to come, for the Great War had exposed the fragility of civilization itself. Its settlement should register no mere Bismarckian triumph totaled up in provinces gained and indemnities levied, but should lay down the foundations of a secure and lasting peace, a peace whose justice would be so evident to all honest souls that the fruit would be reconciliation.

To anyone coming to maturity since the Second World War, it is these expectations which lend to the Peace Conference its most distinctive note. The voices of 1919 seem familiar yet oddly distant. The high ideals: war to end war, general disarmament, a world safe for democracy, the liberation of subject peoples--and assumptions: the victorious progress of democracy, the goodness and peaceableness of the common people once freed of oppression, the efficacy of constitutions and the sanctity of contracts, the inevitability of agreement if discussion is frank and full--have not lost their hold altogether. But the men of Paris, even if charged with hypocrisy or cynicism, as they all were sooner or later, still come across as no worse than second-generation believers in the truths their fathers had distilled from the Enlightenment and called Liberalism.

Clemenceau fitted the mold, after his fashion, assuredly, even though the Conference was not yet over before a junior English financial expert there, John Maynard Keynes, had published a best-seller denouncing the settlement and containing a portrait of him whose brilliance helped to fix him in the public mind ever since as an unregenerate exemplar of the Bad Old Ways and the chief gravedigger of Woodrow Wilson's liberal peace:

> ...Clemenceau silent and aloof...throned, in his gray gloves, on the brocade chair, dry in soul and empty of hope, very old and tired, but surveying the scene with a cynical and almost impish air....
> He felt about France what Pericles felt about Athens--unique value in her, nothing else mattering; but his theory of politics was Bismarck's. He had one illusion--France; and one disillusion--mankind, including Frenchmen, and his colleagues not least....Prudence required some measure of lip service to the "ideals" of foolish Americans and hypocritical Englishmen; but it would be stupid to believe that there is much room in the world, as it really is, for such affairs as the League of Nations, or any sense in the principle of self-determination except as an ingenious formula for rearranging the balance of power to one's own interest.[1]

Keynes was reflecting a widely held view of him, not least of all in France, where Wilsonian leftists and the coteries of ex-premiers alike, if not always for the same reasons, deplored his presence in the Conference. But the bulk of Frenchmen rejoiced in it, confident that their hero, "Père-la-Victoire," would lay a famous hand of iron on foolish Americans and hypocritical Englishmen and compel them to face "les réalités." Neither his supporters nor critics could say with conviction at the end that their opinion had been fully vindicated. The Conference worked its will on all expectations: no prominent figure emerged with an enhanced reputation in the eyes of his constituents. Given the fevered, contradictory hopes of three-dozen nations comprising three-quarters of the world's population, it seems only fair to admit in hindsight that any other outcome would have been astonishing.

Clemenceau knew for a certainty that what could be obtained from the war would fall short of popular expectations: here was the true "réalité." His threat to resign when Poincaré had suggested that an armistice might "hamstring" the victorious troops was founded upon a prevision of this disappointment:

> Since it is to be feared [he wrote to Poincaré] that along the way we will have concessions to make, not to Germany, but to our Allies themselves, and since I am ready to assume the responsibility for all concessions deemed to conform to the higher interests of the country, it is not fitting that the President of the Republic take note in advance, against me and with my supposed consent, of what I was unable to obtain in order to clothe himself in a too easily displayed intransigence when the hour of peril is past.[2]

To a delegation of Radicals which congratulated him on the Armistice and lauded his "intelligence," he retorted, "If I were intelligent or simply a little ambitious, do you know what I'd do? I'd die tonight. That way I'd have a beautiful funeral. But if I wait only until day after tomorrow...."[3] During the evening before the Armistice, a woman he had cared for as a foster father for many years had found him profoundly depressed, tears running down his cheeks:

> Of course, yes, I'm happy, very happy that there's no more bloodshed.--But--I'm afraid!--Yes, France, which could be so beautiful! *Eh bien*!--All those who got themselves killed!--All those who got themselves maimed!--It won't have done any good!--The happier we are, the more I'm afraid.--The greater the disillusion, the more the postwar years frighten me.[4]

And he spoke again of resigning, another of several such hints over the last two months.[5] Not that he really could have gone through with it: to sacrifice the benefits France could reap from his towering prestige and contacts with

Allied leaders would have constituted a desertion. Besides, he could see no one else fit for the job (a touch of pride laced with realism) and already was worrying about the quality of the country's future leadership, so much of it having been sacrificed prematurely on the battlefield.

To reiterate, nothing truly fundamental set him apart from Wilson and Lloyd George, the other grand personages of the moment, if one means to say that they were Western bourgeois gentlemen, believers in reason, shaped by the parliamentary-constitutional systems issuing from the Enlightenment, democrats, anti-militarists, socially conscious reformers of the non-socialist left, impatient meliorists, rejecters alike of class distinctions and class warfare. In Clemenceau's case, while he had long ceased to view democracy as a panacea, he still thought it the wave of the future--a very long future--because, permitting as it does a maximum exercise of individual capacities, it is right, and the greatest might ultimately resides in right.

On the necessity of right to be armed with might, however, he was much clearer and certainly more frank than most Englishmen and Americans. Time and again his differences with them harked back to the emphasis he placed on this truth. America's independence, he reminded Wilson, had been won in the end by force of arms;[6] Napoleon's big battalions had conquered Europe; Prussian might had brought France low in 1870; superior force had ground down the kaiser's legions. Conclusion: A world settlement embodying Justice, Right, or any other virtue praised to heaven since mankind had crawled from the caves would be worth just about what the victors could bring to its enforcement. Here lay the crux of their disagreements about the peace.

All agreed it must be just and that reconciliation was the goal. To Wilson and Clemenceau, justice required that Germany be punished for its transgressions, while Lloyd George assumed that there were just demands which could be severe and yet be accepted by the Germans. But that justice and reconciliation might conflict with each other was a thought which Lloyd George and Wilson resisted in hopes that the settlement would endure without a continuous use of Allied power and thus allow Britain and the United States to revert to their traditional policies of avoiding entangling commitments in Europe.[7] To Clemenceau, on the other hand, the conflict was for the foreseeable future both obvious and unavoidable. As he put it to them:

> What is true is that force cannot establish anything solid if it's not in the service of justice. Everything must be done to be just toward the Germans; but as for persuading them that we are just toward them, that's something else. I believe we can find a way to spare the world a German aggression for a long time; but the German mind [*esprit*] will not change so quickly.[8]

Such being the case, they would have to face up to the problem of enforcement, like it or not. Very many, indeed, of those who sat with him in the Conference found such reminders discomforting. It would be interesting to know how many would have been surprised to learn that he had once written, "A sense of the uselessness of destruction is necessary to awaken pity in us for whatever has life."[9] Or that in spite of everything he still believed it.

About the meaning of the war, Clemenceau found himself on common ground again, although "a war to end war" did go rather too far for him. Like his fellow peacemakers he had made sweeping statements in an effort to fathom the disaster--Civilization, Humanity, the Ideal, the freedom of the world, "the last ragings of unclean force," "a stainless victory,"[10] "the greatest historic labor for justice and right that was ever undertaken by nations down to this day," "a time when no longer, as too often before, covetousness struggles with ambition, but when justice and iniquity themselves contest."[11] Articles written in the heat of battle, perorations before cheering assemblies, and congratulatory letters to one's allies doubtless are not the stuff of sober analysis. But they do show what is in the heart, at least what one *wants* to be true.

Clemenceau later was frank to admit that not until after the fall of the tsar had France fought for the liberation of captive nations such as Poland.[12] But at the same time, the more one expanded the war's meaning, the more the question of responsibility for it intruded, the result being the full flowering of the idea that the origin of a war entails a question of "guilt." Whatever its genesis, whether in the French Revolution's transformation of kings' wars into citizens' wars or the unprecedented scale of this particular conflict, the idea of guilt permeated thinking in 1919. This war mocked everything enlightened Westerners said they believed. It was a crime--the worst of all, a crime against humanity itself--and its perpetrators must bear the consequences. As noted elsewhere, this moral syllogism figured prominently in Clemenceau's mental formation.[13] He doubted not, nor did his fellow victors, that the war had been willed and imposed by Germany. Others certainly were not blameless; he had, after all, delivered himself of more than a few cynical observations about the conduct of international relations in his lifetime. But he believed, as did Wilson and Lloyd George, that no nation or combination had seriously intended to impose a war on Germany to get what they wanted--a judgment that has long since ceased to be contested.[14] The rise and fall of Nazism and the searching post-1945 investigations of Germany's aims in the First World War convincingly exposed the naïveté of most of the assumptions of the "revisionism" of the 1920s and '30s.

But all the same, the 1919 version of Germany's guilt was simplistic. In Clemenceau's case it meshed with a view of German character which, if not altogether alien to Englishmen and Americans soaked in the "hate the Hun" excesses of the propaganda machines of Lord Northcliffe and George Creel, sprang from sources deeper than theirs. Lloyd George, an uncannily perceptive man, admitted that even after months of negotiating he had never fully plumbed his feelings until, while returning together from a treaty-signing, Clemenceau recalled the events of 1870-71. He spoke "with unwonted placidity," but when telling of Jules Favre's breaking down and weeping as he reported to the National Assembly Bismarck's refusal to soften the terms, tears appeared in his eyes "for the first and only time in my intercourse with him....I then understood something of M. Clemenceau's hatred of the Germans." It was that beyond all the disasters they had inflicted, they had treated France with contempt.[15]

He tried, after a fashion, to understand them, but it is striking that his extraordinarily wide circle of foreign friends and close acquaintants included not a single German. He surmised that because the Germans had been civilized later than Romanized Europeans, their character perhaps exhibits barbaric atavisms:

> Since 1871 [he wrote in 1917] I have never met a German without, in the course of the most indifferent conversation, subjecting him to a brief psychological examination. I have always found him brutally implacable toward the weak, base, obsequious, servile toward the strong. False good-naturedness, moral perversity, with the corresponding train of lies and cowardices--that is what I have seen as the indelible trait of the race when I was only seeking a frank and undisguised exchange of views.

He readily admitted their "prodigious art" in exploring science in every way, but he thought them not "intelligent" in the French meaning of the word-- lacking a sense of *mesure*, of the refining qualities found in the worldly wisdom of truly civilized men. Unfortunately--inevitably--war brings out the worst in them: ruthlessness, sadism, blind obedience, and a corresponding swiftness to discouragement when higher authority gives way.[16]

In his speech to the Senate on the Versailles treaty he did qualify somewhat his claim to understand them, remarking that perhaps "the French mind" could comprehend them only via literature and philosophy.[17] Certainly he did not deny all good in Germany, the existence, for example, of a "haute culture allemande" which he (rather condescendingly) thought France should help to preserve.[18] Nor did he--a point which deserves emphasis--deny the Germans' right to their political existence. To critics who complained that he had not broken up Germany, he admitted he was no partisan of her unity; and in fact during the Conference he had pushed hard for an independent Rhineland and had sought to annex that part of the Saar Basin which had belonged to France in 1814. But fundamentally German unity was a fact of life which it would be foolish to deny.[19] The Germans were not yet unified in 1870, yet look what they had accomplished: "What can you do about it? Over there, no matter what, are sixty million men we must get along with."[20] Most unfortunately, his statement came to be paraphrased as "The trouble with the Germans is that there are twenty million too many of them," and genocidal implications read into it, no less--a travesty of his thought and intention.[21] Still, although he didn't think they were beyond redemption, they clearly deserved no indulgence while condemned to work their passage.

Clemenceau's view of the Germans contained enough truth to tempt belief, but it was ladened with stereotypical images and distorted by historical memories, personal experiences, and casual dismissals of contrary evidence. Most of those, for example, who criticized the treaty for harshness thought the peacemakers ought to have given more credence to the "November Revolution" and more encouragement to the infant German Republic. Signature of the treaty did make sincere German republicans terribly vulnerable to recriminations and desertions by basically conservative middle-class elements, and when grave troubles descended later their alienation proved fatal. Although Wilson and especially Lloyd George showed signs of concern about this possibility, Clemenceau remained largely unmoved. He justified some delay in opening the Conference on grounds that time was needed "to let the German Revolution settle down for a while,"[22] but fundamentally he was very sceptical about how deep it ran. In any event he knew something about the fragility of republics and the tenacity of Old Regimes--likely a good deal more, he suspected, than an ex-Princeton professor and late governor of New Jersey.

Hence all the more a misfortune it was that one Count Ulrich Karl Christian von Brockdorff-Rantzau found himself before the Conference on 7 May to receive the draft treaty. In name ("L'hobéreaux," growled Clemenceau[*]) and above all in manner--remaining seated, ignoring protocol without apology, while reading a long, tendentious, accusatory reply--the foreign minister of the German Republic smacked of everything Clemenceau had been saying for months about Junkers and Junkerdom. Lloyd George remarked afterward, "It's hard to have won the war and have to listen to that"--and Wilson, "Really, these fellows are absolutely stupid."[23] (When Karl Renner appeared for Austria later that year, his quiet, dignified courtesy put Clemenceau, quick as always to respond to impressions, in a positively benevolent mood.[24]) Brockdorff in fact was neither a Prussian nor a militarist and had stayed seated because his legs were shaking from emotion.

---

[*] Backwoods nobleman--in French parlance narrow, grasping, and arrogant.

The painful scene all but killed what frail chance still remained for a reasonable dialogue; and misfortune was compounded when Brockdorff's reply thrust forward the guilt question, about which the victors had made a statement 231 articles down in the treaty and crafted as a piece of legal abracadabra to give a moral sanction to the demand for reparation. It had also been inserted in the hope that it might distract the public in the Allied countries from noticing that Germany was not going to be made to pay literally the whole cost of the war after all as Lloyd George and Clemenceau (through Klotz and Loucheur) had led people to expect.[25] Once raised, as it was bound to be, the guilt question could not be ignored, and just as inevitably it prompted justifications which helped none of the parties to the proceedings beyond what they could gain by stoking opinion. The German Republic henceforth bore the mark of Cain and therewith was gratuitously encouraged to behave as Clemenceau had suspected it would no matter what--a classic case of the operation of self-fulfilling prophecies.

II

By the time the Germans were brought onto the scene in May and June, the Conference, which had formally convened in mid-January, had worn down its participants. When Wilson, drained and ailing, sailed for home after the 28 June signing at Versailles, Clemenceau and Lloyd George still faced wearisome palavers about treaties with Austria, Hungary, Bulgaria, and Turkey and defenses of their handiwork before parliaments long grown restless. No one had doubted that the business of peacemaking would take time, but the ordeal far exceeded most expectations held in the heady days of November 1918.

Clemenceau had not given deep thought to peace questions before the Armistice, although in the last weeks of the war he did begin to confer with the study commissions set up in 1916. He never led his ministries in a conventional way, i.e., presiding over regularly scheduled meetings with a cabinet whose folios would be properly stuffed with agenda papers and reports; and during the Conference, seemingly more than ever so far as any important decisions were concerned, he ran the government from under his hat. Five days before the Armistice, Georges Leygues was pouring his worries into his diary: "We have not reflected sufficiently on the problems being posed. Our dossiers are incomplete. *The government improvises too much.*"[26] Not until some time before the end of January did he have a coordinated plan for peace terms in hand.[27] It ought to be added, however, that similar complaints also boiled up among Wilson's and Lloyd George's subordinates, if with somewhat less reason. In Clemenceau's case, while his methods made such cries of alarm inevitable, his attitude toward the coming settlement, certainly in contrast to the American president's, had all along been fundamentally empirical in inspiration: Wilson's famous Points were suitable enough as general principles, but concrete decisions would more clearly be the product of the interplay between realities and Great Power bargaining.

The dimensions of the coming confrontation eluded him at first, as they did everybody. He told Colonel House (14 November) that "preliminary discussion" among the Allies "need not take more than three weeks," with the Conference to last "as long as four months," but by December he was thinking that a year would be needed--a guess still eight months too short, as it turned out.[28] The prospect of Wilson's personally sitting in the deliberations worried him. But when it was finally decided to hold the Conference in Paris rather than Brussels or Geneva, with Wilson participating as a Head of Government, not Chief of State, he rested content: protocol would give a Frenchman, himself, not Wilson--and not Poincaré--the presidency. Moreover, while Wilson no doubt would be hard to deal with inside the Conference, what would happen if he were to stay above the battle on the other side of the Atlantic? He was confident that once face-to-face with him--his favorite method--he could hold his own.

These decisions also helped to cushion failures he experienced in floating an agenda plan and trying to induce Britain and Italy to form a bloc of sorts to contain Wilson. The agenda had some sound merits, e.g., a prior cancellation of the wartime agreements dividing the spoils in advance (a provision which conceivably would have short-circuited disputes over Italy's Adriatic claims and the conflicting promises made to the Arabs in the Middle East) and early settlement via a Preliminary Peace (in accordance with diplomatic tradition) of the principal military and territorial terms before a Final Peace would be negotiated by a congress in which the enemy states would be full participants. But the plan sank without a trace, in considerable part because its untactful soft-peddling of the Fourteen Points and relegation of the establishment of a League of Nations to last place nettled Wilson.[29] The upshot was that the Conference went forward in January under thick clouds of misunderstandings as to its legal standing and purposes which never fully dissipated. For Clemenceau, however, because he was its president and was served by a French-directed secretariat, it meant that he was left with more room to maneuver.

As for the wooing of Britain and Italy, he used the occasion of an Inter-Allied Conference in London (1-3 December)--this despite his flat assurances to Colonel House, whom he was also wooing in hopes of preventing Lloyd George and Wilson from joining forces against *him*, that the meeting was "of no importance whatever" and that he would discuss "no question of any importance with George in London."[30] He allowed Ambassador Paul Cambon and Marshal Foch to put forward a maximum program whose most striking feature was a long-term Allied garrisoning of the Rhineland and its political separation from Germany. Lloyd George was not buying. Clemenceau, who had avoided a personal rebuff by absenting himself and using subordinates on this occasion, let it drop.

Although he was gloomy on his return to Paris, it is hard to believe he had put much hope in winning British support for this strategic design, or indeed that he had intended anything quite as serious as Cambon, a proponent of Quai d'Orsay views, had in fact advanced regarding the containment of Wilson.[31] In light of the defeat which Wilson had just suffered in the November congressional elections plus the concessions he had already made on the Fourteen Points while concluding the Armistice, Clemenceau was beginning to suspect that Lloyd George, not the President (as the Quai d'Orsay was inclined to think) might be the greater obstacle to French desires. Probably he thought the move would serve at least to warn the British (and the Italians, whom he found utterly obsessed by the Adriatic) that if they wanted some things, so did France. Foch's appearance, anyhow, could lead them to appreciate the level of public concern in France about guarantees of security.

His speech in the Chamber of Deputies on 29 December,[32] a fortnight after Wilson's arrival, constituted another warning to the Allies, but also to the French. He made clear that he, not Parliament, was the negotiator and moreover that he would not tell them what he would ask because he might have to give way on some things "in the general interest." He defended the balance-of-power system "condemned by some high authorities"--a reference to Wilson's Guildhall speech on the 28th;[33] if England, Italy, and America had agreed before the war that an attack on one would be an attack on all, the war would not have happened. He would not renounce the alliance system since there should be nothing which could separate the Allies: "For this entente I shall make every sacrifice." (The line won applause, but how many grasped its import?) He would not give up arms and guarantees and would gladly accept "supplementary guarantees," i.e., a League of Nations. If the latter were strong enough, he would sacrifice the former as useless expenditures. He said he would be lying if he asserted that he and Wilson agreed on everything: "There are old injustices to repair. But do you believe we're going to repair them all? I don't believe it because, after all, we're only men."

While praising Wilson, however, he referred to "the noble candor of his mind," a phrase which the opposition seized upon as a mockery. He well knew that in French *candeur* connotes a kind of simple naïveté, not open frankness as in English--which he hastened to affirm was what he had meant. But one is left suspecting that the celebrated phrase was uttered in a burst of that half-sly, half-facetious frankness to which he sometimes gave vent. Certainly it did not win any points among the Americans, who in any event were not at all favorably impressed by his speech. Colonel House found Wilson "disturbed" by the speech and chimed in to tell him that in his opinion "we would have to work with the English rather than with France if we hoped to get the things for which we were striving through."[34]

In closing, Clemenceau frankly admitted to the Chamber that its vote of confidence would be blind because he had not replied in detail. But he warned that if they wanted him out, now was the moment; once the Conference began it would be very difficult to change ministries. The Chamber responded by giving him a 3-to-1 majority, 355 to 119. From that point on he was untouchable, and he meant to stay that way until he finished. His warning of concessions to come had gone largely unheeded, the Wilsonian Left thinking Wilson would prevail, the rest, the large majority, just the reverse.[35]

The normal schedule called for elections in 1918, but they had been suspended for the duration of the war. He decided without opposition to postpone them until after ratification of the German treaty, trusting to his prestige to keep Parliament in line and preferring to deal with men he knew rather than an all-too-likely swarm of unknowns shouting for who-knew-what. (Lloyd George's ill-advised December election concurrently furnished a cautionary example of what could happen in an electorate still suffering from war fever.) Besides, deputies facing elections, not fresh from them, might be more manageable. To the chagrin of several aspirants, notably Briand, Barthou, and Viviani, he chose André Tardieu (formerly High Commissioner to the United States and now closely engaged with him in peace planning) as the only private member of Parliament to be one of the five plenipotentiaries to the Conference; besides himself the others were Pichon, Klotz, and Jules Cambon, secretary-general at the Quai d'Orsay. As negotiations proceeded he sometimes met with the parliamentary commissions, but he dealt only in generalities. The cabinet was scarcely better treated, while the professionals of the Quai d'Orsay unhappily found themselves relegated to the role of mere informants, not close advisers.[36] For these he preferred less hidebound men like Tardieu, Loucheur, and Jeanneney who had gained unique experience in coalition warfare and politics.

In short, he pressed his constitutional powers to the limit and in the end was able to confront Parliament with documents which in effect it had to accept or reject *en bloc*. The members resented their exclusion, all the more because it was imposed by a man who had always defended their prerogatives and who would have been the first to object if he had found himself in their shoes. Perhaps--probably--there was no other way to avoid dragging out the negotiations to an unsupportable length and risking their total failure. As he sadly observed later, he had been able to get by while Wilson, tragically, had not.[37]

He continued press censorship, too, arguing that the country was legally at war until the treaty ratification. Be that as it may, the weapon was too precious to discard. In practice it amounted to a day-to-day manipulation through news censorship and "suggestions" to leading papers about opinions, which nevertheless remained free,[38] the whole intended when occasions arose to support French negotiators and to pressure or (more often, though they failed to appreciate it) to shield the Allies. As for pressure, for example, a French secretary long afterward recalled receiving instructions to encourage public apprehension of his replacement by telling the press he was "being beaten down by his colleagues in the inner council. The next morning he would show the newspaper stories to Wilson and Lloyd George and reproach them for embarrassing him so."[39] An analysis of the French press from January to June 1919 has shown, nevertheless, that apart from *Action Française* and the *Écho de Paris*, newspaper criticism was moderate in tone.[40] The record indicates, in fact, that he tended to favor more freedom for the press than did Wilson and Lloyd George.[41] When the Versailles treaty draft was to be presented to Germany, for example, he favored its immediate publication, but they objected and only a summary was given out. He and Lloyd George also proposed releasing extracts of the minutes of the Council of Four to their parliaments, but Wilson opposed it.

Overall, his main concern, as he said at the opening of the Conference, was to prevent "pitting of one Allied country against another" and the attributing of "any given opinion to a particular statesman and a controversial view to another."[42] His manipulations aroused resentments, of course, and the results he obtained were mixed, but on this issue as on the rest he stood ready to play his strongest card: If Parliament didn't want him or his policies, it had only to say so--on signed tickets in the ballot urns.

III

Domestic problems dogged the negotiators. Clemenceau's were staggering. France was a monster convalescent ward. The most conservative estimates listed 1.3 million young men killed (a four-abreast column from New York to the outskirts of Washington), 360,000 invalided, 740,000 others seriously wounded, 600,000 women widowed, 750,000 children orphaned, over 12,000 square miles of land, towns, and villages plowed up and smashed (equivalent to all of Connecticut and New Jersey), 3,000 miles of railway and 33,000 miles of road wrecked--a litany without end.[43] The financial scene was no less appalling: the franc, literally as good as gold for a century, had lost two-thirds of its purchasing power by 1918. The imposition of currency exchange controls in April 1918 did no more than slow the slide. Battered by soaring reconversion expenses, pie-in-the-sky budgeting, towering debt-service costs eating up nearly half of the Budget, a hasty dismantling of currency controls by the Allies, and a refusal by the United States to open vast credits for reconstruction, by 1920 it had sunk to less than a fifth of its prewar value, by 70% against the pound, and 120% against the dollar. Like others, notably Germany, France paid for the war with borrowings, 140 billion francs' worth through 1918, 21 billion gold francs of it owed to Britain and the United States. And when the franc plummeted in 1919, the government was forced to sell more national defense bonds than it had during the hostilities.

To make matters worse, France's production by 1919 was 30-40% below the level of 1914 and would not reach it again until 1924. The destruction of productive capacity meant importing on a massive scale. Moreover, occupied territories (20% of the tax base) had paid no taxes during the war and would not pay much afterward for some time, while reconstruction costs in the devastated departments added to the debt. The result of all this was that, in contrast to Britain, Germany, and the United States, France's capacity to pay her debts was reduced by difficulties of an altogether different kind and magnitude. It is no wonder that the French could never quite understand why the great attention given to the famous question of Germany's "capacity to pay" for reparation found no echo whenever questions about inter-Allied debts came up.[44]

Not until 1917 had the Senate given way on the income tax, and the laggard implementation of it did nothing to discourage profiteers. Clemenceau, who had a soft spot in his heart for the peasants for furnishing more than their share of front-line soldiers, told Finance Minister Klotz to "cook some fat out of your greasy bourgeois" when he wanted to hike taxes on farmers benefiting from high postwar prices.[45] But when Klotz proposed a capital gains tax in February, howls of "The Boches will pay!" forced him, unsupported by Clemenceau, to beat an ignominious retreat. Since neither of them privately thought Germany likely could or would pay anything approaching the sums being trumpeted in the press--a campaign Klotz and Loucheur abetted by making grossly misleading statements which Clemenceau, to his discredit, let pass without demur[46]--the delays which developed in the reparation negotiations and which were capped by the decision to postpone setting a final figure were not entirely unwelcome and arguably not all that harmful: given enough time, passions might begin to cool down. The delays, however, could also be invoked as an excuse to avoid realistic money measures. And they were. Since even the wisest financial heads (which manifestly did not include Klotz and Clemenceau) were reluctant to court political extinction, the 1919 Budget was voted seven months late and "balanced" by putting war costs in a special account which, when the reparation figures should finally emerge, might be filled with golden eggs from Germany for reconstruction costs or reimbursement of debts to the Allies.

Meanwhile, the government skated along on credits wheedled from the Americans and the English who, while the ink was still wet on the Armistice, had inaugurated the New Age with dry announcements to their shocked ally that they intended presently to close the till. The United States until 1920 did prove to be more forthcoming in fact than in appearance.[47] But given their attitude, it nevertheless was easy to predict that Britain and America would show little interest in an ambitious and innovative plan initially put forward on 19 September 1918 by Clémentel (at Commerce) with help from a remarkable young expert, Jean Monnet. It proposed to continue the Allies' wartime economic cooperation, especially the controls on the supply of raw materials, controls which would be extended to Germany. This would serve in particular to prevent a threatening German economic domination of central and eastern Europe after the war and help to funnel German resources toward rebuilding the devastated areas, thus reducing the role of reparation per se. This "economic union of free peoples," as Clémentel called it, also could be tied to the League of Nations, something Wilson might find attractive. If, however, the United States and Britain refused economic cooperation and a consideration of French requirements, then France would have to demand very high reparation and increase its demands for security.[48] Unfortunately, this "economic union," a first sketch of what would come to fruition (under Monnet's inspiration) after another world war as the European Economic Community, was unceremoniously brushed aside in a race back to the familiar world of laissez-faire leavened with protective tariffs.

IV

Overburdened, absorbed in briefings and negotiations, flogging his seventy-eight-year-old body across a desert of sixteen-hour days, Clemenceau usually found himself unable to do more than help his harried ministers to muddle through as best they could. Even if they had been "eagles," the situation was so unprecedented that governments everywhere were staggering in administrative shell shock. When he did have time, the ministry of war, which he did not dare to put in someone else's hands, was responsibility enough, what with victorious generals to humor and millions of restless men to demobilize while trying to keep enough of them on hand to coerce the Germans and to play the Great Power game in the East.

Shock waves from the Russian Revolution plus a general social effervescence due to the release from wartime tensions and restraints struck the ranks of French socialists and labor leaders, whose forces were rapidly swelling with hundreds of thousands of new recruits. Burdened with his "Top Cop" reputation, Clemenceau had wanted from the outset of his ministry to avoid confrontations with labor, and in 1918, although having to take stern measures during the strike wave which had crested during the Chemin des Dames emergency, he had managed to do so. But the stimuli of rising prices and cross-currents of inchoate hope stirred by Wilson and Lenin promised trouble in 1919. He signaled his concern for labor's role in postwar affairs by making the CGT's general secretary, Léon Jouhaux, a delegate to the Conference and securing passage of collective bargaining (25 March) and eight-hour day (23 April) laws by a nervous Parliament. Although the bills were put through posthaste in hopes of deflating a giant May Day demonstration and did little more than state general principles which decrees would implement by a slow and complex process, he nonetheless regarded them proudly as a personal fulfillment of pledges by the Left dating back to 1848.[49]

For obvious reasons he did not want his or France's standing during the peace negotiations--at their most critical point in April, May, and June-- damaged by trouble in the streets. Despite orders against it, appeals for calm by CGT leaders, and a deployment of forces à la 1906, the May Day demonstration went forward. Some scattered sharp clashes occurred resulting in 2 deaths (one a policeman), 43 police and civilians hospitalized, and 80 prosecuted arrests.[50] Jouhaux resigned, as did the Socialists in sub-cabinet posts, and a rash of strikes followed during May and June in the mining, metal-working, and textile industries. Clemenceau appealed to a CGT delegation to let him finish his work and intimated that patience and non-violence would pay off since the future lay with the workers in view of "the failures of the nobility and the bourgeoisie."[51]

Past disagreements weighed too heavily for his words to be received by most as more than a self-serving ruse. Nevertheless, an international strike planned for 21 July to protest intervention in Russia and Hungary (against Béla Kun's Communist regime) fizzled in France because of the questionable ardor of most of the new union recruits, divisions among labor leaders compounded by their inability to control their followers, high unemployment levels (unlike Great Britain), and because Clemenceau, while taking a very tough line against any threats of violence, promised to speed up demobilization, grant a partial amnesty for political offenses, and crack down on profiteers. He followed up with what was interpreted as a guarantee of his good faith when he induced the resignation (18 July) of Agriculture and Food Minister Victor Boret, a popular target, by leaving him unsupported during a hostile interpellation.[52]

The strike wave subsided, and Jouhaux was able to win a temporary victory over the revolutionary minority in the CGT congress in Lyon (15-21 September). On the whole, Clemenceau got through 1919 with less trouble than might have been expected. But neither he nor labor could take great satisfaction. Strikes returned again in full force in 1920, and both the Socialists and the CGT presently suffered communist split-offs and sharp drops in memberships. As in 1936-37, circumstances undermined labor's advances. The eight-hour day, like the forty-hour week, was advanced at a time when the country needed to produce more and when employers were seeing Reds under beds. Clemenceau, for all his hard-lining about Bolshevism elsewhere, thought (old Radical that he was) that in France the pope was a much more serious menace than Lenin.[53] The 1919 election posters featuring a maniac "Bolshevik" clenching a dagger in his teeth were not the work of the man who at Strasbourg (4 November) called for profit-sharing with the workers, the first premier to do so. But he had also said, "Between them [the Bolsheviks] and us it is a question of force"--and that was what most candidates sailing under his banner preferred to remember.[54]

V

Pressing as France's domestic concerns were, it was solely because of the peace negotiations that he had stayed on after the Armistice. His central purpose in them, simple and undisguised, was twofold: To assure France maximum possible security against Germany and to continue the wartime entente among the victors. Although the elements interlocked, like Wilson, Lloyd George, and Orlando he did not shrink from a threat to break off when he found himself blocked on a point he thought vital to the first.[55] Some thought his demands for security spilled over into vengefulness. An entire absence of such a disposition would have been miraculous in one who in any event had never made claims to sainthood. Lloyd George, however, who went many bruising rounds with him about Germany, afterward felt moved to remark, "There is nothing petty about Clemenceau."[56] For that matter, the records of the conversations of the Big Four as they became public after the Second World War have underscored the essential truth of the diary observation by an American official, Vance McCormick--that they were "big men trying to do the big thing in the proper spirit."[57] In Clemenceau's case they show him clearly to have been no grasping, mean-spirited *revanchard*. His attitude remained consonant with his past, for he had never advocated a war of revenge against Germany, even in Boulanger's heyday. His sense of justice and above all his faithfulness to his word once given--"When he made a promise, no written word was necessary," noted Colonel House, and Lloyd George echoed him[58]--left no room for chicanery at Germany's expense if she were to give evidence of good faith. But he wanted that evidence in deeds, not in fine words on another "scrap of paper."

As for cooperation with the Allies, he proved in the event that he would concede much for the sake of unity. France could not stand alone, even if she broke with her friends in order to snatch guarantees they were unwilling to grant. This truth was terribly painful, not least of all to Clemenceau himself; but to the end of his life he clung to the conviction that peace, and with it France's security, ultimately depended on the determination of the Western democracies to stand together. The sundering of this unity when Britain and the United States returned to their traditional policies embittered his last years and cast a dark cloud over his reputation. Millions in France who once had shouted his name to the sky sullenly accused him of selling the pass to please perfidious Englishmen and Americans.

His basic tactic in the early weeks of the Conference was nearly as obvious as his purpose. Until Wilson took a month's leave in mid-February, the mandate system and the League of Nations, prime concerns for Britain and America, along with Russian affairs and hearings for the minor powers filled the hours. Such being the case, Clemenceau decided, despite mounting impatience in France, to bide his time and show himself conciliatory, notably in regard to the League, where he did virtually nothing to support the French plan (presented by Léon Bourgeois, whom he had sent to the Hague Conference in 1907) which called for an international peacekeeping force or at least a permanent military staff. Bourgeois was understandably upset by this treatment, but Clemenceau's purpose now was to gather bargaining power on the German question, which he had early seen he was going to need in full measure, and to permit events to develop which he hoped would favor the separatist movements in the Rhineland--a hope which proved largely illusory.[59]

Wilson agreed when he left for home that his absence should not hinder an effort to speed German matters along by drafting a preliminary treaty covering military terms. Clemenceau, by now having (predictably) waxed impatient and moreover concerned about the state of public opinion and restlessness in the army, began to push his views seriously on the whole range of German questions. No doubt Wilson's absence encouraged him all the more because he had found it far easier to communicate with Colonel House; as he remarked once, "When I talk with President Wilson I feel just as if I was talking to Jesus Christ."[60] On the eve of Wilson's departure, Lloyd George had expressed a disabused view of what the French premier was up to: "The old tiger wants the grizzly bear back in the Rocky Mountains before he starts tearing up the German hog."[61] Be that as it may, the "speed-up" operation was in no true sense a plot to take advantage of Wilson: after all, he had clearly sanctioned pressing ahead on negotiations about the German case, and anything whatever touching Germany was vital to France. In any event, the whole enterprise finally broke down when 1) the questions raised proved to be too contentious and too linked to a general settlement to be treated in Wilson's absence and 2) when Wilson learned from his experts that any preliminary treaty would have to be ratified by the Senate, a confrontation he had hoped to postpone.

Clemenceau's physical state in these weeks was another cause of difficulty. On 19 February near 8:40 A.M., a young anarchist, Émile Cottin, fired ten shots at his car as it slowed to turn into the boulevard Delessert just below his apartment. Two bullets pierced his clothing and scratched him, but a third struck by his right shoulder blade and lodged in his chest cavity in the mediastinum. Miraculously no vital organ was hit, so it was decided not to risk an operation. To his doctors' consternation he was up and around the next day. (When the pope sent his blessing, he returned his own; Sister Théoneste, his nurse again, was not amused.) He resumed work after a few days' rest, but he tired more easily, developed a wracking cough, and for awhile his power of rapid decision, one of his salient gifts, waned noticeably. Cottin, in the meantime, was condemned to death, but Clemenceau got his sentence reduced to ten years' solitary confinement; he was released in 1924, to Clemenceau's disgust.[62]

Otherwise, his health bore up remarkably well. He kept to his time-honored daily regimen with only slight variations. As he described it to Dr. Grayson, Wilson's physician:

You know, I go home at seven o'clock, eat a little milk and bread, and then go to bed. I wake up between one and three, and then I prop myself up in bed and read until seven. Then I get up for my breakfast and go out and walk around my garden. I also go through morning exercises, deep breathing, etc. In this way I keep from getting old....You know, we doctors can't afford to get old.[63]

On several occasions, however, he relaxed by going incognito to the Opéra-Comique for some light music, e.g., a performance of Rossini's *The Barber of Seville*. But the Conference was never far away; he was heard muttering, "Figaro here, Figaro there--he's a kind of Lloyd George."[64] He had to forego, however, the occasional weekend at Bernouville and his August sojourn in Vichy, which after 1913 had replaced the annual jaunt to Karlsbad.

VI

On Wilson's return (14 March) the hard days began in earnest, and from 24 March the Big Four began to meet regularly in private. Much of the work thus far had taken place in the semi-formal Council of Ten (the chiefs and foreign ministers of Britain, Italy, Japan, the United States, and France) and the commissions, with plenary sessions of the Conference, at which Clemenceau presided with a lightning-fast gavel, merely approving decisions reached elsewhere. In these larger meetings he forced himself to prodigies of patience, speaking infrequently as if to reserve himself, his face a Mongolian mask, eyes nearly closed (leading some to believe he was dozing) but now and then surveying the room when some interesting point was made. Such unnatural restraint when added to the tension imposed by a slowly advancing deafness frequently left him tired and exasperated in private. He was well-briefed and generally well-served by his ministers and experts, whom he nevertheless could treat with an embarrassing rudeness which astonished other delegates. It if suited him to let them address gatherings, he showed no qualms about unceremoniously ignoring their testimony afterward as if to indicate that *he*, of course, was a reasonable man.[65] Although the plenary-session steamrollering drew the smaller powers' ire and the Italians and Japanese in particular were occasionally subjects of sarcastic asides by him, his fairness with the foreign delegations, flashes of humor, and sense of pace when presiding won high praise. In his memoirs Lloyd George went so far as to say that in all his years of public life he never found a man with whom he more enjoyed doing business.[66]

Clemenceau came to a much less charitable opinion of the British prime minister. Resembling him in being a political renegade from the old Celtic lands of the west who had reached the pinnacle through the force of personal gifts matched to extraordinary circumstances, he could admire his vitality, fire, fertility, and marvelous acumen. But he grew wary of "that tireless spinner of words--the kind that leave no trace, not even on the memory of the speaker."[67] "I trusted Lloyd George," he admitted afterward, "and he got away from me."[68] One reason he decided late in 1919 not to retire was concern that his successors might not be up to dealing with the magician from Wales.[69]

If he found Lloyd George unreliable, he found Wilson the opposite, and his regard for him rose correspondingly during the Conference. "I...have learned to appreciate the President," he told Colonel House at the end of May, "for while he is narrow, yet he travels in the same direction all the time while Lloyd George travels in every direction, so inconsistent is he from day to day."[70] His apprehension at the Prophet's approach and the mixture of anxious inquiry, deference, side-door approaches, and sarcastic quips which he used to cope with his presence were almost comical. There was something about Wilson's mind that never ceased to baffle him. In all the hours spent on the Saar question, he later told Mordacq, he had never really understood why Wilson was so stubborn about it.[71] (And for reason: Wilson arbitrarily chose the Saar and Fiume as symbolic tests of principle--while Clemenceau, probably unconsciously, had acquired an emotional attachment to the Saar because it had once belonged to France.) The President's sermonettes dazed him, and he would return home exasperated with the talk, talk, talk and weary from the chore of explaining Europe to him "from A to Z."[72] Lloyd George, who suffered less acutely, left a priceless vignette of a Wilsonian excursion into the empyrean:

> [H]e was developing some theme--I rather think it was connected with the League of Nations--which led him to explain the failure of Christianity to achieve its highest ideals.

"Why," he said, "has Jesus Christ so far not succeeded in
inducing the world to follow His teachings in these matters? It
is because He taught the ideal without devising any practical
means of attaining it. That is the reason why I am proposing a
practical scheme to carry out His aims." Clemenceau slowly
opened his dark eyes to their widest dimensions and swept
them round the Assembly to see how the Christians gathered
around the table enjoyed this exposure of the futility of their
Master.[73]

In time the excursions became less frequent. Clemenceau found that
Wilson's was not really a closed mind and very far from dull. There was even
a certain kinship between their "Jacobin" and "Puritan" mentalities despite
the distance set by circumstance. As he explained to Stephen Bonsal:

Mr. Wilson has lived in a world that has been fairly safe for
Democracy. I have lived in a world where it was good form to
shoot a Democrat. After a few weeks of sparring I became
convinced that your President wanted the same things that I
did, although we were very far apart as to the ways and means
by which we could reach the desired end.[74]

In temperament both men were fighters, albeit with contrasting styles.
Clemenceau came to appreciate this characteristic in him. The stormy
sessions on 28 March over the Saar, a head-to-head confrontation, may well
have marked a watershed in their relations, at least as far as Clemenceau was
concerned, for he found an opponent worthy of his respect. It deserves
relating. During the morning meeting he charged that Wilson was "pro-
German," and when Wilson asked whether he ought not to return to the
United States, he stalked out of the room without a word. That afternoon he
showed up at the meeting, to Wilson's relief. The president then launched
into an eloquent plea calling for stern justice toward Germany but not
vengeance. Dr. Grayson recounted what happened:

The prophet stood as he delivered this exhortation. At one
point Clemenceau moved as if to rise from his chair, and with a
backward sweep of his hand Wilson said fiercely: "Sit down. I
didn't interrupt you this morning when you were speaking."
The tiger shrunk back, but later, when the speech ended, he
got to his feet, his dark eyes burning under white brows. When
he stretched out his arms toward the president, no one knew
what might happen; but the tension ended when he took

Wilson's hand in his, softly patted it, and said: "You are a good man, and a great one."[75]

Other "scenes," if not so dramatic, would follow during the remaining months until Wilson departed, but Clemenceau had received a lasting impression of his courage. He was, also, much too sensitive to remain unmoved by the tragedy slowly enveloping the man and which would climax in his physical-mental breakdown during the struggle with the Senate. In sum, Clemenceau's estimate of Wilson underwent an appreciable change. "How do you like Wilson?" he abruptly asked Lloyd George near the end of the Conference. "I like him," came the answer, "and I like him better now than I did at the beginning." "So do I," he replied.[76]

Among the other figures of the Conference, Clemenceau esteemed none higher than the president's special friend, Col. Edward M. House. The odd thing about this was that he typically scorned easy marks. At their first encounter (23 November 1917) he apparently sensed House's high susceptibility to flattery--and was greatly impressed in return, for House was himself a master of flattery.[77] So he turned on the charm full force and thereafter assiduously fed his desire to play a role, often sending Tardieu around, for example, with information from the inner councils of the government. Without question he fathomed House and used him: "He was a man who made an effort [sic] to be first rate; you can only congratulate him for it. He was the window through which light entered Wilson."[78] Yet he did sincerely like him and--remarkably--never wavered. In his last book he still had nothing but glowing words for "one of the best types of true Americans."[79]

What he gained from House is harder to say. Very likely some of his good opinion reflected a vast relief in finding someone close to Wilson who was ready to listen sympathetically to his views. House filled this role but, ironically, by the time the Conference met his star was fading. Worse still, by pressing him when Wilson was absent from mid-February to mid-March, Clemenceau probably unwittingly encouraged House to overplay his role, the result being the end of his special relationship with Wilson when the latter returned. Clemenceau seemed unaware of the break and certainly over-estimated House's influence during the rest of the Conference. By then

Wilson was not listening to him all that much and was using him mostly as a messenger.[80]

VII

The crisis which opened on Wilson's return reached its climax in the first two weeks of April when agreement on the Saar and the Rhineland loosened the logjam blocking progress on the German treaty. It would barely exceed the truth to say that everything Clemenceau thought and did about the peace--whether the issue was a treaty with Austria, the borders of Bulgaria, the fate of Fiume, a railway in Syria, or help for a stranded Russian admiral fighting Bolsheviks in Siberia--he thought or did with Germany in mind. He could hardly do otherwise. Shorn of her Polish provinces, some border districts, and Alsace-Lorraine, and having lost thirty percent more men than France, Germany still would be fifty percent more populous than France--and growing, while France was not. Moreover, irony of ironies--in this respect so dramatically different from the case at the end of the Second World War--even in defeat Germany had almost entirely escaped physical damage. Her power, actual or potential, well surpassed that of France, and no Frenchman surveying his cemeteries and shattered fields and factories could forget it.

Clemenceau thus faced a very concrete problem. France--not Britain, not Italy, and manifestly not the United States--would be Germany's first target if she were to try to escape and reverse the verdict of the war. Hence French security, in his view, was central to any stable settlement. Since his problem was more urgent than any Wilson had, he was essentially in the position not of taking initiatives to push forward a settlement founded on a disinterested view of things, although he showed himself ready to respond to such initiatives, but of trying to bend or elude the president's principles to meet his needs. Unless Wilson wanted something himself, he could make little headway.

Wilson did want to create a League of Nations, but Clemenceau had found it hard to obtain leverage on this issue. He was not hostile to the League idea,[81] which besides had strong support in France, and the two delegates he named to the drafting commission, Ferdinand Larnaude and Léon Bourgeois, were firm advocates of it. But the kind of League he and most Frenchmen wanted was one with teeth, in essence a continuation of the wartime alliance of victors until such time as Germany had had mended her ways. The French delegates urged strong measures to ensure arms inspection and a rapid organization of national contingents under an international command to meet aggression, but to no avail against Wilson's objections to "militarism." When the text of the Covenant was published on the eve of Wilson's departure in February, the president's stock in France suffered an irretrievable decline. Here was Clemenceau's first break, so to speak, for he had told the Council of Ten (12 February) in all frankness that if the League "gave the guarantees that were expected from it, the military terms [for Germany] would be different from what they would be if no agreement were reached on the various points [in dispute]."[82] The guarantees not having been obtained, he now felt free to present his own program.

A second--crucial--break came when Wilson, fresh from confrontations with his critics at home, returned needing to obtain amendments to the Covenant, in particular one recognizing the Monroe Doctrine. The crisis followed directly. Clemenceau (and Lloyd George, for whom a naval settlement was critical) stalled on the amendments in order to force Wilson to bargain. The game quickly became an intense contest of wills which pushed Wilson's and Clemenceau's nerves and physical resources to the ragged edge. In Wilson's case it was made worse if possible by a severe viral infection which confined him to bed for several days from 3 April on and which probably paved the way for the small stroke he suffered on or about 28 April. (Harold Nicolson, who was present, recalled that when Lloyd George told Clemenceau of Wilson's illness, "Clemenceau rubbed his hands together as if to say: 'Now we can get down to business.'"[83]) At the same time, however, Clemenceau himself came under pressure from both houses of Parliament to hold firm all along the line; it culminated in a motion in the Chamber to question his conduct of negotiations in a secret session, which the government beat down, 345 to 121 (16 April).[84]

The debates in the Council of Four covered all important facets of the German settlement including reparation, but the Saar problem, for reasons already noted, came to assume a disproportionately high symbolic importance. At the height of the struggle Wilson summoned the *George Washington* as a signal that he might pick up and go home. How seriously Clemenceau took the warning is debatable; a semi-official note appeared in *Le Temps* on 7 April giving some hope of relaxation in the French position, but the next day he returned as unbending as ever.[85] The crux of their disagreement was well summed up in an exchange at the close of the session:

> *President Wilson.* I implore you not to hang the peace of the world on the question of the Saar.
> *M. Clemenceau.* No, but the peace of the world requires that we first of all establish justice between us.[86]

Having by now pushed each other to the limit, both men at last gave some ground during the next two days and stitched together a formula to cover the Saar's political status. This agreement opened the gates, and from then on decision began to follow decision. In the meantime Clemenceau, answering a plea from Colonel House, gave out word to the Paris press (15 April) that relations with the United States were just fine and that they would be well advised to lay off criticism of the president--criticism he had pooh-poohed in private but which had angered Wilson and the American delegation to no good end. Fortunately, the Saar compromise, which *Le Temps* published semi-officially the next day, won general approval in the press as evidence that Wilson was indeed willing to accommodate France's views, and it also helped the government to defeat the secret-session motion in the Chamber.[87]

VIII

Of the remaining decisions, the most important--certainly in French eyes, with the arguable exception of the woefully tangled question of reparation--concerned the role of the Rhine in the containment of Germany.[88] Discussion of it had begun in a serious way with Colonel House during Wilson's absence. The great river comprised the most formidable natural strategic barrier to Germany's movement, whether westward to crush France, her principal military opponent, or eastward, where she would not dare to go if the French were in a position to thrust immediately from the bridgeheads toward her vitals. Clemenceau wanted France's military frontier to be fixed in perpetuity on the Rhine. To this end he proposed (for bargaining purposes[89]) that the Rhineland proper (the German territories west of the river) be made into an independent state or states linked to France in a customs union and that Allied troops be stationed permanently at the bridgeheads. He regarded joint occupation, even if the British and Americans were there with only "a battalion and a flag,"[90] as a material guarantee of the continuance of the wartime alliance. He wanted no annexation of the Rhineland despite the calls for it which had begun to sound again from many quarters late in the war, but he did support--clearly enough if very quietly--measures directed by Marshal Foch and the high commissioner there, Paul Tirard, to encourage movements for independence from Germany and friendly ties to France.[91] For this reason, however, he did not put much stock in the Rhenish separatists currently in view because, apart from their questionable standing among the Rhinelanders, their versions of autonomy always contemplated retention of important ties to Berlin.

Lloyd George and Wilson found such views and activity disturbing, to say the least. Above all they wanted "no new Alsace-Lorraines" (a favorite phrase with Lloyd George), something which Clemenceau's solution plainly risked. Compelled by him to admit nonetheless the importance of the Rhine and the gravity of his problem with French public opinion, they decided to offer him treaties guaranteeing military intervention by Britain and America if France were the subject of "unprovoked aggression" by Germany.[92] Although sincerely moved and even amazed by an offer so dramatically at odds with his partners' national traditions, he could not forget how long their armies had taken to come in force to France after 1914; the Rhine line would be needed to buy time. Nor could he ignore admissions by Wilson that he could not guarantee the Senate would approve any such treaty, which he, besides, preferred to term an "understanding."[93] Pressure in France in favor of guarantees "in hand" (i.e., the Rhine), especially from Foch, Poincaré, and the nationalist press, moreover was intense. It was in the toils of this dilemma that he met that moment which he had warned the Chamber of back in December--the one when he would have to make sacrifices in order to maintain the entente with France's allies.

These sacrifices turned out to be less fundamental than tactical, much less serious, in short, than he probably had feared at the height of the struggle.[94] In a complex compromise whose terms he argued point by point for weeks, he gave up a permanent occupation of the Rhine bridgeheads and independence--in the immediate if not necessarily the distant future, anyhow --for the Rhineland. Instead, the bridgeheads would be occupied for fifteen years, decreasing at five-year intervals if Germany were judged to be fulfilling her treaty obligations, with German troops and fortifications to be permanently banned from the Rhineland plus a fifty-kilometer strip along the east bank. For guarantees, in *addition* to the treaties offered and signed by Lloyd George and Wilson, he insisted upon and won an article (44) stating that violation of the demilitarization provision by Germany would be regarded ipso facto as commission of "a hostile act against the Powers signatory of the present Treaty and as calculated to disturb the peace of the world." He also obtained further articles (429 and 430) providing for reoccupation or an extension of the fifteen-year limit if "the guarantees against unprovoked aggression" were "not considered sufficient by the Allied and Associated Governments" or if the Reparation Commission should find that Germany had refused "to observe the whole or part of her obligations...with regard to reparation."[95]

The decisions once made and the terms presented to Germany on 7 May, he had to beat back a last-moment attempt by Lloyd George to moderate them while at the same time he was suffering a decline in French opinion because they appeared too lenient. Worse, he was embarrassed by a show of disobedience from Marshal Foch, who was incensed by the Rhineland solution and with Poincaré's encouragement was feeding a press campaign against him. (Referring to them once when Foch was holding forth in a plenary session after arguing with him publicly over military questions, he walked over to Wilson and muttered, "You must save me from these two fools."[96]). And generals Fayolle, Mangin, and Gérard compounded embarrassment by openly colluding with German separatists in a hasty movement to set up an autonomous Rhenish Republic. Wilson and Lloyd George archly observed that *they* didn't tolerate factious generals. Clemenceau apologized for his errant grandees, who thought with some good reason that they were only carrying out his intentions, and ordered up an investigation. But privately his exasperation with them knew no bounds.[97] As Mordacq heard him say many a time, "Let me tell you, you really have to love your country to continue on with a job like this."[98]

On 28 June, after tense days of uncertainty over whether Germany would sign, the deed was done at the Hall of Mirrors at Versailles where Bismarck had proclaimed the Empire in 1871. And on Bastille Day came the Big Parade, the last of its ilk: contingents from every victorious army, with the *poilus*, cheered to the skies, led through the Arc dc Triomphe by Marshal Pétain on a white horse. "Those of us who saw that day have lived," Clemenceau later remarked.[99] He remembered being profoundly depressed when the delirious crowd surrounded his car afterward: "I wished to die, for I was not born for happiness."[100] For him it was the apogee.

IX

He defended his work after the parliamentary commissions had studied and reported over the summer. Negotiations continued meanwhile on the treaties for Austria, Hungary, Bulgaria, and Turkey. A mood of resignation settled on the country. The debates on the Versailles treaty droned on in Parliament from late August to mid-October, but the passionate interest of the spring had spent itself. People wanted to pick up the threads of ordinary life and to forget. Clemenceau, no longer the invincible hero once the treaty's terms had been made known, was beginning a slow fade into legend. The public did not want to be reminded of past hopes.

What had he done for France in the Conference? By any reasonable measure the provisions directly touching security offered ample protection, certainly for the near future. In addition to the safeguards embodied in the Rhine settlement and the treaties of Guarantee, Germany's army would be reduced to 100,000 and the navy to 15,000 men enlisted for long periods, not conscripted. The Great General Staff would be dismantled and heavy ships and artillery, poison gas, tanks, and the arms trade prohibited.

Of numerous complicated economic provisions, including the return of stolen property, compulsory deliveries of equipment, livestock, and such, those pertaining to the Saar Basin and reparation particularly affected

France. In compensation for destroyed mines, France would get ownership of the Saar mines and the region would be governed by a League of Nations commission for fifteen years, after which a plebiscite would decide its future. Germany could then buy back the mines in districts opting for Germany but with coal deliveries to France to continue as needed.

As for reparation, the subject of innumerable discussions whose meanderings would be superfluous to recount here,[101] it was finally decided that Germany would pay in full for direct damage and war pensions (but not full "war costs"), 20 billion gold marks' worth of it in money or goods by 1 May 1921 with the total remaining amount to be fixed before that date by a Reparation Commission with sweeping powers of investigation; payments would be made in thirty yearly installments or until the debt had been fully met. The provision about fully meeting the debt (Art. 233) as well as one (234) prohibiting reduction of the debt without the unanimous consent of the states represented on the Reparation Commission, which thus gave France a veto, were written in at Clemenceau's insistence as was also, of course, the article (430) permitting reoccupation of the Rhineland if Germany reneged on all or part of her obligation. Thus, although he had had to give up a permanent occupation, he had contrived to regain most of the lost ground by means of the financial clauses while at the same time getting Britain and the United States to offer and initial the treaties of Guarantee.[102]

The general settlement ensured France further elements of strength or at least reasonable hopes for the future. The German colonial empire was distributed as League mandates, with France dividing Togoland and Cameroon with Britain and given special permission to conscript the natives; Clemenceau was worrying about France's low birth rate and had come to appreciate the contribution of black troops from France's African colonies. Poland, Czechoslovakia, and Yugoslavia, carved from German and Austro-Hungarian lands, plus an enlarged Romania all benefited from France's sponsorship of their independence and could be expected to stand with her against their former overlords. This patronage had often cost Clemenceau a good deal of trouble and bouts of exasperation. Ionel Brătianu, the Romanian premier, as arrogant and slippery as he was stubborn, pushed his country's claims for Hungarian territory (principally Transylvania) to the limit and beyond and persistently embarrassed the Conference by defying its orders regarding his army's movements, something which tended to happen all over eastern Europe. Clemenceau was the only one in French circles to take an anti-Romanian stand at the height of the crisis over Romanian operations in Hungary, but to little avail.[103]

A strong Poland was central to French plans for eastern Europe, but division among the Polish leaders, when added to the constraints of having to conciliate British and American views on such subjects as the fate of Danzig, Marienwerder, and Silesia, made for problems.[104] Moreover, desirable as a strong Poland was, he found Poland's claims to large Russian territories inconvenient because they could harm Russo-Polish relations, and thus Franco-Russian relations, once Bolshevism was defeated. Likewise, the dispute between Poland and Czechoslovakia over Teschen was all the more annoying because he was a supporter of both the new states; he sided with the Czechs on this one for economic reasons, but the problem was still unresolved when he left office. Yet despite these aggravations, the fact remained that the settlement found France in a far stronger overall position in eastern Europe than at any time since Napoleon I, while Austria and Hungary, separated and truncated and the former forbidden to be united to Germany, could threaten nobody at all.

Closer to home, the case with Belgium proved to be much more contentious and problematic than expected. Clemenceau had given little attention to Belgium before the war, but her brave conduct, exemplified by King Albert and the archbishop of Malines, Cardinal Mercier, won his outspoken admiration. After the war he believed he had supported her in the Conference as much and as often as he could. But he had found himself under strong pressures from French political, economic, and military interests whose high-handed methods and patronizing attitudes had long characterized French dealings with their relatives to the north. The latter, however, were determined not to be anybody's puppet. They wanted new guarantees of security for themselves and freedom to incorporate Luxembourg, which they feared France would annex.

Clemenceau had no intention of annexing Luxembourg despite domestic pressures to do so, but he did resort to using the Luxembourg question as a lever to obtain Franco-Belgian economic and military accords. The confrontation was only made more painful by the Belgians' naïve and rather inept diplomacy and the personality of Prime Minister Paul Hymans, whose argumentative, hyperlegalistic methods exasperated Clemenceau to the last degree. ("Kill them!" he snarled to Keynes when the Belgian delegation left after a particularly stormy session in early April, adding to Loucheur, "Hymans is even stupider than Brătianu, which I would have thought impossible!"[105]) The result of the pullings and haulings was that when Clemenceau resigned in January 1920 Belgium had a free hand to construct economic ties with Luxembourg but, to her chagrin, minus control of the latter's key railway line, which France got from Germany. And a Franco-Belgian military accord, so important for general Western security, though launched, was far from completed. When added to the manifestly growing reluctance of the British to get further involved in military guarantees in that quarter, this did not bode well for the future.[106]

X

Italy also had turned out to be a problem--one of the first magnitude. A victor state and Great Power (at least by courtesy), she had sacrificed a half-million men in return for small or strongly contested gains and hence might join up with the defeated as an opponent of the settlement. Clemenceau sensibly wanted to avoid alienating her if possible; as he remarked once to Lloyd George and Wilson, "She is like a pretty woman, whom it's better to get along with."[107] But this laudable intention ran afoul of an array of strategic and diplomatic considerations and, unfortunately, personal prejudices.[108] His antipathy toward Catholicism, the Romans, and the Roman Empire--the counterpart of his lifelong love for Greece and the Greeks--colored his perceptions of modern Italy. He made no serious effort to educate himself about her because in truth Italy just didn't interest him. The war did nothing to change his mind. He conceived a low opinion of her performance and intentions and did little to hide it when urging her time and again to do more to relieve the pressure on the Western Front.

Thus, he entered upon the peace negotiations expecting the worst: "After the peace," he had complained to Leygues back in August, "we'll have a world of pains in avoiding a war [!] with Italy; all the decisions will be difficult with them."[109] It did not help, either, that he also harbored a certain disdain for Prime Minister Orlando, whom he thought second-rate, although he did respect his redoubtable foreign minister, Baron Sonnino. Orlando damaged his case with him further, and very seriously, when he ignored his overtures in the SWC meeting in London in December and afterward had let slip opportunities to support him on the Saar and war-crimes trials' questions. It was enough to lead him to wonder aloud to Mordacq if Orlando had intended all along to "march squarely against us."[110]

In light of all these reasons, whatever their wisdom or validity, it is no surprise that when Italy's Adriatic and Turkish claims, fortified by the promises made to her in the Treaty of London (1915) and other wartime agreements, ran headlong into Wilson's principles, Britain's imperial interests, and the needs and ambitions of Romania, Greece, and Yugoslavia, he proved ready to abandon an heretofore neutral stance and side with his stronger, and less uncongenial, partners. Italy's friendship was very important to France, but Britain's and America's were vital. Orlando could have no doubt of it when after suggesting to him a Franco-Italian accord against Britain and the United States he replied, "To what good, my friend, to what good?"[111]

The crisis--which came to a head in mid-April and was capped by an Open Letter from Wilson to the Italian people (23 April) and two days later a return to Rome by Orlando (only for two weeks, it turned out) in order to take counsel--centered on Italy's claims to ports and islands on the eastern coast of the Adriatic (Dalmatia), which were to go to her under the London treaty (to which, of course, the United States was not a party), and claims to the city and environs of Fiume, which were assigned to the Croats under the treaty but which Italy was now claiming because of an Italian majority in the city proper. Back in early March Clemenceau had appeared to be prepared to propose a deal whereby Italy would drop the Dalmation claims in return for Fiume,[112] and at the height of the crisis he did broach it at a meeting with Lloyd George, Orlando, and Sonnino on the morning of the 21st; but Sonnino merely pointed out the obvious, viz., that Wilson "will not give Fiume, nor does he give Dalmatia."[113] By then, however, he and Lloyd George had already made their fundamental position clear enough. They felt honor-bound to stand by the Treaty of London if Italy should insist. It was a convenient position. They could not be accused of disloyalty to their ally, and thus they could hope to preserve some role as mediators; yet in effect they were on Wilson's side since there was no reason to believe that Italy would simply give up on Fiume--any more than would Wilson. "You want Fiume?" Clemenceau chided an Italian journalist. "Why not the moon?"[114]

He and Lloyd George basically agreed with Wilson's position as stated in his Open Letter--Clemenceau even confessed he had been tempted to join Wilson's "adventure[115]--while having doubts about the wisdom of publishing it, but they only succeeded in delaying its appearance by forty-eight hours. None of the three expected its effect in Italy to be as explosive as it proved to be. Clemenceau and Lloyd George thereupon stepped back toward the shade and let Wilson take the heat of the Italian public's wrath.

The three together, however, with Wilson taking the lead, made this difficult situation worse when, in Orlando's absence, they approved (6 May) an immediate landing by Greek troops at the Turkish port of Smyrna (on the Aegean coast of Anatolia) to protect the Greek populace there from being massacred, to assure future Greek possession of the area (although Orlando was given to believe otherwise), and to forestall an imminent landing by the Italians, who were making claims there also.[116] The move not only increased the Italians' alienation, but it also turned out to be a blunder of the first order because it greatly complicated the effort to make a treaty with Turkey; the Treaty of Sèvres was incomplete when Clemenceau resigned in 1920. Moreover, it fed the Turkish revolt led by Mustafa Kemal (Atatürk) which ended in a Greco-Turkish war (1921-22), a massacre and expulsion of the Greeks from Anatolia, and the razing of Smyrna.

Orlando returned to Paris on 6 May, and more schemes were floated to settle the Fiume-Dalmatia deadlock; in late May and early June, Tardieu, with Clemenceau's support, presented one which actually came within hailing distance of solving it.[117] In the end, however, the Conference proved unable to find any solution. Subsequent negotiations between Italy and Yugoslavia plodded on to a settlement of sorts in November 1920 which unravelled nevertheless in a few months.   Not until 1924 was a reasonably stable agreement reached.

To conclude, Clemenceau's conduct of relations with Italy drew heated criticism from the French diplomatic establishment and in particular from the Poincaré-Foch camp, concurrently waxing bitter over his failure to get a permanent hold on the Rhine. Certainly the timing of the Italian crisis was unfortunate for him because he was far more occupied at the moment with the imminent arrival of the Germans to receive their terms on 7 May. His role in the alienating of the Italians was the last straw for the Poincaré-Foch nationalists,[118] proof positive for them of his incapacity, for in their view, in which the Quai d'Orsay concurred, he had muffed the chance to hold on to Italy by using his great prestige among the Italian public (real, if at bottom rather ironical) in order to come forward as the Great Mediator. Whatever the validity of this judgment (which in light of the circumstances at the time does seem overdrawn), it is undeniable that throughout the troubles with Italy he had mostly left the initiative to others, persistently underestimated Italian reactions, kept on thinking everything somehow would be patched up before long, and even left office believing relations were on the mend,[119] notwithstanding the fact that Francesco Nitti, whose leanings toward Germany were no secret, had replaced Orlando as premier in early June. In any event, the postwar period clearly had gotten off to an ominous start in the Mediterranean.   The coming to power of Benito Mussolini and his Fascist thugs in 1922 would more than amply confirm it.[120]

XI

Syria gave Clemenceau a taste of the trouble Orlando had experienced.[121]   Commercial and missionary activity dating back for centuries had made Syria (including Lebanon) a recognized French sphere of influence in the Ottoman Empire.   He cared nothing for the place personally--"storybook stuff," a "medieval matter" fit for a "politique des curés"[122]-- and when he had come to power in 1917 he had told Lloyd George to make whatever terms he wanted with the Turks, but that if he could get France a protectorate over Syria he wouldn't refuse it "as it would please some reactionaries."[123] By the end of the war, however, pressure from *Colonialiste* and Catholic circles was strong. Also, failure to get control of

Syria might fire up nationalist movements among the Muslims of Algeria, Tunisia, and Morocco. And anyhow, since France had helped, albeit modestly, to bring Turkey down, she ought to have some share of the spoils.

Thus, while in London for the SWC meeting in early December 1918 and with memories of the stormy scenes with Lloyd George over the Turkish armistice still fresh,[124] he offered a deal--and thought he obtained it, although nothing was formally signed--in which he would leave the Mosul region of extreme eastern Syria to Britain, which was occupying it anyway, in return for a share of the oil rights there and confirmation of the rest of the zones of influence promised to France in the Sykes-Picot Agreement of 1916. If, however, Wilson were to insist that they scrap Sykes-Picot and instead set up League of Nations mandates, France, supported by Britain, would still end up receiving the promised zones. More to the point, he apparently expected that the surrender of Mosul would earn concessions later from Lloyd George on the Rhineland question.[125] If he had been able to get his way on the Rhine, it is very likely that public interest in the Middle Eastern settlement would have died away. But since he did not, pressure persisted and grew.[126]

And so did the complications. The affair got terribly snarled because of a basketful of contradictory wartime promises Britain had made to the Arabs to pit them against the Turks; because British armies (save for a few French marines in Beirut) currently occupied the area and were prompt to report the strong local opposition to bringing in the French--opposition Clemenceau discounted because Syrian Christian delegations in Paris were assuring him quite to the contrary; and in general because of Lloyd George's dazzling footwork on anything whatever to do with Turkey. For France, the Rhine and central and western Europe were paramount. For Britain, imperial concerns held pride of place, and nothing was more central to these than the fate of the Turks' sprawling domains.

Clemenceau hung firm for Syria--a deal was a deal even if not duly signed and sealed[127]--while Lloyd George and, for different reasons, the Saudi prince Faisal (whom Arab nationalists were backing for the moment) maneuvered in the best tradition of the Eastern Question to keep the French out. The arguments became so heated that on one occasion the prime ministers of the French Republic and His Britannic Majesty's Government nearly came to blows and had to be separated by the President of the United States, who politely scolded them for being "two bad boys" and induced them to shake hands, which finally they did to embarrassed laughter all around.[128] Clemenceau dropped the matter for the time being to avoid further damage to Allied unity. The question returned again in September when the British government, having become gravely concerned over troubles in the Punjab, Egypt, Turkey, and Afghanistan and rumblings in Mesopotamia, decided to pull out the Syrian garrisons and make new proposals (15 September), which in turn became the subject of further unpleasant exchanges. (One wonders how much more acrimonious they would have been had the French been fully apprised of the secret agreement Britain had extracted from the Turks on 12 September to make the former Ottoman lands a British protectorate.[129]) At length the British left the field clear for Clemenceau and Faisal to negotiate head-to-head over Syria's fate while continuing talks on the oil, railway, and pipeline problems.[130]

After more palavers Clemenceau and Faisal met each other halfway: France would in sundry ways under a League of Nations mandate exercise most privileges of a protecting Power in Syria but would not send troops to the interior unless invited. The agreement (6 January 1920) was an accurate reflection of the fact that France and Britain all along had believed that Arab independence, which they had supported in a statement on 7 November 1918, was wholly compatible with tutelary arrangements embodied in protectorates, spheres of influence, and such. They thought the Arabs were not yet fully capable of orderly self-government at the national level.[131] The Clemenceau-Faisal accord nevertheless might have worked had it been reached a year earlier when both men were at the peak of their influence. Instead, Clemenceau retired only a fortnight afterward. His successor, Millerand, concluding that he had given up too much, reverted to a hard line, while poor Faisal upon his return home found himself scorned by the nationalists. By July the French had shot their way to Damascus, Faisal had fled, and the accord was a dead letter.

As for Clemenceau, he had preserved the French "presence," for what it might be worth, but in the bargaining he had kept his bid too high for too long. Syria had cost him his worst moments with Lloyd George, and the legacy would drip poison into Anglo-French relations through the 1920s and '30s and cost De Gaulle and Churchill some of *their* worst moments during the Second World War.

XII

There remained a very large problem which had resisted even temporary solution. The Russian Revolution and its repercussions might alter anything the Conference decided.[132] On this issue as on others of similar gravity, Clemenceau was determined not to become separated from his allies, and as usual this proved to be no simple matter. Even before the Armistice, for example, it had become apparent that he and the British held divergent views of what Russia's future condition and role should be. The British did not hesitate to encourage separatist nationality movements, whose success could ultimately help protect the borders of their realms in Asia and the Middle East and prevent the rebirth of a Great Russia too closely tied, as before the war, to a Germanophobic France.[133] The French, on the other hand, while willing to collaborate with the separatists in order to block the Bolsheviks, held that the best of all possible worlds would contain a (one could hope) democratic Great Russia strong enough to honor the financial obligations the tsarist regime had contracted with French investors and able to guard the east against Germany as an ally of France and friend to a democratic Poland, Czechoslovakia, and Romania. (As has been noted, for this reason they were reluctant, for example, to support Polish claims against Russia until, as it turned out, the defeat of the Whites had destroyed any realistic hopes for at least a non-Bolshevik Great Russia.[134]) In the worst of worlds, an alienated Russia run by Bolsheviks or crypto-tsarist Whites (who contained substantial pro-German elements from the old days) would join hands with a vengeful Germany to overthrow any settlement made at their expense.

In this connection it must be emphasized that to Clemenceau the threat which Bolshevism posed owed little to its supposed ideological appeal in central and western Europe, an attraction he consistently discounted even while now and then brandishing anti-Bolshevism for its political effect at home or on the Allies. Rather, Bolshevism was dangerous because of its ability to provoke enough disorder to hand Germany opportunities to set discontented groups against each other and thereby exert influence in areas where she was no longer checked by the old empires. Germany's present defeat, in short, had by no means dispelled his fear of her eventually gaining the dominance in the east which she had nearly won in the war.

Like most observers at the time, Clemenceau never quite stopped assuming that before long the Bolsheviks would fold; in 1928 he was still predicting it.[135] Although he kept up some unofficial contacts with them, he continued to oppose formal recognition of those "betrayers" of the Allies. He did consent, with great reluctance, to Lloyd George's proposal, taken up by Wilson (21-22 January) to invite them and the White factions to confer at Prinkipo (the Princes' Isles, near Constantinople), but only after threatening to resign rather than have them come to Paris, where he wanted no accredited Bolsheviks spreading their virus among the Socialists and the unions and provoking the Right.[136] The project fell through because of mutual distrust among the Russians, which the French government abetted sub rosa among the Whites, and undermining operations in all the Allied camps including the American. The failure also cooled the Socialists' enthusiasm for Wilson, who never stood so high again in their estimation.

On another tack, meanwhile, and prior to this contretemps, he had ordered (5 December) a polyglot force, eventually numbering some 60,000 French, Algerians, Senegalese, Greeks, and Poles, to go to Odessa (occupied on 19 December) and other Ukrainian and Crimean coastal areas being evacuated by the Germans, its objective being to forestall Bolshevik entry there, protect present and future French economic interests, and (for lack of anything better) to support Ukrainian separatists and General Denikin's White army. Actually, the expedition amounted to a profoundly revised and tardy implementation of an operation originally ordered back on 7 October to revive the Eastern Front against Germany from the Caspian to the White Sea (!) by means of a coordinated action between Franchet d'Esperey's armies and "reconstituted" Romanian and Russian forces.[137]

The affair was a first-class snafu from start to finish.[138] Both Franchet d'Esperey and d'Anselme, the field commander, doubted the wisdom of the enterprise. Its mission, fundamentally defensive, was defined in orders and parliamentary pronouncements so vague and contradictory that the commanders in effect were left to their own calamity-prone devices. Indeed, what *could* they have been expected to do with orders calling for "economic encirclement" of the Bolsheviks and making "common cause with patriotically thinking Russians" so they could "organize their own army" while at the same time "protecting Allied interests" but "rigorously abstaining from all intrusions into internal politics"?[139] The faction-ridden Ukrainians and Whites were pursuing contradictory aims which the uninformed and intolerably arrogant French officers on the spot never really comprehended, while the men of the expedition, mostly homesick survivors of the chronically mismanaged and ignored Salonika campaign, were not exactly burning to risk their necks in this bedlam or, to tell the truth, anywhere at all.

The arrival in Paris of the shocking news of Béla Kun's successful Bolshevik coup in Budapest on 22 March wonderfully concentrated the minds of the Big Four on threats closer to hand and led to angry debates in the French Chamber about the intervention policy which were conducted against a backdrop of growing domestic unrest. On 29 March Clemenceau issued orders for withdrawal of the Odessa force. Having succeeded in uniting the Russians only in a detestation of its presence, the expedition completed a precipitous evacuation of Odessa (6 April) amid appalling scenes of disorder; and later that month the whole affair was wound up when a regiment vegetating at Sevastopol was gotten away under duress while mutinies--shortlived but genuinely alarming--struck some French warships in the Black Sea and subsequently flared from June to October in the fleet's Mediterranean bases and home ports.

The expedition to South Russia comprised, mercifully, the only noteworthy detour in Clemenceau's general course which, for all its conceptual fuzziness, was to give the Whites financial and advisory support in order to keep his hand in the action, salvage what he could from the wreck in the interests of future political and economic influence, and to stay (but watchfully) in tandem with the British, who were more involved with the Whites in the field. Foch, chiming in with Winston Churchill's outspoken advocacy of strong measures, did propose (25 February) an anti-Bolshevik offensive, painted for effect as a crusade, which would employ 250,000 men drawn from the armies of the eastern states. But Clemenceau, who coincidentally was recovering from the assassination attempt, took a dim view of it, and the moment (if there ever was one) passed.[140] The Poles and Czechs were proving keener to quarrel with each other over their new borders than to follow the Marshal to Moscow, and before long the situation in Hungary and Romania's defiance of the Conference's directives about its intervention there turned all such grand projects into pipe dreams.

Despite its manifest failures, Clemenceau's Russian policy never seriously endangered his government. Even many of the Socialists, including Albert Thomas, had supported intervention of some kind, and most were sufficiently sceptical about or even hostile to the Bolsheviks to give him some latitude; and the support of the general public for anti-Bolshevik measures and rhetoric was firm, helped considerably, be it said, by a law passed on 19 September 1918 giving the myriad holders of Russian bonds half credit toward the purchase of national defense bonds.[141] But there were limits, especially after the Odessa fiasco: in July Clemenceau was frank to admit in the Conference that he was having trouble getting any further financial support from Parliament for Russian operation.[142]

In the last analysis, the governing factors in the whole involvement in Russia were the West's lack of men because of distractions elsewhere and insistent cries from the public for rapid demobilization; its lack of reliable information about what was going on there; and its lack of conviction to act decisively. Clemenceau's situation and behavior typified these deficiencies. Himself lacking a deep personal knowledge of or interest in Russian affairs, he paid heed to them only when he had to, never developed a consistent set of views about them, and in the end gradually settled for a low-risk policy of building up the succession states as the Eastern Barrier to Germany, whose affairs *did* interest him, it goes without saying. At the same time these states could serve as a *cordon sanitaire*, a "barbed-wire line" impeding the spread of Bolshevism westward. In December 1919, after six months of steadily winding down French military and financial support of the Whites, he admitted to Lloyd George, who had reached the same conclusion, that he had come to think intervention had been a great mistake.[143]

Indeed it had. It confirmed the Bolsheviks in suspicions they had always harbored about the Western democracies, helped them gain credence among the Russian masses for their claim to be the true defenders of the Motherland, hindered establishment of normal diplomatic relations for four critical years (1920-24) after the Bolsheviks won the civil war, and--a crowning irony--in that interval contributed to bringing about through a rebound effect the very thing Clemenceau had sought to prevent above all: a link-up between Russia and Germany. In 1922 they signed a pact of friendship and collaboration. The Treaty of Rapallo was to be yet another reagent eating at the vitals of the settlement of 1919. Shortly after its signing, German-aided armaments works in Russia secretly began work on the machine that would roll over Europe in a second world war.

XIII

France's ultimate ratification of the Treaty of Versailles was never seriously in doubt. The government won a procedural motion, 262 to 188 (30 September), and the bill itself passed by a vote of 372 to 53 in the Chamber (2 October) and unanimously in the Senate (11 October). Under Parliament's rules, it could not even be amended, but this had not prevented a thorough examination of what Clemenceau had wrought. Most critics, apart from the Socialists, focused on what he had not obtained in securities and guarantees. The list was imposing. Germany had not been broken up; she was not completely disarmed, and the inspection regime was set up under the League of Nations for a fixed term, not permanently under the Allied Military Command; the Rhineland was not separated from her, and the occupation was neither permanent nor coterminous with the reparation period; the 1814 boundary for the Saar was not won, and the plebiscite there would probably favor Germany, as would the one in Upper Silesia (a late concession to Lloyd George); she would not pay full war costs; nobody knew what the final figure would be, but an international commission could be expected to set a figure smaller than the true one for damage and pensions; payments, assuming Germany really could be forced to make them, would lag behind the needed pace of reconstruction; too much depended on commissions operating under an as-yet unorganized League of Nations, making evasion easy; the small new states in the east were a poor substitute for the economic and political unity once supplied by Austria-Hungary and too weak to serve as a barrier to Germany or Russia; Italy had been unnecessarily alienated; the famous Guarantee treaties with Britain and the United States might not be ratified, and even if they were, they promised little more than what those countries were supposedly obligated to do under the League, as they themselves admitted.

Clemenceau defended his handiwork in rambling Chamber and Senate speeches which nonetheless were among his most elevated and self-revealing.[144] The mushy reparation settlement and the failure to win permanently the line of the Rhine affected opinion most adversely. For political reasons, with elections looming, he was evasive on reparation, avoiding mention of the failure to secure economic cooperation or a scaling down of debts from the United States, allowing Klotz and Loucheur to cite fantastically high reparation figures without comment, and even denying that he and they had been willing to accept fixed--and far lower--sums.[145] As for the Rhineland and other guarantees, the truly haunting question that autumn was how they would fare in the United States, where Wilson was locked in a desperate struggle with the Senate. The situation worried Clemenceau to the extent that he misleadingly implied before Parliament that France could unilaterally prolong occupation of the Rhineland should the Guarantee treaties not be ratified.[146] He asserted, and probably believed, that the question was moot: the United States would ratify the Treaty of Versailles because it was "graven on their hearts."[147] It was still all but unthinkable that America really would repudiate her president's signature and turn her back on Europe.

Wilson, for *his* political reasons as well as likely psychological reasons owing to the effects of the severe strokes he suffered after his collapse on 25 September, could not admit that he had incurred any defeats in Paris.[148] Clemenceau, in striking contrast, made no bones about the fact that he had not gotten all he or the country had wanted. But he believed he had obtained all that could be had if ties with the Allies were not to be broken. The nation must face up the challenge ahead. The treaty was only "the beginning of a beginning...a collection of possibilities."[149] Had France been "reduced to vigilance," as his critics complained?   "But life," he replied, "condemns us to it."[150]

XIV

Too many people, worn down by five years of exertions, sufferings, and failed hopes, did not want to be confronted by such truths.   All of Clemenceau's apprehensions about the future had begun to focus upon this weariness.   France, upon whom the peace would so vitally depend, must not give way to resignation and develop a defeatist mentality.   She must keep alive the spirit which had seen her through the war's darkest hours.   He had adamantly insisted upon the occupation of the Rhineland, for example, not simply, nor even in the last resort principally, because of its undeniable military advantages but because, as he told Lloyd George and Wilson, the French needed "a barrier behind which they could begin to raise themselves from their ruins" and because if he were to surrender that guarantee it would "break the vital will [*le ressort vital*] of our people."[151]   They needed now more than ever a civic-minded unity and generosity of spirit, a willingness to sacrifice in peace as they had in war, and not a straggle back to familiar old quarrels, traditional divisions, and their train of sterile recriminations.   Such luxuries arguably had been affordable in the Good Old Days, but in the new age dawning they would be fatal.

These admonitions comprised the central theme of his sole major speech, at Strasbourg on 4 November, before the Chamber elections on 16 and 30 November, although as noted above the strong anti-Bolshevik statement made the greatest impression.   He had insisted that the Chamber elections should precede all the others, but after that he left the electioneering to others and at best exercised only fitful direction.   Briand, leading the opposition, had wanted the Chamber elections delayed until after the local elections, charging that Clemenceau was having himself "plebiscited."   The latter's aloof behavior appeared to belie this interpretation, but the results certainly could be read as a strong endorsement of him.   In any event, the mishmash of majoritarian and proportional representation rules under which this election was held clearly helped to ensure a crushing two-to-one victory for the Bloc National, a collection of coalitions excluding only the Socialists, anti-Clemencist

Radicals, and outright *réactionnaires*. A crowd of novice deputies (369 of 616), many of them war veterans, trooped into town.

Clemenceau was sceptical, uneasy over what this might portend; as Lloyd George had learned from the Coupon Election right after the Armistice, there could be such a thing as winning too big. In circumstances like the present, how govern with an unwieldy, ill-assorted, inexperienced majority? Delicate negotiations were still underway on the Middle East and international finances. Above all, there was the crisis now unfolding because of events in the United States. On 19 November the Senate had rejected ratification of the Versailles Treaty. (A second, final, rejection would come on 19 March 1920.) At Wilson's behest, the loyal Democrats had joined with Republican "irreconcilables" to defeat the treaty because Senator Lodge had attached reservations to it which Wilson considered unacceptable. Clemenceau had been working on Lodge behind the scenes through Ambassador Jusserand in order to make passage possible, but Wilson's intransigence had thrown everything into the cauldron.[152]. Worse yet, the president was now ordering the American delegation to come home, leaving only the ambassador as an official observer.

Clemenceau found Wilson's actions incomprehensible--once in a burst of frustration asking the British ambassador, "What on earth is the Lord Almighty doing that he does not take him to his bosom?"[153] To accept Lodge's reservations, he thought, certainly any of a strictly interpretative character, would be troublesome but far preferable to a flat rejection of the treaty; and presently pro-government papers like the *Journal des Débats* and *Le Temps* began to sound this theme.[154] He pleaded with Frank Polk, the head of the American delegation since Wilson's departure and a man whom he had come to admire, to try to get his recall cancelled and jokingly threatened to have him arrested on trumped-up charges if that was what it would take to keep him on hand.[155] And he pleaded with Wilson via a long telegram to Jusserand on 27 November: Yugoslavia and Romania were on the verge of adhering to the clauses of the Austrian treaty protecting minorities, and the treaty with Hungary was well on the way to completion; the Germans, taking heart from the troubles with the United States, were stalling on exchanging ratifications, refusing to recognize the authority of the disarmament and reparation commissions until the United States appointed representatives to them, and refusing to surrender persons accused of war crimes or to pay compensation for the warships they had scuttled at Scapa Flow back in June. "America would commit bankruptcy at the last moment," he went on, "giving the impression that it was abandoning the cause it has so nobly upheld. Never would France, which felt such deep gratitude and trust for the United States, be able to understand."[156]

Germany's defiance meanwhile led him to propose that a strong note be sent to her threatening military action. But Lloyd George and his cabinet demurred. In the end a toned-down note was dispatched, but the confrontation caste a pall over the prospects of future Anglo-French cooperation.[157] First America and now Britain. And what with France? Where would she find leadership able to cope with them, with the Germans, and with the motley crew in the new Chamber and their elder cousins in the soon-to-be-elected Senate?

Such were his preoccupations and such was the international situation when he stood before the Chamber at its inaugural session on 8 December-- the day the note was sent to Germany and the day before the American delegation's departure. The deputies welcomed him with a stirring ovation. Perhaps it persuaded him, perhaps not. Whatever the case, the next morning he confided to Mordacq that he had made a grave decision. He would let his name be proposed for the presidency of the Republic.[158]

NOTES
CHAPTER XV

1   John Maynard Keynes, *The Economic Consequences of the Peace* (New York: Harcourt, Brace & Howe, 1920), pp. 32-33.

2   Poincaré, *Au service de la France*, 10:382.

3   Treich, *L'esprit de Clemenceau*, p. 95 (dated 19 Nov.).

4   Mordacq, *Clemenceau au soir de sa vie*, 2:277-278, 286. "Mlle. C" (Marie André) was left in the care of her cousin, a nurse in Clemenceau's dispensary in the 1870s. She became crippled, and he tended her several times a week.

5   His peroration on 5 Sept. (JOC, p. 2316)--"To the men who will come, the rest of the labor"--caused a stir.

6   Mantoux, ed., *Les délibérations du Conseil des Quatre*, 1:43.

7   See Marc Trachtenberg, *Reparation in World Politics: France and European Economic Diplomacy, 1916-1923* (New York: Columbia University Press, 1980), pp. 52-53; and David Stevenson, *The First World War and International Politics* (New York: Oxford University Press, 1988), p. 248. Also Trachtenberg, "Versailles after Sixty Years," *Journal of Contemporary History* 17 (1982):497-498 and *passim*.

8   Mantoux, ed., *Les délibérations du Conseil des Quatre*, 1:43 (27 March 1919). See Appendix II below for his full statement.

9   GC, *The Surprises of Life*, p. 186.

10   JOS, 17 Sept. 1918, pp. 603-604.

11   Wilson, *The Papers of Woodrow Wilson*, 45:337 (Clemenceau to Wilson, 21 Dec. 1917), and 47:277-278 (Clemenceau to Wilson, 6 April 1918).

12   GC, *Grandeur and Misery of Victory*, pp. 190-191.

13   See pp. 97-98 above.

14   See the reply to the German Delegation by the Allied and Associated Powers on 16 June 1919 in FRUS, 6:926-930. It is interesting to note that Wilson's view, that Germany in 1914 was on the verge of conquering the world commercially but decided on force as a short cut,

coincided with Clemenceau's almost exactly. See Wilson, *The Papers of Woodrow Wilson*, 53:364 (Diary of Dr. Grayson, 11 Dec. 1918); and HE, 26 April 1915 (pp. 319-320 above).

15   Lloyd George, *War Memoirs of David Lloyd George*, 2:1606.

16   HE, 9 June 1917. See also *Grandeur and Misery of Victory*, pp. 271-293 ("German Insensibility").

17   JOS, 11 Oct. 1919, p. 1623.

18   HE, 18 Oct. 1914. Should one be surprised that he attended a performance of *Die Götterdämmerung* in 1925 and wrote of it in a letter, "The death of Siegfried is an incomparable thing"? GC, *Lettres à une amie*, p. 122.

19   Köhler, in "La révolution allemande 1918/19 et la France," p. 459, notes that he did not approve the attempt, encouraged by Prof. Haguenin, to support Bavarian separatism nor join those who made distinctions between "dangerous Prussians and peaceful Germans" à la Mme. de Staël, "for he had learned to know the Bavarian troops to the point of satiation during the war of 1870."

20   JOS, 11 Oct. 1919, pp. 1621-1622.

21   See Dr. Ernst Meier, "'20 Millionen Deutsche zurviel!' Ein Bietrag zur politischen Schlagwort--und Legendenbildung," *Publizistik*, 1958, Heft #3; also Wormser, *La république de Clemenceau*, p. 360.

22   FRUS, 1:131-132 (House to Sec. of State, 15 Nov. 1918). Later a Quai d'Orsay Note (23 Dec., Pichon Papers) advised going slow so as to give time for "le mouvement de dissociation" to develop in non-Prussian Germany. See Köhler, "La révolution allemande 1918/19 et la France," p. 455.

23   Tardieu, *The Truth about the Treaty*, p. 120; Mordacq, *Le ministère Clemenceau*, 3:263. See also GC, *Grandeur and Misery of Victory*, 106, 157, 399 (oddly, remembering him as standing).

24   Likewise the Bulgarians. See Mordacq, *Le ministère Clemenceau*, 3:300; 4:93, 104-105.

25   When Art. 231 was under discussion, Clemenceau dismissed the problem of "responsibility" as legalisms, "a matter of drafting." See Mantoux, ed., *Les délibérations du Conseil des Quatre*, 1:152 (5 April). Weinberg notes that none of Germany's allies reacted to the "war guilt" clauses in their treaties as did Germany, which became obsessed with them. Gerhard L. Weinberg, "The Defeat of Germany in 1918 and the European Balance of Power," *Central European History* 2 (1969):259-260. The literature on the war-guilt clause is huge. In support of remarks here see especially Trachtenberg, *Reparation in World Politics*, pp. 56-57; Stevenson, *The First World War and International Politics*, pp. 259-260; Robert E. Bunselmeyer,

The Cost of the War, 1914-1919: British Economic War Aims and the Origin of Reparation (Hamden, CT: Archon Books, 1975), pp. 82, 182-184, 221n.; Klaus Schwabe, *Woodrow Wilson, Revolutionary Germany, and Peacemaking, 1918-1919: Missionary Diplomacy and the Realities of Power*, trans. Rita and Robert Kimber (Chapel Hill NC: University of North Carolina Press, 1985), pp. 246, 289-290, 404; and A. Lentin, *Lloyd George, Woodrow Wilson and the Guilt of Germany: An Essay in the Pre-History of Appeasement* (Baton Rouge, LA: Louisiana State University Press, 1984), pp. 101-102.

26   Raphaël-Leygues, *Georges Leygues*, p. 185 (6 Nov. 1918). See also Roy A. Prete and John C. Cairns (commentary), "Since Renouvin: A Reconsideration of French War Aims, 1914-1918," *Proceedings of the Annual Meeting of the Western Society for French History* 10 (1982):467 and *passim*.

27   See Duroselle, *Clemenceau*, p. 726.

28   Charles Seymour, ed., *The Intimate Papers of Colonel House*, 4 vols. (Boston: Houghton Mifflin Co., 1928), 4:208, 213. The Treaty of Trianon (Hungary) was not signed until 4 June 1920 and Sèvres (Turkey) until 10 August.

29   See FRUS, 1:344-371. Eugène Gonda, *La conférence de Versailles: La bataille perdue de Clemenceau, novembre 1918* (Éditions LPF Paris, 1918), though an arresting discussion of this usually neglected project, in my opinion exaggerates the consequences of its rejection.

30   FRUS, 1:333 (House to Sec. of State, 30 Nov. 1918). See also Keith L. Nelson, *Victors Divided: America and the Allies in Germany, 1918-1923* (Berkeley, CA: University of California Press, 1975), p. 289.

31   On the Cambon memorandum of 26 Nov. see Harold I. Nelson, *Land and Power: British and Allied Policy on Germany's Frontiers, 1916-19* (London: Routledge & Paul, 1963), pp. 130-131; and Payne, "The Foreign Policy of Georges Clemenceau: 1917-20," pp. 121-124. Arthur C. Walworth, in *America's Moment, 1918: American Diplomacy at the End of World War I* (New York: W. W. Norton, 1977), pp. 99-109, believes Cambon exceeded his instructions, and finds that both Clemenceau and Balfour worked to overcome Lloyd George's annoyance with Wilson over naval policy in the conviction that good relations with the United States were needed in the interests of Europe's future.

32   JOC, 29 Dec. 1918, pp. 3732-3734.

33   The passage is in Wilson, *The Papers of Woodrow Wilson*, 53:532.

34   *Ibid.*, p. 577 (Diary of Col. House, 31 Dec. 1918).

35   See Pierre Miquel, *La paix de Versailles et l'opinion publique française* (Flammarion, 1972), pp. 60-75.

36   He conferred every morning with Pichon, whom Mordacq described as "a huge worker, full of good sense, moderate, calm, rather conciliatory in temperament [but] sometimes indecisive in difficult moments" (*Le ministère Clemenceau*, 3:118n.). When Pichon's health gave way in the ministry's last months, Philippe Berthelot substituted in these morning conferences. When Pierre de Margerie, Political Director at the Quai d'Orsay, had collapsed from overwork in June 1918, Berthelot had assumed his functions as Adjunct Director. To Berthelot's disappointment, Clemenceau unexpectedly chose Paul Dutasta, ambassador to Switzerland and son of his Toulon publisher-friend, as Secretary-General of the Peace Conference. Clemenceau didn't like Berthelot, distrusted him, and was not inclined to share his views. Duroselle buries the rumor that Dutasta was an illegitimate son of Clemenceau; he was born in 1873, seven years before Clemenceau had met his father. See Duroselle, *Clemenceau*, pp. 374, 798; Auguste Bréal, *Philippe Berthelot*, 3rd ed. (Gallimard, 1937), pp. 153, 188-189; and Gordon A. Craig and Felix Gilbert, eds., *The Diplomats, 1919-1939* (Princeton, NJ: Princeton University Press, 1953), p. 69.

37   Bonsal, "What Manner of Man Was Clemenceau?" p. 75.

38   Miquel's 565 packed pages in *La paix de Versailles et l'opinion publique française* give ample evidence of the freedom of opinion.

39   André Portier (the secretary) to Walworth, 18 Nov. 1959, in Arthur Walworth, *Wilson and His Peacemakers: American Diplomacy at the Paris Peace Conference, 1919* (New York: W. W. Norton, 1986), p. 282n.

40   See J.-B. Duroselle's essay in J. Joseph Huthmacher and Warren I. Susman, eds., *Wilson's Diplomacy: An International Symposium*, The American Forum Series (Cambridge, MA: Schenkman Publishing Co., 1973), p. 34.

41   See Robert A. Burnett, "*L'Homme Libre--L'Homme Enchaîné*: How a Journalist Handled the Press," *Journalism Quarterly* 50 (1973):709 and *passim*.

42   FRUS, 3:579 (Council of Ten, 16 Jan. 1919).

43   Figures vary; those cited here are mainly from Alfred Sauvy, *Histoire économique de la France centre les deux guerres*, vol. 1, *De l'Armistice à la dévaluation de la livre* (Fayard, 1965), pp. 19-38 and annexes.

44   See especially Dan P. Silverman, *Reconstructing Europe after the Great War* (Cambridge, MA: Harvard University Press, 1982), pp. 133-134, 145-146, and *passim*; and Lucien Petit, *Le règlement des dettes interalliés, 1919-1929* (Éditions Berger-Levrault, 1932), pp. 21-24 and *passim*.

45   Stephen Bonsal, *Suitors and Suppliants: The Little Nations at Versailles* (New York: Prentice-Hall, 1946), p. 130. In 1925 he remarked, "The French peasants fought and won the war." Neuray, *Entretiens avec Clemenceau*, p. 28.

46   Duroselle, *Clemenceau*, pp. 770-771, finds this whole charade, which went on through the ratification debates, well nigh unconscionable. Trachtenberg notes that the "Germany will pay" campaign in the spring was not government-inspired but was directed, obliquely, against the government in order to defeat the capital taxation plan. Klotz, incidentally, never said "Germany will pay" but "Germany will pay first." Loucheur, not Klotz, became Clemenceau's veritable adviser on reparation. Trachtenberg, *Reparation in World Politics*, pp. 40-44.

47   France's final debt to the United States came to $3,404,818,945.01, of which $1,434,818,945.01 was in advances after the Armistice. See Benjamin D. Rhodes, "Reassessing 'Uncle Shylock': The United States and the French War Debt, 1917-1929," *Journal of American History* 55 (1969):788. For a full treatment, harshly critical of American policy, see Denise Artaud, *La question des dettes interalliées et le reconstruction de l'Europe, 1917-1929*, 2 vols. (H. Champion, 1978).

48   See especially Étienne Clémentel, *La France et la politique économique interalliée* (Presses Universitaires de France, 1931), pp. 313-318, 337-348; Jean Monnet, *Mémoires* (Fayard, 1976), p. 92; Trachtenberg, *Reparation in World Politics*, pp. 1-18, 27, 34; and *idem*, "Étienne Clémentel and French Economic Diplomacy during the First World War," *French Historical Studies* 10 (1977): 315-341.

49   In 1906 he said he favored the eight-hour day "in principle" but doubted it should be instituted at a stroke; JOC, 19 June, p. 2006. Projects proposed during his first ministry lapsed after its fall. Decrees implementing the 1919 law sector by sector were completed by 1931. See GC, *La mêlée sociale*, pp. 247-255; Mordacq, *Le ministère Clemenceau*, 3:251-253; Wormser, *La république de Clemenceau*, pp. 231-233; and Gary Cross, "*Les Trois Huits*: Labor Movements, International Reform, and the Origins of the Eight-Hour Day, 1919-1924," *French Historical Studies* 14, no. 2 (1985):246-252.

50   See Carrot, *Le maintien de l'ordre en France*, 2:698-699.

51   On 28 May. He later issued a rectification softening his words.

52   On 22 July he won a 289-176 vote of confidence after a hot debate. He had appointed Joseph Noulens, late ambassador to Russia and a notorious foe of the Bolsheviks, as Boret's replacement, which angered the Socialists. See especially Duroselle, *Clemenceau*, pp. 834-837; and Sherwood, *Georges Mandel and the Third Republic*, pp. 31-32.

53   See Martet, *Clemenceau*, p. 332; and Seymour, ed., *The Intimate Papers of Colonel House*, 4:119. Lloyd George thought he disliked the Church even more than Germany. David Lloyd George, *Memoirs of the Peace Conference*, 2 vols. (New Haven, CT: Yale University Press, 1939), 2:911.

472

54   The context of the oft-quoted phrase deserves attention. "Realizations of ideas of social justice," he said, "are only at their beginnings," and no reform should cause fright "if it is founded in public order, a respect for the rights of each." Violence, however, "cannot and will never be tolerated by a government worthy of the name" because "disorder cannot be the principle of life. This is why all attempts to use force which are made in the name of the workers in the shops [ateliers] will meet no fewer obstacles than did the excesses of power of the ancient oligarchies, who succumbed for having believed, as do certain workers' organizations today, that everything was permitted to them." As for the Bolsheviks, he added later, "Between them and us it is a question of force, because while demanding liberty for themselves, they seek to impose on us a dictatorship of absolutism by means of a system of execrable criminal attacks [attentats] in which is exhibited for all to see [s'exalter] the delirium of ferocity which so remarkably distinguishes the ill-emancipated serfs of Russia. It is for us to show that their aggression will not find us defenseless." GC, Discours prononcé...à Strasbourg le 4 novembre 1919, pp. 22, 23, 25.

55   On the Rhineland and Saar questions, 28 March, 8 April, and 2 June.

56   Riddell, Lord Riddell's War Diary, p. 171 (14 Feb. 1920).

57   Vance C. McCormick, Diaries of Vance C. McCormick (Hoover Institution Archives), p. 86 (14 May 1919).

58   Seymour, ed., The Intimate Papers of Colonel House, 4:191; and Lloyd George, Memoirs of the Peace Conference, 2:911.

59   He frankly explained his tactic to the Chamber's Commission of Foreign Affairs; see Watson, Georges Clemenceau, p. 342. See also Poincaré, Au service de la France, 11:112; and McDougall, France's Rhineland Diplomacy, pp. 55-57.

60   David Hunter Miller, My Diary At the Conference of Paris, With Documents, 21 vols. (New York, for the author by the Appeal Printing Co., 1924), 1:254 (16 April 1919).

61   To Philip Kerr, 12 Feb. 1919; from M. L. Dockrill, "Britain, the United States, and France and the German Settlement 1918-1920," in B. J. C. McKercher and D. J. Moss, eds., Shadow and Substance in British Foreign Policy 1895-1939: Memorial Essays Honouring C. J. Lowe (Edmonton, Alb.: University of Alberta Press, 1984), pp. 205-206.

62   See especially Martet, Clemenceau, pp. 36-42; and Mordacq, Le ministère Clemenceau, 3:133-152. For possible effects of this episode on the Russian question, see John M. Thompson, Russia, Bolshevism, and the Versailles Peace (Princeton, NJ: Princeton University Press, 1966), pp. 147-149.

63   Wilson, *The Papers of Woodrow Wilson*, 57:513 (Diary of Dr. Grayson, 20 April 1919).

64   Lentin, *Lloyd George, Woodrow Wilson, and the Guilt of Germany*, p. 122. See also Mordacq, *Le ministère Clemenceau*, 3:106-107.

65   Experts in all the delegations tended to think their chiefs ignorant. Poincaré constantly charged (*Au service de la France*, 11, *passim*) that Clemenceau was uninformed, unable to make coherent explanations, utterly dependent on Tardieu and Mandel, etc. As Renouvin notes in the preface, the bulk of evidence from Mantoux and others contradicts such assertions. In any case, Poincaré's and Clemenceau's mentalities differed dramatically; they seldom could get on the same wavelength.

66   Lloyd George, *War Memoirs of David Lloyd George*, 2:1608. See also Lord Maurice Hankey, *The Supreme Control at the Paris Peace Conference, 1919: A Commentary* (London: George Allen & Unwin Ltd., 1963), p. 32; and for a less favorable view by Lloyd George, Riddell, *Lord Riddell's War Diary*, pp. 171, 397.

67   Bonsal, *Suitors and Suppliants*, p. 131.

68   F. H. Simonds, "Clemenceau, Tardieu, London," *Review of Reviews*, Jan. 1930, p. 61. Simonds knew him.

69   See Mordacq, *Le ministère Clemenceau*, 4:273.

70   Wilson, *The Papers of Woodrow Wilson*, 59:623 (Diary of Colonel House, 30 May 1919).

71   Mordacq, *Le ministère Clemenceau*, 4:257. He thought Wilson's illness at the time may have been the cause. Back in 1867 he had observed that "...it is singularly difficult to dislodge a prejudice which has succeeded in installing itself in one of the recesses of the narrow mind of an Anglo-Saxon." *Le Temps*, 27 Oct. 1867, as quoted in Yves-Henri Nouailhat's essay in *Clemenceau et la justice*, p. 30.

72   Mordacq, *Le ministère Clemenceau*, 3:104.

73   Lloyd George, *Memoirs of the Peace Conference*, 1:142.

74   Bonsal, *Unfinished Business*, p. 69. See also Chastenet, *Histoire de la troisième république*, 5:29.

75   Walworth, *Wilson and His Peacemakers*, pp. 268-269. Lloyd George thought the best way to handle Clemenceau was to "hit him pretty hard at first"--not a bad analysis. *Ibid.*, p. 419.

76   Lloyd George, *Memoirs of the Peace Conference*, 1:144. See also GC, *Grandeur and Misery of Victory*, pp. 169-170; and remarks in Charles

Seymour, "Policy and Personality at the Paris Peace Conference," *Virginia Quarterly Review* 21 (1945):531.

[77] See Mordacq, *Le ministère Clemenceau*, 1:94-95; and Alexander L. and Juliette L. George, *Woodrow Wilson and Colonel House: A Personality Study* (New York: Dover Publications, 1964), pp. 191-192.

[78] Martet, *Le Tigre*, p. 26. Did the effort succeed altogether? A curious comment.

[79] GC, *Grandeur and Misery of Victory*, pp. 148-149.

[80] See Inga Floto, *Colonel House in Paris: A Study of American Policy at the Paris Peace Conference, 1919* (Aarhus: Universitets-forlaget, 1973), pp. 164-214, *passim*.

[81] See, for example, his opening speech to the Conference, FRUS, 3:167-169, and his defense of the treaty, JOC, 25 Sept. 1919, p. 4575; also earlier remarks in HE, 22 Aug., 12 Oct. 1917.

[82] FRUS, 3:974. He believed that "the military terms could not be separated from the political, economic and financial terms" (*ibid.*). Here was fair warning of what he would do during the "speed-up" discussed above, i.e., he would raise the whole range of issues touching Germany once they started talking about military terms.

[83] Nicolson to Walworth, 25 Oct. 1959, in Walworth, *Wilson and His Peacemakers*, p. 286.

[84] See Mordacq, *Le ministère Clemenceau*, 3:212-214, 221.

[85] Clemenceau himself was ready to break off (see n. 55 above). Both pro- and anti-government papers except for the Far Left rallied strongly behind him at the *George Washington* news, which caused a big stir; see Miquel, *La paix de Versailles et l'opinion publique française*, pp. 366-368, but also Wilson, *The Papers of Woodrow Wilson*, 57:63-64n. Tardieu, in *The Truth about the Treaty*, pp. 185-186, asserts that Clemenceau was unmoved. Mantoux says he never heard it mentioned in the Big Four discussions; see his essay in *Centenaire Woodrow Wilson: 1856-1956* (Geneva: Centre européen de la Dotation Carnegie, 1956), p. 19.

[86] Mantoux, ed., *Les délibérations du Conseil des Quatre*, 1:194 (8 April).

[87] See Wilson, *The Papers of Woodrow Wilson*, 57:153-154 (Diary of Colonel House, 15 April 1919); Mordacq, *Le ministère Clemenceau*, 3:222-223; and Walworth, *Wilson and His Peacemakers*, p. 325.

[88] See especially Jere Clemens King, *Foch versus Clemenceau: France and German Dismemberment, 1918-1919* (Cambridge, MA: Harvard University Press, 1960); Walter A. McDougall, *France's Rhineland*

Diplomacy, 1914-1924: The Last Bid for a Balance of Power in Europe (Princeton, NJ: Princeton University Press, 1978), pp. 3-96; Jacques Bariéty, *Les relations franco-allemandes après la Première guerre mondiale, 10 novembre 1918-10 janvier 1925, de l'exécution à négociation* (Pedone, 1977), pp. 26-63; Nelson, *Victors Divided*, pp. 18-23, 80-90, 116-117, and *passim*; and Georges Soutou, "La France et les Marches de l'Est, 1914-1919," *Revue historique* 260 (1978):341-388.

89   See Martet, *Clemenceau*, p. 150.

90   Mantoux, ed., *Les délibérations du Conseil des Quatre*, 1:319 (22 April).

91   See Soutou, "La France et les Marches de l'Est," p. 285.

92   The germ of the idea of a guarantee treaty may have sprung from French sources back in December. David Hunter Miller cabled to Colonel House that "the French idea regarding a League of Nations has as basis the idea that the security of France against any attack should be guaranteed by Great Britain and the United States...." Miller, *My Diary At the Conference of Paris*, 1:26 (3 Dec. 1918).

93   See Loucheur Papers, B12.F12, and his *Carnets secrets*, p. 72; and Bonsal, *Suitors and Suppliants*, pp. 216-217 (conversations with Clemenceau and Tardieu).

94   See Bariéty, *Les relations franco-allemandes*, pp. 62-63; and Watson, "The Making of the Treaty of Versailles," p. 77.

95   FRUS, 13:161, 723, 725. He probably insisted on the clause in Art. 429 prolonging occupation if necessary principally because of his doubts about U.S. Senate ratification of the Guarantee treaty in view of the 1918 elections and the Senate's Round Robin of 3 March 1919. See Pierre Renouvin, "Le destin du pacte d'assistance américain à la France en 1919," *Annales d'études internationaux* [Geneva] 1 (1970):10.

96   Wilson, *The Papers of Woodrow Wilson*, 58:462 (Diary of Dr. Grayson, 6 May 1919).

97   See Mordacq, *Le ministère Clemenceau*, 3:226-231, 265, 298; GC, *Grandeur and Misery of Victory*, pp. 123-136, 205.31: Wilson, *The Papers of Woodrow Wilson*, 60:8-15 (Jeanneney's report); and Robert McCrum, "French Rhineland Policy at the Paris Peace Conference, 1919," *Historical Journal* 21 (1978):623-648. He called Mangin "a real Boulanger" (Poincaré, *Au service de la France*, 11:449), " a bird brain" (Martet, *Le Tigre*, p. 185). On the bad effect on the military of the ambiguousness of the government's policy regarding encouragement of separatists, see Pierre Jardin, "L'occupation française en Rhénanie, 1918-1919, Fayolle et l'idée palatine, " *Revue d'histoirie moderne et contemporaine* 33 (1986):402, 423, and *passim*.

98   Mordacq, *Le ministère Clemenceau*, 3:294.

99   Nobécourt, *L'année du 11 novembre*, p. 415.

100   Benjamin, *Clemenceau dans la retraite*, p. 136.

101   But see below, pp. 534-535.

102   In the Armistice negotiations he had already contemplated a link between the Rhineland and reparation. See Général [Jean-Jules-Henri] Mordacq, *La verité sur l'armistice* (Tallandier, 1929), pp. 69-70, as noted in Robert A. Burnett, "Georges Clemenceau in the Paris Peace Conference, 1919" (Ph.D. diss., University of North Carolina, 1968), p. 31. But see also Trachtenberg, *Reparation in World Politics*, pp. 31-32.

103   See Eva Susan Balogh, "The Road to Isolation: Hungary, the Great Powers, and the Succession States, 1919-1920" (Ph.D. diss., Yale University, 1974), p. 170 and *passim*.

104   See especially Kay Lundgreen-Nielson, *The Polish Problem at the Peace Conference: A Study of the Great Powers and the Poles, 1918-1919* (Odense [Denmark]: Odense University Studies in History and Social Sciences, 59 [1979]), pp. 227-233, 244, 247, 408-412.

105   Loucheur Papers, B12.F12, repr. in *Carnets secrets*, p. 76 (c.4-5 April).

106   A somewhat limited Franco-Belgian military accord was finally signed on 7 Sept. 1920 and a definitive version in Sept. 1926, which Belgium denounced in March 1936. See especially Mordacq, *Le ministère Clemenceau*, 4:254-255; Sally Marks' magistral *Innocent Abroad: Belgium at the Paris Peace Conference of 1919* (Chapel Hill, NC: University of North Carolina Press, 1981), pp. 99-100, 222-224, 305-306, and *passim*; and Duroselle, *Clemenceau*, pp. 794-800, more charitable toward Clemenceau than Marks.

107   Mantoux, ed., *Les délibérations du Conseil des Quatre*, 2:208 (26 May).

108   For matters here and below see especially Duroselle, *Clemenceau*, pp. 780-794, which essentially duplicates his essay, "Clemenceau et l'Italie," in *La France et l'Italie pendant la Première Guerre mondiale*, pp. 492-511, 541-542.

109   Raphaël-Leygues, *Georges Leygues*, p. 159 (30 Aug. 1918).

110   Mordacq, *Le ministère Clemenceau*, 3:242 (25 April, after Orlando's departure for Rome).

111   Orlando's *Memorie*, as quoted in Joel Blatt, "France and Italy at the Paris Peace Conference," *International History Review* [Canada] 8 (1986):35.

112   See Duroselle, *Clemenceau*, p. 788.

113   Count Aldrovandi's diary, in René Albrecht-Carrié, *Italy at the Paris Peace Conference* (New York: Columbia University Press, 1938), pp. 477-478.

114   Blatt, "France and Italy at the Paris Peace Conference," p. 34.

115   To Stephen Bonsal, 29 April 1919, in Bonsal, *Suitors and Suppliants*, pp. 114-115.

116   Whether or how much Sir Basil Zaharoff influenced Clemenceau to support the landing is unclear. See Duroselle, *Clemenceau*, pp. 778, 792; and N. Petsalis-Diomides, *Greece at the Peace Conference, 1919* (Thessalonika: Institute for Balkan Studies, 1978), p. 203n. By the end of 1919 Clemenceau was favoring a Greek withdrawal from Smyrna.

117   See especially Albrecht-Carrié, *Italy at the Paris Peace Conference*, pp. 186-194. Further moves by Clemenceau, but less promising, followed in the last half of 1919.

118   See Blatt, "France and Italy at the Paris Peace Conference," p. 30.

119   See Mordacq, *Clemenceau au soir de sa vie*, 2:63.

120   He took a dim view of Mussolini and his movement: "You'd have to be crazy to undertake what he has done. It will end in a lamentable collapse." Wormser, *Clemenceau vu de près*, p. 273.

121   For the discussion here see especially Andrew and Kanya-Forstner, *The Climax of French Imperial Expansion*, pp. 151-204 and *passim*; Philip S. Khoury, *Syria and the French Mandate: The Politics of Arab Nationalism, 1920-1945* (Princeton, NJ: Princeton University Press, 1987), pp. 36-39; and Jan Karl Tanenbaum, *France and the Arab Middle East, 1914-1920*, Transactions of the American Philosophical Society, vol. 68, pt. 7 (Philadelphia: American Philosophical Society, 1978), pp. 33-43.

122   P. Cambon, *Correspondance*, 3:275 ("C'est de la littérature."); and Bonsal, *Suitors and Suppliants*, p. 50.

123   Roskill, *Hankey, Man of Secrets*, 1:466 (28 Nov.).

124   See p. 401 above. Admiral Calthorpe had negotiated the Armistice of Mudros without consulting the French. But previously Clemenceau had not consulted the English when ordering Franchet d'Esperey to grant terms to the Bulgarians.

125   A highly controversial agreement since it was verbal only. He may have been responding to a hint. Tanenbaum notes that on 27 Nov.

Milner (via Pichon) had warned him that if Sykes-Picot were not changed in some important respects, Britain would not support French policies in western Europe; *France and the Arab Middle East*, p. 23. See especially E. L. Woodward and Rohan Butler, eds., *Documents on British Foreign Policy, 1919-1939* (London: H. M. Stationery Office, 1947-1970), ser. 1, vol. 4:340-341; Lloyd George, *Memoirs of the Peace Conference*, 2:673; Mordacq, *Le ministère Clemenceau*, 4:100-101; Mantoux, ed., *Les délibérations du Conseil des Quatre*, 2:137-141; and Martet, *Clemenceau*, pp. 187-188.

[126] See especially Andrew and Kanya-Forstner, *The Climax of French Imperial Expansion*, pp. 176, 238-239.

[127] He probably had not wanted it signed because this might risk a formal repudiation by the British government under pressure from its "Asiatiques" and because he wanted to avoid stirring up opposition inside and outside the Quai d'Orsay. See *ibid.*, pp. 174-175, 279n.

[128] Wilson, *The Papers of Woodrow Wilson*, 59:321 (Diary of Dr. Grayson, 21 May 1919), 370 (Diary of Edith Benham, 21 May).

[129] See Ahmed S. Ahmedov, "Les antagonismes interalliés sur les problèmes turcs après l'armistice de Moudros jusqu'au traité de Sèvres," *Études balkaniques* [Sofia] 19 (1983):37 and *passim*.

[130] See especially R. W. Ferrier, "French Oil Policy, 1917-30: The Interaction Between State and Private Interests," in *Enterprise and History: Essays in Honour of Charles Wilson*, ed. D. C. Coleman and Peter Mathias (Cambridge: Cambridge University Press, 1984), pp. 245-247. At San Remo, 20 April 1920, France got a 25% participation in the Turkish Petroleum Co., cooperation in Romania, and promises of cooperation elsewhere. Heretofore, France had depended upon the United States for 85% of its oil.

[131] See Elie Kedourie, *England and the Middle East: The Destruction of the Ottoman Empire, 1914-1921* (London: The Harvester Press, 1978), pp. 65, 132-135.

[132] See especially J. Thompson, *Russia, Bolshevism, and the Versailles Peace*; and Hovi, *Cordon sanitaire ou barrière de l'Est?*, pp. 121-217, in particular a memorandum by Clemenceau to Pichon on 23 Oct. 1918, pp. 148-149. The Chamber debated Russian affairs on 29 Dec. 1918 and 16 Jan., 24-29 March, 12, 13, 17 June 1919.

[133] See Richard K. Debo, "Mesentente glaciale: Great Britain, France and the Question of Intervention in the Baltic, 1918," *Canadian Journal of History* 12 (1977):65-86, *passim*; and Ullman, *Anglo-Soviet Relations*, 2:220.

[134] See Hogenhuis-Seliverstoff, *Les relations franco-soviétiques*, p. 43; and George Urbaniak, "French Involvement in the Polish-Lithuanian Dispute, 1918-20," *Journal of Baltic Studies* 16 (1985):54.

135   See Martet, *Clemenceau*, p. 332.

136   See FRUS, 3:647-669, 691-692, *passim*; Payne, "The Foreign Policy of Georges Clemenceau, 1917-1920," pp. 306-308 (letter, Balfour to Lloyd George); and Pichon's statement to the press on 11 Jan. 1919 rejecting dealing with the Bolsheviks, in Wilson, *The Papers of Woodrow Wilson*, 54:28n.

137   The 7 Oct. orders are in France, Ministère de la Guerre, État-Major de l'Armée--Service Historique, *Les armées françaises dans la Grande Guerre*, 102 vols. (Imprimerie nationale, 1922-1937), T. 8, V. 3, Annexes 3, #1378, pp. 120-125. For subsequent modification see the 23 Oct. 1918 memorandum cited in n. 132 above and especially Philippe Masson, *La marine française et la Mer Noire, 1918-1919* (Publications de la Sorbonne, 1982), pp. 27-29, 49-51, 93-95; Hogenhuis-Seliverstoff, *Les relations franco-soviétiques*, pp. 109-112; and Carley, *Revolution and Intervention*, pp. 111-118.

138   Besides works noted above, see especially Paul-J.-L. Azan, *Franchet d'Esperey* (Flammarion, 1949), pp. 239-260; Jean Bernachot, *Les armées françaises en Orient après l'armistice de 1918*, 3 vols. (Imprimerie Nationale, 1970-1972), 1:55-171; Brinkley, *The Volunteer Army*, pp. 113-145 and *passim*; Peter Kenez, *Civil War in South Russia, 1919-1920: The Defeat of the Whites* (Berkeley, CA: Univ. of California Press, 1977), pp. 178-202 and *passim*; J. K. Munholland, "The French Army and Intervention in Southern Russia, 1918-1919," *Cahiers du monde russe et soviétique* 22 (1981):43-66; and Jean Xydias, *L'intervention française en Russie, 1918-1919: Souvenirs d'un témoin* (Éditions de France, 1927).

139   See Bernachot, *Les armées françaises en Orient*, 1:15-17, 67-68; Azan, *Franchet d'Esperey*, p. 240; Terry Lee Smart, "The French Intervention in the Ukraine, 1918-1919: (Ph.D. diss., Univ. of Kansas, 1968), pp. 54-63; John F. N. Bradley, *Allied Intervention in Russia, 1917-1920* (New York: Basic Books, 1968), p. 140; and Pichon's statements in JOC, 29 Dec. 1918, pp. 3714-3719.

140   Hovi, *Cordon sanitaire ou barrière de l'Est?*, and Watson, *Georges Clemenceau*, pp. 372-379, bury a long-persisting thesis that Clemenceau was bent upon a crusade against Bolshevism. The containment of Germany took clear precedence over all other purposes; even his policy toward Béla Kun's regime (March-Aug. 1919) observed this priority (Hovi, pp. 201-202).

141   See Peake, "The Impact of the Russian Revolution Upon French Attitudes and Policies Toward Russia," pp. 230-231; and Carley, *Revolution and Intervention*, p. 129. With Clemenceau, in contrast to his successors, financial considerations, e.g., the tsarist bonds, were not much in evidence in his policy thinking. See J. Thompson, *Russia, Bolshevism, and the Versailles Peace*, pp. 153-155; but also Bradley, *Allied Intervention in Russia*, pp. 162-165.

142   FRUS, 7:25 (5 July 1919).

480

[143] Lloyd George cabinet report, 11 Dec. 1919, discussed in Ullman, *Anglo-Soviet Relation*, 2:313-315, and Hogenhuis-Seliverstoff, *Les relations franco-soviétiques*, pp. 150-151. Clemenceau was ready to deal with Russia economically in January 1920, but Millerand reversed course and supported generals Wrangel and Denikin in the last stages of the civil war. See Marjorie M. Farrar, "Victorious Nationalismus Beleaguered: Alexandre Millerand as French Premier in 1920," *Proceedings of the American Philosophical Society* 126 (1982), no. 6, p. 493.

[144] For his main addresses see JOC, 25 Sept. 1919, pp. 4572-80, and JOS, 11 Oct., pp. 1619-1625; repr. in GC, *Discourse de paix*, publiés par les Amis de Clemenceau (Librairie Plon, 1938), pp. 156-281. Unaccountably, historians have tended to ignore them. On the debates see Emmanuel Beau de Loménie, *Le débat de ratification du traité de Versailles* (Denoël, 1945).

[145] See Trachtenberg, *Reparation in World Politics*, pp. 105-106; and Duroselle's harsh (but justifiable) criticisms in *Clemenceau*, pp. 770-771.

[146] See JOC, 25 Sept. 1919, p. 4552, and JOS, 11 Oct., p. 1625. In *Grandeur and Misery of Victory*, pp. 237-238, he continued to gloss over the point, as did Tardieu in *The Truth about the Treaty*, pp. 211-212.

[147] JOC, 25 Sept. 1919, p. 4579.

[148] See Schwabe, *Woodrow Wilson, Revolutionary Germany, and Peacemaking*, pp. 396-397; and on his mental rigidity due to the strokes, Edwin A. Weinstein, *Woodrow Wilson: A Medical and Psychological Biography* (Princeton, NJ: Princeton Univ. Press, 1981), p. 363 and *passim*.

[149] JOC, 25 Sept. 1919, p. 4578.

[150] JOS, 11 Oct. 1919, p. 1619; also JOC, 25 Sept., p. 4579.

[151] Mantoux, ed., *Les déliberations du Conseil des Quatre*, 2:410 (13 June). Watson emphasizes this point in "The Making of the Versailles Treaty," pp. 79-80 and *passim*. For proof that his fears were not misplaced, see Becker's conclusion in *The Great War and the French People*, p. 327.

[152] See James E. Hewes, Jr., "Henry Cabot Lodge and the League of Nations," *Proceedings of the American Philosophical Society* 114, no. 4 (Aug. 1970), p. 254; and George W. Egerton, *Great Britain and the Creation of the League of Nations: Strategy, Politics, and International Organization, 1914-1919* (Chapel Hill, NC: University of North Carolina Press, 1978), pp. 195-196.

[153] Lord Derby to Lord Curzon, Dec. 1919, in Walworth, *Wilson and His Peacemakers*, p. 556.

154   See Henry Blumenthal, *Illusion and Reality in Franco-American Diplomacy, 1914-1945* (Baton Rouge, LA: Louisiana State University Press, 1986), p. 100.

155   See Walworth, *Wilson and His Peacemakers*, p. 556; and Burnett, "Georges Clemenceau and the Paris Peace Conference," pp. 461-463.

156   Walworth, *Wilson and His Peacemakers*, p. 555.

157   See Michael L. Dockrill and J. Douglas Goold, *Peace Without Promise*: *Britain and the Peace Conferences, 1919-23* (Hamden, CT: Archon Books, 1981), pp. 80-81.

158   Mordacq, *Le ministère Clemenceau*, 4:220. He had first broached the subject on 23 Nov.; *ibid.*, 4:193.

CHAPTER XVI

Evening
(1920-1929)

Clemenceau returned from a conference in London (10-14 December) with his decision confirmed. A cracked rib sustained during a rough Channel-crossing had not damaged his spirits nor prevented him from moving through a long agenda. But the slow progress on Poland's frontiers, the treaty with Turkey, the Adriatic, and reparation--where he won Lloyd George's reluctant consent to a 55-25 apportionment of the French and British shares but not the priority the Chamber had asked for reconstruction costs in the devastated areas--only underscored how much remained to be done. Moreover, the United States Senate's initial rejection (19 November) of the Versailles treaty threatened doom for the Guarantee treaties because Lloyd George, without objections from Clemenceau at the time, had made the Anglo-French treaty contingent on ratification of the Franco-American treaty. (Indeed, as it turned out, after the Senate's second rejection of Versailles, on 19 March 1910, the latter treaty never came to the Senate floor, so both became dead letters.) This first rejection, however, had not greatly surprised Clemenceau, who had long been warned of the possibility by Colonel House, and he even affected to take it rather lightly at the conference, where he was trying to reknit relations with Lloyd George, remarking to the prime minister at one point that "on the whole" he was rather relieved that the United States had dropped out of the peace settlement.[1] (The rejection in March, on the other hand, hit him hard--as well it should have, for despite the warnings, he had remained too sanguine too long.) In short, he found in the state of affairs in the waning weeks of 1919 no end of reasons to think that France would be better served if he stayed on the scene to finish the job.

True, he had promised to resign the premiership after the successive Chamber, Senate, and Presidential elections, which would terminate in mid-January. He repeated the promise categorically in the Chamber when he reported on the London trip,[2] and he reaffirmed his retirement from the Senate in a triumphal farewell visit to the Var (1-4 January). He also decided on his successor as premier: Alexandre Millerand. Mandel had effected a reconciliation after the assassination attempt, and Clemenceau had put him in charge of reintegrating Alsace-Lorraine, where he had done excellent work. A hard-working, able man, Millerand, but lacking in breadth and imagination, he thought. He would need support. With himself at the Élysée as overseer, perhaps making a trip to the United States to reach a financial arrangement complementing one he had just made with Britain, the reef-strewn passage from war to peace could be safely navigated. At the same time, at home he could use the presidency and the Bloc National to work toward establishing a two-party system.[3] After a couple of years at most, he could bow out.

He additionally had let himself be persuaded to stand for the presidency by his family and some of his entourage--Mandel, possibly, and Loucheur, but principally Tardieu.[4] He would not put his name forward publicly, however, nor take any overt action which could be construed as electioneering, with the result that anything his frustrated aides did on his behalf risked an appearance of presumptuousness or a disavowal by their chief. Not until the day before the traditional Preliminary Republican Caucus did he permit a public announcement that his name would be offered, and then only because ballots had to be printed.

The 408-389 Caucus vote on 16 January in favor of Paul Deschanel, the sleek, urbane president of the Chamber, stunned the world. Clemenceau was informed as he left a Peace Conference meeting. For a moment he failed to comprehend, but then he made for his office to face his stricken lieutenants. Very calmly he informed them he would withdraw at once. They pleaded, tallies in hand, that victory the next day at the official National Assembly meeting was certain. He would have none of it: only an overwhelming endorsement would have made possible what he had envisioned for his presidency. The Caucus had freely judged otherwise.

Republican tradition--which he had never ceased flaying Poincaré for ignoring in 1913--plus his sense of personal dignity closed the question. He thanked them, they withdrew, and he went home, alone.

Deschanel was elected the next day--he went insane a few months later and was succeeded by Millerand--while Clemenceau, cheerful as a larking schoolboy, drove off to visit dear Claude Monet, to whom *la grande politique* and Very Important People were utterly inconsequential. On the 18th he tendered his resignation as promised, and on the 20th he presided at the last Peace Conference session of the current series, a nostalgic occasion marked by moving tributes from Lloyd George and others. Afterward, he saw the prime minister off at the station. The latter sought to cheer him up: "The public soon forget." "They will not do it [to you] quite like this in England," he replied--offering what proved to be a poor prediction of what would happen to him in turn two years later.[5]

On the 21st he handed the reins to Millerand. He offered to brief the new premier but was dryly told not to bother. He would not be needed any more.

II

"This time it's the French who're burning Joan of Arc," Lloyd George had cracked when informed of Clemenceau's defeat. Why had he lost? The deed was done by secret ballot in a caucus of politicians of whom a small majority had found one reason or another to vote against him at least in a preliminary canvass. In a general sense the vote no doubt reflected the widespread desire to close out the wartime regime, which Clemenceau symbolized, and return to peacetime ways and institutions--the same desire which would bring down Churchill in 1945. To that extent Lloyd George's quip was an apt description.

But there was more to it than this. Clemenceau had refused to take even minimal precautions. Such aloofness smacked of overweening pride. The office should seek the man, it was said, but the adage had always been honored in the breech by maneuverings worthy of the cardinals of Avignon in a papal conclave. The new Chamber contained a large Catholic contingent, for example. In his speech at Strasbourg (4 November) during the Chamber election campaign, he had extended a small olive branch to them when he praised a formula presented by the Alliance Démocratique and approved by Cardinal Amette stating that "the laicity of the State should be reconciled with the rights and liberties of all citizens regardless of the belief they profess." The lay laws, he said, must be "integrally maintained" and liberty of thought and conscience assured, but beyond that there should be "large horizons of tolerance."[6] Nevertheless, he had refused opportunities to promise renewal of relations with the Vatican, and his reputed intention to apply the lay laws rigidly to Alsace-Lorraine had induced its sizeable Catholic delegation to cast (to its chagrin) a protest vote which it intended to reverse at the official election.[7] In contrast, Deschanel, who had pointed his whole career toward the Élysée, had made certain he got an endorsement from Rome.

Furthermore, he had shut Parliament out of the peace talks and too often had handled Foch, who had many sympathizers, rather tactlessly. His choice of Millerand to succeed himself inevitably had awakened jealousies and animosities among sundry aspirants. His successes had shown up the failures of others, notably Briand, who (with Barthou's help) made himself the maestro of the opposition. Briand knew Clemenceau had at his disposal the Lancken dossier on his contacts with German intermediaries in 1917, including pieces indicating he had continued them without the government's knowledge until at least 13 January 1918;[8] and it was reported back to him that Clemenceau had said, "If I'm elected president for seven years, Briand will be stamping his feet in the cold outside the presidency of the Council."[9] His political future at stake, Briand purred in every receptive ear: common cause with erstwhile Socialist comrades and Radicals sympathetic to Caillaux and Malvy; bland insinuations to Catholics about the scandal of a civil funeral at the Élysée unless, of course, the old man merely lapsed into protracted senility. Clemenceau surely would not confine himself to opening exhibits and bestowing decorations but would govern, withering everyone in his shade, putting his minions in power, and closing the door to anyone who crossed him. For the *patriotardes* who had gotten elected chanting his name, there was the Versailles treaty. Already America was walking away, and *perfide Albion* would surely follow: *la Victoire* was looking more and more like a mess of pottage which an aging idol had gotten in barter for the birthright on the Rhine.

And so forth. It's enough to say that there were reasons enough. He had long resisted entreaties to run. He had let himself be persuaded, hence perhaps in part had not worked to win because he really did not want the office badly enough. He told his intimates that he wanted to continue to live at his apartment, to delegate ceremonial duties, and to be able to visit the countryside and the seashore. And he suspected he was not temperamentally fit for the job: "I shouldn't have waited a week before going off the deep end," he joked afterward.[10] It is hard to disagree: one can scarce imagine a post less suited to him. If Poincaré had failed to make something of it, a man of his temperament would have had no chance whatever. Yet in cold truth he *had* wanted it. He did want a reward, the laurel of his country's highest office for fifty years of service to her, and coming "as if from Heaven." But it didn't come. As he admitted to Sisley Huddleston later, "Well, it was a foolish weakness of an old man to ask for such compensation," and he laughed without bitterness.[11] Yet the desire also had worn a Janus face: "It would be the most beautiful coronation of my life to be beaten by a Deschanel," he had unhelpfully told his aides.[12] Indeed it would. There had always been something of the artist about him.

III

Clemenceau was four months into his seventy-ninth year when he retired, only nine months short of having spent sixty years in public life. Nearly ten years remained to him. It bespeaks the man that he turned them to account. He had always lived a full life. For all his growlings, silences, and incredibly mordant outbursts, he was not one to settle into a slough of self-pitying bitterness at being dismissed--like Bismarck, to whose sad decline he had once devoted some obituary lines.[13] His spirits had always been well-served by remarkable recuperative powers; a good night's sleep or a day in the country could cancel out weeks of accumulated fatigue. "En avant!" he had cried in 1893. On 4 February 1920, barely a fortnight after he walked out of the ministry of war a free man, he went off to Egypt at the invitation of the British government "to see if Cleopatra is still a beauty"[14] and to verify an hypothesis that Greek art had been inspired by the Egyptians. He had planned to take this trip back in 1911 but had cancelled it at the last moment.[15] He unstintingly indulged his passion for ancient history in visits to temples and monuments, while the hospitality of his English hosts wanted nothing in tact and cordiality. It took some arguing, however, to get him to give up an idea of retracing part of the Marchand Expedition's (1896-98) route through the swamps of the Sudan, but he did go beyond Fashoda on the upper Nile. On his return to Cairo, however, he fell seriously ill from a tracheo-bronchial ailment and had to cancel a visit to Palestine.

He returned to Paris in late April. July was spent at Vichy and August at the Bernouville property, which he had decided to sell, and at a Vendée seaside cottage, "Belébat," near Saint-Vincent-sur-Jard, which he had discovered on a trip to the Vendée with Mordacq back in November and which was to become his regular summer retreat. Then on 22 September he left Paris on a six-month journey through South Asia, arriving back on 21 March 1921. He stopped off at Djibouti (his sole visit to a French colony during his lifetime[16]) and then toured India, Ceylon, Burma, Singapore, Java, and Bali as a semi-official guest--an almost royal progress (sometimes by special train) which included a couple of tiger hunts (he shot two, Reuters announced), a trip to the Khyber Pass, and pilgrimages to an endless roster of monuments and holy places. Britain's Indian empire was at its most imposing, but he thought it an anachronism. When asked for his impression of the recently finished viceregal palaces at New Delhi, he replied he was thinking what magnificent ruins they would make someday.[17]

The voyage fulfilled a lifelong dream and stimulated him to start a vastly ambitious book on philosophy, science, and civilization, a kind of grand summing-up of all he knew. He had had such a project in mind for his retirement years for quite some time. On 28 March 1918, while returning with Loucheur from a trip to the front, for example, he had talked about doing a book on Man and the Universe, devoting three years to research and three to writing--after which, he said, he would die in the Vendée "in the company of peasants but above all of dogs, of animals."[18] Despite the daunting dimensions of the project, he saw *Au soir de la pensée* (In the Evening of My Thought) through to completion in two stout volumes, in

1927, the fruit of endless hours of reading, conversing with savants, writing, and rewriting.

IV

As usual, his financial situation was generally less than brilliant. He flatly rejected a purse proposed in Parliament and likewise refused to touch his pensions for parliamentary and ministerial services, turning them over to war charities instead. His trips to Egypt, Asia, and the United States (1922) were largely paid for by his hosts and by borrowing.[19] Nicolas Pietri, a prosperous telecommunications director and businessman to whom he had turned over *L'Homme Libre* in November 1917, became a very close friend, traveling companion, and manager of his finances, which he handled so as to permit his being subsidized when necessary without his knowledge. Sir Basil Zaharoff, the armaments magnate (Vickers-Armstrongs), made him a gift of a Rolls-Royce and the funds for his chauffeur which he accepted only on condition that Pietri retain title to it, and he used it only for trips, not around Paris. Later, after it had become quite shabby, André Citroën gave him a car, but when Citroën refused to accept payment, he sent the money to Citroën's charitable foundation.[20] In 1926, when his landlord proposed a raise in his rent for the rue Franklin apartment, which threatened to force him to move, James Stuart Douglas, the Arizona copper king, who had become a friend of his while serving as director of stores for the American Red Cross in France, secretly bought the whole building and made arrangements to increase his income to meet the new rent. Clemenceau was kept ignorant of the operation until it was too late for him to change it.[21]

Through all these vicissitudes he helped his situation not at all by continuing to be known as a soft touch, now especially among needy ex-*poilus* who regularly found their way to his door. As Stephen Bonsal recalled:

> The way in which he gave away money was often embarrassing to him but as I heard say on one occasion, "It is embarrassing to others too. Let us be fair--even to my bankers. How they squirm, poor devils! They bleat they cannot dishonor the signature of a man who saved France but on the other hand they beg me to have a heart and not compel them to break the banking laws and that apparently is what they do when they cash a check of mine when in some unaccountable way there are no funds on deposit.[22]

Professor Duroselle's researches in Pietri's unedited memoirs have provided invaluable information on his finances in these years.[23] His capital amounted to c.900,000 to a million francs. It was derived totally from the sale of the Bernouville property (August 1923), which he had bought for 40,000 and sold for 250,000; the sale of the Poussin painting, 250,000; and the reconversion of the 100,000 francs he had received for the South American lectures and which he had deposited in Buenos-Aires, coming now to 500,000 due to the rise of the peso. In his last years he got an additional 250,000 francs apiece for his book on Demosthenes and *Au soir de la pensée*, and in the last months a great deal for *Grandeur et misères d'une victoire*. Apart from these last sums, then, he lived through his retirement on about 50-60,000 francs per year in interest. The figures appear much more substantial than was actually the case, however, because of the fall of the franc. In 1926 it was stabilized officially at 22.5% of its 1914 value. Hence the "real" value in prewar gold francs was about 12,000 francs annually, only 25% more than his salary as a senator in those days. And that figure also errs on the side of generosity in terms of what it could actually buy and in light of the fact that the franc before stabilization had sunk far lower.

His memoirs surely would have brought a fortune. Publishers tried to tempt him with highly lucrative advances, but he refused all approaches with *boutades* and flourishes, as he did urgings to return to Parliament--"You shouldn't wait on the stairs after you've left a party."[24] Memoir-writing doubtless held limited natural appeal to a man who had always shown a certain taste for secrecy or mystery about his doings, a trait encouraged by his early exposure to the conspiratorial ways and atmosphere of pre-1870 republicanism. More immediately, he saw dangers in it. In an interview with Alfred Capus in 1920 after his return from Egypt, he observed, "I saw during the war how delicate are the impressions which sustain the morale of a country like France." That "moral force" was still necessary as before: "We must surround it with the same precautions...and eternally extend it toward concord even if we cannot hope to realize it fully." He wished to say or do nothing to awaken passions and hatreds.[25] To another interlocutor, in 1924, he was more explicit: "How could I say certain things which would bring into discussion certain men who are useful to the country? I don't have the desire!" And then he added a self-revelatory statement, speaking (the reporter noted) without a sign of disenchantment or fatigue:

> In my youth I was always angry. The spectacle of society, of its inherent injustices toward life, of men whom I saw driven by their wretched passions--all provoked my spirit [*humeur*]. But I have aged, I've done everything, and my time is too limited for me to expect anything of the world. So, I have buried myself in work. Ideas are the sole object I occupy myself with. I have won a great tranquility of mind. And, first of all, I have reached a conclusion which renders me more tolerant. *I believe that there is no person who can claim to be entirely assured of being right as opposed to everyone else.* Man wears himself out in grand enterprises from which he hopes for every miracle, miracles which they can't bring to him. And, furthermore, man wants to do too much, and in too little time.[26]

Nevertheless, until 1924 he did stay on the fringes of the political scene. In 1921 he wrote a long introduction for Tardieu's *La paix* (The Truth About the Treaty) defending his work, and in October 1921 at Sainte-Hermine and May 1922 at the Lycée Clemenceau in Nantes delivered inspirational speeches to sympathetic audiences. "How do you see me?" he asked the lycée students. "Perhaps like one of those old owls, beating their wings against the wind, nailed by our peasants to the doors of their barns for the crime, according to the writers of fables, of seeing clearly in the night."[27] At Sainte-Hermine he had some hard questions to ask about lack of enforcement of the Versailles treaty, warning, for example, of the risks of reducing Germany's total reparation debt since that "reduces by the same token the guarantees of security [i.e., via the occupation of the Rhineland] whose prolongation is...the sanction against Berlin's failures to honor its obligations." He especially warned against an easy complacency: "For having deserted the duties of the public place, didn't Athens and Rome bring to the abyss the high civilizations they had created?" And again he sounded a note he had struck in *Le Travail* in his youth: "What good will it do to say: *Our fathers were great*, if they, from their graves, judge us to be diminished?"[28]

From the sidelines he encouraged Mandel's and Tardieu's efforts in the Bloc National to ensure a strict observance of the peace treaties. Having no desire to return to journalism, in 1920 he gave his interest in *L'Homme Libre* to Pietri, who insisted in turn on putting it in a trust to be distributed after his (Clemenceau's) death.[29] But in January 1922 he lent his name as "founder" of Tardieu's *L'Écho National*.[30] He sometimes suggested a line to follow, but to Tardieu's disappointment he wrote nary a line. By then it was already obvious that the Bloc could be made into nothing resembling a coherent party. *L'Écho National* did no more than temporarily slow the slide from a hard-line defense of Versailles. It folded on 31 December 1923. When Tardieu later joined a Briand cabinet in 1925, he sent him a terse telegram--"Invincible repugnance for raggedy old slippers. Clemenceau."-- and, to Tardieu's great distress, closed his door on him for good.[31]

V

By all odds Clemenceau's most striking "intervention" was a speaking tour in the United States (18 November-13 December 1922) to plead the cause of France and warn of the dangers of isolationism, a trip he had once hoped to make as president.

General Pershing informally invited him while stopping by for a visit in October 1921, but it was an odd sequence of events in the autumn of 1922 that actually brought about the visit. The publication in the *New York World* of some exceedingly harsh judgments on America's conduct during and after the war by Rudyard Kipling, a friend of Clemenceau, brought a reporter from the *World* to "Belébat" to ask him if he agreed. He said he emphatically did not and added that he was prepared to go to America and say so in person. The *Écho National* at his behest published his reply on 10 September and subsequently his telegrams to the Associated Press and *The Times* of London. Not surprisingly they aroused huge interest and diverse official and unofficial commentaries on both sides of the Atlantic. After much negotiation the results were a contract from the *World* and its affiliated chain for six articles to pay the expenses of a trip and a formal invitation from New York by Colonel House and the newly founded Council on Foreign Relations.[32]

Occurring when it did--a month before an occupation of the Ruhr by France and Belgium (11 January 1923) after Germany's growing financial problems had resulted in her being granted (31 May 1922) a temporary moratorium for reparation payments--the tour aroused immense interest in the United States. Clemenceau, "the Tiger" (a nickname which positively enthralled the press and public), was in American eyes *the* French hero of the war, far surpassing even "Papa" Joffre and Marshal Foch, and the crowds he drew were huge and tumultuous: in New York, Battery Park became packed at daybreak when it was learned he had arrived during the night; in Brooklyn, 200,000 schoolchildren, let out to see the legendary "Tiger," thronged the streets; and in Boston the crowds were even greater. It was much the same elsewhere. Having never been the subject of mass attention and acclaim on such a scale in his own country, he seemed almost frightened of it at times-- and startled, too, by the presence of so many women at his speeches, accustomed as he was to wholly male-dominated political meetings in France--and soon took to staying out of public view whenever he could do so without offending his hosts. International interest was high too, although, ironically, not especially so in the French press, which, perhaps attentive to the Poincaré (*sic*) government's sensibilities, was represented by special correspondents only from *Le Petit Parisien* and (of course) *L'Écho National*.[33]

His tour, involving fourteen major addresses (plus the six articles) and six thousand miles of travel in twenty-six days, took him from New York to Boston, Chicago, St. Louis, Indianapolis, Dayton, Baltimore, Philadelphia, Washington, Chicago (again) and back to New York, and it furnished excellent copy for reporters trailing him to national shrines (including Lincoln's tomb at Springfield, Ill., and the Tomb of the Unknown Soldier for wreath-layings), a Harvard-Yale football game, Chicago's Art Institute and stockyards, the Bronx Zoo's tiger cages, and on a search for his old Manhattan haunts.

While in Washington he visited the invalided, slowly dying Wilson. They spent a few warm minutes together. "We laughed at old memories and it was good to hear that laugh again." When he mentioned the Fourteen Points, Wilson's face lit up. "He's as firm a believer in their ultimate triumph now as he was when he came to Paris," he told a reporter afterward. "Where was there such noble faith in self? And he was so touched when I told him that the chief round of applause at all my speeches comes when I have occasion to mention his name."[34] He came away shaken, however, by the

494

sight of "the great Known Soldier of the War," as he described him to Stephen Bonsal,[35] sitting rigid in the debris of his dream. He would not return the next day despite an invitation: "I felt too strongly that my presence reopened the wound he carried in his heart."[36]

The message he brought to America was clear enough in its main thrust--that the United States must reinvolve itself in Europe's affairs:

> You came too late and you withdrew too soon....Of all your war aims, tell me which you have attained....Remember, a nation may be the prisoner of its own greatness. It cannot choose to be great in history one day and small the next.[37]

And he left believing that his tour had succeeded both in putting France back on the front pages and in answering charges, which were rife at the time, that France intended to rely on force in the future rather than on international sanctions and cooperation. Unfortunately, the occupation of the Ruhr a month afterward rearmed the critics. In an interview with Walter Lippmann during the tour, he had expressed great reservations about such a move: "I fear the Ruhr. The German workers would make nationalist strikes. Shall we send in French soldiers against them?"[38] "If you came back," he said in Washington, "you might help the German democracy to organize some sort of government with which we might become friendly."[39] But as to what forms this "coming back" should take he was not at all precise, at times seeming to call for a resuscitation of the Guarantee treaties, at others speaking of little more than a moral assurance from America to back up a strong Anglo-French agreement about reparation, and on one occasion (in Philadelphia) suggesting a joint American-British-French-German agreement on Franco-German border security which prefigured the Locarno pacts of 1925.[40]

He found himself under even greater pressure to be tactful than perhaps he had anticipated, wanting to both woo and warn his hosts. After his first speeches, for example, he toned down his references to the German threat and put more stress on his hopes for peace: "Reconciliation must come. It must, I tell you. People aren't going to hate each other forever. Germany and France can't fight every fifty years."[41] And he also felt a need to defend the personnel and policies of his own government in public more than he would have liked to do otherwise; observers thought he was, if anything, overly concerned about how his words would be interpreted back home and hence had come off as less "tigerish" than they knew him to be from what he would say at times in private.

Washington, while courteously cordial, unsurprisingly provided him with his least sympathetic audiences. France's reputation was currently at a postwar low, with talk on all sides about alleged French oppression of Germany and desires to dismember her with American help, her failure to repay debts, her secret diplomacy, sabre-rattling, imperialism in the Middle East, and her use of black troops on Rhineland occupation duty--"the Black Horror on the Rhine." He dealt with this last-named issue, which was being widely ballyhooed in the press, from the start of his tour by pointing out that most of the "blacks" were Algerian Arabs anyway, that blacks were accepted as full and honorable members of the French army and had fought with great bravery, and that there had been only one convicted of rape in the Rhineland. His defense earned praise from delegations of American blacks, who also thanked him for France's hospitality to black servicemen during the war.[42]

In addition to his formal address--he declined an assured invitation to the Senate after he learned he would have to ask for it--he dined with Senator Lodge and was honored by a White House luncheon with a distinguished guest list. Accompanied by Ambassador Jusserand, he visited President Harding, who he thought handled the affair with tact but whom he found to be a man of "rather narrow" ideas.[43] Afterward, he ignored an oblique criticism of his charges of American isolationism in a Harding message to Congress and instead pointed out that the four-power pact in the Pacific (of 13 December 1921) which Harding had praised ought to be extended to Europe.[44]

"I am no longer worrying about the American people," he asserted to Lippmann near the end. He knew the limited value of speeches well enough and was neither deluded by cheering crowds nor rendered overly sanguine about the lasting effect of the sentiments aroused when, for example, he embraced General Pershing before the start of his speech in New York to a glittering, overflowing assemblage at the Metropolitan Opera. "His trip," wrote Lippmann, "has convinced him beyond the use of further argument that American needs will force Americans out of artificial isolation."[45] So he said for public consumption, and he may have well believed it, at least so far as he was thinking about the long future.

In the short term, however, his blunt warnings of tragedy to come if America did not take stock had had a hard time being heard over the Jazz Age din. And after his return to France he privately expressed considerable misgivings about what he had seen in America after a fifty-three-year absence: a rampant materialism, "economic meglomania"; unreconstructed racism still, notwithstanding an amazing personal generosity and socially democratic ambience; above all, "an incommensurable pride" replacing a basic modesty he had found before. That pride was terribly dangerous. He had warned, for example, that the United States would almost certainly have to fight Japan, and in that hour she might wish she had friends in Europe. Audiences, he noted, reacted as if they had never thought of such things.[46]

VI

The American tour had a curious sequel--a project for a private meeting with President Hindenburg of the Weimar Republic, for whom Clemenceau had considerable respect as an honorable soldier, to be accompanied by an appeal for peace to be made to the German democrats as (in the words of Stephen Bonsal, who was privy to the affair) "the initial move of a crusade in favor of political and physical disarmament." The project was the fruit of conversations and correspondence with Colonel House about the visit to the United States. House got assurances from Hindenburg regarding Clemenceau's safety, but the French occupation of the Ruhr in January ultimately put an end to the scheme during the summer of 1923. House returned to the charge in August 1924 and June 1925 while visiting Clemenceau; but the latter thought that for him to sanction the concessions being made to Germany, as House desired, was asking too much from him, and that in any event the opportunity, such as had existed, had passed.[47]

The voyage to the United States, to return, had taxed his strength, and he was glad to go back to his quill pens and well-thumbed books. After 1924 he wrapped himself in a public silence broken only by an Open Letter to

President Coolidge (9 August 1926). A great outcry in France in June and July over the decline of the franc and ratification of the Bérenger-Mellon Accord on repayment of the American loans had aroused resentment in the United States. The letter, which apparently was prompted by an anonymous letter he had received calling upon him to speak out, appealed for cancellation of France's war debt in view of Germany's failure to pay anything like what she owed in reparation, a cry of anguish--"France is not for sale, even to her friends"--which he thought could affect current talks. It was received in the American press as a near insult, while Coolidge said the matter was out of his hands. In short, it had no perceptible result. The French may have bled themselves white, but as Coolidge once dryly observed, they'd hired the money, hadn't they?[48]

Steady work on writing projects helped to assuage the bitterness which welled in him whenever he took stock of the latest serving (as he viewed them) of stupidities, weaknesses, betrayals, and rationalizations dished up by his successors. *Au soir de la pensée*, a two-volume, thousand-page corpus "without head or tail" (as he joked) of anthropology, biology, paleontology, physics, epistemology, cosmology, and *Kulturgeschichte* occupied him for six years, half of them in revisions which still left long stretches of it nearly unreadable. Its rambling, overladened sentences groan under the weight of the heaped-together fruits of a lifetime of intermittent study by a prodigiously active man. Only occasionally, in footnotes and asides and more toward the end, where he dealt with Civilization, does one find anything like the pithy style of the best of his earlier writing. *Au soir*'s failings didn't disturb him unduly--the project "amused" him. It was the book he had to write: "All my life I have lived in noise, and now I hear the muffled tread of silence."[49]

Like the philosophes, whom he resembled in his didactic impulse if not in his writing style, Clemenceau was both informed and ignorant enough to dare to offer resumés of whole fields of knowledge.[50] *Au soir*'s science, indeed, was often passé, its philosophy, and for that matter its raison d'être, a reincarnation of the materialist positivism stemming from the Ideologue continuators of the Enlightenment such as Cabanis and Destutt de Tracy whom his father had admired and which Auguste Comte had brought to fullest statement. All knowledge, Comte preached, must be organized in order to demonstrate its unity, and it must lead to a useful, not merely contemplative, end, namely individual and social improvement. Political revolutions, he held, achieve little unless men's ideas have changed through the discovery that altruistic service, not individual egoism, should govern conduct.[51] While Clemenceau endorsed these views, he refused to follow Comte into proposing a new religion in order to reach the masses, who Comte thought needed appeals to emotion. Science and reason, with an assist from the sensibilities awakened by the arts, would have to do the liberating work unaided by an institutionalization of dreams, which he thought was what religion at bottom really is.

The prospect of this work achieving great success any time soon, however, appeared dim. He experienced difficulty in fully reconciling the Darwinian struggle for existence, the world being "a trial of strength," with his democratic republican ideals, especially when he contemplated the nature of man himself and his place in the universe.[52] On the latter score, *Au soir*'s tone was even more somber, if possible, than his turn-of-the-century writings. Man is but "a gleam in the dark storm," a creature who "conceives grandly and persists in living meanly....The victim of Golgotha presiding at the stake! That is the basic fact of human history."[53] And the Universe cares not:

> Regardless of the point in mental evolution which we may have attained, at some time in the indeterminate regions of space into which we are blindly rushing our planetary system is bound to slowly fail us, and the grandest achievements of humanity will be wiped out.[54]

The most striking thing about the book--aside from the fact that it was attempted at all by a man in his eighties who surely had earned repose--was that this "apologetic of death," as a critic called it,[55] stopped short of the despair to which it logically tended. As had happened before, Clemenceau's overmastering will forbade it.

> Every passing day affords me proof that I am renewed through the continuous action of emotional understanding. I intend to cling to it with all the strength of my will. I do not

know much, but I cannot consent to have anemic ignoramuses pretend to prove to me that I do not know what I do know.[56]

And in the end he found refuge again among the Stoics:

> I do not seek to adapt the eternal Cosmos to the especial exigencies of my life, which is no sooner come than gone. We are not gods; that is the great discovery that I allow myself to submit to my contemporaries. May I be permitted, nevertheless, to prefer man's estate to that of the snail, and since I am a man in the course of evolution, to seek to develop my knowledge to the point which will give me the most comprehensive view of my earthly transit?[57]

Man is not the measure--so be it. But he would be a man, for all that.

VII

In the summer of 1925 he put *Au soir* aside to write a short life of Demosthenes which appeared in a collection ("Nobles Vies--Grandes Oeuvres") promoted by Marguerite Baldensperger, the wife of a Strasbourg (later the Sorbonne and Harvard) professor of literature. Thereby hung a tale. Mme. Baldensperger, while in the grip of a serious depression due to the inexplicable death of her eldest daughter, approached him in April 1923 about doing a life of Lincoln. He proposed a Demosthenes instead. As a result of the frequent business contacts, sympathy drew them together and speedily ripened during the summer into an *amitié amoureuse* sealed by a pact: he would help her to live while she helped him to die.[58]

Over the last six years of his life, he wrote her nearly seven hundred letters, most of which were published in 1970 by her son. Interestingly, he never once mentioned her in his other letters, and his intimates, notably Martet and Mordacq, left no trace of her in their writings.[59] Professor Baldensperger, a rare soul, consented to an intimate relationship which restored his wife's mental health while bringing to a man forty years her senior (whom moreover he greatly admired) the feminine affection and attention his bachelor's life had so much lacked.[60] The letters, vibrant with life, reveal again, but more authentically than any of his works or even the recollections of his intimates, the charm, spontaneity, playfulness, sentimentality, and thoughtfulness he so often hid in public; and they have become required reading for anyone who would try to know the man. In the early years they frequently exuded all the anxious ardor of a swain smitten by first love--for love it was, without a doubt; but as time drew on he settled back, calmer and wiser, more like a doting, tenderly possessive father, giving advice, enjoying attention, but conserving his freedom. He conserved enough, in fact, to establish a similar, though much less intense, relationship in his last two years with a young woman, Marcelle Langlois, who served him as a secretary.[61]

Demosthenes was a divertissement, drafted in about five weeks and published in *L'Illustration* (12, 19, 26 December 1925, 2 January 1926) and in February 1926 for the series. He made no run at academic history. Besides, he thought that historians are "funny fellows" who complacently relate the worst horrors and end up excusing everything; he wanted judgments, moral judgments.[62] He wrote the book mostly out of his head, producing a high-toned essay on the character and situation of the great orator who had warned a fading Athens of the peril of Philip of Macedon and suffered exile after trying to forge a coalition of quarreling Greek democracies to oppose the conqueror. Merely to state the theme suggests what everybody saw: Demosthenes/Clemenceau. He would never admit the parallel outright, even in private, but coyly owned that readers might find some "interesting" descriptions of politicians and political habits.[63] One can imagine the pleasure he took in labeling the haughty, cynical Phocion (Caillaux?) a "defeatist." How often in the past he had compared France to Athens. Or had castigated the failings of democracies, "quicker to respond to seductive formulas than to facts."[64] There was, too, the familiar emphasis on will: "He willed, even to the end; that is all one can say. From the first days he could see that military courage lavished itself in vain if civil courage did not dare to employ it."[65]

The book is clogged at times with overwrought disquisitions, a familiar fault which he brushed aside with a remark that he didn't write "for cabdrivers."[66] He nevertheless crafted some passages of real power. His obituary for history's master orator was moving, and not a little suggestive:

> Was it nothing that he reached power without baseness, that he wielded it without fear, and that after his defeat he knew how to resign both it and life without remorse and without regret?[67]

VIII

It was a time for obituaries, a trial especially reserved for the aged. His sister Sophie died in March 1922. In 1926 he lost his two dearest friends: Gustave Geffroy, a steady companion dating back to the Latin Quarter and *La Justice* days; and Claude Monet. He had always numbered artists among his friends and acquaintances--Manet, Carrière, Sisley, Pissarro, Dégas, Cézanne, Toulouse-Lautrec, Raffaëlli, Rodin (whom he helped to gain recognition in the 1880s[68])--and was a leading proponent of the Impressionists in France, where they were much slower in finding acceptance than in Germany or the United States. But Monet was his special love.

As already related, he visited him frequently after 1909, and in retirement he made Sunday outings to Giverny a ritual. Two projects in Monet's regard gave him endless concern and trouble. One was persuading the great painter to undergo an operation for cataracts, which he at last succeeded in bringing about in 1923 with a mutual friend, Dr. Charles Coutéla, doing the surgery. The other was the completion and mounting of the *Grandes Décorations des Nymphéas*, the magnificent water-lilies series at the Orangérie gallery in the Tuileries Gardens.

Back in 1914 Monet had found in a cellar some water-lily paintings he had set aside, and Clemenceau, much taken with them, begged him in the strongest terms to push ahead with them.[69] During a visit to Giverny by Geffroy and Clemenceau a week after the Armistice, Monet proposed giving a couple of paintings to the state in honor of the victory, and it was probably then that the project was born to make a much more important gift: the *Décorations*.[70] The undertaking was quietly launched before Clemenceau left office in 1920. The contract with the state was not signed, however, until 4 June 1922, and further delays followed, with Clemenceau acting as intermediary between the state and his artist friend, whose eye problems, fatigue, recurrent bouts of depression, and continuing changes of mind due to an almost morbid perfectionism, demanded his constant, untiring solicitude. Finally, in January 1925, after Monet suddenly decided not to finish the project and did not tell him of his decision, Clemenceau, past patience and deeply hurt, washed his hands of the affair in an angry letter (7 January) to his old friend.[71]

Fortunately for the two (and for posterity), in late March they reconciled, Monet relented, and the project went forward to a completion--*the* completion probably never would have come--at Monet's death (5 December 1926). Clemenceau was by his bedside at the end, and at his burial he was asked to speak. Words failed him. A graveside photograph showed him a broken-down, shrunken old man.

Toward the end of 1927, the year *Au soir* finally went to press, his sister Adrienne, a gentle woman whose final sufferings much affected him, died of cancer. Only twelve days later, on 5 December, Albert suddenly died of angina. The blow was terrible, the worse for being totally unexpected. Twenty years his junior, Albert was as much a son to him as brother and of all persons the one closest to him. Through the winter of 1927-28 he was depressed, speaking seriously for the first time of death and dying while distractedly supervising *Au soir*'s English translation and burning his papers, which he had intended to leave in Albert's keeping. In May, however, he revived somewhat, having found a new project.

Claude Monet: Les Nymphéas, written for the same series as the *Demosthène*, was a pendant to *Au soir*, a bouquet of essays on art to complete the work on science and philosophy, and like *Au soir* a book he had to write. He found it difficult. Words came hard when dealing with aesthetics, and his brain and body tired with unaccustomed speed under the strain. He saw in Monet's intense concentration on the composition and movement of light a penetration of reality complementing that by science, for example comparing Monet's undulating light to Brownian movement.[72] Monet's painting of the same subjects under changing light conditions, he believed moreover, linked art to science's themes of evolution and relativity.

But as much as he admired Monet's art, it was the example of the man himself, notwithstanding all his exasperating idiosyncracies, which he found most compelling. Monet had given himself wholly to his ideal, a man of action who had triumphantly completed the lonely course he had set from his youth.[73] One detects in Clemenceau's lines a whisper of envy. Monet had fought and won; a life in politics at best wins only transient victories. *Les*

Nymphéas would live long after a treaty at Versailles had gone to ruin. Four months before he died he remarked to Martet, "Only the artists are on the right track. Perhaps you can bring the world a little beauty; you have to give up bringing it reason."[74]

IX

"Belébat," the fisherman's cottage near Saint-Vincent-sur-Jard, provided him a pleasant summer retreat during his last years. As a rule he would go down there for three or four weeks in April and May and two or three months between July and October. He rented the place for 150 francs a year from a local nobleman, who would have him donate the money to needy families in the neighborhood, and also paid the state three francs for the beachfront and one franc to a countess for the dunes. The low, one-story stone structure about twenty-five meters long by five meters wide plus a side porch and sun room contained a bedroom, kitchen-dining room, two guest bedrooms, and a servant's room. (Like the Paris apartment, it has been preserved as a museum, and attracts about 30,000 visitors yearly.) He brought down from Paris some familiar furniture, books, and mementos, and put up several stuffed animal-heads on the walls "for company." When questioned about them once, he cracked: "Believe me, they encourage me. At night, when I get up at the stroke of two to write a bit, if I am drowsy I stare at these brutes and say to them, 'You bunch of idiots, I'm still doing better than you!' Then I get down to work quickly."[75] No sooner, too, had he arrived than he had started a garden on the dunes in front of the house after being told on the best local authority that nothing at all would grow there. The result, which was three years in coming, was a deliberately unorderly mass of plantings of every hue, a miniature triumph both over and with nature and a continuing source of satisfaction and pride.

Strict privacy at "Belébat"--an ancient name of obscure origin and meaning--proved hard to come by. At first it seemed ideal. Since the road stopped short of the place, the last five hundred meters had to be negotiated by donkey cart. To his chagrin, a small hotel (still in operation) presently was erected on the stretch, the donkey path disappeared, and he found himself the subject of tourists' stares and cameras when he ventured outside. And needy or disabled ex-servicemen found their way to his threshold in the

Vendée as steadily as in Paris. To signal that he was in residence but at work and not to be disturbed, he would hoist a beribboned windsock in the shape of a carp, a gift from the Japanese ambassador.[76]

The Baldensperger and Langlois letters belie an impression created by occasional visiting journalists and conveyed even in accounts of some of his intimates that he was an isolated, lonely figure in his last years. In fact, he received a quite steady train of visitors--from Paris and elsewhere at home and abroad and from the neighborhood--and, as was his long-entrenched custom, seldom dined alone at the main meal of the day. But he saw most people by appointment, seldom more than two at a time, and as usual let no one person know all he was doing or whom he had seen. He also enjoyed the company of his servants, who in the old tradition were very underpaid but utterly loyal and discreet: his valet, Albert Boulin, and his wife, Marcelle; his chauffeur, Alfred Brabant; and a cook from the Vendée, Clotilde Benoui, whom he had known since his childhood. Attention had spoiled him a bit; he alternately complained of visitors and of their absence. Yet the image remains, too secure to dispel altogether: an old man at a horseshoe desk in Paris, wearing cloth gloves and an odd, multi-peaked felt cap once given him by a *poilu*, his quill pen scratching away through the quiet night hours; or sitting on a bench in his garden in the Vendée, gazing silently for hours at the sea.

X

The war, Versailles, and its aftermath filled his last months. He had neither wanted nor expected this ending. He had passed another difficult winter in 1928-29. Emma, his elder sister, died in November. Only Paul remained now (he lived to 1946), and their estrangement since the war continued, abetted by his sale of the Le Colombier farm where their father was interred. He had managed to buy back the gravesite, where he planned to be buried in turn.[77] The void opened around him by the train of deaths among his family and friends left him subject to waves of depression. Back in 1924 he had remarked to Mordacq that he had come to the conclusion that only one thing "really exists"--the family, by which he said he meant one's blood relatives and closest friends. They give you trouble and are a distraction sometimes, but when the most difficult hours of your life arrive they are all you have left; only among them do you find true consolation for "the bitternesses of life."[78] And now, one by one, they were disappearing. "I am aging, alas!" he wrote to Marguerite. "The evil is not to die, it's to feel old."[79]

In March Foch died. Clemenceau visited his bier but refused to honor an official invitation to the national funeral; he hated funerals, and the request came from his *bête noire*, Poincaré, currently premier once again. Then, in April, came announcements of a book of conversations with Foch recounted by Raymond Recouly. *Le mémorial de Foch* would rehearse all the complaints the marshal had made of the Versailles settlement and of Clemenceau's treatment of him, and would say just who had done his duty to France.[80] Clemenceau bit his lip: "You don't write polemics on a casket."[81] But the onset of spring had brought him almost glowing health. On 17 April, the day before the *Mémorial* appeared, he announced to Martet, "I was dead. They've resuscitated me. Too bad for them!"[82] Warnings could not dissuade him. He was off and rolling.

He finished a corrected draft of *Grandeur et misères d'une victoire* four days before he died.[83] The *Mémorial* set fire to a decade's accumulated tinder.[84] At times he wrote with furious inspiration, but devastating dry spells would follow. His memory alternately clouded and cleared, while aides searched about for materials. Presentiments of death began to haunt him: "Martet! Martet! give me just six months of life!"[85] Rehearsals of all the old quarrels turned into a dragging agony. The great soldier, so sublime yet so small--"Foch! Foch!...Ah! God!...Men!"[86]

The "finished" book was no memoirs, but twenty-three essays of uncertain internal unity, some on the wartime controversies--the unified command, the Chemin des Dames disaster, English and American manpower problems, the Meuse-Argonne affair, the Armistice--but two-thirds of them on the Treaty and its subsequent "mutilations." In public now, as he had frequently done in private, he expressed his shock at Lloyd George's reply to him during a trip to England to receive an honorary degree at Oxford (22 June 1921) when he had told him that after the Armistice he had found him "an enemy to France": "Well, was it not always our traditional policy?"[87] It was the mutilations, however, which became his real target, and Briand, but above all Poincaré, not Foch--and certainly not Wilson, whom he treated with respect and with few complaints save reminders that he had waited rather long to decide that the world needed to be made safe for democracy. Moreover, the mutilations were important less for what they amounted to as such than for what they boded for the future: *"Germany is arming and France disarming....*Our people have come to this, that they seem to like enduring provocations."[88] A final essay, "The Unknown Soldier," called all before the judgment of those nameless heroes who had done their duty to the end. It was only fitting that the last lines he left to posterity should sound a note which had rung through a lifetime of battles to move his countrymen to action:

> There are nations that are beginning. There are nations that are coming to an end. Our consciousness of our own acts entails the fixing of responsibilities. France will be what the men of France deserve.[89]

XI

The dry leaves of autumn came down. At the end of September at "Belébat" he suffered what was probably a mild stroke, akin to an episode he had experienced around 3 July 1927;[90] his pen fell from his hand and he had to be helped to bed. Once back in Paris he tired easily, his cough became worse, he got fluid in his lungs, and his appetite dwindled. But he drove on harder, hurrying now to finish. On 20 November, his last day of work, his daughter Madeleine came by and persuaded him to get out for a walk in the Bois de Boulogne nearby. He seemed up to form and walked right along. But the next day, about 11:00 A.M., he cried out and fell writhing to the floor. He had been careless of late about his diet, perhaps because during the past few years he had been controlling his diabetes with insulin. (He was one of the first persons to receive it after its discovery in 1922 in Canada, getting it through the diplomatic pouch.[91]) His excretion of toxic chemicals had slowed, and consequently uremia developed. The pain became intense, morphine was administered, and Sister Théoneste and his children were summoned.

In the afternoon of the 22nd he began to lose consciousness for long periods, and the next morning he sank into a coma after another bout of acute pain and a dose of morphine. Shortly after 1:30 A.M. on Sunday, the 24th, the engine refused to run any longer. A few minutes later the word that *Père la Victoire* was no more was passed to the crowd keeping vigil outside.[92]

His will called for private burial without ceremony beside his father. As directed, his iron-topped walking stick and a small casket containing an 1828 edition of Beaumarchais's *Le mariage de Figaro*, a gift from his mother, were put beside him in his coffin along with the remainder of the *poilus'* bouquet. At 2:00 A.M. on the 25th, a short cortege slipped out of Paris for the Vendée. Early in the afternoon that day he was lowered to his grave by some local peasants surrounded by his family and a crowd of friends and reporters who had made their way up the muddy road from Mouchamps to Le Colombier. A cold rain was falling, the Vendée rain he loved. Out of hearing and beyond the horizon, in Paris and all the cities and ports, toll guns boomed.

NOTES
CHAPTER XVI

[1]   Lloyd C. Gardner, *Safe for Democracy: The Anglo-American Response to Revolution, 1913-1923* (New York: Oxford University Press, 1984), p. 270, quoting the Secretary's notes of 11, 12 Dec.

[2]   See JOC, 23 Dec. 1919, p. 5335-5338, his last speech in Parliament. He won a 434-63 vote of confidence.

[3]   See Sherwood, *Georges Mandel and the Third Republic*, pp. 52-53 *passim*. Georges Wormser replaced Mandel as *chef de cabinet* when Mandel won election to the Chamber in Nov.

[4]   See Duroselle, *Clemenceau*, p. 852. For details below see especially Wormser, *La république de Clemenceau*, pp. 392-423, *passim*.

[5]   Lloyd George, *War Memoirs of David Lloyd George*, 2:1607.

[6]   Jean-Marie Mayeur, *Un prêtre démocratique, l'abbé Lemire, 1853-1928* (Castermann, 1968), p. 546; and GC, *Discours prononcé...à Strasbourg le 4 novembre 1919*, pp. 12-13.

[7]   See P. Cambon, *Correspondance*, 3:376; and Maurice Schumann's account of Robert Schuman's recollection in *Georges Clemenceau* (Coll. Génies et Réalités), pp. 253-255. The Chamber voted on 30 Nov. 1920 to renew relations with the Vatican, which was done in May 1921.

[8]   See Wormser, *La république de Clemenceau*, pp. 492-497; and Ribot, *Journal d'Alexandre Ribot*, pp. 280-284. Duroselle (*Clemenceau*, pp. 852-853) doubts the pieces, if authentic, were especially compromising.

[9]   Édouard Bonnefous, *Avant l'oubli: La vie de 1900 à 1940* (Laffont/Nathan, 1984), p. 199. See also Raphaël-Leygues, *Georges Leygues*, p. 219.

[10]   Martet, *Clemenceau*, p. 315.

[11]   Sisley Huddleston, *In My Time: An Observer's Record of War and Peace* (New York: E. P. Dutton, 1938), p. 229. See also pp. 98-99 above.

[12]   Wormser, *La république de Clemenceau*, p. 404. He and Deschanel had fought a duel on 27 July 1894 over the latter's remarks in the Chamber regarding the Norton charges. He cut Deschanel's brow with his epée. See JU, 27-29 July 1894. See also p. 104 above.

13   GC, *Au fil des jours*, pp. 361-376, on Bismarck's memoirs.

14   Altieri, *Nicolas Pietri*, p. 50.

15   André Maurel, *Clemenceau* (Éditions de la Nouvelle Revue Nationale, 1919), p. 55. Maurel was to have accompanied him.

16   See Duroselle, *Clemenceau*, p. 869. My notes about photographs at the Musée Clemenceau indicate a visit to Cambodia (Angkor Wat?), but Mordacq, *Clemenceau au soir de sa vie*, which is the basic source for these years, says nothing on this.

17   Sir James A. Salter, *Personality in Politics* (London: Faber, 1947), p. 192.

18   Hoover Institution, Louis Loucheur Paper, B12.F10, Diary.

19   Prouteau, *Le denier défi de Georges Clemenceau*, pp. 11-74, contains memoirs by his valet, Albert Boulin, which say (p. 58) that he borrowed 25,000 francs from a sister for a trip to the United States in 1922 which he repaid in 1923. Duroselle, *Clemenceau*, pp. 894-895, makes no mention of this supposed loan, which in any event he could have repaid easily from the sums received for his contracted articles plus expense reimbursements from his hosts.

20   See Suzanne-Edith Peuméry, "Clemenceau vu par son valet de chambre [Albert Boulin]," *Historama*, no. 18 (1985), p. 67; Prouteau, *Le denier défi de Georges Clemenceau*, p. 58; and Duroselle, *Clemenceau*, p. 895. Boulin came to him in 1919 from service as Zaharoff's valet. Duroselle, however, says he got the Citroën after his return from Egypt, donating its 10,000 fr. price from the 15,000 fr. he gained (due to the franc's devaluation) from conversion of the remainder of the "rather important" amount of pounds sterling provided for him for the trip to Egypt.

21   See Douglas, "Clemenceau," pp. 29-30; and Robert Paul Browder and Thomas G. Smith, *Independent: A Biography of Lewis W. Douglas* (New York: Alfred A. Knopf, 1986), pp. 11-12, 60. In 1930 the title passed to the Société des Amis de Georges Clemenceau.

22   See Lee Scott Theisen, ed., "Two Kindly Grouches: A Note by Stephen Bonsal on James Douglas and Georges Clemenceau," *Journal of Arizona History* 18 (1977):94-95.

23   Duroselle, *Clemenceau*, pp. 894-895.

24   Letter to Mme. d'Aunay (18 July 1923) on an offer from the Vendée, in Wormser, *Clemenceau vu de près*, p. 254.

25   Capus, "Une visite à M. Clemenceau," *Le Gaulois*, 26 May 1920.

26   Saint-Georges de Bouhélier, "Une visite à M. Clemenceau," *Journal littéraire*, 2 Aug. 1924, p. 2, and 9 Aug., p. 4 (italics added).

27   Recalled by Tardieu in a speech, in HL, 27 April 1931.

28   GC, *Discours prononcé à Sainte-Hermine le 2 octobre 1922*, n.p. (italics in original).

29   See Altieri, *Nicolas Pietri*, pp. 41-42.

30   Wormser, in *La république de Clemenceau*, p. 444n., denies the story that Basil Zaharoff was a shareholder. Michel Clemenceau and his son Pierre were employed by Vickers-Armstrongs after the war.

31   Prouteau, *Le denier défi de Georges Clemenceau*, p. 41 ("vieilles pantoufles éculées").

32   See Wormser, *La république de Clemenceau*, pp. 448-452; Duroselle, *Clemenceau*, pp. 884-886; Hamilton Fish Armstrong, *Peace and Counterpeace from Wilson to Hitler: Memoirs of Hamilton Fish Armstrong* (New York: Harper & Row, 1971), pp. 198-208; and Walter Lippmann, *Public Persons*, ed. G. A. Harrison (New York: Liveright, 1976), pp. 63-66. The Musée Clemenceau has a substantial file of clippings.

33   See J. Kessel, "Le voyage triomphal de M. Clemenceau," *L'Illustration*, 9 Dec. 1922, p. 580.

34   *New York World*, 7 Dec. 1922, by Ferdinand Tuohy, the *World*'s Paris correspondent.

35   Bonsal, "What Manner of Man Was Clemenceau?" p. 73.

36   Mordacq, *Clemenceau au soir de sa vie*, 1:243.

37   As quoted in André Tardieu, *France and America: Some Experiences in Cooperation* (Boston: Houghton Mifflin, 1927), pp. 257-258.

38   *New York World*, 13 Dec. 1922, a long and interesting interview.

39   *Ibid.*, 6 Dec. 1922.

40   *Ibid.*, 10 Dec. 1922.

41   *Ibid.*, 13 Dec. 1922, to Lippmann.

42   In Indianapolis blacks presented him a loving cup. See *ibid.*, 25 Nov. 1922; *New York Times*, 2, 4 Dec. 1922; and Sally Marks, "Black Watch on the Rhine: A Study in Propaganda, Prejudice and Prurience," *European Studies Review* 13 (1983):297-334, *passim*.

43   Mordacq, *Clemenceau au soir de sa vie*, 1:241.

44   See *New York World*, 10 Dec. 1922.

45   *Ibid.*, 13 Dec. 1922.

46   Mordacq, *Clemenceau au soir de sa vie*, 1:247-253.

47   See Bonsal, "What Manner of Man Was Clemenceau?" p. 72; Duroselle, *Clemenceau*, p. 906; and especially Burnett, "Georges Clemenceau in the Paris Peace Conference 1919," pp. 525-526, citing House's diary.

48   Text in GC, *Grandeur and Misery of Victory*, pp. 424-426. Press reactions were summarized in *Literary Digest*, 21 Aug. 1926, pp. 12-13; not all were unfavorable, e.g., the *New York Times*. For the context see Melvyn P. Leffler, *The Elusive Quest: America's Pursuit of European Stability and French Security, 1919-1933* (Durham, NC: University of North Carolina Press, 1979), pp. 138-150; Silverman, *Reconstructing Europe after the Great War*, pp. 196-197; and Rhodes, "Reassessing 'Uncle Shylock,'" *passim*.

49   GC, *In the Evening of My Thought*, 1:6.

50   Martin du Gard, "Clemenceau," asserts that it was Charles Péguy who first saw him as a philosophe.

51   See Zeldin, *France 1848-1945*, 2:596-597; and on Clemenceau's philosophy, Appelbaum, *Clemenceau, Thinker and Writer*.

52   GC,, *In the Evening of My Thought*, 2:284. See Clark, *Social Darwinism in France*, p. 174.

53   GC, *In the Evening of My Thought*, 1:294 ("gleam"), 2:240 ("conceives"), 1:290 ("Golgotha").

54   *Ibid.*, 2:504.

55   D. Draghicesco, "La philosophie de Clemenceau," *Revue mondiale* 199 (1930):294.

56   GC, *In the Evening of My Thought*, 1:299.

57   *Ibid.*, 2:421.

58   GC, *Lettres à une amie, 1923-1929*, ed. Pierre Brive (Gallimard, 1970), p. xiv (on 21 June). Pierre Baldensperger (Brive) died in 1965. For "amitié amoureuse" and discussion of the few political references in the letters see Pierre Dominique, "Lettres de Clemenceau à une amie," *Écrits de Paris*, no. 294 (1970), pp. 68-75. See also Georges Wormser, "Lettres à une amie," *L'Actualité*, 9 April 1970, pp. 35-36.

59   See Duroselle, *Clemenceau*, p. 909.

60   Perhaps about this time he was "ripe" to fall in love. In May 1922 he told Colonel Repington, doubtless in jest, that he had recovered so thoroughly from a recent illness that he was thinking of marriage. See Ryan, "Lieutenant-Colonel Charles à Court Repington," p. 369.   Whether the relationship was also physical is a moot point. For what it's worth (probably not much), a startled Loucheur made the following note (dated 27 March 1918) of a conversation while returning from the front: "His regimen: gymnastics. The flexing muscles--the stretching muscles--'and in addition that conserves the faculty of coitus'!"   Louis Loucheur Papers, B12. F10, Diary. One suspects he was having fun at Loucheur's expense.

61   See Marcelle P.-E. Langlois, "Les dernières heures de Clemenceau," *Histoire de notre temps*, 1967, no. 1, pp. 133-165, extracts from 188 letters. She was hired in 1926 but did not go to the Vendée until Sept. 1927.

62   Martet, *Le Tigre*, p. 23 (1928).

63   Mordacq, *Clemenceau au soir de sa vie*, 2:77.

64   GC, *Demosthenes*, p. 55.

65   *Ibid.*, p. 157.

66   Mordacq, *Clemenceau au soir de son vie*, 2:91.

67   GC, *Demosthenes*, p. 147.

68   He helped get Rodin the commission for the statue of Victor Hugo at the Palais-Royale. Their relations cooled after (it was said) they quarreled in the early 1890s over the attentions of an American model, Selma Everdon; see p. 153 above. He also is said to have persuaded the state to purchase Whistler's *The Artist's Mother* when Whistler was not yet well known in France.

69   Letter from Monet to Geffroy, 20 April 1914, in Wildenstein, *Claude Monet*, 4:79; and Martet, *Clemenceau*, p. 235.

70   See Wildenstein, *Claude Monet*, 4:89.

71   See above, p. 210; also Robert Gordon and Andrew Forge, *Monet*, trans, John Shapley (New York: Henry N. Abrams, 1983), pp. 224-259 and *passim*.

72   See GC, *Claude Monet*, p. 95; and for a foreshadowing of these ideas, *Le grand Pan*, pp. 427-437. See also Julliard's essay in *Clemenceau et la justice*, pp. 106-107.

73   See GC, *Claude Monet*, pp. 75-77. "That was Monet; he threw himself into everything like a man possessed." Martet, *Clemenceau*, p. 214.

74   Martet, *Le Tigre*, p. 286.

75   Benjamin, *Clemenceau dans la retraite*, pp. 69-70.

76   See Duroselle, *Clemenceau*, p. 902, on this gift, which often has been ascribed to the crown prince and future emperor Hirohito.

77   According to *L'Ère Nouvelle*, 26 Nov. 1929. The sale may have occurred c.1914, assuming the authenticity of this report.

78   Mordacq, *Clemenceau au soir de sa vie*, 2:57.

79   GC, *Lettres à une amie*, p. 573 (10 Oct. 1928).

80   Recouly denied that Foch intended to publish posthumously; rather, he had delayed, then died suddenly. Raymound Recouly, *Le mémorial de Foch: Mes entretiens avec le Maréchal* (Éditions de France, 1929), p. iii. Clemenceau thought otherwise. Foch also had mocked his trip to the United States in advance in an interview published in the *New York Tribune*, 18 Oct. 1922. Clemenceau had made no reply. Other books of conversations with Foch, by Charles Bugnet and Charles Le Goffic, also appeared in 1929. Duroselle (*Clemenceau*, pp. 939-940) suspects that the anti-Clemenceau tone of Recouly's book owed more to the author than to Foch.

81   Martet, *Le Tigre*, p. 101 (10 April).

82   *Ibid.*, p. 103.

83   "Misères" has no good English equivalent. It means here wretched, petty troubles or distresses, not exactly "miseries."

84   In 1927 he had started a book addressed to "my American friends" but set it aside, later incorporating it in *Grandeur*. In Oct. 1928 he mentioned (in *Lettres à une amie*, pp. 570, 572) a mysterious project; again, he may have begun something which found its way into *Grandeur*.

85   Martet, *Le Tigre*, p. 154 (13 May).

86   *Ibid.*, p. 276 (16 July); punctuation altered.

87   GC, *Grandeur and Misery of Victory*, p. 113. As Watson says (*Georges Clemenceau*, p. 388), the exchange was jocular, but Clemenceau, "brooding over the evolution of British policy, took it with deadly seriousness."

88   GC, *Grandeur and Misery of Victory*, pp. 391-392 (his italics).

89   *Ibid.*, p. 405.

514

90   See GC, *Lettres à une amie*, pp. 428-437, *passim*. He was sick for two weeks.

91   See Duroselle, *Clemenceau*, p. 1043.

92   See especially Robert, "Un médecin politicien, le docteur Georges Clemenceau," pp. 87-88; Wormser, "Lettres à une amie," p. 36; and HL, 25 Nov. 1929.

CHAPTER XVII

A Life at War

The lives of few public figures in modern history can match Georges Clemenceau's in drama and epic sweep. Moreover, as a grand life in politics as such, it was quite out of the ordinary. What is one to make of a man who spent over five decades in the *métier* at the highest levels, yet who with notoriously few exceptions despised politicians--"the monkeys and pigs who govern us"[1]--and who led his country's government barely five years; who was a decade past the customary retirement age when he reached the summit of his power and fame; and who was called to leadership at that moment "against all parliamentary arithmetic"?[2]

Since he left no proper memoirs and destroyed most of his papers, his own appraisals of his achievements can be found only in stray remarks jotted down by others. In tenor they exhibit a becoming modesty in a man who, although not vain, was undeniably proud. A statement recorded by Mordacq in 1922 typifies the genre:

> I've had everything, in excess. I've been violently criticized, much abused. I've been suspected of all sorts of crimes; I've often even been accused of having sold myself to England. I really should have said to Lloyd George, "Since you've bought me, what are you waiting for to pay me?" On the other hand, they've woven unmerited laurels for me.
>
> Yet, I've done nothing extraordinary; I was there when I was needed. *Voilà tout!*[3]

He was far more inclined to ponder the meaning of life in general than what he himself had done, as witness his last writings or observations--like one to Violet Milner in 1928: "I'm glad to have lived. I do not want to begin again. I should now like to die. Life is a fine spectacle, only we are badly placed for seeing it, and we do not understand what we see."[4] His terse instructions for his unceremonious burial likewise are suggestive, although a family tradition of anonymity in death surely played a role.

It is a striking feature of his case that contemplation of his personality and its expression in action has continued to arouse more interest, as it did in his lifetime, than consideration of his specific achievements. Certainly no assessment should ignore the latter dimension, but the feature noted here provides good reason to give pride of place to the "existential" Clemenceau. His life's meaning is best perceived in his *living*. "A life is a work of art," he once wrote. "There is no more beautiful poem than to live fully."[5] And he defined life as, in essence, struggle. Hence his became a life "at war." Put another way, the dictum "I make war" held for him something well beyond its transient meaning.

In this existential context Georges Clemenceau was a great instrument of the public conscience, above all a great citizen--the title to which he aspired above all others. He was a person of marked individuality, which the liberal society of the nineteenth century did not discourage. By the same token, in being in principles a democratic radical of the Old Left, in habits and demeanor a Victorian country gentleman, and in his earthiness and taste for concrete realities a peasant, he never felt fully at home in twentieth-century industrial, mass society. He was, moreover, a striking example of a breed which after 1914 sadly dwindled toward extinction: a top-rank political figure of very broad and very high culture. Can one readily imagine a late-twentieth century politician spending a cheerful evening after a fall from office (as he did in 1909) with the likes of Paul Dukas, Gabriel Fauré, and Claude Debussy; or engaged in earnest conversation with a colleague (and furthermore surrounded by an intent group of deputies) about the precise rendering and context of a quotation from the classics which had been employed in debate; or in retirement writing books (never mind how profound) about Monet, Demosthenes, and the philosophical implications of the Second Law of Thermodynamics? Talented he was, exceptionally so. His mental processes functioned with superb facility, although his thought usually ran at more speed than depth and his rapid, impressionistic judgments of persons not infrequently served him badly. If he too often allowed himself to become wrought up by petty annoyances or distracted by personal conflicts, he could recover seemingly at will to meet grand situations or sudden emergencies, acting on such occasions, as one of his intimates marveled, with "stupefying ease."[6]

It was often said that he used his talent destructively, that his career was "made of ruins." It must be pointed out, however, that his reputation as a great ministry-wrecker, while deserved, took on from an early date almost mythic proportions. His visibility in such affairs often exceeded his reach. He might deliver the *coup de grâce* in a memorable summation speech, but his followers alone usually comprised only a minority of the hostile majority.[7] In any event, it would be truer to say that he frequently alienated people to no constructive end, pursued foes--Ferry, Delcassé, Briand, Poincaré, the Roman Catholic Church--with near manic relentlessness, preferred to play his own hand rather than build a party or lead a movement, and was no originator of grand, constructive ideas or programs. In this last regard, he accepted with few emendations the intellectual capital bequeathed him by his father: the youthful author of *De la génération des éléments anatomiques* is easily recognizable in *Au soir de la pensée*, the cocky essayist of *Le Travail* in the scarred fighter of *L'Homme Enchaîné*.

But to say that he misapplied or dissipated his talent is to misapprehend where it most concentrated itself. He was an *animateur* who functioned with greatest effectiveness in the roles of critic and teacher. (Save perhaps for his will power, it was this latter role that exhibited his most marked inheritance from his mother.) When he joined the *Dépêche de Toulouse* in 1894, he told Maurice Sarraut he wanted to concentrate on "the education of the people."[8] If he soon found himself writing mostly about politics, it remains true that even in this discourse he continually exercised a didactic impulse. As a critic he brooked few equals, and in brute energy was beyond compare. He exercised, unrelentingly, an extraordinarily strong, finely-tuned power of observation on everyone and everything in its sweep, whether in Parliament, in council, in social gatherings, at the theater, in art galleries, on a battlefield, traveling, or out hunting. From observation flowed his speaking and writing--courageous, often witty, unsparing to the verge of maliciousness, the machine igniting to running speed and snarling off, sometimes on byways but always en route.

He went his own way, surmounting bouts of discouragement and depression, fighting the daily battle to victory or defeat while trying to remain true to what he thought. Blessed with a tough physical constitution and exceptional recuperative powers, which were tested by a growing catalog of ailments capped by diabetes, he was able to push the struggle to an epic length. Being what he was and doing what he did, it would have been no surprise if he had finally failed to reach the very peak in politics. The system made a place for him, for the culture of the Third Republic was nothing if not accommodating; but not in the highest offices, at least for more than a mere sixty-five months, unless he could reconcile himself sufficiently to meeting the conditions--which at bottom he was unwilling to do. If the 1906-9 ministry can be regarded as something of an exception, he still had more or less imposed himself by making himself potentially more dangerous outside a ministerial combination than he might be on the inside. He wanted to make things happen, *faire marcher les affaires*, but the system seemed designed to conserve equilibrium, adapted with almost biological intricacy to the requirements of what has been dubbed "the cellular society."[9] It had no ready room for him at the top until it needed a character to rise above it and whose persona linked it to a glorious past--to the Great Revolution, and more the Revolution of 1792, of *la Patrie en danger*, than of the constitution-makers of 1789. As he said, he had the good fortune to be present when his moment arrived. He was seventy-six, more than a decade older than Winston Churchill would be when *his* moment came, but--maybe the most striking thing about him, truly awe-inspiring--he still was ready to seize and to use it to the very limit.

Only slightly less remarkable was how he spent his last years after the cheering stopped. The defeat of 1920 no more stalled the machine than had those of 1871, 1893, 1900, 1909, and 1916. He filled his final passage with voyages, reading, contemplation, correspondence, gardening, conversation, and writing, writing, writing. And the end came, as it should, in battle, with rest at last in an unnamed grave.

"All great men are humbugs," he joked once to Bonar Law.[10] We think we know what he meant, certainly if he were only out to puncture their pomposities or to blow away the fog of indiscriminate praise that usually comes to envelop them. There is, however, a characteristic he may have had in mind if only subconsciously, one which Professor Duroselle has well described:

> ...all great men tend to be narrowminded, to oversimplify and to possess overriding personal convictions....A great statesman cannot also be a subtle intellectual, fond of distinctions, and so preoccupied with judging all aspects of a question that absolute certainty is denied him. Bismarck, Hitler, Adenauer, Clemenceau, De Gaulle, Lincoln, Wilson, Palmerston, Churchill--each of these men, for good or evil, was in his way *a true fanatic*, and for this reason, each left his mark not only upon his country but upon the world.[11]

In his willingness to do battle, he surely ranked near the head of any such list, and in his case what has been noted as the "Manichean" character of political argument in France[12]--e.g., us/them, order/movement, *révolutionnaire/réactionnaire*, Catholic/anticlerical, patriot/emigré, worker/bourgeois-- suited his naturally confrontational character to perfection. By this criterion, Clemenceau's foremost entitlement to greatness comes from his honoring--in superb style and for a lifetime--a commitment to fight for his ideas, for a better life as he conceived it for his fellow man.

II

As for what he concretely accomplished, his claim is by any ordinary standard secure, if on the whole less compelling. His achievements might be conveniently summed up by considering his role in four fields of activity: in bringing democracy to France; in promoting Radicalism and helping to found the Radical-Socialist party; in conducting the last year of the Great War; and in negotiating the peace. Two episodes, however, deserve at least passing preliminary mention, namely, his fight to obtain justice for Dreyfus, and his first ministry (1906-1909).

Once engaged, he conducted the Dreyfus battle bravely and on the whole skillfully, although in time he hared off too much into a strident anticlericalism and long before the end was preaching that gospel only to the converted. His bitterness over the pardon became too deep and longnourished; it made him appear--unjustly, really--self-righteous, lacking in humanity, and vindictive. Nevertheless, his writings on the Affair remain one of the signal achievements in the history of journalism.

As for his first ministry: it met with more failure than success, certainly if measured by what it set out to do. It is true that its chances were parlous at best, for the unity of the Left was a great mirage, rhetoric notwithstanding, and the Radicals in particular were undergoing at this juncture something akin to an identity crisis. Judgments on the ministry have been harsh and not infrequently colored by a certain animus. The epithet "Clemenceau the strike-breaker," for example, has entrenched itself even in otherwise balanced histories, and one suspects that, like Keynes' image of him at the Peace Conference, it will somehow live on forever.

It is fair to say, nevertheless, that Clemenceau was too combative by nature to function with optimum effectiveness in the circumstances of those years, which demanded high-wire balancings of firmness and conciliation. One wonders if a Briand would have done better. Quite probably so, although it has been remarked that in Briand's first ministry (which immediately followed Clemenceau's) his handling of labor questions closely resembled Clemenceau's--while, typically, reaping less blame.[13] Clemenceau showed evidences of statesmanship during his ministry, notably in his handling of foreign affairs, but he left an impression which hindered his recall to office except *in extremis*. That he was recalled at all nevertheless reflected a verdict that he had not failed altogether.

III

In regard to Clemenceau's role in bringing democracy to France, one must grant at the outset that any single individual could play only a modest part in so formidable an enterprise. Clemenceau deserves a respectable place among the fathers of French democracy during its most crucial passage since the Revolution. Historical research has done great service in pointing up how slow the democratizing process was and how much remained to be done when the Third Republic made its debut, especially in the countryside.[14] Such an appreciation is bound to shed a more sympathetic light on the oft-remarked "defensiveness" of Republicans under the Third-- how much they feared and fought remnants of the old authoritarian order of the French State, particularly in its Bonapartist guise, with its taste for

Caesarist leadership and penchant for viewing government as essentially a matter of firm administration. It is easy to overlook the obvious fact that all the leaders of the Third Republic until at least the turn of the century had grown up under the July Monarchy or the Second Empire and to a man had experienced personally or in their family some degree of political repression. Obviously, too, they could never forget that the Republic had been filched (or so they believed) in 1830 and strangled in 1851, and that the country had elected an overwhelming majority of monarchists in 1871.[15]

Clemenceau shared all these experiences and memories and was a preeminent exemplar of this defensive stance. Even after he quietly dropped constitutional revision as a result of the Boulanger affair, he was ever to be found defending the Republic, however "mediocre" its institutions (as he characterized them at Strasbourg in 1919[16]), from the latest assault of the "praetorians" of the Old Order, behind whom he seldom failed to glimpse the black legions of Rome. And fate made him late in life the chief defender of the Republic from the assault from abroad, for the regime surely would have foundered, as it did in 1940, if France had lost the war. His experience in conducting this latter defense confirmed his belief in the end that institutions are less important as such than the character of those running them. At Strasbourg he expressed doubt that the government really needed stronger executive powers: "The very simple truth...is that what ails executive power is less an insufficiency of its means of action than the too frequent deficiency of the characteristics needed to meet the responsibilities of office."[17]

In carrying out the democratizing mission, certainly during the first two decades of the Republic, Gambetta and Ferry--the former as the greatest inspirer and organizer of the early Republic, the latter for his work in building the all-important educational system for the enterprise--must rank well ahead of Clemenceau, who held no office and attached his name to no major legislative act. What he did do, better than anyone else and long after most of the founding fathers had disappeared, was to goad the enterprise on, constantly reminding those in power of what the ideals were (not least in importance, pricking their consciences about imperialism), taking them to task for faint-heartedness, and telling them that despite the temptation to believe that the word "Republic" was a talisman guaranteeing that the country's ills would be cured (a belief he had appeared to hold in his youth), a true republic must be *made*, and above all its values lived, if it were to be sustained.

Of all such values, Republicans usually assigned the highest place to the liberty of the individual. Certainly Clemenceau did. But he was--before Juarès' heyday, at any rate--the single most persistent (if usually unheeded) advocate in Parliament of the view that liberty for most men is meaningless in effect if they cannot organize to protect and further their economic interests and obtain protection against the major risks of existence-- unemployment, accident, disease, and a penniless old age. Without such assurance, the liberty of the individual is useful only to "the strongest," whose oppression of the weak, he never tired of saying, is humanity's oldest story. That he held such views, it must be added, makes all the more puzzling the "stupefying" absence (in Duroselle's words) of anything in *Au soir de la pensée* on social and economic affairs.[18]

The work went slowly, although more was done before the Popular Front, or for that matter before 1914, than is usually admitted; even Clemenceau was willing, in old age, to give his late Opportunist foes some overdue credit. To conclude, his role in implanting democratic ways and institutions was important, above all in cumulative effect, but subject to limitations, inherent or self-generated.

IV

Clemenceau is beyond dispute a towering figure in the history of French Radicalism and of the Radical-Socialist party, the Third Republic's most important party and certainly the most representative of its political culture. As such he assumes a certain historical significance, even if the Radicals as a party have ceased to play a role at all comparable to the one they filled from the 1870s to the 1950s. This much said, difficulties appear, for as a Radical he was at once typical and atypical. As noted elsewhere, he belonged to Radicalism's national organization, the Parti républicain radical et radical-socialiste, for less than a year (1909). By itself this proves little, for Radicals characteristically paid no more than polite deference to the national entity; it was the local committees which commanded their interest. It does, nevertheless, point up a feature mentioned before, namely, his lack of sustained interest in party building and organization. He did devote himself to them in the early 1880s and to some extent before then, but his activity waned in the wake of the Boulanger affair.

Boulangism split the Radicals. The majority, gradually and with regrets, went into opposition to the movement, an important effect of which was to push them into a basically defensive posture about the form of the regime. Constitutional revision, poisoned by Boulangism's exploitation of it, began to evaporate from the Radicals' programs, including Clemenceau's, hence sliding them closer to the Opportunists, who had opposed Boulanger all along. The Panama affair gave another shove in this direction, for its elimination of a number of the older Radical stalwarts, which the Boulanger affair had begun to do already, cleared the way for the arrival of a new generation of Radicals who wanted to get into power and who hence saw little merit in the kind of intransigence Clemenceau had exemplified.

The difficulties Clemenceau encountered in the Boulanger and Panama affairs, however, cannot be held fundamentally responsible for his failure to engage much in party affairs after the early 1890s. At most they propelled him in a direction consonant with his experience and natural inclination. His observation of American parties as a young man had implanted a scepticism about their worth. Sooner or later they degenerate into mere vehicles serving the ambitions of their members rather than the public good. Such, at any rate, was a view he frequently expressed during most of his career.[19] He liked to speak not of parties, but of movements which come together on an issue or to meet a grand occasion and whose apparatus and leadership is not permanent.[20] Because he never gave elaborate definition to what he meant, one is left suspecting that at bottom it amounted to a rationalization of the leader-loner role he assumed through most of his public life. Party discipline through free-form association around an ideal amounted in practice to no discipline at all. So far as he was concerned, that might be regrettable, but he did not appear to think that another mode of operation was in the long run preferable. In this connection his dismissal of Marxism, well-anchored though it was in philosophical disagreements, owed much to his rejection of the discipline it prescribed, it if did not always practice. A Jaurès could accept it while conserving an intellectual independence and working for change within party confines; Clemenceau could not--and hence could not altogether fathom Jaurès.

The more one ponders Clemenceau's career, the more one is struck by the impact on it of the Boulanger affair. It burned him badly. His judgment fell under suspicion, his reputation suffered as he squirmed away from the movement, his following divided to the benefit of the Moderates on one side and the new Socialist formations on the other, and it made him personally more of a target than ever. When the Panama scandals ripened and burst, he received painful retribution. It was disappointed Boulangists who despised him as a deserter who were mainly responsible for his defeat in 1893. Falling upon him as it did, when he was at what should have been the peak of his career and in mature possession of his faculties, the Boulanger affair and its malevolent offspring, the 1893 disaster, scarred his soul and set him in a role he followed for the rest of his days: a solitary fighter, knowing only temporary allies, imposing his leadership by sheer force of will and talent whenever the fortunes of the hour might open a way.

He remained, withal, the greatest spokesman of Radicalism in his time, and as such a preeminent founder of the party which took its name. But he was not a participant in its official councils nor, in many respects, its socio-political milieu. Although he was, as were so many Radicals, a man of provincial qua rural origins--roots which profoundly affected him, giving him a deep love of the soil and an easy camaraderie with peasants which showed itself most dramatically in his rapport with the peasant-dominated infantry of the Great War--he spent most of his life in Paris and was, with his quick, sarcastic wit and his love of change, color, and cultural pursuits, as "Parisian" as any native. His Parisian side alienated him from the bulk of post-1900 Radicals; likewise his authoritarian spirit, which grated on their easy-going, accommodative ways. Their "Republic of the Pals" manifestly was not his natural habitat. As did the bulk of Radicals in due course, he transferred his electoral seat to a southern, country district, but he ignored as much as he prudently could the purely local concerns of his constituency, the infighting among party committees and such which became the meat and drink of so many Radicals. Rather, it was in the sphere of ideas--ideology, if one will, although the word implies more rigidity than Radicalism thought desirable, valuing liberty of thought as highly as it did--that he was as representative a Radical as one could find.

Any resumé of the Radicals' beliefs or predispositions readily bears this out.[21] In historical discourse, for example, a reverence for the Enlightenment, but that of Voltaire more than Rousseau; likewise a reverence for the Great Revolution, à la Michelet, without class conflict, of 1792 somewhat more than 1789 or the Jacobin Republic and the Terror, and a persistent evocation of "our fathers" of that epoch, Danton and Carnot more than Mirabeau or, for the most part, Saint-Just and Robespierre; a detestation of Bonapartism and the Second Empire; little mention (unlike the Socialists) of 1848 or the Commune, but a ready reference to the *Seize mai* crisis (1877) and the Dreyfus Case; in political philosophy democratic, but after Boulanger retreating from populism to a defense of parliamentarianism; in economics and social theory protective of the small man and small enterprise, disliking industrialism and the grand bourgeoisie, but rejecting class warfare (or even the word "class") and Marxist theory in general; ambivalent about the state, wanting to use it to protect the citizen and bring him benefits, but deeply suspicious of its power, methods, and agents, especially high functionaries; in sentiment patriotic and nationalistic, tempered by a distrust of the professional army and by a universalist, humanitarian impulse inherited from the fathers of the Declaration of the Rights of Man; and finally--many would say, above all--anticlerical, regarding Roman Catholicism as the institutionalized ignorance of the ages, the greatest obstacle to that progress and enlightenment which surely will flow from the advance of Science.

Clemenceau followed in these tracks with remarkably few detours. After 1893 he was less doctrinaire, more inclined to adopt an empirical stance on particulars and seldom expressing a sentimentalized view of "the people." (In 1898 he was heard twitting John Morley, the keeper of the Liberal flame: "Where are you now politically? As for me, I am a nihilist. I have no set views!"[22]) His dropping of constitutional revision and his election to the Senate, that braking institution *par excellence*, gave clear evidence of a chastened view of democracy. His anti-clericalism continued unabated until the War, when admiration for the heroic conduct of priests and monks in the services led him to moderate its expression. In this connection it is worth noting about his life that it exactly coincided with the rise (from the 1840s) triumph, and decline of the anticlerical crusade; by the 1930s the crusade was in virtual eclipse, whereupon the Radicals began a long decline from which they have not recovered. Clemenceau's anticlericalism, however, stopped short of the extravagances of undiluted Combism. Providing church and state were kept rigidly separated, he would try to avoid taking measures which could be fairly deemed oppressive. Besides, he thought time was working against the Church and that it eventually would fade into irrelevancy.

To sum up, Clemenceau was arguably the most important single founder and persistent advocate of post-Second Empire Radicalism. As such he spoke for millions of ordinary Frenchmen who were unable to feel at home in Roman Christianity or Marxism but who wanted a government more democratic in spirit and more concerned with their welfare than that advocated by moderate Republicans of various stripes. It was one of the recurrent ironies of his life that Radical speechmakers seldom mentioned his name after he was gone. More often it has been Moderates and even Conservatives who invoke it--not in praise of his Radicalism, of course, but as a "man of order," the *Père la Victoire* of the Great War who prosecuted leftist "defeatists" like the Radicals Malvy and Caillaux, a foe of Marxism, and the man who had said at Strasbourg, "Between them [the Bolsheviks] and us it is a question of force." Charles de Gaulle, for one, was never laggard in paying his respects.[23]

V

About Clemenceau's role in the last year of the war, opinion has been all but unanimous that he furnished an outstanding example of wartime leadership in a democracy. That France emerged from the trial still a liberal, democratic society was no small tribute to him and to the labors of his fellow Republicans over the preceding forty years. Around 1911 he had remarked to Léon Abensour that "the French people are profoundly conservative, and at present more than ever. They know what they have and intend to keep it. What they have is the Republican regime."[24] Nevertheless, one need not venture far afield in French history to begin to appreciate the high risks which democratic institutions had run during this protracted, excruciating ordeal. If his civilian leadership had faltered and sagged toward defeat, it is altogether possible, even probable, that the military would have stepped in to take control with or, if it should come to that, without the leave of Parliament or the president.

Clemenceau is one of a very select group of historical personages who could claim that once upon a time they had "saved" their country. It cannot be proved, of course, that France would have lost the war if he had not been called. Despite her victory in Russia, Germany by late 1917 was suffering greater strain than was generally realized, and her allies were tottering. She might have lost eventually no matter what, or at best earned a stand-off. But at that moment her cause was still far from hopeless, for the Allies were in very deep trouble: Russia was all but out of it, and Italy staggering; Britain's armies were hemorrhaging in Flanders at a frightful rate; the United States was still literally and figuratively three thousand miles from being a present military menace; while France was bled-out, physically battered, and in the throes of a rumbling crisis of confidence. No method can definitively answer speculative questions, but it is always wise to heed what the parties to a dispute *thought* was the case, and in this instance they agreed: both sides believed that the spring of 1918 would bring victory within Germany's reach, closer than at any time since September 1914, and that for the Allies a French collapse would be fatal.

To press the case a step further, contemporary opinion on *both* sides came to attribute to Clemenceau a decisive role in preventing this collapse. All things considered, there seems little reason to question that perception. If he had failed, if his leadership had proved unequal to the challenge, who else *was* there at the time, civilian *or* soldier, who could have retrieved a situation as desperate as it was certain to be at *that* moment? France would have crumpled up; and in short order, doubtless, the cause of the Allies would have toppled into the wreckage. Such, for whatever it's worth, was the opinion of the ex-Crown Prince of Germany, whom an English correspondent, Henry Wales, interviewed in June 1920 at Wieringen, Holland. Clemenceau, he mused, was responsible "more than all the others" for France's victory, adding, "If we had had a Clemenceau, a man of his stature and of the courage of this Frenchman, I wouldn't be on this horrid little island, because we would not have lost the war."[25]

A catalog of particulars of Clemenceau's wartime performance, most of which have been discussed elsewhere, shows many more points of strength than weakness. On the domestic front, the vitally important problem of morale could not be met with quick solutions. As late as the Chemin des Dames crisis (early June) it was worrisome. In time he succeeded by employing various means. He stated difficulties frankly, refusing to sugar-coat, thus complimenting the people by not treating them like a flock of children. At the same time he manipulated a stern censorship in order to stem panic and protect relations with the Allies, but he was canny enough and sufficiently self-confident to allow free political criticism of himself and his government. He showed himself ready to be ruthless in order to get obedience, but he was selective in his targets, thus avoiding petty tyrannizing. He used the arrest of Caillaux to get across a message, for example, but he was able to dissipate a threatening witch-hunting atmosphere--which to some degree he had helped to generate in the autumn of 1917--by leaving cases in regular channels.

Finally, and arguably first in importance in affecting the public consciousness, he ran great risks to his personal safety in order to focus the country's attention on the suffering *poilus*, and he somehow was able to do this without appearing to be a headline-hunter. His success in raising the country's morale was hard-earned and in the end undeniable, a singular triumph. If, as someone put it after the war, he "belonged to that type of man ...for whom other men are willing to be killed,"[26] it reflected not just the kind of person he was but what he had managed to achieve in the early months of his ministry.

In administering affairs, he avoided playing the role of sole actor, interfering in every decision under the illusion that since he was ultimately responsible he must do it all. To husband his energy for larger matters, he mostly left his ministers alone to do their jobs, a wise and necessary mode of operation for a man his age. Coordination was not all it should have been, however, because of his disdain for necessary bureaucratic procedures and collective consultation, his love of rapid action, his taste for secrecy, and the general unpredictability of his reactions. He did need, and found, a few subordinates (notably Mordacq) who could steer him out of troubles in which some of his personality traits could land him. He struck a fine balance, too, with his generals, sharply watching and questioning them while not slipping into a belief--not uncommon among civilian war-leaders--that he was a military expert, hence leaving them free to act in their professional capacity.

Lastly, it bears repeating that in all these matters he acted within existing constitutional confines. On 10 February 1918, for example, he obtained decree powers to regulate production and distribution of foodstuffs. But he did so by means of a law passed by Parliament even though he could have simply gone ahead and used existing decree powers. He thus showed his respect for Parliament. So confident was he of his hold that he felt he could dispense with asking for full powers for this or that and neither sought nor used the lavish grants of extraordinary powers which governments obtained from the 1930s on when times were difficult.[27] In the summer of 1918 he alluded to this method, albeit with a modesty invited by the occasion, when he answered a compliment on his performance by saying, "I have done nothing, save to allow France to fight."[28] Fundamentally, his dominance, which in effect approached dictatorship, was in essence a moral dominance. For this reason, if for no other, his premiership acquired and has retained a high reputation as an exemplar of democratic leadership in time of war.

In foreign relations and on questions of strategy he kept his attention focused on the big issues, although his outbursts and his intense activity in a host of matters sometimes left on others a different impression. Georges Leygues, echoing in his diary complaints frequently heard from Poincaré and others concerned with foreign policy, remarked that "he does not study *les questions extérieures*, [but] treats and resolves them relying on instinct and his prejudices."[29] He put great emphasis, nevertheless, upon inter-Allied cooperation. He could quarrel with Lloyd George, for example, when he had to, but he knew how to keep disagreements from ballooning out of control or poisoning relationships. In dealing with the intricate problem of unity of command, he exploited his Anglophilic reputation and connections to good effect among the English and was fortunate to have enough knowledge of America to understand its problems and at bottom, notwithstanding his bouts with Pershing, its sensitivities. He cultivated the British commanders, Haig in particular, and this greatly helped to smooth the tortuous path he followed toward Foch's appointment. The problem of command in the Mediterranean, however, never found a satisfactory solution and to the very end generated nasty altercations with the British and Italians.

The Westerner-Easterner division about strategy likewise never was resolved to everybody's satisfaction and doubtless never could be because of all the hypothetical questions involved. But the weight of opinion rested (and has remained) with the Westerners, with whom Clemenceau sided from the start. In 1918 he had a powerful case, for it was the Germans who that year would get off the first shot to try to win, and *they* could win only by defeating the Allies in the West. The Allies arguably could win via the East, but they *first* had to avoid defeat in the *one* place where they could suffer *irretrievable* disaster. He never let himself be deflected from this analysis, and his stubbornness in its defense was critical in winning Lloyd George's eventual acquiescence.

Finally, when Germany and her allies began to cave in, he (and Foch) knew when it was time to call a halt--always a problem in the conduct of war. It was a controversial decision then, and even more so later on when German power waxed again in a far more malevolent form. Nevertheless, whatever the merits of a policy of grinding the Third Reich into the dust, the case favoring leniency in 1945 was much less persuasive than that which occurred in 1918. Germany by now had indeed lost the war, and everybody there knew it, even those who could not yet bring themselves to admit it. Given the exhaustion of both sides after the costly fighting in the fall of 1918, the prospects of another terrible winter with starvation now stalking the lands of the Central Powers, the likelihood of a desperate defense of German soil aided by the succession of strong river lines from the Rhine eastward, the probability that Allied leftists would raise an uproar if Germany's willingness to accept the Fourteen Points were brushed aside, the present or incipient chaos throughout central and eastern Europe, and the spectre of Bolshevism hovering everywhere over the shambles, it seemed sensible, let alone humane, to accept Germany's conditional surrender, which was what the "armistice" amounted to. Doubtless a desire to prevent the United States' leverage from increasing as her forces grew while others' declined also entered his, and Lloyd George's, thinking, but there is no evidence that it was as persuasive as the reasons cited.[30]

On the debit side of the ledger, the fumbling over policy on Russia might be assigned first place--unless it belongs to his failure to take truly effective measures against inflation and profiteering; financial policy left much to be desired. Until the summer of 1918 he had, partly by luck, kept clear of direct involvement in the Russian Revolution. The Czech Legion's revolt pushed things over the edge. Involvement did not assume truly damaging proportions before the Armistice, but by then he and his partners were too far into the quagmire to get free without a struggle. Meanwhile, his tactlessness in dealing with the sensitive Italians laid up trouble for the future, and the same was true of his run-ins with Foch and Poincaré as the war wound down. Likewise his throwing his weight around in the Pershing-Argonne affair, although the result was less hurtful to the future. Whatever he gained in these embroilments was not worth the eventual cost.

In strategy, while he had excellent reasons to push the Western view, he was perhaps too slow, or privately reluctant, to appreciate what the Salonika force could accomplish by attacking the opposing alliance's weakest members, and he stinted his support for it too long. The veterans of Franchet d'Esperey's army never wholly forgave him for it, nor for closing down their drive toward Vienna and Bavaria in the last weeks because of his new plans for an Eastern front in Romania and Russia. His handling of the Czernin affair likewise probably damaged chances for breaking the Central Powers apart, or so opinion has usually asserted. On balance, however, particularly when one examines the context of the affair, the criticism he reaped appears overdrawn, for reasons explained elsewhere. Failure to take a hard stance undeniably would have risked his domestic standing at a moment when the Germans were applying intense pressure.

To cite a final case, somewhat the same conditions applied to his failure to publish a more precise agenda of war aims. As noted before, he underestimated the damage such declarations could do to German and Austrian morale. If his silence served his purpose of keeping French minds on the business at hand and avoiding disputes at home and abroad about hypothetical matters, it also fostered suspicions of French ambitions which were unjustified in most respects and which sapped his negotiating positions at the Peace Conference. He never succeeded in dispelling these suspicions, and they lingered on, unhappily for France, long into the post-Conference years.

Looking back over his performance, one finds on balance no reason to disagree with his remark that if he had died at the Armistice he would have gone out a hero. The crowds at the Place de l'Opéra roared the heartfelt thanks of a profoundly grateful nation. He had entered into legend, and what followed could not efface it, whatever the oracles have had to say about the peace that failed.

VI

Of the Paris Peace Conference, whose labors closed his public life and whose tarnished reputation rubbed off on his own: It failed to bring more than a truce to a world through which the war virus has coursed since time out of mind. On an appallingly burdened situation it laid more burden still, which those charged with making something of it in the 1920s and '30s only compounded by their misperceptions, confusion, and collective flights from responsibility. About the best one can say of Clemenceau's contribution is that what was done might well have been worse but for him. He proved to be a first-rate negotiator, in any event, and of all the *grands hommes* of the hour he had the keenest appreciation of the factor which could best forestall another slide into the abyss--namely, cooperation among the great Western democracies.

He knew the treaties, that "collection of possibilities," would need revision, for his whole philosophy taught that nothing human is permanent, certainly not victory in a war. But he viewed the kind of "revision" undertaken in the last decade of his life as a prescription for disaster. It was the crowning mercy of his life that he did not live to witness Germany's remilitarization of the Rhineland in 1936 while a feckless French government and its sclerotic army stood by, impotent. It was the move which opened the road to all the catastrophes which followed--just as he had predicted it would to Charles Seymour in 1925: "But if Germany is allowed to fortify the Rhineland, then she would move against Bohemia, will be free to raise the issue of the Sudetenland, settle the question of *Anschluss* [with Austria], and take off in any direction she may decide."[31]

He was an old man, barely a generation removed from the Congress of Vienna and the oldest figure of note on the scene,[32] in temper sceptical and disabused, symbolizing in his presidency of the Areopagus the ancient sad truth that in war old men make the decisions while the young pay the price. He put forward no grand vision of the future which could answer the yearnings of the coming generation. The lesson he had learned and lived-- that life is a perpetual struggle toward a distant, often dimly perceived good-- brought no solace at an hour when the world was weary with struggle and wanting to believe that the debacle had not made a cynical joke out of two centuries of belief in progress. Wilson presented a vision but cracked under the strain of trying to square it with the demands of his office and of a world in which force, not reason, was still the final argument; Lloyd George spoke well of visions, and even better about what Britain wanted; Clemenceau thought he knew more than they about the way of the world with visions.

Only in the 1970s did it become possible, because of the rules of access, to study the inner workings of the French government during the Conference and the early 1920s. (The destruction or dispersal of much material in the Quai d'Orsay's archives in World War II will never permit as full an examination as is possible in many other countries.) Research thus far tends to underscore several features of the period.

Probably first in importance is the impression one receives of the difficulties of France's situation. These go much deeper than judgments founded on the usual recitals of figures of lives lost or the visual evidence of ruined towns and acres of wooden crosses. Contemporaries heard and saw and were moved. But they also saw a huge military establishment, radiant with the aureole of victory, standing at the Rhine in a defeated Germany wracked by violence and starvation. Not visible, even to Frenchmen, was the underlying reality: that France was "a power in full retreat."[33] She could not face the future alone. She needed Britain and the United States but could not risk becoming dependent on them. By herself unable to crush or even to contain Germany, France conceivably might turn to her. Clemenceau did not overlook even this possibility, for he used the diplomatic mission in

Berlin in the spring and summer of 1919 to take soundings, especially about financial arrangements. But it became clear that any agreement acceptable to Germany would only push France toward dependence once again.[34]

The only viable solution he saw, hence, was to scrape together somehow "a collection of possibilities"--close ties with the succession states in the east, pledges (however dubious) of military assistance from the United States and Britain, reparation payments, promises of financial aid and loans from friends, some scheme to put France's military frontier at the Rhine...whatever. And raise the birth rate. As he told the Senate, "The treaty does not say that France must undertake to have children, but it is the first thing which should have been written in it. For if France turns her back on larger families, one can put all the clauses one wants in a treaty...[but] France will be lost because there will be no more Frenchmen."[35]

A second impression, corollary and consequence of the first, is that French policy had no grand design issuing in a rigid bill of particulars. As noted elsewhere, Clemenceau dealt with questions quite freely, knowing when and how to be stubborn while also understanding and respecting his partners' needs. He wanted timely decisions, but because his natural impatience comported ill with the niceties of diplomatic procedure and because he lacked the training and instincts of a lawyer, he could be cavalier about the fine print. This flexibility, which ran counter to conventional public perceptions of him--perceptions due in part to the fact that André Tardieu's *The Truth About the Treaty* (1921), for which Clemenceau wrote a long preface, sought for political reasons to portray him as tough and Millerand (by extension) as weak[36]--strikingly manifested itself, for example, in the arguments about reparation.

Clemenceau early on may have wanted Germany to pay the "cost" of the war (whatever he thought that meant) and disbelieved talk of Germany's inability to pay it.[37] But when the debate was fully joined he showed an almost casual willingness to raise or lower figures and (in private) was frank in expressing doubts that Germany would ever pay the bill in full, whatever it was. As a rule he preferred lower figures--contrary to what has usually been said--since they might be surer of collection and because of in the lower ranges the famous "play of percentages" increased France's share. Britain, to be sure of getting very much, had to argue for a vast expansion of "damage" so that things such as sunken ships and soldiers' pensions could count. Clemenceau could go high too, however, in order to frighten his partners back toward helping French reconstruction with loans or to persuade them to agree with him on other elements of security.

At the same time, like Lloyd George he eventually concluded that any fixed sum even remotely acceptable to Germany would fall far short of what the public expected. The upshot was that no final figure was set in the treaties even though everyone agreed in principle that it should be, and the whole thing was tied into the complicated formula on the Rhineland occupation, a somewhat fortuitous linkage.[38] As viewed by Clemenceau, the connection did have a particular merit. As he told a cabinet meeting on 25 April 1919: "We have the right to reoccupy or prolong [the occupation] if we are not paid. I make a prediction: Germany will go into bankruptcy [*faire faillite*] and we will stay where we are, with the alliance [i.e., the Guarantee treaties]. Note that down on my tomb when I've died."[39] He chose not to point out, however, that Allied consent would be necessary.

A third impression, related to the second, is that Clemenceau was more intent upon staying in the Rhineland than has been commonly supposed, notwithstanding his much-publicized clashes with Foch. Because France's power was limited, it made sense to economize, and he chose the Rhine, not reparation, as the point of focus: the Rhine was more important and permanent than promises of money. When he left office he continued to argue that to all intents and purposes France really *had* gained the Rhine for her strategic frontier. It was not a specious argument, for through very tough bargaining he had created a substantial number of loopholes permitting the extension of the fifteen-year occupation scheme just in case the Guarantee treaties were not ratified.[40] But keeping the Rhine would demand careful work by his successors--and not a little luck, for what Britain and the United States would do would have great bearing. How would they be likely to interpret "refuses to observe the whole or part of her [Germany's] obligations," or "hostile act," or "unprovoked aggression" ten or twenty years hence?

Clemenceau's focus on the Rhine was the natural consequence of the importance he assigned to the containment of Germany if peace were to have a chance. Recent studies of his policy toward Russia appear to reinforce this conclusion by demonstrating the distinctly secondary role in it of ideological anti-Bolshevism. His stance on Russia and on Bolshevism fundamentally was governed by his perception of their relationships to German power, present or future. If anything, he and France's political and military leadership after him overrated the likelihood of a Russo-German alliance to break out of the framework of the peace treaties. His comment in a letter to Nicolas Pietri upon receiving news of the Rapallo treaty (16 April 1922) between Germany and Russia, that "one would have to be devoid of all intelligence not to understand that the economic alliance entails the military alliance," typified these fears which, though by no means groundless--for Germany subsequently did obtain in Russia facilities which helped her to evade the armaments and training clauses of Versailles--were on the whole exaggerated, as almost always proved to be the case in France on anything touching the German question.[41]

One might conclude here by noting that recent research has heavily underscored the magnitude of the problems faced by Clemenceau's successors. Even before he left office the British and Americans, not to mention the Italians, were in plain retreat from the settlement, yet it had been erected upon the assumption that their cooperation would continue. He could gloss over what was happening in order to get his parliament's consent, but the edifice was visibly crumbling. Moreover, the settlements woefully lacked enforcement devices. Even granting the advantages conferred by full occupation of the defeated states, the settlement after World War II showed much less regard for the hoary prerogatives of sovereignty, or at all events they took the responsibilities of investigation and oversight more seriously, having in mind what happened after 1919.

Germany tried to evade the Versailles terms from the start, which was only to be expected--and who could blame her for trying? The weakness of the enforcing mechanisms only encouraged her while further sapping the will of the enforcers. Furthermore, the daunting complexities of the economic and financial clauses, when added to the existent problems of war recovery on all sides, overtaxed the expertise of the day. In France's case these difficulties loomed all the larger because of the deadlines set down in the treaties, which in effect gave her until 1925 to make the most of the favors she enjoyed.[42] All in all, one has to think that Clemenceau's reputation would have fallen much further than it had already if, ironically, he had won his bid for the presidency and stayed on even for a year.

One cannot leave the subject without taking note of his failure to inspire confidence in France in the treaties. Nobody else stood as good a chance as he did to win his countrymen to their support. Because he could not do this alone, however, it was all the more important that he win over men like Foch and Poincaré--and this he failed to do. If he had associated Parliament more with his work and treated Foch and Poincaré with greater subtlety and tact, he might have fostered the kind of domestic understanding of difficulties ahead and a disposition to support the country's leadership that his successors would badly need. He did not do these things, and--sad to say--met with a pettiness and hostility from Foch and Poincaré which did them no credit either. Foch in particular appears never to have appreciated how Clemenceau had protected him from Lloyd George's and Wilson's anger whenever he threatened to disobey their collective orders.[43] Nevertheless, more trust--or less mistrust--on all sides surely would have helped the country's prospects as it headed into the stormy seas ahead. But to avoid the ultimate foundering of the peace, would it have sufficed?

To be blunt about it, a true "peace of reconciliation," one so generous that it would dissolve away any serious desire in Germany to seek revenge, was a political impossibility in 1919. All the sufferings of the war had not succeeded in extirpating the war virus; indeed, for the moment they only thrust most people back to vengeance dressed in sincerely anguished cries for "justice." Public opinion would have swiftly repudiated any Allied leader who showed himself unwilling to lay a heavy hand on Germany. Clemenceau viewed a peace of reconciliation as a possible long-term outcome of a process which would first involve establishment once again of a balance of power in Europe--the key to which for the present would be the containment of Germany--after which organs of international cooperation could gradually assume the role of keeping the peace. But "balance of power" *narrowly construed* was not what he had in mind. The peace should embody justice so far as was humanly possible under the circumstances in order to hold the victorious coalition together. As he put it in *Grandeur and Misery of Victory*:

> ...there were only two possible kinds of peace for us to contemplate: the maintaining of military domination, which our coalition would retain in its own hands after wresting it from the Germans, or else a grouping of States banded together to represent abstract justice in Europe, and capable of forming an impassable barrier to the unruly outbursts of the spirit of conquest. In other words, to keep everything in *statu quo ante*, and to expose ourselves to a repetition of the same experience, or in some form or another to maintain the victorious alliance, one of the grand advantages of which was that in no circumstances could it become a force for domination.[44]

Wilson scorned talk of balance of power, although he by no means consistently ignored considerations of balance in practice, while Lloyd George took such a narrow view of it that, to Clemenceau's horror and disgust, he was soon running away from cooperation with an "overmighty" France and defending it by saying that it was "always our traditional policy."[45] As Clemenceau remarked to Violet Milner in the mid-1920s, Britain's balance-of-power policy was understandable in the days of Louis XIV and Napoleon, "but after four years together in the trenches, not to know the difference between the French and the Germans is amazing."[46]

To admit the impossibility of reconciliation in 1919 is not to say that the treaties of themselves made another war inevitable--an altogether facile judgment which has long disfigured sensible discussion. The boundaries they established, for example, have held up remarkably well despite the heated criticism they provoked at the time and all the disruptions that surfaced in the wake of a second conflagration. The Locarno pacts of 1925, although it is easy to overestimate their implications, furnish some grounds for believing that a way out was being found. And if the arrival on the scene of Adolf Hitler had much to do with the coming of the Second World War (surely a reasonable proposition!), one is left to wonder if he would have been anything but a footnote in the history of the Weimar Republic had not the

Great Depression thrown everything (not least of all German politics) into the cauldron again.

Still, one is left with the war virus, and its presence qualifies all arguments over the might-have beens of 1919. Clemenceau lived his life in the shadow of wars past, present, and future between France and Germany. That shadow is gone. One can no more imagine them going to war with each other now than one can imagine the United States and Mexico or Britain and Spain or Italy and Austria setting off for their old battlefields. Granted that intra-European pacification owes much to the restraining presence of atomic and biological weapons, a military dominance by extra-European superpowers who balance each other, and so on: the fact remains that the Second World War did do much toward the purging of the war virus from the vitals of Western society, a purgation which the First World War began.[47] In the case of France and Germany it also drastically reduced the attractiveness and viability of war by bringing defeat to both and to Germany an end to national unification for two generations. Harsh as it may seem, and sad to admit, the stinking, gas-soaked, rat-infested gehennas of the Western Front, by breeding a salutary deep dread of another attack of the ancient plague, were necessary in helping to move mankind appreciably closer to what must occur if it is to survive at all, namely, extinction of the war madness.

The peace made in 1919 could have been a wiser one. But who would care to argue that the product of the labors of Wilson, Lloyd George, Clemenceau, and their collaborators hurt the chances of driving the plague from the world more than would have a *Diktat* from the hands of Wilhelm II, Ludendorff, and their Habsburg acolytes? Notwithstanding the all-too-human faults and limitations of the Allied leaders, who today would regret that these men and the forces they led managed to prevent *that* eventuality?

No small part of the credit for this contribution to world peace, however modest it may appear in retrospect in a troubled age, must be put to the account of an indomitable, fierce old man at the Ministry of War of the French Republic in 1918.

VII

Clemenceau's burial place is not easy to find. At Saint-Vincent-Sterlanges, a hamlet a few kilometers north of Chantonnay on the La

Rochelle-Nantes national highway, one turns east for three kilometers to the *bocage* village of Mouchamps (pop. 2,300) on the Petit Lay. Some 2.3 kilometers farther east on departmental road D13 is a sign on the left, "Le Colombier 3k," pointing to a narrow road which twists on up to a gentle ridge with long vistas on all sides. At a junction on the ridge one turns right and continues on to the Le Colombier farm, where the road ends. At the farm entrance there is a terse official marker on the left indicating a gate into an enclosure (c.100 X 30 meters) parallel to the road and containing planted rows of trees. On the far side of the enclosure stands a rough-finish granite stele bearing a bas-relief of a helmeted Athena leaning on a point-down spear, her head bowed. Beyond and below the stele, in the shade of a giant cedar Liberty Tree planted by Benjamin in 1848, one discovers two low iron grillworks in a cut-back portion of a wooded bank leading down to the Petit Lay. The Athena's spearpoint is directly aligned with the one on the right.[48]

There are no names or inscriptions. Save for the marker by the road and a small sign near the gate pointing to a path along the bank to the gravesite, one would not know what this place is. The trees rustle; the creek below tumbles on its way. In a pasture across the stream cattle graze. From the farmyard drift sounds of poultry, a barking dog, and children at play.

NOTES
CHAPTER XVII

1   Martin du Gard, *Les mémorables (1918-1923)*, 1:10n.

2   Philippe Bernard and Henri Dubief, *The Decline of the Third Republic, 1914-1938*, trans. Anthony Forster (New York: Cambridge University Press, 1985), p. 60.

3   Mordacq, *Clemenceau au soir de sa vie*, 1:215.

4   Milner, *My Picture Gallery*, p. 70.

5   GC, *Au fil des jours*, p. vii.

6   See Jean Martet, "Qui était Clemenceau?" *Revue de Paris*, 15 Dec. 1929, pp. 931-937, a superior sketch.

7   See Ellis, *The Early Life of Georges Clemenceau*, pp. 84-85, for an analysis of his "topplings" down to 1893. Only after the elections of 1885 did he have enough votes to combine with the Right to form a hostile majority. Ellis finds his role to have been "crucial" only in the falls of Rouvier (1887), Tirard (1888), and Freycinet (1892). After 1902 he played very prominent roles in the falls of Combes (1905), Briand (1913), and Ribot (via Malvy, 1917), and his role was crucial in forcing Caillaux out in 1912. It goes without saying that his criticisms helped in varying degrees to undermine all of the other ministries.

8   Martin du Gard, *Les mémorables (1918-1923)*, 1:9-10n.

9   Zeldin, *France 1848-1945*, 2:1169. Possibly a more accurate, at any rate less pejorative, label than Stanley Hoffmann's "stalemate society" or Michel Crozier's "société bloqué."

10   Thomas Jones, *Whitehall Diary*, vol. 1: *1916-1925*, ed. Keith Middlemas (London: Oxford University Press, 1969), p. 155 (30 April 1921).

11   Duroselle's essay in Huthmacher and Susman, eds., *Wilson's Diplomacy* p. 114 (italics added).

12   Tony Judt, *Marxism and the French Left: Studies on Labour and Politics in France, 1830-1981* (Oxford: Clarendon Press, 1986), p. 3.

13   See p. 256 above; and J.-B. Duroselle, *La France et les français, 1900-1914* (Éditions Richelieu, 1972), p. 347. Millerand, whose handling of the 1920 strikes resembled his--indeed if anything more stern--likewise drew

less lasting personal blame.   See Farrar, "Victorious Nationalismus Beleaguered," pp. 483-488.

14   E.g., Eugen Weber's remarkable *Peasants into Frenchmen: The Modernization of Rural France, 1870-1914* (Stanford, CA: Stanford University Press, 1976).

15   See, e.g., Nicolet, *L'idée républicaine en France*, pp. 146, 159.

16   He *was* impressed by the fact that the Republic's institutions had weathered the trials of the Great War, and at Strasbourg (1919) and Ste.-Hermine (1921) he asserted that the regime (*sic*) was now beyond dispute.   His statement in his preface to Tardieu's *The Truth About the Treaty*, p. viii, that France's institutions are "the best in the world" is an exception that proves the rule.

17   GC, *Discours prononcé...à Strasbourg le 4 novembre 1919*, p. 18. The phrase is "trop fréquente carence des caractères à la hauteur des responsibilités."

18   Duroselle, *Clemenceau*, p. 937.

19   For a good example see HL, 24 July 1913; also 3 Dec. 1913 and 12 June 1914.

20   See p. 221 above.   This stance was not atypical, reflecting as it does some basic problems in French organization life.   See Warwick, "Ideology, Culture, and Gamesmanship in French Politics," pp. 636, 648, and *passim*.

21   See especially Jean Touchard, *La gauche en France depuis 1900* (Éditions Seuil, 1977), pp. 13-88, *passim*; and Jean-Thomas Nordmann, ed., *La France radical* (Gallimard: Julliard, 1977), *passim*.

22   Milner, *My Picture Gallery*, p. 116.

23   See Nathan C. Leites, *On the Game of Politics in France* (Stanford, CA: Stanford University Press, 1959), pp. 17-18.   See also Berstein, *Histoire du Parti Radical*, 1:54-55, 93; and p. 472 above.

24   Abensour, *Dans la cage du Tigre*, pp. 112-113.

25   From *L'Ère nouvelle*, 25 Nov. 1929.

26   William Martin, *Statesmen of the War in Retrospect, 1918-1928* (New York: Minton, Balch & Co., 1928), p. 323.

27   See Domestici-Met, "Le deuxième gouvernement de Clemenceau," pp. 1138-1139.

28   Milner, *My Picture Gallery*, p. 69.

29   Raphaël-Leygues, *Georges Leygues*, pp. 127-128 (1 May 1918). In shutting out Poincaré from a role in foreign affairs he contravened a constitutional practice dating back to Grévy's presidency. This change lasted through the rest of the Third Republic. See Domestici-Met, "Le deuxième gouvernement de Clemenceau," pp. 1115-1117.

30   See especially Charles S. Maier, "Wargames: 1914-1919," *Journal of Interdisciplinary History* 18 (1988):843.

31   Charles Seymour, *Geography, Justice, and Politics at the Paris Peace Conference of 1919* (New York: American Geographical Society, 1951), pp. 10-11. Two important recent studies--James T. Emmerson, *The Rhineland Crisis, 7 March 1936: A Study in Multilateral Diplomacy* (Ames, IA: Iowa State University Press, 1977) and Robert J. Young, *In Command of France: French Foreign Policy and Military Planning, 1933-19\40* (Cambridge, MA: Harvard University Press, 1978)--present less harsh judgments on France's performance in this crisis than the one offered here, for which see John C. Cairns, "March 7, 1936, Again: The View from Paris," *International Journal* 20 (1965):230-246.

32   Nearest to his age (b. 1841) were Pašić of Yugoslavia (1845), Balfour (1846), and Saionji of Japan (1849). Wilson (1856), Orlando (1860), and Lloyd George (1863) were decidedly younger.

33   McDougall, *France's Rhineland Diplomacy, 1914-1924*, p. 4.

34   On the overtures by Prof. Émile Haguenin and René Massigli see especially Köhler, "La révolution allemand 1918/19 et la France," pp. 459-463; and Marc Trachtenberg, "Reparation at the Paris Peace Conference," *Journal of Modern History* 51 (1979):42-44, 54.

35   JOS, 11 Oct. 1919, pp. 1625-1626. It became a frequent theme with him.

36   See Trachtenberg, *Reparation in World Politics*, p. 102.

37   E.g., his remarks to Lord Bertie in *The Diary of Lord Bertie*, 2:307 (2 Dec. 1918).

38   See Trachtenberg, "Reparation at the Paris Peace Conference," p. 83 and *passim*. On the limitations on politicians in dealing with financial and monetary matters, notably because of the state of economic theory at the time, see Silverman, *Reconstructing Europe after the Great War*, pp. 9-11, 114, and *passim*.

39   Bariéty, *Les relations franco-allemandes après la Première guerre mondiale*, p. 62.

40   See Schwabe, *Woodrow Wilson, Revolutionary Germany, and Peacemaking*, pp. 282-283, a lucid exposé.

41   Letter (22 April 1922) in Wormser, *La république de Clemenceau*, p. 445. See especially Renata Bournazel, *Rapallo: La naissance d'un mythe. La Politique de la peur dans la France du Bloc National* (Fondation nationale des sciences politiques/Armand Colin, 1974), pp. 210-211, 227.

42   See Bariéty, *Les relations franco-allemandes après la Première guerre mondiale*, pp. 753-754. On enforcement problems see especially Sally Marks, *The Illusion of Peace: International relations in Europe, 1918-1933* (New York: St. Martin's Press, 1976), pp. 26-54. On financial and economic complications see especially Walter A. McDougall, "Political Economy versus National Sovereignty: French Structures for German Economic Integration after Versailles," *Journal of Modern History* 51 (1975):4-23, 56-81, an outstanding short discussion; also Leffler, *The Elusive Quest*; Charles S. Maier, *Recasting Bourgeois Europe: Stabilization in France, Germany, and Italy in the Decade after World War I* (Princeton, NJ: Princeton University Press, 1975); and Stephen A. Schuker, *The End of French Predominance in Europe: The Financial Crisis of 1924 and the Adoption of the Dawes Plan* (Chapel Hill, NC: University of North Carolina Press, 1976).

43   See especially Wormser, *Clemenceau vu de près*, pp. 217-221, citing in particular Foch's refusal on 17 April to transmit a dispatch to the Germans and his refusal on 16 June to march on Berlin if the Germans did not sign.

44   GC, *Grandeur and Misery of Victory*, p. 186.

45   See p. 505 above.

46   Milner, *My Picture Gallery*, p. 69 (c.1925-1926). For a defense of Lloyd George's views see especially Kenneth Owen Morgan, *Consensus and Disunity: The Lloyd George Coalition Government 1918-1922* (New York: Oxford University Press, 1979), pp. 115-116, 133-134. On Clemenceau's and Wilson's clashing perceptions of means and ends in the treatment of Germany see especially Lloyd E. Ambrosius, "Wilson, Clemenceau, and the German Problem at the Paris Peace Conference of 1919," *Rocky Mountain Social Science Journal* 12 (1975):69-80, a penetrating summary.

47   See especially F. H. Hinsley, "The Rise and Fall of the Modern International System," *Review of International Studies* [Great Britain] 8 (1982):1-7.

48   The grave's location was not within easy view of the reporters present at the burial, which may have given rise to the story, widely repeated, that he was buried standing up facing Germany. The stele, a copy of a statue in Athens which Clemenceau liked, was done at his request by the sculptor François Sicard, a friend.

APPENDIX I

The Dreyfus Case

This editorial, "C'est dommage," appeared in *L'Aurore* on 7 January 1898, three days prior to the trial of Major Esterhazy and six days before *L'Aurore* published Zola's "J'accuse...!" It states succinctly and with cold passion what Clemenceau thought the Dreyfus Case was about.

It's a Pity

It's a pity that all Frenchmen are not in agreement in demanding impartial justice for all.

It's a pity that republicans can be found who invoke *raison d'état* and who consent, while living under a free government, to maintain the iniquities of royal tyranny.

It's a pity that men who made a name for themselves calling for social justice are today spending their share of authority in trying to persuade France that the arbitrary practices which they themselves once condemned are excusable in certain cases, and that one can tolerate their being used against others when one does not feel oneself threatened.

It's a pity that so many who think otherwise let themselves be frightened by the insults of cynics and do not dare to declare themselves openly as champions of justice and truth.

It's a pity that the government has, by a series of inexplicable acts, encouraged the thought that it can veil the truth and violate justice with impunity in order to hide the mistakes of some people in high places.

It's a pity that in acting thus the ministers have lost all right to public confidence and no longer show themselves to us, whatever the political

546

nuances which separate us, to be faithful guardians of the primordial rights of any citizen in a civilized society.

It's a pity that they should be allowed to lay their hands on the guarantees assuring the life, honor, and liberty of citizens.

It's a pity that a minister of war dares to protect unlawfully a man accused of espionage.

It's a pity that self-professed patriots can proudly cover Esterhazy, the uhlan, with their protection and that public indignation does not mete out justice to these men.

It's a pity that our patriotism should be one of words and not action.

It's a pity that the citizenry gives up instead of reacting against the authorities who betray their duty.

It's a pity that the name of Jew, of Protestant, of freethinker, or of Catholic seems to be to us a justification for violence exercised against those who do not share our beliefs.

It's a pity that the lofty virtue of tolerance should now be banished from the French spirit.

It's a pity that, in this general disarray, we have come to the point of calling each other "sellouts," in the face of Europe which is judging us, and are looking only for financial reasons to explain the actions of our fellows, while systematically closing our minds to any suspicion of disinterestedness.

It's a pity that the idea has not occurred to anybody--as it would have to everybody a century ago--that one can defend victims because of the simple need to do justice, or even, if I dare pronounce the word, from a spirit of generosity.

It's a pity that we should no longer hold it noble to oppose the injustice of the strong.

It's a pity that antique French bravery, driven from public life, should be trod into the depths of souls.

It's a pity that noble sentiments should be hidden and the bad rise.

It's a pity that the spirit of chivalry seems lost in all the ranks of the French nation.

It's a pity that France, at first the soldier of God, later the soldier of man, should be so brutally awakened from its dream of the ideal.

It's a pity that, our ancestors having been so great, we should be so much less.

For it was a noble country, this universal homeland of justice for all, loved by all who aspired to the right, feared by all who abused force.

Look upon what we have done, and say with me that it's a pity.

APPENDIX II

The Paris Peace Conference

Clemenceau made the following two statements during meetings of the Council of Four on 27 and 28 March 1919 near the beginning of the "crisis" of the conference (to mid-April). He was responding to Lloyd George's "Fontainebleau Memorandum," which sought to moderate some of the proposed terms, and to President Wilson's objections to French claims in the Saar Basin. They comprise a particularly concentrated and striking expression of some fundamental features of his point of view during the Conference. It should be borne in mind, however, that he is arguing a case here and thus is not, for the moment, dealing in qualifications or nuances. This text, quoted by permission, is a translation from the notes of the interpreter in *Les Délibérations du Conseil des Quatre (24 mars-28 juin 1919)*. Notes de l'Officier Interprête Paul Mantoux (Éditions du centre national de la recherche scientifique, 1955), 1:42-44, 69-71.

I said yesterday that I altogether agree with Mr. Lloyd George and President Wilson about the way to treat Germany; we should not abuse our victory; peoples must be treated with care and with a fear of provoking a revolt by an offended national conscience.

But I shall venture one fundamental objection. Mr. Lloyd George is too frightened of the consequences of a possible resistance by the Germans refusing to sign the treaty. I should point out that they gave up without waiting until our troops entered Germany, fearing no doubt the atrocious reprisals we were incapable of. This time we should expect that they will resist: they will argue, they will argue every point, they will talk of refusing their signature, they will play upon incidents like that which just occurred in Budapest [Béla Kun's coup] and those which could occur tomorrow in Vienna; they will contest or refuse everything they can refuse. You've probably read in yesterday's papers Count Bernstorff's interview: he speaks with the arrogance of a conqueror.

But we must not fear them more than necessary. We should take heed of the possible danger; but we should also, after having gained the victory at the price of so many sacrifices, assure ourselves of its fruits.

After all, the Germans' resistance has not always been what it was expected to be. You've taken their whole navy; nevertheless, they had clung to it and their emperor told them: "Our future is on the water." The possibility of a desperate resistance by the Germans was envisaged when we deprived them of their fleet; you remember the observations concerning this by Marshal Foch when we drew up the armistice terms. In point of fact, nothing has happened. We're now taking their merchant fleet--to supply them, it's true. But they foresaw the case of their not being supplied, for the *Berliner Tageblatt* wrote today that in this case Germany would take measures to live in spite of the blockade.

I come now to President Wilson's precept [viz., that they should not give Germany powerful reasons to want to take revenge], which I accept, but which I do not apply to the Germans except with a certain reserve. One must not--President Wilson says--give the Germans the feeling of an injustice being done to them. Agreed, but what we will find just here, in this room, will not necessarily be accepted as such by the Germans.

People are astonished that France should be opposed to the immediate admission of Germany to the League [*Société*] of Nations. Yesterday, again, I received a new dossier on the atrocities committed in France. We have, unfortunately, learned to know the Germans at our expense, and we know that they are a people which submits to force in order to itself impose force on the world. I shall remind Mr. Lloyd George of a conversation I had with him seven or eight years ago at Karlsbad; I made known to him my anxieties about the future of Europe and I spoke to him about the German danger. Mr. Lloyd George was hoping Germany would be wise: he has, unfortunately, been put right.

The Germans are a slavish [*servile*] people which needs force to support an argument. Napoleon said before he died: "Nothing permanent is founded on force." I'm not so sure, because it's enough to look at the great nations of Europe and the United States to have doubts. What is true is that force cannot establish anything solid if it's not in the service of justice. Everything must be done to be just toward the Germans; but as for persuading them that we are just toward them, that's something else. I believe we can find a way to spare the world a German aggression for a long time; but the German mind [*esprit*] will not change so quickly. Look at the German Social Democrats who used to call themselves brothers of our socialists and yours: we've seen them serving the imperial government and they are today serving [Philip] Scheidemann [an S.D. leader] surrounded by the old bureaucratic personnel of the Empire, with [Count Brockdorff-] Rantzau at its head.

Observe that nobody, in Germany, makes a distinction between the just and unjust demands of the Allies. There is no resistance stronger than that manifested against giving Danzig to Poland. Nevertheless, to undo the historic crime committed against the Polish nation, we are obliged, in calling this nation back to life again, to give it the means to live. We should not forget the crimes committed in particular by Germany against Poland, after the great crime of its partition: in the nineteenth century and, so to speak, by scientific methods. We remember children being whipped for praying to God in Polish, peasants expropriated, driven from their lands in order to make room for occupants of the German race.

We have perhaps, all of us, similar expropriations on our consciences from a more or less distant past; but it's a question there of deeds which have taken place before our very eyes and those who have committed them are standing before us. The Social Democrats are with them, for they have supported their government during four years of war.

I pay homage to Mr. Lloyd George's spirit of equity when he expressed the desire to give Poland the fewest possible German subjects. But I do not accept the sentence [in the Memorandum] where he says that, in the question of communications between Danzig and the interior, one must set aside every strategic consideration. If we followed this counsel, we would leave a sad legacy to our successors. We must accept the inevitable impediments [*accrocs*] to the principle of the right of self-determination of peoples if we wish to safeguard the principle itself.

An example haunts my thought, that of Austria. There is talk of disarming all of us; I certainly want that; believe me, the spirit of conquest which has been found in the French people in times past is dead forever. But if we reduce our armaments and if, at the same time, Austria goes and adds seven million people to the population of Germany, the power of our German neighbors grows in a way which is menacing to us. Is it an offense against the rights of peoples to say to the Austrians: "We require only that you remain independent. Do what you want with this independence; but you must not join a German bloc and take part in a plan for German revenge"?

My principles are yours; I discuss only the application. May I say to President Wilson: Do not believe that the principles of justice which will satisfy us will satisfy the Germans. I know them: I've taken it upon myself, since 1871, to go almost every year to Germany; I wanted to know the Germans and, at certain moments, I have hoped that one could find a way to bring our two peoples together. I can tell you that their idea of justice is not ours.

After the greatest effort and the greatest sacrifices in shed blood that history has ever seen, we must not compromise the result of our victory. The League of Nations is offered to us as a means to give us the security we need: I accept this means; but the League of Nations cannot give military sanctions to its decrees; one must find this sanction elsewhere. I should point out that on the sea this sanction is ready: Germany no longer has a navy. We need an equivalent on land. I have no prejudices as regards modalities. I beg you to understand my state of mind, as I am trying to understand yours. America is far away, protected by the Ocean. England couldn't be reached by Napoleon himself. You are, both of you, safe; we are not.

No man is farther removed than I am from the militarist spirit. I'm ready to do anything to reach a solution which would be better than the military solution. But we can't forget that, in our great crisis, military men did a great deal to save us. Don't commit the fault of not taking advice from them at a time like this. In the day of danger and trial they'll say to us: "It's not our fault if you haven't listened to us."

A last word. We have reason to fear bolshevism in the enemy's land and to avoid provoking its development; but we shouldn't spread it at home.

There is a sentiment of justice between allies which must be honored. If this sentiment were violently thwarted, be it in France, be it in England, a great danger could result from it. It's well to want to treat the vanquished with care [*ménager*]; but we must not lose sight of the victors. If a revolutionary movement should occur somewhere because our solutions appeared unjust, may it not be in our own countries. I want to give here only a simple indication.

I take note of President Wilson's words and excellent intentions. He eliminated sentiment and memory: that's where I have a reservation about what he has just said. The president of the United States ignores the basis [*fond*] of human nature. The reality of the war cannot be forgotten. Americans did not see this war up close during the first three years; as for us, during that time, we lost a million and a half men. We have no more manpower. Our English friends, who lost less than we, but enough to have suffered greatly also, will understand me.

Our trials have created in this country a deep feeling about the reparations which are due us; and it's not only a question of material reparation: the need for moral reparation is no less great. The doctrines which have just been invoked would make it possible, if they were interpreted in full rigor, to refuse us Alsace-Lorraine as well. In reality, the Saar and Landau are part of Lorraine and Alsace.

Our great enemies of 1815, against whom we fought for so many centuries, the English, insisted, after Napoleon's fall, that Prussia not take the Saar Basin. A gesture of generosity toward a people which has suffered so much would not be in vain. It's an error to believe that the world is led by abstract principles. These are accepted by certain parties, rejected by others --I'm not speaking of supernatural doctrines, about which I've nothing to say; but I deem that there are no human dogmas, only rules of justice and good sense.

You seek to do justice to the Germans. Don't believe they will ever pardon us for it; they will seek only the chance for revenge; nothing will destroy the rage of those who wanted to establish their domination of the world and who believed themselves so close to succeeding.

I shall never forget that our American friends, like our English friends, came to aid us at a time of supreme danger, and I will tell you the argument I hold in reserve for the French, if I do not manage to convince you. I shall say to them: "Suppose the English and the Americans had posed conditions before coming to our rescue: would you have accepted them?"

I betray my argument to you, I put myself in your hands, in order to prove to you how keenly I feel about how much we owe you. But you will do justice to humanity in recognizing a sentiment which is something different from your principles but which is no less deep.

Likewise, when those young men Lafayette and Rochambeau went to aid Americans fighting for their independence, it is not cold reason, it's not some deeds of war, after all pretty ordinary, which created the memory which clings to their intervention; it's an impression, a deep sentiment which has linked our two nations forever. The world is not led by pure principles.

I'm old. In a few months I'll have left political life forever. My disinterestedness is absolute. As Mr. Lloyd George said the other day, there is no finer role than to succumb while defending a just cause. I hope for no finer end; I don't hope for a finer end for anybody. I shall support before Parliament the conclusions we shall arrive at together. But here, between us, let me tell you that you will lose a chance to seal one more link to the chain of affection which joins France to America.

I shall not change your opinion, I'm afraid: you consider yourself bound by your word. I should like to note, nonetheless, that these 350,000 people [in the Saar Basin], of whom at least 150,000 are French, do not constitute a nation. You don't want to make an exception to the principle? You'll certainly be obliged to by the facts. How take the Germans of Karlsbad without destroying Bohemia itself? Populations which have thrown themselves at each other for centuries have remained mixed together as if in a battle. In the Balkans you can't make a Greece which doesn't contain Bulgarians, a Serbia which doesn't contain Albanians.

I respect your sentiment, which is very honorable. Your role is a great one. But you are going against your goal. You will not sow hatred; but you will meet bitterness and regrets. That's why it's necessary to arrive at justice, not mathematical justice, but one which takes account of sentiment.

You are ready to do justice to us from an economic point of view; I thank you for that. But economic necessities are not everything. The history of the United States is a glorious history, but short. A hundred years for you is a very long time; for us, it's not much. I've known men who saw Napoleon with their own eyes. We have our conception of history which is not altogether the same as yours.

I ask you simply to think about what I have just said when you are alone and to ask yourself in good conscience if it doesn't contain a piece of the truth.

APPENDIX III

Chronology, 1906-1909

1906

March 10

A horrible explosion at Courrières, near Lens, kills 1,200 miners; ultimately 20,000 troops are sent to keep order during two months of strikes in the Nord and Pas-de-Calais.

March 14

Sarrien's ministry; Clemenceau is minister of the interior.

April 11-17

Paris postal strike, leading to a nationwide wave of strikes.

May 1

Huge demonstrations in Paris in favor of the eight-hour day met by a massive concentration of police and troops.

May 6, 20

General elections a victory for the Left, especially the Radicals.

June 12-21

Great debate between Clemenceau and the Socialists (unified in 1905 as the "Section française de l'Internationale Ouvrière").

July 12

Dreyfus declared innocent by the Court of Cassation and restored to the army; Picquart promoted to general.

August 15

Pius X condemns the *associations cultuelles*, reopening the religious question after Clemenceau had suspended contested property inventories to avoid bloodshed.

Oct. 13

The General Confederation of Labor (CGT) adopts the Charter of Amiens endorsing anarcho-syndicalism.

Oct. 18, 25	Sarrien resigns; Clemenceau's government formed.
Nov. 5	Clemenceau's ministry approved in the Chamber, 376-94.
Dec. 7	The Chamber votes to nationalize the Western Railway.
Dec. 11	Msgr. Montagnini, the Vatican's liaison agent, expelled for political spying and his papers seized.

1907

Jan.	Passage of legislation designed to circumvent papal obstruction of the Separation Law.
Feb. 7	The income tax bill presented to the Chamber.
March-April	Agitation among teachers and postal workers demanding rights to strike and join the CGT is met by some suspensions and firings.
March 8-9	Electrical workers cut off power in Paris.
March 12	Explosion of the battleship *Iéna* prompts a naval inquiry by Parliament.
March 16	A man killed in a dockers' strike at Nantes.
March 25	Oudjda (Morocco), near the Algerian border, occupied after the murder of a French doctor at Marrakech.
May-June	Distress in the Midi vineyards due to catastrophic price declines prompts huge rallies leading to mass resignations of mayors, rioting, arson, and mutiny in a regiment (17th Inf.) sent to keep order.
May 7-14	Heated interpellations on the teachers' and postal workers' agitation and counter-measures.
July-Sept.	The winegrowers' movement subsides as a result of persuasion, forceful action, a law against wine frauds, and the discrediting of Marcelin Albert ("The Redeemer"), who had accepted travel

	money from Clemenceau following a private meeting.
Aug. 7	Forces land at Casablanca after murders of nine foreign workers. Mawlay Abd al-Hafid launches civil war against Sultan Mawlay Abd al-Aziz.
Aug. 13	The Socialists endorse the general strike and insurrection in the event of capitalist-inspired war; the Radicals in distress over relations with them because of Hervéism (anti-patriotism).
Aug. 31	The Anglo-Russian Entente is signed.
Sept.-Dec.	Pacification efforts extended from Casablanca inland as the sultan's situation deteriorates.

1908

Jan.-March	Pacification of the Casablanca region largely achieved.
Jan.-May	Long debates on the income tax bill.
March	Interpellations on Senate commission delays of the workers' pensions bill and on civil service unions issues.
April 7	Passage of church property legislation effectively ends the religious issue revived by the Dreyfus Affair.
May 2-Aug. 4	A bitter strike of navvies and sandpit workers near Paris (Draveil, Vigneux, Villeneuve-Saint-Georges) costs six lives.
June 25	The ministry wins a 128-125 vote in the Senate on passage of the Western Railway bill.
July 30-31, Aug. 3	A "general strike" in Paris provoked by the Draveil strike deaths fails; several CGT leaders arrested for incitement, but the government resists calls to dissolve the CGT.
Sept. 14	Mawlay Abd al-Hafid provisionally recognized as sultan of Morocco.

Sept. 25	Several Foreign Legion deserters at Casablanca are seized from German consular officials aiding their escape.
Oct. 6	Austria-Hungary annexes nominally Turkish Bosnia-Herzegovena following a deal between Izvol'skii (Russia) and Aehenthal (Austria) at Buchlau; the ensuing international crisis lasts until March 1909, when Germany pressures Russia into dropping support of Serbia's protests about the annexation.
Oct. 19	Thomson, minister of marine, resigns after a string of naval accidents.
Nov. 3-10	Sudden Franco-German tension over the Casablanca Deserters Affair; the dispute is sent to the Hague Tribunal, which rules (22 May 1909) mostly in France's favor.

1909

Jan. 14	A revised version of the workers' pensions bill sent to the Senate.
Feb. 9	Treaty with Germany confirming French political and police roles in Morocco but calling for economic cooperation there.
March 9	The Chamber passes the income tax bill, but the Senate elects a commission hostile to it.
March 12-20, May 11-21	Strikes of post-and-telegraph workers; disciplinary measures rekindle the civil service unions issue.
March 25	A second naval inquiry launched.
May 19-July 3	Merchant seamen's strike.
June 11	The Chamber passes the courts-martial reform bill, a legacy of the Dreyfus Affair.
June 11-July 15	The ministry wins a 184-vote majority in a series of interpellations on general policy.
July 9	The Senate passes the railway pensions bill after a decade of delay.

July 20   The ministry falls, 176-212 (many supporters had left on a junket to Scandinavia), after heated exchanges between Clemenceau and Delcassé during debate on the report of the commission investigating naval administration.

APPENDIX IV

Clemenceau's Ministerial Memberships

NB. Imputed party or group affiliation varies in different sources, particularly between Radical/Radical-Socialist and Radical/Republican Left.

Sarrien
(14 March-25 Oct. 1906)

Ministers

Pres. of the Council, Justice: Jean Sarrien (Dep., Rad.).

Foreign Affairs: Léon Bourgeois (Sen., Rad.).

Interior: Georges Clemenceau (Sen., Rad.-Soc.).

Finance: Raymond Poincaré (Sen., Rep. Left).

War: Eugène Étienne (Dep., Rep. Left).

Marine: Gaston Thomson (Dep., Rad.-Soc.).

Education, Fine Arts, and Religion: Aristide Briand (Dep., Ind. Soc.).

Public Works, Posts, Telegraphs, and Telephones: Louis Barthou (Dep., Rep. Left).

Commerce, Industry, and Labor: Gaston Doumergue (Dep., Rad.-Soc.).

Agriculture: Joseph Ruau (Dep., Rad.).

Colonies: Georges Leygues (Dep., Rad.).

Under-Secretaries of State

Interior: Albert Sarraut (Dep., Rad.-Soc.).

Fine Arts: Henri Dujardin-Beaumetz (Dep., Rad.-Soc.).

Posts, Telegraphs, and Telephones: Alexandre Bérard (Dep., Rad.-Soc.).

I Clemenceau
(25 Oct. 1906-24 July 1909)

Ministers

Pres. of the Council, Interior: Georges Clemenceau (Sen., Rad.-Soc.).

Justice: Edmond Guyot-Dessaigne (Dep., Rad.). Died 31 Dec. 1907.

Foreign Affairs: Stephen Pichon (Sen., Rad.-Soc.).

Finance: Joseph Caillaux (Dep., Rep. Left).

War: Gen. Georges Picquart (non-parl.).

Marine: Gaston Thomson (Dep., Rad.-Soc.). Resigned 19 Oct. 1908 under fire.

Education, Fine Arts, and Religion: Aristide Briand (Dep., Ind. Soc.) until 4 Jan. 1908.

Public Works, Posts, Telegraphs, and Telephones: Louis Barthou (Dep., Rep. Left).

Commerce and Industry: Gaston Doumergue (Dep., Rad.-Soc.) until 4 Jan. 1908.

Agriculture: Joseph Ruau (Dep., Rad.).

Colonies: Raphaël Milliès-Lacroix (Sen., Rad.-Soc.).

Labor and Social Security: René Viviani (Dep., Ind. Soc.).

Under-Secretaries of State

Interior: Albert Sarraut (Dep., Rad.-Soc.). Resigned 17 June 1907 because of political considerations in his constituency during the Midi winegrowers' revolt.

War: Henry Chéron (Dep., Rad.).

Fine Arts: Henri Dujardin-Beaumetz (Dep., Rad.-Soc.).

Posts, Telegraphs, and Telephones: Julien Simyan (Dep., Rad.-Soc.).

Changes

20 July 1907

> Under-Secretary at Interior: Adolphe Maujan (Dep., Sen. [1909], Rad.-Soc.), replacing Sarraut.

4 Jan. 1908

> Justice and Religion: Aristide Briand (Dep., Ind. Soc.), replacing Guyot-Dessaigne.

> Education and Fine Arts: Gaston Doumergue (Dep., Rad.-Soc.), replacing Briand.

> Commerce and Industry: Jean Cruppi (Dep., Rad.), replacing Doumergue.

22 Oct. 1908

> Marine: Alfred Picard (non-parl.), replacing Thomson.

II Clemenceau
(16 Nov. 1917-20 Jan. 1920)

*   No prior wartime service
** Debut

Ministers

Pres. of the Council, War: *Georges Clemenceau (Sen., Rad.-Soc.).

Justice: Louis Nail (Dep., Rad.-Soc.).

Foreign Affairs: *Stephen Pichon (Sen., Rad.-Soc.).

Interior: *Jules Pams (Sen., Rad.).

Finance: Louis Klotz (Dep., Rad.-Soc.).

Marine: *Georges Leygues (Dep., Rad.).

Education and Fine Arts: *Louis Lafferre (Dep., Rad.-Soc.) to 27 Nov. 1919. Defeated in Nov. 1919 election.

Public Works and Transport: Albert Claveille (non-parl.).

Commerce and Industry, Posts, Telegraphs, and Telephones, Merchant Marine: Étienne Clémentel (Dep., Rad.) to 27 Nov. 1919. Defeated in Nov. 1919 election.

Agriculture and Food: **Victor Boret (Dep., Ind. Soc.). Resigned 18 July 1919 under fire.

Colonies: **Henry Simon (Dep., Rad.-Soc.).

Labor and Social Security: **Pierre Colliard (Dep., Ind. Soc.) to 2 Dec. 1919. Defeated in Nov. 1919 election.

Armaments and War Production: Louis Loucheur (non-parl.; elected to Chamber in Nov. 1919).

Blockade and Liberated Territories: Charles Jonnart (Sen., Rep. Left). Resigned 23 Nov. 1918 for reasons of health.

Under-Secretaries of State

Presidency of the Council, War: **Jules Jeanneney (Sen., Rad.).

Interior: **Albert Favre (Dep., Rad.-Soc.).

Finance: **Charles Sergent (non-parl.).

War (Manpower and Pensions): **Louis Abrami (Dep., Rep. Left).

Military and Naval Aviation: Louis Dumesnil (Dep., Rad.-Soc.). Resigned, 9 Jan. 1919.

Medical Services: Justin Godart (Dep., Rad.-Soc.). Resigned 1 Feb. 1918 under fire.

Military Justice: **Édouard Ignace (Dep., Rad.).

Marine (Submarine Warfare): **Jules Cels (Dep., Rad.-Soc.).

Shipping and Merchant Marine: **Henry Lémery (Dep., Rad.-Soc.). Resigned 28 Nov. 1918.

Agriculture and Food: **Ernest Vilgrain (non-parl.).

Changes: Ministers

23 Nov. 1917

Blockade and Liberated Territories: Albert Lebrun (Dep., Rep. Left), replacing Jonnart. Resigned 6 Nov. 1919 at Clemenceau's request for running on a ticket with Louis Marin, who had voted against the Versailles Treaty.

20 July 1919

Agriculture and Food: Joseph Noulens (Dep., Rad.), replacing Boret.

6 Nov. 1919

Liberated Territories: **André Tardieu (Dep., Rep. Left), replacing Lebrun.

26 Nov. 1919

Industrial Reconstruction: Louis Loucheur (Rep. Left), his former post having been terminated.

27 Nov. 1919

Education and Fine Arts: Léon Bérard (Dep., Rep. Left), replacing Lafferre.

Commerce and Industry, Posts, Telegraphs, and Telephones: **Louis Dubois (Dep., Progressist), replacing Clémentel.

2 Dec. 1919

Labor and Social Security: **Paul Jourdain (Dep., Bloc Nat.), replacing Colliard.

Changes: Under-Secretaries of State

5 Feb. 1918

Medical Services: Louis Mourier (Dep., Rad.-Soc.), replacing Godart.

19 Nov. 1918

Public Works, Transport, and Merchant Marine: Jules Cels (Dep., Rad.-Soc.), his former post having been terminated and Lémery having resigned.

6 Dec. 1918

Demobilization: **Louis Deschamps (Dep., Rad.).

5 Feb. 1919

Finance (Disposition of Surplus Materiel): Paul Morel (Dep., Rad.) to 27 Nov. 1919. Defeated in Nov. 1919 election.

27 Nov. 1919

Finance (Disposition of Surplus Materiel): **Yves Le Troquer (Dep., Ind. Soc.), replacing Morel.

Posts, Telegraphs, and Telephones: Louis Deschamps (Dep., Rad.).

BIBLIOGRAPHY

Archives

The principal biographical repository is the Musée Clemenceau, 8 rue Franklin, Paris 75116, a block from the Trocadéro metro station. It is open on Tuesday, Thursday, Saturday, Sunday, and holidays, 2:00-5:00 p.m., and closed in August. The administration will consider applications for additional hours in the workroom-library and access to the private dossiers. The workroom contains a large number of books on Clemenceau and his times, the bulk of his newspaper contributions, including both censored and uncensored copies of *L'Homme Enchaîné*, and extensive files of clippings.

Because Clemenceau destroyed most of his papers before he died, the bulk of his letters must be sought in the correspondence of others. The dossiers at the Musée Clemenceau were briefly described for the first time in J.-B. Duroselle, *Clemenceau* (1988), pp. 955-957. To date (1989) access to them has been very restricted, and publication from their contents almost entirely confined to the Duroselle biography and the works of Georges Wormser, particularly in *La république de Clemenceau* (1961) and *Clemenceau vu de près* (1979). Clemenceau materials in other archives have been identified and used extensively by Duroselle and David R. Watson, *Georges Clemenceau: A Political Biography* (1974), the former quite exhaustively as regards French archives, the latter on British repositories in particular.

The misleadingly titled Fonds Clemenceau at the archives of the Service historique de l'Armée at Vincennes is the largest single body of archival materials, but it contains no personal papers, only official documents, 1917-1920, and has been fully open only since 1972.

Writings by Clemenceau

No single comprehensive bibliography exists, but one essentially complete may be constructed from Hector Talvart and Joseph Place, *Bibliographie des auteurs modernes de langue français, 1801-1962* (1928-1964),

570

Hugo P. Thieme, *Bibliographie de la littérature française de 1800 à 1930* (1933), and J.-B. Duroselle, *Clemenceau*. Gustave Geffroy, *Georges Clemenceau, sa vie, son oeuvre*, new ed. (1930) and Georges Wormser, *La république de Clemenceau* together list most of his newspaper collaborations. The most important of these:

> *La Justice*, 1880-1897 (especially after 3 Oct. 1893)
> *La Dépêche* (Toulouse), 1894-1906
> *L'Aurore*, 1897-1899, 1903-1906
> *Le Bloc* (a weekly), 1901-1902
> *L'Homme Libre*, 1913-14
> *L'Homme Enchaîné*, 1914-1917

There are two collections of speeches, *Discours de guerre* and *Discours de paix* (see below). A number of his speeches and reports were printed as pamphlets; most of these plus notices of prefaces for others' books--the most important for André Tardieu's *La paix* (1921)--appear in the printed catalogs of the Bibliothèque Nationale.

His books are collections of articles, sketches, stories, and essays published first in the press and reissued by himself or others under his direction. Except for his play, *Le voile du bonheur*, the same is true of his novel, *Les plus forts*, and *Demosthène, Claude Monet, Au soir de la pensée* (selected pages), and *Grandeur et misères d'une victoire*, which appeared serially in *L'Illustration* before being published as books.

Books

American Reconstruction, 1865-1870, with the Impeachment of President Johnson. Edited with an Introduction by Fernand Baldensperger. Translated by Margaret MacVeagh. New York: Lincoln MacVeagh-Dial Press, 1928. Reprint with Foreword and Notes by Otto H. Olsen: Da Capo, 1969.

Au fil des jours. É. Fasquelle, 1900. Miscellaneous portraits and travel pieces.

Au pied du Sinai. Illustrations de Henri de Toulouse-Lautrec. H. Floury, 1898. Rev. ed. by Éditions Georges Crès, 1920. Eng. trans.: *At the Foot of Sinai*. Introduction by Dr. A. Coralnik. Translated by E. V. Earle. New York: Bernard G. Richards, 1922. Sketches of East European Jewry.

Au soir de la pensée. 2 vols. Plon-Nourrit, 1927. Eng. trans.: *In the Evening of My Thought*. 2 vols. Translated by Charles Miner Thompson and

John Heard, Jr. Boston: Houghton Mifflin, 1929. His intellectual testament.

Aux embuscades de la vie: dans la foi, dans l'ordre établi, dans l'amour. Bibliothèque-Charpentier, 1903. Eng. Trans.: *The Surprises of Life.* Translated by Grace Hall. New York: Doubleday, Page, 1920. Human character in conflict with itself and society.

Claude Monet. Les Nymphéas. Librairie Plon, 1928. Eng. trans.: *Claude Monet: The Water Lilies.* Translated by George Boas. Garden City, NY: Doubleday, Doran, 1930. Essays on his friend and his art.

Contre la justice. Affaire Dreyfus III. P.-V. Stock, 1900. 102 articles, 12 Dec. 1898-31 March 1899.

Dans les champs du pouvoir. Payot, 1913. Articles 5 May-13 July 1913 on the Three Years' Service Law controversy.

De la génération des éléments anatomiques. J.-B. Ballière et fils, 1865. New ed. with introduction by M. Ch. Robin, by G. Ballière, 1867. His doctoral dissertation

Demosthène. Plon-Nourrit, 1926. Eng. trans.: *Demosthenes.* Translated by Charles Miner Thompson. Boston: Houghton Mifflin, 1926.

Des juges. Affaire Dreyfus IV. P.-V. Stock, 1901. 40 articles, 1 April 1899-11 May 1899.

Discours de guerre, publiés par la "Société des Amis de Georges Clemenceau." Librairie Plon, 1934. New ed., Presses Universitaires de France, 1968.

Discours de paix, publiés par la "Société des Amis de Georges Clemenceau." Librairie Plon, 1938.

Discours pour la liberté. Cahiers de la Quinzaine, 1903. His 17 November 1903 Senate speech on church-state relations plus excerpts.

Discours prononcé à Saint-Hermine le 2 octobre 1921. Payot, 1921.

Discours prononcé par M. Georges Clemenceau, Président du Conseil, Ministre de la Guerre, à Strasbourg le 4 novembre 1919. Imprimerie Lanz, Blanchong, 1919.

Figures de Vendée. Avec 52 eaux-fortes originales de Charles Huard. Maurice Méry, 1903. Rev. and expanded ed. by Plon-Nourrit, 1930. Short stories and sketches of his native province.

La France devant l'Allemagne. Edited by Louis Lumet and Jean Martet. Payot, 1916. New ed., 1918. Eng. trans.: *France Facing Germany: Speeches and Articles by G. Clemenceau.* Translated by Ernest Hunger Wright. New York: E. P. Dutton, 1919.

Le grand Pan. Charpentier et Fasquelle, 1896. New ed. by Bibliothèque-Charpentier, 1919. Divers sketches and stories with an important introductory essay.

Grandeur et misères d'une victoire. Plon-Nourrit,1930. Eng. trans.: *Grandeur and Misery of Victory*. Translated by F. M. Atkinson. New York: Harcourt, Brace, 1930. Essays on wartime and postwar controversies.

La honte. Affaire Dreyfus VII. P.-V. Stock, 1903. 65 articles, 24 Sept. 1899-3 Nov. 1901.

L'iniquité. Affaire Dreyfus I. P.-V. Stock, 1899. 162 articles, 25 Dec. 1894-20 July 1898.

Injustice militaire. Affaire Dreyfus VI. P.-V. Stock, 1902. 78 articles, 23 Aug. 1899-17 [?] Dec. 1899.

Justice militaire. Affaire Dreyfus V. P.-V. Stock, 1901. 83 articles, 12 May-22 Aug. 1899.

La leçon de la Russie. Floury, 1915. Articles praising the Duma's role in the war.

Lettres à une amie, 1923-1929. Édition établie et présentée par Pierre Brive. Gallimard, 1970. Letters to Marguerite (Mme. Fernand) Balsensperger edited by her son.

La mêlée sociale. Bibliothèque-Charpentier, 1895. New ed., 1919. Largely on social problems, with preface.

Notes de voyage dans l'Amérique de Sud: Argentine, Uruguay, Brésil. Hachette, 1911. Eng. trans.: *South America Today: A Study of Conditions, Social, Political, and Commercial in Argentina, Uruguay, and Brazil*. New York: G. P. Putnam's Sons, 1911.

Les plus belles pages de Clemenceau. Recueillies et annotées par Pascal Bonetti. Méricourt, n.d.

Les plus forts, roman contemporain. Fasquelle, 1898. Eng. trans.: *The Strongest*. Garden City, NY: Doubleday, Page, 1919. His only novel.

Sur la démocratie. Neuf conférences de Clemenceau rapportées par Maurice Ségard. Larousse, 1930. Notes from the 1910 lectures in South America.

Vers la réparation. Affaire Dreyfus II. P.-V. Stock, 1899. 135 articles, 21 July 1898-11 Dec. 1898.

Le voile du bonheur. Pièce en un acte. Musique de scène de Gabriel Fauré. Représentée pour la première fois sur la scène du théâtre de la

Renaissance (Théâtre Gémier), le 4 novembre 1901. New ed. by *La Petite Illustration*, No. 461, 4 Jan. 1930 (Théâtre: No. 248, pt. 2). Eng. Trans.: *The Veil of Happiness*. New York: Private Printing for the Members of the Beechwood Players, 1920. His only play, for which Charles Pons wrote music for the 1911 production.

Translation

Mill, John Stuart. *Auguste Comte et le positivisme*. Traduit par le docteur Georges Clemenceau. Germer-Ballière, 1968. There were six editions down to 1898.

Prefaces

Bernhardi, Gen. Friedrich von. *Notre avenir*. Translated by Emile Simonnot. Louis Conrad, 1915.

Brulat, Paul. *L'Affaire Dreyfus. Violence et raison*. P.-V. Stock, 1898.

Byron, Lord George Gordon. *Lettres de Lord Byron*, trad. par Jean Delachaume. Calmann-Lévy, 1911.

Destrée, Jules. *L'effort britannique: Contribution de l'Angleterre à la guerre européenne (août 1914-février 1916)*. G. Van Oest, 1916. In GC, *Discours de guerre*, pp. 58-60.

Jacquet, Louis. *L'alcool, étude économique générale*. Masson, 1912.

Les massacres d'Arménie. Mercure de France,1896.

Tardieu, André. *La paix*. Payot, 1921. Eng. trans.: *The Truth about the Treaty*. Foreword by Edward M. House. Introduction by Georges Clemenceau. Indianapolis: The Bobbs-Merrill Company, 1921.

Articles (cited in the text)

"Letter to John Durand." *Revue de littérature comparée* 12 (April 1932):420-422.

"Quelques considerations sur la séparation des Églises et de l'État." *La Grande Revue*, 1 May 1903, pp. 263-271.

"Reponse à l'enquête sur les responsabilités de la presse." *Revue politique et littéraire (Revue bleue)*, 11 Dec. 1897, pp. 740-741.

Selected General Bibliography

Primary and secondary sources and both books and articles are listed together here for convenience of reference from the Notes. A few items not mentioned in the Notes nevertheless made a contribution significant enough to merit inclusion here. As in all cases above, place of publication is Paris unless otherwise stated; reprint dates are not usually cited. As a rule, general histories and reference works are not listed. Newspaper articles are mentioned only if cited by title in the Notes. Asterisks (*) indicate items of special interest in any study of Clemenceau. For the *Journal Officiel* see "Glossary of Abbreviations."

*Abensour, Léon. *Dans la cage du Tigre. Clemenceau intime.* Souvenirs 'un Ancien secrétaire. Éditions Radot, 1928.

_____. "Un grand projet de Georges Clemenceau." *La Grande Revue*, Feb. 1930, pp. 531-550.

Adam, George Jeffrey. *The Tiger: Georges Clemenceau, 1841-1929.* New York: Harcourt, Brace, 1930.

*Adam de Villiers, Georges. *Clemenceau parle: Conversations inédites.* Éditions Tallandier, 1931.

Ageron, Charles-Robert. "Clemenceau et la question coloniale." In *Clemenceau et la justice* (q.v.), pp. 69-84.

_____. "Jules Ferry et la colonisation." In François Furet, ed., *Jules Ferry, fondateur de la République* (q.v.), pp. 191-206.

Agulhon, Maurice, "En relisant la 'Mêlée sociale' (Clemenceau et l'idée socialiste dans les débuts de la Troisième République)." In *Clemenceau et la justice* (q.v.), pp. 85-92.

Ahmedov, Ahmed S. "Les antagonisme interalliés sur les problèmes turc après l'armistice de Mudros jusqu'au traité de Sèvres." *Études balkaniques* [Sofia] 19 (1983):27-48.

*Ajalbert, Jean. *Clemenceau.* Librairie Gallimard, 1931. He was at *La Justice* in the 1880s and was a friend.

Albert, François. "Les paradoxes d'une carrière: L'homme libre et son parti." *L'Ère Nouvelle*, 24 Nov. 1929. He was the former secretary general of *L'Homme Libre*.

Albert, Pierre; Feyel, Gilles; and Picard, Jean-François. *Documents pour l'histoire de la presse nationale aux XIXe et XXe siècles.* Centre national de la recherche scientifique, 1977.

Albertini, Rudolf von. "Die Diskussion um die franzosiche Steuerreform 1907-1909." *Schweizer Beiträge zur Allegemeinen Geschichte* 13 (1955):183-201.

Albrecht-Carrié, René. *Italy at the Paris Peace Conference.* New York: Columbia University Press, 1938.

Aleksič-Pejkovič, Ljiljana. "La Serbie et les rapports entre les puissance de l'Entente (1908-1913)." *Balkan Studies* [Thessalonika] 6 (1965):305-344.

Allain, Jean-Claude. "Clemenceau et Caillaux." In *Clemenceau et la justice* (q.v.), pp. 121-130.

_____. *Joesph Caillaux.* 2 vols. Imprimerie Nationale, 1978-81. Vol. 1: *Joseph Caillaux, le défi victorieux (1863-1914)* (1978); Vol. 2: *L'oracle, 1914-44* (1982). Important.

Allard, Paul. *Les dessous de la guerre révélés par les Comités secrets.* Les Éditions de France, 1935.

_____. *Les favorites de la IIIe républicque.* Les Éditions de France, 1942.

Allizé, Henri. *Ma mission à Vienne (mars 1919-aôut 1920).* Librairie Plon, 1933.

*Altieri, Louis. *Nicolas Pietri, l'ami de Clemenceau.* Albin Michel, 1965.

Amaury, Francine. *Histoire du plus grand quotidien de la IIIe république: Le Petit Parisien, 1876-1944.* 2 vols. Presses Universitaires de France, 1972.

Ambrosius, Lloyd E. "Wilson, Clemenceau and the German Problem at the Paris Peace Conference of 1919." *Rocky Mountain Social Science Journal* 12 (1975):69-80. A penetrating summary.

_____. "Wilson, the Republicans, and French Security after World War I." *Journal of American History* 59 (1972):341-352.

Amdur, Kathryn. *Syndicalist Legacy: Trade Unions and Politics in Two French Cities in the Era of World War I.* Champaign, IL: University of Illinois Press, 1986.

Améline, Henri, ed. *Depositions de témoins de l'enquête parlementaire sur l'insurrection du 18 mars, classés et resumées par Henri Améline.* 3 vols. E. Dentu, 1872.

Andler, Charles. *Vie de Lucien Herr (1864-1926).* Éditions Rieder, 1931.

Andreani. "La fondation du parti radical-socialiste." *Revue politique et parlementaire,* Jan. 1952, pp. 33-41.

Andrew, Christopher, and Kanya-Forstner, A. S. *The Climax of French Imperial Expansion, 1914-1924.* Stanford, CA: Stanford University Press, 1981.

_____. "The French 'Colonial Party': Its Composition, Aims, and Influence." *Historical Journal* [Cambridge] 14 (1971):99-128.

Andrieux, Louis. *A travers la république*. Payot, 1926.

*_____. "Georges Clemenceau." *North American Review*, Feb. 15, 1907, pp. 371-382.

*Applebaum, Samuel Isaac. *Clemenceau, Thinker and Writer*. New York: Columbia University Press, 1948. The only book devoted exclusively to the subject.

Arago, Étienne. *L'Hôtel de Ville de Paris au 4 septembre et pendant le siège. Reponse à M. le comte Daru et aux Commissions d'enquête parlementaire*. J. Hetzel, n.d. [1874].

Armstrong, Hamilton Fish. *Peace and Counterpeace from Wilson to Hitler: Memoirs of Hamilton Fish Armstrong*. New York: Harper & Row, 1971.

Artaud, Denise. *La question des dettes interalliées et la reconstruction de l'Europe, 1917-1929*. 2 vols. H. Champion, 1978.

Ashley, Susan A. "The Failure of Gambetta's Grand Ministère." *French Historical Studies* 9, no. 1 (Spring 1975), pp. 105-124.

_____. Howorth, Jolyon (commentary). "The Radical Left in Parliament, 1879-1902." *Proceedings of the Annual Meeting of the Western Society for French History* 11 (1983):307-315, 327-331.

Astruc, Gabriel. *Le pavillon des fantômes, souvenirs*. B. Grasset, 1929.

Auclair, Marcelle. *La vie de Jaurès, ou la France d'avant 1914*. Éditions du Seuil, 1954.

Audouin-Rouzeau, Stéphane. "Les soldats et la nation de 1914 à 1918 d'après les journaux de tranchées." *Revue d'histoire moderne et contemporaine* 34 (1987):66-86.

Auffray, Bernard. *Pierre de Margerie (1861-1942) et la vie diplomatique de son temps*. Klincksieck, 1976.

Augarde, Jacques. "Le general d'Amade, pacificateur de la Chaouia." *Revue historique des Armées*, 1987, no. 1, pp. 24-32.

Aulard, A.; Bouvier, E.; and Ganem, A. *Histoire politique de la Grande Guerre*. Librairie Aristide Quillet, 1924.

Avril, P. "Les origines du radicalisme: II.-Les crises du XXe siècle." *Les Cahiers de la République*, no. 3 (1951), pp. 72-79.

Azan, Paul-J.-L. *Franchet d'Esperey*. Flammarion, 1949.

Baal, Gérard. "Jaurès vu par les radicaux." *Société d'études jaurèsiennes, Bulletin*, no. 94 (1984), pp. 33-40.

_____. "Un salon dreyfusard, des lendemains de l'Affaire à la Grande Guerre: La marquise Arconati-Visconti et ses amis." *Revue d'histoire moderne et contemporaine* 28 (1981):433-463.

Bailey, Thomas A. *Woodrow Wilson and the Great Betrayal*. Chicago: Quadrangle Books, 1963.

_____. *Woodrow Wilson and the Lost Peace*. New York: Macmillan, 1944.

*Baldensperger, Fernand. "Clemenceau dans la retraite. Souvenirs et documents inédits." *Revue de défense national* 12 (1951):446-457.

* _____. "L'initiation américaine de G. Clemenceau." *Revue de littérature comparée* 8 (1928):127-154.

Baldick, Robert. *The Siege of Paris*. New York: Macmillan, 1964.

Balogh, Eva Susan. "The Road to Isolation: Hungary, the Great Powers, and the Succession States, 1919-1920." Ph.D. dissertation, Yale University, 1974.

Bankwitz, Philip C. F. *Maxime Weygand and Civil-Military Relations in Modern France*. Cambridge, MA: Harvard University Press, 1967.

Bariéty, Jacques. "L'appariel de presse de Joseph Caillaux et l'argent allemand (1920-32)." *Revue historique* 247 (1972):375-406.

_____. *Les relations franco-allemandes après la Première guerre mondiale, 10 novembre 1918-10 janvier 1925, de l'éxécution à négociation*. Redone, 1977. Exceptionally important.

_____. "Les reparations allemandes après la Première guerre mondiale: Objet ou prétexte à une politique rhénane de la France (1919-1924)." *Société d'histoire moderne, Bulletin*, a. 72, ser. 15, no. 6, pp. 21-33.

*Barrès, Maurice. *Leurs figures*. Émile Paul, n.d. [1902].

_____. *Mes cahiers*. 9 vols. Plon, 1929-1931.

*Barthou, Louis. "Sous les griffes du Tigre." *Les Annales*, no. 2348 (15 Dec. 1929), pp. 543-545.

Barzun, Jacques. "Tiger in the Night." *New Republic*, 6 Dec. 1943, pp. 824-826.

*Bastoul, Berthe. *Clemenceau vu par un passant inconnu*. Avignon: Maison Aubanel Père, 1938. Little known but insightful.

*Bauër, Gérard. "Lorsque Clemenceau dirigeait 'L'Aurore.'" *Nouvelles littéraires, artistiques et scientifiques*, 30 Nov. 1929.

Baumont, Michel. "Abel Ferry et les étapes du contrôle aux armées, 1914-1918." *Revue d'histoire moderne et contemporaine* 15 (1968):162-208.

Baylen, Joseph O. "An Unpublished Note on Général Georges Boulanger in Britain, June 1889." *French Historical Studies* 4, no. 3 (Spring 1966), pp. 344-347.

Beau de Loménie, Emmanuel. *Le débat de ratification du triaté de Versailles*. Denoël, 1945.

_____. "L'échec de Clemenceau à la présidence de la République." *Miroir de l'histoire*, no. 47 (1953), pp. 1288-1300.

_____. *Les responsabilités des dynasties bourgeoises*. 3 vols. Denoël, 1943-1954.

Bechtel, Guy. *1907: La grande Révolte du Midi*. Edition Robert Laffont 1976.

Becker, Jean-Jacques. *Le Carnet B: Les pouvoirs publics et l'antimilitarisme avant la guerre de 1914*. Klincksieck, 1973.

_____. *The Great War and the French People*. Translated by Arnold Pomerans. New York: St. Martin's Press, 1986.

_____. *1914: Comment les Français sont entrés dans la guerre: Contribution à l'étude de l'opinion publique, printemps-été 1914*. Presses de la Fondation nationale des sciences politiques, 1977.

_____. "L'opinion publique française en 1917." *Historiens-Géographes*, no. 315 (1987), pp. 1497-1514.

Bédé, Jean-Albert. "Paris et Clemenceau." *Renaissance* [New York] 1 (1943):391-406.

Bellanger, Claude, et al., eds. *Histoire générale de la presse française*. Vol. 2: *De 1871 à 1940*. Presses Universitaires de France, 1972.

Bellesort, André, *La société française sous Napoléon III*. Librairie Académique Perrin, 1932.

*Benjamin, René. *Clemenceau dans la retraite.* Librairie Plon, 1930. Conversations with the novelist.

Benoist, Charles. *Souvenirs de Charles Benoist.* 3 vols. Librairie Plon, 1932-1934. See also Sybil.

Berger, Marcel, and Allard, Paul. *Les secrets de la Censure pendant la Guerre.* Éditions des Portiques, 1932.

Bernachot, Jean. *Les armées françaises en Orient après l'armistice de 1918.* 3 vols. Imprimerie Nationale, 1970-1972.

Bernain de Ravisi, Mme. *Sous la dictature de Clemenceau: Un forfait judiciare: Le procès Paul-Meunier, Judet-Brossard.* André Delpeuch, 1926.

Bernard, Philippe, and Dubief, Henri. *The Decline of the Third Republic, 1914-1938.* Translated by Anthony Forster. New York: Cambridge University Press, 1985.

Berstein, Serge. *Histoire du Parti Radical.* Vol. 1: *La recherche de l'age d'or, 1919-1926.* Presses de la Fondation nationale des sciences politiques, 1980.

_____. "Le parti Radical et les élections de 1919." *Société d'histoire moderne, Bulletin,* 74, no. 10 (1975), pp. 2-8.

_____. "Le Parti radical-socialiste durant la Première Guerre mondiale." In Patrick Fridenson, ed., *1914-1918, l'autre front.* Les Éditions Ouvrières, 1977.

Bertaut, Jules. *Figures contemporaines. Chroniqueurs et polémistes.* E. Sansot, 1906.

Bertie, Lord [Francis Levinson]. *The Diary of Lord Bertie.* 2 vols. Edited by Lady Algernon Gordon Lennox. New York: George H. Doran, 1924.

Billy, André. "Clemenceau homme de lettres." *Le Figaro littéraire,* 23 Feb. 1970, p. 25.

_____. *Les écrivains de combat.* Les Oeuvres représentatives, 1931.

Binion, Rudolph. *Defeated Leaders: The Political Fate of Caillaux, Jouvenel, and Tardieu.* New York: Columbia University Press, 1960.

Blanche, Jacques-Émile. "Clemenceau écuyer de haute école et écrivain hippique." *Les Nouvelles littéraires,* 14 Dec. 1929, p. 4.

Blanqui, Louis-Auguste. *Critique sociale.* 2 vols. F. Alcan, 1885.

Blatt, Joel. "France and Italy at the Paris Peace Conference." *International History Review* [Canada] 8 (1986):27-40.

Bliss, Tasker H. "The Evolution of the Unified Command." *Foreign Affairs* 1, no. 2 (Dec. 1922), pp. 1-30.

Blum, John M. *Woodrow Wilson and the Politics of Morality*. Boston: Little, Brown, 1956.

Blum, Léon. *Souvenirs sur l'Affaire*. Gallimard, 1935.

Blumenthal, Henry. *Illusion and Reality in Franco-American Diplomacy, 1914-1945*. Baton Rouge, LA: Louisiana State University Press,1986.

Boisrouvray, Xavier du. "Nantes en 1846, d'après la relation d'un Suédois, le baron Karl Frederick Palmstierna." *Société archéologigue et historique de Nantes de de Loire-Atlantique, Bulletin* [Nantes] 116 (1979-1980):37-57.

Bompard, Maurice. *Mon ambassade en Russie (1903-1908)*. Librairie Plon, 1937.

Bonnefous, Édouard. *Avant l'oubli: La vie de 1900 à 1940*. Laffont/Nathan, 1984.

_____. *Histoire politique de la troisième république*. 7 vols. 3rd ed. Presses Universitaires de France, 1965-1968.

Bonsal, Stephen. *Heyday in a Vanished World*. New York: W. W. Norton, 1937.

_____. *Suitors and Suppliants: The Little Nations at Versailles*. New York: Prentice-Hall, 1946.

_____. *Unfinished Business*. Garden City, NY: Doubleday, Doran, 1944.

*_____. "What Manner of Man Was Clemenceau?" *World's Work* 59 (Feb. 1930):72-75, 110. By an American friend in close touch.

Bouchardon, P. "L'affaire Bolo Pacha." *Historia* [France] 19 (1956):557-566.

Bournazel, Renata. *Rapallo: naissance d'un mythe. La politique de la peur dans la France du Bloc National*. Fondation nationale des sciences politiques/Armand Colin, 1947.

Bourrin, Ennemond-Claude. *Pas de clémence pour un inclément: Georges Clemenceau*. Restitution aux vainqueurs de l'armée d'orient de la gloire légitime dont ils ont été frustrés malgrés l'armistice du 29 septembre 1918. Nice: Imprimerie Universelle, 1968.

Boussel, Patrice. *L'Affaire Dreyfus et la presse*. Armand Colin, 1960.

Bouvier, Jean. *Les deux scandales de Panama*. René Julliard, 1964.

Bradley, John F. N. *Allied Intervention in Russia, 1917-1920*. New York: Basic Books, 1968.

_____. "France, Lenin and the Bolsheviks in 1917-1918." *English Historical Review* 86 (1971):783-789.

_____. "L'intervention française en Sibérie (1918-1919)." *Revue historique* 234 (1965):375-388.

*Brandes, Georg. *Correspondance de Georg Brandès: Lettres choisies et annotée par Paul Krüger*. 2 vols. Copenhagen: Rosenkilde og Bagger, 1952-1966. Letters to the Danish critic.

_____. "Sketch of Clemenceau." *The Contemporary Review* 84 (1903):656-674.

Bréal, Auguste. *Philippe Berthelot*. 3rd. ed. Gallimard, 1937.

Bredin, Jean-Denis. *The Affair: The Case of Alfred Dreyfus*. Translated by Jeffrey Mehlman. New York: George Braziller, 1986. Outstanding work.

_____. *Joseph Caillaux*. Hachette, 1980.

Breteuil, Marquis Henri de. *La haute société, journal secret (1886-1889)*. Atelier Marcel Jullian, 1979.

Brinkley, George A., Jr. "Allied Policy and French Intervention in the Ukraine, 1917-1920." In Taras Hunczak, ed., *The Ukraine, 1917-1921: A Study in Revolution*. Cambridge, MA: Harvard University Press, 1977, pp. 323-351.

_____. *The Volunteer Army and Allied Intervention in South Russia, 1917-1921*. Notre Dame, IN: University of Notre Dame Press, 1966.

Brisson, Adolphe. *Portraits intimes. Deuxième Série*. 3rd ed. Armand Colin, 1904.

Brogan, Denis W. *France under the Republic: The Development of Modern France (1870-1939)*. New York: Harper & Bros., 1939.

Browder, Robert Paul, and Smith, Thomas G. *Independent: A Biography of Lewis W. Douglas*. New York: Alfred A. Knopf, 1986.

Brown, Alice F. "The Love Story of Georges Clemenceau." *Mentor* 16 (Oct. 1928):17-19. By a cousin of Mary Plummer.

Brown, Bernard E. "Pressure Politics in France." *Journal of Politics* 18 (1956):702-19.

Bruhat, Jean; Dautry, Jean; and Tersen, Émile. *La Commune de 1871*. 2nd ed. Éditions Sociales, 1970.

Brulat, Paul. *Lumières et grandes ombres: Souvenirs et confidences*. B. Grasset, 1930.

Brunschwig, Henri. *French Colonialism, 1871-1914: Myths and Realities*. Translated by W. G. Brown. New York: Frederick A. Praeger, 1966.

Bruntz, George C. *Allied Propaganda and the Collapse of the German Empire, 1918*. Hoover War Library Publications, no. 13. Stanford, CA: Stanford University Press, 1938.

*Bruun, Geoffrey. *Clemenceau*. Cambridge, MA: Harvard University Press, 1944. Outdated but insightful.

Bugnet, Charles. *En écoutant le maréchal Foch (1921-1929)*. B. Grasset, 1929.

_____. *Rue St.-Dominique et G. Q. G., ou les trois dictatures de la guerre*. Librairie Plon, 1937.

Buican, Denis. *Histoire de la génétique et de l'évolutionnisme en France*. Presses Universitaires de France, 1984.

Bunselmeyer, Robert E. *The Cost of the War, 1914-1919: British Economic War Aims and the Origin of Reparation*. Hamden, CT: Archon Books, 1975.

Buré, Émile. "Camille Pelletan et Georges Clemenceau." *L'Ordre*, 17 July 1933.

_____. "Clemenceau et la classe ouvrière: Reponse à R. de Marmande de 'Syndicats.'" *L'Ordre*, 14 Aug. 1938. Buré was a sometime friend and colleague.

_____. "Clemenceau et la Commune." *Revue hebdomadaire*, 12 April 1930.

_____. "M. Georges Clemenceau, homme de lettres." *L'Éclair*, 23 June 1924.

Burnett, Philip Mason. *Reparation at the Paris Peace Conference, from the Standpoint of the American Delegation*. New York: Columbia University Press, 1940.

*Burnett, Robert A. "Georges Clemenceau in the Paris Peace Conference, 1919." Ph.D. dissertation, University of North Carolina, 1968.

_____. "*L'Homme Libre-L'Homme Enchaîné*: How a Journalist Handled the Press [at the Paris Peace Conference]." *Journalism Quarterly* 50 (1973):708-715.

Burns, Michael. *Rural Society and French Politics: Boulangism and the Dreyfus Affair, 1886-1900*. Princeton, NJ: Princeton University Press, 1984.

Bury, John P. T. *Gambetta's Final Years: 'The Era of Difficulties,' 1877-1882*. New York: Longman, 1982.

Busch, Briton Cooper. *Britain, India, and the Arabs, 1914-1921*. Berkeley, CA: University of California Press, 1971.

Caillaux, Joseph. *Agadir, ma politique extérieure*. A. Michel, 1919.

_____. *Devant l'histoire: Mes prisons*. 2nd ed. Éditions de la Sirène, 1920.

*_____. *Mes mémoires*. 3 vols. Plon, 1942-1947.

Cairns, John C. "March 7, 1936, Again: The View from Paris." *International Journal* 20 (1965):230-246.

Calhoun, Arthur Fryar. "The Politics of Internal Order: French Government and Revolutionary Labor, 1898-1914." Ph.D. dissertation, Princeton University, 1973.

Callwell, Maj.-Gen. Sir Charles E. *Field-Marshal Sir Henry Wilson: His Life and Diaries*. 2 vols. London: Cassell, 1927.

*Cambon, Jules. "Georges Clemenceau." *Revue des deux mondes*, 15 Dec. 1929, pp. 16-24.

Cambon, Paul. *Correspondance, 1870-1924*. 3 vols. Bernard Grasset, 1940-1946.

Capus, Alfred. "M. Georges Clemenceau." *Revue hebdomadaire* 22 Feb. 1919, pp. 421-439.

*_____. "Une visite à M. Clemenceau." *Le Gaulois*, 26 May 1920.

Carley, Michael J. "The Origins of the French Intervention in the Russian Civil War, January-May 1918: A Reappraisal." *Journal of Modern History* 48 (1976):413-439.

584

_____. *Revolution and Intervention: The French Government and the Russian Civil War, 1917-1919.* Kingston and Montreal: McGill-Queen's University Press, 1983.

Carls, Stephen Douglas. "Louis Loucheur: A French Technocrat in Government, 1916-1920." Ph.D. dissertation, University of Minnesota, 1982.

Carr, Philip. "Clemenceau." *Fortnightly Review* 126 (1926):401-413.

Carré, Dr. Adrien. "Conférence sur Clemenceau." *Société archéologique et historique de Nantes et de Loire-Atlantique, Bulletin,* 116 (1979-80):11-25.

Carrot, Georges. *Le maintien de l'ordre en France.* 2 vols. Thèse Droit, Nice, 1982. Toulouse: Presses de l'Institut d'études politiques, 1984.

Castex, Henri. *Les Comités secrets: la "Grande Guerre" pour rien?* Éditions Roblot, 1974.

_____. *Les Comités secrets: 1917, la paix refusée, un million de morts inutiles.* Librairie Gedalge, 1972.

_____. *La Guerre parlé: Les comité secrets--la fin du second pouvoir--"le gouvernement de Chantilly."* Éditions du Mont-Cenis, 1971.

Catalogue de l'exposition Georges Clemenceau, 1841-1929, organisée au musée du Petit-Palais, 1979-1980. Les Presses artistiques, 1979.

Centenaire Woodrow Wilson: 1856-1956. Geneva: Centre européen de la Dotation Carnegie, 1956.

Challener, Richard D. *The French Theory of the Nation in Arms (1866-1939).* New York: Columbia University Press, 1955.

Chamberlain, Joseph. *A Political Memoir, 1880-1892.* London: Batchworth Press, 1953.

Chapman, Guy. *The Dreyfus Case: A Reassessment.* London: Rupert Hart-Davis, 1955.

_____. *The Dreyfus Trials.* New York: Stein & Day, 1972.

_____. *The Third Republic of France: The First Phase, 1871-1894.* London: Macmillan, 1962.

Charle, Christophe. *Les élites de la république (1880-1900).* Librairie Arthème Fayard, 1987.

Charles-Roux, François. *Souvenirs diplomatiques. Rome-Quirinal. Février 1916-février 1919.* A. Fayard, 1958.

Charlton, Donald Geoffrey. *Positivist Thought in France During the Second Empire.* Oxford: Clarendon Press, 1959.

Chastenet, Jacques. *La France de M. Fallières: Une époque pathétique.* Arthème Fayard, 1949.

_____. *Gambetta.* Fayard, 1968.

_____. *Histoire de la Troisième République.* 6 vols. Hachette, 1952-63.

_____. *Raymond Poincaré.* Julliard, 1948.

Chevalier, Pierre. *La séparation de l'Église et de l'École: Jules Ferry et Léon XIII.* Fayard, 1982.

Chichet, Étienne. *Feuilles volantes: Quarante ans de journalisme.* Nouvelles Éditions Latines, 1935.

Choury, Maurice. *Les origines de la Commune, Paris livré.* Éditions Sociales, 1960.

Churchill, Winston S. *Amid These Storms: Thoughts and Adventures.* New York: Scribner's, 1932.

*_____. *Great Contemporaries.* New York: G. P. Putnam's Sons, 1937.

Claris, Edmond. *Souvenirs de soixante ans de journalisme, 1895-1955.* José Millas-Martin, 1958.

Clark, Linda L. *Social Darwinism in France.* University, AL: University of Alabama Press, 1984.

*"The Clemenceau Case." *The World* (N.Y.), 14 March 1892. An interview with Mme. G. Clemenceau.

Clemenceau et la justice. Actes du Colloque de décembre 1979 organisé pour le cinquantenaire de la mort de G. Clemenceau. Série "France XIX-XXᵉ," no. 15. Université de Paris 1. Publications de la Sorbonne, 1983. Essays by 17 specialists.

*"Clemenceau et les enfants-assistés." *L'Hôpital et l'aide sociale à Paris* 6 (1965):641-643.

Clemenceau, Madeleine [Mme. Michel], and Goublet, Juliette. *Georges Clemenceau: Sa vie racontée à Jeunesse de France.* Aurillac: Éditions du Centre, 1966.

586

Clemenceau, Michel. "La vie ardente de Georges Clemenceau." Conférence faite aux anciens combattants de la Seine-Maritime le 11 novembre 1957. Musée Clemenceau MS.

*Clemenceau-Jacquemaire, Madeleine. "Memories of My Father." Translated by H. I. Eager. *Delineator* [N.Y.], Feb. 1921, pp. 19ff.

*_____. *Le pot de basilic.* J. Tallandier, 1928. A novel with characters and settings from her family background.

Clémentel, Étienne. *La France et la politique économique interalliée,* Presses Universitaires de France, 1931.

Coblentz, Paul. *Georges Mandel.* Éditions du Belier, 1946.

Coffman, Edward M. *The War to End All Wars: The American Military Experience in World War I.* New York: Oxford University Press, 1968.

Cole, Hubert. *Laval: A Biography.* New York: G. P. Putnam's Sons, 1963.

Combarieu, Abel. *Sept ans à l'Élysee avec le président Émile Loubet.* Librairie Hachette, 1932.

Combes, Émile. *Mon ministère: Mémoires 1902-1905.* Librairie Plon, 1956.

Contamine, Henry. *La Revanche, 1871-1914.* Éditions Berger-Levrault, 1957.

Cooper, M. B. "British Policy in the Balkans, 1908-09." *Historical Journal* [Cambridge] 7 (1964):258-279.

Corday, Michel. *L'envers de la guerre: Journal inédit, 1914-1918.* 2 vols. Flammarion, 1932.

*Cordier, Gaston, and Soubiran, André. "La thèse d'un étundiant en médecine hors série: Georges Clemenceau (13 mai 1865)." *La Presse médicale* 73, no. 52 (1 Dec. 1965), pp. 3029-3034.

Corra, Émile. "Clemenceau positiviste." *Revue Positiviste internationale* 24 (1929):348-352.

Coutéla, Charles. "Georges Clemenceau, la médecine et les médecins." *La Presse médicale* 73, no. 24 (1965), pp. 1435-1438.

Crafts, N. F. R. "Economic Growth in France and Britain, 1830-1910: A Review of the Evidence." *Journal of Economic History* 44 (1984):49-67.

Craig, Gordon A., and Gilbert, Felix, eds. *The Diplomats, 1919-1934.* Princeton, NJ: Princeton University Press, 1953.

Cresson, G.-L. *Cent jours du siège à la Préfecture de Police.* Plon-Nourrit, 1901.

Crisp, Olga. "The Russian Liberals and the 1906 Anglo-French Loan to Russia." *Slavonic and East European Review* 39 (1961):496-511.

Cromwell, Richard S. "Russia's Collapse in World War I: The Military and Economic Impact on the Central Powers." *East European Quarterly* 7 (1973):265-284.

Cross, Gary. "Les Trois Huits: Labor Movements, International Reform, and the Origins of the Eight-Hour Day, 1919-1924." *French Historical Studies* 14, no. 2 (Fall 1985), pp. 240-268.

Crozier, Philippe. "L'Autriche et l'avant guerre." *Revue de France* 1 (1921):268-308, 560-589; 2 (1921):325-358, 576-617.

Cyon, Élie de. *Histoire de l'entente Franco-Russe 1886-1894: Documents et souvenirs.* 2nd ed. Lausanne: B. Benda, 1895.

Damé, Frédéric. *La Résistance; les maires, les députés de Paris, et la comité central du 18 au 26 mars, avec pièces officielles et documents inédits.* Alphonse Lemerre, 1871.

Dansette, Adrien. *L'Affaire Wilson et la chute du Président Grévy.* 2nd ed. Perrin, 1936.

_____. *Les affaires de Panama.* 2nd ed. Librairie Académique Perrin, 1934.

_____. *Le boulangisme.* Librairie Arthème Fayard, 1946.

Daudet, Léon. *La vie orageuse de Clemenceau.* Albin Michel, 1938. Inferior to his other writings touching on Clemenceau, on which see Duroselle, *Clemenceau.*

Dautry, Jean, and Schéler, Lucien. *Le Comité Central Républicain des vingts arrondissements de Paris (septembre 1870-mai 1871).* Éditions Sociales, 1960.

Debidour, A. *L'Église catholique et l'État sous la troisième république (1870-1906).* 2 vols. Félix Alcan, 1909.

Debo, Richard K. "Mesentente glaciale: Great Britain, France and the Question of Intervention in the Baltic, 1918." *Canadian Journal of History* 12 (1977):65-86.

_____. *Revolution and Survival: The Foreign Policy of Soviet Russia, 1917-18.* Toronto: University of Toronto Press, 1979.

Decaux, Alain. *Blanqui l'insurgé*. Librairie Académique Perrin, 1976.

Defrasne, (Colonel) J. "La guerre psychologique pendant le premier conflit mondial." *Revue historique de l'Armée* 13, no. 3 (1957), pp. 63-85.

Derfler, Leslie. *Alexandre Millerand: The Socialist Years*. The Hague: Mouton, 1977.

Desachy, Paul. *Une grande figure de l'affaire Dreyfus: Louis Leblois*. Éditions Rieder, 1934.

Desagneaux, Henri. *Journal de guerre 14-18*. Denoël, 1971.

Devos, Jean-Claude, and Nicot, Jean. "La censure de la presse pendant la guerre de 1914-1918." Comité des travaux historiques et scientifiques. *Actes du 105ᵉ Congrès national des Sociétés savantes, Caen, 1980. Section d'histoire moderne et contemporaine*. Vol. 1: *La diffusion du savoir de 1600 à nos jours. Questions diverses*, pp. 343-364.

Dickmann, Fritz. "Die Kriegsschuldfrage auf der Friedenskonferenz von Paris 1919." *Historische Zeitshcrift* 197 (1963):1-101.

Dietrich-Erdmann, Karl. "Clemenceau, l'Allemagne et le problème d'une paix de droit." In *Clemenceau et la justice* (q.v.), pp. 183-188.

Dietz, J. "Jules Ferry: Son première présidence du conseil." *Revue politique et parlementaire*, 10 Aug. 1935, pp. 96-109.

_____. "Jules Ferry: La révision de la constitution et le scrutin de liste." *Revue politique et parlementaire*, 10 Nov. 1935, pp. 515-532; 10 Dec. 1935, pp. 101-117.

*Dimnet, Ernest. "Georges Clemenceau, Writer and Philosopher." *Nineteenth Century* 61 (1907):611-617.

Dobie, Edith. "Clemenceau's Accession to Power in 1917." *Southwestern Social Science Quarterly* [Austin] 12 (1931):61-76.

Dockrill, Michael L. "Britain, the United States, and France and the German Settlement 1918-1920." In B. J. C. McKercher and D. J. Moss, eds., *Shadow and Substance in British Foreign Policy, 1895-1939: Memorial Essays Honouring C. J. Lowe*. Edmonton, Alberta: The University of Alberta Press, 1984.

_____ and Goold, J. Douglas. *Peace Without Promise: Britain and the Peace Conferences, 1919-23*. Hamden, CT: Archon Books, 1981.

Dogan, Mattei. "Le personnel parlementaire sous la 3ᵉ république." *Revue française de science politique* 3 (1953):319-348.

Dolléans, É. *Histoire du mouvement ouvrier (1871-1920)*. 2 vols. 4th ed. Colin, 1953.

*Domestici-Met, Mario-José. "Le deuxième gouvernement de Clemenceau, 1917-1920: Contribution à l'étude du chef de gouvernement en régime parlementaire." *Revue du droit public et de la science politique en France et à l'étranger* 102 (1986):1097-1151.

Dominique, Pierre. "Lettres de Clemenceau à une amie." *Écrits de Paris*, no. 294 (1970), pp. 68-75. Review of the volume of letters to Marguerite Baldensperger.

Dommanget, Maurice. *Auguste Blanqui au debut de la IIIe république (1871-1880)*. Mouton, 1971.

_____. *Blanqui et l'opposition révolutionnaire à la fin du Second Empire*. A. Colin, 1960.

_____. *Blanqui, la guerre de 1870-71 et la Commune*. Donat-Montchrestien, 1947.

_____. *Les idées politiques et sociales d'Auguste Blanqui*. Marcel Rivière, 1957.

Doty, C. Stewart. "Parliamentary Boulangism after 1889." *The Historian* 32 (1970):250-269.

Douglas, Lewis W. "Clemenceau." In Lord Longford [Frank Pakenham] and Sir John Wheeler-Bennett, eds., *The History Makers: Leaders and Statesmen of the 20th Century*. New York, St. Martin's Press, 1973, pp. 8-33.

Draghicesco, D. "La philosophie de Clemenceau." *Revue mondiale* [formerly *Revue des revues*] 199 (1930):287-300.

Dreux, Robert. "Clemenceau et Viviani." *L'Ordre*, 23 Nov. 1938.

Dreyfus, Alfred, and Dreyfus, Pierre. *The Dreyfus Case*. Translated and edited by Donald C. McKay. New Haven, CT: Yale University Press, 1937.

*Dreyfus, Mathieu. *L'Affaire: Telle que je l'ai vécue*. Bernard Grasset, 1978.

*Drieu la Rochelle, Pierre. "Paroles d'outre-tombe." *Revue hebdomadaire*, 7 Dec. 1929, pp. 5-17. Interview in 1923 which he forbade being published until after his death.

Dubief, H.; Garmy, R.; and Kriegel, A. "Legs Hélène Brion." *Le Mouvement social* 44 (1963):93-100.

Dubly, Henry-Louis. *La vie ardente de Georges Clemenceau.* 2 vols. Lille: "Mercure de Flandre," 1930. A few good observations and a section on religion; otherwise worthless.

Ducray, Camille. *Clemenceau.* Payot, 1918. Some material on his education.

*Duroselle, Jean-Baptiste. *Clemenceau.* Fayard, 1988. The standard, and the first full scholarly treatment in French.

_____. "Clemenceau et la 'Paix de Droit.'" In *Clemenceau et la justice* (q.v.), pp. 171-181.

_____. "Clemenceau et l'Italie." *La France et l'Italie pendant la Première Guerre mondiale* (q.v.), pp. 492-511, 541-542.

_____. "Clemenceau vu par Orlando." *Revue politique et parlementaire* 63, no. 712 (1961), pp. 26-34.

_____. *La France et les Français, 1900-1914.* Éditions Richelieu, 1972.

Dutton, David J. "The Balkan Campaign and French War Aims in the Great War." *English Historical Review* 94, no. 370 (1979), pp. 97-113.

_____. "Paul Painlevé and the End of the Sacred Union in Wartime France." *Journal of Strategic Studies* 4 (1981):46-59.

Edwards, E. W. "The Far Eastern Agreements of 1907." *Journal of Modern History* 26 (1954):340-355.

_____. "The Franco-German Agreement on Morocco, 1909." *English Historical Review* 78 (1963):483-513.

Egerton, George W. *Great Britain and the Creation of the League of Nations: Strategy, Politics, and International Organization, 1914-1919.* Chapel Hill, NC: University of North Carolina Press, 1978.

Ellingson, Douglas Wayne. "The Politics of the French Chamber of Deputies, 1881-1889." Ph.D. dissertation, University of Minnesota, 1977.

*Ellis, Jack D. *The Early Life of Georges Clemenceau, 1841-1893.* Lawrence, KA: The Regents Press of Kansas, 1980. A study emphasizing psychological considerations from an Eriksonian perspective.

Elwitt, Sanford. *The Third Republic Defended: Bourgeois Reform in France, 1880-1914.* Baton Rouge, LA: Louisiana State University Press, 1986.

Emmerson, James T. *The Rhineland Crisis, 7 March 1936: A Study in Multilateral Diplomacy.* Ames, IA: Iowa State University Press, 1977.

Engel-Janosi, Friedrich. "Die Friedensaktion des Frau Hofrat Szeps-Zuckerkandl im Fröhjahr 1917." *Archiv für Osterreichische Geschichte* 125 (1966):257-268.

Engels, Friedrich, and Lafargue, Paul and Laura. *Correspondance (1868-1895).* 3 vols. Éditions Sociales, 1956-1959.

*Erlanger, Philippe. *Clemenceau.* Grasset, Paris-Match, 1968. Non-scholarly but quite well informed.

Escholier, Raymond. *Souvenirs parlés par Briand.* Hachette, 1932.

Esher, Reginald Baliol Brett, 2nd Viscount. *Journals and Letters of Reginald, Viscount Esher.* Edited by Maurice V. Brett and Oliver, Viscount Esher. 4 vols. London: I. Nicholson & Watson, 1934-1938.

Estèbe, Jean. *Les ministres de la République, 1871-1914.* Presses de la Fondation nationale des sciences politiques, 1982.

Euloge, Georges-André. *Histoire de la police et de la gendarmerie: Des origines à 1940.* Plon, 1985.

"The Fall of M. Clemenceau." *Fortnightly Review* 92 (1909):197-203.

*"Les familles Clemenceau et Gautreau." *Société de l'histoire, du protestantisme français. Bulletin historique et littéraire* 78 (1929):440-444.

Farley, John. *The Spontaneous Generation Controversy from Descartes to Oparin.* Baltimore: The Johns Hopkins University Press, 1977.

Farrar, Majorie M. "Victorious Nationalismus Beleaguered: Alexandre Millerand as French Premier in 1920." *Proceedings of the American Philosophical Society* 126, no. 6 (1982), pp. 481-519.

Fayolle, Maréchal [Marie-Émile]. *Cahiers secrets de la Grande Guerre.* Edited by Henry Contamine. Plon, 1964.

Ferrier, R. W. "French Oil Policy, 1917-30: The Interaction Between State and Private Interests." In D. C. Coleman and Peter Mathias, eds., *Enterprise and History: Essays in Honour of Charles Wilson.* Cambridge: Cambridge University Press, 1984, pp. 237-262.

Ferro, Marc. *The Great War, 1914-1918.* Translated by N. Stone. London: Routledge & Kegan Paul, 1973.

Ferry, Abel. *Les carnets secrets (1914-1918) d'Abel Ferry.* Bernard Grasset, 1957.

_____. *La guerre vue d'en bas et d'en haut.* 3rd ed. Bernard Grasset, 1920.

Ferry, Jules. *Lettres de Jules Ferry, 1846-1893.* Calmann-Lévy, 1914.

Fest, Wilfried. *Peace or Partition: The Habsburg Monarchy and British Policy, 1914-1918.* New York: St. Martin's Press, 1978.

Fiaux, Louis. *Histoire de la guerre civil de 1871.* G. Charpentier, 1879. Especially on the 18 March uprising.

Fiechter, Jean-Jacques. *Le socialisme français: De l'affaire Dreyfus à la Grande Guerre.* Geneva: Librairie Droz, 1965.

Fischer, Fritz. *Germany's Aims in the First World War.* New York: W. W. Norton, 1967.

Floto, Inge. *Colonel House in Paris: A Study of American Policy at the Paris Peace Conference, 1919.* Aarhus: Universitets-forlaget, 1973.

Flourens, Émile. *La France conquise: Édouard VII et Clemenceau.* Garnier Frères, 1906. By a former foreign minister; illustrative of the lingering hostility toward him.

Foch, Maréchal [Ferdinand]. *Mémoires pour servir à l'histoire de la guerre 1914-1918.* 2 vols. Librairie Plon, 1931. Disappointing.

Fowler, W. B. *British-American Relations, 1917-1918: The Role of Sir William Wiseman.* Princeton, NJ: Princeton University Press, 1969.

France. Ministère de la Guerre. État-Major de l'Armée--Service historique. *Les armées françaises dans la Grande Guerre.* 102 vols. Imprimerie Nationale, 1922-1937.

_____. Ministère des Affaires étrangeres. Commission de publication des documents relatifs aux origines de la guerre de 1914. *Documents diplomatiques français (1871-1914).* 3 series. Imprimerie Nationale, 1929-1959. Especially for 1906-1909.

La France et l'Italie pendant la Première guerre mondiale. Actes du Colloque tenu à l'université des Sciences sociales de Grenoble...28, 29, 30 septembre 1973. Grenoble: Presses Universitaires de Grenoble, 1976.

Freycinet, Charles de. *Souvenirs, 1848-1893.* 2 vols. 4th ed. Charles Delagrave, 1912-1913.

Fulton, L. Bruce. "Ernest Constans and the Presidency of the French Republic, 1889-92." *Australian Journal of Politics and History* 30 (1984):31-45.

_____. "France and the End of the Ottoman Empire." In Marian Kent, ed., *The Great Powers and the End of the Ottoman Empire*. Winchester, MA: Allen & Unwin, 1984, pp. 141-171.

Fussell, Paul. *The Great War and Modern Memory*. New York: Oxford University Press, 1975.

Furet, François. "Jules Ferry et l'histoire de la Révolution française: Le polémique autour du livre d'Edgar Quinet, 1865-1866." In François Furet, ed., *Jules Ferry, fondateur de la République* (q.v.), pp. 15-22.

_____. ed. *Jules Ferry, fondateur de la République*. Colloque de l'École des hautes études en sciences sociales, 1982, présenté par François Furet. Civilisations et Sociétés, no. 72. Éditions de l'École des hautes études en sciences sociales, 1985.

*Gabriel-Robinet, Louis. "Clemenceau journaliste." *Les Annales* 64, no. 80 (1957), pp. 5-20.

*Gaillard, Abbé. "L'Aubraie des Clemenceau." *Revue du Bas-Poitou*, no. 1 (1930), pp. 1-11.

Gaillard, Jeanne. "Le conseil municipal et municipalisme parisien (1871-1890)." *Société d'histoire moderne, Bulletin* 81, no. 13 (1982), pp. 7-16.

_____. "Le radicalisme pendant la commune d'après les papiers de la Ligue d'Union républicaine des Droits de Paris." *Société d'histoire moderne, Bulletin*, no. 1, 1966, pp. 8-14.

Galérant, Dr. Germain. "L'odieuse legende de la mort du président Félix Faure." *Histoire des sciences médicales* 19 (1985):175-182.

Gallo, M. "Quelques aspects de la mentalité et du comportement ouvriers dans les usines de guerre 1914-18." *Mouvement social*, no. 56 (July-Sept. 1966), pp. 3-33.

Gambiez, General Fernand. "Allocution d'ouverture." *Les fronts invisibles: Nourrir-fournir-soigner*. Actes du Colloque international sur la logistique des armées au combat pendant la première guerre mondiale, organisé à Verdun les 6, 7, 8 juin 1980, organisé par le Comité national du Souvenir de Verdun, Université de Nancy II, communications réunies par Gérard Canini. Nancy: Presses Universitaires de Nancy, 1984.

_____. "Le combattant de 1918." *Revue historique de l'Armée* 24, no. 4 (1968), pp. 7-16.

Ganiage, Jean. *L'expansion coloniale de la France sous la IIIe république, 1871-1914.* Payot, 1968.

Gardner, Lloyd C. *Safe for Democracy: The Anglo-American Response to Revolution, 1913-1923.* New York: Oxford University Press, 1984.

Garvin, James Louis. *The Life of Joseph Chamberlain.* 3 vols. London: Macmillan, 1932-1934.

*Gatineau-Clemenceau, Georges. *Des pattes du Tigre aux griffes du destin.* Les Presses du Mail, 1961. A black-sheep grandson (Thérèse's son) hangs out some family wash. Must be approached with caution.

Gauthier, Robert, ed. *"Dreyfusards!" Souvenirs de Mathieu Dreyfus et autres inédits.* Julliard, 1965.

Geffroy, Gustave. *L'enfermé.* 2 vols. Rev. ed. Éditions G. Crès, 1926. Biography of Auguste Blanqui.

*_____. *Georges Clemenceau, sa vie, son oeuvre.* Avec des pages choisies et annotées par Louis Lumet. New ed. Librairie Larousse, n.d. [1932]. By a longtime intimate friend, a prominent art critic. Contains a valuable list of newspaper collaborations.

George, Alexander L. and Juliette L. *Woodrow Wilson and Colonel House: A Personality Study.* New York: Dover Publications, 1964.

Georges, Bernard, and Tintant, Denise. *Léon Jouhaux, cinquante ans de syndicalisme.* Presses Universitaires de France, 1962.

Georges Clemenceau. Collection Génies et Réalités. Hachette, 1974. Essays by Jacques Chastenet, Maurice Schumann, J.-B. Duroselle et al.

"Georges Clemenceau et la guerre. Essai bibliographique." *Revue d'histoire de la guerre mondiale* 8 (1930):51-62.

Gheusi, Pierre-Benjamin. *Cinquante ans de Paris: Mémoires d'un témoin.* 3 vols. Plon, 1939-1941.

Gilbert, Martin. *Winston S. Churchill.* Vol. 4: *The Stricken World, 1916-1922.* Boston: Houghton Mifflin, 1975.

Girard, Louis. "Jules Ferry et la génération des républicains du Second Empire." In François Furet, ed., *Jules Ferry, fondateur de la Republique* (q.v.), pp. 49-58.

*Goblet, René. "Souvenirs de ma vie politique." *Revue politique et parlementaire* 136 (1928):357-389; 137 (1928):177-197, 345-373; 139

(1929):5-20, 183-208, 359-374; 140 (1929):5-17; 141 (1929):5-29, 171-194; 145 (1930):337-358; 149 (1931):177-196.

Godin, Pierre. "Qu'eut fait Clemenceau." *L'Homme Libre*, 15 June 1951. Godin was formerly Directeur du Cabinet civil for Clemenceau.

Goguel-Nyegaard, François. *La politique des partis sous la IIIe république.* 2 vols. Éditions du Seuil, 1946.

*Gohier, Urbain. *La vraie figure de Clemenceau.* Éditions Baudinière, 1932. Hostile portrait by a former colleague at *L'Aurore* during the Dreyfus Affair.

*Gola, A.-G. *Clemenceau et son sous-préfet: Souvenirs et entretiens.* Fontenay-le-Comte: Imprimerie Moderne, 1937.

Goldberg, Harvey. *The Life of Jean Jaurès.* Madison, WI: University of Wisconsin Press, 1966.

Gombault, Georges. [Article on the ending of the censorship.] *L'Oeuvre*, 13 Oct. 1919.

Goncourt, Edmond and Jules de. *Journal des Goncourt--Mémoirs de la vie littéraire.* 4 vols. É. Fasquelle, 1891-1907.

Gonda, Eugène. *La conférence de Versailles: La bataille perdue de Georges Clemenceau, novembre 1918.* Éditions LPF Paris, 1981. The failed attempt to adopt the French plan for the conference including a Preliminary Peace.

Gordon, Robert, and Forge, Andrew. *Monet.* Translated by John Shapley. New York: Henry N. Abrams, 1983.

*Gosse, Edmund. "The Writings of M. Clemenceau." *Edinburgh Review* 229 (1919):253-270.

Graham, James Q., Jr. "The French Radical and Radical-Socialist Party, 1906-1914." Ph.D. dissertation, The Ohio State University, 1962.

Grasset, Colonel A. "Clemenceau, Foch et l'unité de commandement." *L'Illustration*, 3 May 1930, pp. 2-4. Author was a member of Clemenceau's *cabinet militaire*, Nov. 1917-1919.

Great Britain. Foreign Office. *British Documents on the Origins of the War, 1898-1914.* 22 vols. London: His Majesty's Stationery Office, 1926-38. Especially for 1906-1909.

Griffen, David Eugene. "Adolphe Thiers, the Mayors, and the Coming of the Paris Commune of 1871." Ph.D. dissertation, University of California, Santa Barbara, 1971.

Grigg, John. *Lloyd George: From Peace to War, 1912-1916.* Berkeley, CA: University of California Press, 1985.

Die Grosse Politik der Europäischen Kabinette, 1871-1914. Johannes Lepsius, Albrecht Mendelssohn Bartholdy, and Friedrich Thimme, eds. 40 vols. Berlin: Deutsche Verlagsgesellschaft für Politik, 1922-1927. Especially for 1906-1909.

Groussac, Paul. *M. Clemenceau et la République Argentine.* Librairie Champion, 1911. Extract from the *Revue politique et littéreaire (Revue Bleue)* of 11 Nov. 1911.

Grupp, Peter. "Eugène Étienne et la tentative de rapprochemente franco-allemand en 1907." *Cahiers d'études africaines* 15 (1975):303-311.

Guépin, Dr. A., and Bonamy, Dr. E. *Nantes au XIXe siècle: Statistique topographique, industrielle et morale.* Reédition précédée de "De l'observation de la ville comme corps social," par MM. Ph. Le Pichon et A. Supiot. Nantes: Centre de recherche politique, Université de Nantes, 1981.

Guillen, Pierre. *L'expansion, 1881-1898.* Vol. 3 of *Politique étrangère de la France,* dirigée par Jean-Baptiste Duroselle. Imprimerie Nationale, 1984.

Guinn, Paul. *British Strategy and Politics, 1914 to 1918.* Oxford: The Clarendon Press, 1965.

Guiral, Pierre. "Le style de Georges Clemenceau: L'écrivain et l'orateur." In *Clemenceau et la justice* (q.v.), pp. 93-99.

Guyot, J.-C. "Lorsque Clemenceau visitait le front." *Aux Carrefours de l'histoire,* no. 1 (July-Aug. 1957), pp. 55-57.

Haig, Douglas. *The Private Papers of Douglas Haig, 1914-1919.* Edited by Robert Blake. London: Eyre & Spatiswoode, 1952.

Halévy, Daniel. *Clemenceau.* Les Amis d'Édouard, no. 149. Abbéville, F. Paillart, 1930.

Halpern, Paul G. *The Mediterranean Naval Situation, 1908-1914.* Cambridge, MA: Harvard University Press, 1971.

Hamilton, K. A. "Great Britain, France, and the Origins of the Mediterranean Agreements of 16 May 1907." In *Shadow and Substance in British Foreign Policy, 1895-1939: Memorial Essays Honouring C. J. Lowe.* Edited by J. C. McKercher and D. J. Moss. Edmonton: University of Alberta Press, 1984, pp. 115-146.

Hankey, Lord [Maurice]. *The Supreme Command, 1914-1918.* 2 vols. London: George Allen & Unwin, 1961.

_____. *The Supreme Control at the Paris Peace Conference 1919: A Commentary*. London: George Allen & Unwin, 1963.

Harding, James. *The Astonishing Adventure of General Boulanger*. New York: Charles Scribner's Sons, 1971.

Harrigan, Patrick. *Mobility, Elites, and Education in French Society of the Second Empire*. Waterloo, Ontario: Wilfred Laurier University Press, 1980.

Hause, Steven C., with Kenney, Anne R. *Women's Suffrage and Social Politics in the Third French Republic*. Princeton, NJ: Princeton University Press, 1984.

Hayes, Carlton J. H. *A Generation of Materialism, 1871-1900*. The Rise of Modern Europe Series, William L. Langer, ed. New York: Harper & Brothers, 1941.

Headlam-Morley, Sir James. *A Memoir of the Paris Peace Conference, 1919*. Edited by Agnes Headlam-Morley, Russell Bryant, and Anna Cienciala. London: Methuen, 1972.

Helmreich, Paul C. *From Paris to Sèvres: The Partition of the Ottoman Empire at the Peace Conference of 1919-1920*. Columbus, OH: The Ohio State University Press, 1974.

Hemmings, F. W. J. *Émile Zola*. 2nd ed. Oxford: Clarendon Press, 1966.

Herbillon, Colonel Émile E. *Le général Alfred Micheler, d'après son correspondance et ses notes*. Librairie Plon, 1934.

_____. *Souvenirs d'un officier de liaison pendant la guerre mondiale: Du général en chef au gouvernement*. 2 vols. Jules Tallandier, 1930.

Hewes, James E., Jr. "Henry Cabot Lodge and the League of Nations." *Proceedings of the American Philosophical Society* 114, no. 4 (1970), pp. 245-255.

Hinsley, F. H. "The Rise and Fall of the Modern International System." *Review of International Studies* [Great Britain] 8 (1982):1-8.

Hoffman, Robert Louis. *More Than a Trial: The Struggle Over Captain Dreyfus*. New York: The Free Press, 1980.

Hoffmann, Stanley. *Decline or Renewal: France Since the 1930s*. New York: The Viking Press, 1974.

Hogenhuis-Seliverstoff, Anne. *Les relations franco-soviétiques, 1917-1924*. Publications de la Sorbonne, 1981.

Holt, Edgar. *The Tiger: The Life of Georges Clemenceau, 1841-1929.* London: Hamilton, 1976. Journalist; respectable non-scholarly work.

Homberg, Octave. *Les coulisses de l'histoire: Souvenirs, 1898-1928.* Arthème Fayard, 1938.

Homem-Christo, F. de. *Les porte-flambeaux.* Éditions Fast, n.d. [1918].

Hostetter, Richard J. "The Anti-War Policy of the French Socialist Party (S. F. I. O.) 1905-1914: A Study of Patriotism Expressed Through the Ideas of the General Strike and Insurrection." Ph.D. dissertation, University of California, 1947.

Hovi, Kalervo. *Cordon sanitaire ou barrière de l'Est? The Emergence of the New French Eastern European Policy, 1917-1919.* Turku: Turin Yliopisto, 1975.

Hubert, Lucien. "A la commission sénatoriale des affaires étrangerès (1915-1918)." *Revue d'histoire diplomatique* 81 (1967):233-253.

Huddleston, Sisley. *In My Time: An Observer's Record of War and Peace* New York: E. P. Dutton, 1938.

*Hugues, Pierre d'. "M. Clemenceau et la bureaucratie." *La Grande Revue*, Dec. 1929, pp. 258-265.

Huthmacher, J. Joseph, and Susman, Warren I., Jr., eds. *Wilson's Diplomacy: An International Symposium.* The American Forum Series. Cambridge, MA: Schenkman, 1973. Contributions by Arthur S. Link, J.-B. Duroselle et al.

Hutton, Patrick H. "Popular Boulangism and the Advent of Mass Politics: In Interpretation of the Boulangist Movement in France, 1886-90." *Journal of Contemporary History* 11 (1976):85-106.

_____. "The Role of the Blanquist Party in Left-Wing Politics in France, 1879-90." *Journal of Modern History* 46 (1974):277-295.

*Hyndman, Henry M. *Clemenceau, the Man and His Time.* New York: Frederick A. Stokes, 1919. By a founder of British Marxism who knew him personally. Only for its personal recollections.

Irvine, William D. *The Boulanger Affair Reconsidered: Royalism, Boulangism, and the Origins of the Radical Right in France.* New York: Oxford University Press, 1989.

Isorni, Jacques. *Philippe Pétain.* 2 vols. La Table rond, 1972-1973.

Jacobson, Jon. "Review Article: Strategies of French Foreign Policy after World War I." *Journal of Modern History* 55 (1983):78-95.

Jardin, André, and Tudesq, André-Jean. *Restoration and Reaction, 1815-1848*. Translated by Elborg Forster. Cambridge: Cambridge University Press, 1983.

Jardin, Pierre. "L'occupation française en Rhénanie, 1918-1919, Fayolle et l'idée palatine." *Revue d'histoire moderne et contemporaine* 33 (1986):402-426.

Jauffret, Jean-Charles. "Armée et pouvoir politique: La question des troupes spéciales chargées du maintien de l'ordre en France de 1871 à 1914." *Revue historique* 270, no. 547 (1983), pp. 97-144.

Jaurès, Jean. *Oeuvres. Textes rassemblés, présentés et annotés par Max Bonnafous*. 9 vols. Éditions Rieder, 1931-1939.

*_____. "Préface aux *Discours parlementaires*: 'Le socialisme et le radicalisme en 1885,' présentation de Madeleine Rebérioux." Geneva: Slatkine Reprints, 1980.

Jeanneney, Jean-Noël. "L'affaire Rochette: Clemenceau, sa politique et les juges." In *Clemenceau et la justice* (q.v.), pp. 153-159.

_____. *L'argent caché: Milieux d'affaires et pouvoirs politiques dans la France du XXe siècle*. Arthème Fayard, 1981.

_____. "Jacques Millerand parle d'Alexandre Millerand." *Histoire* 8 (1979):108-115.

*Jerrold, Laurence. "M. Clemenceau." *Contemporary Review* 90 (Nov. 1906):679-686. One of a number of insightful articles in this periodical, 1906-1909.

_____. *The Real France*. London: John Lane, 1911.

Jessup, Philip. *Elihu Root*. 2 vols. New York: Dodd, Mead, 1938.

Jobert, Aristide. *Souvenirs d'un ex-parlementaire (1914-1919)*. Éditions Eugène Figuière, 1933.

Johnson, Douglas. *France and the Dreyfus Affair*. New York: Walker, 1967.

Johnston, W. M. "The Origins of the Term 'Intellectuals' in French Novels and Essays of the 1890s." *Journal of European Studies* 4 (1974):43-56.

Jones, R. B. "Anglo-French Negotiations, 1907: A Memorandum by Sir Alfred Milner." *Institute of Historical Research, Bulletin* 31, no. 84 (1958), pp. 224-227.

Jones, Thomas. *Whitehall Diary*. Vol. 1: *1916-1925*. Edited by Keith Middlemas. London: Oxford University Press, 1969.

600

Joughin, Jean T. *The Paris Commune in French Politics, 1871-80*. Baltimore: The Johns Hopkins University Press, 1955.

Jouvenel, Robert de. *La république des camarades*. Bernard Grasset, 1914.

*Judet, Ernest. *Le véritable Clemenceau*. Berne: Ferdinand Wyss, 1920. Savagely hostile account by an old enemy who was convicted of collaboration with the Germans; documentation.

Judt, Tony. *Marxism and the French Left: Studies on Labour and Politics in France, 1830-1981*. Oxford: Clarendon Press, 1986.

_____. *Socialism in Provence, 1871-1914: A Study in the Origins of the French Left*. Cambridge: Cambridge University Press, 1979. Especially for the Var.

Julliard, Jacques. "La C. G. T. devant la guerre (1900-1914)." *Mouvement social*, no. 49 (Oct.-Dec. 1964), pp. 47-62.

*_____. *Clemenceau, briseur de grèves: L'affaire de Draveil-Villeneuve-Saint-Georges, présentée par Jacques Julliard*. Collection Archives Julliard, 1965.

_____. "Clemenceau et les intellectuels." In *Clemenceau et la justice* (q.v.), pp. 101-112.

_____. "Clemenceau, journaliste de l'Affaire." *Les écrivains et l'Affaire Dreyfus*. Textes réunis par Gérald Leroy. Actes du colloque organisé par le Centre Charles Péguy et l'Université d'Orléans, 29, 30, 31 octobre 1981, pp. 167-176.

*Kahn, Gustave. "M. Clemenceau littérateur." *La Nouvelle Revue*, 15 March 1903, pp. 267-272.

Kaiser, David E. "Germany and the Origins of the First World War." *Journal of Modern History* 55 (1983):442-474.

Kalvoda, Josef. *The Genesis of Czechoslovakia*. East European Monographs, no. 209. New York: Columbia University Press, 1986.

Kaspi, André. *Le temps des américains: Le concours américain à la France en 1917-1918*. Publications de la Sorbonne, 1976.

Kayser, Jacques. *L'action républicaine de M. Poincaré avec un article de M. Georges Clemenceau*. A. Delpeuch, 1929. The article is from *Le Bloc*, 15 March 1902, "Le Poincarisme."

_____. *Les grandes batailles du radicalisme, des origines au portes du pouvoir, 1820-1901*. Rivière, 1962.

*_____. "Note sur Clemenceau et le parti radical." *Les Cahiers de la République* 2, no. 9 (Sept.-Oct. 1957), p. 100.

Kedouri, Elie. *England and the Middle East: The Destruction of the Ottoman Empire, 1914-1921*. London: The Harvester Press, 1978.

Keiger, John F. V. *France and the Origins of the First World War*. New York: St. Martin's Press, 1983.

_____. "Jules Cambon and Franco-German Detente, 1907-1914." *Historical Journal* [Cambridge] 26 (1983):641-659.

Kenez, Peter. *Civil War in South Russia, 1919-1920: The Defeat of the Whites*. Berkeley, CA: University of California Press, 1977.

Kennan, George F. *Soviet-American Relations, 1917-1920*. 2 vols. Princeton, NJ: Princeton University Press, 1956-58.

Kent, Marian. *Oil and Empire: British Policy and Mesopotamian Oil, 1900-1920*. New York: Barnes & Noble, 1976.

Kessel, J. "Le voyage triomphale de M. Clemenceau." *L'Illustration*, 9 Dec. 1922, pp. 580-582. The trip to the United States.

Kettle, Michael. *The Allies and the Russian Collapse, March 1917-March 1918*. Vol. 1 of *Russia and the Allies, 1917-1920*. Minneapolis, MN: University of Minnesota Press, 1981.

Keynes, John Maynard. *The Economic Consequences of the Peace*. New York: Harcourt, Brace & Howe, 1920.

Khoury, Philip S. *Syria and the French Mandate: The Politics of Arab Nationalism, 1920-1945*. Princeton, NJ: Princeton University Press, 1987.

*King, Jere Clemens. *Foch Versus Clemenceau: France and German Dismemberment, 1918-1919*. Cambridge, MA: Harvard University Press, 1960.

_____. *Generals and Politicians: Conflicts Between France's High Command, Parliament, and Government, 1914-18*. Berkeley, CA: University of California Press, 1951.

*Kirby, Luella M., and Lenz, Carolyn B. "Wife of Clemenceau Was a Wisconsin Girl." *Wisconsin Then and Now* 16, no. 4 (1969), pp. 6-7.

Klotz, Louis-Lucien. *De la guerre à la paix, souvenirs et documents*. Payot, 1924. By the minister of finance, 1917-1920.

Köhler, Hennig. "La révolution allemande 1918/19 et la France: Problèmes et perspectives politiques en France entre l'armistice de Rethondes et la paix de Versailles." *Francia* 8 (1980):455-463.

Kokovtsov, Count V. M. *Out of My Past: The Memoirs of Count Kokovtsov.* Translated by L. Matveev. Edited by H. H. Fisher. Hoover War Library Publications, no. 6. Stanford, CA: Stanford University Press, 1935.

Kolz, Arno W. F. "Note: British Economic Interests in Siberia During the Russian Civil War, 1918-1920." *Journal of Modern History* 48 (1976):483-491.

Kosyk, Wolodymyr. *La politique de la France à l'égard de l'Ukraine, mars 1917-février 1918.* Publications de la Sorbonne, 1981.

Kranzberg, Melvin. *The Siege of Paris, 1870-1871: A Political and Social History.* Ithaca, NY: Cornell University Press, 1950.

*Krebs, Albert. "Le mariage de Clemenceau." *Mercure de France* 324, no. 1104 (1955), pp. 634-650.

*_____. "Le secret de Clemenceau révélé par les souvenirs d' Auguste Scheurer-Kestner." *Sociéte industrielle de Mulhouse: Bulletin trimestrial,* no. 735 (1969), pp. 67-86. His unsuccessful suit for the hand of Hortense Kestner; long extracts from his letters.

_____, and Wormser, André. "Clemenceau, Scheurer-Kestner et la revendication de l'Alsace-Lorraine." In *Clemenceau et la justice* (q.v.), pp. 3-22.

Kriegel, Annie. *Aux origines du communisme français, 1914-1920.* 2 vols. Montan, 1964.

Krizman, Bogdan. "Austro-Hungarian Diplomacy Before the Collapse of the Empire." *Journal of Contemporary History* 4 (1969):97-115.

Krumeich, Gerd. "Poincaré und der 'Poincarismus.'" *Francia* 8 (1980):427-454.

Kulstein, David T. "The Attitude of French Workers Towards the Second Empire." *French Historical Studies* 2 (1961-1962):356-376.

Kupferman, Alfred. "Les campagnes défaitistes en France et en Italie: 1914-1917." In *La France et l'Italie pendant la Première guerre mondiale* (q.v.), pp. 246-259.

_____. *Laval, 1883-1945.* Balland, 1987.

_____. "L'offensive morale allemande contre la France (novembre 1914-novembre 1917)." *Revue d'Allemagne* 4 (1972):887-906.

_____. "L'opinion française et le défaitisme pendant la Grande Guerre." *Relations internationales*, 1974, no. 2, pp. 91-100.

_____. "Le rôle de Léon Daudet et de *L'Action française* dans la contre-offensive morale, 1915-1918." *2e Colloque Maurras, Aix-en-Provence 1970, Études maurrassienes*, 1973, t. 2, pp. 121-145.

*Lacombe, Pierre de. "L'enigme de Clemenceau." *Revue française de psychanalyse* 12 (1948):297-309. Aside from Ellis (q.v.), the only serious attempt at a psychological study.

Lafargue, Général [André]. *Foch et la bataille de 1918*. Arthaud, 1975.

La Gorce, Paul-Marie de. *The French Army: A Military-Political History*. Translated by K. Douglas. London: Weidenfeld & Nicolson, 1963.

Lane, Robert E. *Political Thinking and Consciousness: The Private Life of the Political Mind*. Chicago: Markham, 1969.

Langer, William L. *The Franco-Russian Alliance, 1890-1894*. Cambridge, MA: Harvard University Press, 1929.

_____. "Russia, the Straits Question, and the European Powers, 1904-8." *English Historical Review* 44 (1929):59-85.

*Langlois, Marcelle-P.-E. "Les dernières heures de Clemenceau." *Histoire de notre temps*, no. 1 (1967), pp. 133-165. Extracts from 188 letters to one of his secretaries.

Lanoux, Armand. *Bonjour Monsieur Zola*. Amiot-Dumont, 1954.

Lansing, Robert. *The Big Four and Others of the Peace Conference*. Boston: Houghton Mifflin, 1921.

_____. *War Memoirs of Robert Lansing, Secretary of State*. London: Rich & Cowan, 1935.

Larkin, Maurice. *Church and State after the Dreyfus Affair: The Separation Issue in France*. New York: Harper & Row, 1973.

_____. "'La République en danger?' The Pretenders, the Army and Déroulède, 1898-1899." *English Historical Review* 100 (1985):84-105.

Laroche, Jules. *Au Quai d'Orsay avec Briand et Poincaré, 1913-1926*. Hachette, 1957.

Lasswell, Harold D. *Power and Personality*. New York: Viking Press, 1962.

Launay, Jacques de. *Secrets diplomatiques, 1914-1918*. Brussels: Brepola, 1963.

604

Laure, Général E. *Le Commandement en Chef des armées françaises du 15 mai 1917 à l'Armistice*. Éditions Berger-Levrault, 1937.

*Lautier, Eugène. "Clemenceau." *L'Homme Libre*, 25 Nov. 1929.

Lauzanne, Stephane. *Great Men and Great Days*. Translated by L. B. Williams. New York: D. Appleton, 1921.

Lavergne, Bernard. *Les deux présidences de Jules Grévy*. Préface de Pierre Renouvin. Notes et commentaires de Jean Elleinstein. Librairie Fischbacher, 1966. Diary by a parlementarian close to Grévy.

Lazare, Bernard. *Une erreur judiciare: La verité sur l'affaire Dreyfus*. Brussels: Imprimerie Monnom, 1896.

Leblois, Louis. *L'affaire Dreyfus: L'iniquité, la réparation; les principaux faits et les principaux documents*. Librairie Aristide Quillet, 1929.

Le Blond, Maurice. *La crise du Midi*. Bibliothèque-Charpentier, 1907. The winegrowers' revolt in 1907.

Le Clère, Bernard, and Wright, Vincent. *Les préfets du Second Empire*. Armand Colin, 1973.

*Lecomte, Georges. *Georges Clemenceau: The Tiger of France*. Translated by Donald Clive Stuart. New York: D. Appleton, 1919. By a friend; for anecdotes only.

Lederer, Ivo J. *Yugoslavia at the Paris Peace Conference: A Study in Frontiermaking*. New Haven: CT: Yale University Press, 1963.

Lefèvre, Frédéric. "An Hour with Georges Clemenceau." *Living Age*, 15 Aug. 1927, pp. 351-355.

Leffler, Melvyn P. *The Elusive Quest: America's Pursuit of European Stability and French Security, 1919-1933*. Chapel Hill, NC: University of North Carolina Press, 1979.

Lefranc, Georges. *Le mouvement socialiste sous la troisième république*. 2 vols. 2nd ed. Payot, 1977.

*Lefranc, Jean. "Clemenceau, souvenirs et portrait." *Revue politique et parlementaire* 141 (1929):331-345.

Le Goffic, Charles. *Mes entretiens avec Foch, suivis d'un entretien avec le général Weygand*. Éditions Spec, 1929.

Leites, Nathan C. *On the Game of Politics in France*. Stanford, CA: Stanford University Press, 1959.

*Lémery, Henry. "Clemenceau comme je l'ai vu." *Histoire de notre temps*, no. 6 (1968), pp. 159-177. By an under-secretary of state in his wartime cabinet.

_____. *D'une république à l'autre: Souvenirs de la mêlée politique, 1894-1944*. La Table rond, 1964.

Lentin, A. *Lloyd George, Woodrow Wilson and the Guilt of Germany: An Essay in the Pre-History of Appeasement*. Baton Rouge, LA: Louisiana State University Press, 1984.

Lépine, Louis. *Mes souvenirs*. Payot, 1929. By the longtime prefect of police.

*Letrait, J.-J. "Clemenceau et le Var." *Société d'études scientifiques et archéologiques de Draguignan, Bulletin*, new ser. 9 (1964):38-47.

Levin, Norman Gordon. *Woodrow Wilson and World Politics*. New York: Oxford University Press, 1968.

*Lévy, Claude. "Un journal de Clemenceau: *Le Bloc* (janvier 1901-mars 1902)." *Revue d'histoire moderne et contemporaine* 10 (1963):105-120.

Lewinsohn, Dr. Richard. *The Mystery Man of Europe: Sir Basil Zaharoff*. Philadelphia: J. B. Lippencott, 1929.

Lhopital, Commandant [René-Michel-Marie]. *Foch, l'armistice et la paix*. Plon, 1938.

Liens, Georges. "L'opinion à Marseille en 1917." *Revue d'histoire moderne et contemporaine* 15 (1968):54-78.

Liesner, Thelma. *Key Economic Statistics, 1900-83: Main Industrial Countries, United Kingdom, United States, France, Germany, Italy, Japan*. New York: Facts on File Publications, 1985.

Link, Arthur S. *The Higher Realism of Woodrow Wilson and Other Essays*. Nashville, TN: Vanderbilt University Press, 1971.

Lippmann, Walter. *Public Persons*. Edited by G. A. Harrison. New York: Liveright, 1976.

Lipschutz, Léon. "Trois lettres inédits de Clemenceau sur l'affaire Dreyfus." *Les Cahiers naturalistes* 14 (1968):182-188.

*Lloyd George, David. *Memoirs of the Peace Conference*. 2 vols. New Haven, CT: Yale University Press, 1939.

_____. *War Memoirs of David Lloyd George*. New ed. 2 vols. London: Oldhams Press, n.d. [1938].

Logue, William. *From Philosophy to Sociology The Evolution of French Liberalism, 1870-1914.* De Kalb, IL: Northern Illinois University Press, 1983.

Long, James William. "Russian Manipulation of the French Press, 1904-1906." *Slavic Review* [Seattle] 3 (1972):343-354.

Loubère, Leo A. "French Left-Wing Radicals: Their Economic and Social Program Since 1870." *American Journal of Economics and Sociology* 26 (1967):189-203.

_____. "The French Left-Wing Radicals: Their Views on Trade-Unionism, 1870-1898." *International Review of Social History* [Assen] 7 (1962):203-230.

_____. "Left-Wing Radicals, Strikes, and the Military, 1880-1907." *French Historical Studies* 3 (1963):93-105.

_____. *Radicalism in Mediterranean France: Its Rise and Decline, 1848-1914.* Albany, NY: State University of New York Press, 1974.

*Loucheur, Louis. *Carnets secrets, 1908-1932.* Présenté et annotés par Jacques de Launay. Brussels: Brepola, 1962. Selections from the Papers.

_____. "Le commandement unique." *L'Illustration*, 24 March 1928, pp. 272-276. An eyewitness.

_____. Papers. Archives. Hoover Institution on War, Revolution, and Peace, Stanford University.

Louis, Georges. *Les carnets de Georges Louis.* 2 vols. Éditions Rieder, 1926.

Ludendorff, General [Erich]. *My War Memories, 1914-1918.* 2 vols. 2nd ed. London: Hutchinson, n.d. [1919].

Lundgreen-Nielson, Kay. *The Polish Problem at the Paris Peace Conference: A Study of the Great Powers and the Poles, 1918-1919.* Odense [Denmark]: Odense University Studies in History and Social Science, vol. 59, 1979.

Lyautey, Hubert. *Un Lyautey inconnu: Correspondance et journal inédits, 1874-1934*, publié par André Le Révérand. Perrin, 1979.

McCormick, Donald. *Peddler of Death: The Life and Times of Sir Basil Zaharoff.* New York: Holt, Rinehart & Winston, 1965.

McCormick, Vance C. Diaries of Vance C. McCormick. Archives. Hoover Institution on War, Revolution, and Peace, Stanford University.

McCrum, Robert. "French Rhineland Policy at the Paris Peace Conference, 1919." *Historical Journal* [Cambridge] 21 (1978):623-648.

McDougall, Walter A. *France's Rhineland Diplomacy, 1914-1924: The Last Bid for a Balance of Power in Europe*. Princeton, NJ: Princeton University Press, 1978.

_____. "Political Economy versus National Sovereignty: French Structures for German Economic Integration after Versailles," with Comments by Charles S. Maier, Klaus Schwabe, and Gordon Wright. *Journal of Modern History* 51 (1979):4-23, 56-81. An outstanding discussion.

Maehl, William H. "Germany's War Aims in the East, 1914-17: Status of the Question." *The Historian* 34 (1972):381-406.

Maier, Charles S. *Recasting Bourgeois Europe: Stabilization in France, Germany, and Italy in the Decade after World War I*. Princeton, NJ: Princeton University Press, 1975.

_____. "Wargames: 1914-1919." *Journal of Interdisciplinary History* 18 (1988):819-849.

Maier, Lothar. "Die Lloyd George-Koalition und die Frage einem Kompromissfriedens 1917/1918." *Historische Zeitschrift*, 1983, Beiheft 8: 47-87.

*Malartic, Yves. "Comment Clemenceau fut battu aux élections législatives à Draguignan en 1893." *Provence historique* [Marseille] 12 (1962):112-138.

Malvy, Louis-Jean. *Mon crime*. E. Flammarion, 1921.

Mandell, R. D. "The Affair and the Fair: Some Observations on the Closing Stages of the Dreyfus Case." *Journal of Modern History* 39 (1967):253-265.

Mamety, Victor S. *The United States and East Central Europe, 1914-1918: A Study in Wilsonian Diplomacy and Propaganda*. Princeton, NJ: Princeton University Press, 1957.

Manevy, Raymond. *La presse de la IIIe république*. J. Foret, 1955.

Mantoux, Etienne. *The Carthaginian Peace, or The Economic Consequences of Mr. Keynes*. Charles Scribner's Sons, 1952.

*Mantoux, Paul, ed. *Les délibérations du Conseil des Quatre (24 mars-28 juin 1919)*. Notes de l'Officier Interprète Paul Mantoux. 2 vols. Éditions du Centre national de la recherche scientifique, 1955.

_____. "Le President Wilson au Conseil des Quatre." In *Centenaire Woodrow Wilson* (q.v.).

Marcellin, L. *Politique et politiciens.* 4 vols. Renaissance du Livre, n.d. Numerous editions. "Inside" stories.

Marchand, René, ed. *Un livre noir: Diplomatie d'avant-guerre d'après les documents des archives russes, novembre 1910-juillet 1914.* 3 vols. Librairie du Travail, 1922-1934.

Marks, Sally. "Black Watch on the Rhine: A Study in Propaganda, Prejudice and Prurience." *European Studies Review* 13 (1983):297-334.

———. *The Illusion of Peace: International Relations in Europe, 1918-1933.* New York: St. Martin's Press, 1976.

———. *Innocent Abroad: Belgium at the Paris Peace Conference of 1919.* Chapel Hill, NC: University of North Carolina Press, 1981. A magistral work.

———. "The Myths of Reparations." *Central European History* 11(1978):231-255.

Marmande, M. R. de. *L'intrigue florentine.* 2nd ed. Éditions de la Sirène, 1922. The Métivier affair in the Draveil strike, 1909.

Marshall, George C. *Memoirs of My Service in the World War, 1917-18.* Boston: Houghton Mifflin, 1976.

*Martel, Charles. "Souvenirs de 'La Justice,' journal de M. Clemenceau." *La Grande Revue*, 25 Oct. 1909, pp. 726-739.

*Martet, Jean. "Avec Georges Clemenceau." *Les Annales*, no. 2348 (15 Dec. 1929), pp. 547-555. Martet was his secretary, 1916-1929.

———. "Clemenceau." *L'Illustration*, special number, 30 Nov. 1929, pp. 603-604.

———. *Georges Clemenceau.* Translated by Milton Waldman. New York: Longmans, Green, 1930. [Cited as Martet, *Clemenceau.*] Contains the bulk of *Le silence de M. Clemenceau* and *M. Clemenceau peint par lui-même.*

*———. *M. Clemenceau peint par lui-même.* Albin Michel, 1929.

———. *La mort du Tigre.* Albin Michel, 1930.

*———. "Qui était Clemenceau?" *Revue de Paris* 15 Dec. 1929, pp. 931-937.

*———. *Le silence de M. Clemenceau.* Albin Michel, 1929.

*———. *Le Tigre.* Albin Michel, 1930.

Martin, Louis. "Dans l'intimité de Clemenceau." *Le Pontissalier* [Haut-Doubs], 14 June 1958. Musée Clemenceau. By a former personal secretary, 1913-1914.

Martin, William. *Statesmen of the War in Retrospect, 1918-1928.* New York: Minton, Balch, 1928. The former French chief of protocol.

Martin du Gard, Maurice. "Clemenceau." *Nouvelles littéraires*, 30 Nov. 1929, p. 1.

_____. *Les mémorables (1918-1923).* Flammarion, 1957.

Masson, Philippe. *La marine française et la Mer Noire (1918-1919).* Publications de la Sorbonne, 1982.

Mauclair, Camille. *Servitude et grandeur littéraires.* 6th ed. Librairie Ollendorff, n.d.

Maunoury, Henry. *Police de guerre (1914-1919).* Éditions de la Nouvelle revue critique, 1937.

Maurel, André. *Clemenceau.* Éditions de la Nouvelle revue nationale, 1919.

_____. *Les écrivains de la Guerre.* La Renaissance du Livre, 1917.

*_____. "Souvenirs intimes sur Clemenceau." *Revue de France*, 15 Dec. 1929, pp. 706-738. An old newspaper colleague.

May, Arthur J. *The Passing of the Hapsburg Monarchy, 1914-1918.* 2 vols. Philadelphia: University of Pennsylvania Press, 1966.

Mayer, Arno J. *The Political Origins of the New Diplomacy, 1917-1918.* New Haven, CT: Yale University Press, 1959.

_____. *Politics and Diplomacy of Peacemaking: Containment and Counterrevolution at Versailles, 1918-1919.* New York: Alfred A. Knopf, 1967.

Mayeur, Jean-Marie. *Un prêtre démocrate, l'abbé Lemire, 1853-1928.* Castermann, 1968.

_____, and Rebérioux, Madeleine. *The Third Republic from Its Origins to the Great War, 1871-1914.* Translated by J. R. Foster. Cambridge: Cambridge University Press, 1984.

Mazédier, René. *Histoire de la presse parisienne de Théophraste Renaudot à la IVe république, 1631-1945.* Éditions du Pavois, 1945.

Mazgaj, Paul. *The Action Francaise and Revolutionary Syndicalism.* Chapel Hill, NC: University of North Carolina Press, 1979.

Meier, Dr. Ernst. "'20 Millionen Deutsche zuviel!' Ein Beitrag zur politischen Schlagwort--und Legendenbildung." *Publizistik*, 1958, Heft no. 3.

Méjan, L.-V. *La séparation des Églises et de l'État: L'oeuvre de Louis Méjan.* Presses Universitaires de France, 1959.

*Méric, Victor. *A travers la jungle politique et littéraire, Ier serie.* Librairie Valois, 1930. The son of Sen. Méric of the Var, whose defeat Clemenceau obtained in 1909, was prosecuted for defamation of the army in 1907-1908.

Mermeix [Gabriel Terrail]. *Les coulisses du boulangisme.* Rev. ed. Chez Léopold Cerf, 1890.

Messimy, Général [Adolphe]. *Mes souvenirs.* Librairie Plon, 1937.

Meunier-Surcouf, Charles. "Notes personnelles, 1916-1917." MS., Musée Clemenceau.

*Michon, Georges. *Clemenceau.* Marcel Rivière, 1931. Generally hostile biography by a Socialist historian; documented.

Miller, David Hunter. *My Diary At the Conference of Paris, With Documents.* 21 vols. New York, for the author by the Appeal Printing Company, 1924.

*Milner, Lady [Viscountess Violet Georgina]. "Clemenceau intime." *Revue des deux mondes*, 15 Feb. 1953, pp. 611-619. An intimate friend and correspondent since the 1890s.

_____. *My Picture Gallery, 1886-1901.* London: John Murray, 1951.

*Milner, Lord [Alfred]. "Memorandum to the Cabinet by Lord Milner on His Visit to France, Including the Conference at Doullens, March 26th, 1918." *New Statesman*, 23 April 1921, pp. i-iv.

Miquel, Pierre. *La paix de Versailles et l'opinion publique française.* Flammarion, 1972.

_____. *Poincaré.* Librairie Arthème Fayard, 1961.

Mirbeau, Octave. *Les écrivains: Deuxième série, 1895-1910.* E. Flammarion, n.d. [1925-1927]. Mirbeau knew him well.

Mitchell, Allan. "Crucible of French Anticlericalism: The Conseil Municipal de Paris, 1871-1885." *Francia* 8 (1980):395-405.

_____. *The German Influence in France after 1870: The Formation of the French Republic.* Chapel Hill, NC: University of North Carolina Press, 1979.

Molinier, Sylvain. *Blanqui*. Presses Universitaires de France, 1948.

Monger, George. *The End of Isolation: British Foreign Policy, 1900-1907*. London: Thomas Nelson & Sons, 1963.

*Monnerville, Gaston. *Clemenceau*. Fayard, 1968. Well-informed but no notes. Valuable for the secret sessions of the Senate, 1915-1917. Author was formerly president of the Senate.

Monnet, Jean. *Mémoires*. Fayard, 1976.

Monod, François. *Musée Clemenceau: Guide descriptif*. Librairie Larousse, n.d.

*Mordacq, Général [Jean-Jules-Henri]. *L'armistice du 11 novembre 1918: Récit d'un témoin*. Plon, 1937. He was Clemenceau's *chef de cabinet militaire*, 1917-1920.

_____. *Clemenceau*. Éditions de France, 1939. Disappointing.

*_____. *Clemenceau au soir de sa vie (1920-1929)*. 2 vols. Plon, 1933.

*_____. *Le ministère Clemenceau: Journal d'un témoin*. 4 vols. Plon, 1930-1931.

*_____. *La vérité sur l'armistice*. Tallandier, 1929.

*_____. *La vérité sur le commandement unique*. New ed. Éditions Albert, n.d. [1934].

*Moreau, Jacques. *Clemenceau en Bloc*. Préface de Jean Martet. Éditions J. Tallandier, 1931. Good selections.

Morgan, Kenneth Owen. *Consensus and Disunity: The Lloyd George Coalition Government 1918-1922*. New York: Oxford University Press, 1979.

Morice, Charles. *Quarante ans de journalisme, presse, et parlement: Souvenirs et anecdotes*. 4 vols. Unpublished ms. at the Bibliothèque Nationale.

*Morizet, A. *De l'incohérence à l'assassinat! Trente mois de ministère radical*. Préface de Marcel Sembat et une lettre de Maurice Allard. L'Humanité, 1909. A sample of the kind of virulence he aroused on the Far Left, 1906-1909.

Mueller, Gordon H. "Rapallo Reexamined: A New Look at Germany's Secret Military Collaboration with Russia in 1922." *Military Affairs* 40 (1976):109-117.

Munholland, J.-K. "The French Army and Intervention in Southern Russia, 1918-1919." *Cahiers du monde russe et soviétique* 22 (1981):43-66.

Napo, Félix. *1907: La révolte des vignerons*. Toulouse: Privat, 1971.

Nelson, Harold I. *Land and Power: British and Allied Policy on Germany's Frontiers, 1916-19*. London: Routledge & Paul, 1963. Important work.

Nelson, Keith L. *Victors Divided: America and the Allies in Germany, 1918-1923*. Berkeley, CA: University of California Press, 1975.

Néré, Jacques. *Le boulangisme et la presse*. Librairie Armand Colin, 1964.

Neton, Albéric. *Delcassé*. Académie diplomatique internationale, 1952.

*Neuray, Fernand. *Entretiens avec Clemenceau*. Préface de Léon Daudet. Éditions Prométhée, 1930.

Nevakivi, Jukka. *Britain, France and the Arab Middle East, 1914-1920*. London: Althone Press, 1969.

Neville, Robert G. "The Courrières Colliery Disaster,1906." *Journal of Contemporary History* 13 (1978):33-52.

Nevins, Allan. *Henry White: Thirty Years of American Diplomacy*. New York: Harper & Brothers, 1930.

*Newhall, David S. "Georges Clemenceau, 1902-1906: 'An Old Beginner.'" 2 vols. Ph.D. dissertation, Harvard University, 1963. Copies at Harvard and the Musée Clemenceau.

Nicolet, Claude. *L'idée républicaine en France (1789-1924): Essai d'histoire critique*. Gallimard, 1982.

_____. "Jules Ferry et la tradition positiviste." In François Furet, ed., *Jules Ferry, fondateur de la République* (q.v.), pp. 23-48.

Nicolson, Harold. *Peacemaking 1919*. Boston: Houghton Mifflin, 1933.

Nicot, Jean. "Psychologie du combattant français de 1918." *Revue historique de l'Armée* 28 (1972):61-74.

Nintchitch, Momtchilo. *La crise bosniaque (1909-1909) et les Puissances européennes*. 2 vols. Alfred Costes, 1937.

Nobécourt, R.-G. *L'année de 11 novembre (1918)*. Robert Laffont, 1968.

Noble, George Bernard. *Policies and Opinion at Paris, 1919*. New York: Macmillan, 1935.

Nolde, Baron Boris. *L'alliance franco-russe: Les origines du système diplomatique d'avant guerre.* Librairie Droz, 1936.

Nord, Philip G. *Paris Shopkeepers and the Politics of Resentment.* Princeton, NJ: Princeton University Press, 1986.

_____. "The Party of Conciliation and the Paris Commune." *French Historical Studies* 15, no. 1 (Spring 1987), pp. 1-35.

Nordmann, Jean-Thomas, ed. *La France radicale.* Gallimard/Julliard, 1977.

_____. *Histoire des radicaux, 1820-1973.* La Table rond. 1974.

Nouailhat, Yves-Henri. "Clemenceau et la démocratie américaine." In *Clemenceau et la justice* (q.v.), pp. 23-38.

Noulens, Joseph. *Mon ambassade en Russie soviétique.* 2 vols. Plon, 1933.

Nouschi, Marc. "Les forces navales françaises et le problème turc." *Revue historique des Armées*, no. 158 (March 1985), pp. 62-70.

*O'Brien, Jeanne Gilmore. "Les racines républicaines de la famille Clemenceau." In *Clemenceau et la justice* (q.v.), pp. 39-44. Very important.

Opinion publique et politique extérieure. Colloque organisé par l'École française de Rome [et al.], Rome, 16-20 février 1981. Vol. 2: *1915-1940.* École française de Rome, 1984.

Ormesson, Wladimir d'. *Qu'est-ce qu'un Français? Essai de psychologie politique: Clemenceau, Poincaré, Briand.* Éditions Spes, 1934.

Osterreich-Ungarns Aussenpolitik von der Bosnischen Krise 1908 bis zum Kriegsausbruch 1914. Diplomatische Aktenstücke des Osterreichisch-Ungarische Ministeriums des Aussen. 8 vols. Selected by Ludwig Bittner et al. Edited by Ludwig Bittner and Hans Uebersberger. Vienna: Osterreichischen Bundesverlag für Unterricht, Wissenschaft und Kunst, 1930. Especially for the Bosnian crisis.

Oxford and Asquith, Earl of [Herbert Henry Asquith]. *Memories and Reflections, 1852-1927.* 2 vols. Boston: Little, Brown, 1928.

Painlevé, Paul. *Comment j'ai nomme Foch et Pétain.* F. Alcan, 1924.

Paléologue, Maurice. "Comment le service de trois ans fut rétabli en 1913." *Revue des deux mondes*, 1 May 1935, pp. 67-94; 15 May 1935, pp. 307-344.

_____. *Au Quai d'Orsay à la veille de la tourmente: Journal 1913-1914.* Librairie Plon, 1947.

———. *Un grand tournant de la politique mondiale (1904-1906)*. Librairie Plon, 1934.

Palmer, Alan W. *The Gardeners of Salonika*. New York: Simon & Schuster, 1965.

Panichas, George A., ed. *Promise of Greatness: The War of 1914-1918*. New York: John Day, 1968.

Papayanis, Nicholas. "Alphonse Merrheim and the Strike of Hennebont: The Struggle for the Eight-Hour Day in France." *International Review of Social History* [Neth.] 16 (1971):159-183.

———. *Alphonse Merrheim: The Emergence of Reformism in Revolutionary Syndicalism, 1871-1925*. Boston: M. Nijhoff, 1985.

Parias, L.-H., ed. *Histoire du peuple française*. Vol. 4: *De 1848 à nos jours*, by Georges Duveau. Nouvelle Librairie de France, 1953.

Parsons, Edward B. *Wilsonian Diplomacy: Allied-American Relations in War and Peace*. St. Louis: Forum Press, 1978.

Partin, Malcolm O. *Waldeck-Rousseau, Combes, and the Church: The Politics of Anticlericalism, 1899-1905*. Durham, NC: Duke University Press, 1969.

Paul, Harry W. "The Debate over the Bankruptcy of Science in 1895." *French Historical Studies* 5, no. 3 (Spring 1968), pp. 299-327.

Paul-Boncour, Joseph. *Recollections of the Third Republic*. 3 vols. Translated by George Marion, Jr. New York: Robert Speller & Sons, 1957.

*Payne, David Sylvester. "The Foreign Policy of Georges Clemenceau: 1917-1920." Ph.D. dissertation, Duke University, 1970.

Paz, Maurice. "Clemenceau, Blanqui's Heir: An Unpublished Letter from Blanqui to Clemenceau Dated 18 March 1879." *Historical Journal* [Cambridge] 16 (1973):604-615.

———, ed. *Lettres familières d'Auguste Blanqui et du docteur Louis Watteau*. Marseille: Institut historique de Provence, 1976.

Peake, Thomas Rhea. "The Impact of the Russian Revolutions upon French Attitudes and Policies Toward Russia, 1917-1918." Ph.D. Dissertation, University of North Carolina, 1974.

Pedroncini, Guy. "Clemenceau et le général Pétain, novembre 1917-mars 1918." In *Clemenceau et la justice* (q.v.), pp. 161-167.

_____. "Le Haut Commandement français et le front italien (1917-1918)." In *La France et l'Italie pendant la Première guerre modiale* (q.v.), pp. 555-578.

_____. *Les mutineries de 1917.* Presses Universitaires de France, 1967.

_____. *Pétain, général en chef, 1917-1918.* Presses Universitaires de France, 1974. Exceptionally important work.

_____. "Trois maréchaux, troi stratégies?" *Guerres mondiales et conflits contemporains* 37, no. 145 (1987), pp. 45-62.

*Pelletan, Camille, et al. *Célébrités contemporaines.* A. Quantin, 1884. Especially for his oratory.

* _____. "La crise du parti radical." *La Revue (Ancienne Revue des Revues)*, 15 May 1909, 145-164.

Perreux, Gabriel; Ducasse, André; and Meyer, Jacques. *Vie et mort des français 1914-19.* Hachette, 1962.

Perrod, Pierre-Antoine. "Autour d'une correspondance inédite: Stephen Pichon et ses amis." *Revue des sciences morales et politiques* 139 (1984):43-62.

Pershing, John J. *My Experiences in the World War.* 2 vols. New York: Frederick A. Stokes, 1931.

Persil, R. *Alexandre Millerand (1859-1943).* Société d'Éditions françaises et internationales, 1949.

Peter, Jean-Pierre. "Dimensions de l'Affaire Dreyfus." *Annales: Économies, Sociétés, Civilisations* 16 (1961):1141-1167.

Petit, Lucien. *Le règlement des dettes interalliés (1919-1929).* Éditions Berger-Levrault, 1932.

Petsalis-Diomidis, N. *Greece at the Peace Conference, 1919.* Thessalonika: Institute for Balkan Studies, 1978.

*Peuméry, Suzanne-Edith. "Clemenceau vu par son valet de chambre." *Historama* [France], no. 18 (1985), pp. 64-58. Recollections by Albert Boulin.

*Philip, Jean (senateur). "Souvenirs d'un parlementaire desabusé." *La France active,* no. 149 (May-June 1935), pp. 23-32; no. 150 (July-Aug. 1935), pp. 20-29; no. 151 (Sept.-Oct. 1935), pp. 17-31. He wrote for *L'Aurore* and was *chef de cabinet* at the Interior ministry in 1906.

Pierrefeu, Jean de. *G. Q. G., Secteur 1.* 2 vols. G. Crès, 1922.

616

*Pincetl, Stanley, Jr. "A Letter of Clemenceau to His Wife by Balloon." *French Historical Studies* 2, no. 4 (1962), pp. 511-514. During the siege of Paris, 1870-1871.

Pingaud, A. *Histoire diplomatique de la France pendant la grande guerre.* 3 vols. Éditions "Alsatia," 1938-1940.

Pinkney, David. *Decisive Years in France, 1840-1847.* Princeton, NJ: Princeton University Press, 1986.

*Pinon, René. "Clemenceau et l'Autriche." *Revue politique et parlementaire* 194 (1948):154-162.

Pisani-Ferry, Fresnette. *Jules Ferry et le partage du monde.* Bernard Grasset, 1962.

Pontal, Gaston. *L'article 10 du Code d'instruction criminelle.* Carcassone: L. Bonnefous et fils, 1941.

Poidevin, Raymond. "La politique extérieure de Jules Ferry, 1883-1885." In François Furet, ed., *Jules Ferry, fondateur de la République* (q.v.), pp. 207-222.

_____. *Les relations économiques et financières entre la France et l'Allemagne de 1898 à 1914.* Colin, 1969.

*Poincaré, Raymond. *Au service de la France: Neuf années de souvenirs.* 11 vols. Plon-Nourrit, 1926-1933; Plon, 1974.

Ponty, Janine. "La presse quotidienne et l'affaire Dreyfus en 1899. Essai de typologie." *Revue d'histoire moderne et contemporaine* 21 (1974):193-220.

Porch, Douglas. *The March to the Marne: The French Army, 1871-1914.* New York: Cambridge University Press, 1981. Impressive revisionist study.

Power, Thomas F., Jr. *Jules Ferry and the Renaissance of French Imperialism.* New York: King's Crown Press, 1944.

Pratt, Julius W. "Clemenceau and Gambetta: A Study in Political Philosophy." *South Atlantic Quarterly* 10 (1921):95-104.

Prete, Roy A., with a commentary by John C. Cairns. "Since Renouvin: A Reconsideration of French War Aims, 1914-1918." *Proceedings of the Annual Meeting of the Western Society for French History* 10 (1982):461-71, 482-484.

Prévost, Marcel. "Clemenceau et l'Académie." *Revue de France,* 15 Dec. 1929, pp. 739-742.

Price, Roger. *The French Second Republic: A Social History*. Ithaca, NY: Cornell University Press, 1972.

_____, ed. *Revolution and Reaction: 1848 and the Second French Republic*. New York: Barnes & Noble, 1975.

Le proès Zola, devant la Cour d'assises de la Seine et la Cour de cassation (7 février-23 février, 31 mars-2 avril 1898). Comte-rendu sténographique "in-extenso" et documents annexes. 2 vols. Aux Bureaux du "Siècle," 1898.

"Les projets de M. Clemenceau." *Le Cri de Paris*, no. 677 (1910).

Prost, Antoine; and Rosenzveig, Christian. "La Chambre des députés (1881-1885): Analyse factorielle des scrutins." *Revue française des sciences politiques* 21 (1971):5-49.

*Prouteau, Gilbert. *Le dernier défi de Georges Clemenceau*. France-Empire, 1979. Especially "Introduction à Georges Clemenceau," by Albert Boulin, his valet.

Quillard, Pierre. "Georges Clemenceau." *Mercure de France*, July 1898, pp. 5-14.

Raffalovitch, A. *L'abominable vénalité de la presse, d'après les documents des archives russes (1897-1917)*. Librairie du Travail, 1931.

Raiga-Clemenceau, Dr. André. "La thèse de doctorat du docteur Georges Clemenceau (mai 1869)." *Nouvelles archives hospitalières* 46, no. 1 (1974), pp. 21-24. The author is a grandson of Clemenceau's sister Emma.

* _____. "Le vrai caractère de Clemenceau." *Nouvelles archives hospitalières*, 1973, no. 2, pp. 44-48; no. 3, pp. 66-72; no. 4, pp. 88-96.

Ralston, David B. *The Army of the Republic: The Place of the Military in the Political Evolution of France, 1871-1914*. Cambridge, MA: The M. I. T. Press, 1967.

*Raphaël-Leygues, Jacques. *Georges Leygues, "le père" de la marine (Ses carnets secrets de 1914 à 1920)*. Éditions France-Empire, 1983. Leygues was navy minister, 1917-1920.

Rebérioux, Madeleine. "L'évolution de Jaurès après 1905: Un problème d'interpretation." *Société d'études jaurèsiennes, Bulletin* 4, no. 11 (Oct.-Dec. 1963), pp. 10-13.

_____. "Jaurès devant les radicaux et le radicalisme." *Société d'études jaurèsiennes, Bulletin*, no. 94 (1984), pp. 27-32.

_____. *La République radicale? 1898-1914*. Éditions du Seuil, 1975.

*Recouly, Raymond. *Le mémorial de Foch: Mes entretiens avec le Maréchal.* Éditions de France, 1929. The book which provoked Clemenceau to write *Grandeur et misères d'une victoire.*

Reinach, Joseph. *Histoire de l'affaire Dreyfus.* 7 vols. La Revue blanche, 1901-1911.

Rémond, René. *L'anticlericalisme en France de 1815 à nos jours.* Fayard, 1976.

Renouvin, Pierre. *L'armistice de Rethondes, 11 novembre 1918.* Gallimard, 1968.

_____. "Les buts de guerre du gouvernement français (1914-1918)." *Revue historique* 235 (1966):1-38.

_____. "La conduite de la guerre en 1918." *Revue historique de l'Armée* 24, no. 4 (1968), pp. 17-26.

_____. "Le destin du pacte d'assistance américain à la France en 1919." *Annales d'études internationales* [Geneva] 1 (1970):9-22.

_____. *Les formes du gouvernement de guerre.* Presses Universitaires de France, 1925.

_____. "L'opinion publique en France pendant la guerre 1914-1918." *Revue d'histoire diplomatique* 84, no. 4 (1970), pp. 289-336.

Repington, Lieut.-Col. Charles à Court. *The First World War, 1914-1918.* 2 vols. London: Constable, 1920.

Rhodes, Benjamin D. "Reassessing 'Uncle Shylock': The United States and the French War Debt, 1917-1929." *Journal of American History* 55 (1969):787-803.

Ribot, Alexandre. *Journal d'Alexandre Ribot et correspondances inédites, 1914-1922.* Librairie Plon, 1936.

Richardson, Joanna. *The Courtesans: The Demi-Monde in Nineteenth-Century France.* Cleveland: World Publishing Co., 1967.

Riddell, Lord [George Allardyce Riddell] *Lord Riddell's Intimate Diary of the Peace Conference and After, 1918-1923.* New York: Reynal & Hitchcock, 1934.

_____. *Lord Riddell's War Diary, 1914-1918.* London: Ivor Nicholson & Watson, 1933.

Ridley, F. F. *Revolutionary Syndicalism in France.* New York: Cambridge University Press, 1971.

*Rieux, Calixte de. "Clemenceau et le parti radical." *Les Cahiers de la République*, no. 8 (July-Aug. 1957), pp. 93-108.

*Rinaudo, Yves. "Clemenceau vu d'en bas: L'air et la chanson." *Revue d'histoire moderne et contemporaine* 32 (1985):324-341.

_____. "Une sensibilité politique de gauche: Le Var rural au début du XXe siècle." *Provence historique* [Marseille] 32 (1982):361-377.

_____. *Les vendanges de la république: Les paysans du Var à la fin du XIXe siècle*. Lyon: Presses Universitaires de Lyon, 1982.

*Robert, Dr. Louis. "Un médecin politicien, le docteur Georges Clemenceau." *Berry médical*, no. 61 (1953), p. 63-106. By one of his doctors.

Roche, Émile. *Avec Joseph Caillaux: Mémoires, souvenirs et documents*. Publications de la Sorbonne, 1980.

_____. *Caillaux que j'ai connu*. Librairie Plon, 1949.

Rochefort, Henri. *Les aventures de ma vie*. 5 vols. Paul Dupont, 1896.

Rocolle, Pierre. *L'hécatombe des généraux*. Éditions Lavauzelle, 1980.

*Romane-Musculus, Paul. "Genéalogie des Gautreau, ascendants maternels de Georges Clemenceau." *Revue du Bas-Poitou*, no. 2-3 (1952-53), pp. 110-117.

Roskill, Stephen. *Hankey, Man of Secrets*. 3 vols. New York: St. Martin's Press, 1970-1974.

Rosny aîné, J. H. [J. H. H. Boëx]. *Torches et lumignons: Souvenirs de la vie littéraire*. "La Force française," 1921.

Rothwell, Victor H. *British War Aims and Peace Diplomacy, 1914-1918*. New York: Oxford University Press, 1971.

Rudelle, Odile. "Clemenceau et le souvenir de l'Année terrible, 1870-1887." In *Clemenceau et la justice* (q.v.), pp. 45-58.

_____. *La République absolue: Aux origines de l'instabilité constitutionelle de la France républicaine, 1870-1889*. Publications de la Sorbonne, 1982. Important work.

Rudin, Harry R. *Armistice 1918*. New Haven, CT: Yale University Press, 1944.

Rufin, Georges. "L'opinion publique en 1917 dans l'arrondissement de Tournon." *Revue d'histoire moderne et contemporaine* 15 (1968):79-96.

Ruinaut, J. "Autour de Clemenceau (d'après de recentes publications)." *Revue des questions historiques*, 1 July 1930, pp. 76-89.

Ryan, W. Michael. "Lieutenant-Colonel Charles à Court Repington: A Study in the Interaction of Personality, the Press, and Power." Ph.D. Dissertation, University of Cincinnati, 1976.

*Saatmann, Inge. *Parlament, Rüstung und Armee in Frankreich 1914/18*. Dusseldorf: Droste Verlag, 1978. Indispensable for the Senate Army Commission's work.

Saint-Georges de Bouhelier. "Une visite à M. Clemenceau." *Journal littéraire*, 2 Aug. 1924, pp. 1-2; 9 Aug., p. 8.

Salter, Sir James A. *Personality in Politics*. London: Faber, 1947.

Sanders, Richard W. "The Labor Policies of the French Radical Party, 1901-1909." Ph.D. dissertation, Duke University, 1971.

Saunders, David. "Britain and the Ukrainian Question (1912-1920)." *English Historical Review* 103 (1988):40-68.

Sauvy, Alfred. *Histoire économique de la France entre les deux guerres*. Vol. 1: *De l'Armistice à la dévaluation de la livre*. Fayard, 1965.

*Scantrel, Yves [Suarès]. "M. Clemenceau." *La Grande Revue*, 10 Aug. 1909, pp. 574-83. A superior sketch.

Schaper, Bertus Willem. *Albert Thomas: Trente ans de réformisme social*. Assen, Neth.: Van Gorcum, 1959.

Scherer, André, and Grunewald, Jacques, eds. *L'Allemagne et les problèmes de la paix pendant la première guerre mondiale: Documents extraits des archives de l'Office allemand des Affaires étrangères*. 2 vols. Presses Universitaires de France, 1962-1966.

Scheurer-Kestner, A. *Souvenirs de jeunesse*. Bibliothèque-Charpentier, 1905.

Schillinger, Philippe. "Un projet français d'intervention économique en Russie (1918)." *Relations internationales*, no. 1 (May 1974), pp. 115-122.

Schmieder, Eric. "La Chambre de 1885-1889 et les affaires du Tonkin." *Revue française d'histoire d'Outre-Mer* 53 (1968), no. 192-193, pp. 153-214.

Schmitt, Bernadotte. *The Annexation of Bosnia, 1908-1909*. London: Cambridge University Press, 1937.

Schuker, Stephen A. *The End of French Predominance in Europe: The Financial Crisis of 1924 and the Adoption of the Dawes Plan.* Chapel Hill, NC: University of North Carolina Press, 1976.

Schwabe, Klaus. *Woodrow Wilson, Revolutionary Germany, and Peacemaking, 1918-1919: Missionary Diplomacy and the Realities of Power.* Translated by Rita and Robert Kimber. Chapel Hill, NC: University of North Carolina Press, 1985. Masterful.

Seager, Frederic H. *The Boulanger Affair: Political Crossroad of France, 1886-1889.* Ithaca, NY: Cornell University Press, 1969.

Seymour, Charles. *Geography, Justice, and Politics at the Paris Peace Conference of 1919.* New York: American Geographical Society, 1951.

_____, ed. *The Intimate Papers of Colonel House.* 4 vols. Boston: Houghton Mifflin, 1928.

_____. "Policy and Personality at the Paris Peace Conference." *Virginia Quarterly Review* 21 (1945):517-534.

Shanafelt, Gary W. *The Secret Enemy: Austria-Hungary and the German Alliance, 1914-1918.* Boulder, CO: East European Monographs, 1985.

*Sherwood, John M. *Georges Mandel and the Third Republic.* Stanford, CA: Stanford University Press, 1970.

Silberstein, Gerard E. "Germany, France and the Casablanca Incident, 1908-1909: An Investigation of a Forgotten Crisis." *Canadian Journal of History* [Saskatoon] 11 (1976):331-354.

Silvera, Alan. *Daniel Halévy and His Times: A Gentleman-Commoner in the Third Republic.* Ithaca, NY: Cornell University Press, 1966.

Silverlight, John. *The Victors' Dilemma: Allied Intervention in the Russian Civil War.* New York: Weybright & Talley, 1970.

Silverman, Dan P. *Reconstructing Europe after the Great War.* Cambridge, MA: Harvard University Press, 1982.

Simon, Maron J. *The Panama Affair.* New York: Charles Scribner's Sons, 1971.

Simonds, F. H. "Clemenceau, Tardieu, London." *Review of Reviews,* Jan. 1930, pp. 59-61.

Siwek-Pouydesseau, Jeanne. *Le corps préfectoral sous la troisième et quatrième république.* Presses de la Fondation nationale des sciences politiques, 1969.

Slater, Catherine. *Defeatists and Their Enemies: Political Invective in France, 1914-1918*. New York: Oxford University Press, 1981.

Smart, Terry Lee. "The French Intervention in the Ukraine, 1918-1919." Ph.D dissertation, University of Kansas, 1968.

Smythe, Donald. *Pershing: General of the Armies*. Bloomington, IN: Indiana University Press, 1986.

Soria, Georges. *Grande histoire de la Commune*. 5 vols. Livre Club Diderot, 1970-1971.

Sorlin, Pierre. *Waldeck-Rousseau*. Librairie Armand Colin, 1966.

Soutou, Georges. "La France et les Marches de l'Est, 1914-1919." *Revue historique* 260 (1978):341-388. Very important.

_____. "Problèmes concernant le rétablissement des relations économiques franco-allemandes après la première guerre mondiale." *Francia* 2 (1974):580-596.

Spears, Sir Edward L. *Assignment to Catastrophe*. 2 vols. London: Heinemann, 1954.

Spector, Sherman. *Rumania at the Paris Peace Conference: A Study of the Diplomacy of Ioan I. C. Brătianu*. New York: Bookman Associates, 1962.

Stead, Philip John. *The Police of France*. New York: Macmillan, 1983.

Stearns, Peter N. *Revolutionary Syndicalism and French Labor: A Cause Without Rebels*. New Brunswick, NJ: Rutgers University Press, 1971.

Steed, Henry Wickham. *Through Thirty Years, 1892-1922: A Personal Narrative*. 2 vols. Garden City, NY: Doubleday & Page, 1925.

Steglich, Wolfgang, ed. *Die Friedensversuche der kriegsführenden Mächte im Sommer und Herbst 1917: Quellenkritische Untersuchungen, Akten und Vernehmungsprotokolle*. Stuttgart: Franz Steiner, 1984.

_____. *Die Friedenspolitik der Mittelmächte 1917-18*. Wiesbaden: F. Steiner, 1964.

Sternhell, Zeev. *Maurice Barrès et le nationalisme français*. Éditions Complexe, 1985.

_____. "Paul Déroulède and the Origins of Modern French Nationalism." *Journal of Contemporary History* 4, no. 4 (1971), pp. 46-70.

Stevenson, David. *The First World War and International Politics*. New York: Oxford University Press, 1988.

_____. *French War Aims Against Germany, 1914-1919*. Oxford: Clarendon Press, 1982. The best on the subject.

Stevenson, Frances [Louise (Stevenson) Lloyd George, Countess]. *Lloyd George; A Diary by Frances Stevenson*. Edited by A. J. P. Taylor. New York: Harper & Row, 1971.

*Stock, P.-V. *Mémorandum d'un éditeur: Deuxième série*. Librairie Stock, 1936. Publisher of his collections of Dreyfus Case articles.

*_____. *Mémorandum d'un éditeur: Troisième série. L'Affaire Dreyfus anecdotique*. Éditions Stock, Delmain et Boutelleau, 1938.

Stone, Judith F. "Political Culture in the Third Republic: The Case of Camille Pelletan." *Proceedings of the Annual Meeting of the Western Society for French History* 13 (1986):217-226.

_____. *The Search for Social Peace: Reform Legislation in France, 1890-1914*. Albany, NY: State University of New York Press, 1985.

Stone, Norman. *Europe Transformed, 1878-1919*. Cambridge, MA: Harvard University Press, 1984.

Strauss, Paul. "Souvenirs: Gambetta et Clemenceau." *Le Temps*, 9 Nov. 1930.

_____. *Les fondateurs de la République, souvenirs*. La Renaissance du Livre, 1934.

Suarez, Georges. *Briand: Sa vie, son oeuvre, avec son journal et de nombreux documents inédits*. 6 vols. Plon, 1938-1952.

*_____. *Clemenceau: Soixante années d'histoire de France*. 2 vols. Les Éditions de France, 1932. A revised and expanded edition of the work below. Informed, but without notes and full of imagined conversations, etc.

_____. *La vie orgueilleuse de Clemenceau*. Éditions de France, 1930.

*Sybil [Charles Benoist]. "M. Georges Clemenceau." *Revue politique et littéraire (Revue bleue)*, 14 Sept. 1889, pp. 321-326. An important early sketch.

Tabouis, Geneviève. *The Life of Jules Cambon*. Translated by C. F. Atkinson. London: Jonathan Cape, 1938.

*Talmeyr, Maurice. "Clemenceau, Degas et Cie." *Le Figaro*, 17 Dec. 1930.

Tanenbaum, Jan Karl. *France and the Arab Middle East, 1914-1920.* Transactions of the American Philosophical Society 68, Pt. 7. Philadelphia: American Philosophical Society, 1978.

_____. *General Maurice Sarrail, 1856-1929: The French Army and Left-Wing Politics.* Chapel Hill, NC: University of North Carolina Press, 1974.

Tardieu, André. *France and America: Some Experiences in Cooperation.* Boston: Houghton Mifflin, 1927.

_____. "La France et l'Allemagne, 1906-1909." *Revue des deux mondes,* 1 July 1909, pp. 65-98.

_____. "M. Clemenceau et le risque américain." *L'Illustration,* 20-27 March 1920, pp. 179-180. On the failure of the U.S. Senate to ratify the Versailles treaty.

*_____. *The Truth about the Treaty.* Foreword by Edward M. House. Introduction by Georges Clemenceau. Indianapolis: The Bobbs-Merrill Company, 1921.

*Tchernoff, J. [Iouda]. "Georges Clemenceau sous le second empire." *Opinion: Journal de la semaine,* 18 July 1908, pp. 15-17.

_____. *Le parti républicain au coup d'état et sous le second empire, d'après des documents et des souvenirs inédits.* A. Pedone, 1906.

Tenot, Eugène, and Dubost, Antonin. *Les suspects en 1858: Étude historique sur l'application de la loi de sûreté générale: Emprisonements--Transportations.* Armand Le Chevalier, 1869.

Terraine, John. "'An Actual Revolutionary Situation': Germany in 1917." *History Today* 28 (1978):14-22.

_____. "The Aftermath of Nivelle." *History Today* 27 (1977):426-433.

_____. *To Win a War: 1918, the Year of Victory.* Garden City, NY: Doubleday, 1981.

*Théaux, Marcel. "Les idées philosophiques de M. Clemenceau." *Mercure de France,* 1 April 1906, pp. 354-366.

*Theisen, Lee Scott, ed. "Two Kindly Grouches: A Note by Stephen Bonsal on James Douglas and Georges Clemenceau." *Journal of American History* 18 (1977):93-98.

Thomas, Edith. *Louise Michel, ou la Velléda de l'anarchie.* Gallimard, 1971.

Thomas, Marcel. *L'Affaire sans Dreyfus.* Arthème Fayard, 1961.

Thompson, John M. *Russia, Bolshevism, and the Versailles Peace.* Princeton, NJ: Princeton University Press, 1966.

Thorson, Winston B. "Freycinet's Egyptian Policy in 1882." *The Historian* 4 (1942):172-92.

Tillman, Seth P. *Anglo-American Relations at the Paris Peace Conference of 1919.* Princeton, NJ: Princeton University Press, 1961.

Tirard, Paul. *La France sur le Rhin: Douze années d'occupation rhénane.* 4th ed. Librairie Plon, 1930.

Toland, John. *No Man's Land: 1918, The Last Year of the Great War.* Garden City, NY: Doubleday, 1980.

"Le 'tombeur' de Clemenceau." *Journal du Peuple,* 26 Jan. 1920.

Tombs, Robert. *The War Against Paris, 1871.* Cambridge: Cambridge University Press, 1981.

Touchard, Jean. *La gauche en France depuis 1900.* Éditions Seuil, 1977.

Tournès, Gen. René. *La crise du commandement unique: Le conflit Clemenceau-Foch-Haig-Pétain.* Bossard, 1931.

Trachtenberg, Marc. "Étienne Clémentel and French Economic Diplomacy during the First World War." *French Historical Studies* 10, no. 2 (Fall 1977), pp. 315-341.

_____. "Reparation at the Paris Peace Conference," and Comments by Charles S. Maier, Klaus Schwabe, Gordon Wright, Walter McDougall. *Journal of Modern History* 51 (1979):24-85.

_____. *Reparation in World Politics: France and European Economic Diplomacy, 1916-1923.* New York: Columbia University Press, 1980. Exceptionally important.

_____. "Versailles after Sixty Years." *Journal of Contemporary History* 17 (1982):487-506.

Trani, Eugene P. "Woodrow Wilson and the Decision to Intervene in Russia: A Reconsideration." *Journal of Modern History* 48 (1976):440-461.

Trask, David F. *The United States in the Supreme War Council: American War Aims and Inter-Allied Strategy, 1917-1918.* Middletown, MA: Wesleyan University Press, 1961.

Travers, Tim. *The Killing Ground: The British Army, the Western Front and the Emergence of Modern Warfare, 1900-1918.* London: Allen & Unwin, 1987.

*Treich, Léon. "Chez Clemenceau." *Revue hebdomadaire*, 23 April 1927, pp. 482-491.

*_____. *L'esprit de Clemenceau.* 5th ed. Gallimard, 1925. Anecdotes and witticisms, real or alleged.

_____. *Vie et mort de Clemenceau.* Éditions de Portiques, 1929.

Tuchman, Barbara. *The Proud Tower.* New York: Bantam Books, 1966.

Tudesq, André-Jean. *Les grands notables en France (1840-1849): Étude historique d'une psychologie sociale.* 2 vols. Presses Universitaires de France, 1964.

Ular, Alexandre. *Inside Russia Today.* London: W. Heinemann, 1905.

Ullman, Richard H. *Anglo-Soviet Relations, 1917-1921.* 3 vols. Princeton, NJ: Princeton University Press, 1961-1973.

United States of America. Department of State. *Papers Relating to the Foreign Relations of the United States. The Lansing Papers, 1914-1920.* 2 vols. Washington, D.C.: United States Government Printing Office, 1939-1940.

_____. *Papers Relating to the Foreign Relations of the United States. Paris Peace Conference. 1919.* 13 vols. Washington, D.C.: United States Government Printing Office, 1942-1947.

Urbaniak, George. "French Involvement in the Polish-Lithuanian Dispute, 1918-1920." *Journal of Baltic Studies* 16 (1985):52-63.

Valentin, Michel. "Clemenceau, précurseur de la médecine de travail." In *Clemenceau et la justice* (q.v.), pp. 59-66.

Valiani, Leo. *The End of Austria-Hungary.* New York: Alfred A. Knopf, 1973. Translated from the Italian edition of 1966.

Vallat, Xavier. "Pourquoi le 'Tigre' ne logea pas à l'Élysée." *Écrits de Paris,* Oct. 1970, pp. 43-54.

Vandiver, Frank E. *Black Jack: The Life and Times of John J. Pershing.* 2 vols. College Station, TX: Texas A. & M. University Press, 1977.

Varenne, Francisque. "Une célèbre collaboration: Georges Clemenceau-Georges Mandel." *Miroir de l'histoire,* no. 37 (1953), pp. 73-80.

*_____. "Clemenceau devant ses électeurs du Var." *Revue politique et parlementaire* 209 (April-June 1949):19-28.

_____. "La défaite de Georges Clemenceau à Draguignan en 1893." *Revue politique et parlementaire* 215, no. 646, pp. 255-259.

*_____. *Mon patron Georges Mandel.* Éditions Défense de la France n.d. [1947].

Vassili, Count Paul [Ekaterina Radziwill]. *France from Behind the Veil: Fifty Years of Social and Political life.* New York: Funk & Wagnalls, 1914.

Vaughan Ernest. *Souvenirs sans regrets.* Félix Juven, 1902. Author founded *L'Aurore.*

Vercors [Jean Bruller]. *Cent ans d'histoire de France.* Vol. 1: *L'apogée de la République ou Moi, Aristide Briand: 1862-1932: Essai d'autoportrait.* Plon, 1981.

*Vidal-Naquet, Pierre. "Joseph Reinach: Vers la grace de Dreyfus." *Passé Present,* no. 2 (1983), pp. 107-131. Previously unpublished extract from Reinach's *Journal.*

Vigier, Philippe. *La séconde république dans la région alpine: Étude politique et sociale.* 2 vols. Presses Universitaires de France, 1963. For Gustave Jourdan.

Vincent, C. Paul. *The Politics of Hunger: The Allied Blockade of Germany, 1915-1919.* Athens, OH: Ohio University Press, 1985. The post-Armistice blockade was manipulated by both sides, with tragic results for the populace.

Walworth, Arthur C. *America's Moment, 1918: American Diplomacy at the End of World War I.* New York: W. W. Norton, 1977.

_____. *Wilson and His Peacemakers: American Diplomacy at the Paris Peace Conference, 1919.* New York: W. W. Norton, 1986. A truly outstanding study.

Wandycz, Piotr S. *France and Her Eastern Allies, 1919-1925.* Minneapolis: University of Minnesota Press, 1962.

Warner, Geoffrey. *Pierre Laval and the Eclipse of France.* New York: Macmillan, 1968.

Warwick, Paul. "Ideology, Culture and Gamesmanship in French Politics." *Journal of Modern History* 50 (1978):631-659.

*Watson, David R. "Clemenceau and Blanqui: A Reply to M. Paz [q.v.]." *Historical Journal* [Cambridge] 21 (1978):387-397.

_____. "Clemenceau, le socialisme et le nationalisme." In *Clemenceau et la justice* (q.v.), pp. 113-117.

628

*_____. *Georges Clemenceau: A Political Biography*. London: Eyre Metheun, 1974. The first truly scholarly full-length treatment; especially good as a guide through the politics of his times.

*_____. "A Note on Clemenceau, Comte and Positivism." *Historical Journal* [Cambridge] 14 (1971):201-204.

*_____. "The Making of French Foreign Policy During the First Clemenceau Ministry, 1906-1909." *English Historical Review* 86 (1971):774-782.

_____. "The Making of the Treaty of Versailles." In Neville Waites, ed., *Troubled Neighbors: Franco-British Relations in the Twentieth Century*. London: Weidenfeld & Nicolson, 1971.

Watt, Richard M. *Dare Call It Treason*. New York: Simon & Schuster, 1963. The French spy scandals in World War I.

Weber, Eugen. *France, Fin de Siècle*. Cambridge, MA: Harvard University Press, 1986.

_____. *The Nationalist Revival in France, 1905-1914*. Berkeley, CA: University of California Press, 1959.

_____. *Peasants into Frenchmen: The Modernization of Rural France, 1870-1914*. Stanford, CA: Stanford University Press, 1976.

Weil, Bruno. *Panama*. Translated by Albert Lehman. 7th ed. Éditions Bernard Grasset, 1934.

Weill, Georges. "Les gouvernements et la presse pendant la guerre." *Revue d'histoire de la guerre mondiale* 11 (April 1933):97-118.

Weinberg, Gerhard L. "The Defeat of Germany in 1918 and the European Balance of Power." *Central European History* 2 (1969):248-260. Excellent.

Weinstein, Edwin A. *Woodrow Wilson: A Medical and Psychological Biography*. Princeton, NJ: Princeton University Press, 1981.

Weinstein, Harold R. *Jean Jaurès: A Study of Patriotism in the French Socialist Movement*. New York: Columbia University Press, 1936.

Weygand, Général [Maxime]. "Le maréchal Foch et l'armistice." *Revue des deux mondes*, 1 Nov. 1938, pp. 1-29.

_____. *Mémoires*. 3 vols. Flammarion, 1950-1957.

Wheeler-Bennett, John W. *Brest-Litovsk: The Forgotten Peace, March 1918*. New York: St. Martin's Press, 1966.

*Wicart, A. "Clemenceau, orateur." *Annales politiques et littéraires*, 10 Aug. 1935, pp. 128-131. By one of his doctors.

*Wildenstein, Daniel. *Claude Monet.* 4 vols. Lausanne-Paris: La Bibliothèque des Arts, 1974-1985. Numerous extracts from their correspondence.

Wilder, Amos. "At the Nethermost Piers of History. World War I, A View from the Ranks for Jules Deschamps." In George A. Panichas, ed., *Promise of Greatness* (q.v.), pp. 345-357.

Williams, John. *The Home Fronts: Britain, France, and Germany, 1914-1918.* London: Constable, 1972.

*Williams, Wythe. *The Tiger of France: Conversations with Clemenceau.* New York: Duell, Sloan & Pearce, 1949. Unreliable on details, but good anecdotal material and observations from a *New York Times* correspondent and friend.

Williamson, Samuel R., Jr. *The Politics of Grand Strategy: Britain and France Prepare for War, 1904-1914.* Cambridge, MA: Harvard University Press, 1969. Important work.

Wilson, Keith M. *The Policy of the Entente: Essays on the Determinants of British Foreign Policy, 1904-1914.* Cambridge: Cambridge University Press, 1985.

Wilson, Stephen. *Ideology and Experience: Antisemitism in France at the Time of the Dreyfus Affair.* Rutherford, NJ: Fairleigh Dickinson University Press, 1982.

*Wilson, Woodrow. *The Papers of Woodrow Wilson.* Edited by Arthur S. Link. Princeton, NJ: Princeton University Press, 1966-[1989]. Through vol. 60 (1-17 June 1919).

*Wolfe, Robert. "The Parisian Club de la Révolution of the 18th Arrondissement, 1870-1871." *Past and Present*, no. 39 (April 1968), pp. 81-119.

Wolff, Theodor. *Through Two Decades.* Translated by E. W. Dickes. London: Heinemann, 1936.

Woodward, David R. "Did Lloyd George Starve the British of Men Prior to the German Offensive of 21 March 1918?" *Historical Journal* [Cambridge] 27 (1984):241-252.

_____. *Lloyd George and the Generals.* Newark, DE: University of Delaware Press, 1983.

_____. "The Origins and Intent of David Lloyd George's January 5 War Aims Speech." *The Historian* 34 (1971):22-39.

Woodward, Ernest Llewellyn, and Butler, Rohan, eds. *Documents on British Foreign Policy, 1919-1939*. London: His Majesty's Stationery Office, 1947-1970. Vols. on 1919-1920.

Woollcott, Alexander. *While Rome Burns*. New York: The Viking Press, 1934.

*Wormser, Georges. "Au sein du cabinet de guerre de Clemenceau," *Histoire de notre temps*, no. 1 (1967), pp. 113-131.

*_____. *Clemenceau vu de près*. Hachette-Littéraire, 1979. Contains numerous extracts from the files of the Musée Clemenceau.

_____. *Gambetta dans les tempêtes*. Éditions Sirey, 1964.

*_____. *Georges Mandel, l'homme politique*. Plon, 1967.

_____. "Lettres à une amie." *L'Actualité*, 9 April 1970, pp. 35-36.

*_____. *La république de Clemenceau*. Presses Universitaires de France, 1961. Indispensable study by a former member of his staff and close friend. Regrettably lacks an index, which makes it difficult to use because of its peculiar organization.

*_____. *Le septennat de Poincaré*. Fayard, 1977. For 1913-1920.

*Worsfold, W. Basil. "Lord Milner and the Unified Command: A Chapter in the History of the Great War." *United Empire* [London], May-June 1929, pp. 237-244, 316-324.

Wright, Gordon. *Raymond Poincaré and the French Presidency*. Stanford, CA: Stanford University Press, 1942.

Wright, Capt. Peter E. *At the Supreme War Council*. London: Everleigh Nash, 1921.

Wright, Vincent. "La loi de sûreté générale de 1858." *Revue d'histoire moderne et contemporaine* 16 (1969):414-430.

Xydias, Jean. *L'intervention française en Russie, 1918-1919: Souvenirs d'un témoin*. Éditions de France, 1927.

Yates, Louis A. R. *The United States and French Security, 1917-1921*. New York: Twayne Publishers, 1957.

Young, Robert J. *In Command of France: French Foreign Policy and Military Planning, 1933-1940*. Cambridge, MA: Harvard University Press, 1978.

Zeldin, Theodore. *France 1848-1945*. 2 vols. Oxford: Oxford University Press, 1973-77.

Zévaès, Alexandre [Bourson]. *Au temps du boulangisme*. Gallimard, 1930.

* _____. *Clemenceau*. René Julliard, n.d. [1949]. The author, a longtime member of Parliament, wrote numerous books on the Third Republic; widely informed but not always reliable.

* _____. "Clemenceau et Jaurès." *Revue politique et parlementaire* 204 (June 1951), pp. 230-241.

_____. *Tony Révillon, 1831-1898*. Arthème Fayard, 1950.

*Zuckerkandl, Berthe [Berta] Szeps. *Clemenceau, tel que je l'ai connu*. Algiers: Éditions de la Revue Fontaine, 1944. The author was the sister of Paul Clemenceau's wife.

_____. *My Life and History*. Translated by John Sommerfield. New York: Alfred A. Knopf, 1939.

INDEX

NB. As a rule, subheadings reading, e.g., "in 1906-09" group casual references for the sake of convenience and do not necessarily include all matters falling within the stated period, for which consult other subheadings. Titles and military ranks given here ordinarily do not reflect promotions subsequent to the matters dealt with in the text. Because of space considerations full baptismal French names or initials are not given.

Turkey, 6, 7, 8, 275, 276, 389, 401,
402, 419, 427, 449, 453, 454,
455-56, 457, 469, 483, 560.
See also Constantinople.
Turkish Petroleum Company, 487.
Turmel, Louis (1866-1919), 368.
Two Years' Service Law, *see*
Military Service laws.
Tyler, John (1790-1862), 5.

U

"Uhlan Letters" (Esterhazy), 200.
Ukraine, 381, 383, 384, 459, 460.
Ular, Alexandre (pseud.): *Inside
Russia Today* (1905), 241.
Unified command, *see* Western
Front, unification of
command on.
Unifiés, see Socialists (post-1905).
Union républicaine radicale et
radicale-socialiste, 347,
405.
Union sacrée (1914-17
governments), 307, 310, 312,
331, 334, 338, 340.
United Company of Merchants of
England Trading to the East
Indies, 8.
United States of America, 82,
180, 189, 243, 343, 375, 407,
431, 433, 471, 478, 501, 527,
539, 553;
in the 1840s, 4, 5, 9;
residence in (1865-69), 37,
42-53, 111, 320, 523;
his popularity in, 360, 493;
in 1906-09, 243;
in 1914-17, 324, 325, 343,
353, 466;
in 1917-18, 370, 385, 390,
395-96, 397, 401, 413;
use of manpower of
(1917-18), 333, 343, 346,
380-81, 384, 387-88, 390,
412-13, 505;
in 1919-20, 437, 466;
attitudes in 1919 of, 422,
429, 433, 434;

isolationism of, 325, 463,
492, 493-94, 495, 496,
536, 552;
speaking tour in (1922), 46,
47, 55, 484, 489, 492-96,
509, 513;
character of, 56, 57, 324,
420, 473, 495, 554-55.
See also Allies; Coolidge;
Guarantee, treaties of;
Versailles, Treaty of;
Wilson, Woodrow.
Unknown Soldier, tribute to, 506;
Tomb of the, 493.
Uruguay, 295.

V

"V., comtesse," 153.
Vaillant, (Marie) Édouard
(1840-1915), 264.
Valmy, battle of (1792), 353.
Var (department), 141, 142, 170,
177, 180, 233, 238, 268, 484;
Republican tradition in,
132, 222;
elected in (1885), 132, 144;
elected in (1902), 222-23;
elected in (1909), 298.
See also Draguignan.
Vatican, the, 225, 226, 253, 486,
508, 558.
Vaughan, Ernest, 191, 193, 201,
208, 212, 238, 308.
Vauthier, Louis (b. 1815), 126.
Vendée (department), 14, 15, 19,
20, 26, 31, 33, 53, 184, 187,
190, 210, 269;
character of, 1, 3, 10-12, 15,
197, 388;
practices medicine in, 55,
77;
his retirement in, 488,
503-504, 512;
his burial in, 507, 539-40,
544.
Vercingetorix (c. 72-46 B.C.), 11.
Verdun, battle of (1916), 263, 317,
323, 327, 353, 356, 363.